D0771951

UNDERSTANDING YOUR USERS

A Practical Guide to User Research Methods

UNDERSTANDING YOUR USERS

A Practical Guide to User Research Methods

Second Edition

Kathy Baxter, Catherine Courage,
and Kelly Caine

AMSTERDAM • BOSTON • HEIDELBERG • LONDON
NEW YORK • OXFORD • PARIS • SAN DIEGO
SAN FRANCISCO • SINGAPORE • SYDNEY • TOKYO
Morgan Kaufmann is an imprint of Elsevier

Acquiring Editor: Todd Green
Editorial Project Manager: Lindsay Lawrence
Project Manager: Punithavathy Govindaradjane
Designer: Kelly Huang

Morgan Kaufmann is an imprint of Elsevier
225 Wyman Street, Waltham, MA 02451, USA

Copyright © 2015, 2005 Elsevier Inc. All rights reserved.

No part of this publication may be reproduced or transmitted in any form or by any means, electronic or mechanical, including photocopying, recording, or any information storage and retrieval system, without permission in writing from the publisher. Details on how to seek permission, further information about the Publisher's permissions policies and our arrangements with organizations such as the Copyright Clearance Center and the Copyright Licensing Agency, can be found at our website: www.elsevier.com/permissions.

This book and the individual contributions contained in it are protected under copyright by the Publisher (other than as may be noted herein).

Notices

Knowledge and best practice in this field are constantly changing. As new research and experience broaden our understanding, changes in research methods, professional practices, or medical treatment may become necessary.

Practitioners and researchers must always rely on their own experience and knowledge in evaluating and using any information, methods, compounds, or experiments described herein. In using such information or methods they should be mindful of their own safety and the safety of others, including parties for whom they have a professional responsibility.

To the fullest extent of the law, neither the Publisher nor the authors, contributors, or editors, assume any liability for any injury and/or damage to persons or property as a matter of products liability, negligence or otherwise, or from any use or operation of any methods, products, instructions, or ideas contained in the material herein.

ISBN: 978-0-12-800232-2

British Library Cataloguing-in-Publication Data
A catalogue record for this book is available from the British Library

Library of Congress Cataloging-in-Publication Data
A catalog record for this book is available from the Library of Congress

For information on all Morgan Kaufmann publications, visit our website at www.mkp.com

IN PRAISE OF *UNDERSTANDING YOUR USERS, SECOND EDITION*

"The first edition became my 'go-to' book for mastering user requirements gathering. Ten years later, this second edition is even better. Don't leave your office without it!"

—**Joe Dumas,** Editor in Chief, *Journal of Usability Studies*

"Do you believe in driving while blindfolded? That's what you're doing if you design and market a technological product without studying your target users and tasks. This book is a comprehensive handbook on the "why" and "how" of user research, illustrated with vivid real-world examples. Don't drive your design project while blindfolded. Get this book, read it, and follow its prescriptions. It will repay its cost many times over."

—**Jeff Johnson,** author of *GUI Bloopers 2.0* and *Designing with the Mind in Mind*

"Very authoritative, this work combines expertise from industry and academia, with lots of specific guidelines, tips and examples, and with pointers to other readings for deeper insights. Useful for students and practitioners alike, this should be on everyone's bookshelf. The authors do a great job of explaining the importance of business-side stakeholders (C-suite, marketing, sales, development) and how to speak their language."

—**James D. Foley,** Professor, College of Computing, Stephen Fleming Chair in Telecommunications, Georgia Institute of Technology

"Understanding Your Users is a thorough guide to user experience for designers both technical and non-technical. Instructors, students and practitioners will find this book very useful to your success as an user experience expert."

—**Juan E. Gilbert, Ph.D.,** Andrew Banks Family Preeminence Endowed Chair, Computer & Information Science & Engineering Department, University of Florida

"Understanding Your Users is handbook of practical wisdom for the serious human centered design practitioner. This second edition includes updated content around emerging best practices. It is a must have in any design team's library."

—**Janaki Kumar,** Head of Strategic Design Services, America, Design and Co-Innovation Center, SAP Labs Palo Alto

"With the massive expansion of digital products, new processes for faster development cycles, and competition that can appear out of nowhere in days, the product design has become the major differentiator, and key to success. Understanding your end user is more important than it ever has been, how they really work, and how your assumptions match up to their reality. This book takes tried and true methodology and shows how any or all of it can be applied to your products now."

—**Jeremy Ashley,** VP, Oracle Cloud UX

"A great introductory book for anyone wishing to understand and engage in traditional user research methods. The language is clear and straightforward, allowing the reader to try and use the methods on their own project. Each method is accompanied with an extensive bibliography allowing the curious mind to further delve into any of the described methods. Samples of forms, letters and examples enhance the practical nature of the book, making this title a staple for the beginning practitioner."

—**Joseph Kramer** is a Service Design Lead at Fjord—Design and Innovation from Accenture Interactive

"The difference between product success and failure often comes down to the user experience. Baxter, Courage, and Caine share the methods you need to better understand your users so that you can design delightful experiences."

—**Craig Villamor,** Chief Design Architect at Salesforce.com

CONTENTS

PART 3 THE METHODS 191

PREFACE

What Is New in This Edition: Ten Years of Progress

A lot has changed in the ten years since the first edition of this book was published. One of the biggest changes is the shift from a focus on "usability" to "user experience." "Usability" is an attribute of a system or user interface (UI). It refers to the effectiveness, efficiency, and satisfaction with which users can achieve tasks when using a product. "User experience," on the other hand, is human-centered and is the co-creation of an interaction between a person or persons and a product. User experience includes "usability" *and* all aspects a user encounters when dealing with a product or service from the branding to the motion and audio design to customer support. It is about how the product or service makes the user *feel*. You can see this change reflected in job titles (e.g., from "Usability Engineer" in the 1990s and early 2000s to "User Experience Researcher" today) and professional organizations (e.g., the "Usability Professionals Association" changed their name to "User Experience Professionals Association" in 2012). The result of the change in focus means that a User Experience Researcher (UER or UXR) must conduct research beyond the UI and think about all of the elements influencing a user's experience. This change is reflected most prominently in our new title: "Understanding Your Users: A Practical Guide to *User Research*," but you'll see smaller reflections of this throughout the book.

A second change in the profession is the popularity of *agile development processes* and similar lightweight, iterative, project-based approaches. Created in 2001, Agile is a rapid development process used by a cross-functional team that ideally works together closely and meets daily. While agile development does include continuous customer or stakeholder involvement, the competing requirement to iterate quickly in small operable chunks, means it can be difficult to incorporate user research into the process. This makes conducting early user research to understand user requirements critical because there may be less time in later cycles to conduct longer-term research. To address this development, we added content around the importance of and techniques to enhance interactions with stakeholders and product teams.

A third development is the increasing variety of technology and contexts where research is needed. For example, products that were considered science fiction ten years ago such as wearables (e.g., smart watches, Google Glass), self-driving cars, and increasingly complex consumer medical devices (e.g., contact lens that measures blood glucose in tears) are now here or within reach. This means that the research we conduct is less often inside a usability lab and more often in context. It means we must understand not just whether users can find the feature they want and whether it meets a real user need, but also how people *around those* using the device(s) feel and respond to it. It is this highly complex interplay of technology development at breath-taking speeds and the human response to it that makes conducting valid, reliable, and ethical research much more challenging today. With this in mind, we refreshed the chapter on ethics, updated the example scenarios we use throughout the book and included additional details about conducting user research in the user's context.

A fourth development is the dramatically increased availability of tools that enable remote user research. These tools range from tools created specifically to make the job of a user researcher easier, to general purpose communication tools like Skype or Google Hangouts that now make conducting interviews across the country as convenient as conducting them in the user researcher's home city. Throughout the chapters, we introduce these tools, provide links to example tools, and include discussions of the pros and cons of using these types of tools in your research.

Besides updating the book to meet these shifts in practice and the profession of user experience research, we removed two methods that are less frequently used (i.e., Wants and Needs Analysis, Group Task Analysis). We replaced these with other methods that were not included in the first edition, but have since become increasingly used to learn about users (e.g., Social Sentiment Analysis, Experience Sampling Methodology, Diary Studies, crowdsourcing). Another significant change we made, based on feedback primarily from students, was to add a chapter on evaluation methods (i.e., heuristic evaluation, cognitive walkthroughs, usability testing, eye tracking, Rapid Iterative Testing and Evaluation, desirability testing, remote testing, and live experiments). Students and professors told us they loved the first edition, but for it to be more useful in introductory courses on user research, it should include a chapter on evaluating a product's usability. We agree and feel this increases the scope of the book from just user requirements methods to cover the entire spectrum of user research. We also added a section to discuss special user types one should consider in their research (e.g., older users, children, physically challenged). Finally, in the spirit of modernization, we have updated all of the methods to reflect the most recent understanding about ways to collect data validly and reliably and refreshed the references accordingly.

To make the book easier to use, we ceased relegating data analysis methods to appendices and instead incorporated one detailed data analysis method per chapter. For user research methods where more than one data analysis method can be used, we outlined those methods briefly and pointed readers to additional details within other chapters. We hope this provides a more pleasant, straightforward, self-contained reading experience. Another way we improved usefulness was by incorporating example data collection instruments, tools, worksheets, and notetaking samples throughout the book. We anticipate these examples and tools will be especially useful to those readers who are new to user experience research and/or are working in contexts where these types of examples are not readily available.

Finally, we wanted to make sure the book was fun and immediately practical. Abi Jones' cartoons provide delightful pictures when words wouldn't do and add levity. With the help of incredibly talented case study authors, we have included all new case studies that provide practical examples of these methods in action in a variety of contexts from software development to banking to medical devices.

How to Use This Book

This book is designed to be a comprehensive, easy-to-read, "how-to" guide on user research methods. It teaches many distinct user research methods and also covers pre- and post-method considerations, such as recruiting, facilitating activities or moderating, negotiating with product development teams/customers, and getting your results incorporated into the product. To help illustrate the material and methods presented in this book, we refer to a fictitious mobile travel app called "TravelMyWay.com" throughout the book.

This book has five main parts:

Part 1: What You Need to Know Before Choosing an Activity

Often people are not aware of all the factors they should consider before choosing a requirements activity. Chapters 1 through 5 will introduce you to user research methods and the factors you need to consider. They cover such critical topics as:

- The difference between user requirements and other types of requirements
- Getting buy-in from the product team to conduct user research
- Product/domain research
- Learning who your end user really is, including creating personas and scenarios
- Special user types
- Legal and ethical issues
- Creating an environment to conduct user requirements activities
- Choosing the best method based on your research question(s) and resources

Part 2: Get Up and Running

Once you have decided to conduct a user research activity, the preparation process begins. Much of the preparation that must be done is the same regardless of the activity you conduct. Chapters 6 and 7 focus on this groundwork so that you are fully prepared to execute your activity. This work includes:

- Creating a proposal and protocol for your activity
- Recruiting
- Piloting your activity
- Welcoming the participants
- Moderating the activity

Part 3: The Methods

Chapters 8 through 14 focus on user research methods. Each chapter focuses on a different method and variations on that method. For each of these methods, you will learn how to prepare for the activity step by step, conduct the activity, and analyze the data. Materials, templates, and checklists are provided to get you using the techniques in no time! Lessons learned and method modifications are discussed as well so that you can adapt a method to suit your needs and avoid making costly mistakes. The methods covered are:

- Diary studies
- Interviews
- Surveys
- Card sorting
- Focus groups
- Field studies
- Evaluations methods

In addition, research experts have provided real-world case studies that are presented at the end of each chapter, to show each method in action.

Part 4: Wrapping Up

Once you have conducted an activity and analyzed the data, your job isn't done. You must communicate results clearly to your product team/customer or else the data are worthless. In Chapter 15, we discuss how to effectively report and present your results to ensure they are incorporated into the product.

Part 5: Appendices

We also include appendices with additional information that will be of great value as you begin your user requirements methods. The appendices are:

- Requirements for creating a participant recruiting database (Appendix A)
- A report template for your findings (Appendix B)
- Glossary of terms (Appendix C)
- A bibliography of references (Appendix D)

Targeted Readers

This book has something to offer whether you are new to user experience or a seasoned professional.

New to User Experience

You may be a designer, a member of a product development team, or a computer science professor who has heard about 'user studies' but hasn't conducted one yourself, or you may have a role in sales or marketing and have been asked to start thinking about or own 'user experience.' Regardless of your job title or level of knowledge of user experience, this book will enable you to effectively run a variety of user research activities to ensure that your users' needs are represented in your product. Because this book is designed as a how-to guide, we take you through every aspect of the activity, from preparation to presentation of the results.

Students

Students from a variety of fields such as Human-Centered Computing, Human Computer Interaction (HCI), Human Factors, Psychology, and Computer Science need to understand user research methods. This book may be used as a textbook for a course, as a supplement to coursework, thesis work, or in preparation for a peer-reviewed publication that reports results from a user research activity. Because we focus not only on theoretical concepts about user research, but also include practical tips and examples from industry, this book will be useful to you as you transition from student to professional.

User Experience Research Professional

If you are a seasoned user research professional in industry or academia, this book can provide you with some additional user research activities that you may not be familiar with. UER professionals are always looking to add new methods to their toolbox. In addition, this book can act as a reference guide for some of those methods you may not have conducted in a while or point to modifications of a method you had never thought of. Finally, we have packed the book with research to demonstrate shortcomings and strengths of the different methods, as well as case studies so you can see how your peers are executing these methods.

User Experience Promoter

Many of us within product development organizations are faced with the task of promoting the importance of user experience and user research. Perhaps, you are a VP of Customer Experience or are in Sales or Marketing and want to advocate for your customers and therefore promote the need to conduct user research. This book will help provide you with some ammunition. The real-world case studies located within the chapters demonstrate how these methods have been used successfully within companies to improve their products.

ABOUT THE AUTHORS

Kathy Baxter is a Staff User Experience Researcher and UX Infrastructure Manager at Google. Since 2005, she has conducted research that spans the company from Ads to Enterprise Apps to Search and has managed the Global User Experience Infrastructure Team. Prior to 2005, she worked as a Senior User Experience Researcher for eBay and Oracle.

She received her MS in Engineering Psychology and a BS degree in Applied Psychology from the Georgia Institute of Technology. She has presented papers and taught courses to the Human Factors and HCI community around the world, as well as worked on the CHI, EPIC, and early UPA conference committees over the years. She also actively volunteers in events to get more girls and young women involved science, technology, engineering, art/design, and math (STEAM) careers. Of all her accomplishments, she is most proud of her amazing daughter, Hana!

Catherine Courage is Senior Vice President of the Citrix Customer Experience Group. Her team's mission is to create world-class products and services that drive adoption and loyalty. Catherine is an active writer and speaker on design and user experience. Her work has been featured by Harvard Business Review, The Wall Street Journal, Fast Company and TEDxKyoto. Catherine was selected by the Silicon Valley Business Journal as one of Silicon Valley's 40 Under 40, and one of Silicon Valley's 100 Most Influential Women. She also made Forbes list of Top 10 Rising Stars at the World's Most Innovative Companies.

Catherine is an advisor to two entrepreneurial groups, Citrix Startup Accelerator and C100, and is a board member of the California College of the Arts and the Leukemia and Lymphoma Society. She holds a Masters of Applied Sciences, specializing in Human Factors, from the University of Toronto. When she's not working, you'll find her swimming, biking, and running in preparation for her next triathlon.

Kelly Caine is the director of the Humans and Technology Lab at Clemson University, where she leads research in human factors, human-centered computing, privacy, usable security, health informatics and human-computer interaction. She is a thought-leader who has been invited to speak around the world, has published dozens of peer-reviewed papers and is regularly cited by media such as the AP, Washington Post, NPR, and New York Times. Kelly enjoys teaching students to become scientists, and has designed and taught courses on research methods for understanding people and their relationship with technology at universities and in industry.

Prior to joining Clemson, she was Principal Research Scientist in the School of Computing at Indiana University and a UX researcher at Google (where she and Kathy first met!). She holds degrees from the University of South Carolina (B.A.) and the Georgia Institute of Technology (M.S. and Ph.D.). When work doesn't get in the way, she is an adventurer, world-traveler, and avid equestrienne.

ACKNOWLEDGMENTS

In many ways, the second edition of this book was both easier (more fun!) and harder to write than the first. It was easier and more fun because a colleague and friend, Kelly Caine, joined us! Also, we had an additional 10 years of experience each to draw upon. It was harder because we had to coordinate across the country, time zones, companies, and schedules. With so many more obligations, the success of this collaboration in so little time is a testament to our passion for our field and the incredible support team we had helping us.

First of all, we thank Meg Dunkerley, Heather Scherer, Lindsay Lawrence and Todd Green from Morgan Kaufmann for their cheerful and unrelenting assistance throughout the writing and editing process. We also thank our reviewers, Michael Beasley, Dan Russell, and Suzanna Rogers for the very helpful peer reviews. We know it was a lot of work! We are also very thankful for the incredibly talented authors who shared their expertise about user research methods via case studies: Apala Lahiri Chavan, John Boyd, Hendrik Mueller & Aaron Sedley, Jenny Shirey, Arathi Sethumadhavan, Lana Yarosh and Pamela Walshe & Nick Opderbeck. We know readers are going to love hearing about your experiences. We'd also like to thank Abi Jones for her fabulous cartoons throughout and Kelly Huang for her incredible cover design! Finally, we thank Ariel Liu and Jim Foley for their last minute reviews and feedback and especially Sara Snow for a thorough subject matter expert edit and copy edit. On a personal note, we would like to individually thank friends and family.

I am grateful for the patience of my husband, Joe, and especially my daughter, Hana, as I sat for hours at the computer. I hope I have made them as proud of me as I am of them! I must also thank my mother for always believing in and supporting everything I have done in my life. Thank you for being the example I want to set for my daughter! Of course, my deepest gratitude to Kelly and Catherine for joining me on this epic adventure to write a book (again)! And, finally, I'd like to thank several coworkers for their valuable insights on specific sections of the book including Mario Callegaro, Hilary Hutchinson, Patri Forwalter-Friedman, Adam Banks, and Ilmo van der Löwe.

Kathy Baxter

Thank you to my husband, Ian. His support through words and actions made this second edition possible. And thank you to my family, friends and coworkers who continue to inspire and encourage me to do my best work. And to my fabulous co-authors Kathy and Kelly who were a joy to work with and made the impossible possible!

Catherine Courage

I would like to thank all of my family and friends for their support; I am in awe of the patience and kindness you all display when I spend my "free time" writing. I would especially like to thank Micah. My gratitude for the balance you bring to life is boundless. I would also like to thank my mom and dad for their truly unconditional love. Your love and support have given me the confidence to take on challenges (like coauthoring a book!) without fear.

I am also indebted to the many scholars, teachers and colleagues from whom I learned how to conduct research, especially Dan Fisk, Wendy Rogers, Robin Jeffries, James Evans and Mac McClure. I am also very thankful for the hundreds of students and research participants who have taught me the practical aspects of research and inspired me to want to put this knowledge in a form that is useful to others.

Finally, I would like to thank Kathy and Catherine for showing me the ropes of what it takes to co-author a book. You two are so fun to work with, helpful, patient, thoughtful, smart and knowledgeable! I could not have asked for better partners in this experience.

Kelly Caine

PART 

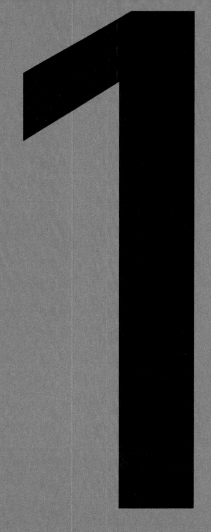

WHAT YOU NEED TO KNOW BEFORE CHOOSING AN ACTIVITY

CHAPTER 1

Introduction to User Experience

What Is User Experience?

If you are reading this book, you already have some idea about, or at least interest in, User Experience (UX). However, you likely arrived at this book and this field via a different path from the colleague sitting next to you or the classmate across the country who is taking the same online human-computer interaction (HCI) or human factors class as you. User experience practitioners and students come to UX from a diverse range of backgrounds, including computer science, psychology, design marketing, business, anthropology, and industrial engineering (Farrell & Nielsen, 2014). This diversity is an advantage; our community adopts the best practices and benefits from the knowledge of all of these disciplines. However, it also means that there is not one singular activity, style, or approach that defines UX.

There are many definitions of UX (see http://www.allaboutux.org/ux-definitions). The User Experience Professionals Association (UXPA) defines it as "Every aspect of the user's interaction with a product, service, or company that make up the user's perceptions of the whole. User experience design as a discipline is concerned with all the elements that together make up that interface, including layout, visual design, text, brand, sound, and interaction. Usability Engineering works to coordinate these elements to allow for the best possible interaction by users."

TIP

If you are talking to people who are not familiar with UX and need an easy way to help them understand what you do, tell them you "help make technology easy for people to use." It is not a perfect definition by any means, but people get the gist. Kelly discovered this after she got tired of blank stares when telling people her various job titles. She conducted a little user research on her friends, family members, and airplane seatmates to discover a one-line description for what she does. "I help make technology easy for people to use" always worked and usually made people say, "Wow, that's great! We need more people like you."

Whereas usability is about creating problem-free interactions, user experience is much broader and holistic. Usability is objective and product-based (i.e., a product is usable), whereas user experience is subjective and human centered (i.e., a person and a product co-create the user experience). Very often, user experience research seeks to gather "user requirements" for the design of technologies (e.g., mobile devices, websites, wearable technologies, software) or evaluate the usability of an existing technology.

User requirements refer to the features/attributes a product should have or how it should perform from the users' perspective. **User-centered design** (UCD) is an approach for collecting and analyzing these requirements. This chapter introduces the basic concepts behind UCD, introduces **stakeholders** and their requirements, and tells you how to get buy-in for your user research activities.

Who Does User Experience?

Lots of people from many different backgrounds do work in user experience (see Figure 1.1). In industry, there are a variety of titles for UX practitioners, including (Farrell & Nielsen, 2014):

- User experience designer
- User experience researcher
- Information architect
- Interaction designer
- Human factors engineer
- Business analyst
- Consultant
- Creative director
- Interaction architect
- Usability specialist

At the executive level, the titles include (Manning & Bodine, 2012):

- Chief customer officer
- Chief client officer
- Chief experience officer
- VP of user experience

Fundamentally, UX research is about understanding people, the domain, and technology. In that sense, while we have written this book from the perspective of UX research, the methods we describe can be used in any situation where you want to understand more about human behavior, perceptions, ideas, needs, wants, and concerns and how those play out in various contexts and with various technologies.

At a Glance

> User-centered design
> A variety of experiences
> Getting stakeholder buy-in for your activity

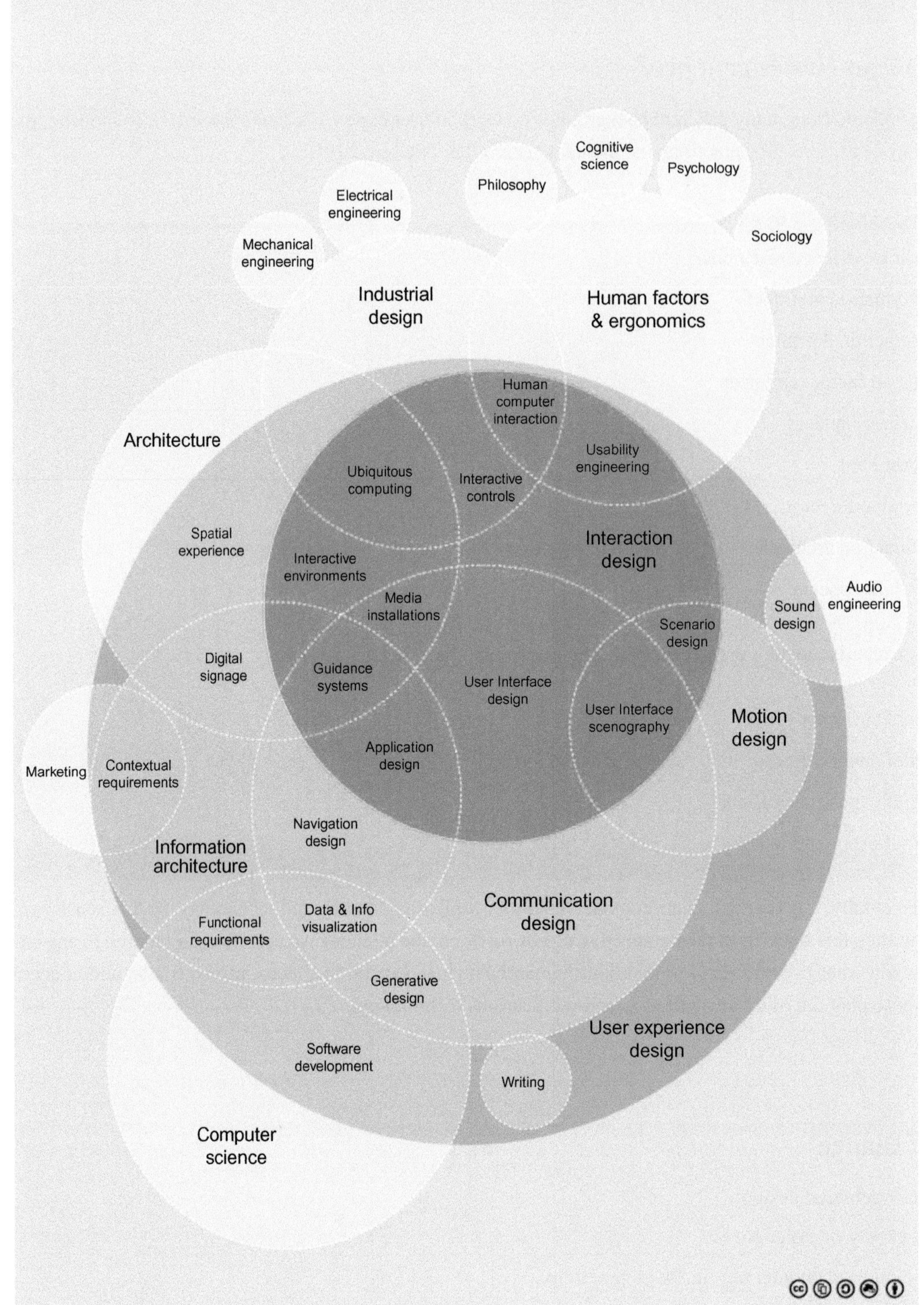

Figure 1.1: The disciplines of User Experience (www.envis-precisely.com). This work is licensed under the Creative Commons Attribution-Share Alike 30 Unported License. To view a copy of this license, visit http://Creativecommons.org/licenses/ by-sa/30 or send a letter to Creative Commons, 171 Second Street, Suite 300, San Francisco, California, 94105, USA. *From http://upload. wikimedia.org/wikipedia/commons/d/d5/Interaction-Design-Disciplines.png.*

Suggested Resources for Further Reading

There are many colleges and universities with master's and PhD programs in human-centered computing, HCI, engineering psychology, information sciences, etc., that offer coursework that will prepare you for a career in User Experience. If you do not have a degree in these or a related field, the books below can offer an introduction to many of the concepts discussed in this book.

- Norman, D. A. (2013). *The design of everyday things: Revised and expanded edition*. Basic Books.
- Lidwell, W., Holden, K., & Butler, J. (2010). *Universal principles of design, revised and updated: 125 ways to enhance usability, influence perception, increase appeal, make better design decisions, and teach through design*. Rockport Pub.
- Rogers, Y. (2012). HCI theory: Classical, modern, and contemporary. *Synthesis Lectures on Human-Centered Informatics*, *5*(2), 1–129.
- Johnson, J. (2014). *Designing with the mind in mind: Simple guide to understanding user interface design guidelines* (2nd ed.). Morgan Kaufmann.
- Weinschenk, S. (2011). *100 things every designer needs to know about people*. Pearson Education.

User-Centered Design

UCD is a product development approach that focuses on end users. The philosophy is that the product should suit the user, rather than making the user suit the product. This is accomplished by employing techniques, processes, and methods throughout the product life cycle that focus on the user.

A Note About Terminology

Some of our colleagues (and even some of us!) do not like the word "user." It has negative associations (e.g., drug "users"), can create subjective distance, and certainly does not convey the complexity and depth of people and their experiences. Don Norman (2006) wrote, "Words matter. Talk about people: not customers, not consumers, not users." We agree. However, UX is the term of the trade, so we use it and its components (user and experience) throughout the book.

Principles of User-Centered Design

There are three key principles of UCD (Gould & Lewis, 1985): an early focus on users and tasks, empirical measurement of product usage, and iterative design.

An Early Focus on Users and Tasks

The first principle focuses on the systematic and structured collection of users' experiences. That is the focus of this book. We will teach you how to effectively collect users' experiences using a variety of methods.

To maximize the quality of the user experience of a product, the user should be involved from the product's inception. The earlier the user is involved, the less repair work needs to be done at the final stages of the life cycle (e.g., after a usability test). The UCD process should begin with user experience gathering. By collecting user experiences, you can gain an understanding of what your users really want and need, how they currently work or how they would like to work, and their mental representations of their domain. This information is invaluable when creating a superior product.

Empirical Measurement of Product Usage

The focus here is on classical usability: ease of learning and effective, error-free use. This can be assessed early in the life cycle via usability testing of prototypes. Metrics such as errors, assists, and task completion rates gauge this. In a usability test, users are given a prototype or the final product and asked to complete a series of typical tasks using the product. This activity allows you to identify usability issues with your product. Then, changes are made to improve the product before its release. We describe usability evaluation in Chapter 14.

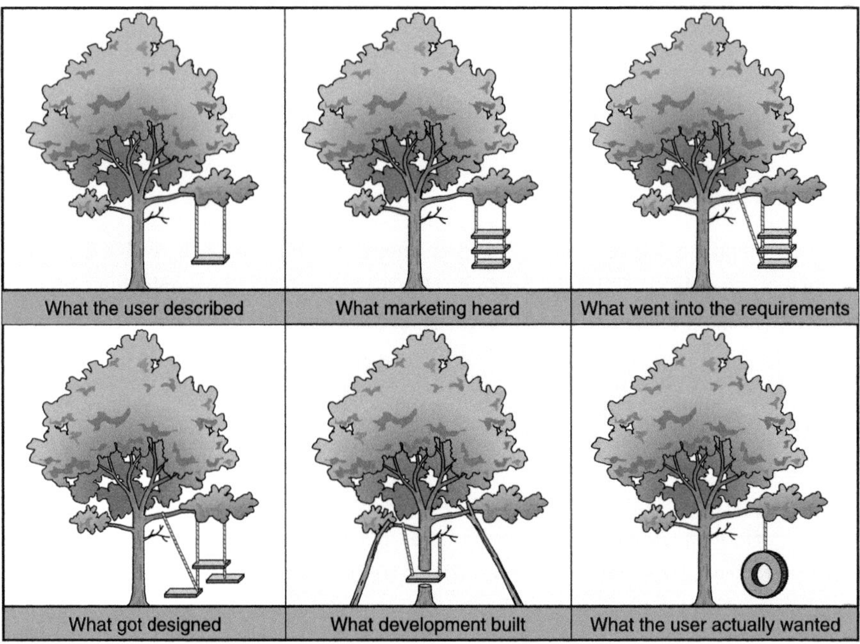

Image based on cartoon #5 at http://www.usability.uk.com/

Iterative Design

The final principle recommends that experiences are collected and the product is designed, modified, and tested repeatedly. The idea of iterative design is to fail early; it is much easier to change the user interface of an early prototype than a deployed system. This could mean that you and your team start with **paper proto-**

types and iterate at that stage multiple times and only then move on to an interactive prototype. You do not go through the development cycle once; you continue to iterate and fine-tune with each cycle until you get it right. No one gets all the information the first time, no matter how expertly you execute each user research activity.

Incorporating UCD Principles into the Product Development Life Cycle

This book offers research techniques for every stop in the product development life cycle, but it is unlikely you will have the time, resources, or even need to do every one of them. To be successful, it is *your* job to identify the critical research questions facing your team, company, or academic lab and then to identify the method(s) necessary to answer those questions. Stone (2013) wrote, "To me, great UX research is four things—in this order—timely, believable, actionable, and surprising. Timely because we need to learn to work at the same pace as product teams, otherwise our direct impact on the product will suffer. Believable comes from thinking hard about the context of use and structuring your tasks to capture this context. Actionable comes from knowing the decisions the product team is facing, and being on the same page with them.... Surprising comes from understanding how to observe and report on user behavior better than anyone else on your team. This is the only trick I know. Do excellent work and do it fast, and people will notice and thank you for it."

Figure 1.2 illustrates the ideal product life cycle with these UCD processes incorporated. The 'Concept' phase (Stage 1) encompasses an early focus on users. The 'Design' phase (Stage 2) incorporates an early focus on users and empirical measurement. The 'Develop' and 'Release' phases (Stages 3 and 4) tend to focus on empirical measurement. Sample activities in each phase are discussed in this section.

Stage 1: Concept

This is the idea phase of your product. You are:

- Developing user experience goals and objectives
- Creating user profiles and personas
- Executing user experience research activities, such as interviews and field studies

Stage 2: Design

At this stage, you begin using the information collected in Stage 1 to create iterative designs. Some user research activities include:

- User walkthroughs of low-fidelity prototypes (e.g., paper)
- Heuristic evaluations
- Execution of user experience research activities, such as focus groups and card sorts

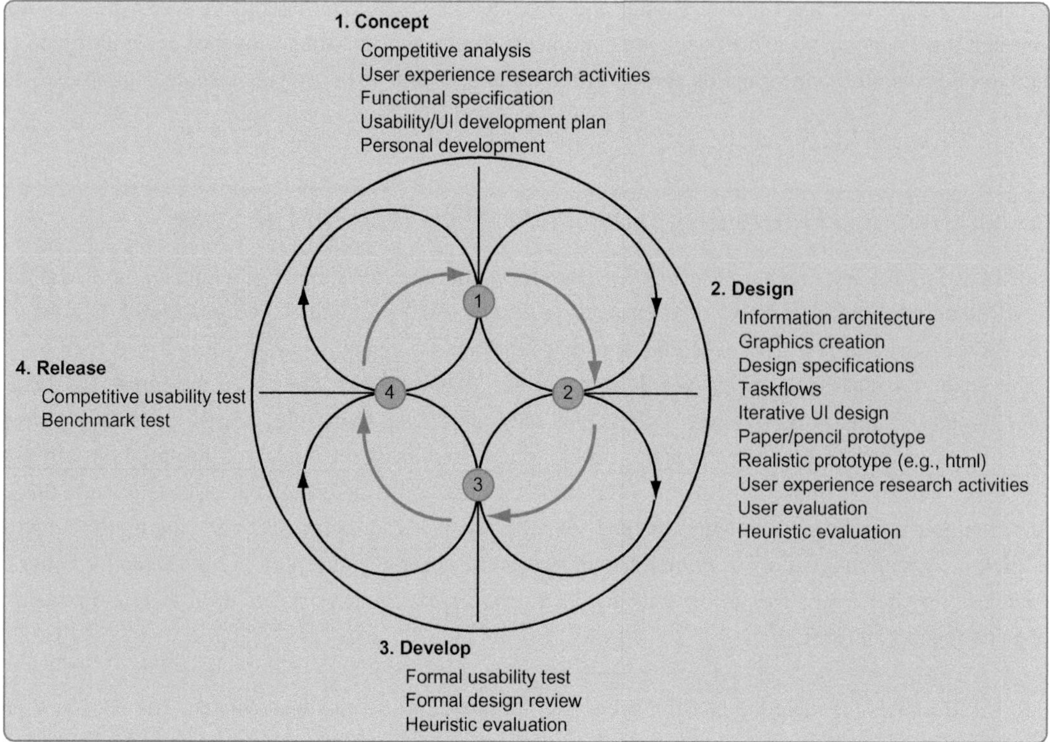

Figure 1.2: Product lifecycle with UCD processes incorporated.

Stage 3: Develop

The developers or engineers now begin to create the product. Some usability activities include:

- Preparation, planning, and execution of pre-product release **heuristic evaluations**
- Preparation, planning, and execution of pre-product release usability testing

Stage 4: Release

The last stage is when your product is released to the public or customer or within your organization. This stage often blends both user experience research activities with other types of empirical measurements. In software environments, formal usability tests are typically executed on the live code. In addition, user experience research collection for the next product release often begins at Stage 4, to gauge users' feedback on the product that has been released in the real world. Some Stage 4 activities include:

- Usability testing
- Surveys or interviews to gain feedback on released code
- Field studies to see the product being used in its environment

The third principle of UCD—"iterative design"—is employed throughout the entire cycle, as well as within each stage of the process. For example, you may do a field visit in the concept phase. This activity will begin your user experience research data collection, but may also open up new questions prompting you to run a follow-up activity such as individual interviews. You will then use the results of the interviews to go back and revise and refine or iterate your user experience research document based on your new data.

Design Thinking

If your colleagues have not adopted a UCD process, you have a larger issue on your hands. Conducting a few user research activities will not lead to a cure. One option is to consider "design thinking."

If your company, client, or academic advisor does not understand the value of user research, design thinking can be a great way to get them to see the necessity. Design thinking is an approach to innovation that can be applied to all areas of business and practice. It does not refer to a formal step-by-step process, but to a framework and a mind-set. It is focused on a bias toward action, a human-centered viewpoint, and a mode of continual experimentation. The core idea is that by deeply understanding user needs, opportunities for innovation will emerge. These ideas can be further refined through rapid prototypes and iterations with users to result in breakthrough outcomes. The process of collecting user requirements is an integral part of this approach. The design thinking approach provides greater context so people understand why understanding users is so critical to creating great products and services. The Hasso Plattner Institute of Design (Stanford d.school) has done a good job of popularizing this approach in the d.school classes and its executive boot camps. You will now find similar workshops offered by other academic institutions and consultants. With a day or two of training, you can get a team to understand the criticality of user empathy.

Suggested Resources for Additional Reading

If you are interested in building a design thinking culture, check out:

- Hasso Plattner Institute of Design: http://dschool.stanford.edu/.
- "Building a Culture of Design Thinking at Citrix": http://www.mixprize.org/story/reweaving-corporate-dna-building-culture-design-thinking-citrix.

You may also decide to employ a change management strategy in order to affect organization structure, processes, and culture. This is no small task. These books provide detailed guidance:

- Bias, R. G., & Mayhew, D. J. (Eds.). (2005). *Cost-justifying usability*. San Francisco: Morgan Kaufmann.
- Schaffer, E. (2004). *Institutionalization of usability: A step-by-step guide*. New York: Addison-Wesley.
- Sharon, T. (2012). *It's our research: Getting stakeholder buy-in for user experience research projects*. Morgan Kaufmann.

A Variety of Requirements

Thanks to a growing awareness of user experience, many product teams now realize the importance of understanding their users and the consequences that result when users are unable to utilize products with maximum ease and pleasure. As a result of this awareness, many companies and academic labs have incorporated some of the UCD process into their product or scientific life cycles. For many though, user experience still begins and ends with the usability test.

There is a clear difference between usability testing and user experience research. Usability testing determines whether a given solution is usable—easy to use in an error-free manner. User experience research provides insight into the many possible solutions and allows a team to select and investigate the best solution from the users' perspective. The difference between a good designer and the outstanding designer is the latter's vision of solutions. Without user research, your vision is seriously limited.

Although usability testing is a critical part of an effective UCD life cycle, it is only one component of the UCD. This book is focused primarily on the user experience research stage, which often receives less attention than usability testing, but is equally important. User experience research can be used to gather "user requirements" for the design of technologies. By user requirements, we mean the features/attributes the product should have or how it should perform. Requirements can come from a variety of sources—marketing, product development, end users, purchasing decision-makers, calls for proposals, etc. All sources have valid requirements and they must be taken into consideration by the team. For example, if you are building a mobile app for booking travel, some user requirements might include the following:

- The mobile app must be available on iOS, Android, and Windows phones.
- Users must register with the site before making purchases.
- The site must be available in English, Spanish, and French.
- The site should appeal to all demographics of users.
- Users should not require training.

We next describe the different types of requirements you may encounter, with a focus on industry settings. The advice here can be applied to other settings such as nonprofits or academia by considering the perspectives represented on your team (e.g., you may not have sales requirements, but you still have stakeholders). In all cases, by understanding a product's "competing" requirements, you can better position the user requirements for inclusion.

The Product Team's Perspective

In industry settings, the product team is composed of everyone who has a stake in building, deploying, and selling the product. The requirements-gathering phase is the period when the product team must do its initial research to determine the direction of the product. They must collect requirements from a variety of sources (e.g., sales, marketing, managers in your company, customers, end users) and use this information to determine what functionality will be included in the product. This stage is critical in creating a basis for the design. Poor requirements collection will impact the remaining stages of the product life cycle depicted in Figure 1.2. You will end up with a misguided product that will not sell or will be unusable and useless to the users and/or the company that purchases it.

There are a variety of different requirements that factor into product development, and there is often confusion between them. Figure 1.3 illustrates some of the many requirements and sources that a product team must deal with.

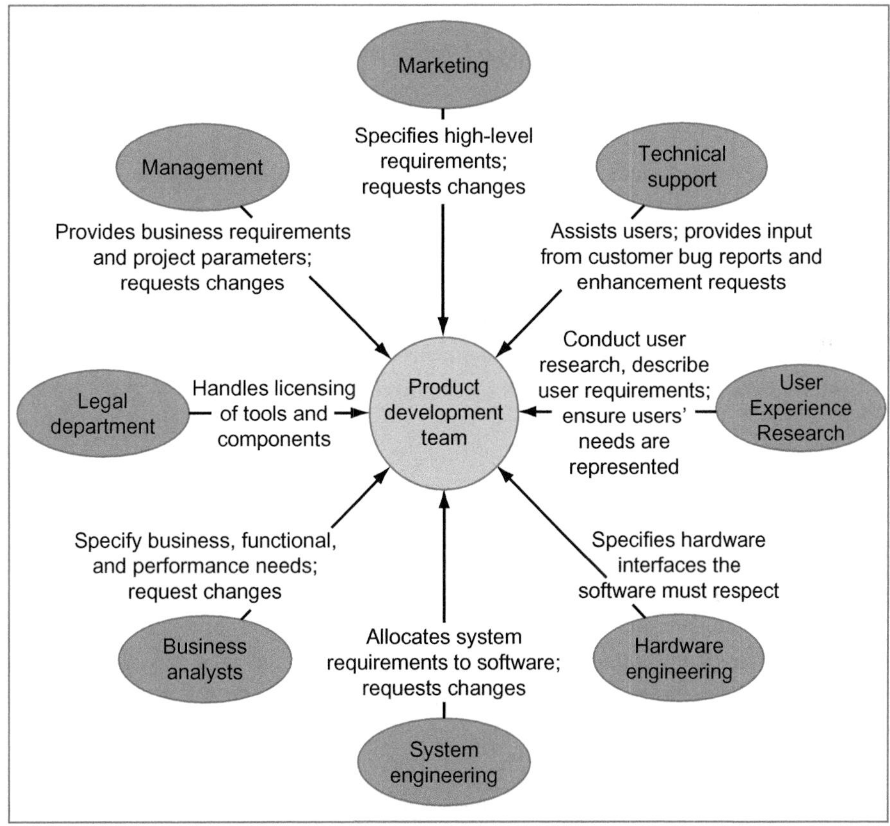

Figure 1.3: Requirements sources (image based on Weigers, 1999).

We often encounter teams who say, "We have already collected our user requirements," but in reality, they have collected functional or marketing requirements, not actual user requirements. Below, we discuss business, marketing, and sales requirements because they are often confused with user requirements. It is important to note that each of these is important, but not a user requirement. There may be overlap, but it is critical for all of the different sources of requirements to be independently collected and then prioritized as a group. You cannot assume that what the salesperson wants to see in the product is the same as what the end user wants to see in the product. To collect the different requirements effectively, you must be able to distinguish among them.

DILBERT © 2003 Scott Adams. Used By permission of UNIVERSAL UCLICK. All rights reserved.

Business Requirements

The people who are considering purchasing your product have requirements for that product. These people are typically corporate professionals or executives. They are often referred to as "the decision-makers." Their requirements often reflect the current business practices of their company or new practices they want to adopt to employ cost savings. They want to make sure the product matches their requirements. If you want to keep these customers, being aware of their business requirements is very important. Sometimes these requirements overlap with the users' requirements, but often, business requirements are higher-level and/or more technical. In academia, the "decision-maker(s)" may be your advisor or thesis committee.

Marketing and Sales Requirements

The marketing and sales departments want to ensure the product sells and their requirements reflect this goal. They may have requests for features or functions that they think customers want, that competitors have or do not have, etc. Marketing requirements tend to be at a high level that lacks detail. Marketers are not interested in sending a message about the minute details of the product; they want to send high-level messages to potential customers that will lure them to the product. For example, for a travel app, they may have a requirement that the app should have more airline choices than all other competitors or that it will find the lowest guaranteed airfare.

The sales representatives are in the field with customers day-in and day-out, so the requirements they have are frequently based on what they are hearing from their customers during product demos. Keep in mind that they are usually demonstrating the product to purchasing "decision-makers" and not end users. They may have requirements such as "It needs to be fast" or "It needs to look like the number one travel app in the marketplace." It is important to remember that these requirements may be very customer-specific and not applicable or scalable to other current (or future) customers.

Sales and marketing departments do not typically collect detailed information regarding what users must be able to do with the product, how they must be able to use it, and under what circumstances they must be able to use it; however, some marketing and sales requirements do represent a form of end user requirement. Consequently, you will likely see some overlap between the user requirements and what sales and marketing have uncovered. The reality is that if the product does not do what users want, it does not matter how usable it is. Marketing and sales folks often talk to end users, and sometimes, they even talk to them about usability, even if only at a high level. Mostly, they talk to users about features and capabilities. This is valuable information. Its weakness is that the information they collect is often incomplete, and they almost always collect it in "demo mode" (i.e., selling rather than listening). They may try to understand users, but because it is not their primary goal, they do not have time or motivation to gather true user requirements. In addition, they may encourage new features to be included in the product because the latest technology is easier to sell, not because users actually want it or will end up using it.

User Requirements

Whether you are working in academia, in private industry, or at a nonprofit, you will have stakeholders with their own goals to meet. Those stakeholders have to keep in mind the needs of a government agency that is funding the grant for your research (e.g., NIH), or private donors, or shareholders in your company. It is everyone's job to balance user needs against business, reporting, or sales needs. But before a product or service is complete, you want to make sure that end users can actually use it and that it contains the features they need. If you ignore this important goal, increased training and support or decreased user productivity will lead to unsatisfied users. That can harm future development efforts, your scientific success, and future sales or decrease renewed licenses or product upgrades. It can also lead to a poor reputation, unhappy funders, or no new customers.

As was discussed above, you may think you understand what the end users want and need because other sources have told you on their behalf. This is the number one mistake that product teams make. In reality, purchasing decision-makers, sales, and marketing may think that users interact with the product in a certain way, but because they (decision-makers, sales, and marketing) are not the true end users, they are frequently mistaken. In other cases, they receive information from one single source that has spoken to the end user, but much gets lost in the translation and interpretation by the time the information gets to you. Figure 1.4 illustrates many of these problematic communication paths from which the product team receives "user information."

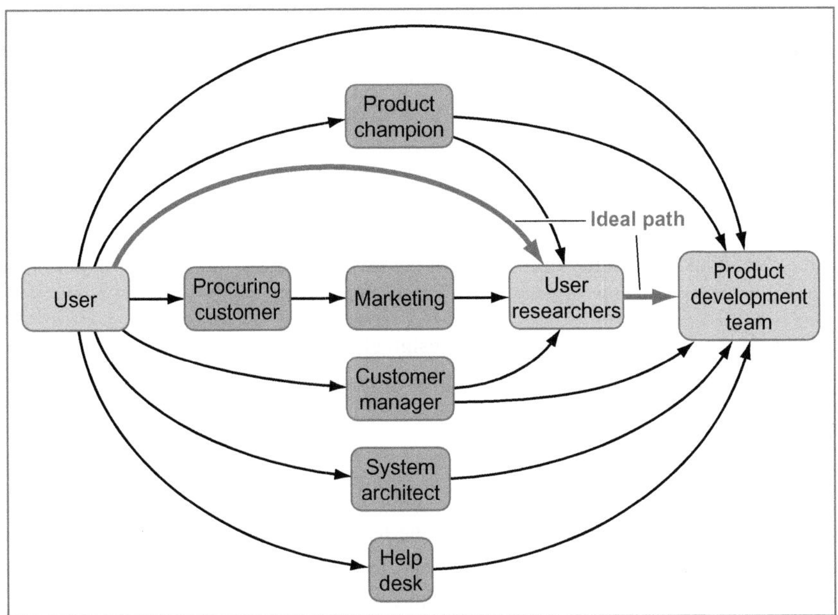

Figure 1.4: Communication paths from the user to the product team (image based on Weigers, 1999).

As a result, you must talk to the actual users—the people who will use the product at the end of the day—to gain an understanding of their perspective and needs. This understanding includes their tasks, goals, context of use, and skills.

By addressing your users' requirements, you can create a product that fulfills their needs. This fulfillment will in turn:

- Increase sales and market share due to increased customer satisfaction and increased ease of use
- Decrease training and support calls that result from user interfaces that do not match the users' needs
- Decrease development time and cost by creating products that contain only the necessary functionality

Getting Stakeholder Buy-In for Your Activity

If you are lucky, the stakeholders you are working with already know the value of user research. However, we have found that many times, the evidence about how user experience research drives innovation, acceptance, productivity, and profit has not made its way to all stakeholders. Therefore, one key skill you need as a user experience professional is to be able to effectively convince people of the importance of user research.

UX brings a huge amount of value to a project beyond just financial benefits. However, when you need to convince stakeholders to buy in to your activity, money often talks. Good UX leads to increased productivity, increased user satisfaction, decreased errors, decreased training costs, decreased support costs, increased sales, savings on redesign costs, increased audience/traffic, and better online reviews (Bias & Mayhew, 2005). Here are some specific pieces of evidence for you to use to help demonstrate the value of UX:

- Understanding UX is critical to innovation. "Innovation is not invention. Innovation may involve invention, but it requires many other things as well—including a deep understanding of whether customers need or desire that invention" (Keeley, Walters, Pikkel, & Quinn, 2013).
- The quality of a firm's customer experience strongly relates to loyalty measures such as willingness to consider the company for another purchase, likelihood to switch business, and likelihood to recommend to friends and family. These factors are strongly related to yearly revenue (Burns, Manning, & Petersen, 2012).
- Improving customer experience, even in small ways, "can translate into billions of dollars of incremental revenue per year.... No industry is totally immune from the revenue impact of customer experience" (Manning & Bodine, 2012).
- Integrating UX early can save a huge amount of redesign effort in the long run. Sun demonstrated that $20,000 of upfront UX research could have saved $152 million (Rhodes, 2000).

Arguments and Counterarguments

Along the way, you may encounter arguments for avoiding user experience research. In Table 1.1, we present the most common arguments we have encountered and suggestions for how to handle them. On the left side of the table, there are statements you can quote directly, and on the right side are explanations of the rationale behind each quote.

Table 1.1: Arguments Against Doing UX Research and How to Counter Them

"We don't have time for such a study." or "We're already behind schedule."	
"We can scale the project to the time available. We could have some preliminary information to you in as little as a day." "Even if we cannot get the information in time to influence the upcoming release of the product, we can use data we collect now for future releases." "A little time now may save us a lot of time later. Inaccurate user experiences are responsible for up to 60% of the errors in software production alone (Weinberg, 1997)." "Poor user experience research practices can lead to delays. Sixty-three percent of large software projects significantly overran various estimates when planning and many of these relate to poor UX (Lederer & Prasad, 1992)."	A little information is better than no information. You want information to make an impact as soon as possible, but do not let this prevent you from collecting information altogether. It is fast and easy to show cases where products went wrong and could have been saved by conducting user research. See Hackos and Redish (1998) for a plethora of case studies. See also Johnson (2008), *GUI Bloopers 2.0, Chapter 8, Management Bloopers*. There were 24 different reasons for the inaccuracies in the estimates, and the four with the highest responsibility were related to a lack of poor user experience gathering (Marcus, 2002).
"We don't have money for such a study."	
"We can conduct a study for very little money." "The return on investment for creating a good user experience is very high. In a 2011 study, customer experience accounted for between $31 million and $1.2 billion of revenue." "Our competitors know the value of user research." "Incorporating ease of use into your products actually saves money. For every dollar spent to resolve a problem during product design, $10 would be spent on the same problem during development, and multiply to $100 or more if the problem had to be solved after the product's release." "We don't have money NOT to conduct such a study. The maintenance costs of unmet user needs can account for 80% of lifecycle costs."	Discount techniques are cheap. Start small and demonstrate value to build upon. User experience is an investment in future revenue (Forrester's North American Technographics Customer Experience Online Survey, Q4, 2011 (US)). Understanding your users provides a competitive edge. It is far more economical to consider user needs in the early stages of design than it is to solve them later. Robert Pressman calculated the cost at design, development, and release in *Software Engineering: A Practitioner's Approach* (IBM, 2001 via Marcus, 2002). Eighty percent of software life-cycle costs occur during the maintenance phase. Most maintenance costs are associated with "unmet or unforeseen" user requirements and other usability problems (Pressman, 1992 via Marcus, 2002).
"It's not our problem if users are stupid."	
"You are not the user. Just because people aren't like you (e.g., don't know every keyboard shortcut by heart or can't recall 25 different 30-character passwords) doesn't mean they are stupid. Not everyone has had the same experiences and training as you."	Findings from user research can help show stakeholders (often engineers) that even other very smart people do not use products the same way they do. The key to countering this argument is to help stakeholders realize they are not a good representation of the people who will be end users.
"Users don't know what they want," or "If you asked users what they wanted, they would have said a faster horse."	
"It's not the job of the users to be able to articulate exactly what they want or need. It's my job to study how people behave and what they need. I elicit relevant information from them and translate that into useful, actionable information."	Understanding users is a skill that takes training and practice, just like all the other roles in product development. Users should not be mistaken for designers. It is the UX team and the product team who are responsible for providing potential solutions.
"We don't want to ruin any potential deals or make the customer unhappy by pointing out what our product doesn't do."	
"When systems match user needs, satisfaction often improves dramatically." "In all of our years of conducting user research and usability tests, we have never caused our company to lose a deal or caused a customer to be unhappy with our products. User experience research improves relationships with customers because they see your company is trying to understand them and their needs."	In a 1992 Gartner Group study, usability methods raised user satisfaction ratings for a system by 40% (Bias & Mayhew, 2005). If customers perceive that the product development or sales team is not meeting their needs, this will lead to unhappy customers and frustrated developers or salespeople.

Continued

Table 1.1: Cont'd

"Sales owns the customers."	
"We are all responsible for creating a user experience that is pleasant and satisfying for users." "If sales does not have time to help us find participants, we can figure that part out on our own." "It's our research."	Other stakeholders may fear that you will undermine their position and authority. Reassure them that UX has different goals from sales and your work will help them achieve their goals. In the end, if you cannot get access to customers, there are other ways of accessing end users (refer to Chapter 6, page 139). See Sharon (2012), *It's our research getting stakeholder buy-in for user experience research projects*, for a thorough introduction to helping the team take ownership of UX.
"You'll make promises we can't keep."	
"We will not make any promises to customers. We will listen and collect data only. The team will make decisions about how this information will be used in the product."	Participants understand that you are seeking their input and will not expect you to immediately create a magical product that fits all their desires, and you will not promise to either.
"You'll let out confidential information."	
"We have all our participants sign a non-disclosure agreement." "We will develop a standard script and pass it by everyone for review prior to using it with any participants."	If it is obvious to your participants what you are working on based on your questions, non-disclosure agreements (NDA; refer to Chapter 3, page 76) can be put in place to keep them quiet.
"We have information already. Why collect more?" or "I've been in this business for a decade. I think I know what our customers want."	
"That information is good and we do not intend to replace it. However, we need additional information to supplement what you have already learned." "The methods we use and goals we have are different from those that were used to collect that information. We want to make sure we have unbiased, empirical data."	Show how the information you plan to collect will be different. For example, you want to interview actual end users, not purchasing decision-makers; or you want to learn how users currently complete tasks, not get feedback on a prototype. The product team may have already conducted their own "focus groups," the marketing department may have already interviewed potential users, or the sales team may have already conducted their own "site visits," but these teams have different goals.
"We are introducing a different process, so don't waste your time studying the current process."	
"We need to understand the user's current environment, even if it will change to understand what challenges we may end up facing when changing the process." "We need to understand how people currently work, so we can leverage the good and leave the bad behind."	You also want to understand a transfer of training. You could end up designing something that is incompatible with current practices. You also need to understand the ripple effect of your changes. You may end up inadvertently affecting other groups/systems/customers.
"This product/process/service is completely new. There is nothing to observe."	
"If the potential users do not exist, who will buy the product?" "There is always someone or something we can learn from to inform your designs."	How was a need for the product determined in the first place? There has to be a manual or automated process currently in place. Look for the non-obvious.
"Everyone does it differently so there is no point studying a few users."	
"There will be individual differences. This is why we want to study a range of users and environments." "Studying even five users can reveal 80% of the most critical issues users may encounter."	The differences may also be smaller than everyone assumed. If the differences are large, knowing that is important. Studying "a few" users can be useful (Nielsen, 2000).
"We're changing just one part of the system/product/environment. We don't need to study more than that."	
"The most successful systems are developed when all parts integrate seamlessly—and this cannot happen if we only consider each part in isolation."	Systems are much more interrelated than most people realize. You need to understand the context that the change fits into. Users do not work in isolation.
"We don't need this method. The product is only for our own organization. Plus, the time you'll take with our employees isn't billable."	
"The productivity hit is actually twice as bad when an unusable product is implemented in your own organization. Employees are less productive and they depend on the support of people in your organization to help them."	Frame the time as an investment. Time that is spent now will save time, and thus costs later. Try to schedule participants during time that employees are not at their max productivity. For example, are there some people who are between contracts?

Preventing Resistance

The best way to combat resistance is to avoid it all together. There are two ways to accomplish this:

- Get stakeholder involvement.
- Become a virtual team member.

Get Stakeholder Involvement

One of the key themes that is reiterated throughout this book is "getting your product team (or stakeholders) involved." You want them to feel ownership over the activities that you conduct. You want to have their agreement and buy-in that user experience activities will benefit their product. If they do not believe in what you are doing or are skeptical, then they will likely be hesitant to implement your recommendations after the execution of your activity. To gain acceptance of user research, you need to involve them in all stages of the activity—from the preparation stages to the recommendations stage.

Become a Virtual Team Member

If you are not organizationally a member of the product team, you will want to virtually become a member. From the moment you are assigned to the project, you will want to work to become an active, recognized member of the product development team. You want to be perceived as part of the team; otherwise, it is too easy to be forgotten in the distribution of critical information or in a meeting that is deciding directions without critical input that you can provide.

If you work in a consulting capacity, the product development team may view you as an outsider. Even if you are a dedicated resource to that product, the developers or management may not view you as a team member because of your unique skill-set. Deliverables such as your activity proposals and activity findings may not be taken with the same sense of ownership if you are not seen as "one of them." The product team may even feel that you are not knowledgeable enough about the product to be taken seriously. Clearly, this is a detriment to your work.

The ideal situation is when you can become a virtual member of their team. You need to be as knowledgeable about the product and the factors that feed into the process as possible. You want to be perceived as someone who contributes to developing solutions for the product, rather than just identifying problems with existing solutions. This may require you to develop technical expertise and attend weekly staff meetings that do not always apply to user research and design. You will need to gain the respect and trust of the team, and this takes time. You are not there to sabotage their hard work; you are there to help them develop the best product they can. To do this, you need to understand how user research fits into the big picture. Of course, user research is critical for a successful product, but you must be willing to acknowledge that the users' needs are not the only requirements.

The earlier you can get involved, the better. The more time you spend with the team and the more familiar you become with the product, the more the team will respect you and your effort.

What Is Next?

Now that you know what user experience is, who does UX research, the principles of UCD, the stakeholders you will work with, and how to get buy-in for your research, it is time to start planning your user research activity. In the following chapters, we will teach you what you need to do before you choose a research activity, what ethical and legal issues you should consider, how to set up space in which to conduct user research, and how to choose and prepare for your user research activity.

CHAPTER 2

Before You Choose an Activity: Learning About Your Product Users

Introduction

When starting work on a new project, your first objectives are to learn about the product (if it already exists), domain, and (target) users. It is key for you to ascertain as much as possible about any existing products and domain in terms of functionality, competitors, and customers so you do not duplicate work or spend time generating knowledge that already exists. This is done by using the product yourself; reading customer support comments, social sentiment analysis, log files, and web analytics; speaking with your marketing department; conducting a competitive analysis; and getting feedback from early adopters or partners (e.g., trusted testers). In addition, you need to assess what is currently understood about the users and begin to create user profiles. This information will enable you to choose appropriate user research activities, so you can ultimately improve your product. In this chapter, we will detail how to collect product information from a variety of sources and how to make sense of the information readily available to you. We will also discuss how to create user profiles, personas, scenarios, guiding principles, and antiprinciples and how to use these as design tools, so you can maximize the impact of your research. Finally, we discuss special user types that you should keep in mind when designing your product: international users, challenged users, children, and older adults.

At a Glance

> Existing research
> Learn about your product
> Learn about your users
> Special populations
> Pulling it all together

Existing Research

It is a rare situation when people cannot learn something about their product domain by conducting a literature review. A search of a database dedicated to academic publications like Google Scholar can often yield insights that can jump-start your product development. You may be able to access some articles and patents for free, but other resources such as copyright-protected articles, will require a fee. You or your institution may be a member of an organization that provides access to certain resources. For example, if you are an ACM member, you have access to the ACM portal. If you work for a university, you will have access to many publications via your library.

Even if you do not have a membership, the process of searching can inform you of alternative terminology, related topics/domains, and new ways of thinking about your product. For example, when Kathy began working on a new domain (e-discovery) for Google, she began by doing a Google Scholar search for "e-discovery" and found some research articles. A general web search helped her identify alternative terms (e.g., ESI, digital forensics, spoliation) to do further searches on and expanded her understanding of the domain. Journal articles on your topic can also identify standardized questions for your future research.

Learn About Your Product

Before you even begin working with a single user, you need to understand the domain you are working in. We cannot stress enough how important it is to do your homework before jumping into one of the user research activities described in this book. You may be extremely pressed for time and think you can learn the domain while you are collecting data from users. Big mistake! You will need to answer many questions for yourself. What are the key planned or available functions of the product? Who are the competitors? Are there any known issues with the product? Who are the product's perceived users? In addition to helping you collect effective requirements, this knowledge will also earn you necessary respect and trust from the product team (refer to Chapter 1, "Become a Virtual Team Member" section, page 19).

We hope that the product team you are working with is composed of experts in the domain and that they have done their homework as well, but this is not always the case. Particularly with new products, the product team is learning about the users and the domain at the same time as you. It is important to interview the product team and learn everything you can from them, but you must also supplement that information with data from other sources. In addition, the more you know about the product and domain, the more respect you get from the product team. If you are new to the domain, you may never know as much as an expert product manager; however, there are always some fundamentals they will expect you to know or to pick up quickly. In the very beginning, you can get away with being naive, but with time, **stakeholders** will expect you to understand what they are talking about.

Keep in mind that this section of the chapter is not intended to tell you what to do *instead* of conducting user research. It is intended to tell you about some of the research you will want to conduct *before* you even consider running a user research activity.

If you do not have a background in **usability** or **user experience research**, you will need to be aware of some of the founding principles. You need to understand what questions can be answered by a user experience research activity and what questions a design professional should answer.

Suggested Resources for Further Reading

There are many colleges and universities with master's and PhD programs in human-computer interaction (HCI), engineering psychology, information sciences, and similar. If you do not have a degree in these or a related field, the books below can offer an introduction to the concepts discussed in this book:

- Norman, D. A. (2013). *The design of everyday things: Revised and expanded edition.* Basic Books.
- Lidwell, W., Holden, K., & Butler, J. (2010). *Universal principles of design, revised and updated: 125 ways to enhance usability, influence perception, increase appeal, make better design decisions, and teach through design.* Rockport Pub.

- Rogers, Y. (2012). HCI theory: classical, modern, and contemporary. *Synthesis Lectures on Human-Centered Informatics*, *5*(2), 1–129.
- Johnson, J. (2014). *Designing with the mind in mind: Simple guide to understanding user interface design guidelines* (2nd ed.). Morgan Kaufmann.
- Weinschenk, S. (2011). *100 things every designer needs to know about people*. Pearson Education.

Data are out there that can help you learn a lot about your product, if it currently exists. If it does not, you may be limited to a literature review and a **competitive analysis** (see page 32). In this section, we tell you how you can use log files, marketing, customers, and general research to help you become a domain expert.

At a Glance

> Use your product
> Networking
> Customer support comments
> Social network analysis
> Log files and web analytics
> Your marketing department
> Competitors
> Early adopter or partner feedback

Use Your Product

The best way to learn about your product is to use it (if it already exists). In the case of a travel app, you should search for a hotel and flight, make a reservation, cancel your reservation, ask for help, etc. Stretch the product to its limits. Be sure to note possible pain points so you spot them if your participants encounter them as well. It will be easier to identify patterns if you have some ideas of what to look for.

Networking

You are surrounded by people who know about your product and domain; you just have to get to know them. If you work at a company, start by finding out if it has ever conducted user research in the past (in-house or hired a vendor). Read any existing research reports to see if there are known issues and/or existing user requirements. Meet the content writers for the company. These are the folks who create the user manuals and online help (for websites and web applications). Ask them what is difficult to document. Is it because it is difficult to articulate, or is the product itself too complicated to explain?

If you work in academia, or if your company offers training courses, attend classes and speak with the folks who teach the courses. What is hard to teach? What types of question are users asking? What tips (not documented) are the instructors offering?

Customer Support Comments

If you are working on a product that already has an existing version and your company has a help desk or customer support group, you can learn a great deal about your product by visiting that department. If you work independently, you can often find customer comments available online.

People rarely call or e-mail with compliments to tell a company how wonderful their product is, so customer calls pertain to issues you should become familiar with. If you can access logs of customer questions, problems, and complaints over time, you will see trends of difficulties users are encountering. Perhaps the user's manual or help is not helpful enough. Perhaps the product has a bug that was not captured during quality assurance (QA), or perhaps users do not like or cannot figure out a feature the product team thought every user had to have. This can give you a sense of where you will need to focus your efforts to improve the product.

Users may not be able to accurately describe the problem they are having or may misdiagnose the cause. Likewise, customer support may not have experience with the product under consideration. Although this should never be the case, it often is. If your support staff is not very familiar with the product in question, they may also misdiagnose the cause of the customer's problem or may not capture the issue correctly. This means that once you have a log of customer feedback, you may need to conduct interviews or field studies with users to get a full understanding of the issues.

Social Sentiment Analysis

People could be talking about your product and brand right now! According to the Pew Research Center's Internet and American Life Project, 73% of American online adults use social media (as of September 2013). Ninety-five percent of people say they share bad product experiences online and 45% share bad customer service experiences via Facebook, Twitter, and other platforms (Costa et al., 2013). However, 87% say they share good customer service interactions online, too. So whether you know it or not, you have a presence on social media.

Does your company have a Facebook or Google Plus page? A Twitter feed? If so, speak with the people at your company whose job it is to respond to user comments, often called "community managers" or the like. Whether you have a formal presence on a social networking site or not, do a search of the various sites and see what people have said. Using a tool like *Radian6*, *Crimson Hexagon*, *Sysomos*, or *Clarabridge*, you can analyze the sentiment of those comments. Using these tools, you can:

- Learn what users are saying right now
- Learn what users say they like and do not like about your product/service

- Learn emerging trends or topics
- See where your users are that are talking about you
- Track how your customer base is changing over time and in response to campaigns

Figure 2.1 shows a photo of the Clemson University Social Media Listening Center as an example of what you might see. These tools can take a first pass at detecting positive and negative sentiment, but many will be labeled as "unknown." You will have to manually review those and mark them as positive or negative. Good tools will learn based on your feedback, but be wary of sarcasm and slang, as many tools are unable to accurately categorize them.

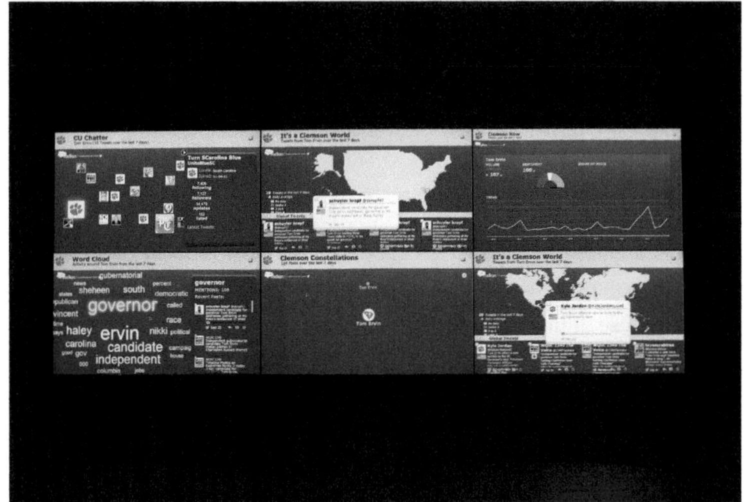

Figure 2.1: Social sentiment monitoring at Clemson University. *Photo courtesy of the Clemson University Social Media Listening Center.*

Log Files and Web Analytics

If you are responsible for the usability of a website, web server **log files** may provide an interesting perspective for you. When a file is retrieved from a website, server software keeps a record of it. The server stores this information in the form of text files.

The information contained in a log file varies but will typically include the source of a request, the file requested, the date and time of the request, the content type and length of the transferred file, the referring page, the user's browser and platform, and error messages. Figure 2.2 shows a sample of a server log file.

Services like Google Analytics are available that capture user behavior across your site by implanting code on the website. There are also analytics tools to give more insight into what happens within pages (e.g., Crazy Egg, ClickTale) by recording user actions within a page in a more fine-grained way. However, you may need to work

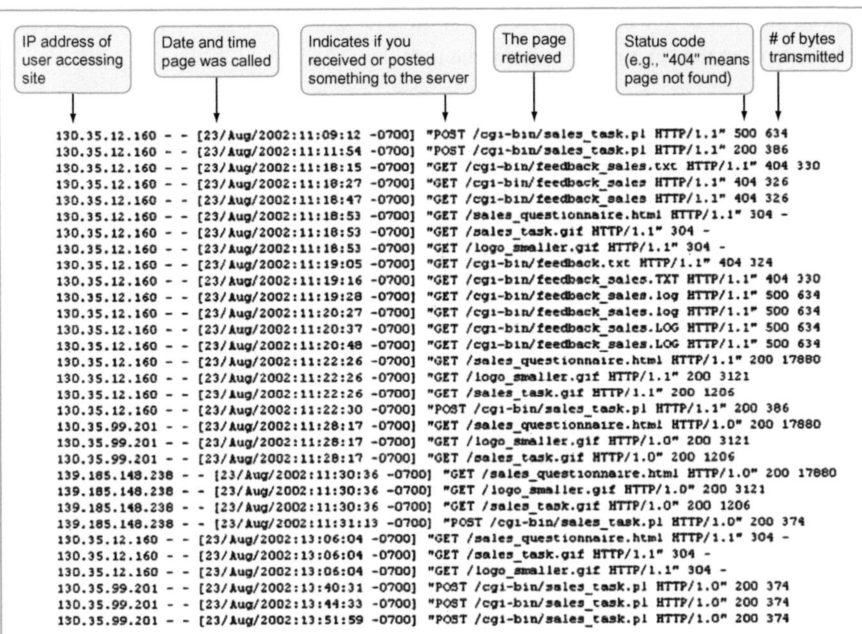

Figure 2.2: Sample server log file.

with your organization's IT department to collect log data, store it, and extract it in order to conduct user research or usability analysis. Information that can be captured includes the following:

- Unique ID for each visitor so you can see who is returning.
- Click path (i.e., the pages users visit and the sequence in which they visit them).
- Time spent per page.
- Where visitors leave the site (what page).
- Actions taken (e.g., purchases made, downloads completed, information viewed).

There are some issues or limitations that you should be aware of when interpreting the data you collect from log files:

- The log files often contain an **Internet Protocol** (IP) address temporarily assigned by an **Internet service provider** (ISP) or a corporate **proxy** server. This prevents unique identification of each user. Be aware that under some circumstances (e.g., children, certain countries), IP addresses are considered personally identifiable information (PII). It is good practice to remove any potentially identifiable information from log files prior to analysis.
- Browser **caching** leaves gaps in the recorded **click stream**. If a page is cached, the log files do not record the second, third, or hundredth time it is visited during the user's stay at your site. Depending on your tools, you may or may not be able to capture the pages called when the back browser button is used. Consequently, the last

page recorded in the log file may not be the last page viewed, if the user exited on a previously cached page. As a result, you cannot be sure what the "exit page" was for the user.

- Log files record when a request was made for a page but not when the transfer was completed. Also, if a user spends 30 minutes on a single page, you do not know why. Did the user walk away or look at another site or program, or was the user viewing the page the entire time?
- You cannot be sure whether the user completed his or her goal (i.e., purchasing, downloading, looking for information) if you do not know the user's goal. Perhaps the user wanted to buy three CDs but could find only one. Perhaps the user was looking for information and never found it.

You can work with your IT department to address *some* of these issues, but it takes time and knowledge of *what you need* versus *what can be captured.* External companies like *WebTrends* (www.netiq.com/webtrends/default.asp) can be hired to help if you are unfamiliar with this. These companies are a great source of basic usage data once you have a website running (e.g., number of page views per hour or per day, what page the user came from, how the user got there, time spent on the homepage, number of excursions to other pages, time spent on each page, ads clicked on).

Examining the time users spend per page is a more meaningful measure than the number of **page views** per page. When analyzing time data in a log file, it is best to use **median** or trimmed mean rather than average times because they are less susceptible to **outliers.** You must look at your distribution and decide if throwing out clear high and low outliers will make a mean useful or if you really need a median. Unfortunately, if you are using web analytics tools, you probably will not get to see the variance in values. However, there is typically a cap on high outlying time values because if a user spends more than half an hour inactive, it will get counted as an exit and excluded from the time-on-page calculation.

Probably the most interesting data for you will be click-path analysis, segmenting users based on behavior on your site and then comparing those user types, seeing how users got to your site, and analyzing what they searched for. However, it is best to study log files and web analytics over a long period to discover data that complement or spur studies in greater depth. For example, you can identify areas of a site for further testing, look for seasonal trends, and see how redesigns in your site affect user behavior.

TIP

The "big data" you can capture from log analysis can offer incredible insights about user behavior, but it can never tell you about the user's context or motivation. In other words, it can give you the *what* but not the *why.* In order to understand user goals, context, and whether or not they were successful at what they were trying to do, you must triangulate the data with other sources. For example, if you can conduct a **survey** (see Chapter 10) in the midst of customers using your product and you can tie that to the logs of their actions, you can get a more complete picture.

Suggested Resources for Additional Reading

- Beasley, M. (2013). *Practical web analytics for user experience: How analytics can help you understand your users*. Morgan Kaufmann.
- Jansen, B. J. (2009). Understanding user-web interactions via web analytics. *Synthesis Lectures on Information Concepts, Retrieval, and Services*, 1(1), 1–102.
- Rodden, K., Hutchinson, H., & Fu, X. (2010, April). Measuring the user experience on a large scale: user-centered metrics for web applications. In *Proceedings of the SIGCHI conference on human factors in computing systems* (pp. 2395–2398). New York: ACM.

Your Marketing Department

Frequently, your company's marketing department will conduct focus groups or **competitive analysis** (see next section) to determine the need for a product and how best to promote and place it. Although this information is meant to drive sales, it is an excellent source to learn about the product, as well as potential customers and competitors.

Marketing information should not be confused with user requirements. The data from the marketing department *can* reflect the end users' needs, but not always. Marketing collects information about the value and perceived worth of a product, whereas user research professionals collect information about how something is used and how the product's worth is realized.

Additionally, the information you collect from the marketing department is only part of the information needed when creating a user profile. It is often missing contextual information about circumstances and environment that can affect a user's decision to use and how to use your product. This is often the case for products that are to be used by corporations rather than an individual (e.g., human resources applications versus a website designed to sell books to the public). In the case of corporate products, the marketing department is typically interested in the business needs of the marketplace (i.e., companies that could be potential buyers) rather than the end users. Regardless, this information can be very helpful to you when you are starting out.

When you contact the marketing department, you may want to ask them questions, such as:

- Where are you collecting your data?
- Who are our competitors?
- What is the profile of the people you have spoken with, and how did you find them?
- What activities have you conducted (e.g., focus groups, surveys)?
- When is your next activity scheduled?
- Have you conducted a **competitive analysis**?
- What are the requirements you have collected?

Competitors

You can learn a lot from your competitors. A **competitive analysis** lists the features, strengths, weaknesses, user base, and price point for your competitors. It should include not only first-hand experience with the product(s) but also user reviews and analysis from external experts or trade publications.

This can be an effective way to gain an advantage over your competitors. It is beneficial to conduct a competitive analysis when you are creating an entirely new product or simply entering a new product domain. It can also be a great strategy if your product is failing, but your competitor's product is thriving. It is wise to periodically check out your competition to see where you stand with the rest of the pack. Some companies have product analysts whose primary job is to keep tabs on the competitors and the market. Get to know this person and learn everything he or she knows. If the product does not have a product analyst, this is something that you can do.

TIP

When leveraging your competitor's successes, keep in mind copyright laws and intellectual property rights. If you are not sure where the line is between public domain and intellectual property, consult a lawyer or your company's legal department.

Do not limit yourself to direct competitors. You should also examine **surrogate products.** These products may or may not compete directly with your product, but they have similar features to your product and should be studied to learn about your strengths and weaknesses. For example, if you are adding a shopping cart to your travel app, check out companies that have shopping carts, even if they do not compete with you (e.g., online book stores). Some people make the mistake of thinking their product or service is so innovative that no one else does it; therefore, they skip competitive analysis. No product is so revolutionary that there is not someone out there from which to learn.

Traditional competitive analysis focuses more on cost, buying trends, and advertising. A usability competitive analysis is more concerned with the user experience (e.g., user interface, features, user satisfaction, overall usability). The goals of both types of competitive analyses are to learn from your competitors and to snag a strategic advantage. Below, we will concentrate on conducting a usability competitive analysis.

To identify your competitors, speak with the product team and sales or marketing department, conduct a web search, read trade magazines, and conduct user surveys, interviews, or focus groups. Market analysts and researchers (e.g., CNET, ZDNet, Gartner, Anderson, Forrester Research, IDC) can be a great way to collect information about your product's market space and competitors. These companies identify and analyze emerging trends in products and their impact on business.

Keep in mind primary competitors as well as secondary competitors. A secondary competitor can be a smaller company with a less threatening product offering, one having only a few features in common with your product, or one competing indirectly with your product. For example, the brick-and-mortar travel agency does not compete directly with your online travel company, but it is an alternative that should not be ignored.

Once you have identified your competitors, you should ascertain their:

- Strengths
- Weaknesses
- Customer base (profile of users, size of customer base, loyalty, etc.)
- Availability
- Functionality and unique features
- Reputation
- Requirements (hardware, software, etc.)

If a product can be bought off the shelf or is an easily accessible website, this should not be a problem. However, some products or services are sold only directly to companies. Many major software companies state in their licensing agreement that you are not allowed to conduct competitive tests against their product. They also state that you cannot show the installation of the product (or the product in use) to a competitor company. Check with your legal department for advice before proceeding.

If you are able to evaluate the competitor product yourself, you should identify a set of core tasks with which to compare your product (if you have one at this stage) and the competitor's. This is particularly important if you plan to include functionality from the other product, because you may learn that a function does not work well. Take numerous screenshots or photos and record your interaction as you conduct the evaluation.

Whether or not you are able to access the product yourself, interviews (Chapter 9, page 220), surveys (Chapter 10, page 266), focus groups (Chapter 12, page 340), and evaluations (Chapter 14, page 432) will be valuable ways to learn about users' perceptions of the product. By conducting these kinds of activities with users of your competitor's products, you can learn about the strengths, weaknesses, and key features of these products. In a competitive analysis, the majority of your effort should be spent mining the competitor's product for ideas (e.g., functionality, user interface style, widgets, task structure, terminology).

There are a number of companies available to measure the usability or user satisfaction of a website (e.g., Bizrate Insights, OpinionLab, User Focus). They can do this for your site or for your competitor's site. These companies send actual or target customers to any website (i.e., yours or a competitor's) and then collect qualitative, quantitative, and behavioral data as users pursue actual tasks in a natural environment, such as their own homes and offices. Most companies allow clients to easily analyze both the quantitative and qualitative data gathered during an evaluation. This approach can be quite beneficial, but it is often expensive and requires that users can easily access the website. If the web-based product must be purchased or is behind a **firewall**, you will have to provide the users with access. In the case of a competitor that sells licensed software, this option is more difficult and more expensive. For example, you may need to send participants to a dummy page where they get assigned a dummy product key, and proceed from there.

As you conduct your competitive analysis, it is helpful to create a grid comparing your product against the competitor's (see Table 2.1). List the key features, design strengths and weaknesses, usability scores or issues, or anything you can learn. Tracking this information over time will show you how your product compares and how the market may be changing.

Table 2.1: Grid comparing TravelMyWay.com against three competitors

	TravelMyWay.com	TravelTravel.com	WillTravel.com	Corner travel store
Unique features	Client recommendations Chat board	Customer loyalty program	Travel agent on call	Personalized service
Design strengths	Short three-step process Shows price comparison	Useful travel guides Customer and expert ratings	Shows price comparison Travel alerts and recommendations	Frequent customer program Phone access or in person
Design weaknesses	Must know three-letter airport code			
	Customer support/help is hidden	Cluttered display with too many options		
		Confusing search UI	Search results are inconsistent and not reliable	No web access
Customer base	2,500 users	500,000 users	150,000 users	Customer size unknown
Satisfaction score	68	72	Not available	Not applicable
Requirements	Section 508 compliant Accessible on all browser types	Internet Explorer only Flash required	Accessible on all browser types	No requirements
Core features				
Research locations	×	×	×	✓
Air travel	✓	✓	✓	✓
Rental car	✓	✓	✓	✓
Hotel reservations	✓	×	✓	✓
Train tickets	✓	✓	×	✓
Bus tickets	×	✓	×	✓
Travel packages	✓	✓	✓	✓

Early Adopter or Partner Feedback

Frequently, companies will align themselves with a small number of customers, sometimes referred to as "trusted testers," in the early stages of development. These customers may play an active role in the design of the product and become partners in the process. They may implement early versions of the product on a small scale in their own companies. This relationship is beneficial to all parties. The customers get to help design the product to meet the needs of their own companies. On the other side, the product team gets early feedback to "fail fast" and iterate, as well as ask early adopters for references when selling the product to others.

The feedback early adopters provide can be enlightening because the product can be implemented and used in a real-world setting (as opposed to testing in the lab). You can leverage these existing relationships to learn about the product space and some of the product's known issues. However, when you are ready to move on to the next stage and collect user requirements, be wary of basing your user requirements on the few early adopters as they may not be representative of *all* of your user base. You should obtain user requirements from a variety of users (refer to Section "Learn About Your Users" below).

Learn About Your Users

At a Glance

> User profile
> Personas
> Scenarios

The single most critical activity in developing a quality product is to understand who your users are and what they need and to document what you have learned. This begins by developing a **user profile**—a detailed description of your users' attributes (e.g., job title, experience, level of education, key tasks, age range, etc.). These characteristics will typically reflect a range, not a single attribute (e.g., ages 18-35). A user profile will help you understand who you are building your product for and will help you when recruiting for future user research activities.

Once you have developed a thorough user profile, you can develop **personas** (exemplars of your end user) and **scenarios** (a day in the life of your end user).

- Personas are designed to help keep specific users in focus during design discussions.
- Scenarios help you test your system and build functionality into your product that users will actually want to use.

Table 2.2: Comparison of user profiles, personas, and scenarios

Document	Definition	Purpose	Content
User profile	Detailed description of your users' attributes	To ensure that you know who you are developing your product for and who to recruit for research activities	• Demographic data • Skills • Education • Occupation
Persona	A fictional individual created to describe the typical user based on the user profile	To represent a group of end users during design discussions and keep everyone focused on the same target	• Identity and photo • Status • Goals and tasks • Skill set • Requirements and expectations • Relationships
Scenario	Story that describes how a particular persona completes a task or behaves in a given situation	To bring your users to life, test to see if your product meets the users' needs, and develop artifacts for research activities (e.g., tasks for usability tests and day-in-the-life videos for focus groups)	• Setting • Actors • Objectives or goals • Sequence of events • Result

Table 2.2 compares these three types of user documents. You may have very little information to develop these initially—that is why you conduct user requirements activities. As you conduct user research activities, you will collect information to feed back into the user profiles, personas, and scenarios. Figure 2.3 illustrates the relative time to spend at each stage of the cycle. Please note its iterative nature; you should always feed the results of requirements activities back into your initial understanding of your users. User profiles, personas, and scenarios are discussed in detail in the following sections.

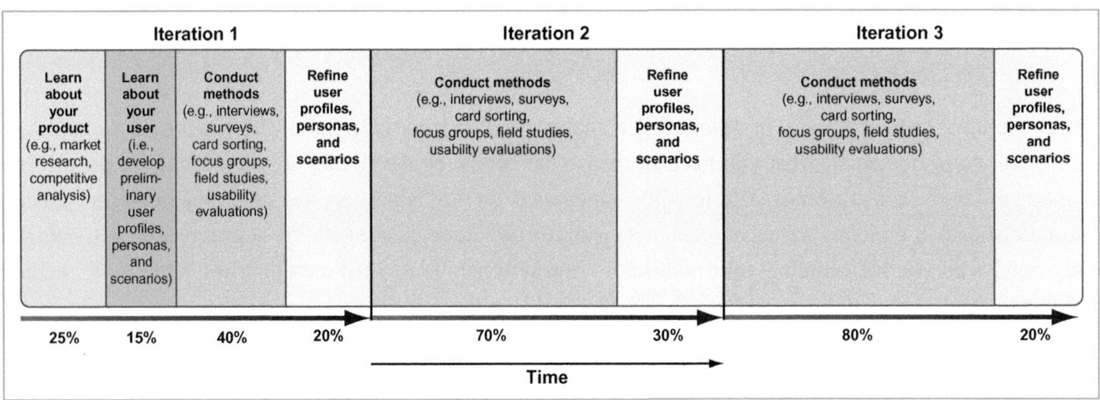

Figure 2.3: Illustration of the relative time to spend at each stage of the life cycle. This is the ideal case with multiple iterations.

Keep in mind as you learn about your users that you should not focus on only the "best" or most experienced users. Someone who is considered an expert on a system may not be an expert on all parts of the system. It is much more likely that an individual will leverage only key areas of the product over and over while ignoring other parts. You should consider a range of users to ensure that your product works for the majority of your user population. The only way to know if your product works for the majority of your user population is by doing research. Depending on your user type or product, this may require a satisfaction survey of your users (see Chapter 10, page 266) or field study observations (see Chapter 13, page 380) or a usability evaluation (see Chapter 14, page 432).

Step 1: User Profile

At a Glance

> Finding information to build your user profile
> Understanding the types of users
> Creating a user profile

The first step in understanding your users is to create a user profile.

Finding Information to Build Your User Profile

It is vital to get the right users for your research; otherwise, not only are the data you collect worthless, they can actually harm your product, your credibility, and the credibility of the research. But who are your users? What are their goals?

You should begin by developing a user profile. For example, the typical user might be between 18 and 35 years of age; have job titles like "travel specialist," "travel agent," or "travel assistant" and work for travel agencies with fewer than 50 employees.

Creating a user profile is an iterative process. You will likely have some idea of who your users are at first, but this will probably not be detailed and may even be just a guess. But it is a place to start. The example above is just our first, best guess of who our travel agent user might be. You can capture the initial information to build your user profile from the following:

- Product managers
- Functional specifications
- Industry analysts
- Marketing studies
- Market analysts
- Customer support
- Competitive benchmarking and analysis
- Census bureau
- Surveys

Understanding the Types of Users

You need to define what you mean by "user." Most people consider the individuals who will interact directly with the product as their users, but you may need to consider other individuals as well:

- The manager of your direct user
- The system administrator who configures the product for the direct user
- People who receive artifacts or information from the system
- People deciding whether they will purchase your software
- People who use competitors' products (you want to convert them to use your product)

Try to categorize your users into one of three categories: primary, secondary, and tertiary. **Primary users** are those individuals who work regularly or directly with the product. **Secondary users** use the product infrequently or through an intermediary. **Tertiary users** are those who are affected by the system or the purchasing decision-makers. All of these individuals have an interest in the product. This does not mean that you have to conduct user requirements activities with the secondary and tertiary users, but you should at least know who they are. If the tertiary decision-makers do not purchase your product, the primary users will never use it. If the secondary system administrators cannot figure out how to customize and implement the product, the primary users will have a painful experience with it.

It is also important to realize that a single user may have several roles, and sometimes, these roles can have contradictory needs. For example, many online auction users are both buyers and sellers. Buyers want to pay the least they can, while sellers want to get as much as they can, and a single auction site must support both these contradictory roles without harming either. Additionally, the product should behave similarly for both roles—users should not have to learn a different interaction model, navigation, terminology, etc., based on their role. Only the information presented and some of the functions available should be different.

Creating a User Profile

There are several characteristics you need to consider to develop a thorough user profile. We provide an *ideal* list of characteristics below, but you will likely not have access to all of this information. As you do further research and conduct additional user requirement activities, you will fill in these blanks, but you may never find the answers to some of the questions. Ideally, you should determine not only the typical or most frequent level for each of the characteristics but also the range and the percentage of users who fall along that range. As a final note, some of the characteristics on page 39 are more important than others in regard to your product and situation. Prioritize the characteristics and spend the majority of resources capturing information on those key characteristics for your product. For example, if a human resources administrator enters the wrong social security number into a financial application, an employee might not get paid. This is terrible, but if a medical professional enters the wrong social security number in an electronic chart, a patient might get the wrong medication. This is much more serious, so it is important to understand not only the tasks a user does but also the consequences of a possible error. Figure 2.4 shows a sample user profile. The US Census (census.gov) and Pew Research Center (www.pewinternet.org/) have well-tested questions and options for capturing demographic data, so we recommend referring to their surveys when designing yours:

Travel Agent (primary) Characteristic Ranges	
Age:	25-40 years (Average: 32 years)
Gender:	80% female
Job Titles:	Travel agent, Travel specialist, Travel associate
Experience Level:	0-10 years (Typical: 3 years)
Work Hours:	40 hours per week; days and times depend on the company
Education:	High school to Bachelor's degree (Typical: some college)
Location:	Anywhere in the U.S. (Predominantly mid-west)
Income:	\$25,000-\$50,000/year; depends on experience level and location (Average: \$35,000/year)
Technology:	Some computer experience; high-speed Internet connection
Disabilities:	No specific limitations
Family:	Single or married (Predominantly married with one child)

Figure 2.4: Sample user profile for a travel agent.

- *Demographic characteristics*—age, gender, location, socioeconomic status
- *Occupation experience*—current job title, years at the company, years of experience at that position, responsibilities, previous jobs and job titles
- *Company information*—company size, industry
- *Education*—degree, major, courses taken
- *Computer experience*—computer skills, years of experience
- *Specific product experience*—experience with competitors' products or other domain-specific products, usage trends
- *Tasks*—primary tasks, secondary tasks
- *Domain knowledge*—the users' understanding of the product area
- *Technology available*—computer hardware (monitor size, computing speed, etc.), software, other tools typically used
- *Attitudes and values*—product preferences, fear of technology, etc.
- *Learning style*—visual learner, audio learner, etc.
- *Criticality of errors*—in general, the possible consequences of a user's error

Once you determine the range of responses for each of the characteristics and the percentage of users along that range, you will want to categorize your users into groups based on their similarities. Some groupings you may use are the following:

- Age (e.g., child, young adult, adult, older adult)
- Experience (e.g., novice, expert)
- Attitudes (e.g., first adopters, technophobe)
- Primary task(s) (e.g., buyer, seller)

You can use an **affinity diagram** to organize the characteristics into groups (see Chapter 12, Focus Groups, page 363). The groups should be significantly different from each other in order to justify them as different user types.

As with many things, this is more of an art than a science, and there are rarely clearly marked boundaries that put every user in one group or another. Having multiple stakeholders take part in the affinity diagram exercise can help when creating these groups and also assures stakeholder buy-in from the very beginning (refer to Chapter 1, "Getting Stakeholder Buy-in for Your Activity" section, page 16).

Now that you have a handle on your user population, you can develop personas, scenarios, and a recruitment screener (refer to Chapter 6, "Recruiting Participants" section, page 126).

Step 2: Personas

At a Glance

> Benefits of personas

> Things to be aware of when creating personas

> Creating a persona

"According to my Zip Code, I prefer non-spicy foods, enjoy tennis more than golf, subscribe to at least one news-oriented periodical, own between thirty and thirty-five ties, never buy lemon-scented products, and have a power tool in my basement, but none of that is true."

© The New Yorker Collection 1993 Roz Chast from cartoonbank.com. All rights reserved

Alan Cooper developed a method called "Goal-Directed Design" in which **personas** are a key part. Personas were first introduced to the world in Cooper's 1999 book *The Inmates are Running the Asylum*.

Benefits of Personas

Personas take a user profile and then fill in details to create a "typical" user. A persona is simply a fictional individual created to describe a specific user. Since you cannot possibly speak with every end user, you must create a model that can represent those end users.

There are many benefits to using personas. Because it can be difficult to feel connected to an abstract description of something, personas give your users life and help team members feel connected to them. They also get everyone on the same page by encouraging all team members to think about the same persona, instead of each individual working toward his or her own vision of who the end user is. Trying to build a product for the generic "user" is like trying to hit a moving target. Without a specific target to focus on, "the user" can change from the expert to the novice to your grandmother, all in the midst of a single conversation. Designing for a small set of personas will assure greater success of hitting that target. A persona can be used in meetings as a discussion tool (e.g., Zhiwei would never use that feature), in cognitive walk-throughs, **storyboarding,** role-playing, and other user research activities. Finally, personas can also help new team members quickly learn who the end user is. You should create at least one persona per user type (e.g., one for the travel agent, one for the travel customer).

Things to Be Aware of When Creating Personas

You may want to develop multiple personas for each user type. This will help you cover the range of characteristics for each user type. For example, if one of your user types is a "novice travel agent," you may want to create multiple "novice" personas: one at a small company, one at a large company, one who received formal training, one who was self-taught, etc. By limiting your vision to just one persona, you may end up filtering out valuable data from end users who do not match that one profile. For example, if we did not create a persona for the self-taught travel agent, team members might assume all travel agents receive formal training and make all their design decisions based on that fact. Having multiple personas for each user type will prevent people from building the product around a single user and help develop a product that works for all of your users. However, you should keep the set of personas manageable. It is a balancing act. If you have too many personas to represent one user type, they will simply blur together in everyone's mind and diminish their benefits. You want your personas to be memorable. Only create as many personas as needed based on significant behavioral differences.

You must also make sure that the personas you devise are specific to the product or feature you are developing. As we mentioned above, not all users use all parts of a product or system; therefore, it is unrealistic to assume that the same persona will work for all parts of your product.

As a final note, we want to stress that personas should never replace conducting user research activities with your end users. Personas should be based on the data from user research activities and not simply describe the ideal user the team *wants* to have.

Creating a Persona

There are several components to a persona. You can add as much detail to each of these areas as you have, but you may not be able to fill in all areas at first. The details will come from the information in your user profile. Just as developing a user profile is an iterative process, so is persona development. As you conduct user requirement activities, you should take what you learn to validate and beef up your personas. When creating a persona, it should be fictional but describe attributes from real users. Provide details and maintain authenticity. The list below is an idealized list—you may not have all the information below (fill in what you can):

- *Identity*. Give this user a first and last name. Provide an age and other demographic data that would be representative of the user profile.
- *Status*. Is this a primary user, secondary user, tertiary user, or **antiuser** of your system?
- *Goals*. What are these user's goals, particularly those related to your specific product or competitor products?
- *Skill set*. What is the background and expertise of your user? This includes education, training, and specialized skills. Again, do not limit yourself to details related to your specific product.
- *Tasks*. What are the basic or critical tasks the user conducts? What are the frequency, importance, and duration of those tasks? More detailed task information is included in scenarios (see below).
- *Relationships*. Understanding with whom the user associates is important. Including relationships in the persona keeps you thinking about secondary and tertiary stakeholders.
- *Requirements*. What does your user need in order to use your product or be successful using it (e.g., high-speed Internet connection, specific mobile phone OS, specific training or education)? Including quotes will really drive those needs home.
- *Expectations*. How does the user think the product works? How does the user organize the information in his or her domain/job?
- *Photograph*. Include a photo in your persona to put a human face to your end user.

TIP

It is helpful to give your personas disabilities of one kind or another. Even though a minority of your users may have disabilities at any given time, designing for people with disabilities will tend to help everyone, and building accessibility into a product starts with thinking about users.

Just as there are several types of user profiles, there are several types of personas: primary user, secondary user, tertiary user, and the antiuser (or **negative users**). The primary, secondary, and tertiary users have been described. An antiuser is one who would not buy or use your product in any way. You want to keep this persona in mind to warn you when you are getting off track. For example, if you are designing a product for an expert user but find more and more instruction text, tutorials, and help dialogues creeping into the product, you should check your antiuser persona (a novice user in need of a "walk up and use" product) to see whether this product would now work for him or her. If so, you are on the wrong track. You want to be sure that you are designing for the primary user while considering the secondary and tertiary users. Figure 2.5 shows a persona for a travel agent.

Name: Alexandra Davis

Age: 32

Job: Travel agent at TravelMyWay.com for the past three years

Work hours: 8 am to 7 pm (Mon–Sat)

Education: B.A. Literature

Location: Denver, Colorado

Income: $45,000/yr

Technology: PC, 1024 × 768 monitor, T1 line

Disabilities: Wears contacts

Family: Married with 8-year-old twin daughters

Hobbies: Plan trips with her family

Goals: Double her productivity every year, travel to every continent at least once by age 35.

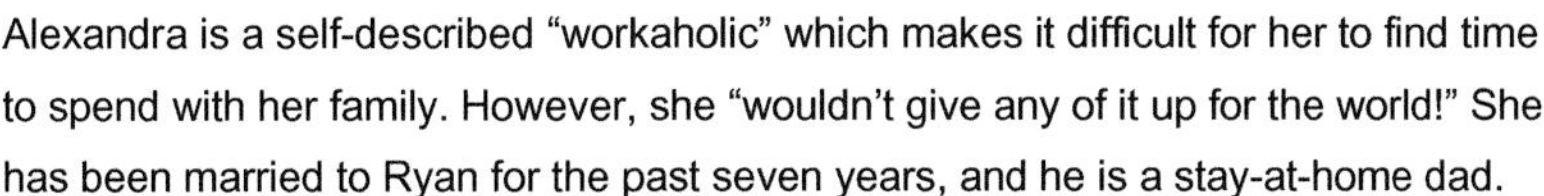

Alexandra is a self-described "workaholic" which makes it difficult for her to find time to spend with her family. However, she "wouldn't give any of it up for the world!" She has been married to Ryan for the past seven years, and he is a stay-at-home dad.

She loves the perks she gets working for TravelMyWay.com. She is able to travel all over the world with her family at a substantially reduced rate. This is very important to her, and she would not work those kinds of hours without such perks.

Alexandra began working as a travel agent right after college. She has used every system out there and is amazed at how difficult they are to use. Speed is the name of the game. "Clients don't want to sit on the phone and listen to typing for five minutes while I look up all the available five-star hotels in Barbados. I need that information with few keystrokes and all on one screen. Don't make me page through screen after screen to see the rates for all the hotels."

Alexandra loves helping clients design their dream vacations! She helps to take care of all of their travel needs, including choosing destinations, booking airfares, arranging car rentals, booking hotels, and arranging tickets for attractions. Clients often send Alexandra postcards and pictures from their destinations because they are so grateful for all her help. She appreciates the fact that TravelMyWay.com offers clients the opportunity to do it all themselves or to seek out the help of a professional. She feels that travel agents are sorely under-appreciated. "Of course people can make travel reservations on any website today. There are tons of them out there, and they all offer pretty much the same deals. But if you do not know anything about your destination, you could easily pick a bad hotel because their advertising literature is out of date, or you could pay too much because you do not know what to ask for. Travel agents do so much more than book flights!"

Figure 2.5: Sample persona for a travel agent. ©*Getty Images. Reprinted with permission.*

Things to Be Aware of When Using Personas

There are a few risks one should be aware of when creating and using personas. The first is that any time one distills a lot of data down to a generalized description, some data will be lost. You will miss out on the exceptions or edge cases that can be important to consider. If you base recruiting off of your personas, you may end up excluding valid users who do not neatly fit into one of your personas. This limiting of data is something to be aware of and regularly evaluate.

Just as your product may change over time, so may your users and their needs. As a result, your personas must be updated to reflect those changes or you risk designing your product around inaccurate data.

If multiple teams across your organization are also developing personas, share your data. It is likely that the same people who are using your product are also using other products from your company. By collaborating, you can develop richer personas that highlight cross-product use rather than potentially contradicting each other.

Personas should never replace ongoing user research. They are a helpful tool, but they can never replace the actual voice of your user throughout the development process.

Step 3: Guiding Principles/Antiprinciples

Most products begin with some kind of design document or spec that states the goal or purpose of the product and planned functionality to meet that goal. Despite this, teams can still end up with different understandings about what the product should do. To address this, it is helpful to list the **guiding principles** (GPs) for the product. This is a qualitative description of the principles the product stands by. Similarly, **antiprinciples** (APs) should be documented to explicitly state what this product does not intend to address. If you find your product can be described by any of the APs, you know you are off track. Although the APs can be the opposite of the GPs, they oftentimes include unique considerations. For example, an AP might be "ad-generating revenue." You are unlikely to have "negative ad revenue" or similar in your GPs. See Table 2.3 for an example.

Table 2.3: Example guiding principles and antiprinciples for TravelMyWay.com

Principle	**Definition**	**How to measure**
Guiding principles		
Easy to use	Customers can book a flight with 100% success rate without training or use of online help	Usability studies
Fast	Provide complete flight search results under 30 s	Log analysis
Complete	Show flight ticket information from every airline	Data feed
Lowest price	We offer the lowest price available among all of our competitors	Market analysis
The best	Highest satisfaction rating among travel apps	Surveys
Antiprinciples		
Ad-filled	Ads take up more than 10% of the screen real estate	UI evaluation
Untrustworthy	Customers are not sure they are getting the best price from our site	Surveys
Too smart	Site makes decisions for the user without the user's consent	Usability testing, surveys
Unprofessional	Use of hipster phrases, slang, or funny phrases in error messages and other communication	UI evaluation, surveys

Brainstorm

With your user personas in hand, the team should brainstorm all of the words and phrases they would like to hear users, marketing, and/or those reviewing your product to say when describing it. These will be your GPs. The Microsoft product reaction cards (Benedek & Miner, 2002) are a great way to jumpstart the process, but do not limit yourself to just those words. We have found that writing each word or phrase on a sticky note and taking turns to call them out before posting them on the whiteboard is fast, and it makes it easy to group similar concepts. In the end, you ideally want no more than 10 GPs to remember. You want these to be easy to remember so everyone can adhere to them during product development. A laundry list of principles will be unwieldy to manage.

Define It to Measure It

Whatever your principles are for your product, they need to be measurable. In all likelihood, one of the GPs of your product will be "easy to use," but what *exactly* does that mean? No training or help documentation for any of your features? Primary tasks are completed within a certain time frame or number of steps? A 100% task success rate in usability testing? You need to be specific in your definitions so that you can measure if your product is meeting the GPs or not.

Repeat for Antiprinciples

Conduct another team brainstorm using sticky notes, but this time, identify all of the words and phrases you do *not* want to hear your users, marketing, and/or reviewers say about your product. These are your APs. Again, group similar concepts, and keep the number of antiprinciples under 10 so it is manageable. It is equally important to define your APs so they, too, can be measured. One of the important benefits of APs is that they can prevent feature creep. You may find stakeholders suggesting the inclusion of features in the product just because it is technically impressive, sounds like a good idea, or is a pet project of someone in management. Evaluating every new feature against the GPs/APs offers a neutral method for assessing what should be included or not. It makes it a lot easier to say "No" when you can follow that up by saying, "This not only doesn't fit into one our guiding principles; it is actually one of our antiprinciples."

Evaluate

Unfortunately, it is common for teams to put a lot of effort into brainstorming and documenting the GPs/APs and not follow through with the evaluation step. With each version of your product, you should revisit your GPs/APs to make sure they are still relevant. Products, user needs, markets, competitors, and business goals all evolve over time, so your GPs/APs should, too. You may be able to evaluate your product against your GPs/APs prior to launch (e.g., usability testing, focus groups), but you may have to wait until after launch (e.g., log analysis, surveys), so put check points into your development timetable to do the evaluations.

Step 4: Scenarios

At a Glance

> Benefits of a scenario
> Things to be aware of when creating scenarios
> Creating scenarios

Scenarios, often referred to as "use cases," are stories about the personas you created and should fit into the guiding principles you identified. A good scenario begins with a persona and then adds more detail based on your user requirements activities. The story describes how a particular persona completes a task or behaves in a given situation. It provides a setting; has actors, objectives or goals, and a sequence of events; and closes with a result.

Benefits of a Scenario

Scenarios are another way to bring your users to life during product development. They can be used to test a system during early evaluation. Is this a system that meets your users' needs? Does it satisfy the goals and fit in the user's workflow? You can also use scenarios to create "day-in-the-life" videos. These are useful artifacts for focus groups (refer to Chapter 12, page 340).

Things to Be Aware of When Creating Scenarios

Scenario development can be time-consuming. It is not necessary to create a library of scenarios that cover every conceivable task or situation the end users might encounter. Focus on developing scenarios for the primary tasks users will encounter, and then, if there is time, move to secondary tasks. Never let user profiles, personas, or scenarios replace user research activities with actual users. You need data from real users to build your product and to keep your profiles, personas, and scenarios fresh. People change over time. Their needs, expectations, desires, and skills are not permanent, so your scenarios should not be either.

Creating Scenarios

Scenarios normally include descriptions about the following:

- The individual user (i.e., the persona)
- The task or situation
- The user's desired outcome/goal for that task
- Procedure and task flow information
- A time interval
- Envisioned features/functionality the user will need/use

You may also want to include exceptions. What are some of the rare events that happen? (Remember, frequency does not equate to importance!) By understanding the extreme or infrequent situations users encounter, you may identify situations where your product would be obsolete or even problematic. You could also identify key features that would benefit your end users.

Using the list of tasks in the user profile and/or persona, choose the critical tasks and begin creating scenarios with your stakeholders. In one scenario, describe the ideal way the persona might complete a given task. In another scenario, describe a problem (or problems) the persona might encounter while completing this task and how the persona would react. Continue building a set of scenarios for each of your personas until you feel you have covered the functionality of your product and the tasks/situations users encounter. As with user profiles and personas, you should use the information from user requirement activities to validate your scenarios and add more information to them.

Scenarios should not describe individual widgets. For example, you should avoid things like "and then Nikhil selected his preferred hotel from the droplist" or "Nikhil scrolled to the bottom of the page and clicked the 'Submit' button." Instead, you should describe the basic actions, like "Nikhil selected his preferred airline" or "Nikhil submitted the information." Below is an example of a very simple scenario:

> **Shikoh needs to plan a vacation for her family. She decides to check out the TravelMyWay app and do both the research and reservations there. She begins by researching the top family-friendly destinations as recommended by TravelMyWay app customers. She wants to compare the travel time, travel costs, hotel costs, hotel availability, and amusement activities for each destination. For each of those criteria, Shikoh gave a weighting to help her make her decision. She finally settled on the destination that required the least travel time, cheapest travel costs, moderate hotel costs, good availability, and a large selection of activities for the whole family. From that spot, Shikoh begins searching for the flights and hotels that meet her criteria. She decides to save those results for later because she wants to be sure the whole family is in agreement before she makes the reservations with her credit card.**

Scenarios can be more sophisticated depending on the information you have collected. Often, they will start out small—based on the information you were able to collect initially—and then expand to give more detail as you gather data from user research activities.

To make scenarios more consistent among each other and more complete, a template is recommended for each scenario. One possible template is provided below (McInerney, 2003). The sections include the following:

- *Title*. This provides a general description of the situation. Avoid being too specific or character-driven. For example, "Sally needs to research locations for a family vacation" should be worded instead as "Research vacation locations."
- *Situation/task*. In a paragraph or two, describe the initial situation, the challenge facing the user, and the user's goal. Do not discuss how the user will accomplish his or her goal yet—that is covered next.

- *Method to address the situation.* In either a bullet list or a task flow diagram, describe how the users cope with the situation. There are many ways in which the user could accomplish a given task. The task flow should show the different possibilities in about 5-15 steps. This section should be generic and technology-neutral (do not include specific design elements). The specific technology is discussed next.
- *Execution path.* In a narrative form, describe how the task is completed and the user's goal is reached. Now, you can discuss specific features or technology used. You will likely have multiple "Execution path" sections—one for each possible way of accomplishing the task shown in the "Method to address the situation" step. Alternatively, you may want to illustrate how different designs would accomplish each task. This section should be updated as design decisions are made. The other parts of the scenario will remain relatively unchanged over time.

Suggested Resources for Additional Reading

Check out Chapter 9 of *The Inmates are Running the Asylum* for a classic discussion of personas. Adlin and Pruitt wrote an entire book devoted just to persona creation and use.

- Cooper, A. (1999). *The inmates are running the asylum*. Indianapolis, IN: Sams.
- Adlin, T., & Pruitt, J. (2010). *The essential persona lifecycle: Your guide to building and using personas*. Morgan Kaufmann.

To learn more about scenarios and their role in design, check out the following:

- Carroll, J. M. (2000). *Making use: Scenario-based design of human-computer interactions*. Cambridge, MA: MIT Press.
- Rosson, M. B., & Carroll, J. M. (2002). *Usability engineering: Scenario-based development of human-computer interaction*. San Francisco, CA: Morgan Kaufmann.

Special Populations

International Users

Many global companies based in the United States develop products first for the United States and then think about how they might need to change that product for outside of the United States. At a minimum, this involves **internationalization** and **localization** or **globalization** (a combination of internationalization and localization). Internationalization is the process of developing the infrastructure in your product so that it can *potentially* be adapted for different languages and regions without requiring engineering changes each time. Localization means using the infrastructure created during internationalization to adapt your product to a specific language and/or region by adding local-specific components and translating text. This means adapting your product to support different languages, regional differences, and technical requirements. But it is not enough to simply translate the content and localize things like currency, time, measurements, holidays, titles, and standards (e.g., battery size, power source). If you rely on third-party sources for content or functionality, you need to adapt it or find alternative sources if they are not available for the country of interest. You also must be aware of any regulatory compliance that applies to your product/domain (e.g., taxes, laws, privacy, accessibility, censorship).

But even if you get all of that covered, you have not focused on the user. It is just as important to understand the user needs of your population and any cultural differences as it is to get the language, technical platform, and legal issues covered. It is unlikely that your product is going to work for every single person in the United States because the population in the United States is so diverse. The differences in context, background, technology, income, needs, etc., mean that a one-size-fits-all product will not support every person in the United States. The same is true for countries in the rest of the world. You cannot make assumptions about needs of users in China as a whole, much less a region as broad as Asia, and yet, many companies do. Once a product is localized, works on the major platforms for the region, and is in compliance with all laws and regulations, many companies think they are done. To truly support the users in a particular country or region, you must use the same techniques in this book to identify user profiles, scenarios, and needs of those users. You should spend as much time and effort developing your product for any country/region outside of the United States as you did developing it for the United States.

You will likely need to work with a researcher or at least recruiting vendor in the country of interest in order to get access to participants, incentives, and facilities to conduct the research. A vendor in the country can help not only with conducting the research (or conduct it for you), but they can also inform you about cultural issues you may not be aware of prior to the study. Being culturally aware in advance of the study will not only make your study go much more smoothly and help with the reliability and validity of the data collection, but can also help you avoid offending your participants.

Ethical Considerations for International Research

If you plan to conduct IRB-approved research in other countries, be sure to plan for additional review time. Research conducted outside a researcher's home country is subject to additional review, including certifying translations of consent forms and other documents to the local language, letters of agreement from local officials, and reviews of ethical procedures from local researchers.

Suggested Resources for Additional Reading

IBM and Microsoft offer detailed information to help with the technical aspects of globalizing software and applications.

- IBM Globalization website: http://www-01.ibm.com/software/globalization/
- Microsoft Globalization Step-by-Step guide for applications: http://msdn.microsoft.com/en-us/goglobal/bb688110.aspx

Apala Lahiri Chavan and Girish Prabhu have edited a collection of interviews with researchers about conducting research in emerging markets that readers will find helpful when preparing to conduct international research. Apala is also the contributor for this chapter's case study.

- Chavan, A. L., & Prabhu, G. V. (Eds.). (2010). *Innovative solutions: What designers need to know for today's emerging markets*. CRC Press.

Accessibility

The best products and services adhere to the guidelines of **universal design** or **inclusive design.** The term "universal design" was coined by Ronald L. Mace (1985). It means that your product or service enables everyone to access and use regardless of one's age, abilities, or status in life. Universal design is important because everyone has limitations at some point or another that makes accessing products or services difficult, and design that is inclusive is easier for everyone to use (Story, Mace, & Mueller, 1998):

- *Hearing impaired:* People working in loud environments (e.g., construction sites) or those listening to music cranked up are going to have a difficult time hearing any audio signal from your product.
- *Visually impaired:* Glare from the screens on mobile devices can make seeing anything, particularly low-contrast content, extremely difficult.
- *Color-blind:* If your content depends on color-coding for interpretation, it will be lost when your users view it on displays with limited colors or print it out in black and white.
- *Limited dexterity:* In cold winter climates, manipulating smartphones and tablets with gloves can be tricky unless you have purchased special gloves for that purpose.
- *Physically challenged:* Few people have gone their whole lives without an injury that limits their movements. Parents carrying a child or heavy groceries tie up the use of their arms. Pushing a stroller, bike, walker, or rolling luggage prevents the use of stairs and pose a challenge with curbs.
- *Mentally challenged:* Anyone that has suffered from sleep deprivation, is under the influence of medication, or dealt with short-term memory issues may not be able to comprehend your product or information in the same way you intended.
- *Illiterate:* You may be able to read content in your language fluently, but the moment you step into a store, restaurant, or country where information is displayed in a different language, you become illiterate.

When you are conducting user research, you need to think about the full range of users, recruiting a broad range of ages, abilities, and statuses. The designer(s) for your product might be using the latest computers and monitors with the highest speed Internet connection, but there will be a segment of your user population that does not. What does your product look like for them? Can they even access it?

The Center for Universal Design offers seven principles for universal design (Copyright © 1997 NC State University, The Center for Universal Design):

1. *Equitable use:* The design is useful and marketable to people with diverse abilities.
2. *Flexibility in use:* The design accommodates a wide range of individual preferences and abilities.
3. *Simple and intuitive use:* Use of the design is easy to understand, regardless of the user's experience, knowledge, language skills, or current concentration level.
4. *Perceptible information:* The design communicates necessary information effectively to the user, regardless of ambient conditions or the user's sensory abilities.
5. *Tolerance for error:* The design minimizes hazards and the adverse consequences of accidental or unintended actions.
6. *Low physical effort:* The design can be used efficiently and comfortably with minimum fatigue.
7. *Size and space for approach and use:* Appropriate size and space are provided for approach, reach, manipulation, and use regardless of user's body size, posture, or mobility.

Suggested Resources for Additional Reading

The Center for Universal Design provides several resources to help those wanting to create products and environments that are accessible to all.

- The Center for Universal Design (1997). *The Principles of Universal Design*, Version 2.0. Raleigh, NC: North Carolina State University. Retrieved from http://www.ncsu.edu/ncsu/design/cud/about_ud/udprinciples.htm

The Web Accessibility Initiative (http://www.w3.org/WAI/) provides guidelines and tutorials for developing accessible online sites and services, as well as instruction for how to evaluate web accessibility.

The *Universal Design Handbook, 2nd edition*, covers not only accessibility design recommendations but also globalization, making this an excellent resource for thinking about *all* of your users.

- Preiser, W. F., & Smith, K. (Eds.). (2010). *Universal design handbook*, 2nd ed. McGraw Hill Professional.

Children

Increasingly, children are being exposed to tablets before they are able to read, and some elementary school children are getting their parents' hand-me-down smartphones. If you are creating consumer products, there is a good chance children are using your products whether you intend them to or not. These are your future power users and a huge opportunity for you, so you would do well to at least consider children in your product development process. However, there are a number of things you need to be aware of when conducting research with children:

- *Nondisclosure agreements:* Anyone under the age of 18 in the United States cannot sign legal documents. A legal guardian must sign NDAs on behalf of the children. You will also need to explain what confidentiality means in terms the child can understand.
- *Informed consent:* Not only must parents be informed about the details of the study to consent on behalf of their child(ren), but also, you are ethically obligated to explain to children their rights prior to any study (see

Chapter 3, "Ethical and Legal Considerations") in words that the child can understand. Although parents must consent to the study, it is up to the *child* to decide whether or not he or she wants to participate and when he or she wishes to withdraw. Parents and children must be informed of this prior to the start of the study.

- *Incentives:* Identify appropriate incentives for the age of your participants. A Visa gift card may not be as enticing for a child as a gift card to a toy store. Discuss the incentive with the parents in advance to ensure that the parents will not object to it. Nothing is worse than handing a gift to a child at the end of a study only to have a parent take it away.
- *Cognitive ability:* Children will not have the same cognitive abilities or focus as the adults you typically conduct research with. Keep this in mind when designing the length of your study and tasks.
- *Regulations:* Depending on the country, there are stricter regulations around personally identifiable information (PII) than for adults. This is certainly true in the United States.
- *Instructions:* Children should be informed that this is not a test and that there are no right or wrong answers. *They* are not being evaluated; the product is. Just as adult participants may need to be reminded of this during the study, so must children.
- *Eye tracking:* If you are conducting an evaluative study using an eye tracker, you must ensure that it is safe for children with no long-term exposure concerns, inform the parents during the screening process that an eye tracker will be used, and get both the parents' and child's consent. Be aware that some mobile eye trackers can actually cause nausea so you are obligated to advise both child and parent of the risk during recruitment.

Older Users

As we age, we experience changes in our cognitive and physical capabilities and limitations. While some abilities increase (e.g., verbal, wisdom), other abilities tend to decline (e.g., visual acuity). These changes mean you should consider the age of your target users and of your participants. Specifically, you should include older adults in your participant sample if you plan for older people to use your product. And with older adults (65 years and above) representing 13% of the population in 2010 and estimated to represent 19% in the United States by 2030 based on trends in the data (Department of Health and Services, 2010), it is likely that your product will be used by older people.

Just like other populations (e.g., children), there is a huge variation in what it means to be an older adult. "To compare a person who is 60 to a person who is 90 is not unlike comparing a 13-year-old to a 45-year-old" (Fisk, Rogers, Charness, Czaja, & Sharit, 2009). In aging research, there are three categories of "older adult:"

- The "young old"—65-74
- The "old"—74-84
- The "oldest old"—85+

TIP

The performance of older adults is typically more variable than that of younger adults. Therefore, if you are engaged in research where you are collecting quantitative data about older adults' behavior, you will typically need a larger sample size to achieve statistical significance.

When selecting older adult research participants for a study, you should carefully consider what inclusion/exclusion criteria are appropriate. Criteria could include the following:

- *Cognitive status (and impairments)*—older adults, especially those in the "old" and "oldest old," are more likely to have a cognitive impairment than younger adults. You can screen for cognitive impairment status using the Mini-Mental State Examination (MMSE; Folstein, Folstein, & McHugh, 1975).
- *Health status*—the majority of older adults have at least one chronic health condition (AARP, 2009). You may be interested in perceived health status (how older adults feel about their health) or the number and specific types of health conditions your participants live with.
- *Living situation*—while many older adults are "community dwelling," meaning they live in their own home or apartment, many live in communities or institutions that provide various levels of care. While retirement communities typically offer convenience services such as yard maintenance, assisted living facilities may offer more extensive services, such as meal preparation and transportation assistance. Nursing homes offer skilled medical care on a daily basis.

Declines in speed of processing and working memory associated with aging mean that older adults will likely take longer to complete a study (Fisk et al., 2009). A guideline is to plan for a study protocol to take about one and a half times as long with an older adult as with a younger adult. If a study takes an hour for a younger adult, it will likely take an hour and a half for an older adult to complete.

TIP

Because of changes in visual acuity, we recommend using 14-point font for study materials for older adults, although almost everyone will appreciate it!

Suggested Resources for Further Reading

- Fisk, A. D., Rogers, W. A., Charness, N., Czaja, S. J., & Sharit, J. (2009). *Designing for older adults: Principles and creative human factors approaches* (2nd ed.). Boca Raton, FL: CRC Press.
- Pak, R., & McLaughlin, A. C. (2010). *Designing displays for older adults*. Boca Raton, FL: CRC Press.

Pulling It All Together

In this chapter, we have covered various sources you can turn to in order to learn more about your product domain and end users. Doing your homework is critical to the success of your product! It provides a solid foundation from which to build your future research activities and can save you a great deal of time and money further down the road.

CASE STUDY: *THERE IS "CULTURAL" METHOD IN THE MADNESS*

Apala Lahiri Chavan, Institute of Customer Experience, Human Factors International, Puducherry, India

There are many long-established and well-validated methods developed in the Western world to understand user motivations and unarticulated needs (e.g., in-depth interviews, focus groups, think-aloud protocols). In fact, they are so well accepted that practitioners use them worldwide. Yet these methods do not always work well in other cultures and, therefore, need to be adapted.

It might seem odd to think that there are cultures where observation, think-aloud testing, and in-depth interviews are ineffective. But Asian users, for example, prefer more context in communication (Hall, 1989). They are more hesitant to make negative comments and are sensitive to cues of the hierarchy and subtext of communication. In addition, group dynamics affect Asian users more than users in most Western countries.

The adaptation of methods requires sensitivity to the triggers that enable communication within a culture. We must understand the root cause of hesitancy in communication, which can be different as we move between countries, or even across the river within a country (such as in India)!

In order to decide what triggers to use, we need to do our homework. This involves doing secondary research about that specific culture, speaking with local researchers, and forming a hypothesis about possible triggers that will work within that culture. Then we need to test whether our hypothesis is correct by pilot testing with local researchers. This pilot session is critical since this helps us design the final research method(s).

I developed the Bollywood usability testing method in 2001 (Plocher & Chavan, 2002) to deal with the challenge that "foreign" user research methods did not work well in India. Since then, we have used a range of methods for ecosystem research in various cultures. In this case study, I highlight some of the recent work we have done in India and Africa.

Rasas: India

Rasas are the essences of our emotions that exist in both the body and the mind. The central objective of classical Indian art and drama is to create the appropriate "rasa" for the spectators to communicate or suggest a kind of knowledge that cannot be clearly expressed in words.

We incorporated the nine rasas that are most well known in India (Figure 2.6) in the form of cultural probes for a project in India to explore the emotions people felt when interacting with ATMs for the first time. These rasas were love, joy, anger, peace, courage, sadness, disgust, wonder, and fear.

This culture probe was designed as a set of cinema "emotion tickets," carrying the omnipresent Bollywood theme forward (see Figure 2.7). Each rasa was expressed (in the emotion ticket) through images and dialogues from familiar Bollywood films (Chavan & Munshi, 2004). The "emotion tickets" were designed in a way that participants could identify a rasa (emotion) when interacting with an ATM and also note some details about the

Figure 2.6: The nine most well-known rasas.

Interview Enhancement & Cultural Probes

"I feel emotionally drained. Like my Bank Account"

Love Joy Wonder Courage Calmness Anger Sadness Fear Disgust

Rasas

"Emotion tickets," using images and dialogues from Bollywood films, were used to create a *rasa*—the essence of an emotion—in participants while interacting with new technology. The result was innovation ideas for new ATMs.

We needed to explore the emotions people felt when interacting with ATMs for the first time.
'Rasas' or the essence of various emotions is what we decided to use for the research. We used the ancient Indian Theory of Performance which looks at the use of nine basic emotions (or Rasas) in theatre and dance. This culture probe was designed as a set of cinema 'emotion tickets'. These tickets were categorized to express the nine rasas. Each rasa was expressed through images and dialogues from Bollywood films. Each user was given a booklet with a set of emotion tickets and asked to carry these around with them. Users were expected to articulate their feelings when interacting/using any financial service and/or technology, by recording it using the appropriate rasa. The analysis led to the creation of an emotion map that helped us determine the dominant emotions felt by people when interacting with ATMs

Which research method suits your business? Reach us to find out.

hfi@humanfactors.com

Human Factors International

www.humanfactors.com

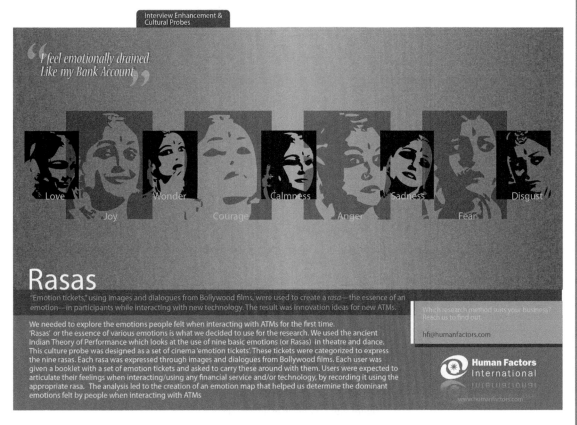

Figure 2.7: Using rasas as culture probe.

context of the interaction. Each user was given a booklet with a set of emotion tickets and asked to carry these around with them for 2 weeks (see Figure 2.8).

Participants were expected to articulate their feelings when interacting with any financial service and/or technology, by recording it using the appropriate rasa. We asked two questions: When? How? For example, "You laughed at money or technology. When? How?" Participants were instructed to answer these two questions every time they experienced one of the nine rasas.

At the end of two weeks, we collected the emotion tickets and analyzed them. The analysis led to the creation of an emotion map (see Figure 2.9) that helped us identify the dominant emotions people felt when interacting with ATMs and hence what innovations would make sense for a new design for these localized ATMs.

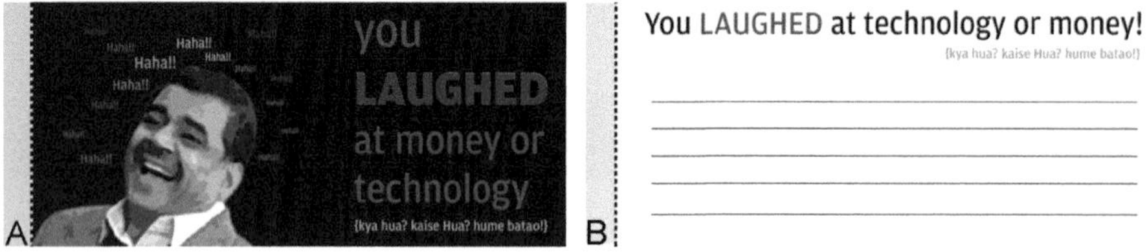

Figure 2.8: The emotion tickets.

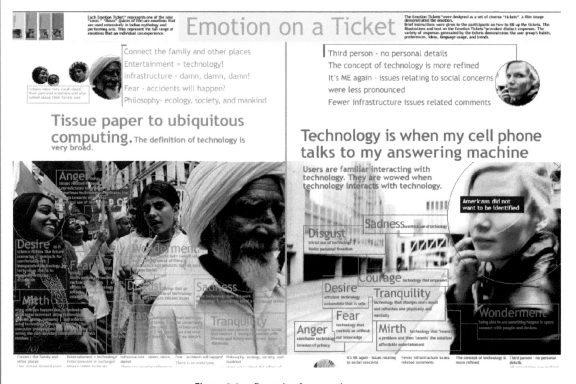

Figure 2.9: Example of an emotion map.

The Auto Rickshaw Radio: A New Representation for the Semantic Differential Scale

The semantic differential scale is used for measuring the *meaning* of things and concepts (Snider & Osgood, 1969). Participants indicate where they feel a product or experience lies on a 7-point scale between polar adjectives (e.g., strong-weak, good-bad). We noticed, over several projects done in India, that the semantic differential scale seemed to be a major stumbling block for participants, especially for semiliterate users. Whenever the semantic differential scale was presented, there was a tendency to select one of the two extreme options and nothing in between. This was very different from the experience these participants had expressed while using the product in question. So, in spite of an experience that was not black and white, everyone seemed to want to pick one of the two extremes.

After much probing and reflection, we realized that for these users, the concept of a difference in degree (moving from negative to positive) being represented by a horizontal straight line did not make sense. The feeling was that if the different points in the scale represented different degrees of an attribute, then they could not appear to be on the same (horizontal) level. Hence, a control was devised that resembled the volume control knob on a radio, with which all users were familiar. Transitioning from a low to high volume on a radio was very similar to what they needed to do when expressing the degree of an attribute (positive or negative) via the semantic differential scale. This alternative, nonlinear representation significantly improved comprehension among the participants. The stark difference in how the participants went from selecting one of the options at the two ends of the scale to wanting to fine-tune to a granular level was very insightful (Figure 2.10).

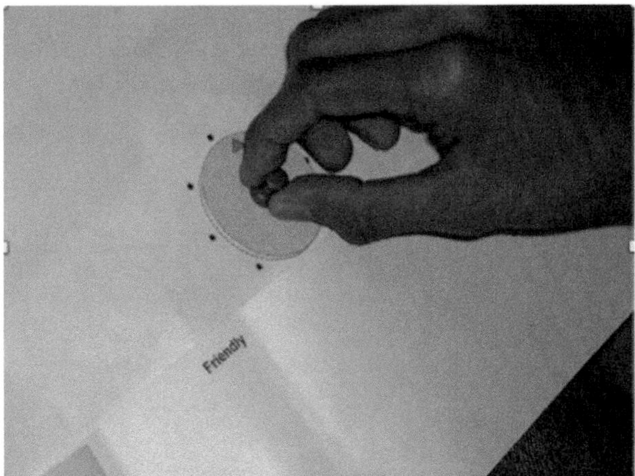

Figure 2.10: The volume control knob representing the semantic differential scale.

The Animal Picture Board: Kenya

We conducted research on the adoption and usage of financial institutions in rural Kenya to advise our client about innovative, localized strategies for various banking channels such as the bank branch, the ATM, mobile banking, and the contact center. See Figure 2.11.

Figure 2.11: Researching in rural Kenya.

We needed people to talk about their deep associations with different financial institutions/mechanisms, whether formal or informal. Since Kenya, like most of Asia, is a hierarchical and collectivist culture (Geert & Jan, 1991), we realized there was a strong likelihood they would have the same inhibitions we observed in Asia, where talking openly with a stranger would be a problem. Even though we would have a local researcher moderating the sessions, the fact that we (an Indian and South African research team) were going to be present would make it difficult for them to articulate what they really wanted to say. So we wondered, "What would resonate with these participants, triggering instant associations and hence instant responses without any 'interference' by the analytical part of the brain?" We observed that Kenya had a long and deep connection with wildlife. Wildlife was an area of shared knowledge in Kenyan culture.

We designed a method using images of animals common in Kenya on a board and asking questions around that picture board (see Figure 2.12). We tested this (and other methods) with our two local researchers as the pilot participants. The pilot sessions helped clarify the local association with each animal and tweak some of the pictures of the animals.

Figure 2.12: Using the animal picture board and coffee evaluation scale.

In the study, we asked participants about the different kinds of financial mechanisms they used (e.g., a money lender, an informal neighborhood group where they lend money to each other, the formal bank). We then asked which animal they associated with each financial mechanism and why.

The responses came without hesitation. "The cheetah is like this particular service, and the elephant reminds me of this institution." Each person would make particular associations quickly. Responses reflected deep-seated patterns rather than being manufactured for us.

There were several interesting patterns that emerged from this exercise. For example, the elephant was repeatedly associated with a specific local bank. The reason was that participants felt this bank was strong and reliable like an elephant, and hence, they felt a sense of security and comfort in engaging with this bank.

On the other hand, many participants associated the cheetah with a new mobile transaction service. They felt this service was fast (in terms of time taken to complete a transaction) like the cheetah, but was also "cunning" like the cheetah. The cheetah, while appearing less intimidating than the lion or the leopard, had the speed to attack and kill its prey while seeming to appear out of nowhere. They also stated that the cheetah was always supposed to attack sneakily, from behind. So for the new mobile transaction service, while they greatly appreciated the speed with which they could make payments and receive money from across large distances, there was a hidden side to using this service. This was the gradual realization that they were, as a result of using this mobile transaction service, spending their money faster and on things that perhaps they did not really need. They felt that this was the "cunningness" of this service where and did not realize when they signed up that there was a flip side to the convenience of instant access. This duality made them apprehensive and not totally comfortable with the service.

Bizarre Bazaar: South Africa

This is a variation of an "informance" or informative performance method (i.e., a set of techniques in which actors and/or researchers study what is known about consumers and role-play with potential consumers) that has tested well with Asian users in our 15 years of ecosystem research and usability testing across Asia.

We used this recently in South Africa, when working on a banking project. We needed to understand low-income users' motivational drives and blocks regarding mobile banking. The bank had introduced mobile banking, but adoption was minimal. We had to figure out why.

We were in the (supposedly) dangerous township of Umlazi near Durban. We knew that just asking the participants why they were not using mobile banking or specific mobile banking features/functions would be a challenge. Once again, since this specific segment was relatively collectivist and was also very uncomfortable being asked questions by "outsiders," the chances of participants feeling comfortable enough to share the real reasons of their low adoption of mobile banking were slim.

So we decided to use the Bizarre Bazaar. Participants were asked to compare a range of options and specify which ones they would select. When asked directly, participants usually responded by saying they would select all options, even though on further questioning, it became clear that reaction was far from reality! Hence, the Bizarre Bazaar method was designed to make participants experience a situation that is common in their everyday lives: bargaining with a vendor when buying a product or service (in cultures where bargaining during buying/selling is normal practice). This converts the seemingly difficult task of having to compare options and indicate preference into an experience that mimics everyday life and helps to activate involuntary reflexes based on a familiar situation. The method also uses the strong intrinsic block most of us feel to part with cash. This block trumps the participants' drive to say what the researchers want to hear and surfaces in collective and hierarchical contexts.

In this study, we wrote the name of every mobile banking function available to the participants (via the bank), on small pieces of paper. Then we put these pieces of paper in a basket/bowl used by market vendors to display their wares to customers. We placed this basket/bowl with the pieces of paper in front of the participant and told them to imagine that they were in their neighborhood bazaar and had chanced upon a vendor selling mobile banking features/functions (see Figure 2.13). Which features would they buy? To make the simulation complete, we handed each participant 300 rand in cash (just for the exercise). They would need to make the first move by offering the amount of cash they felt was appropriate for any feature/function they liked and wanted to buy. As the participant offered cash for a feature/function, the research moderator acted like the vendor and asked for a higher price. In the course of the "bargaining," we were able to probe and understand which features were considered valuable and useful and why.

Figure 2.13: Performing the Bizarre Bazaar.

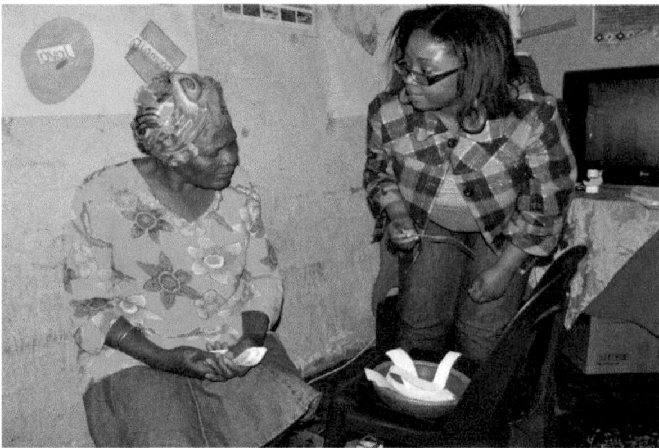

The cash acted as the anchor for the conversation about what was preventing participants from using mobile banking in general. More specifically, however, it helped them talk about which features they would actually use every day and in what situations they would use them. The insights from this exercise helped us come up with ideas for new concepts and improvements, and also helped us determine which features could be dropped.

Lessons Learned

I have learned several lessons using these fun and innovative techniques:

1. **It is possible to be so engrossed in the thrill of creating a "clever" method that one overlooks the "human" angle.**
   When we were conducting ecosystem research in Kenya, the Bizarre Bazaar method was part of our repertoire. However, as we started the session with our first very low-income participant, we realized that the act of handing over cash as a mere artifact for research when that entire amount could have fed the family for a week would be cruel and heartless on our part. So we decided to change course, even though that meant we could not create a "clever" technique as replacement for the first day's research.

2. **One needs to be very careful when constructing a hypothesis about a culture, based on secondary data on the Internet.**
   A decade ago, when I was in China for my first ethnographic research study in Shanghai, several of the research methods I had constructed were all based on the assumption that China was a very hierarchical culture. None of the methods, therefore, involved activities with the children in the family (since the assumption was that they do not play any significant role in decision-making). However, when conducting the pilot sessions with our local researchers, it emerged that due to the one-child policy, China was not as hierarchical in 2003 (at least within the family) as it had been in the 1960s, when most of the data regarding cultural dimensions were gathered. Since much of the cultural data on the Internet are based on old research, the data did not always reflect current cultural values.
   Even more important was the fact that since there was only one child in each family, the child was actually a *very* important decision-maker! Based on this insight, we had to change our research methods to include activities with the children. Subsequently, we decided that, in addition to piloting our methods with local researchers, we also needed to include local researchers in our early discussions before actually creating any customized method(s).

3. **When using customized methods, include multiple methods that explore the topics/issues being researched.**
   It is only by analyzing participant response to *all* the methods that one can come to a reliable conclusion about the insights gathered from the research. Multiple methods help validate the insights of each method.

To Conclude

In today's globalized world, where product and service ideas surface in one part of the world (e.g., mobile banking) but are expected to be adopted globally, the local voice is more important than ever (Chavan & Prabhu, 2010). Without clarity about the deep motivators and barriers that exist within the local ecosystem, providing the local "soul" to a global idea becomes impossible.

An important question to ask is whether the insights that one gets from the use of these interactive, culturally customized methods actually lead to any advantages over the conventional research methods. Research insights obviously depend upon the skill and experience of the research team. No amount of customized methods can substitute for skill and experience! However, what has worked distinctly better about these methods than the conventional methods are the following:

1. **Reduction in the time needed to get insights**
   The time it takes to get participants to the level of open sharing using the right triggers in a customized technique versus a more conventional question and answer approach is usually 30-40% *shorter*.

2. **Qualitatively better insights**
   The quality of insights is deeper with these customized methods. For example, the duality represented by the "cheetah perspective" with the mobile payment was not something that any of the previous qualitative research conducted by the client had unearthed. Would we have been able to uncover this without having used the animal picture board? It is not likely.

3. **Actionable insights**
   As with any insight, regardless of the method, if it cannot lead to any specific action, it is of little use. Once again, in the "cheetah" example, we were able to ask detailed probing questions to understand what problems speed solved, why it was important, and how it made them feel. Similarly, the discomfort with the cheetah's cunning unlocked a veritable Pandora's box of issues around perceived disempowerment and discriminatory treatment by foreign banks and the resulting distrust. The insights obtained from the use of the animal picture board led to conceptualizing specific features (ranging from incremental to disruptive innovation) for the client's offerings to this segment of users.
   And last, but not least, it is a great advantage to use these methods because the participants enjoy them as much as the interviewer. It becomes a fun hour or two they spend together!

CHAPTER 3

Ethical and Legal Considerations

Introduction

Before conducting any kind of user activity, there are a number of ethical and legal considerations you must be aware of. You are responsible for protecting the participants, your company, and the data you collect. These are not responsibilities that should be taken lightly. This chapter applies to *all* readers. Even if you are doing "just a little research," if it involves human participants, this chapter applies to you. In this chapter, we will inform you of what you need to know before conducting a user activity to make sure you collect valuable data without legal or ethical harm. These are general guidelines but you need to be aware of your local laws, practices, and regulations.

Policies vs. Laws vs. Ethics

People often conflate their company's policies, laws, and ethical guidelines. It is important to understand the differences. **Policies** are set forth by your company, often with the goal of ensuring employees do not come close to breaking laws or just to enforce good business practices. For example, many companies have privacy policies stating how they handle customer data. The specifics of those policies may differ among companies. California is the only state that requires a company to post their privacy policy if it is collecting personal information from any California resident; however, it is best practice to post one's privacy policy, regardless of where the customers reside.

Laws are rules set forth by the government, and everyone must comply with them, regardless of where they work. United States tax laws, for example, mandate how much a company may pay an individual per year before the company must file forms with the Internal Revenue Service (IRS). This is important to know and track if you plan to provide incentives (cash or otherwise) to participants in your studies. **Nondisclosure** or **confidentiality agreements** (NDAs or CDAs) are legally binding agreements that protect your company's intellectual property by requiring participants to keep what they see and hear in your study confidential and hand over the ownership of any ideas, suggestions, or feedback they provide. We will discuss these in a little more detail later (see Figure 3.1).

An **informed consent form** is an agreement of your ethical obligations to the participant (see Figure 3.2). It may not be legally binding, but it is absolutely ethically binding. Keep in mind that you likely cannot develop *one* informed consent form for all studies since not every study is identical. You should evaluate the risks to the participants and the elements you need to inform them of for *every* study. Another example of an ethical obligation is to be transparent about how a participant's data will be handled. Who will be able to see it within the company (e.g., just the researcher, the entire development team, anyone in the company who is interested)? Will the participant's name and other identifiable information be associated with their data (e.g., video of the session, transcript from the interview)? There is not a law requiring you to inform participants of this and your company may not have a policy about this, but research ethics state you should inform them.

<Company letterhead>

Confidentiality Agreement

Thank you for agreeing to give us your feedback on **<describe project non-specifically>**. The concepts you will be exposed to, and the information concerning them, are confidential and have not been released to the public. In exchange for participating in our design process and for seeing these unreleased concepts, you agree to keep the information you see or hear confidential until **<name of company>** releases that information to the public. You agree not to disclose this information to any third parties or use the information for any purpose other than this development process.

This agreement will cover discussions we intend to have with you on **<date, place>**.

To indicate your acceptance of these terms and your agreement to keep them confidential, please sign below (and return a copy to us if this agreement is being signed before our meeting).

We greatly appreciate your participation in our design process. Only by learning the needs of people like you can **<company name>** design systems that are useful. Thank you for your participation.

Signature ________________________________ **Date** ____________

Printed name ______________________________

Signature for **<company name>** ________________ **Date** ____________

Figure 3.1: Basic nondisclosure agreement.

Ethical Considerations

Having strong ethical standards protects the participants, your company, and your data. Every company/organization that gathers data from people should have a set of policies and practices in place for ethical treatment. If your company does not, then you should implement them for your group or organization. Remember: you are acting as the user's advocate. It is your responsibility to protect the participants' physical and psychological well-being when they have kindly volunteered to help you by sharing their time, experience, and expertise. In the case where the participant is a customer, you have the added responsibility of protecting and promoting the customer's relationship with your company. A poor experience in your usability activity could result in lost revenue. You can be certain that your company will not support future usability activities once that has occurred.

As a final (but important) consideration, you *must* protect the data you are collecting. You do not want to bias or corrupt the data. If this happens, all of your time, money, and effort will be wasted when the data have to be

Statement of Informed Consent

Purpose:

You have been asked to participate in a <**insert activity**> for <**insert product or project name**>. By participating in this activity, you will help us make our product easier to learn and use. This activity is meant to help us develop our product; it is not intended to test your individual performance in any way.

Evaluation Procedure:

You will be asked to <**insert summary statement of task(s) participants will accomplish**>. While you work, I will videotape your interactions and record your comments.

Confidentiality:

We will use the data you give us, along with the information we collect from other participants, to develop our product. To ensure confidentiality, we will not associate your name with your data. This session will be videotaped.

Breaks:

There <**will/will not**> be a scheduled break. However, you may take a break at any time.

Freedom to Withdraw:

You may withdraw from the activity at any time without penalty.

- -

If you agree to these terms, please indicate your acceptance by signing below:

Signature: ______________________________

Printed name: ______________________________

Date: ______________________________

Figure 3.2: Sample informed consent form.

discarded. The data you use in making design decisions must be valid and reliable or you risk doing more harm than good; poor data can result in bad design decisions. With this being said, if data are compromised, it is always possible to recruit more participants and collect more data, but it is much harder to restore the dignity of a participant who feels coerced or ill-treated or to correct a damaged business relationship. So keep in mind that the participants' well-being is always your top priority. Figure 3.3 illustrates this priority by placing the participant at the highest point.

In this section, we discuss some of the key ethical considerations to keep in mind when running any usability activity.

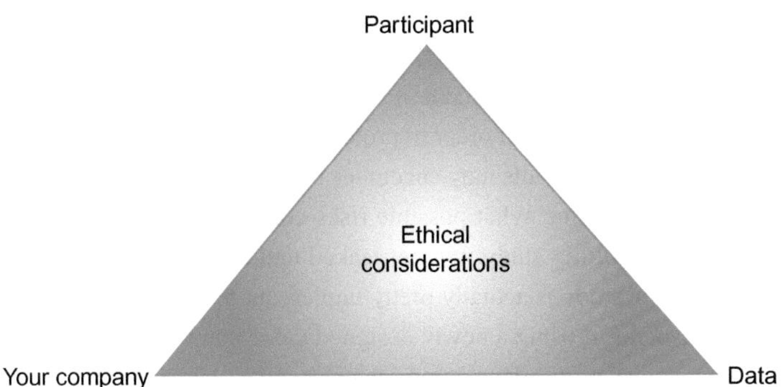

Figure 3.3: Triad of ethical considerations.

Suggested Resources for Additional Reading

For more detail about any of the points below, please refer to the APA's *Ethical Principles of Psychologists and Code of Conduct*. You can also download a free copy at http://www.apa.org/ethics/code/index.aspx.

Each major research association has their own code of ethics; however, you will find they have the same basic tenets in common. Below are a few websites where you can learn more:

- American Psychological Association: www.apa.org/ethics/code/index.aspx
- American Anthropological Association: www.aaanet.org/committees/ethics/ethcode.htm
- American Sociology Association: www.asanet.org/about/ethics.cfm
- Association for Computing Machinery: www.acm.org/about/code-of-ethics

At a Glance

> Do no harm
> The right to be informed
> Permission to record
> Create a comfortable experience
> Appropriate language
> Anonymity vs. confidentiality
> The right to withdraw without penalty
> Appropriate incentives
> Valid and reliable data
> Acknowledge your true capabilities
> Data retention, documentation, and security
> Debrief

Do No Harm

At the core of all ethical guidelines are the principles of **beneficence** and **nonmaleficence**. That is a fancy way of saying that your research must be beneficial and do no harm. But in order to protect your participants from harm, you must first understand all of the potential risks your participants may encounter in your study. Right now, you are probably thinking, "It's a card sorting study for a website. What possible risks could there be?!" The risks could be perceived by the participant (e.g., "The video of my study will get leaked and everyone will laugh at it") or actual (e.g., the product is so hard to use that the study is actually pretty unpleasant to use). The risks can be benign (e.g., boredom), physical (e.g., thumb discomfort using a newly designed game controller), emotional (e.g., anxiety about account security in a phishing study), or worrisome (e.g., the participant learns of a new feature being developed that causes him or her to be concerned after the study). You must find a way to mitigate all of the risks, real and perceived, and address them in your informed consent to the participant. Using the example of the game controller, if there really is no way you can redesign the controller to avoid the thumb discomfort, then first, you should help mitigate it by limiting the time the participant uses it (e.g., short test sessions, frequent breaks). Second, you must notify participants of the risk at the beginning of the study and inform them that they are free to take a break or quit at any time they feel discomfort. Be aware that it is also possible that removing an intervention you introduced in your study can cause harm (e.g., giving participants an easier tool for their jobs then removing it after the study).

The Right to Be Informed

It is only when the participants fully understand the risks and what is going to happen in the study that they can be willing (not deceived) participants. For example, since it is not uncommon for participants to worry that many people are going to see the video of their study and possibly laugh at their mistakes, you should inform all participants (not just the ones who ask) how you will control access to the video and data.

Participants have the right to know the purpose of the activity they are involved in, the expected duration, procedures, use of information collected (e.g., to design a new product), incentives for participation, and their rights as a participant of the study (e.g., freedom to withdraw without penalty). You should also inform participants that the purpose of the study is to evaluate the product, *not them*, and any difficulty they encounter is a reflection on the product, *not them*. This information should be conveyed during the recruitment process (refer to Chapter 6, Preparing for Your User Requirements Activity, "Recruitment Methods" section, page 139) and then reiterated at the beginning of the activity when the informed consent form is distributed and signed by the participants. The participants sign this form to acknowledge being informed of these things and agreeing to participate. If you are working with participants under the age of 18, a parent or guardian must sign the informed consent form; however, the minor must still be verbally informed of the same information "in terms they can understand" and provide their consent. If the minor does not consent, it does not matter that the parent has already agreed.

Deception should be avoided unless the benefits greatly outweigh any potential harm. You may not want to reveal every aspect of your study up front to avoid biasing the participant's response, but the participant should not be tricked into participating if you believe he or she never would have agreed to sign up had he or she known the details of the study. For example, if you want to conduct a **brand-blind study** (i.e., the creator of the product is not identified) or **sponsor-blind study** (i.e., you do not wish to reveal that you are conducting an analysis of your competition's product), a third-party recruiting for your study could provide participants with a list of possible companies (including yours and your competitors) that are conducting the study. The participants should then be asked if they have any concerns or issues with participating in studies by any of those companies. At the end of the study, the evaluator should reveal the true sponsor.

If participants have a misperception about the purpose of the activity (e.g., believing that it is a job interview), the participant must be corrected immediately and given the opportunity to withdraw. Participants should also have the opportunity to ask questions and to know whom to contact with further questions about the study or their rights.

Permission to Record

It is common to record research studies as it allows stakeholders who could not attend to see what happened, and it allows researchers to focus on what is happening without having to take copious notes during the study. Before recording the voice or image of any individual, you must obtain permission. This can be accomplished with the consent form in Figure 3.2. The recording must not be used in a manner that could cause public identification or harm. Inform participants during recruitment that they will be audio or video recorded. Some individuals are not comfortable with this, so you do not want to wait until the participant arrives to find that out. Although it is rare, we have had a couple of participants leave before the activity even began because they refused to be recorded. If you would like to use recordings of a participant beyond your research team, you must seek additional permission. For example, if you would like to show a video of participants in a study at a research conference, you could let participants "opt in" to a recording by adding the following to your consent form or permission to record form:

Please select ONE of the following options for use of audio/video recordings by initialing your preference below:

- **If you are willing to allow us to use a recording of any portion of your interview, please initial here___. If you have initialed here, we may use a portion of your interview in a presentation, for example, but you will never be identified by name.**
- **If you would prefer that we use information from your audio/video recording only in transcribed form (rather than as an audio or video clip), please initial here ___.**

On the flip side, with the use of remote evaluations, you must inform users that they are not allowed to record the sessions or take any screenshots. Remember to include this in your **NDA** (refer to "Legal Considerations" section on page 76 to learn more about nondisclosure agreements).

"You don't mind if we record this, do you?"

Cartoon by Abi Jones

Create a Comfortable Experience

Participants in your study should never feel uncomfortable, either physically or psychologically. This includes simple things like offering regular bathroom breaks, beverages, and comfortable facilities. And of course, this includes treating the participants with respect at all times. If your study involves minors, keep the tasks age or skill appropriate and keep the sessions shorter to allow for shorter attention spans. If your user research activity involves any type of completion of tasks or product use (e.g., having users complete tasks on a competitor product), you must stress to the participant that the *product* is being evaluated, not them. Using a particularly difficult or poorly designed product can be stressful. If a participant performs poorly, never reveal that his or her answers are wrong or that something was done incorrectly. You need to be empathetic and remind participants that any difficulties they encounter are not a reflection on their own abilities but on the quality of the product they are using. For example, if participants blame themselves for their difficulties (e.g., "I am sure the way to do this task is obvious but I am never good at this kind of thing"), you can reply, "Not at all! The difficulty you are having is the fault of the website, not you. If you were at home and would normally quit at this point, please don't hesitate to say so!"

Appropriate Language

Part of treating participants with respect is to understand that they are not "subjects." Historically, this was how participants were described. It was not meant pejoratively, but the *APA Publication Manual* referred to earlier recommends that you replace the impersonal term "subjects" with a more descriptive term when possible. You do not want to use the participants' names for reasons of anonymity (see below); however, *participants, individuals*, or *respondents* are all better alternatives to "subjects." Of course, you would never address a participant by asking, "What do you think, Subject Number 1?" You should also show the same respect when speaking about them in their absence or in documentation. Never make light of participants (e.g., stakeholders laughing at participants in the observation room or after the study). The people who agree to provide you with their time and expertise are the foundation of a successful study. Without them, nearly every activity listed in this book would be impossible.

We strongly recommend that readers review the sixth edition of the *APA Publication Manual* to better understand language bias, both written and spoken.

Anonymity vs. Confidentiality

Anonymity and **confidentiality** are also terms that people often conflate. To keep a participant's participation in your study completely anonymous means not having any personally identifying information (PII) about them. Since we typically conduct screeners to qualify participants for our studies, we know their names, e-mail addresses, etc. Instead, we typically keep their participation confidential. We do not associate a participant's name or other personally identifiable information with his or her data (e.g., notes, surveys, videos) unless the participant provides such consent in writing. Instead, we use a participant ID (e.g., P1, participant 1). It is important to protect a participant's privacy, so if you are unable to provide anonymity, at a minimum, you must keep his or her participation confidential.

If the participants are employees of your company, you have a special obligation to protect their anonymity from their managers. Never show videos of employees to their managers (refer to Chapter 7, During Your User Research Activity, "Who Should NOT Observe" section, page 162). This rule should also apply to their colleagues. You should also be aware that the requirements around handling the personally identifiable information of minors differs per country.

The Right to Withdraw

Participants should feel free to withdraw from your activity *without penalty* at any point in the study. If a participant withdraws partway through the study and you do not pay the person (or pay only a fraction of the original incentive), you are punishing him or her. If you are conducting an economic behavioral study, a participant's choices during the study actually impact the size of their incentive. However, in most HCI studies, you are obligated to pay all participants the full incentive, whether they participate in the full study or not. One way to make this crystal clear to participants is by providing them with their incentive as soon as they arrive at the lab. As you inform the participants of their rights as stated in your informed consent form, you can point out, "I have already provided your incentive, and that is yours to keep, regardless of how long you participate in the study." In all of our years of conducting user research, the authors have never had a case of a participant taking advantage of the situation by arriving to get his or her incentive and then just leaving.

Appropriate Incentives

You should avoid offering excessive or inappropriate incentives as an enticement for participation as such inducements are likely to coerce the participant (refer to Chapter 6, Preparing for Your User Requirements Activity, "Determining Participant Incentives" section, page 127). We realize the incentive is part of the reason why most people participate in research activities, but the incentive should not be so enticing that anyone would want to participate regardless of interest. The main reason for participation should be interest in influencing your product's design. In other words, do not make participants an offer they cannot refuse. This is context-dependent so the amount of the incentive you offer in the United States will be different from the amount you offer in India, for example, and the amount you offer for a highly skilled worker (e.g., doctor, lawyer) may be different from what you offer a general Internet user. This is an especially important point to understand if conducting international research where the amount you offer for one hour of participation in the United States is equivalent to a month's salary in another country. You may feel you are doing a service by offering such an excessive incentive. This is not only coercive, however; you also risk pricing out other local companies with your inflated incentives.

The incentives should also be accountable (i.e., no cash). In other words, you need to be able to track that the incentive was given to the participant. This is not an ethical guideline but is good practice in any company. You could offer AMEX gift checks, Visa gift cards, or other gifts. You will need to investigate what type of incentive is most appropriate for each country or region you are conducting research in (e.g., mobile top-up cards, M-Pesa). Do not forget to track the amount you provide per participant (see earlier tax discussion).

You should speak with your legal department before recruiting paying customers and offering them any incentives for your studies. Many companies, especially those in the enterprise space, do not provide monetary incentives to paying customers, or they may prefer to offer only logo gear of nominal value (e.g., t-shirts, mugs) to avoid the appearance of offering bribes for business. Make sure you know your company's policies. You should *never* offer incentives to government officials. To many people's surprise, US public school teachers and state college/university employees are considered government employees. If you are developing a product for teachers, you obviously will want to include them in your study, so you may need to speak with your legal department to determine how to provide a benefit of some kind for these participants. Outside of the United States, it can be much trickier to know who a government employee is, so check with your legal department when planning to do studies outside your home country.

One question that many people have is how to compensate for longitudinal or multipart studies. If you are concerned about high drop-off or participants not completing all parts of your study, you can break your study into smaller pieces with smaller incentives. You can decide which and how many of the pieces of the study you want to invite participants to complete, and they can decide which ones to opt into. One concern here is the appearance of coercion to complete the study. Make sure that your incentive structure does not unduly influence participants from withdrawing from the study. For example, if you set up an incentive scheme where participants would receive $1 per day every day for five days and then an additional $100 if they completed all five days, this might prevent them from feeling they could withdraw from the study after two days. A better strategy would be to pay them $20 per day for each day and then a $5 bonus if they completed all five days.

Valid and Reliable Data

The questions you ask participants and your reactions to their comments can affect the data you collect. In every activity, you must ensure that the data you collect are free from bias, accurate, **valid**, and **reliable**. You should never collect and report data that you know are invalid or unreliable. If you suspect that participants are being dishonest in their representation, regardless of their reasons, you should throw away their data. You must inform **stakeholders** about the limitations of the data you have collected. And of course, you must *never* fabricate data.

Along the same lines, if you learn of someone who is misusing or misrepresenting your work, you must take reasonable steps to correct it. For example, if in order to further an argument, someone is inaccurately quoting partial results from a series of studies you conducted, you must inform everyone involved of the correct interpretation of the results of the study. If people question the integrity of your work, your efforts are all for naught.

You should remove yourself from situations in which a conflict of interest may affect your actions. For example, it is ill-advised for one to personally collect feedback on their own designs because objectivity is affected. Although many companies hire individuals to act as both designer and researcher with the expectation that they will evaluate their own designs, this is unwise. Due to your bias, your results will not be valid. However, if you find yourself in the situation where you are doing research on your own designs, be aware of your own bias. By recognizing this, you can attempt to mitigate it. If possible, try to put some temporal distance between the design phase and the research phase, for example. Alternatively, set up your study so you have less influence over the results (e.g., quantitative survey data require less interpretation than qualitative interview data).

Acknowledge Your True Capabilities

You should provide services, make recommendations, and conduct research *only* within the boundaries of your competencies. In your job role, this may require you to seek out additional training or resources. You should always inform individuals of the boundaries of your knowledge and skills, should you be placed in a situation that is outside your areas of expertise. For example, if you are asked to run a usability evaluation and you know nothing about usability, you should not attempt to wing it. If you do not have the time to learn what is necessary to run the activity, you should contract it out to a professional who can.

We provide the training and tools in this book to help you learn how to conduct user research, but we also encourage you to supplement this with additional courses and mentoring.

Finally, you should not delegate work to individuals who you know do not have the appropriate training or knowledge to complete the task. This also means you cannot hand over your ethical responsibilities to a third party. Anyone that you hire to recruit participants or conduct studies for your company should adhere to the same ethical standards you observe. If a vendor is unhappy about your requirement to provide a list of potential sponsors during the screening stage for a brand-blind study or to pay participants in full even if they withdraw partway through a study, find another vendor. If a vendor warns you that a certain user type will be difficult to recruit and thus may need to be "creative," ask what "creative" means. Turning a blind eye to how a vendor recruited those users is engaging in unethical behavior and is putting the participants, your company, and your data at risk.

Data Retention, Documentation, and Security

Retain the original data collected (e.g., screeners, raw notes, videos) only for as long as it is required by your organization, industry, country, or region. This may be the period of time that you are working on a particular version of the product or it may be several years. You will want to retain the data in case you need to reference it at a later date for clarification purposes. It can also be very useful to provide continuity in the event that someone must take over research support for the product. In academic settings, the funder of your research (e.g., the

National Science Foundation) and/or the IRB likely have rules about how long you must keep your data after a study has been completed. After that, to protect user confidentiality, you should destroy it. In the meantime, you are responsible for ensuring the data are secure and only those that need access have it. One strategy Kelly uses in most of her work is to de-identify data as soon as possible after collection. Once participants have been paid, there is rarely a reason to need to know their real name, birthday, address, or phone number. Even if you do have to collect this information, you should not store it with study data. Instead, keep any of this personal information stored separately. That way, even if others were able to access your data, they would not be able to match participants' study data to their names.

It is important to accurately record the methods of any study you conduct (refer to Chapter 15, Concluding Your Activity, "Reporting Your Findings" section, page 463). This will allow anyone to understand exactly how you collected the data and what conclusions were drawn. This history is also critical for all stakeholders—and especially anyone who is new to the product team. You would be amazed at how often a "brand new" idea really is not brand new. Those reports can prevent repetition of the same mistakes every time a new team member comes on board.

Debrief

If a participant was not aware of the full intent of the study (i.e., its purpose) before it began, you should attempt to debrief him or her about the nature, results, and conclusions of the study. Typically in a user research activity, the participants are told why the information is being collected (e.g., to help design a usable product, to learn more about a domain, to collect user requirements), so this is not an issue. However, in the case of a customer, this could mean asking participants at the end of the study whether they wish to be contacted regarding the results of the activity once the product has shipped. You should also give participants a way to redress any concerns they may have if they feel they have been deceived or poorly treated. For example, offer to allow them to speak with your manager or, if the issue is more serious, your company's legal department.

Legal Considerations

It is very important for you to protect your company whenever you run any kind of research activity. You do this not only for ethical reasons but also to protect your company from being sued. By following the basic rules of ethics discussed above, you should avoid such circumstances.

In addition to protecting your company from lawsuits, you also want to protect the confidentiality of your products. As a company, you do not typically want the world to know too early about the latest and greatest products you are developing. In most cases, this information is deemed highly confidential. When you run user research activities, you are exposing people outside of your company to a potential or existing product. It may not be the product itself, but ideas relating to that product. Regardless, it is imperative that your participants keep the information they are exposed to confidential so that it cannot be used to create competitor products. In order to protect your company's product, you should have all participants sign an NDA. This form is a legal agreement in which the participant signs and thereby agrees to keep all information regarding the product and session confidential for a predefined period. It does not stop a participant from leaking the confidential information, but it provides your company with legal recourse in the event it happens. This agreement also typically states that any ideas or feedback the participant provides becomes the property of your company. You want to avoid participants later requesting financial compensation for an idea they provided in your study, regardless of whether it really was the source of your great new product enhancement. Work with your legal department to create an agreement that is appropriate for your purposes and to ensure that it will protect your company. Ideally, it should be written in terms a layperson can understand, but you are still obliged to explain the terms of the agreement (especially when the participant is a minor) and answer any questions. Although a parent or guardian must sign an NDA on behalf of a minor, the minor must still understand what is being asked of them and the consequences of violation.

Figure 3.1 shows a sample NDA to help you get a sense of the kind of information that this document should contain. Again, we do not advise that you take this document and start using it at your company. It is imperative that you have a legal professional review any NDA that you decide to use.

TIP

Make sure that any document you give to participants (legal or otherwise) is easy to read and understand. Handing participants a long, complicated document full of legal terms will unnecessarily frighten them, and some may refuse to sign without having a lawyer review it.

Although it is written with the assumption that you are conducting the study in person with the participant, some of the methods in this book can be conducted remotely (e.g., diary study, survey, remote usability test). Regardless of whether you are face to face with the participant or not, all of the legal and ethical issues discussed here apply. In remote studies, you will likely need to provide the following:

- An e-mail address or phone number where participants can contact you with any questions before and after a study. You need to answer those questions as completely as you would in an in-person study and do it quickly.
- Clear informed consent laying out all of the participants' rights, purpose of the study, permission to record (if applicable), how their data will be handled, risks, and benefits.
- Mechanisms to avoid risk. Going back to the example of the game controller potentially causing thumb discomfort, you may need to create time limits to prevent participants from using the controller for too long and make it easy for them to take breaks as needed.
- Online NDA for participants to click and accept or easy mechanism for them to read, sign, and return the NDA. Remember that not everyone has access to a scanner, so you if you are forced to use paper documents, provide a self-addressed stamped envelope for participants to mail you their NDA.
- Ability to quit the study at any point while still easily receiving their incentive.
- Appropriate incentive that the participant can quickly and easily receive. For example, if you are conducting a diary study with different groups of participants over several weeks, participants should not have to wait until

your entire study is complete before receiving their incentive. Instead, you need to provide the incentive (ideally) as soon as participants begin the study or shortly after they finish their participation.

- Debrief mechanism following the study if there is anything you hid from the participants (e.g., study sponsor).

Pulling It All Together

In this chapter, we have introduced you to the legal and ethical issues to take into consideration when conducting a user research activity. By treating participants legally and ethically, you will protect them, your company, and your data—all of which are critical for successful user research. This involves *always* obtaining informed consent from your participants, and to do that, you must verify that participants:

- Understand what it means to participate
- Comprehend and agree to any risks
- Understand how their personal data will be protected
- Have a meaningful chance to ask questions
- Are able to seek redress if they are unhappy
- Know they can withdraw without penalty at any point in time

Without the participants, you could not conduct your study. Remember the participants in your study must be treated with the utmost respect. This applies to *all* methods described in this book.

CHAPTER 4

Setting Up Research Facilities

Introduction

You may already have access to a **usability** lab at your company or your client's site. If so, it was most likely built with the intent of conducting one-on-one usability evaluations. Will this lab work for all types of user experience research? Yes and no. For individual activities (e.g., interviews, solo card sort), your current setup may be fine. However, it is unlikely that a "standard" usability lab is able to accommodate group activities (e.g., group card sort). Since standard labs are typically the size of an office, they are just too small. It may also be inadequate for simulating home environments if you are interested in evaluating video games, Internet-connected TVs, or other products that are more likely to be used in a casual home environment instead of a formal office setting.

If you are conducting user requirements gathering, you may be wondering whether a permanent space needs to be built to conduct these activities. The answer is no. It is great if you have the budget, but it is not absolutely necessary. If you want to observe users in their own environment (e.g., field studies) or collect data from a lot of users (e.g., surveys, diary studies), then a usability lab is unnecessary. However, labs are excellent for card sorting, interviews, and focus groups. In this chapter, we discuss the options for setting up facilities to conduct a user requirements activity. We look at the pros and cons for each option, as well as what you should be aware of when making your selection.

TIP

Wherever you conduct user research activities, be sure to create and post some signs outside the room indicating that an activity is in session and whether or not people may enter the room. If you can secure the door to prevent entry, that is even better. This will prevent people from barging in and disrupting your session.

At a Glance

> Using your company's existing facilities
> Renting a marketing or hotel facility
> Building a permanent facility

Using Your Company's Existing Facilities

If your budget is razor-thin, your only option may be to use your organization's existing space (e.g., conference room, classroom), but that is actually not a problem! If you are conducting a group activity, then when choosing a room for your session, you must obviously ensure it can comfortably accommodate all of the participants, plus one or more moderators. It should be flexible enough to allow multiple activity configurations. For example, it should allow everyone to sit around one large table for **brainstorming** with enough room for you, an optional notetaker, and a whiteboard or flip charts at the front of the room (see Figure 4.1 for two possible configurations).

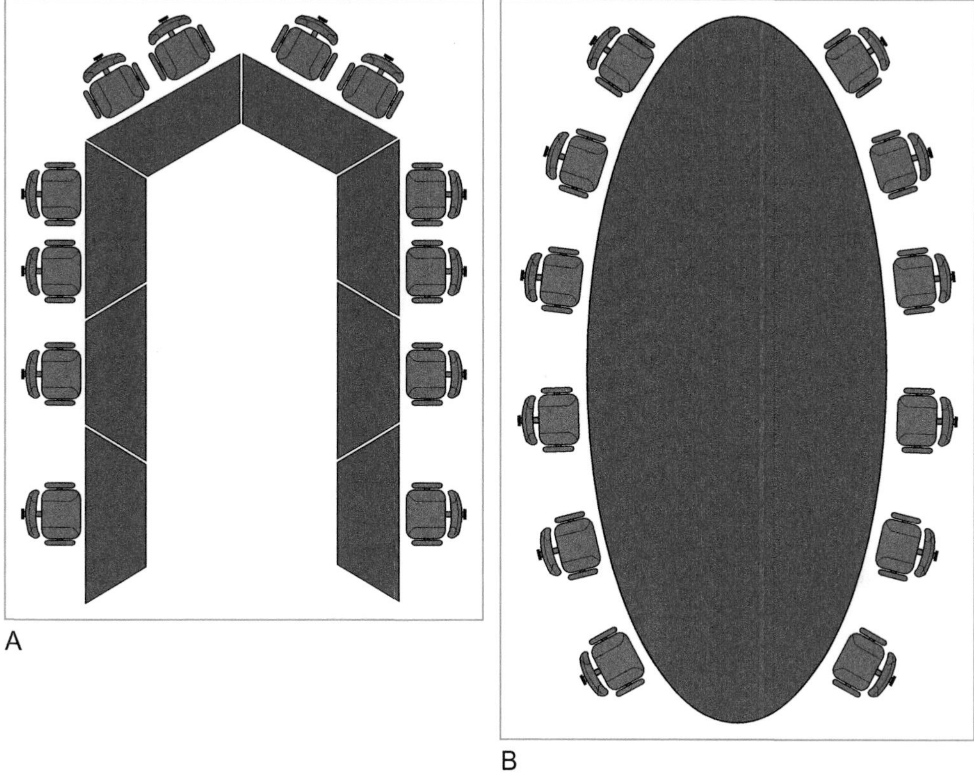

Figure 4.1: Table setup for a focus group or group card sort. The "U" shape allows all participants to see each other easily—as well as the moderator—but an oval shape will work as well.

This arrangement will accommodate a group card sorting activity (Chapter 11, page 304) and a focus group (Chapter 12, page 340). It should also allow you to bring in smaller tables for a group of three participants for triad interviews (see Figure 4.2 for two possible configurations). A large conference room is the most likely candidate for these purposes.

Individual activities (e.g., interviews) can be conducted in a conference room, or you may choose a more intimate location that is quiet, such as an empty office. Whatever location you choose, it does not need to be permanently devoted to user activities. As long as you can get access to the room when needed, and no one disturbs your activities, there is no reason why a good conference room or office should be locked up when not in use for their primary purpose.

When using your company's existing facilities, you may be tempted to leave enough space in the back of the room for observers, but you must resist this temptation. It is important to keep the observers in a room that is separate from the participants. The participants will feel very self-conscious if there are people in the room who are not taking part in the activity but simply watching them. Instead, you can transmit an image of the session live to a TV in the next room, use a video-conferencing tool for people to dial into from another room, or record the activity for later viewing by product team members. A **mobile lab** or **portable lab** is ideal for situations when you must move between rooms.

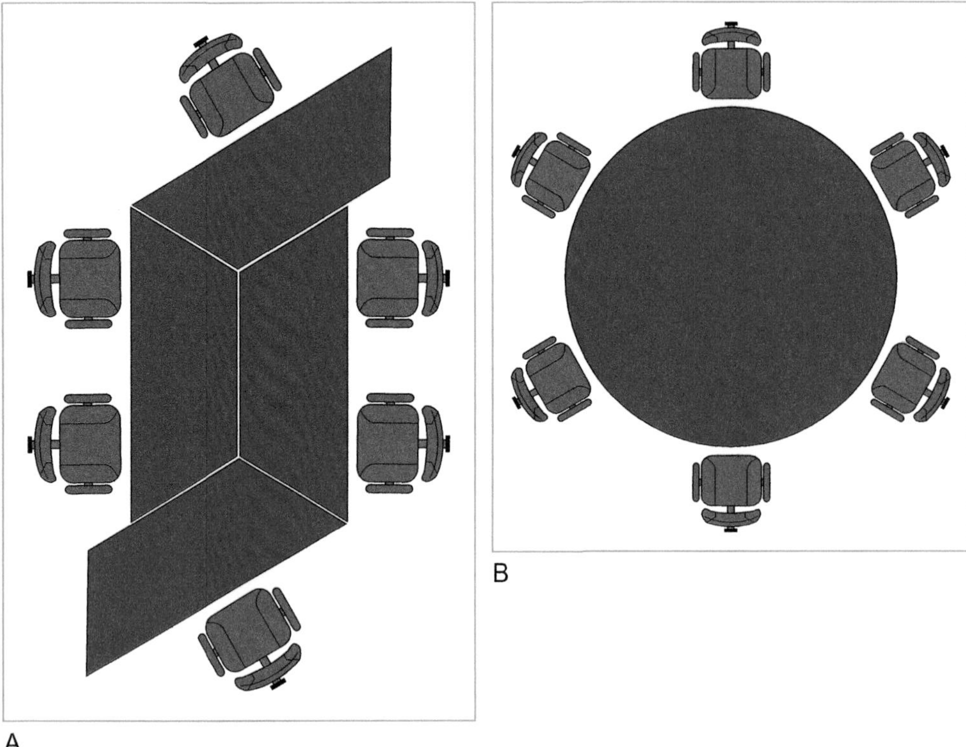

Figure 4.2: Table setup for a focus group, triad interview, or small group card sort. A round table works just as well, but these configurable tables can be expanded for larger groups.

It also works well for studies in the field. A laptop with a web camera and screen-capture or video-recording software is all that is really needed. An additional laptop for notetaking, video camera and tripod, and external mic (to pick up quiet participants or in noisy environments) can be very helpful but are not strictly necessary.

A videographer to control the camera will be necessary if the participants will be moving around (refer to Chapter 7, During Your User Requirements Activity, "Recording and Notetaking" section, page 171).

Portable Lab Equipment

- Laptop with web camera (required if conducting an evaluation)
- Screen-capture software or video-recording software (required if conducting an evaluation)
- Video camera and tripod to record participant(s) (strongly recommended)
- Laptop for notetaking (optional)
- External microphone (optional)

Renting a Marketing or Hotel Facility

If you have a little more budget and you prefer not to conduct studies in a conference room or classroom, you can often rent a room from a marketing research vendor. Rooms are available in most major cities in the United States and the Western world. One benefit of this option is that the activity is being held on neutral territory. You may also be able to hire one of the employees of the vendor to help conduct the study. Participants may feel free to be more honest in their statements if they are not sitting in the middle of the company's conference room.

These firms are typically set up for focus groups with one camera and an observation room. These full-service facilities may offer focus group moderators for an additional fee. They will also typically recruit participants and provide food for your session. If you do not conduct user research activities frequently and cannot acquire the funds for a permanent lab, this is a good option. You can find market research companies in your area through one of the sources below:

- Quirk's Researcher SourceBook™ (a directory of marketing research and market research companies) (http://www.quirks.com/directory/sourcebook/index.aspx)
- AAPOR/WAPOR Blue Book (http://www.aapor.org/Blue_Book1.htm#.U58DgWSSx2k)
- ESOMAR Directory of Research (http://directory.esomar.org/)
- MRA Blue Book Marketing Research Services Directory (http://www.bluebook.org/)
- AMA Marketing Resource Directory (http://marketingresourcedirectory.ama.org/)

If you do not have marketing research vendors in your area, you may wish to go to the nearest hotel and reserve a meeting room. As was noted in "Using Your Company's Existing Facilities," you should not have observers in the same room as the participants, and you will need to set up video equipment to record the session. Some hotels will not let you bring in your own video camera, requiring you to use their services for a fee, so make sure you ask about this when making the reservation.

Building a Permanent Facility

Usually, the most difficult thing to convince a company of is to give you a permanent space to build your lab. The budget to purchase the equipment is usually easier to get approved, but committing a space that could otherwise be used as a conference room or a set of offices is quite difficult. However, there are several benefits to having a dedicated usability lab:

- It tells/reminds people in your company that they have a research group—one important enough in the company's agenda to get their own lab (hopefully in a prominent location near the main entrance so that participants can get to it easily).
- You do not have to ask someone for permission to use the facility to conduct your research activity or worse, get evicted from the room by a higher-ranking individual.

- You do not have to transport the audio-video equipment and other materials from one room to another because you can keep them there permanently. Not only will this save your back and time, but it will prevent damaging equipment during as well.
- You will have your *own* room in which to analyze data, post **affinity diagrams** and session artifacts without fear of someone removing them, or hold design discussions. You will also have a ready location to hold meetings and brainstorms.

Components of a Devoted User Research Facility

If your company is supportive of creating a permanent room devoted to user research, you are in luck! You should not feel overwhelmed, however, by the daunting task of figuring out what equipment you should choose. There are many audiovisual installation companies that can help you assess your needs (and your budget) and build the lab of your dreams—but you should at least be knowledgeable about the equipment available and its purpose.

At a Glance

> Equipment for your facility:

User Room

- At least one table
- At least two chairs
- One-way mirror (optional)
- Adjustable lighting
- Video cameras or web camera
- Microphones
- Computer and monitor
- Screen-capture software
- Soundproofing
- Mixer
- Datalogging software
- Equipment cart

Observation Room

- Tables and chairs for stakeholders to take notes
- Television/video monitor
- Magnetic whiteboards or wall surfaces that you can tape paper to
- Storage space

Technology often drops in price over time, and you may be able to find the equipment on discount websites. But do keep in mind that often you get just what you pay for, so saving money in the short term may cost you in the long term.

Caution

It is obvious to state that technology changes. Use this chapter as a starting point, but also do research on what is new to the market. This chapter is meant simply to be a starting point.

TIP

"Preowned" equipment *may* be an option via online auction sites. Some large companies periodically update their equipment, and when they do, they want to get rid of their old equipment. Other companies, when hitting on hard times, have had to sell their lab equipment and disband their research group. However, these most likely will not come with any warranties or guarantees. Remember, you get what you pay for.

Lab Layout

We recommend having a "user" room and an "observation" room in your lab configuration (see Figure 4.3). If you are unable to build this type of layout, but you do have access to a second room, you can stream the sessions over a local network or the Internet.

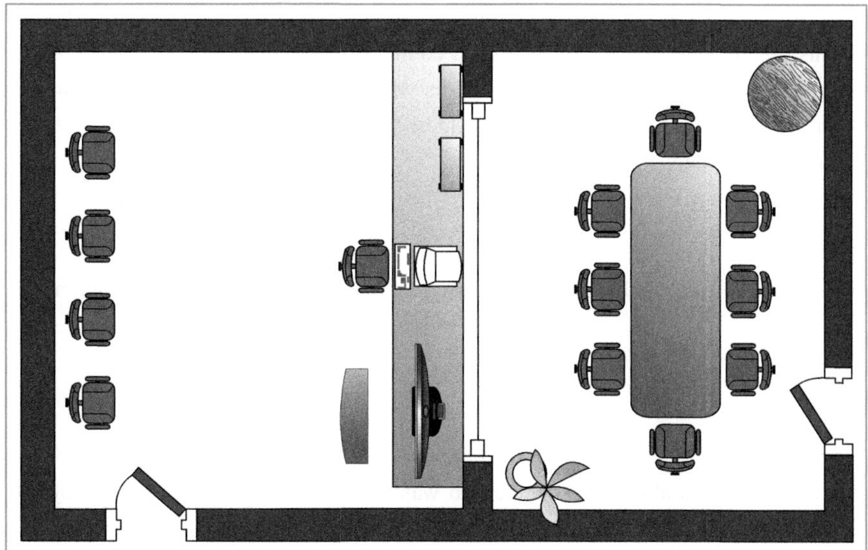

Figure 4.3: Typical two-room lab layout.

Tables

Figure 4.4 shows a lab at Google that can be used for individual interviews, group discussions, and eye-tracking usability studies. Large group activities are typically done in one of the large conference rooms on campus. Configurable tables for the user room, as sketched in Figures 4.1 and 4.2, are extremely useful. These tables have rollers with locks on them so they can be pushed from one arrangement to another quickly and easily and then locked in the chosen position. Standard tables for the observation room allow **stakeholders** to comfortably sit and take notes while observing your studies.

Figure 4.4: Google's multipurpose usability lab.

Chairs

Try to find chairs that are stackable (for storing in tight places) and easy to move. The chairs should be well made so that participants, researchers, and observers can sit comfortably for one to two hours. If the participants are uncomfortable, you will not be getting their best. Chairs with armrests are not only more comfortable but also take up more room. If you are in a tight space, you might be better off skipping the armrests, but keep in mind that comfortable participants are happy participants.

Couch

If there is enough space, it is nice to have a couch in the user room to conduct interviews and mobile evaluations comfortably.

One-Way Mirror

If you have the luxury of dividing a space into two halves—a user half and an observer half—a one-way mirror is optional. Obviously, this allows stakeholders to watch a session without being seen by the participants. Unfortunately, it can be expensive to purchase and install a one-way mirror (the cost depends on the size of the room and the construction required). It can also decrease the soundproofing. A cheaper and easier solution is to install televisions or monitors and run cables to transmit the live feed.

Remember that if you use a one-way mirror, you will need to keep the observation room dark. You can have low levels of light, and it will still be extremely difficult for participants to see through. However, keep in mind that reflective surfaces (e.g., television screens, laptop screens, white paper, white clothes) in the observation room can sometimes be seen even when the lights are very low. Figures 4.5 and 4.6 show the observation rooms for Citrix and Google, respectively.

Figure 4.5: Citrix's observation room.

Figure 4.6: Google's observation room.

TIP

If you have a separate room where observers can watch from behind a one-way mirror, paint the walls of this room a dark color. This reduces reflection and makes it more difficult for participants to see observers through the glass. The goal is not to conceal that people are observing the study (you should inform participants of this at the start of the study); however, it will prevent participants from being distracted when they see observers walking in and out of the room.

Adjustable Lighting

Because the activities in the lab will vary, different levels of lighting may be necessary. Dimmer switches, and lights that can be turned on independently throughout the room, will allow you to provide as much or as little light as needed. You should also provide dimmer switches in the observation room so that very low levels of light can be achieved to ensure the participants will not see the observers during a user research activity. Task lighting can be very helpful for solo card-sorting tasks and to avoid glare when evaluating mobile devices.

Video Cameras

Purchasing a high-definition (HD) video camera that has pan/tilt control (i.e., allowing horizontal and vertical movement) will be an excellent investment; however, this will also require a separate control system. Alternatively, a sturdy tripod with two-way pan/tilt control can be used for less.

The ideal location of video cameras is wherever they give you the best range of desired angles. Whether that is on the ceiling, wall, or a crane arm depends on the layout of the room, furniture, and equipment. For example, ceiling-mounted cameras are extremely useful when conducting group activities or a mobile evaluation. Good-quality dome cameras have remote pan/tilt/zoom capabilities and are perfectly silent (see Figure 4.7). Of course, you will not be able to use the cameras in other rooms or in field studies.

If you have a couch, you can also consider a crane to mount the camera, giving you the flexibility to shoot over the participant's shoulder during card sorting or mobile evaluations. Document cameras can also be used for mobile studies but they are less flexible, as the participant must keep the mobile device on the table.

Microphones

Microphone placement depends on the type of activity being recorded. Ideally, microphones should be small and unobtrusive. Omnidirectional table microphones are often best for in-room studies. They go virtually unnoticed by participants, which is ideal when you do not want to make people self-conscious about being recorded. Lavalier microphones are ideal for the moderator in group sessions when he or she is often on the move. They offer improved audio quality, but they require a mixer to receive the wireless signal. Mics can be connected directly to an audio recorder or computer, but for good sound quality, the lab will need an audio processor to combine the signals from all mics and computer inputs for recording, streaming, and local observation.

Figure 4.7: Photo of a dome camera in a Google lab.

Computer and Monitors

A laptop or single workstation will likely be sufficient in the user-half of the lab. An additional laptop or workstation in the observation room allows a colleague to take notes during the activity. At the very least, ensure that plenty of outlets are installed so that stakeholders can bring in laptops to take their own notes during a session.

Screen-Capture Software

You can purchase software that captures the image on a computer hard drive while a participant works. Products like TechSmith's *Morae®* and *Camtasia®*, Hyperionic's *HyperCam™*, MatchWare's *ScreenCorder*, and SmartGuyz's *ScreenCam®* allow you to edit the images to create a highlight video (a visual summary of actions the user made or comments the user said). Many of these tools have free trial versions, so you can see which one best suits your needs.

Soundproofing

Whether or not you have a separate control room, it is wise to have soundproofing in your lab. At a minimum, it blocks out conversations from the hallway or surrounding offices. In addition, it keeps the confidential discussions within the lab. If you do have an observation room (e.g., control room), soundproofing is necessary between this room and the participant's room, so that the participants do not hear any discussions in the control room between the observers.

To ensure quality soundproofing, double-glass one-way mirrors with a bit of space for air between the two mirrors will work well.

The cost of soundproofing will vary depending on the size of the room and the materials used. Having separate entrances to the two rooms will also ensure that sound does not travel through the door. Double walls between the control room and the users' room, with a little space between the walls, also ensures good soundproofing. Regardless of the quality of soundproofing, it is always a good idea to ask the observers to be as quiet as possible.

Mixer

A video mixer/multiplexer will allow multiple inputs—from cameras, computers, or other inputs—to be combined into one mixed image. Some mixers will also allow the creation of "picture in picture" (PIP) overlays. The output from a video mixer can be fed either directly into a screen (e.g., in the observation room) or into a recording device locally. If you are only looking to create a PIP (e.g., of a computer input with the user's face overlaid), some screens/TVs have this option built in. Figure 4.8 shows the control room for the Citrix labs. All of the equipment for all of the labs is centralized in this one room.

Figure 4.8: Control room for the Citrix labs.

Datalogging Software

Special software for taking notes during the session is not required, although it is extremely valuable to have a program that time stamps each entry to match the corresponding video. If you want to create a highlights tape to showcase particular user comments, you can check the datalog and then go to the exact section of the recording.

There are actually quite a few datalogging products available, but as their availability changes over time, we recommend you do a web search for "usability datalogging software" to find the latest ones and read reviews for them. These tools support customizable functions that allow you to create codes for specific user actions (e.g., each time a participant references a specific topic). This allows faster notetaking and allows you to categorize behavior for easy analysis. Some tools come with analysis functions, while other tools allow the data to be exported to a spreadsheet or statistical analysis program.

Unfortunately, some datalogging applications available today are really designed more for usability testing than for requirements gathering activities. Make sure you do your homework and insist on a free trial period before investing in any application. Some things to look for in a datalogging application:

- Automatic clip extraction of digital recordings based on comments and codes
- Free form text notetaking *and* structured coding
- Searching digital video files

In the majority of cases, a simple text editor or spreadsheet (most will give you time stamps) will do just fine to record users' comments and unique events.

TIP

Label those cords on both ends! Most cords look alike. If a piece of equipment is misbehaving or needs to be replaced, you do not want to spend an hour tracing back every cord to figure out which one is the one you need. You can buy special zip tags for this purpose, but masking tape and a permanent marker work just as well.

Television/Computer Monitor

If observers are watching from another room, a television or monitor is necessary to show what you are recording. Make sure it is large enough for everyone to see and the resolution is high quality so they can see what the participant sees.

Equipment Cart

If you have been unable to convince your company to give you a space that is yours alone, you may wish to move the equipment out to prevent curious individuals from altering your settings or unintentionally breaking your hard-earned equipment. You will need a sturdy, high-quality equipment cart on wheels. Do not try to save money by buying a cheaper cart only to have all your equipment crash to the floor! The best kinds have a built-in power strip so you only need one outlet to power all of your equipment. You can keep the equipment permanently stored on the cart, so when it comes time to relocate, you simply unplug the cables and roll away. Even if you have a dedicated space, an equipment rack is a convenient way to organize all of your equipment neatly (see Figure 4.9 for the equipment storage rack in one of Google's labs). A door on the cart also hides all that potentially scary-looking equipment from view.

Magnetic Whiteboards or Walls That You Can Tape Paper to

Some conference room walls are covered in carpet or fabric to provide a level of soundproofing. Unfortunately, this makes it almost impossible to tape anything to it. Additionally, some walls are so dense that you cannot use push-pins. For capturing brainstormed ideas, affinity diagramming, displaying paper prototypes, etc., you will need a

Figure 4.9: Equipment storage rack in a Google lab.

surface from which you can hang paper. Unless you have a whiteboard to write on or a smooth surface to tape paper to, you will need multiple easels. Painting the walls in whiteboard paint is ideal; however, you will still likely need to type up what was written on the board. For this reason, we find it faster and easier to just capture text on paper flip charts and take them back to our desks to retype or have someone else copy text from the board during the session.

TIP

Use your cell phone to take a picture of the work just in case anything happens to the originals before you can transcribe the notes.

Space for Refreshments

It is always nice to offer at least a light snack and drinks during long group sessions, especially those conducted during dinnertime. Obviously, you need to be sure there is enough room to set the refreshments out of the way so they do not get bumped into while allowing participants to easily access them.

Storage Space

Storage space (e.g., closet, cabinet) is often forgotten when designing a lab. Space is at a premium and you may be thinking it is more important to use that space for additional observers. A small storage closet or cabinet with a lock will allow you to keep all of your materials (e.g., sticky notes, easels, flip charts, markers, incentives) and additional chairs locked away so that others do not "borrow" them. Ideally, you want this in or next to your lab so you do not have to haul chairs or an armful of materials back and forth between sessions. Also, if you must move your equipment out of the lab from time to time (see "Equipment Cart" discussion), the storage closet is a convenient place to lock it away.

TIP

Regardless of what kind of equipment you are using or where you are conducting your research, schedule time to conduct pilot studies to ensure you are familiar with every piece of equipment and everything is working as expected. There are few things worse than realizing five minutes before a study is scheduled to begin that a video camera battery is dead and there is no place to plug in the charger or the screen-recording software keeps crashing when you launch it.

Pulling It All Together

User research activities can be quick and easy to run and do not require expensive, high-tech usability labs. We have offered solutions for any budget, as well as resources to build the lab of your dreams!

CHAPTER 5

Choosing a User Experience Research Activity

Introduction

Now that you have gotten stakeholder buy-in, learned about your products and users, considered legal and ethical considerations, and arranged any facilities you may need, you are ready to choose the user experience research method that is best suited to answer your research question.

This chapter provides an overview of the methods presented in this book and a decision aid for choosing which methods will best help you answer your user experience research questions.

What It Takes to Choose a Method

Get the Right People Involved

If you are a consultant, you may join a project the moment the need for user experience research is recognized. If you work for a large company, your job may be to ensure that user experience research is used to drive all new product decisions. If you are a student, you may propose to do user research as part of your thesis or dissertation, or if you are a faculty member, you may propose to do user research as part of an application for funding. Who you need to get involved will depend on your situation. In industry, you often need to get **stakeholder** input (see Chapter 1, "Getting Stakeholder Buy-in for Your Activity" section, page 16) in addition to buy-in from the product team, whereas on a thesis or dissertation project you need to get input from committee members. Either way, you need to find out what stakeholders want to get out of the user research you are going to plan and conduct. Depending on your preferences and the stakeholders' availability, a meeting may be the most effective way to get input from everyone who needs to be involved and thinking about the project. The goal of the meeting should be to answer the question: what do we want to know at the conclusion of the user experience research?

Ask the Right Questions

Once you have input from stakeholders, you need to transform everyone's input into questions that can be answered via user research. There are some questions that cannot be answered and others that should not be answered via user research. User research is not intended to answer questions about business decisions (e.g., companies to acquire to expand product offerings, timing of feature releases) or marketing (e.g., how to brand your offering, market segmentation, how much people are willing to spend on your offering). Market research is about understanding what people will buy and how to get them to buy it. User research is about understanding how people think, behave, and feel in order to design the best interaction experience. This includes questions such as the following:

- What do users want and need?
- How do users think about this topic or what is their mental model?
- What terminology do users use to discuss this topic?
- What are the cultural or other influences that affect how a user will engage with your product?
- What are the challenges and pain points users are facing?

Know the Limits

Now that you know what the fundamental questions are that you should seek to answer during your user research, you need to understand what limits there are that will further guide your decisions. The most common limits we see in user research are time, money, access to appropriate users or participants, potential for bias, and legal/ethical issues. While at first, these limits can seem problematic, we like to think of them as constraints that help guide the choice of a particular research methodology. For example, if you are conducting research about a socially sensitive topic, it is important to be aware that **social desirability bias** will likely be at play, and therefore, you need to choose a method that decreases the likelihood of this bias (e.g., anonymous survey rather than in-person interviews). If you have six months to inform the redesign of your company's washer and dryer models, you may choose to spend a few weeks conducting field studies across the country with different demographic groups of potential customers. However, if you have only six weeks to complete *all* of your research, a one-week diary study may be more appropriate. The key here is that whatever method you choose should be based on your research question and scaled to the size you can accomplish given your constraints. Knowing these limits in advance will help you choose the best method for your research question, timeline, budget, and situation (see Figure 5.1).

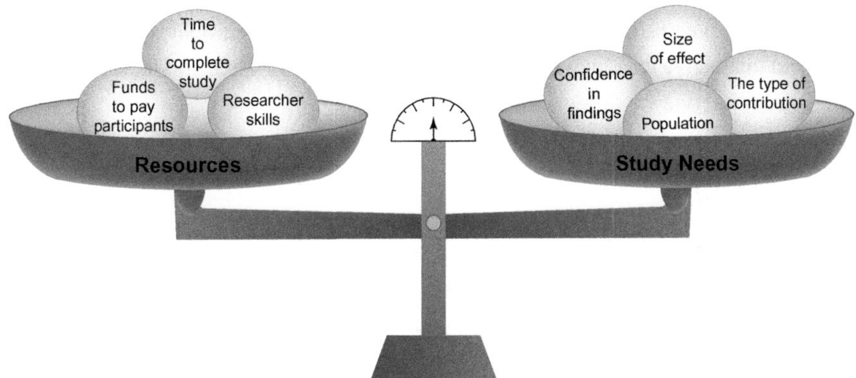

Figure 5.1: Weighing resources with study needs.

The Methods

One of the myths surrounding user research is that it takes too much time and money. This is simply not true. There are activities that fit within every time frame and budget. While some can be designed to take months, others can be conducted in as little as two hours. Each type of activity provides different information and has different goals; we will help you understand what each of these is. Regardless of your budget or time constraints, in this book, you can find a user experience activity that will answer your questions and improve the quality of your product. The methods we cover are:

- Diary studies
- Interviews

- Surveys
- Card sorts
- Focus groups
- Field studies
- Evaluation (e.g., usability tests)

We chose these methods for two reasons. First, each offers a different piece of the picture that describes the user. Second, using these methods, or a mix of these methods, you will be able to answer or **triangulate** an answer to almost any user research question you may encounter. In this section we provide a brief description of each method.

Diary Studies (Chapter 8)

Diary studies ask participants to capture information about their activities, habits, thoughts, or opinions as they go about their daily activities. These allow a researcher to collect *in situ*, typically longitudinal, data from a large sample. Diaries can be on paper or electronic and can be structured (i.e., participants are provided with specific questions) or unstructured (i.e., participants describe their experience in their own words and their own format). Both quantitative and qualitative data may be collected. Diary studies are often conducted along with other types of user research, such as interviews.

Interviews (Chapter 9)

Interviews are one of the most frequently used user research techniques. In the broadest sense, an interview is a guided conversation in which one person seeks information from another. There is a variety of different types of interviews you can conduct, depending on your constraints and needs. They are incredibly flexible and can be conducted as a solo activity or in conjunction with another user experience activity (e.g., following a card sort). Interviews can be leveraged when you want to obtain detailed information from users individually.

The end result of a set of interviews is an integration of perspectives from multiple users. If you conduct interviews with multiple user types of the same process/system/organization, you can obtain a holistic view. Finally, interviews can be used to guide additional user research activities.

Surveys (Chapter 10)

Surveys ask every user the same questions in a structured manner. Participants can complete them in their own time and from the comfort of their home or work. Since they can be distributed to a large number of users, you can typically collect much larger sample sizes than with interviews or focus groups. In addition, you can get feedback from people around the world; response rates can vary from 1% (charity surveys) to 95% (census surveys).

Card Sort (Chapter 11)

A card sort is most often used to inform or guide the development of the information architecture of a product. For example, it can help determine the hierarchy in applications. It can also provide information when deciding how to organize displays and controls on an interface.

To conduct the technique, each participant sorts cards describing objects or concepts in a product into meaningful groups. By aggregating the grouping created by several users, we can learn how closely related each of the concepts are. This method tells us how a product's features should be structured to match the users' expectations about how those features are related. This technique can be conducted with individuals or with a group of users working individually.

Focus Groups (Chapter 12)

In a focus group, six to ten users are brought together for an hour or two to provide information in response to a series of questions or to provide their subjective response to product demonstrations or concepts. Often, participants are given tasks to complete with prototypes of the product so they may have a better frame of reference from which to speak. Presenting the questions or product to a group sparks group discussion and can provide more information than interviewing individuals alone.

Focus groups are best suited for idea generation rather than formal evaluation and analysis. You can also discover problems, challenges, frustrations, likes, and dislikes among users; however, you cannot use focus groups to generalize the exact strength of users' opinions, only that they are adverse to or in support of a concept or idea. If conducted well, a focus group can provide a wealth of useful information in a short period.

Field Studies (Chapter 13)

The term "field study" encompasses a category of activities that can include contextual inquiry, on-site interviews, simple observations, and ethnography. During a field study, a researcher visits users in their own environments (e.g., home or workplace) and observes them while they are going about their daily tasks. Field studies can last anywhere from a couple of hours to several days depending on the goals and resources of your study.

Using this technique, a UX professional gains a better understanding of the environment and context. By observing users in their own environment, you can capture information that affects the use of a product (e.g., interruptions, distractions, other task demands) and additional context that cannot be captured or replicated in a lab environment. Field studies can be used at any point during the product development life cycle but are typically most beneficial during the conceptual stage.

Evaluation Methods (Chapter 14)

Evaluation methods (e.g., usability tests) are a set of methods that focus on uncovering usability issues and determining whether new or redesigned products or services meet certain criteria. There are two general categories of evaluation methods: inspection methods, where trained UX/HCI professionals inspect an interface to assess its usability, and testing methods, where UX professionals observe users as they interact with a product or service. Evaluation criteria can include task success, time on task, page views, number of clicks, conversion, user satisfaction, ease of use, and usefulness. In addition, a list of issues uncovered is typically produced with proposed design improvements.

Focus Group, Individual Interviews, or Surveys?

Focus groups are excellent if you are looking for multiple points of view in a short period. They can be used in the middle or at the end of the development cycle. They can also be a great activity to help you gather initial requirements or requirements that can be of benefit at a later stage of development. For example, a focus group can help you understand surprising or contradictory results obtained via surveys (see Chapter 10, page 266) or identify reasons why user satisfaction is so poor with your product. Individual interviews (see Chapter 9, page 220) are a better choice than focus groups when you need to collect information that is too sensitive for group discussion. You may also choose to use an interview when you need to collect information so detailed that a respondent would be required to write an essay if responding via a survey. Participants are much more likely to give an essay-length response than write one. In individual interviews, you are able to follow up on responses and clarify participants' statements, which is not possible in a survey. Furthermore, you can spend more time understanding a single participant's needs, thoughts, and experiences in an interview than in a focus group. You can also cover more topics and do not have to worry about participants influencing each other's responses. In a focus group, you are typically limited in the number of questions you can ask and the depth of discussion with each participant because you want to hear from each participant equally.

One-on-one interviews can take significant time to conduct and more resources than a survey. However, there may be times when you need to collect large samples of data to feel more confident that the results you have obtained can be applied to the user population as a whole (not just the people you interviewed). This is not typical of most product development, but it may be the case, for example, in government-regulated industries. Since the goal is usually not to obtain **statistically significant** results with a focus group (or even several focus groups), you cannot be sure that the proportion of responses to a question or topic in a focus group will match the proportion in the general population. In other words, if eight out of ten participants in a focus group state that they want a particular feature, you cannot extend that to say 80% of all users want that same feature. If you are looking for statistically significant results that can be generalized to the population as a whole, surveys with a representative sample of your population are a better choice.

Differences Among the Methods

These methods also differ in terms of whether they address questions about behaviors or attitudes; include end users and if so, what they ask those end users to do; originate from different theoretical perspectives; collect words or data in numbers; and include where they are performed. We outline each of these considerations below. For an overview of how these methods differ along these dimensions, see Table 5.1.

Table 5.1: Summary of differences between methods

Method	Behavioral vs. attitudinal	Research and participant roles	Qualitative vs. quantitative	Lab vs. contextual	Formative vs. summative	Sample size
Diary study	Either	Self-report	Either	Contextual	Formative	Medium to large
Interviews	Attitudinal	Self-report	Qualitative	Either	Formative	Small to medium
Survey	Either	Self-report	Quantitative	Either	Formative	Large
Card sort	Behavioral	Observation	Quantitative	Lab	Formative	Small
Focus group	Attitudinal	Self-report	Qualitative	Lab	Formative	Medium
Field study	Either	Observation	Either	Contextual	Formative	Medium
Evaluation	Behavioral	Observation or expert review	Either	Either	Either	Small to medium

Note: This table presents a generalized summary of the most typical variation of each method. All methods can be/are adapted on each of these characteristics.

Behavioral vs. Attitudinal

While attitudes or beliefs and behaviors are related, for a variety of reasons, they do not always match (Fishbein & Ajzen, 1975). Because of this, it is important for you to decide which of these two, behaviors and attitudes, you are most interested in studying. If you want to know how people feel and talk about an organization or symbol, you are interested in their attitudes. If you want to know whether more people will click on a button that says "purchase flight" or "take me flying," you are interested in behaviors. Some measures such as surveys are more appropriate for measuring attitudes, whereas other methods such as field studies allow you to observe behaviors. However, be certain to remember that attitudes and behavior *are related*; even if you or your stakeholders are primarily interested in behaviors for one study, you cannot disregard attitudes; attitudes can drive behaviors over the long term.

Research and Participant Roles

Related to issues of attitude and behavior are the roles of the researcher and participant in the research. Some methods rely entirely on **self-report,** which means that a participant provides information from memory about him or herself and his or her experiences. In contrast, other methods collect **observations.** Observational studies rely on the researcher watching, listening, and otherwise sensing what a participant does, rather than asking him or her to report what he or she does or thinks. Finally, some methods do not involve participants at all and instead rely on the experience of experts. These types of studies are called **expert reviews.**

Lab vs. Contextual

Conducting studies in a lab environment (see page 87) allows you to control many potential **confounds** in your study and is useful for isolating how one variable impacts another. However, the lab environment lacks contextual cues, information, people, and distractions that participants will have to contend with when they use your product in real life. When you are considering methods, realize that some methods, such as field studies, allow you to understand the users' context. Others, such as lab-based usability tests, provide control over these contextual factors, so you can focus on the product in isolation.

Qualitative vs. Quantitative

Qualitative suggests data that include a rich verbal description, whereas **quantitative** suggests data that are numeric and measured in standard units. Qualitative data, such as open-ended interview responses, can be quantified. For example, you could use a content analysis to determine the number of times a certain word, phrase, or theme was expressed across participants. However, the root of the difference between these approaches is deeper and related to disciplinary traditions potentially making quantifying qualitative data unappealing. To answer many research questions thoroughly, you need to combine these approaches.

TIP

As you consider the type of method to use, think carefully about what you want to be able to say at the conclusion of the study. Do you want to be able to present how many times something happened or how people responded? That is a quantitative approach. Do you want to provide a rich description of participants' experiences? That is a qualitative approach.

Formative vs. Summative

Formative evaluations are conducted during product development or as a product is still being formed. The goal is to influence design decisions as they are being made. In formative research, you can figure out what participants think about a topic, determine when a feature is not working well and why, and suggest changes based on those findings. **Summative evaluations** are conducted once a product or service is complete. The goal is to assess whether the product or service meets standards or requirements. In summative research, you can determine whether a product is usable by some standard measure, such as number of errors or time on task.

Number of Users

While some types of studies require a large participant population to provide the most useful information (e.g., surveys), others can be conducted with a relatively low **N** and still provide significant value (e.g., usability tests). Determining how many users you need for any study can seem like a daunting task. For any study, there are a number of considerations that come into play when you are trying to determine sample size, such as available resources (e.g., time to complete study, funds to pay participants, number of prototypes), size of the effect you are looking for, the population you would like to extrapolate your findings to, the confidence you need to have in your findings, the type of contribution you would like to make, and your experience, comfort, and preferences for determining sample size. There are a number of straightforward ways, however, that can help you determine how many participants you need, including power analysis, saturation, cost or feasibility analysis, and heuristics.

TIP

While serving on program committees for academic conferences and as a reviewer for journals, Kelly has seen a number of peer reviews that cite "small" sample size as a reason for rejecting a paper from publication. These reviewers often write the phrase "this sample size seems small." From a statistical perspective, it is never a valid criticism to say a sample size "seems small." Sample size can be inadequate to determine whether there is a reliable effect at a certain level of confidence, but this requires a statistical determination rather than a reviewer's gut feeling. What reviewers who use this phrase often mean is that "in my experience, the data properties are so variable that this sample size cannot capture the inherent variation and therefore not support the inferences you're drawing." A more helpful response that could help authors improve their paper and/or future methods would be to suggest including a power analysis in their results (or proposal) or that they meet some other objective criteria such as expert recommendation or community standard for sample size for the type of study they report or propose.

Power Analysis

For quantitative studies where you will draw statistical inferences, you can determine how many participants you need using a power analysis. A power analysis considers the type of statistical test you plan to conduct, the significance level or confidence you desire (more confidence = lower power), the size of the effect you expect (bigger effect = more power), the level of "noise" in your data (more noise or higher standard deviation = lower power), and the sample size (N; higher sample size = more power). If you know three of these factors, you can determine the fourth, which means you can use this type of analysis to determine the sample size you would need to be able to confidently and reliably detect an effect.

There are a number of ways to calculate power including the following:

- By hand
- Using online calculators
  - https://www.measuringusability.com/problem_discovery.php
  - http://www.surveysystem.com/sscalc.htm
  - http://www.resolutionresearch.com/results-calculate.html
  - http://hedwig.mgh.harvard.edu/sample_size/js/js_parallel_quant.html
- In stats packages
  - SAS
  - SPSS

If you would like to use a power analysis to determine the number of participants for an upcoming study but are not comfortable using the methods above, we recommend the following:

- Consult *Quantifying the User Experience* (especially Chapter 7, Sauro & Lewis, 2012) for a historically grounded and thorough description and explanation of sample size calculations for formative research.
- Take a statistics class. Classes are offered at local technical colleges, at universities, and in specialized UX stats workshops.
- Hire a consultant with expertise in quantitative analysis. Many universities have statistical consultants and/or biostatisticians on staff who will perform a power analysis for you for a reasonable fee.

TIP

Large sample sizes allow you to discover things that occur rarely or to detect small differences between groups. With small sample sizes, you are limited to finding only large effects/differences or participant characteristics that a large proportion of users have. One reason why small sample sizes are often justifiable in user research is because we are looking to find the biggest problems that the most people will encounter because those are the highest priority to fix. For example, if you observe a usability problem during a usability test with a small sample size, the question to ask is how severe or common the problem is, not whether any users will encounter it; they very likely will.

Saturation

For qualitative studies, it may not be possible to determine in advance how many participants you will need. Unlike many quantitative approaches, in some qualitative approaches, the qualitative researcher is analyzing data throughout the study. Data saturation is the point during data collection at which no new relevant information emerges. While reaching saturation is the ideal, because it is not possible to predict in advance when saturation will be reached, this method may be hard to justify to other stakeholders or make study logistics difficult.

Cost/Feasibility Analysis

While power analysis and saturation are the ideal ways to determine the number of participants to recruit for a study, in reality, we often find that researchers are not able to fulfill this ideal. Instead, life comes into play: you have a limited budget with which to remunerate participants, you have five days within which to meet with participants, you have to collect all data for your dissertation over the summer, and your lab does not have funding for you to travel to meet participants in more than three locations. In these situations, two methods you can use to determine sample size are cost and feasibility analyses.

Cost or ROI Analysis

Sometimes, the one constraint you know going into a project is how much money you have to spend. Under these circumstances, a cost analysis can help you determine how many participants you can recruit for your study. The simplest, most basic, least-informed analysis is

$$\frac{(\text{total \$ available to pay participants})}{(\text{\$ per participant})} = \text{number of participants}$$

Feasibility Analysis

Besides monetary costs, there are often other constraints as you plan a study. Constraints include time to complete the study, participant availability, and number of participants that exist (e.g., the population of fighter jet pilots is much more limited than the number of mobile phone owners). For physical products, you must also consider the number of prototypes, bandwidth, number of researchers available, space, equipment (e.g., fMRI machine), and client requirements.

Using a feasibility analysis, you can use the constraints you know to guide the number of participants you sample. For example, let us say your client wants to know how technology could be used to improve the local hospital emergency room discharge process. They ask you to conduct focus groups and want to get the perspective of patients, providers, and hospital administrators. As you work with the client, a major constraint is imposed: you only have time and location resources to conduct four focus groups. You explain that this constraint will limit the reliability and depth of your results, but the client explains that this is the only option. You agree that some data are better than no data.

You can use this constraint to guide how you configure the focus groups. There are only eight hospital administrators in the entire hospital, so these can all fit in one group. Similarly, there are only 30 EHR doctors and nurses, so you can sample around 30% of them in one focus group. However, there are tens of thousands of patients, so you know you should devote at least two groups to them. Alternatively, you could present the option to the client to only study the perceptions of patients, devoting all four focus groups to patients only. This, you argue, would allow you to get a more reliable understanding of the patient perspective. If this portion of the study goes well, you think it might be possible to do a follow-up study with the doctors and nurses and administrators.

Heuristics

There are two types of heuristics for determining sample size: previous similar or analogous studies (or "local standards") and recommendations by experts.

Previous Similar or Analogous Studies (Local Standards)

To find out the local standards in your organization or community, ask colleagues how many participants they have used for studies similar to the one you are planning. If you plan to publish your work, read recently published papers from the venue where you plan to submit your work to determine community norms.

Recommendations by Experts

Experts are people who have worked in a field with success for a long time. Because of their expertise, they are often trusted as sources of information about a topic. For convenience, we have compiled a table that summarizes sample size recommendations based on expert opinion for each type of study we discuss in this book. This is presented in Table 5.2. This summary presents only a range and suggested sample size and does not detail the reasoning, justification, or description that exists in the cited reference. Please refer to the original source for more information, and use these recommendations from experts with care.

Table 5.2: Heuristics for number of participants for each study type

Method	Range (suggested)	Reference
Diary study	5-1200 (30)	Hektner, Schmidt, & Csikszentmihalyi (2007)
Interview - Qualitative - Quantitative	 12-20 (20) 30+	 Guest, Bunce, & Johnson (2006) Green & Thorogood (2009)
Survey	60+; "the number of participants should always be higher than the number of questions in the survey"	Sears & Jacko (2012)
Card sort	15-30 (15)	Tullis & Wood (2004)
Focus groups	4-12 (6-8) per group; 3-4 groups per type of participant	Krueger & Casey (2000)
Field study - Grounded theory - Ethnography	 20-30 30-50	 Creswell (1998) Morse (1994); Bernard (2000)
Evaluation/usability test - Quantitative - Qualitative - Think aloud	 15-30 (30) 3-15 (5[1]-10) 5	 Nielsen (2000); FDA (2014) Nielsen (2000); Hwang & Salvendy (2010) Nielsen (1994)

[1]Given a straightforward task; per design iteration.

Sampling Strategies

In an ideal world, a user research activity should strive to represent the thoughts and ideas of the entire user population. Ideally, an activity is conducted with a representative random **sample** of the population so that the results are highly predictive of the entire population. This type of sampling is done through precise and time-intensive sampling methods. In reality, this is rarely done in industry settings and only sometimes done in academic, medical, pharmaceutical, and government research.

In industry user research, **convenience sampling** is often used. When employed, the sample of the population used reflects those who were available (or those you had access to) at a moment in time, as opposed to selecting a truly *representative* sample of the population. Rather than selecting participants from the population at large, you recruit participants from a convenient subset of the population.

The unfortunate reality of convenience sampling is that you cannot be positive that the information you collect is truly representative of your entire population. We are certainly not condoning sloppy data collection, but as experienced user research professionals are aware, we must strike a balance between rigor and practicality. For example, you should not avoid doing a survey because you cannot obtain a perfect sample. However, when using a convenience sample, still try to make it as representative as you possibly can. Other nonprobability-based sampling strategies we see used are **snowball sampling**, where previous participants suggest new participants, and **purposive sampling**, where participants are selected because they have a characteristic of interest to the researcher. One problem with snowball sampling is that you tend to get self-consistent samples because people often know and suggest other potential participants who are similar to themselves.

Figure 5.2 presents a graphical representation of general guidelines about how many participants are required for each type of study by study contextualization. An overview of sample size considerations is provided in this chapter, and a thorough discussion of number of participants is provided in each methods chapter.

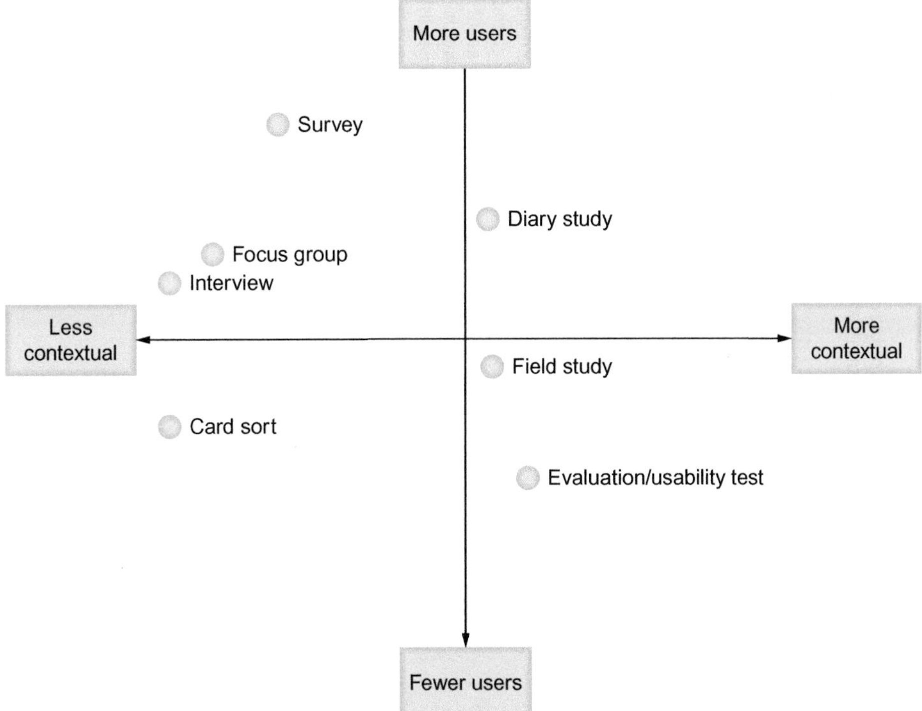

Figure 5.2: Graphical representation of number of participants required by context. *Inspired by Quesenbery and Suzc (2005).*

Choosing the Right Method

As you can see, these seven sets of methods provide you with a variety of options. Some techniques can be intensive in time and resources (depending on your design) but provide a very rich and comprehensive data set. Others are quick and low-cost and provide the answers you need almost immediately. Each of these techniques can provide

Table 5.3: Comparison of user research techniques presented in this book

Method	Purpose	Ideal research need/goal	Advantages	Disadvantages
Diary studies (Chapter 8)	Collect *in situ* data, typically over a long period of time	• Gather longitudinal data from a large sample • Gather structured, quantitative data from large sample; obtain statistical significance • Understand infrequent tasks or things that you might not be able to see, even if you observed the user all day or you do not want to interrupt natural behavior	• Researcher does not need to be present for data collection • Avoids many disadvantages of typical self-report studies because queries are presented in context and without long time delays	• Depending on the format (e.g., paper, SMS), data may need to be entered and coded by hand • Automated data collection such as via a mobile app may not be available to certain members of a population (e.g., if they do not own a smartphone) • Participants may choose not to provide some data you would find valuable because they are not cognizant of it or just do not want to tell you
Interviews (Chapter 9)	Collect in-depth information in a user's own language	• Get information about attitudes, beliefs, feelings, and emotional reactions • Get answers to open-ended questions (i.e., when you do not have a good idea of the most likely set of answers a user would like to select from) • Gather detailed and in-depth responses • Learn information about sensitive topics that people may feel uncomfortable sharing in a group setting	• Easy for participants because of conversational nature • May ask open-ended questions without fear of increasing nonresponse rate • Participants can think and speak deeply about the topic in their own words • Flexible; you can ask follow-up questions and delve into details on interesting topics • Can be used with populations who are illiterate	• Self-report data have drawbacks including memory biases and social desirability bias • Analysis of audio or transcribed data can be very time-consuming, especially if questions and answers are unstructured • It can be very time-consuming to conduct enough interviews to know if the data are representative of your entire population
Surveys (Chapter 10)	Quickly collect broad self-report data from a large number of users in a structured format	• Learn the percentage of people who will choose among a set of answers when you have a good idea of the most likely answers a user would like to select from • Gather structured, quantitative data from large sample; statistical significance	• Collect information from a large number of users simultaneously • Quick and easy to organize the data because they are structured • Relatively inexpensive if your needs are met with a convenience sample	• It is difficult to create good questions that elicit the answers you are interested in; must ask questions in language users will understand • Must pretest all survey questions • Should not ask many open-ended questions as this may make the nonresponse rate higher • No opportunity to follow up on interesting/unexpected findings • Can be expensive if it is important to get a representative sample of your population via probability sampling

Table 5.3: **Comparison of user research techniques presented in this book—Cont'd**

Method	Purpose	Ideal research need/goal	Advantages	Disadvantages
Card sort (Chapter 11)	Identify how users group information or objects	• Understand how users group concepts • Want the users' mental model to drive the information architecture of the product • Gather feedback about the content, terminology, and organization of your product	• Relatively simple technique to conduct • If run as group or online, can inexpensively collect data from several users at once	• Unless combined with another method (e.g., interview), no opportunity to understand why participants grouped things the way they did
Focus groups (Chapter 12)	Assess the attitudes, opinions, and impressions of groups; understand disagreements within groups	• Understand how a group, rather than an individual, thinks and talks about a topic • Gather data from participants, but there is a power differential between the researcher and the participants • Learn about the language your participants use to describe your topic of interest • Answer "why" questions about previously obtained quantitative data that can be used to identify solutions for old and new problems	• Creates a free, naturalistic conversation and feedback within the group, mimicking the way people talk about things with peers • Collect data from several users simultaneously • Group discussion often sparks new ideas • Ample opportunities for follow-up questions • Can be used with populations who are illiterate	• Not appropriate for measuring frequency of occurrence of attitudes or preferences of individuals • Should not be used when exploring sensitive topics • Data analysis can be time-consuming
Field studies (Chapter 13)	Learn about the users' tasks and context in-depth	• Gather user behavior, but the user will not be able to describe relevant issues because of issues with memory, social desirability, acquiescence, and prestige response bias • Understand how the user works or behaves, the context of the tasks undertaken, and the artifacts used to support those tasks (e.g., checklists, forms to fill out, calendars) • Gather experiences that have become automatic, which is, as a result, difficult to articulate	• Can observe what people actually do, rather than what they say they do • Get to see users' actual environment • Can collect a plethora of rich data • High ecological validity	• Logistics are challenging • May visit on an unusual day, leading to misunderstanding of "normal" events • Participants may act differently because you are observing them • It is typically impossible to conduct enough interviews to know if the data are representative of your entire population
Evaluation (Chapter 14)	Evaluate designs based on specific criteria	• Evaluate an existing design in terms of ease of use and potential for errors • Determine whether your product or service meets usability criteria (e.g., time on task, errors) • Gather experiences that have become automatic, which is, as a result, difficult to articulate	• Very effective for making small changes that have a big impact on speed of use, number of errors, etc. • Need relatively few users to participate in order to get useful data to act upon	• Because this step comes toward the end of the product life cycle, changes are often incremental

different data to aid in the development of your product or service. Your job as a researcher is to understand the trade-offs being made—in cost, time, accuracy, representativeness, etc.—and to present those trade-offs as you present the results and recommendations. It is important that you choose the correct activity to meet your needs and that you understand the pros and cons of each. In Table 5.3, we outline each of the activities proposed in this book and review what it is used for and present its advantages and disadvantages. If you are unfamiliar with these research methods, this table might not make sense to you right now. That is OK. Think of the tables in this chapter as a reference to use as you read the book or as you are deciding which method is right for your research question.

In addition to teaching you how to conduct each of these methods, this book can help you choose the best method(s) for your research question. Table 5.2 gives examples of various research needs and matches those with appropriate methods to use in each case. Use this table to help you determine which method is right for your research question.

PART 2

GET UP AND RUNNING

CHAPTER 6

Preparing for Your User Research Activity

Introduction

Presumably, you have completed all the research you can before involving your end users (refer to Chapter 2, page 24) and you have now identified the user research activity necessary to answer some of your open questions. In this chapter, we detail the key elements of preparing for your activity. These steps are critical to ensuring that you collect the best data possible from the real users of your product. We cover everything that happens or that you should be aware of prior to collecting your data—from creating a proposal to recruiting your participants.

At a Glance

> Creating a proposal
> Deciding the duration and timing of your session
> Recruiting participants
> Tracking participants
> Creating a protocol
> Piloting your activity

Creating a Proposal

A proposal is a road map for the activity you are about to undertake. Whether you are a student writing a thesis or dissertation proposal, a nonprofit employee, or a corporate UX researcher, the idea behind creating a proposal is the same: to place a stake in the ground for everyone to work around. Proposals do not need to take long to write but can provide a great deal of value by getting everyone on the same page. In the following sections, we focus primarily on creating a business proposal because academic institutions and the like will have varied specific requirements. However, the general principles apply to all types of proposals.

At a Glance

> Why create a proposal?
> Sections of the proposal
> Sample proposal
> Getting commitment

Why Create a Proposal?

As soon as you and the team decide to conduct a user research activity, you should write a proposal. A proposal benefits both you and the product team by forcing you to think about the activity in its entirety and determining what and who will be involved. You need to have a clear understanding of what will be involved from the very beginning, and you must convey this information to everyone who will have a role in the activity.

A proposal clearly outlines the activity that you will be conducting and the type of data that will be collected. In addition, it assigns responsibilities and sets a time schedule for the activity and all associated deliverables. This is important when preparing for an activity that depends on the participation of multiple people. You want to make sure everyone involved is clear about what they are responsible for and what their deadlines are. A proposal will help you do this. It acts as an informal contract. By specifying the activity that will be run, the users who will participate, and the data that will be collected, there are no surprises, assumptions, or misconceptions.

TIP

If you are conducting multiple activities (e.g., a card sort and focus group for the same product), write a separate proposal for each activity. Different activities have different needs, requirements, and timelines. It is best to keep this information separate.

Sections of the Proposal

There are a number of key elements to include in your proposal. We recommend including the following sections.

History

The history section of the proposal is used to provide some introductory information about the product and to outline any user research activities that have been conducted in the past for this product. This information can be very useful to anyone who is new to the team.

Objectives, Measures, and Scope of the Study

This section provides a brief description of the activity you will be conducting, as well as its goals, and the specific data that will be collected. It is also a good idea to indicate the specific payoffs that will result from this activity. This information helps to set expectations about the type of data that you will and will not be collecting. Do not assume that everyone is on the same page.

Method

The method section details how you will execute the activity and how the data will be analyzed. Often, members of a product team have never been a part of the kind of activity that you plan to conduct. This section is also a good refresher for those who are familiar with the activity but may not have been involved in this type of activity recently.

User Profile (aka "Participants")

In this section, detail exactly who will be participating in the activity. It is essential to document this information to avoid any misunderstandings later on. You want to be as specific as possible. For example, do not just say "students;" instead, state exactly the type of student you are looking for. This might be the following:

- Between the ages of 18 and 25
- Currently enrolled in an undergraduate program
- Has experience booking vacations on the web

It is critical that you bring in the correct user type for your activity. Work with the team to develop a detailed user profile (refer to Chapter 2, "User Profile" section, page 37). If you have not yet met with the team to determine the user profile, be sure to indicate that you will be working with them to establish the key characteristics of the participants for the activity. Avoid including any "special users" that the team thinks would be "interesting" to include but are outside of the user profile.

Recruitment

In this section, describe by whom and how the participants will be recruited. Will you recruit them, or will the product team do this? Will you post an advertisement on the web, use social media, or use a recruitment agency? Will you contact current customers? How many people will you recruit?

You will need to provide answers to all of these questions in the recruitment section. If the screener for the activity has already been created, you should attach this to the proposal as an appendix (see "Developing a Recruiting Screener" section, page 129).

Incentives

Specify how participants will be compensated for their time and how much they will be compensated (see "Determining Participant Incentives" section, page 127). Also, indicate who will be responsible for acquiring these incentives. If the product team is doing the recruiting, you want to be sure the team does not offer inappropriately high incentives to secure participation (refer to Chapter 3, "Appropriate Incentives" section on page 73 for a discussion of appropriate incentive use). If your budget is limited, you and the product team may need to be creative when identifying an appropriate incentive.

Responsibilities and Proposed Schedule

This is one of the most important pieces of your proposal—it is where you assign roles and responsibilities, as well as deliverable dates. Be as specific as possible in this section. Ideally, you want to have a specific person named for each deliverable. For example, do not just say that the product team is responsible for recruiting participants; instead, state that "John Brown from the product team" is responsible. The goal is for everyone to read your proposal and understand exactly who is responsible for what.

The same applies to dates—be specific. You can always amend your dates if timing must be adjusted. It is also nice to indicate approximately how much time it will take to complete each deliverable. If someone has never before participated in one of these activities, he or she might assume that a deliverable takes more or less time than it really does. People most often underestimate the amount of time it takes to prepare for an activity. Sharing time estimates in your proposal can help people set their own deadlines. In some cases, you may even want to include hours and cost. For example, if you are a consultant or your team uses a charge back model to other groups within the company, this level of detail will be important.

Once the preparation for the activity is under way, you can use this chart to track the completion of the deliverables. You will be able to see at a glance what work is outstanding and who is causing the bottleneck. In the next section, we provide a guide to help you determine how much time to plan for each phase of preparation.

TIP

If possible, propose activities on Tuesdays, Wednesdays, and Thursdays on regular, nonholiday weeks. Mondays, Fridays, and holiday weeks have the highest participant no-show rates.

Preparation Timeline

Table 6.1 contains approximate times based on our personal experience and should be used only as a guide. If you are new to research, the length estimate will likely be much longer. For example, it may take you double the time to create the questions, conduct the study, and analyze the data. In addition, the length of time for each step depends on a variety of factors, such as responsiveness of the product team, access to users, and resources available.

Table 6.1: Preparation timeline

When to complete	Approximate time to complete	Activity
As soon as possible	1-2 weeks	• Learn about your user • Meet with team to identify goals, research questions, and constructs to measure • Meet with team to identify desired population
After identification of questions and user profile	1 week	• Create and distribute study proposal • Determine data analysis method
After the proposal has been agreed by all stakeholders	1-2 weeks	• Word questions/script/tasks appropriately and distribute to colleagues for review

Continued

Table 6.1: Preparation timeline—Cont'd

When to complete	Approximate time to complete	Activity
After the questions are finalized	2 weeks	• Conduct pilot test and make any necessary changes • Identify sample and recruit participants • Acquire incentives (optional) • Prepare any documentation (e.g., consent form) • Create study materials (e.g., script, questionnaire)
After a successful pilot	A few hours to several days	• Conduct the study and distribute incentives
Analyze data and create report/ presentation	1 day to several days A few days to 2 weeks	• Clean data (if necessary) • Analyze data • Create documentation to communicate findings

Sample Proposal

The best way to get a sense of what a proposal should contain and the level of detail is to look at an example. Figure 6.1 offers a sample proposal for a card sorting activity to be conducted for our fictitious travel app. This sample can be easily modified to meet the needs of any activity.

TravelMyWay.com

CARD SORT PROPOSAL

Jane Adams
User Researcher

Introduction and History

TravelMyWay.com is a website that will allow travelers to book their travel online at discount prices. The key features for the first release will include:

- Searching for and purchasing airline tickets
- Searching for and booking hotels
- Searching for and booking rental cars

A Focus Group Analysis was conducted for this product in February of this year. Student participants brainstormed features that they want and need in an ideal discount travel site. The report of this activity can be found on the TravelMyWay.com internal user research webpage. The results of the Focus Group Analysis will be used to create cards for a Card Sort activity.

Figure 6.1: Example of a card sort proposal.

This document is a proposal for a group Card Sort activity, which will be conducted in the User Research Laboratory with students currently enrolled in college. The Card Sort will be carried out through the coordinated efforts of the TravelMyWay.com product team and the User Research and Interface Design team.

Objectives, Measures, and Scope of Study

Card sorting is a common usability technique that discovers a user's mental model of an information space (e.g., a website, a product, a menu). It generally involves representing each piece of information from the information space on an individual card and then asking target users to arrange these cards into groupings that are meaningful to them.

This activity has two objectives:

- To help establish the high-level information architecture for the main functions of TravelMyWay.com for student users
- To learn about any problematic terminology in TravelMyWay.com

The following data will be collected:

- Students' categorization schemas for travel objects and actions
- Category naming information
- Alternative terminology identified by participants
- Demographic information for each respondent (e.g., university, frequency of travel, web experience)

The information collected from this activity will be used to architect the TravelMyWay.com website specifically targeted toward students.

Method

Cards

There will be a set of objects represented on cards for participants to sort into categories. A term and a corresponding definition will be printed on each card, along with a blank line for participants to write an alternate/preferred term for the definition.

Procedure

The card sort will be conducted in the usability lab on the evenings of March 25th and 27th. *<Sometimes the specific dates have not been determined at the time of the proposal. You should at least make a guess—e.g., the end of March>*

- After signing consent and nondisclosure agreements, participants will be given the set of "object" cards.
- Participants will first read each card and make sure they understand the meaning of each term and definition. The test administrator will clarify any unfamiliar terms.
- Participants may rename any card they wish by writing the new term on the blank line.

Figure 6.1 – Cont'd

Continued

- Next, participants will sort the cards into "groups that make sense to them." Participants will be informed there is no wrong way to sort the cards, no limit to the number of groups or cards in a group, and to work individually.
- Blank cards will be included in the set for participants to include any concept they feel is missing from the set.
- After sorting the cards, participants will give each group a name describing the group.
- Finally, participants will staple or clip groups together and give them to the administrator.

After the session is completed, the data will be analyzed using cluster analysis software. The User Research and Interface Design team will conduct the analysis and provide design recommendations to the product team.

User Profile

Participants must meet the following criteria in order to participate:

- Be a student currently enrolled in one or more college classes
- Be at least 18 years of age
- Not work for a TravelMyWay.com competitor

Recruitment

User research intern, Mark Jones, will perform the recruiting for the Card Sort. An advertisement will be posted on a local web-based community bulletin board to solicit potential participants. Participants will be screened using the screener questionnaire (*you should attach this to the proposal if it has been created*), and a total of 17 participants will be scheduled (15, plus 2 in case of attrition).

Compensation

Participants will receive $75 in AMEX gift cards for their participation. These incentives will be paid for and acquired by the User Research and Interface Design group.

What the user research team needs from the TravelMyWay.com team

The user research team requires the following commitments from the TravelMyWay.com product team:

- Work with user research team to develop objects list with definitions
- Attendance by at least one member of the product team to observe each session
- Review and approve user profile (see above)
- Review and approve screener
- Review and approve study proposal (this document)

Figure 6.1 – Cont'd

What the user research team will provide

The user research team is committed to providing the following:

- User researcher, Jane Adams, to conduct the study
- User research intern, Mark Jones, to recruit participants
- Acquisition and distribution of incentives for participants
- Detailed study plan (this document)
- Data collection and analysis
- Summary report with recommendations
- Presentation to your staff/manager

Proposed Schedule

	Work package	*Owner*	*Estimated time to complete*	*Date forecast*	*Status*
1	Provide object terms and definitions	Jane (UI team) and Dana (Product team)	2 days	March 1	COMPLETED March 3
2	Request incentives for 17 participants	Jane (UI team)	1 hour	March 1	COMPLETED March 1
3	Book laboratory space	Jane (UI team)	1 hour	March 1	COMPLETED March 1
4	Meet with UI team to finalize proposal	Jane (UI team) and Terry (Product team)	1 hour	March 20 (firm)	As of March 27, not yet completed
5	Recruit 17 participants (15 + 2 extra for attrition)	Mark (UI team)	1 week	Mar 17–21	TBD
6	Print labels for cards and create card sets	Jane and Mark (UI team)	6–10 hours	Mar 17–Apr 21	TBD
7	Conduct session 1	Jane (UI team)	1 hour	March 25 6:00–8:00 *<ifknown>*	TBD
8	Conduct session 2	Jane (UI team)	1 hour	March 27 6:00–8:00 *<if known>*	TBD
9	Analyze data and produce high-level findings for OSS team	Jane (UI team)	1 week	Mar 28–Apr 4	TBD
10	Create draft report	Jane (UI team)	1 week	Mar 28–Apr 4	TBD
11	Review and comment on report	Jane (UI team) and Terry (Product team)	1 week	Apr 4–11	TBD
12	Publish final report	Jane (UI team)	1–2 weeks	Apr 10–21	TBD

Figure 6.1 – Cont'd

Getting Commitment

Your proposal is written, but you are not done yet. In our experience, if **stakeholders** are unhappy with the results of a study, they will sometimes criticize one (or more) of the following:

- The skills/knowledge/objectivity of the person who conducted the activity
- The participants in the activity
- The tasks/activity conducted

Being a member of the team and earning their respect (refer to Chapter 1, "Preventing Resistance" section, page 19) will help with the first issue. Getting everyone to sign off on the proposal can help with the last two. Make sure that everyone is clear, before the activity, about all aspects of the study to avoid argument and debate when you are presenting the results. This is critical. If there are objections or problems with what you have proposed, it is best to identify and deal with them now.

You might think that all you have to do is send the proposal to the appropriate people. This is exactly what you do *not* want to do! Never e-mail your proposal to all the stakeholders and assume they read it. In some cases, your e-mail will not even be opened. The reality is that everyone is very busy and most people do not have the time to read things that they do not believe to be critical. People may not believe your proposal is critical. It is your job to help them understand that it is.

Instead, organize a meeting to review the proposal. It can take as little as 30 minutes to review the proposal as a group. Anyone involved in the preparation for the activity or who will use the data should be present. At this meeting, you do not need to go through every single line of the proposal in detail, but you do want to hit several key points. They include the following:

- *The objective of the activity*. It is important to have a clear objective and to stick to it. Often in planning, developers will bring up issues that are out of the scope of the objective. Discussing it up front can keep the subsequent discussions focused.
- *The data you will be collecting*. Make sure the team has a clear understanding of what they will be getting.
- *The users who will be participating*. You really want to make this clear. Make sure everyone agrees that the user profile is correct. You do not want to be told after the activity has been conducted that the users "were not representative of the product's true end users"—and hence, the data you collected are useless. It may sound surprising, but this is not uncommon.
- *Each person's role and what he or she is responsible for*. Ensure that everyone takes ownership of roles and responsibilities. Make sure they truly understand what they are responsible for and how the project schedule will be impacted if delivery dates are not met.
- *The timeline and dates for deliverables*. Emphasize that it is critical for all dates to be met. In many cases, there is no opportunity for slipping.

TIP

Add a cushion to your deliverable dates. We often request deliverables a week before we absolutely need them. Then, if deliverables are late (which they often are), it is OK.

Although it may seem overkill to schedule *yet another* meeting, meeting in person has many advantages. First of all, it gets everyone involved, rather than creating an "us" versus "them" mentality (refer to Chapter 1, "Preventing Resistance" section, page 19). You want everyone to feel like a team going into this activity. In addition, by meeting, you can make sure everyone is in agreement with what you have proposed. If they are not, you now have a chance to make any necessary adjustments and all stakeholders will be aware of the changes. At the end of the meeting, everyone should have a clear understanding of what has been proposed and be satisfied with the proposal. All misconceptions or assumptions should be removed. Essentially, your contract has been "signed." You are off to a great start.

Deciding the Duration and Timing of Your Session

You will need to decide the duration and timing of your session(s) before you begin recruiting your participants. It may sound like a trivial topic, but the timing of your activity can determine the ease or difficulty of the recruiting process; it may be easier to recruit people for an hour block after work hours than an hour block during regular work hours, for example. For individual activities, we offer users a variety of times of day to participate, from early morning to around 8 pm. We try to be as flexible as possible and conform to the individual's schedule and preference. This flexibility allows us to recruit more participants.

For group sessions, it is a bit more challenging because you have to find one time to suit all participants. The participants we recruit typically have daytime jobs from 9 am to 5 pm, and not everyone can get time off in the middle of the day. We have found that conducting group sessions from 5-7 pm and 6-8 pm work best. We like to have our sessions end by 8 pm or 8:30 pm, as we have found that, after this time, people get very tired and their productivity drops noticeably. Because most people usually eat dinner around this time, we have discovered that providing dinner shortly *before* the session makes a huge difference. Participants appreciate the thought and enjoy the free food, and their blood sugar is raised so they are thinking better and have more energy. As an added bonus, participants chat together over dinner right before the session and develop a rapport. This is valuable because you want people to be comfortable in sharing their thoughts and experiences with each other. The cost is minimal (about $60 for two large pizzas, soda, and cookies), and it is truly worth it. For individual activities that are conducted over lunch or dinnertime, you may wish to do the same. The optimal times will depend on the working hours of your user type. If you are trying to recruit users who work night shifts, these recommended times may not apply.

User research activities can be tiring for both the moderator and the participant. They demand a good deal of cognitive energy, discussion, and active listening to collect effective data. We have found that two hours is typically the maximum amount of time you want to keep participants for most user research activities. This is particularly the case if the participants are coming to your activity after they have already had a full day's work. Even two hours is a long time, so you want to provide a break when you see participants getting tired or restless. If you need more than two hours to collect data, it is often advisable to break the session into smaller chunks and run it over several days or evenings. For some activities, such as surveys, two hours is typically much more time than you can expect participants to provide. Keep your participants' fatigue rate in mind when you decide how long your activity will be.

Recruiting Participants

Recruitment can be a time-consuming and costly activity. The information in this section can help you recruit users who represent the population of interest and can save you time, money, and effort.

TIP

Never include supervisors and their own employees in the same session. Not only are these different user types, but employees are unlikely to contradict their supervisors. Additionally, employees may not be honest about their work practices with their supervisors present. Finally, supervisors may feel it necessary to "take control" of the session and play a more dominant or expert role in the activity to save face in front of their employees. The issues are similar when you mix user types of different levels within a hierarchy, even if one does not report directly to the other (e.g., doctor and nurse).

At a Glance

> How many participants do I need?
> Determining participant incentives
> Developing a recruiting screener
> Creating a recruitment advertisement
> Recruitment methods
> Preventing no-shows
> Recruiting international participants

- Recruiting special populations
- Online services
- Crowd sourcing

Determining Participant Incentives

Before you can begin recruiting participants, you need to identify how you will compensate people for taking time out of their day to provide you with their expertise. You should provide your participants with some kind of incentive to thank them for their time and effort. The reality is that it also helps when recruiting, but you do not want your incentive to be the sole reason why people are participating. You should not make the potential participants "an offer they cannot refuse" (refer to Chapter 3, "Appropriate Incentives" section, page 73).

We are often asked, "How much should I pay?" Based on our experiences and discussions with academics and professionals, incentive amounts can vary from $25 to $125 per hour based on many factors, including budget, location, user type, length of study, complexity of study, and more. We cannot provide strict guidance about how large an incentive you should offer. In the San Francisco Bay Area, we typically pay $100 per hour, whereas in Clemson, South Carolina, we typically pay participants $10-20 per hour. We may vary incentives based on the user type as well; for example, we may pay orderlies $50 for a two-hour study, but pay physicians $200 for the same session.

We recommend that you speak with colleagues at organizations similar to yours to see what the norm is. Offering too little can result in no participation for your studies. However, offering large incentives may encourage dishonest individuals to participate in your study. They may not be truthful about their skills. Make the incentive large enough to thank people for their time and expertise but nothing more.

Generic Users

When we use the term "generic users," we are referring to people who participate in a user research activity, but have no ties to your company, university, or nonprofit organization. They are not customers or employees of your company or organization. They have typically been recruited via an advertisement or an internal database of potential participants, and they are representing themselves, not their company, at your session (this is discussed further in "Recruitment Methods"). This is the easiest group to compensate because there is no potential for conflicts of interest. You can offer them whatever you feel is appropriate. Some standard incentives include:

- One of your company products for free (e.g., a piece of software)
- A gift card (e.g., to an electronics store, to a department store) or a movie pass
- Charitable donations in the participant's name

Cash is often very desirable to participants, but it can be difficult to manage if you are running a large number of studies with many participants. In our experience, we have found a gift card to be a great alternative to cash. Gift cards can be used like a credit card. Participants can spend them at any place that takes credit cards, and they are convenient to manage. One thing to be aware of is that some gift cards charge convenience fees. You have to choose a card that does not have these charges. Or you can opt for an e-certificate for a specific store with a wide variety of options, like Amazon, as they typically do not have fees.

One thing to keep in mind is that you want to pay everyone involved in the *same* session the same amount. We sometimes come across situations where it is easy to schedule the first few participants but difficult to schedule the last few. Sometimes we are forced to increase the compensation in order to entice additional users. If you find yourself in such a situation, remember that you must also increase the compensation for those you have already recruited. A group session can become very uncomfortable and potentially confrontational if, during the activity, someone casually says, "This is a great way to make $100" to someone who you offered a payment of only $75. You do not want to lose the trust of your participants and potential end users—that is not worth the extra $25.

For highly paid individuals (e.g., CEOs), you could never offer them an incentive close to their normal compensation. For one study, a recruiting agency offered CEOs $500 per hour, but they could not get any takers. In these cases, a charitable donation in their name sometimes works better. For children, a gift card to a toy store or the movies or a pizza parlor tends to go over well (just make sure you approve it with their parents first).

Customers or Your Own Company Employees

If you are using someone within your company as a participant, you may not be able to pay them as you would a generic end user. We often use company logo gear, or "swag," for these kinds of participants as a token of thanks. This is also often the case in corporate accounts with business users. Paying customers could represent a conflict of interest because this could be perceived as a payoff. Additionally, most activities are conducted during business hours, so the reality is that their company is paying for them to be there. The same is true for employees at your own company. Thank customer participants or internal employees with a company logo item of nominal value (e.g., mug, sweatshirt, keychain).

If sales representatives or members of the product team are doing the recruiting for you, make sure they understand what incentive you are offering to customers and why it is a conflict of interest to pay customers for their time and opinions. We recently had an uncomfortable situation in which the product team was recruiting for one of our activities. They contacted a customer that had participated in our activities before and always received swag. When the product team told them their employees would receive $150, they were thrilled. When we had to inform the customer that this was not true and that they would receive only swag, they were quite offended. No matter what we said, we could not make the customer (or the product team representative) understand the issue of conflict of interest, and they continued to demand the payment. After we made it clear that this would not happen, they declined to participate in the activity. You never want the situation to get to this point.

Students

In some academic settings, students are encouraged to participate in research activities as a way to learn about the research process. Sometimes called a "participant pool," this group of students may be available to participate in user research studies as part of credit for a course or for extra credit. Ethically, whenever students are offered this opportunity, an alternative such as a writing assignment must be offered so students are not coerced to participate in studies to get extra credit.

Developing a Recruiting Screener

Assuming you have created a user profile (refer to Chapter 2, "User Profile" section, page 37), the first step in recruiting is to create a detailed phone screener. A screener is composed of a series of questions to help you recruit participants who match your user profile for the proposed activity.

Screener Tips

There are a number of things to keep in mind when creating a phone screener. They include the following:

- Avoid screening via e-mail
- Work with the product team
- Keep it short
- Use test questions
- Request demographic information
- Eliminate competitors
- Provide important details
- Prepare a response for people who do not match the profile

Avoid Screening via E-mail

With the exception of surveys, it is ideal for you to talk to participants before scheduling their session for a number of reasons. Firstly, you want to get a sense of whether or not they truly match your profile, and it is difficult to do this via e-mail. Secondly, you want to make sure the participants are clear about what the activity entails and what they will be required to do (see "Provide Important Details" section, page 131). However, this may not always be practical. If you cannot speak with potential participants, we recommend a questionnaire like Google Forms, rather than e-mail. It is much easier to see at a glance in one spreadsheet who qualifies and who does not. The questionnaire is also an easy way to ensure you get the information you need consistently.

Work with the Product Team

We cannot emphasize too strongly how important it is to make sure you and the team are aligned on who the right users are for this study. Your screener is the tool to help with this. Make sure the product team helps you develop it. Their involvement will also help instill the sense that you are a team working together, and it will avoid anyone from the product team saying "You brought in the wrong user" after the activity has been completed.

Keep It Short

In the majority of cases, a screener should be relatively short. You do not want to keep a potential participant on the phone for more than 10 minutes. People are busy, and they do not have a lot of time to chat with you. You need to respect their time. Also, you are very busy and the longer your screener is, the longer it will take you to recruit your participants.

"I'm not trying to sell you anything, sir. I'm doing market research, and all I ask is two or three hours of your time to answer a few thousand questions."

© The New Yorker Collection 2000 J. B. Handelsman from cartoonbank.com. All rights reserved

Use Test Questions

Make sure that your participants are being honest about their experience. We are not trying to say that people will blatantly lie to you (although occasionally they will), but sometimes, people may exaggerate their experience level, or they may be unaware of the limitations of their knowledge or experience (thinking they are qualified for your activity when, in reality, they are not).

When recruiting technical users, determine that they have the correct level of technical expertise. You can do this by asking test questions. This is known as knowledge-based screening. For example, if you are looking for people with moderate experience with HTML coding, you might want to ask "What is a Common Gateway Interface (CGI) script and how have you used it in the past?" Like other user research activities, creating a good test question will require you to know the domain well.

Request Demographic Information

Your screener can also contain some further questions to learn more about the participant. These questions typically come at the end, once you have determined that the person is a suitable candidate. For example, you might want to know the person's age and gender. Depending on your study needs, this information may be used to exclude them from participation. For example, if you are studying a new input device on a mobile phone among older adults, you will not include younger participants in your research activities. You can also use this demographic information to balance the diversity of your population of participants. In some academic situations, you are not able to collect this information until the time of the study. Be sure you know your policies in this area.

Eliminate Competitors

If you work for a company, always, always find out where the potential participants work before you recruit them. You do not want to invite employees from companies that develop competing products (i.e., companies that develop or sell products that are anywhere close to the one being discussed in the study). Assuming you have done your homework (refer to Chapter 2, page 24), you should know who these companies are. Similarly, depending on your circumstances, you want to avoid members of the press, regardless of whether they will sign a nondisclosure agreement (NDA) or not. You might imagine that, ethically and legally, this would never happen, but it does. We once had a situation where an intern recruited someone from a competitor to participate in an activity; as luck would have it, the participant cancelled later on. If you find out that you have recruited a competitor before the study begins, call the participant and explain that you must cancel. Apologize for any inconvenience but state that you must cancel the appointment. People will usually understand.

Sending the participants' profiles to the product team after recruitment is also a good double-check. The team may recognize a competitor they forgot to tell you about. If you are in doubt about a company, a quick web search can *usually* reveal whether the company in question makes products similar to yours.

Provide Important Details

Once you have determined that a participant is a good match for the activity, you should provide the person with some important details. It is only fair to let the potential participants know what they are signing up for (refer to Chapter 3, to learn more about how to treat participants). You do not want there to be any surprises when they show up on the day of the activity. Your goal is not to trick people into participating, so be up front. You want people who are genuinely interested. Here are some examples of things you should discuss:

- *Logistics:* Time, date, and location of the activity.
- *Incentives:* Tell them exactly how and how much they will be compensated.
- *Group versus individual:* Let them know whether it is a group or individual activity. Some people are painfully shy and do not work well in groups. It is far better for you to find out over the phone than during the session. We have actually had a couple of potential participants who declined to participate in a session once they found out it was a group activity. They simply did not feel comfortable talking in front of strangers. Luckily, we learned this during the phone interview and not during the session, so we were able to recruit replacements. Conversely, some people do not like to participate in individual activities because they feel awkward going in alone.
- *Recording:* Tell people in advance if you plan to record the session. Some people are not comfortable with this and would rather not participate. Others will want to make sure they dress well, look nice, etc.

- *Appointment time:* Emphasize that participants must be on time. Late participants will not be introduced into an activity that has already started (refer to Chapter 7, "The Late Participant" section, page 176).
- *ID:* If your company requires an ID from participants before entry, inform them that they will be required to show an ID before being admitted into the session (see "The Professional Participant" section, page 151).
- *Legal forms:* Inform them that they will be required to sign a consent and NDA, if applicable, and make sure that they understand what these forms are (refer to Chapter 3, "Legal Considerations" section, page 76). You may even want to fax the forms to the participants in advance.

Prepare a Response for People Who Do Not Match the Profile

The reality is that not everyone is going to match your profile, so you will need to reject some very eager and interested potential participants. Before you start calling, you should have a response in mind for the person who does not match the profile. It can be an uncomfortable moment, so have something polite in mind to say, and include this in your screener so you do not find yourself lost for words. We often say, "I'm sorry, you do not fit the profile for this particular study, but thank you so much for your time." If the person seems to be a great potential candidate, encourage him or her to respond to your recruitment postings in the future.

Sample Screener

Figure 6.2 is a sample screener for the recruitment of students for a group card sorting activity. This should give you a sense of the kind of information that is important to include when recruiting participants.

TravelMyWay.com Card Sort
Recruitment Screener
March 25 and 27, 6:00–8:00 pm

Start of Call

Hello, this is ____________ from TravelMyWay.com's research group. I'm responding to your e-mail regarding the research activity for students. Let me tell you a little about the activity, and then if you're interested, I'll need to ask you a few questions. Is that OK? Great!

This will be a **group activity**, where you would be helping us design a travel website. The activity will begin at 6:00 pm on either Tuesday, March 25, or Thursday, March 27, and will last for about one hour. This takes place at TravelMyWay.com in San Francisco. <*Describe the location briefly.*> Participation is on a paid basis.

Are you interested in participating?

- **Yes**—ask the next series of questions.
- **No**—thank the person and then end the call.

Figure 6.2: Example of a recruitment screener.

Great! I have a few questions to ask you to see whether you fit the profile of the individuals we need for this session. After talking with you, I will take your information back to the team for review, and then I will call you back to let you know whether your background is a good fit, and to schedule you.

I. Background information

Name: ____________________________ Daytime Phone: ___________________________

E-mail: __________________________________

1. Have you participated in TravelMyWay.com usability testing before?____ Ye s ____ No
   If yes, when/what activity? ______________________________ *<If yes, check the participant database for comments and to determine how much they have been paid this calendar year.>*
2. Are you currently enrolled as a student? ____ Yes ____ No *<If no, end the call.>*
   _____ Undergraduate ______Graduate
3. At which college or university? ___________________________ *<Participants should be from a mix of schools.>*
4. Department/Major? _____________________________________ *<Participants should be from a mix of departments/majors.>*
5. Are you a full-time or part-time student? _______Full ______Part *<Informational only.>*
6. Have you booked travel on the web before? ____ Yes ____ No *<If no, end the call.>*
7. How many trips have you booked in the last 12 months? _______ *<If less that two, end the call.>*
8. Are you currently employed outside of your school? ____Yes ____ No
   If yes, company name: ____________________________ *<Must not be TravelMyWay.com competitor—e.g., CheapTravel.com.>*
   Job title: _____________________________________ *<Informational only.>*

II. Computer Experience

9. How long have you been using the web? _______ *<If less than six months, disqualify.>*
10. How long have you been using a computer? _______ *<If less than one year, disqualify.>*

III. Confidentiality agreement, permission to tape, and verify identity

[*If the participant meets all criteria, please ask the additional questions that follow.*]

I also have some questions to make sure you understand and are comfortable with our procedures before you come in:

- Are you willing to sign a standard consent form, which acknowledges that you agree to participate, and confidential disclosure form, which states you agree not to share the details of the session with anyone for a period of three years?
  _____ Yes _____ No *<If no, disqualify.>*

Figure 6.2 – Cont'd

Continued

- Are you willing to be videotaped? (The video's purpose is so we can go back and capture more detailed notes. Videos are seen internally only by members of the product and user research teams who are interested in what you have to say.)
  _____ Yes _____ No *<If no, disqualify.>*
- The compensation is $75 in American Express gift cards (used like travelers checks). In order to pay you, we will require that you show us a government-issued ID. We are required to make sure that the name on the gift card matches the name of the person we are paying. *<Make sure that the name the person has given you will match the name on the driver's license.>* Are you willing to bring your driver's license or a passport?
  _____ Yes _____ No *<If no, disqualify.>*

Based on the screener answers in sections (I, II, & III) choose one of the following responses:

It looks like your profile is a match for this activity, and if you'd like, I'll go ahead and schedule you for a time.

or

It looks like you might fit the profile for this study, but I will have to check with the product team before I can know for sure. I will check with the team and get back with you as to whether or not we can go ahead and schedule you for this study.

or

I'm sorry, you do not fit the profile for this particular study, but thank you so much for your time.

IV. Availability

For which session(s) would you be available?

Tuesday, March 25 @ 6:00 pm ___available ___not available ___not sure

Thursday, March 27 @ 6:00 pm ___available ___not available ___not sure

Thank you for taking time to share your information. I will now take your information to the team and will call you soon to let you know whether you would be a match for this particular study.

V. Scheduling

It looks like your profile is a match for this activity, and I'd love to schedule you for a time.

<Schedule participant and verbally confirm date and time.>

Great! Let me give you some information about where to go, and I will follow that up with an e-mail confirmation along with a map to TravelMyWay.com.

- *Participation contact:* Mark Jones, Phone: 555-555-6655
- *Location:* 123 Fake Street, San Francisco, CA 94105
- *Directions:* Hwy 280 (North or South, depending on where they're coming from) to King Street exit. Go straight and take a left on Third Street to Harrison. You can park in the lot on your right, or in any parking garage for free.

Figure 6.2 – Cont'd

Other Instructions:

- Wait in lobby of the building to be escorted to session room.
- Participants will be escorted in starting at 5:40 pm for light dinner/snacks (so come early!). *<Inquire whether they are vegetarian, if you feel comfortable asking this.>*
- Allow plenty of time, as traffic can be very bad! Because we will begin the activity right at 6:00 pm, late arrivals may not be able to join the session, as it would delay everyone else. *<Emphasize this.>*
- Also, on some occasions we need to cancel sessions. We don't expect this, but if this does happen you will be contacted as soon as possible before your session.
- Please remember your driver's license, or we cannot let you into the session!
- I will call you again just before your scheduled appointment to remind you of the evaluation and confirm your attendance. If for some reason you need to cancel or reschedule, please call me as soon as possible! Thank you and we look forward to seeing you on *<Insert time & date>*!

Figure 6.2 – Cont'd

Creating a Recruitment Advertisement

Regardless of the method you choose to recruit your participants, whether it is via social media, a web posting, or an internal database of participants (discussed later in "Recruitment Methods"), you will almost always require an advertisement to attract appropriate end users. Depending on your method of recruiting, you or the recruiter may e-mail the advertisement, post it on a website or social media, or relay its message via the phone. Potential participants will respond to this advertisement or posting if they are interested in your activity. You will then reply to these potential participants and screen them.

There are several things to keep in mind when creating your posting.

At a Glance

> Provide details

> Include logistics

> Cover key characteristics

> Do not stress the incentive

> State how they should respond

> Include a link to your in-house participant database

Provide Details

Provide some details about your study. If you simply state that you are looking for users to participate in a user research study, you will be swamped with responses! This is not going to help you. In your ad, you want to provide some details to help narrow your responses to ideal candidates, for example, seeking HTML5 experts between the ages of 45 and 65 years.

Include Logistics

Indicate the date, time, and location of the study. That way, those who are not available will not respond. You want to weed out unavailable participants immediately.

Cover Key Characteristics

Indicate some of the key characteristics of your user profile. This will prescreen appropriate candidates. These are usually high-level characteristics (e.g., job title, company size). You do not want to reveal all of the characteristics of your profile because, unfortunately, there are some people who will pretend to match the profile. If you list all of the screening criteria, deceitful participants will know how they should respond to all of your questions when you call.

For example, let us say you are looking for people who:

- Are over 18 years of age
- Have purchased at least three airline tickets via the web within the last 12 months
- Have booked at least two hotels via the web within the last 12 months
- Have booked at least one rental car via the web within the last 12 months
- Have experienced using the TravelMyWay.com website or app
- Have a minimum of two years' web experience
- Have a minimum of one year computer experience

In your posting, you might indicate that you are looking for people who are over 18, enjoy frequent travel, and have used travel apps.

Do Not Stress the Incentive

Avoid phrases like "Earn money now!" This attracts people who want easy money and those who will be more likely to deceive you for the cash. Incentives are meant to compensate people for their time and effort, as well as to thank them, not entice them to do something they otherwise would hesitate to do. An individual who is attending your session only for the money will complete your activity as quickly as possible and with as little effort as possible. That kind of data can do more harm than good. Trust us.

State How They Should Respond

We suggest providing a generic, single-purpose e-mail address (e.g., studyname@yourdomain.com) for interested individuals to respond to rather than your personal e-mail address or phone number. If you provide your personal contact information (particularly a phone number), your voice mail and/or e-mail inbox will be jammed with responses. Another infrequent but possible consequence is being contacted by desperate individuals wanting to participate and wondering why you have not called them yet. By providing a generic e-mail address, you can review the responses and contact whomever you feel will be most appropriate for your activity.

It is also nice to set up an automatic response on the e-mail account, if it is used solely for recruiting purposes. Keep it generic, so you can use it for all of your studies. Here is a sample response:

> **Thank you for your interest in our study! We will be reviewing interested respondents over the next two weeks, and we will contact you if we think you are a match for our study.**
>
> **Sincerely,**
>
> **The TravelMyWay.com Team**

Include a Link to Your In-House Participant Database

If you have an in-house participant database (see below to learn more), you should point participants to your web questionnaire, at the bottom of your ad.

Be Aware of Types of Bias

Ideally, you do not want your advertisement to appeal to certain members of your user population and not others. You do not want to exclude true end users from participating. This is easy to do unknowingly based on where you post your advertisement or the content within the advertisement.

For example, let us say that TravelMyWay.com is conducting a focus group for frequent travelers. To advertise the activity, you have decided to post signs around local colleges and on college webpages because students are often looking for ways to make easy money. As a result, you have unknowingly biased your sample to people who are in these college buildings (i.e., mostly students), and it is possible that any uniqueness in this segment of the population may impact your results. Make sure you think about bias factors when you are creating and posting your advertisement.

Another type of bias is referred to as **nonresponder bias**. This is created when certain types of people do not respond to your posting. There will always be suitable people who do not respond, but if there is a pattern, then this is a problem. To avoid nonresponder bias, you must ensure that your call for participation is perceived equally by all potential users and that your advertisement is viewed by a variety of people from within your user population.

One kind of bias that you are unable to eliminate is **self-selection bias**. You can reduce this by inviting a random sample of people to complete your survey (i.e., a survey pop-up appears for every 10th visitor who comes to your website), rather than having it open to the public, but the reality is that not all people you invite will want to participate. Some of the invited participants will self-select to not participate in your activity.

Sample Posting

Figure 6.3 is a sample posting to give you a sense of how a posting might look when it all comes together.

Attention Frequent Travelers!

Interested in participating in an activity to help design a discount travel website?

We will be conducting a research study on March 25 and 27 at the TravelMyWay.com Usability Labs in San Francisco, CA (King Street exit). Participation will involve approximately one hour of your time on one day and is on a paid basis.

To participate in the study, you should meet the following requirements:

- Enjoy frequent travel
- Have experience with travel websites
- Be over 18 years of age

If you are available and would like to be part of this activity, please reply via e-mail to travel_usabilty@travelmyway.com with the subject line "Travel study."

You also must include:

- **Your name**
- **Age**
- **Indicate the travel website that you have experience with**
- **Phone number**

We will contact you within the next two weeks if you are an appropriate match.
If you are also interested in participating in future research activities at TravelMyWay.com, please complete the form located at http://travelmyway.com/usability.htm.

Figure 6.3: Example of a recruitment ad.

TIP

After a potential participant has been screened, sending the completed screener to the product team for their approval **before** the participant is scheduled can be a good idea. This works well in cases in which the qualifications are particularly complex or when you want to make sure the product team agrees that the participants were truly potential users.

Recruitment Methods

There are a variety of methods to attract users, and each method has its own strengths and weaknesses. If one fails, then you can try another. In this section, we will touch on some of these methods, so you can identify the one that will best suit your needs.

At a Glance

> Advertise on community bulletin board sites and via social networks
> Create an in-house database
> Use a recruiting agency
> Make use of customer contacts

Advertise on Community Bulletin Board Sites and Via Social Networks

Web-based community bulletin boards (e.g., craigslist.org) allow people to browse everything from houses to jobs to things for sale (see Figure 6.4). We have found them to be an effective way to attract a variety of users. We will typically place these ads in the classified section under "Jobs." You may be able to post for free or for less than $100, depending on the area of the country you live in and the particular bulletin board. The ad is usually posted within 30 minutes from when you submit it. One of the advantages of this method is that it is a great prescreen

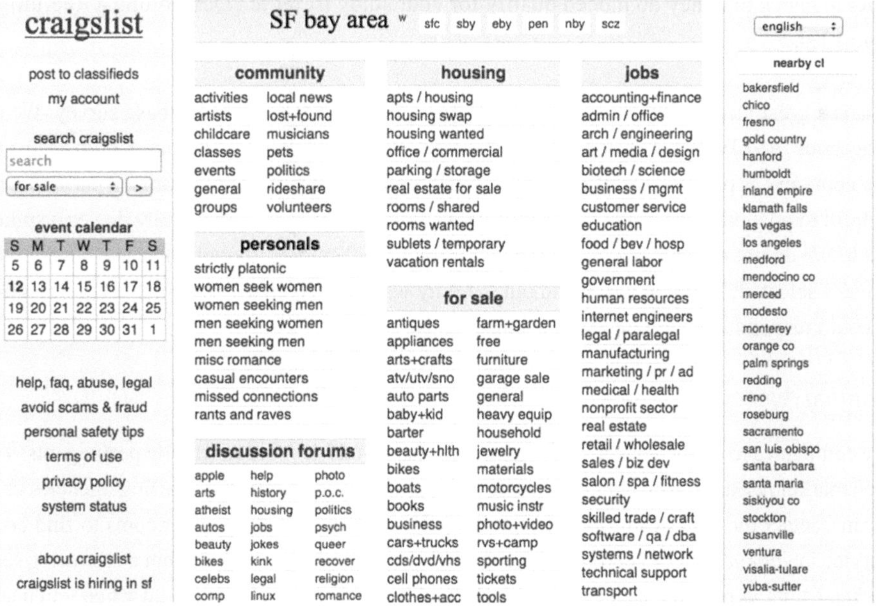

Figure 6.4: Craigslist in the San Francisco Bay Area (www.craigslsit.org)

if you are looking for people who use the web and/or computers. If they have found your ad, you know they are web users! However, you should be aware that this has become such a popular source for study recruitment, particularly in tech areas like the San Francisco Bay Area, Seattle, New York, Atlanta, and Austin, that "professional" participants lurk on those sites. These are individuals that spend a significant portion of their time participating in studies and may not be completely honest in screeners so they can increase their chances of being selected.

If you are looking for people who are local, use a site that is local to your area. Sites such as your local newspaper website or community publications are good choices. If you do not have access to any web publications in your area or if you want people who do not have web experience, you could post your advertisement in a physical newspaper or even on paper on real bulletin boards.

Create an In-House Database

You can create a database within your organization where you maintain a list of people who are interested in participating in user research activities. This database can hold some of the key characteristics about each person (e.g., age, gender, job title, years of experience, industry, company name, location, etc.). Prior to conducting an activity, you can search the database to find a set of potential participants who fit your user profile.

Once you have found potential participants, you can e-mail them some of the information about the study and ask them to e-mail you if they would like to participate. The e-mail should be similar to an ad you would post on a web community bulletin board site (see Figure 6.3). State that you obtained the person's name from your in-house participant database, which he or she signed up for, and provide a link or option to be removed from your database. For those who respond, you should then contact them over the phone and run through your screener to check that they do indeed qualify for your study (refer to "Developing a Recruiting Screener" section, page 129).

Social media is a great mechanism for getting people to sign up and take your database survey. We use sites like Google+, Facebook, and Twitter. Today, most companies have official pages on all three, both as just the company (e.g., google.com) and as product-specific pages (e.g., Chrome). So if you need to attract a particular product user, it is very helpful to post on those product pages. It helps with legitimacy, and we really do see a spike in sign-ups when we do it. We do not recommend social media for individual studies, though, because people will post questions like "Was I selected?" "When will I find out?" "Why wasn't I selected?" With hundreds of sign-ups, there is no way we could respond to everyone about a single study.

Use a Recruiting Agency

You can hire companies to do the recruiting for you. They have staff devoted to finding participants. These companies are often market research firms, but depending on your user type, temporary staffing agencies can also do the work. You can contact the American Marketing Association (www.marketingpower.com) to find companies that offer this service in your area. It can certainly be extremely helpful. We have found that a recruiting service is most beneficial when trying to recruit a user type that is difficult to find. They are also great when you need to conduct a **brand-blind** and/or **sponsor-blind** study (i.e., when you do not want participants to know who is conducting the study or for whom the product was created).

For example, we needed to conduct a study with physicians. Our participant database did not contain physicians, and an electronic community bulletin board posting was unsuccessful. As a result, we went to a recruiting agency and they were able to get these participants for us.

An additional benefit to using recruiting agencies is that they usually handle the incentives. Once you have a purchase order with the company, you can include money for incentives. The recruiting agency will then be responsible for paying the participants at the end of a study. This is one less thing for you to worry about.

You might ask, "Why not use these agencies exclusively and save time?" One of the reasons is cost. Typically, they will charge anywhere from $100 to $200 to recruit each participant (not including the incentives). The price varies depending on how hard they think it will be for them to attract the type of user you are looking for. If you are a little more budget-conscious, you might want to pursue some of the other recruiting options, but keep in mind that *your* time is money. A recruiting agency might be a bargain compared to your own time spent recruiting.

Also, in our experience, participants recruited by an agency have a higher no-show rate and are more likely to be professional participants. One reason for this is that not all agencies call to remind the participants about the activity the day before (or on the day of) the study. Additionally, using a recruiting agency adds a level of separation between you and the participants—if you do the recruiting yourself, they may feel more obligated to show up. Your experience will vary depending on the vendor and your specific needs, so do your homework!

Some recruiting agencies need more advance notice to recruit than we normally need ourselves. Some agencies we have worked with required a one-month notice to recruit so they had enough resources lined up. The smaller the agency, the more likely this will be the case. Consequently, if you need to do a quick, lightweight activity, an agency might not be able to assist you, but it never hurts to inquire.

Lastly, we have found that agencies are not effective in recruiting very specialized user types. Typically, the people making the calls will not have domain knowledge about the product you are recruiting for. Imagine you are conducting a database study and you require participants who have an intermediate level of computer programming knowledge. You have devised a set of test questions to assess their knowledge about programming. Unless these questions have very precise answers (e.g., multiple-choice), the recruiter will not be able to assess whether the potential participant is providing the correct answers. A participant may provide an answer that is close enough, but the recruiter does not know that. Even having precise multiple-choice answers does not always help. Sometimes, the qualifications are so complex that you simply have to get on the phone with candidates.

Regardless of these issues, a recruiting agency can be extremely valuable. If you decide to use one, there are a few things to keep in mind.

"We need to find a new recruiter."

Cartoon by Abi Jones

At a Glance

> Provide a screener
> Ask for the completed screeners to be sent after each person is recruited
> Ensure they remind the participants of your activity
> Avoid the professional participant
> Keep in mind that you cannot add them to your database

Provide a Screener

You will still need to design the phone screener and have the product team approve it (see above to learn more). The recruitment agency will know nothing about your product, so the screener may need to be more detailed than usual. Indicate what the desired responses are for each question and when the phone call should end because the potential participant does not meet the necessary criteria. Also provide a posting, if they are going to advertise to attract participants.

Be sure to discuss the phone screener with the recruiter(s). Do not just send it via e-mail and tell them to contact you if they have any questions. You want to make sure they understand and interpret each and every question as it was intended. Make sure you do this, even if you are recruiting for users with a non-technical profile. You may even choose to do some role-playing with the recruiter. Only when the recruiter begins putting your screener to work will you see whether he or she really understands it. Many research firms will employ a number of people to make recruitment calls. If you are unable to speak with all of them, then you should speak with your key point of contact at the agency and go through the screener.

Ask for the Completed Screeners to Be Sent After Each Person Is Recruited

This is a way for you to monitor who is being recruited and to double-check that the right people are being signed up. You can also send the completed screeners along to members of the product team to make sure they are happy with each recruit. This has been very successful for us in the past.

Ensure They Remind the Participants of Your Activity

It sounds obvious, but reminding participants of your activity will drastically decrease the no-show rate, as will sending them a calendar invite when you schedule them. Sometimes, recruiting agencies recruit participants one to two weeks before the activity. You want to make sure they call to remind people on the day before (and possibly again on the day of) the activity to get confirmation of attendance. It is valuable to include reminder calls in your contract with the recruitment agency, which also states that you will not pay for no-shows. This increases their motivation to get those participants in your door.

Avoid the Professional Participant

Yes, even with recruitment agencies, you must avoid the "professional participant." A recruitment agency may call on the same people over and over to participate in a variety of studies. The participant may be new to you but could have participated in three other studies this month. Although the participant may meet all of your other criteria, someone who seeks out research studies for regular income is not representative of your true end user. They will likely behave differently and provide more "polished" responses if they think they know what you are looking for.

You can insist that the recruitment agency provide only "fresh" participants. To double-check this, chatting with participants at the beginning of your session can reveal a great deal. Simply ask, "So, how many of you have participated in studies for the ABC agency before?" People will often be proud to inform you that the recruiting agency calls on them for their expertise "all the time."

TIP

Include a screener question that asks whether a person has participated in a user research study or a market research group in the last six months, and if so, how many. If the answer is more than one, you should consider disqualifying that person.

Keep in Mind that You Cannot Add Them to Your Database

You may be thinking that you will use a recruiting agency to help you recruit people initially and then add those folks to your participant database for future studies. In nearly all cases, you will not be able to do this. Most recruiting agencies have a clause in their contract that states that you cannot enlist any of the participants they have recruited unless it is done via them. Make sure you are aware of this clause, if it exists.

Make Use of Customer Contacts

Current or potential customers can make ideal participants. They truly have something at stake because, at the end of the day, they are going to have to use the product. As a result, they will likely not have problems being honest with you. Sometimes, they are brutally honest.

Typically, a product team, a sales consultant, or **account manager** will have a number of customer contacts with whom they have close relationships. The challenge can be convincing them to let you have access to them. Often, they are worried or concerned that you may cause them to lose a deal or that you might upset the customer. Normally, a discussion about your motives can help alleviate this problem.

Start by setting up a meeting to discuss your proposal (see "Getting Commitment" section, page 124). Once the product team member, sales consultant, or account manager understands the goal of your user research activity, they will hopefully also see the benefits of customer participation. It is a "win-win" situation for both you and the customer. Customers love to be involved in the process and have their voices heard, and you can collect some really great data. Another nice perk is that it can cost you less, as you typically provide only a small token of appreciation rather than money (see "Determining Participant Incentives" section, page 127).

Despite your efforts, it is possible that you will be forbidden from talking with certain customers. You will have to live with this. The last thing you want is to make an account manager angry or cause a situation in which a customer calls your company's representative to complain that he or she wants what the user research group showed him or her, not what the representative is selling. The internal contacts within your company can be invaluable when it comes to recruiting customers—they know their customers and can assist your recruiting—but they have to be treated with respect and kept informed about what you are doing.

If you decide to work with customers, there are several things to keep in mind.

At a Glance

> Be wary of the angry customer

> Avoid the unique customer

> Recruiting internal employees

> Allow more time to recruit

> Make sure the right people are recruited

Be Wary of the Angry Customer

When choosing customers to work with, it is best to choose those who currently have a good relationship with your company. This will simply make things easier. You want to avoid situations that involve heavy politics and angry customers. The last thing you or your group needs is to be blamed for a spoiled business deal. However, deals have actually been *saved* as a result of intervention from the user research professionals—the customer appreciated the attention he or she was receiving and recognized that the company was trying to improve the product based on his or her feedback. If you find yourself dealing with a dissatisfied customer, give the participants an opportunity to vent; however, do not allow this to be the focus of your activity. Providing 15 minutes at the beginning of a session for a participant to express his or her likes, dislikes, challenges, and concerns can allow you to move on and focus on the desired research activity you planned.

When recruiting customers, if you get a sense that the customer may have an agenda, plan a method to deal with this. Customers often have gripes about the current product and want to tell someone. One way to handle this is to have them meet with a member of the product team in a separate meeting from the activity. The user research needs to coordinate this with the product team. It requires additional effort, but it helps both sides.

Avoid the Unique Customer

It is best to work with a customer that is in line with most of your other customers. Sometimes, there are customers who have highly customized your product for their unique needs. Some companies have business processes that differ from the norm or industry standards. If you are helping the product development team conduct user research for a "special customer," this is fine. If you are trying to conduct user research that is going to be representative of the majority of your user population, you will not want to work with a customer that has processes different from the majority of potential users.

Recruiting Internal Employees

Sometimes, your customers are people who are internal to your company. These can be the hardest people of all to recruit. In our experience, they are very busy and may not feel it is worth their time to volunteer. If you are attempting to recruit internal participants, we have found it extremely effective to get their management's buy-in first. That way, when you contact them, you can say, "Hi John, I am contacting you because your boss, Sue, thought you would be an ideal candidate for this study." If their boss wants them to participate, they are unlikely to decline.

Allow More Time to Recruit

Unfortunately, this is one of the disadvantages of using customers. Typically, customer recruiting can be a slow process. There is often corporate red tape that you need to go through. You may need to explain to a number of people what you are doing and whom you need to participate. You also need to rely on someone within the company to help you get access to the right people. The reality is that although this may be your top priority, in most cases, it is not theirs, so things will always move more slowly than you would like. You may also have to go through the legal department for both your company and the customer's in order to get approval for your activity. NDAs may need to be changed (refer to Chapter 3, "Legal Considerations" section, page 76).

Make Sure the Right People Are Recruited

You need to ensure that your internal recruiter or recruiting agency contact is crystal clear about the participants you need. In most cases, the contact will think you want to talk to the people who are responsible for purchasing or installing the software. If you are in fact seeking end users, be sure the person understands that you want to talk to the people who will be *using* the software after it has been purchased and installed. It is best not to hand your screener over to the customer contact. Instead, provide the person with the user profile (refer to Chapter 2, "User Profile" section, page 37) and have him or her e-mail you the names and contact information of people seeming to match this profile. You can then contact them yourself and run them through your screener to make sure they qualify.

It is important to note that companies often want to send their best and brightest people. As a result, it can be difficult to get a representative sample with customers. You should bring this issue up with the customer contact and say, "I don't want only your best people. I want people with a range of skills and experience."

Also, do not be surprised if the customer insists on including "special" users in your study. Often, supervisors will insist on having *their* input heard before you can access their employees (the true end users). Even if you do not need feedback from purchasing decision-makers or supervisors, you may have to include them in your activity. It may take longer to complete your study with additional participants, but the feedback you receive could be useful. At the very least, you have created a more positive relationship with the customer by including those "special" users.

Preventing No-Shows

Regardless of your recruitment method, you will encounter situations where people who have agreed to participate do not show up on the day of the activity. This is very frustrating. The reason could be that something more important came up, or the participant might have just completely forgotten. There are some simple strategies to try and prevent this from occurring.

Provide Contact Information

Participants are often recruited one to two weeks before the activity begins. When we recruit, participants are given a contact name, e-mail, and phone number and told to contact this person if they will not be able to make the session for any reason. We understand that people do have lives and that our activity probably ranks low in the grand scheme of things. We try to emphasize to participants that we really want them to participate, but we will understand if they cannot make the appointment. We let them know that we really appreciate when people take the time to call and cancel or reschedule; it allows us an opportunity to find someone else or to at least make good use of our time instead of waiting around for someone who is not going to show up. We want them to know that it is the people who do not appear who cause the most difficulty.

Remind Them

The day before, and on the day of the activity, contact the participants to remind them. Some people just simply forget, especially if it is on a Monday morning! A simple reminder can prevent this.

Try to phone people rather than e-mail them, because you need to know whether or not they will be coming. If you catch them on the phone, you can get this immediately. Also, you can reiterate a couple of very important points to them. Remind them that they must be on time for the activity *and* they must bring a valid ID (if required), or they will *not* be admitted to the session. If you send an e-mail, you will have to hope that people read it carefully and take note of these important details. Also, you will have to wait for people to respond to confirm. Sometimes, people do not read your e-mail closely, and they do not respond (especially, if they know they are not coming). If participants cannot be reached by phone and you must leave a voice mail, remind them about the date and time of the session and all of the other pertinent details. Ask them to call you back to confirm their attendance.

Over-recruit

Even though you have provided your participants with contact information to cancel and you have called to remind them, there are still people who will not show up. To counteract this problem, you can over-recruit participants. It is useful to recruit one extra person for every four or five participants needed; some colleagues even double recruit—two people for every one needed!

Sometimes, everyone will show up, but we feel this cost is worth it. It is better to have more people than not enough. When everyone shows, you can deal with this in a couple of ways. If it is an individual activity, you can run the additional sessions (it costs more time and money but you get more data) or you can call and cancel the additional sessions. If participants do not receive your cancellation message in time and they appear at the scheduled time, you should pay them the full incentive for their trouble.

If everyone shows up for a group activity, we typically keep all participants. An extra couple of participants will not negatively impact your session. If there is some reason why you cannot involve the additional participants, you will have to turn them away. Be sure to pay them the full amount for their trouble.

Recruiting International Participants

Depending on the product you are working on and its market, you may need to include participants from other countries. You cannot assume that you can recruit for *or* conduct the activity in the same manner as you would in your own country. Below are some pieces of advice to keep in mind when conducting international user research activities (Dray & Mrazek, 1996):

- Use a professional recruiting agency in the country where you will be conducting the study. It is highly unlikely you will know the best places or methods for recruiting your end users.
- Learn the cultural and behavioral taboos and expectations. The recruiting agency can help you, or you can check out several books specifically for this. (Refer to "Suggested Resources for Additional Reading" section on page 148 for more information.)
- If your participants speak another language, you will need a translator, unless you are perfectly fluent. Even if your user speaks your language, you will need a translator. The participants will likely be more comfortable speaking in their own language or could have some difficulty understanding some of your terminology, if they are not fluent. There are often slang or technical terms that you will miss out on, despite being well-versed in the foreign language.

- If you are doing in-home studies in some countries in Europe, not only is it unusual to go to someone's home for an interview or other activities, but it is also unusual for guests to bring food to someone's home. Since you are a foreigner, or because the study is unusual, bringing food will likely be accepted.
- Punctuality can be an issue. For example, you must be on time when observing participants in Germany. In Korea or Italy, however, time is somewhat relative—appointments are more like suggestions and very likely will not begin on time. Keep this in mind when scheduling multiple visits in one day.
- Pay attention to holiday seasons. For example, you will be hard-pressed to find European users to observe in August, since many Europeans go on vacation at that time. Also, countries with a large Islamic population will likely be unavailable during Ramadan.

Recruiting is just the tip of the iceberg when it comes to conducting international field studies. You cannot simply apply a user research method in a foreign country in the same way that you would in your own country.

Suggested Resources for Additional Reading

Here are some additional resources you may find valuable when preparing for international user studies:

- Chavan, A. L., & Prabhu, G. V. (Aug 16, 2010). *Innovative solutions: What designers need to know for today's emerging markets.*
- Quesenbery, W., & Szuc, D. (Nov 23, 2011). *Global UX: Design and research in a connected world.*

Recruiting Special Populations

There are a number of special considerations when recruiting special populations of users. These populations can include such groups as children, the elderly, and people with disabilities. This section discusses some things to consider. Sometimes, special populations require more time to recruit, so factor that into your plan.

Transportation

You may need to arrange transportation for people who are unable to get to the site of the activity. You should be prepared to arrange for someone to pick them up before the activity and drop them off at the completion of the activity. This could be done using taxis, or you could arrange to have one of your employees do it. Also, if it is possible, you should consider going to the participant rather than having him or her come to you.

Escorts

Some populations may require an escort. For example, in the case of participants under the age of 18, a legal guardian must accompany them. You will also need this guardian to sign all consent and confidential disclosure forms. You may also find that adults with disabilities or the elderly may require an escort. This is not a problem. If the escort is present when the user research session is being conducted, simply ask him or her to sit quietly and not interfere with the session. It is most important for the participant to be safe and feel comfortable (refer to Chapter 3, "Ethical Considerations" section, page 67). This takes priority over everything else.

Facilities

Find out whether any of your participants have special needs with regard to facilities as soon as you recruit them. If any of your participants have physical disabilities, you must make sure that the facility where you will be holding your activity can accommodate people with disabilities. You should ensure that it has parking for the handicapped, wheelchair ramps, and elevators and that the building is wheelchair-accessible in all ways (bathroom, doorways, etc.). Also keep in mind that the facility may need to accommodate a dog if any of your participants use one as an aid.

If you are bringing children to your site, it is always a nice idea to make your space "kid-friendly." Put up a few children's posters. Bring a few toys that they can play with during a break. A few small touches can go a long way to helping child participants feel at ease.

Online Services

There are many vendors available to conduct studies on your online product. A simple web search for "online usability testing" will highlight those vendors. They can conduct research methods like surveys, card sorting, and usability evaluations online. Most provide their own panel of participants for your study. These are most likely **nonprobability-based samples** and may be rife with professional participants (refer to Chapter 10, "Probability Versus Nonprobability Sampling" section, page 271). Some allow you to conduct the research yourself using their tools and your own participants (e.g., from your customer database), so be sure to ask.

If they are recruiting, you must indicate your desired user profile and provide a script for the participants to follow. They also may require you to provide a link to your site/product, upload a prototype, or provide other content (e.g., names of your features in your product for card sorting). The vendor then e-mails study invitations to members of their panel that meet your user profile. Within hours, you can get dozens of completed responses, sometimes with videos of the participants' think-aloud commentary. Be aware that, although participants may be under an NDA, there is a greater risk of confidential product details being leaked. If this is not a concern for you, the online data collection is an excellent way to get feedback quickly from a large sample across the country.

Crowd Sourcing

Amazon's Mechanical Turk, or MTurk (mturk.com), is a popular method for quick recruiting and getting quick feedback from a large sample on microtasks (i.e., tasks that take a few seconds to a couple minutes to complete). Depending on the length and complexity of your tasks, each completed response can cost less than a dollar (sometimes just pennies!). This is an affordable way to get feedback from a large sample fast! MTurk participants are slightly more demographically diverse than standard Internet samples and significantly more diverse than typical American college samples (Buhrmester, Kwang, & Gosling, 2011); however, like other research panels, MTurk has a set of "professional participants" known as "super-Turkers" that spend 20+ hours/week completing tasks (Bohannon, 2011). You can include some screener questions, but this method is really best for basic tasks that are applicable across a broad spectrum of users, not highly trained or domain-specific users. To ensure more reliable and valid responses, include ways to check that participants are reading your tasks and responding completely (e.g., throw out responses that are too quick, look for **straight lining,** include test questions, minimum character count for open-ended questions) (Kittur, Chi, & Suh, 2008). If possible, make it just as easy for participants to provide valid responses as it is to try to "cheat" the system (Buhrmester et al., 2011; Casler, Bickel, & Hackett, 2013).

Suggested Resources for Further Reading

Bolt, N., Tulathimutte, T., & Merholz, P. (2010). *Remote research.* New York: Rosenfeld Media.

Kittur, A., Chi, E., & Suh, B. (2008). Crowdsourcing for usability: Using micro-task markets for rapid, remote, and low-cost user measurements. *Proceedings of the CHI 2008 conference*. ACM.

Tracking Participants

When recruiting, there are a number of facts about the participants that you need to track. To help you accomplish this, set up a database that lists all of the participants that you contact. This can be the beginning of a very simple participant database. You will want to track such things as:

- The activities they have participated in
- The date of the activity
- How much they were paid
- Any negative comments regarding your experience with the participant (e.g., "user did not show up," "user did not participate," "user was rude")
- Any positive comments (e.g., "Nikhil was a great contributor")
- Current contact information (e-mail address, phone number)

At a Glance

> Tax implications

> The professional participant

> Create a watch list

Tax Implications

If any participant is paid over $600 in one calendar year in the United States, your organization will be *required* to complete and submit a 1099 tax form ($600 threshold based on time of publication). Failure to do so can get your organization into serious trouble. To track this, you will need to know how much each participant has been paid each calendar year. If you want to avoid submitting tax forms, as soon as an individual reaches the $550 mark, move him or her to a watch list (see below), because when he or she hits $600, you will have to complete the forms. This list should be reviewed prior to recruiting. Keep in mind that you must account for the retail value of swag you give participants, just as if they were cash or gift cards. If you have a small set of users providing ongoing feedback on one of your products (e.g., a wearable computing device) and the individuals get to keep it after the study is over, you must account for the full retail value of that device, *not* what your company paid for it. If the retail price of that device will be $600 or more, you will have to submit the tax forms.

The Professional Participant

Believe it or not, there are people who seem to make a career out of participating in user research activities and market research studies. Some are just genuinely interested in your studies, but others are genuinely interested in the money. You definitely want to avoid recruiting the latter.

We follow the rule that a person can participate in an activity once every three months or until he or she reaches the $600/year mark (see "Tax Implications" section above). Unfortunately, there are some people who do not want to play by these rules. We have come across people who have changed their names and/or job titles in order to be selected for studies. We are not talking about subtle changes. In one case, we had a participant who claimed to be a university professor one evening and a project manager another evening—we have compiled at least nine different aliases, phone numbers, and e-mail addresses for this participant! The good news is that these kinds of people tend to be the rare exceptions.

By tracking the participants you have used in the past, you can take the contact information you receive from your recruits and make sure that it does not match the contact information of anyone else on your list. When we discover people who are using aliases, or who we *suspect* are using aliases, we place them on a watch list (see below).

We also attempt to prevent the alias portion of the problem by making people aware during the recruiting process that they will be required to bring a valid government-issued ID (e.g., driver's license, passport). If they do not bring their ID, they will not be admitted into the activity. You need to be strict about this. It is not good enough to fax a photocopy or send an e-mail of the license before or after the activity. The troublesome participant described above actually altered her driver's license and e-mailed it to us to receive the incentive she had been denied the night before.

Create a Watch List

The watch list is an important item in your recruiting toolbox. It is where you place the names of people you have recruited in the past but do not want to recruit in the future. These people can include those who:

- Are close to or have reached the $600 per calendar year payment limit (you can remove them from the watch list on January 1st)
- Have been dishonest in any way (e.g., used an alias, changed job role without a clear explanation)
- Have been poor participants in the past (e.g., rude, did not contribute, showed up late)
- Did not show up for an activity

The bottom line is that you want to do all you can to avoid bringing in participants who do not help the research goals. Again, in the case of our troublesome participant, she managed to sweet-talk her way into more than one study without a driver's license ("I left it in my other purse" and "I didn't drive today"). As a result, we posted warning signs for all researchers in our group. We even included her picture. See Figure 6.5 for an example of a "Warning" poster.

Attention All User Researchers
DO NOT ALLOW THIS PERSON IN!
Call Security immediately (444-3333)

CALIFORNIA
DRIVER LICENSE
EXPIRES 3-4-05
Dan Adams
123 Main St.
Downtown, CA
92123
3440-4-9698-80021

It has been discovered that this person has been participating in studies under a variety of names and job titles. Their motivation is unknown. They are not to be recruited or admitted into the building for any reason.

Aliases for "Dan Adams" (we believe his true name is Dan Aiken):

Last names used:
Aiken, Adams, Marks, Jones, Johnson

First names used:
Dan, Danny, Don, Damien, Joe, Brian

E-mails:
danadams@mailmail.com, daiken@yipee.com, jones@talkbox.com, bj@gig.com, marks@downtown.com, danny@supersite.com

Phone numbers:
555-859-8493, 555-849-8593, 500-859-3832, 500-533-3432
Other miscellaneous 1-877 numbers

Companies he claims to be from:
A2 Consulting, PS9 Associates, Aiken and Partners

Figure 6.5: Example of a warning poster.

Creating a Protocol

A protocol is a script that outlines all procedures you will perform as a moderator and the order in which you will carry out these procedures. It acts as a checklist for all of the session steps and may be required if you are seeking Institutional Review Board (IRB) approval for your study (see Chapter 3, page 66).

The protocol is very important for a number of reasons. First, if you are running multiple sessions of the same activity (e.g., two focus groups), it ensures that each activity and each participant is treated consistently. If you run several sessions, you tend to get tired and may forget details. The protocol helps you keep the sessions organized and polished. If you run the session differently for each activity, you will impact the data that you receive for each session. For example, if the two groups receive different sets of instructions, each group may have a different understanding of the activity and hence produce different results.

Second, the protocol is important if there is a different person running each session. This is never ideal, but the reality is that it does happen. The two people should develop the protocol together and rehearse it.

Third, a protocol helps you as a facilitator to ensure that you relay all of the necessary information to your participants. There is typically a wealth of things to convey during a session, and a protocol can help ensure that you cover everything. It could be disastrous if you forgot to have everyone sign your confidential disclosure agreements—and imagine the drama if you forgot to pay them at the end of the session.

Finally, a protocol allows someone else to replicate your study, should the need arise.

Sample Protocol

Figure 6.6 is a sample protocol for a group card-sorting activity. Of course, you need to modify the protocol according to the activity you are conducting, but this one should give you a good sense of what it should contain.

TravelMyWay.com Card Sort Protocol

Before participant arrives:

- Lay out food
- Turn on background music while people are comingin and getting settled
- Distribute name tags, pens, consent form/NDA
- Make sure you have protocol, cards, envelopes, staples, rubber bands, extra pens, and incentives

Figure 6.6: Example of a protocol.

Continued

After participant arrives:

- Ask for ID
- Offer something to drink and eat
- Explain about video, observers behind the one-way mirror, and breaks
- Explain NDA/consent form and name tags
- Collect signed paperwork and ask assistant to make copies
- Begin recording
- Explain who we are and the purpose of the activity
- Indicate that we are not members of the development team. We did not develop the content we will be working with today, so feel free to be honest.

Facilitator says:

"We are in the process of designing a travel website targeted at college and university students. Today, you are here to help us develop the structure of the interface. There are several pieces of information or objects that we would like for you to group into meaningful piles. This will help us to group the information in our product so that it is easy to find.

I am going to present each of you with a stack of cards. On each card is a term and a corresponding definition. I would like for you to review each card and tell me if the definition does not make sense or if you disagree with the term we have provided. For example, you might say 'I have heard of this before but I call it something else.' At that point, I will ask if there is anyone else who calls this object by a different name. I would like for you to make any changes to the definition or the term directly on the card. Also, if you do not use this object or if you have never heard of it before, please write 'I never use this' or 'I have never heard of this before' directly on the card.

After you have reviewed all of the terms, please sort the objects together into meaningful groups. There is no limit to the number of groups or number of cards in a group. Also, we'd like you to work individually. There are NO wrong answers. If you believe that an object *needs* to be in more than one group, you can create a duplicate using one of the blank cards.

Once you have divided all of your cards into groups, please use the blank cards to give each group a meaningful name. This could be a word or a phrase. If you need more blank cards, please let me know. Also please let me know if you have any questions!"

<Do a quick sorting example on the whiteboard. If people understand, then hand out the set of cards and let them begin to sort. Sit quietly at the front of the room and answer any questions.>

Finishing Up

- As people begin to finish their sorts, ask them to staple each group together and place them in a pre-marked envelope. If a group is too big to be stapled, use a rubber band.
- As participants finish, thank them for their time, pay them, and escort them back to the lobby.
- Be sure to collect each participant's visitor's badge.

Figure 6.6 – Cont'd

Piloting Your Activity

A pilot is essentially a practice run for your activity. It is a mandatory element for any user research activity. These activities are complex, and even experienced user researchers need to conduct a pilot. You cannot conduct a professional activity without a pilot. It is more than "practice;" it is debugging. Run the activity as though it is the true session. Do everything exactly as you plan to for the real session. Get a few of your colleagues to help you out. If you are running a group activity that requires 12 people, you do not need to get 12 people to participate in the pilot. (It would be great if you could, but it usually is not realistic or necessary.) Three or four colleagues will typically help you accomplish your purpose. We recommend running a pilot about three days before your session; this will give you time to fix any problems that crop up.

Conducting a pilot can help you accomplish a number of goals.

Is the Audiovisual Equipment Working?

This is your chance to set camera angles, check microphones, and make sure that the quality of recording is going to be acceptable. You do not want to find out after the session that the video camera or tape recorder was not working.

Clarity of Instructions and Questions

You want to make sure that instructions to the participants are clear and understandable. By trying to explain an activity to colleagues ahead of time, you can get feedback about what was understandable and what was not so clear.

Find Bugs or Glitches

A fresh set of eyes can often pick up bugs or glitches that you have not noticed. These could be anything from typos in your documentation to hiccups in the product you plan to demo. You will obviously want to catch these embarrassing oversights or errors before your real session.

Practice

If you have never conducted this type of activity before, or it has been a while, a pilot offers you an opportunity to practice and get comfortable. A nervous or uncomfortable facilitator makes for nervous and uncomfortable participants. The more you can practice your moderation skills, the better (refer to Chapter 7, "Moderating Your Activity" section, page 165).

The pilot will also give you a sense of the timing of the activity. Each activity has a predetermined amount of time, and you need to stay within that limit. By doing a pilot, you can find out whether you need to abbreviate anything.

Who Should Attend?

If this is the first time you have conducted this type of activity, it is advisable to have someone experienced in your pilot session. He or she will be able to give you feedback about what can be improved. After the pilot, if you do not feel comfortable executing the activity due to inexperience as a moderator, you will seriously want to consider having someone experienced (a colleague or consultant) step in for you. You can then shadow the experienced moderator to increase your comfort level for next time. Members of the product team or your advisor, if you are a student, should attend your pilot session. They are a part of your team for this activity, so you want them to be involved in every step—and this is an important step. Even though they have read your proposal (see "Getting Commitment" section, page 124), they may not have a good sense of how the activity will "look." The pilot will give them this sense. It also gives the product team members one last chance to voice any concerns or issues. Be prepared for some possible critical feedback. If you feel their concerns are legitimate, you now have an opportunity to address them.

Ironically, the pilot is the one session to which you may feel uncomfortable inviting team members because you may be nervous and because events do go awry at pilots. But if you explain the nature and purpose of pilots to the team and set their expectations, they can help you without causing you to feel threatened.

Pulling It All Together

Preparation is the key to a successful user research activity. Be sure to get the product team involved in the preparation immediately, and work together as a team. In this chapter, we have covered all the key deliverables and action items that you and your product team will need to complete in order to prepare for a successful user research activity.

CHAPTER 7

During Your User Research Activity

Introduction

In the previous chapter, you learned how to lay the groundwork and prepare for any activity. In this chapter, we cover the fundamentals of executing a successful user research activity. Because user research activities can occur in the lab or in the field, in person, or via e-mail, audio chat, or video chat, how much you, as the researcher, have to do "during" an activity can differ greatly depending on which activity you have chosen (see Table 7.1). For example, during an online survey, you simply keep an eye on the quality of the data as they flow in. On the other hand, during an in-person focus group, you are responsible for greeting participants, keeping participants energetic, ensuring you are eliciting quality discussion, and making sure all your recording equipment is functioning properly. It takes a lot more preparation and energy *during* a focus group than it does *during* a survey!

Besides differences between activities, there are also different choices you can make about what will happen during your activity. For example, you can choose to conduct your session with only one person at a time (individual) or with many people at a time (group). You can choose to conduct a session face-to-face (in person) or via a mediated communication channel, such as video chat (remote). You can choose to conduct your activity in a space specifically set up for user research activities (lab) or in the home or office of a participant (field). Finally, you can choose for your portion of the activity to be at the same time as the participant, allowing interaction (synchronous), or at different times (asynchronous).

Because there are so many options, some of the recommendations in this chapter will not fit exactly with every activity as you have designed it. See Table 7.2 for a quick guide about which sections of this chapter are most applicable to each activity type. We have focused most of our discussion on activities that can be tricky and require high levels of researcher participation *during* the activities, which are usually those that are in person, are synchronous, and occur in groups. However, all of the recommendations can be used as a guide no matter what type of activity you are conducting. For example, if you are conducting your research activity remotely (e.g., remote card sort), you will need to vary the way you welcome participants, get informed consent, and provide incentives to fit your format. Even though you will not meet participants in person, you will still need to welcome them, get informed consent, and pay them. In this case, instead of welcoming participants in person verbally, you will need to do this by displaying text on a welcome screen; instead of having participants sign a paper consent form, have them read and agree to the form online; instead of handing participants a gift card, give them a code that lets them spend their incentive online right away or let them know that you will mail them a gift card immediately.

Table 7.1: Level of researcher activity during a typical study by type

Study type	Level of activity
Diary study	Low
Interview	High
Survey	Low
Card sort	Medium
Focus group	High
Field studies	Medium
Evaluation	Medium

Table 7.2: A quick guide to what you need to do during each type of user research activity

	Diary study	Interview	Survey	Card sort	Focus group	Field studies	Evaluation
Invite observers	No	Yes	No	Yes	Yes	Yes	Yes
Welcome participants	Yes	Yes	No	Yes	Yes	Yes	Yes
Moderate the activity	No	Yes	No	Maybe	Yes	Maybe	Maybe
Record and notetake	No	Yes	No	Yes	Yes	Yes	Yes
Deal with late and absent participants	Yes	Yes	No	Yes	Yes	Yes	Yes

Inviting Observers

By the term "observer," we mean someone who does not have an active role during the activity. For example, you may want to invite a developer who has a difficult time understanding that users approach an interaction differently than she does. Strive to invite **stakeholders** to view live user research sessions in a way where their presence will not distract, disrupt, and/or intimidate participants (e.g., behind a one-way mirror, sitting quietly in the back of a room, via a webcam). When it is not possible or practical to invite observers to view a live session (e.g., diary studies), be sure to collect data in a way that will allow stakeholders to hear the participants' voice and understand their perspective. To learn about setting up a way for observers to view user research sessions, see Chapter 4 on page 82.

TIP

One of the most effective ways to help stakeholders and others who may not usually interact with the users better understand the users and their needs is to have them attend or view a recording of a session where they get to see and hear the users. Sometimes seeing and hearing even one user can be more meaningful and transformative in terms of perspective than reading an entire user research report.

In addition to helping observers understand user needs, another advantage of inviting observers is team building. You are all part of a "team," so stakeholders should be present at the activities, too. Also, it helps stakeholders understand what you do and what value you bring to the team—and that builds credibility. It is also wise to record sessions and make these recordings available for any stakeholders who may not be able to attend, as well as for your own future reference.

When you invite observers to a live session, it is a good idea to set expectations up front:

- Tell the observers to arrive early and enter in a manner that is respectful and unobtrusive.
- If observers are in a room near the participant, they may need to be quiet and still. Often, rooms divided by a one-way mirror might not be fully soundproof or not dark enough to hide all movements. When using a video link, this may not be a requirement.
- Observers should turn off their cell phones. Answering calls will disturb participants and other observers. It can be difficult to get busy people (especially executives) to turn off their phones, but if they understand that their phone can interfere with the comfort of participants, colleagues, and equipment, they will usually oblige.

When you invite observers to a remote session:

- Instruct observers to remain quiet during the session and remind them to turn off their cell phone ringers and for those using video or audio conference software, to mute their microphones and phones.
- Always introduce everyone in the room, even if the participant cannot see everyone (e.g., in an audio-only interview or a video chat where you are the only person visible). If you do not introduce everyone in the room and someone speaks up (e.g., a designer, product manager or engineer pipes up to answer a participant's question), you will have lost the participant's trust.

TIP

For group activities in the lab, we usually order extra food so there is enough left over for the observers to enjoy after the session. The promise of cookies is usually enough incentive for the observers to hang around until the very end!

Who Should NOT Observe?

In general, do not allow anyone who is in a supervisory or managerial role over a specific participant to observe that participant. If participants believe that their boss is watching, it can dramatically impact what they do or say. For example, in a field study, if participants know their boss is watching them, they may say that they do things according to what the company policy dictates rather than how they perform in practice. Explain to managers or supervisors that their presence may intimidate the participant and that you will summarize the data for them (without specific participant names). We find that with this explanation, they typically understand and accept your request not to observe. If you are unable to avoid this situation for political reasons (e.g., a high-profile customer insists on observing), you may have to allow the supervisor to observe and then scrap the data. For ethical reasons, let the participant know he or she will be observed by the supervisor before you start the session.

Welcoming Your Participants

Welcoming Participants to a Lab Session

If participants are meeting you at a lab or other similar location, ask them to arrive about 15 minutes before the session is due to begin (30 minutes if you are serving a meal). This allows enough time for participants to get some food, relax, and chat. In the case of a group session, it also provides a buffer in case some participants are running late. We tell participants during recruitment (refer to Chapter 6, "Recruitment Methods" section, page 139): "The session starts at 6:00 pm; please arrive 30 minutes ahead of time in order to eat and to take care of administrative details before the session starts. Late participants will not be admitted into the session." Playing music during this time can provide a casual atmosphere and is more pleasant than the sound of uncomfortable silence or of forks scraping plates.

TIP

Once your participants are in the room where the activity will take place, you should not leave them alone. Participants may get lost if wandering the halls during a break or in your absence, and you will waste time trying to find them. Also, for security reasons, it is not wise to allow nonemployees to roam the premises.

If it is a group session, during this presession period, post a colleague in the lobby with a "Welcome" sign on a flip chart to greet and direct participants as they arrive. Such a sign might read "Welcome participants of the TravelMyWay App focus group. Please take a seat and we will be with you shortly." This sign lets participants know they are in the right place and directs them in case the greeter is not present. If your location has a receptionist, to avoid confusion, provide the receptionist with your participant list and make sure the receptionist asks all participants to stay in a specified location. If your location does not have a receptionist, put up a large sign that specifies where participants should wait in case people arrive while others are being escorted to the activity location. It saves time and effort to bring participants to the session location in groups of four or five. To avoid making multiple trips back and forth, ask participants if they need to use the bathroom along the way. If possible, have a receptionist or greeter ask participants to show ID and sign a nondisclosure agreement (NDA) while they are waiting to meet you.

Welcoming Participants in the Field

If you are meeting participants in the field (e.g., their home or office), you should also arrive early so participants are not waiting for you! If you are visiting a participant at his or her home, arrive in the area early, but do not go to his or her door until right on time. He or she may have arranged his or her day around you, so do not expect him or her to be available before the appointment time.

Introducing the Session

Once your participant or participants have arrived, or you have arrived in the field, you should welcome them, introduce yourself, give them an overview of the session, tell them the overall goals, let them know about any observers who will be watching the session and have them sign the NDA and consent form. You should also outline any ground rules you have for the session and set up expectations. For example, ask participants to turn off their cell phones.

Consenting Participants

Once you are sure participants understand the plan for the session and their part in it, you are ready to begin the consent process. Remember that the consent process involves more than just having participants sign a form. Instead, it is a conversation between you and the participants that results in the participants understanding the goals of the session and plan for the session and their willingness and knowledgeable agreement to participate. Once you are sure the participants know the plan, are comfortable with the plan, and want to participate, have them sign two copies of the NDA and consent form—one for you and one for them. This is also a good time to revisit the NDA, if they signed it in advance, and to make sure participants understand that they are agreeing to keep any information about the session confidential.

Providing Incentives

We recommend providing the incentives you agreed to provide (see Chapter 6, "Incentives" section, page 118) as part of your consent process. That way, participants are more likely to believe you when you tell them that they are free to leave at any time without penalty. It is a good idea to ask participants to sign a simple receipt acknowledging they have received the incentive (see Figure 7.1).

User Research Incentive Receipt

Please sign below to indicate that you have received an incentive for your participation in session.

	Amount $		
Name (Print)			
Name (Signed)			
Researcher Name		**Date**	

Figure 7.1: Example of a simple incentive receipt.

Developing Rapport

When conducting any kind of user activity, ensure that your participants are comfortable and feeling at ease before you begin collecting data that you will use. When conducting an individual activity, start out with some light conversation. Comment on the weather; ask whether the person had any trouble with traffic or parking. Be sure to carve out a bit of time, even if it eats into your hour, to make the participant comfortable. Keep it casual. When you sit down to begin the session, start with an informal introduction of yourself and what you do. Ask the participant to do the same. Also, find out what you should call the person, and then, use first names if appropriate.

Warm-Up Exercises

Ensuring that participants are at ease is extremely important for group activities. Each person will typically need to interact with you and everyone else in the room, so you want to make sure they feel comfortable. In addition to developing rapport with participants, you may also want to conduct some warm-up exercises. One method we use is to give people colorful markers and name tags or name tents and ask them to write their names and draw something that describes their personality. For example, if I like to ride horses, I might draw a saddle on my name tag. During this time, the moderators should also create name tags for themselves.

Once everyone has finished, we ask the participants to describe their drawing for the group. The moderators should go first and explain what they have drawn on their own name tags and why. This will help to put the first participant at ease when he or she describes his or her name tag and so on around the room. Any type of warm-up activity that gets people talking will do.

The name tag activity is great because it serves a twofold purpose: it helps everyone relax, and it helps you get exposure to each person's name. You should use people's names as much as possible throughout the session to make the session more personal.

You can use any kind of warm-up activity that you feel works best for you. Your goal should be to get everyone talking and to get those creative juices flowing. Fifteen minutes should be plenty of time to accomplish this. Here are a few example warm-up exercises we have used in the past:

- In a group setting, ask people to introduce themselves and say one interesting thing about themselves.
- Ask people what they like and dislike about the current product they are using.
- Ask general, easy-to-answer questions about the topic that is the focus of the study. For example, if you are studying the TravelMyWay mobile app, you might ask participants, "What are your three favorite mobile phone apps? Why?"

Moderating Your Activity

Excellent moderation is key to the success of any activity. The moderator is responsible for setting expectations, keeping track of time, maintaining control over the session, and providing motivation. Even when participants are provided with instructions, they do not always know exactly what you are looking for, so it is your job to remind and guide them. Also, since many times these activities are scheduled in the evening and people are tired after work, it will be your job to keep them energized. A moderator must keep the participants focused, keep things moving, make sure everyone participates equally, and ultimately ensure that meaningful data are collected.

Moderation of a group is more complex, but moderation is also important for individual activities. There are a few rules that apply to both types, such as staying focused and keeping the activity moving. Some common individual and group moderating scenarios are discussed below. Table 7.3 provides some suggested statements in response to different moderation situations.

TIP

It is ideal for the moderator to have some domain knowledge, particularly if a complex topic is being discussed. If you have domain knowledge, this will enable you to follow up and delve deeper into important issues and to give little attention to things that are unrelated or unimportant to the discussion. One way to learn about the topic in advance is to consult a **subject matter expert** (SME).

Table 7.3: Moderation tips: what to say when you want to ...

Set expectations	"If you ask me questions, I may not really answer you or I may be vague. If I'm doing that, I'm not being unfriendly; I'm just trying to stay neutral."
Turn a question around	"I'm not sure, but tell me more about what you're thinking here ..." "What matters is your experience, which we can learn from. Tell me more about what you're experiencing here ..."
Prompt a silent/ nonresponsive participant	"What are you trying to do right now?" "What are you thinking right now?" "What is going through your mind right now?"
Provide reassurance and build engagement	"There are no wrong answers here; you're here to help us." "If we didn't see what areas work well or not so well for you, we wouldn't learn anything." "Please know that your candor is appreciated. Nothing you say will hurt anyone's feelings. You're here to help us make the product better for yourself and future users." "This is just the kind of feedback we want to hear ..."
Redirect or cut feedback short	"This is all very helpful to see and hear. Just for the sake of time, I'm going to ask you to go to the next task/go back to ..." "Let's move on for now. I wanted to ask you about what you did earlier ..." "Let's stop this here and we can come back to it later. Read the next scenario ..." "I'm interested in hearing more about this. I do want to make sure we cover everything we have planned, so if there is time, let's come back to this at the end of the session ..."
End a session early	"You went through everything faster than expected, so we're going to get you out of here early." "That's actually all I had for you today, so you'll get some time back in your day! Thank you so much for your feedback."

Source: Adapted from Tedesco & Tranquada (2014) Appendix A: What to Say. *The Moderator's Survival Guide.*

Moderation Strategies

At a Glance

> Be approachable and positive
> Ask questions
> Stay focused
> Keep the activity moving
> You are not a participant
> Keep the participants motivated and encouraged
> No critiquing
> Everyone should participate; no one should dominate
> Practice makes perfect
> Find your own style

Be Approachable and Positive

Participants should feel at ease around you, the moderator. Be personable and approachable; remember to smile and look them in the eyes. You may be tired and have had a terrible day, but you cannot let it show. You need to emanate a positive attitude. Before the session begins, chat with participants. You do not need to talk about the activity, but participants often have questions about your job, the product, or the activity. Getting to know the participants will help you get a sense for the type of people, and it will put them at ease and get them comfortable speaking to you.

Ask Questions

Remember that you are not the expert in the session. The participants are the experts, and you should make them aware of that. Let them know that you will be stopping to ask questions and get clarification from time to time. The participants will undoubtedly use acronyms and terminology with which you are unfamiliar, so you should stop them and ask for an explanation rather than pushing on. There is no point collecting data that you do not understand.

You also want to make sure that you capture what the user is *really* saying. Sometimes, the best way to ensure that you understand someone is to listen reflectively ("active listening"). This involves paraphrasing what the participant has said in a nonjudgmental, nonevaluative way and then giving the participant a chance to correct you if necessary.

At other times, you will need to probe deeper and ask follow-up questions. For example, Vivian may say, "I would never research travel on my phone." If you probe further and ask "Can you explain that a little more?" you may find out that it is not because Vivian thinks it would be a bad idea to research travel on her phone; it is just that she never conducts travel research because she spends all of her vacation time at her condo in the Florida Keys.

Stay Focused

Do not let participants go off on a tangent. Remember that you have a limited amount of time to collect all of the information you need, so make sure that participants stay focused on the topic at hand. Small diversions, if relevant, are appropriate, but try to get back on track quickly. A good strategy for getting participants back on track is to say something like "That is really interesting. Perhaps we can delve into that more at the end of the session, if we have time."

Another strategy is to visually post information that will help keep people on track. For example, if you are running a focus group, write the question on a whiteboard. If people get off topic, *literally* point back to the whiteboard and let them know that although their comments are valuable, they are beyond the scope of the session. You can also periodically repeat the question to remind people what the focus of the discussion is.

Keep the Activity Moving

Even when people stay focused on the goal or question presented in the activity, they sometimes go into far more detail than necessary. You need to control this; otherwise, you might never finish the activity. It is OK to say "I think I now have a good sense of this topic, so let's move on to the next topic because we have a lot of material to get through today." After making a statement such as this once or twice during the session, people will typically get a sense of the level of detail you are going after. You can also let them know this up front in your introduction, by saying, "We have a lot to cover today, so I may move along to the next topic in the interests of time."

You Are Not a Participant

It is critical that you elicit thoughts and opinions from participants without interjecting your own thoughts and opinions about the topic. Be patient and let participants answer the questions; do not try to answer for them. Also, do not offer your opinions because that could bias their responses. This may sound obvious, but sometimes, the temptation can be very hard to resist. It may be particularly difficult in an interview session when participants ask you for your opinion about a product or ask for your help with a task. A good response to use in this case is "You're the expert here. I'm interested in hearing about what you think." If you fall into the trap of inserting your opinion, you will end up with results that represent *your* thinking instead of that of the users.

Keep the Participants Motivated and Encouraged

User research activities can take anywhere from five minutes to months to complete. On average, an in-person, moderated user research activity lasts one to two hours. This is quite a long period of time for a person or a group of people to be focused on a single activity. You must keep people engaged and interested. Provide words of encouragement as often as possible. Let them know what a great job they are doing and how much their input is going to help your product or understanding of a topic. A little acknowledgment goes a long way! Also, keep an eye on your participants' energy levels. If they seem to be fading, you might want to offer them a break or offer up some of those leftover cookies or coffee to help give them the necessary energy boost. You want everyone to have a good time and to leave the activity viewing it as a positive experience. Try to be relaxed, smile often, and have a good time. Your mood will be contagious.

No Critiquing

As the moderator, you should never challenge what participants have to say. This is crucial, since you are there to learn what *they* think. You may completely disagree with their thoughts, but you are conducting user research and you are not the user in this situation. You may want to probe further to find out why a participant feels a certain way, but at the end of the day, remember that, in this session, he or she is the expert, not you. We often include a statement like this at the beginning of a session:

Remember, there are no right or wrong answers here. We are not evaluating you. All ideas are correct, and we welcome all your thoughts and comments.

Practice Makes Perfect

Moderating activities is not easy and requires practice. We still find that we learn new tricks and tips and also face new challenges with each session. We recommend that people new to moderating groups watch videos of the activity they will be conducting and observe how the facilitator interacts with the participants. Next, they should shadow a facilitator. Being in the room as the activity is going on is a much richer experience than watching a video. Also, a beginner should practice with colleagues who are experienced moderators. Set up a pilot session so you can practice your moderating skills before the real activity. Have your colleagues role-play. For example, one person can be the dominant participant, one can be the quiet participant, and one can be the participant who does not follow instructions. You can record the sessions and watch them with an experienced moderator to find out how you can improve. Another great idea is to be a participant in user research activities. Find a local facility that runs and/or recruits for them and contact them to get on their participant list. That way, you can observe professional moderators at work. Finally, be sure to practice answering questions that are likely to come up while you are moderating a study. For example, when moderating a study on software, users would frequently ask if a certain feature was enabled. Instead of saying yes or no, we would say, "This is the out-of-box product," which was enough information for them to be happy, but did not give any more details than necessary.

Find Your Own Style

There is no one moderation style that works for everyone. For example, some people can easily joke with participants and use humor to control the overbearing ones: "If you don't play well with the others, I will have to take your pen away!" Other people are not as comfortable speaking in front of groups and have difficulty using humor in these situations. In those cases, trying to use humor can backfire and might come across as sarcasm. Find an experienced moderator to emulate—one whose personality and interaction style is similar to yours.

Additional Moderating Strategies

For additional information on moderating strategies, we recommend the following book:

Tedesco, D., & Tranquada, F. (2013). *The Moderator's Survival Guide*. Morgan Kaufmann.

In this excellent, practical book, Tedesco and Tranquada recommended strategies such as "friendly face," "inquisitive mind," "down to business," "student," and "by the book." They also note that some strategies are more appropriate for certain types of participants. For example, for shy participants, try a friendly face strategy, whereas for a gregarious participant, try a down-to-business strategy. They also discussed how some strategies work best in some phases of the research. For example, in the formative research phase, they suggested trying the inquisitive mind strategy.

Using a Think-Aloud Protocol

A think-aloud protocol is the process of having participants speak what they are thinking as they complete a task. This technique not only is typically used for usability tests but also can be quite beneficial for certain user research activities where you are working with one person at a time—for example, individual card sorts (refer to Chapter 10, page 266) and field studies (refer to Chapter 13, page 380).

Using a think-aloud protocol, you get an understanding of why the user is taking the actions that he or she takes and the person's reactions to and thoughts about what he or she is working with. For example, in the case of a card sort, you can learn about why the person groups certain cards.

Before asking participants to think aloud, it is helpful to provide an example, preferably one that reflects what they will be working with. If they will be completing tasks on a mobile phone, for example, demonstrate an example with a phone-based task. Remember that the instructions to the participant should model what you want them to do. So if you want them to describe expectations, model that for them. If you want them to express feelings, model that for them. During the demonstration, the facilitator works through the task and the participant observes him or her using the protocol. Below is an example of a think-aloud protocol demonstration using a mobile phone to send an SMS text (adapted from Dumas and Redish, 1999):

> **As you participate today, I would like you to do what we call "think out loud." What that means is that I want you to say out loud what you are thinking as you work. Let me show you what I mean. I am going to think out loud as I try to send a text message on this mobile phone. OK, I am looking at the home screen of the phone. I would expect there to be an icon that says "text" or "messages" right here on the home screen, but I don't see that here. I'm confused by that. I'm going to look in other places for it. I think I'll try to click on this icon of a callout bubble because that seems like it might be related to talking, like "I talk, the other person talks." Okay, now that that is open, I see an icon that says "text messages." I'm glad to see that there because that is what I was expecting to see.**
>
> **Do you see what I mean about thinking out loud? Now let's have you practice by telling me out loud how you would send an e-mail on this phone.**

It may help participants to describe to them that you want to hear *what they are thinking as they interact with a product* rather than *their opinion about a product.* For example, while you do want to know what they are trying to accomplish, what they are looking at, and what they expected, you are not interested in other things they may want to tell you, for example, how they think other people will feel about an interface. When participants understand what you are looking for and say things like, "I am looking for a way to book an airline ticket using this mobile app, but I was expecting it to be in the 'purchase' tab," give them positive feedback in the form of an "mm hmm." If they get off track and say something like "I don't think most people will think this color green is attractive. You should change it," redirect them to the task, and ask, "Tell me what you expected to see here."

If you are recording the session, you may find that participants need to be reminded to speak up. Many participants talk quietly as if it were a private conversation instead of a recorded session. If they are quiet, we say, "That was just what I want you to do, but remember you are speaking to the microphone, not just to me. You may have to talk a bit louder. Don't worry; I will remind you if I can't hear you."

Think-aloud protocols are not without their limitations. For example, people are limited in what they themselves can understand and convey about their own thought processes and motivations (Boren & Ramey, 2000;

Nisbett & Wilson, 1977). In addition, having people participate in a think-aloud protocol takes resources away from the task they are performing, thus reducing the cognitive capacity people will have to devote to the task itself. Despite these limitations, think-aloud protocols are often a very useful technique.

Debrief Participants

At the conclusion of the study, you should thank participants, give them a chance to ask any questions they may have, tell them about the goals of the study, and provide any incentive you have agreed to provide, if you have not already provided this during the consent process (see Chapter 6, "Incentives" section, page 118).

Recording and Notetaking

There are a few options when deciding how to capture information during your activity.

At a Glance

> Take notes

> Use video or audio recording

> Use screen-capture software

> Combine video/audio/screen recording and notetaking

Take Notes

Taking notes on a laptop and taking notes by hand on paper are two obvious options. One of the benefits of taking notes during the session is that you can walk away from the activity with immediate data and begin analysis (see Figure 7.2 for sample notes from an interview). You are also signaling to the participants that you are noting what is being said. It is good to show the participants that you are engaged in the activity, but they might be offended if you are not taking notes when the participants feel they are saying something particularly noteworthy. When taking notes on a laptop, there is also the possibility that participants may think you are doing something else on the laptop, like checking your e-mail, rather than paying attention to them. If you are a touch typist, you can avoid this by looking at the participants, rather than your screen while you take notes on a laptop.

A potential problem with taking notes is that you can get so wrapped up in being a stenographer that you have difficulty engaging the participants or following up. You could also fail to capture important comments because the pace of a discussion can be faster than your notetaking speed. If you choose to take notes yourself during a session, develop shorthand so that you can note key elements quickly (see Figure 7.3 for some sample shorthand). Also, do not try to capture every comment verbatim—paraphrasing is faster and sufficient for most purposes. If you need verbatim quotes, consider using video or audio recording.

For some activities, such as focus groups, the moderating is so consuming that it is simply not possible for you to take effective notes. In that case, a better option is to have a colleague take notes for you.

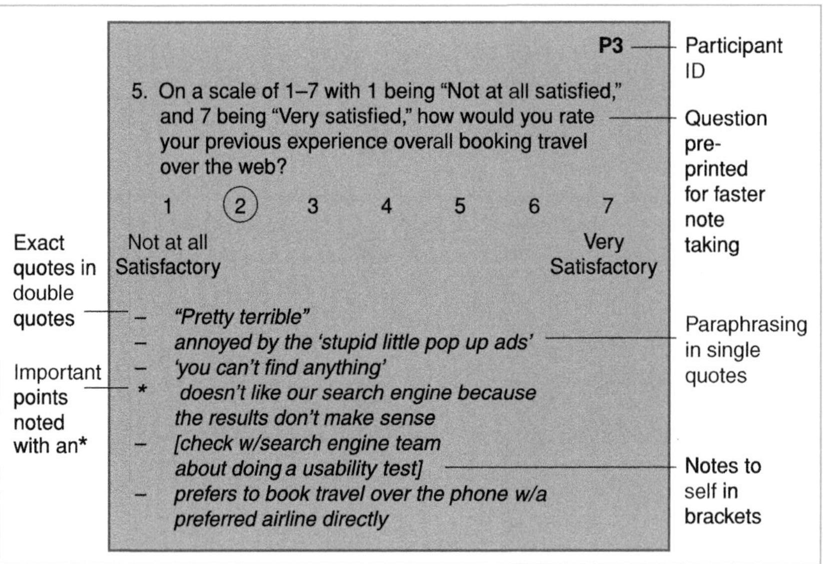

Figure 7.2: Excerpt of notes taken during an interview.

Participant #1: P1
Because: b/c
With: w/
Within: w/i
By the way: btw
At: @
As a matter of fact: aamof
Not applicable: N/A
No comment: NC

Figure 7.3: Sample shorthand for notetaking.

A notetaker can be in the same room with you, watching a live video stream, or watching from behind the one-way mirror if you have a formal lab setup (refer to Chapter 4, "Building a Permanent Facility" section, page 85). It can also help to have an additional pair of eyes to discuss the data with and come up with insights that you might not have had yourself.

If the notetaker is in the same room, you may or may not want to allow the person to pause the session if they get behind in the notes or are not understanding what a participant says. This can be very disrupting to the session, so ideally, you want an experienced notetaker who will not require this. The person should not attempt to play court stenographer: you are not looking for a word-by-word account, only the key points or quotes. The moderator should keep the notetaker in mind and ask participants to speak more clearly or slowly if the pace becomes too fast.

Another way to facilitate notetaking is to prepare a notetaking template in advance of the research activity. If you have specific ideas about what you are looking for, you can include placeholders in the template that serve both to remind you to note comments and/or behaviors relevant to a particular topic and to organize your notes so it is

FIELD STUDY NOTES

PARTICIPANT:

DATE:

LOCATION:

LOCATIONS VISITED

- ☐ Check-in counter
- ☐ Check-in kiosk
- ☐ Baggage drop-off
- ☐ Security line
- ☐ Bathroom
- ☐ Restaurant
- ☐ Baggage claim
- ☐ ______
- ☐ ______
- ☐ ______
- ☐ ______
- ☐ ______
- ☐ ______
- ☐ ______

FRUSTRATIONS ENCOUNTERED

Frustration	Time to resolve
______	______
______	______
______	______
______	______
______	______
______	

OTHER NOTES

Figure 7.4: Sample notetaking form.

easier to find this information for analysis. For example, Figure 7.4 shows a template for notes for a field study of mobile app users at an airport. If you do not know in advance what you are looking for (i.e., in more exploratory work), then you can use a template that is more generic (see Figure 7.5).

Finally, it is also helpful when you can get any of the stakeholders viewing the activity to take notes. This can add further richness to the data you collect and helps more people feel like they are actively contributing and therefore invested in the results.

TIP

Like the activity moderator, the notetaker needs to have domain knowledge, particularly if a complex topic is being discussed. If the notetaker understands what he or she is writing, it is much easier to condense what is said. Also, an awareness of the domain means that the notetaker will have an understanding of what is important to capture versus things that are known or unrelated.

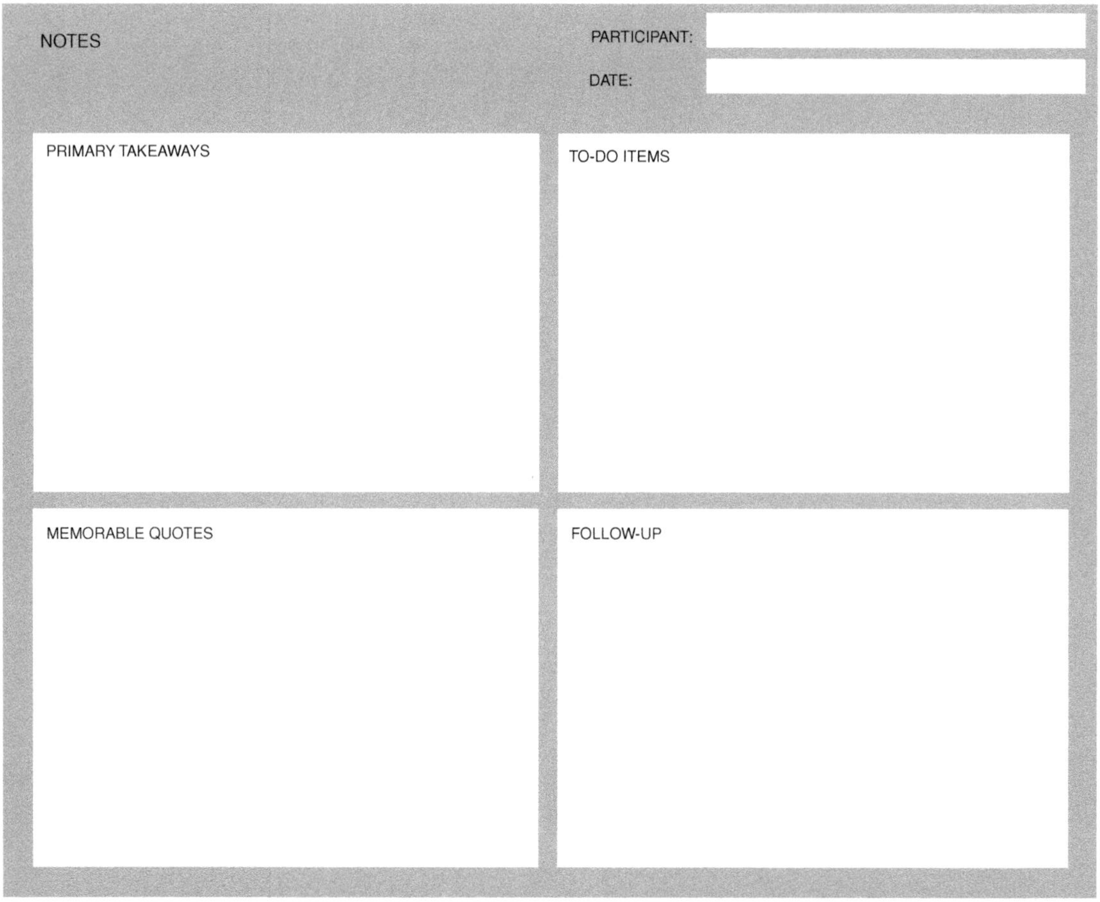

NOTES

PARTICIPANT:

DATE:

PRIMARY TAKEAWAYS

TO-DO ITEMS

MEMORABLE QUOTES

FOLLOW-UP

Figure 7.5: Sample generic notetaking template.

Use Video or Audio Recording

The benefits of recording are numerous. First, if you are moderating solo and do not have a notetaker, you can focus solely on following up on what the participants say and use your energy to motivate them and understand what they are telling you instead of taking notes. The recordings also capture nuances in speech and context that you may not capture when taking notes (e.g., the participant's instant message window kept popping up causing the participant to pause his or her speech). Video recording also has the benefit of showing you the participant's (as well as your own) body language. You can also refer back to the recordings as often as needed and, in some cases, analyze these data directly.

If you choose to rely solely on video or audio recording and not to take notes during the session, you must either listen to the recording and make notes or send the recording out for transcription. Transcription can be very expensive and can take a long time to complete. Depending on the complexity of the material, the number of speakers, and the quality of the recording, it can take four to six times the duration of the recording to transcribe (e.g., a one-hour interview can take four to six hours to transcribe). There are many online services that offer transcription services. In 2014, we found prices ranging from $1 to $3 per minute of audio, meaning that the cost to transcribe a single two-hour interview can run between $120 and $360.

We recommend getting transcripts of the session *only* when you need a record of who said what (e.g., for exact quotes or documentation purposes) or for scientific research where this level of detail is required (e.g., for a content analysis, you need verbatim participant quotes). Regulated industries (e.g., Food and Drug Administration) may also require such documentation.

Finally, you should be aware that recording the session can make some participants uncomfortable, so they may be less forthcoming. Let the participants know *when you recruit* them that you plan to record. If a person feels uncomfortable, stress his or her rights, including the right to confidentiality. If the person still does not feel comfortable, then you should consider recruiting someone else or just relying on taking notes. In our experience, this outcome is the exception rather than the rule.

Finally, it is a good idea to have a policy about how long you plan to keep video files. Will you keep them only until you have presented recommendations to stakeholders and then delete them? Will you keep them for a one-year period no matter the status of the study at that point? If you work in academia, if your study receives funding from some agencies (e.g., National Science Foundation), or is approved by an IRB, you may be required to keep the recordings for a specified period. Refer to Chapter 3, "Data Retention, Documentation, and Security" section on page 75 for more information.

VIDEO TIPS

- If you choose to video record, there are several things to keep in mind. If you are in the lab, you may be able to record from a separate room (i.e., behind a one-way mirror). If you are not in the lab or if this is not possible, have someone who already has a role in the activity also take on the responsibility for the video to avoid introducing additional people into the room.
- It is not necessary to have someone behind the camera the entire time—that will only serve to distract. Simply set up the video camera to get a shot that includes what is important (e.g., in a card sort, the cards; in an interview, the participant's face), and leave it until you are required to do something with it (e.g., stop the recording).
- If you are conducting a group activity, the cameraperson should focus on the group as a whole rather than zooming in on each individual. Attempting to focus in on each speaker is difficult with large groups, and anyone watching the video afterward will get motion sickness.

Use Screen-Recording Software

When your activity involves having users interact with an artifact such as a website or mobile app, it is often desirable—some would say essential—to record not only what the participant is doing but also what is happening on screen. There are many screen-recording tools (both commercial and open-source) available for use during in-person and remote sessions, such as the following:

- Adobe ConnectNow (www.adobe.com)
- CamStudio (camstudio.org)
- GoToMeeting (www.gotomeeting.com)
- Morae (www.techsmith.com/morae.html)
- Skype (www.skype.com)

Be sure to try out your screen-recording software in advance of your study. Sometimes, this software will interfere with the performance of the interface you are testing, especially when the software is in a prototype state.

Combine Video/Audio/Screen Recording and Notetaking

As with most things, a combination is usually the best solution. Having a colleague take notes for you during the session while it is being recorded is the optimal solution. That way, you will have the bulk of the findings in notes, but if you need clarification on any of the notes or user quotes, you can refer back to the recording. This is often necessary for group activities because so many people are speaking and because conversations can move quickly. An audio or video recording of the session will allow you to go back and get clarification in areas where the notes may not be clear or where the notetaker may have fallen behind. In addition, although it is rare, recordings do fail, and your notes are an essential backup.

Dealing with Late and Absent Participants

You are sure to encounter participants who are late or those who simply do not show up. In this section, we discuss how to prevent or deal with these situations.

At a Glance

> The late participant

> You cannot wait any longer

> Including a late participant

> The no-show

The Late Participant

You are certain to encounter late participants in both group and individual activities. While many of these issues do not apply to remote activities, other issues, such as technical issues that delay the start of remote sessions, do arise. We do our best to emphasize to participants during the recruiting phase that being on time is critical—and if they are late, they may not be able to participate in the session. We emphasize this again when we send them e-mail confirmations of the activity and when we call to remind them about the session the night before. It is also a good idea to make them aware of any traffic, parking, or setup issues that may require extra time and provide them with parking passes via mail and instructions for setting up their computer to use remote software in advance, if needed. Or, if you are on-site, be sure they are clear about where you will be located if you are not going to them.

However, through unforeseen traffic problems, getting lost, and other priorities in peoples' lives, you will often have a participant who arrives late despite your best efforts. Thanks to cell phones, many late participants will call, text, or e-mail you to let you know they are on their way or are still getting their computer up and running. If it is a group activity and you have some extra time, you can try to stall while you wait for the person to show up. If it is an individual activity, your ability to involve a late participant may depend on the flexibility of your day's schedule. We typically schedule a one-hour cushion between participants, so a late participant presents less of a problem. For group sessions, we will typically build in a 15-minute cushion knowing that some people will arrive late. It is not fair to make everyone wait too long just because one or two people are late. If it is an evening session and we are providing food, we ask participants to arrive 30 minutes earlier than the intended session time to eat. This means that if people arrive late, it will not interfere with your activity. They will just have less time (or no time) to eat.

You Cannot Wait Any Longer

In the case of a group activity, at some point, you will need to begin your session whether or not all of your participants are present. The reality is that some participants never show, so you do not want to waste your time waiting for someone who is not going to appear.

After 15 minutes, if a participant does not appear, leave a "late letter" (see Figure 7.6) in the lobby with the security guard or receptionist. For companies that do not have someone employed to monitor the lobby on a full-time basis, you may wish to arrange ahead of time to have a colleague volunteer to wait in the lobby for 30 minutes or so for any late participants. Alternatively, you can leave a sign (like the "Welcome" sign) that says something like, "Participants for the TravelMyWay App Focus Group: the session began at 5 pm and we are sorry that you were unable to arrive in time. Because this is a group activity, we had to begin the session. We appreciate your time and regret your absence."

You should provide an incentive in accordance with the policy you stated during recruitment. If you do not plan to pay participants if they are more than 15 minutes late, you should inform them of this during recruitment. However, you may wish to offer a nominal incentive or the full incentive to participants who are late as a result of bad weather, bad traffic, or other unforeseeable circumstances. Just decide prior to the activity, inform participants during recruiting, and remain consistent in the application of that policy. Make sure you tell whomever is waiting to greet the late participants to ask for identification before providing the incentive (refer to Chapter 6, "The Professional Participant" section, page 151) and have the participant sign a receipt (see Figure 7.1).

As an added courtesy, you may wish to leave the late participant a voice mail on their cell phone and home or work phone. State the current time and politely indicate that because the person is late, he or she cannot be admitted to the session. Leave your contact information and state that the person can receive an incentive (if appropriate) by coming back to your facility at his or her convenience and showing a driver's license (if ID is one of your requirements) and/or reschedule for another time.

Dear Participant:

Thank you for signing up for tonight's group activity. Unfortunately, you have arrived too late to participate in this evening's session. The session was scheduled for <*insert start time*>, and we delayed the start time until <*insert last check time*> hoping to include as many people as possible. However, at <*insert last check time*> we had to begin the session. We have a lot of material to cover in a short time, and it would be disruptive to stop and repeat the instructions for late arrivals once we have started. Doing so would slow down the entire group, pushing the end of the session beyond <*insert end time*>. We hope you understand that it would be unfair to those who arrived on time if we asked them to stay beyond their committed time.

We understand that many circumstances such as traffic, work, and home life can cause a delay in arrival. We regret that we have to turn away those who struggled to get here this evening, but it is the only fair thing we can do for the entire group. To thank you for taking the time to try and make it to the session we would like to compensate you with <*insert incentive*>.

We are sorry that you were unable to join us this evening, but we hope that you will consider participating in a user activity in the future. We really do value your input.

Sincerely,
<*Your name, job title, phone, e-mail*>

Figure 7.6: Example of a letter for latecomers.

Including a Late Participant

There are some situations where you are unable to turn away a late participant. These situations may include a very important customer who you do not want to upset or a user profile that is very difficult to recruit and you need every participant you can get.

Again, for individual sessions (e.g., interviews), we typically have about an hour cushion between participants so a latecomer is not that big a deal. For group sessions, it is a little more difficult to include latecomers. If they arrive just after the instructions have been given, you (or a colleague) can pull them aside and get them up to speed quickly. This is by no means ideal, but it can usually be done fairly easily and quickly.

If the participant arrives, the instructions have been given, and the activity itself is well under way, you can include him or her, but you may have to discard his or her data. Obviously, if you know you are going to throw away the person's data, you would only want to do this in cases where it is politically necessary to include the participant, not for cases where the participant is hard to get. In cases where participants are hard to come by, make sure you reschedule the participant(s). Keep in mind that if you reschedule them, the participants who are late once are more likely to be late again or be no-shows.

The No-Show

Despite all of your efforts, you will encounter no-shows. These are the people who simply do not show up for your activity without any warning. We have found that for every 10 participants, one or two will not show up. This may be because something important came up and you are the lowest priority or the person may have just completely forgotten. Chapter 6 discusses a number of measures that you can take to deal with this problem, for example, calling participants the night before the study (refer to Chapter 6, "Preventing No-Shows" section, page 146).

Dealing with Awkward Situations

Just when you think you have seen it all, a participant behaves in a way you could never have expected! The best way to handle an awkward situation is by preventing it all together. However, even the best-laid plans can fail. What do you do when a user throws you a curve ball? If you are standing in front of a group of 12 users and there is a room of eight stakeholders watching you intently, you may not make the most rational decision. You must decide before the situation ever takes place how you should behave to protect the user, your company, and your data. Refer to Chapter 3, Legal and Ethical Considerations on page 66 to gain an understanding of these issues.

In this section, we look at a series of several uncomfortable situations and suggest how to respond in a way that is ethical and legal and that preserves the integrity of your data. Unfortunately, over the last several years, we have encountered every single one of these awkward situations. They have been divided by the source of the issue (i.e., participant or product team/observer). We invite you to learn from our painful experiences.

TIP

If you find yourself in an awkward situation and you cannot decide whether a participant should be paid, err on the side of caution, and pay up. In most cases, a disruption in your study is not the fault of the participant, so they should not be penalized. Even if the person *is* the cause of the awkward situation, saving $100 is not worth the potential for confrontation. In an academic setting, your IRB may require you to remunerate participants regardless of the situation.

Extra Caution Required with Customers

If you are working with paying customers and an awkward situation arises, you need to treat the situation with utmost care. For example, if you discover during a session that a participant is not the correct user type and that person is *not* a customer, you can typically explain the situation, tell the participant that, due to the error, his or her involvement will not be required, and pay him or her. However, if the person is a customer, it is not always that easy. Typically, you will need to involve the person in the session somehow. Turning away or dismissing a customer who is excited about being involved in your activity could potentially damage your relationship with that customer. You may not be able to use the data you collect, but it is more important to include the customer than risk harming your relationship.

When working with customers, we typically try to have extra product team members available and a backup plan in place so that if something goes wrong (e.g., recruitment of a customer who is the wrong user type, a customer with an agenda that differs from your planned activity), we ask product team members to attend to the customers. For example, in a group session, if a customer is disruptive or the wrong user type, we have a colleague or product team member conduct a separate session with the user while the main session continues.

In most cases, participants are not sure exactly what they are going to be doing as a part of your activity, so they happily go along with whatever you propose. So just remember that keeping your customer happy will have to take precedence. If you have thought through the potential problems in advance, you should be able to have a happy customer and good data.

At a Glance

> Participant issues
- The participant brings company
- The participant's cell phone rings continuously
- The wrong participant is recruited
- The participant gets extremely frustrated
- The participant notices technical issues
- The participant has a conflict of interest
- The participant thinks he is on a job interview
- The participant gets lost trying to find the study location
- The participant refuses to be video recorded
- The participant wants to take photos and video to share his or her experience online
- The participant is confrontational with other participants
- The participant is not truthful about her identity
- The participant refuses to sign NDA and consent forms
- The participant is under the influence

> Product team/observer issues
- The team changes the product midstudy
- Observers make themselves known

Participant Issues

The Participant Brings Company

Situation: A participant shows up in the lobby escorted by friends or family (e.g., an elderly woman shows up with her son, who wanted to make sure she was not being scammed, a child is driven to the location by his or her parent). When you greet the participant, she says, "This is my son. He drove me here. Can he join us?"

Response: If the participant is an adult, politely say, "We prefer for guests to wait in the lobby." If this distresses the participant, then you may want to allow it. If you do, make sure the guest signs an NDA and ask the guest to sit quietly in the back of the room so as not to influence the participant or interrupt the session. In the case of a child who has her parent with her, common sense and law require that the parent be allowed to be in the same room as his or her children, if he or she requests it. Just as for other guests, make sure the parent signs an NDA and knows to sit quietly so as not to influence the child's performance.

The Participant's Cell Phone Rings Continuously

Situation: The participant is a very busy person (e.g., doctor, database administrator). She is on call today and cannot turn off her cell phone for fear of losing her job. Throughout the session, her phone vibrates, interrupting the activity. Each call lasts only a couple of minutes, but it is clear that the participant is distracted. This user type is really hard to come by so you hate to lose her data. Should you allow the activity to continue, or ask her to leave?

Response: It is obvious that the user is distracted, and it will not get better as the session continues. If this is an individual activity, you may choose to be patient and continue. However, if this is a group session where the user is clearly disturbing others, have a collaborator follow the participant out during the next call. When she finishes her call, ask her to turn the phone off because it is causing too much distraction. If this is not possible, offer to allow her to leave now and be paid.

You should inform potential participants during the screening process that they will have to turn their cell phones off for the duration of the activity (refer to Chapter 6, "Developing a Recruiting Screener" section, page 129). If the potential participant will be on duty the day of the session and cannot comply with the request, do not recruit him or her. When the participants arrive for the activity, ask everyone to turn their cell phones off. They agreed to give you one or two hours of their time and you are compensating them for it. It is not unreasonable to insist they give you their full attention, especially if you made this request clear during the screening process.

TIP

A humorous way to get users to comply is to ask everyone who has a cell phone to get it out and show it to the person on their right. After you have seen everyone who has a phone, ask them—on the count of three—to turn them off! Users sometimes groan at the trick but find it amusing. Too many participants, when asked to turn off a phone if they have one, will either ignore the request by saying it is already off or will genuinely think it is off when it is not.

The Wrong Participant Is Recruited

Situation: During an activity, it becomes painfully obvious that he does not match the user profile. The participant has significantly less experience than he originally indicated or does not match the domain of interest (e.g., has the wrong job to know about anything being discussed). It is not clear whether he was intentionally deceitful about his qualifications or misunderstood the research in the initial phone screener. Should you continue with the activity?

Response: Is the participant different on a key characteristic? If you and the team agree that the participant is close enough to the user profile to keep, continue with the activity and note the difference in the report.

If the participant is too different, your response depends on the activity. If it is a group activity where the participants do not interact with one another (e.g., a group card sort), note the participant and be sure to throw his data out. If it is a group activity that involves interaction among the participants, you will have to remove the participant from the session because the different user type could derail your session entirely. Take the participant aside (you do not want to embarrass him in front of the group) and explain that there has been a mistake and apologize for any inconvenience you may have caused. Be sure to pay the participant in full for his effort.

If it is an individual activity, you may wish to allow the participant to continue with the activity to save face and then terminate the session early. It may be necessary to stop the activity on the spot if it is clear that the participant simply does not have the knowledge to participate and to continue the activity would only embarrass the participant further. Again, pay the participant in full; he or she should not be penalized for a recruiting error.

The Participant Gets Extremely Frustrated

Situation: During the study, the participant becomes extremely frustrated because he or she cannot answer your questions or cannot complete a task you have asked him or her to do. He or she begins verbally beating him or herself up about his or her inability to "do anything right." Should you stop the session immediately and dismiss him or her?

Response: First, do not blame yourself. Participants bring their own frustrations to the session and these are not your fault. If the participant's frustration is clearly something that does not have to do with the session, you may want to end the session early. If the participant's qualifications are the issue, see above. Either way, you may want to offer the participant a different set of questions or tasks—that is, he or she will be easily able to answer or complete—before you wrap up the session so that he or she leaves feeling good, rather than helpless.

The Participant Notices Technical Issues

Situation: You introduce a prototype during the study that is supposed to be working well enough to be evaluated. However, the prototype crashes in the middle of the session and you cannot get it restarted. The participant obviously notices the technical issues and does not know how to react.

Response: Remember that you, as the moderator, should set expectations. Immediately reassure the participant that he or she did not do anything wrong and tell him or her what will happen next. If you feel certain that you or a colleague will be unable to get the prototype working again within the time for the session, you have a couple options. If you have a lower-fidelity prototype, such as a paper prototype, you may revert to that. Alternatively, you may want to turn the session into an impromptu interview if you think the participant could provide useful input. Finally, you may simply end the session early. Pay the participant the full amount; it is not his or her fault the technology failed.

The Participant Has a Conflict of Interest

Situation: When you greet a participant at her home for a field study, you see her name badge hanging on the key holder by the front door. You recognize the name of the company as a competitor. Should you conduct the session anyway?

Response: If the participant turns out to work for a competitor, is a consultant who has worked for a competitor and is likely to return to that competitor, or is a member of the press, you need to terminate the session immediately. Remind the person of the binding confidentiality agreement and pay her. Put her on the watch list immediately (refer to Chapter 6, "Create a Watch List" section, page 151).

Follow up with the recruiter to find out why this participant was recruited (refer to Chapter 6, "Recruitment Methods" section, page 139). Review the remaining participant profiles with the team/recruiting agency to make sure that no more surprises slip in. If the project is particularly sensitive, you may need to review and approve each user with the team as he or she is recruited.

The Participant Thinks He Is on a Job Interview

Situation: The participant arrives in a suit and brings his résumé, thinking he is being interviewed for employment at your company. He is very nervous and asks about available jobs. He says that he would like to come back on a regular basis to help your company evaluate its products. He even makes reference to the fact that he needs the money and is grateful for this opportunity to show his skills.

Response: This situation can be avoided by clarifying up front when the participant is recruited that this is *not* a job interview opportunity and in no way constitutes an offer of employment (refer to Chapter 6, "Developing a Recruiting Screener" section, page 129). If the participant attempts to provide a résumé at any point in the conversation, stop the activity and make it clear that you cannot and will not accept it. If you do accept it, you may further the participant's confusion about the session and receive follow-up phone calls or e-mails from the participant "to touch base about any job opportunities."

If you have already started the activity when you discover that the participant believes he is on a job interview, you need to be careful not to take advantage of a person who is obviously highly motivated but for the wrong reasons. In this case, the activity should be paused and you should apologize for any misunderstanding and make it clear that this is not a job interview. Reiterate the purpose of the activity and clarify that there is no follow-up opportunity for getting a job at your company that can be derived from his participation. The participant should be asked whether he would like to continue now that the situation has been clarified. If not, the participant should be paid and leave with no further data collection.

The Participant Gets Lost Trying to Find the Study Location

Situation: You have reserved a study location that has special features that you need to provide context to the issue you are studying. You only have this space for a limited time, so you are sure to provide excellent directions and a map to your study location. A participant is very late to his individual interview session at the location. You call the participant's cell phone but do not get an answer. Just then, you hear a knock on the door. Instead of just your participant, you see two security guards with your participant. One security guard says, "We found this guy wandering around. He says he's here to see a 'magic' house. Is he yours?" How do you respond to the security guards? Should you cancel the session with the participant? Should you use his data?

Response: Thank the security guards for escorting the participant to your location. Briefly explain to them that you expect more participants to be coming and you sincerely appreciate their help pointing any other lost participants to the location because you know it is very difficult to find. Let the participant hear you so he knows you understand how difficult it is to find the location and, by inference, that you understand that he did nothing wrong. Once the guards have gone, have the participant sit down and talk with him. How is he feeling? Is he stressed out because of the interaction with the guards? If so, offer to reschedule the session. If the participant refuses, offer the incentive right away and remind him that he does not need to continue with the session. If he still wants to participate in the study because he feels his ordeal would be wasted otherwise, do not refuse him this comfort. Go on with either the study as planned or a less stressful, shortened version. At the conclusion of the session, thank the participant for coming and participating, despite the difficulty finding the location. If the participant was obviously affected by the experience, you may need to discard the data. However, if the participant easily calmed down and you conducted the study as planned, you may be able to include it, as long as you check it against your other data and it seems to fit. To prevent this in the future, speak with participants on the phone and stress that the building is difficult to find (e.g., not on GPS) and that it is very important that they follow the directions you provide or they *will* get lost.

The Participant Refuses to Be Video Recorded

Situation: During recruiting and the pretest instructions, you inform the participant that the session will be video recorded. The participant is not happy with this. She insists that she does not want to be video recorded. You assure her that her information will be kept strictly confidential, but she is not satisfied. Offering to turn the video recording off is also not sufficient for the participant. She states that she cannot be sure that you are not still taping her and asks to leave. Should you continue to persuade her? Since she has not answered any of your questions, should you still pay her?

Response: Although this rarely occurs, you should not be surprised by it. It is unethical to coerce the participant to stay and be recorded in a way that makes her uncomfortable. However, you may want to ask if she would be willing to be audio recorded instead. This is not ideal but at least you can still capture her comments. Alternatively, if the user type is difficult to find and/or if you are dealing with a customer, you may wish to rely on notes and assure her you are not video or audio recording. If she still balks, tell her that you are sorry she does not wish to continue but that you understand her discomfort. You should still pay the participant. If you have a list of participants to avoid, add her name to this list (refer to Chapter 6, "Create a Watch List" section, page 151).

To avoid such a situation in the future, inform all participants during the phone screening that they will be audio- and/or videotaped and must sign a confidentiality agreement (refer to Chapter 6, "Developing a Recruiting Screener" section, page 129). Will this be a problem? If they say that it is, they should not be brought in for any activity.

The Participant Wants to Take Photos and Videos to Share His or Her Experience Online

Situation: You greet a participant in the lobby. Upon seeing you, she immediately pulls out her cell phone, snaps your photo, and says how excited she is about visiting your workplace and giving feedback about your products. Before you can get in a word, she says, "I love your products and can't wait to share what I learn today with my followers!" You realize what she means is that she plans to post the photo she has just taken of you on social media. How should you react?

Response: Tell the participant politely to please stop taking photos, recording, and/or broadcasting. Once she has done this, explain to her that she will have to read and sign an NDA if she has not already and that this requires that she cannot share anything confidential that you show her or discuss with her. You should explain to her that she should not even share the questions or topic of the study because those can reveal unexpected insights. If your company has a designated place where photos are permitted (e.g., company sign, lobby), take the participant there at the conclusion of the study and offer to take her photo. Remind her that she may share this photo, but no other details about the study. It is up to you if you want to request that she delete the photo she snapped of you when you greeted her. Keep in mind that if you do not ask her to delete it, you will have no control over what the participant writes about it or who she shares it with.

The Participant Is Confrontational with Other Participants

Situation: While conducting a group session, one of the participants becomes more aggressive as time goes by. He moves from disagreeing with other participants to telling them their ideas are "ridiculous." Your repeated references to the rule "Everyone is right—do not criticize yourself or others" is not helping. Unfortunately, the participant's attitude is rubbing off on other group members, and they are now criticizing each other. Should you continue the session? How do you bring the session back on track? Should you remove the aggressive participant?

Response: Take a break at the earliest opportunity to give everyone a chance to cool off. Since you are the focus of most participants at this moment, you will need a colleague to assist you. Have the colleague quietly take the participant outside of the room and away from others to dismiss him. The colleague should tell the participant that he has provided a lot of valuable feedback, thank him for his time, and pay him. When you restart the session, if anyone notices the absence of the participant, simply tell the group that he had to leave early. It is never easy to ask a participant to leave, but it is important not only to salvage the rest of your data but also to protect the remaining participants in your session.

The Participant Is Not Truthful About Her Identity

Situation: You recognize a participant from another activity you conducted but the name does not sound familiar. You mention to her that she looks familiar and ask whether she has participated in another study at your company. She denies that she has ever been there before, but you are convinced she has. Should you proceed with the test or pursue it further?

Response: Unless you are conducting an anonymous study, ask every participant for an ID when you greet him or her. If a participant arrives without some form of ID, apologize for the inconvenience and state that you cannot release the incentives without identification. If it is possible, reschedule the activity and ask the participant to bring an ID next time.

When recruiting, you should inform participants that you will need to see an ID for tax purposes, as well as for security purposes (refer to Chapter 6, "Developing a Recruiting Screener" section, page 129). In the United States, the Internal Revenue Service requires that companies complete a 1099 form for any individual who receives more than $600 from you in a year. For this reason, you need to closely track whom you compensate throughout the year. During recruitment, you may say to participants:

> **In appreciation for your time and assistance, we are offering a $100 gift card. For tax purposes, we track the amount paid to participants, so we will be asking for an ID. We also require an ID when issuing a visitor's badge. If you can simply bring your driver's license with you, we will ask you to present it upon arrival.**

Repeat this in the phone or e-mail confirmation you provide to participants. For participants being dishonest about their identity (in order to participate in multiple studies and make additional money), this will dissuade them from following through. For honest participants, it reminds them to bring their ID with them, as opposed to leaving it in the car or at home.

If the information provided does not match the information on the driver's license, you will have to turn the participant away. Then, copy the information from the ID next to the "alternative" information provided by the participant. Place both identities on your watch list (refer to Chapter 6, "Create a Watch List" section, page 151).

The Participant Refuses to Sign NDA and Consent Form

Situation: You present the usual NDA and consent form to the user and explain what each form means. You also offer to provide copies of the forms for the participant's records. The participant glances over the forms but does not feel comfortable with them, particularly the NDA. Without a lawyer, the participant refuses to sign these documents. You explain that the consent form is simply a letter stating the participant's rights. The NDA, you state, is to protect the company since the information that may be revealed during the session has not yet been released to the public. Despite your explanations, the participant will not sign the NDA. Should you continue with the activity?

Response: Absolutely not. To protect yourself and your company, explain to the participant that without her signature, you cannot conduct the activity. Since the participant is free to withdraw at any point in time without penalty, you should still provide the incentive. Apologize for the inconvenience and escort her out. Be sure to place her on your watch list (refer to Chapter 6, "Create a Watch List" section, page 151).

Prevent this situation by informing participants during recruitment that they will be expected to sign a confidentiality agreement and consent form (refer to Chapter 6, "Developing a Recruiting Screener" section, page 129). Always e-mail participants a copy of the forms for them to review in advance. Some participants (particularly VPs and above) cannot sign NDAs. Their company may have a standard NDA that they are allowed to sign and bring with them. In that case, ask the participant to e-mail you a copy of his or her NDA and then forward it to your legal department for approval in advance.

If the legal department approves of his or her NDA, you may proceed. However, if a participant states during the phone interview that he or she cannot sign any NDA, thank the person for his or her time but state that the person is not eligible for participation.

The Participant Is Under the Influence

Situation: You greet a participant in the lobby. He seems very happy to be at the session, smiling continuously as you walk to the testing room and prepare for the activity. As you begin a task that requires the participant to interact with a laptop computer and think aloud, you notice that he is staring at the screen in an unusual way and seems transfixed. When you prompt him to say out loud what he is thinking, he responds, "The mouse trails you've added here are really cool!" However, there are no mouse trails in the user interface. You realize that the participant may be under the influence of alcohol or drugs. Should you confront the person about whether he is under the influence? Do you continue the session? If so, should you use the data?

Response: Unless you are specifically studying altered performance (e.g., a driving simulator where you want to understand the affects of drunk driving), you should end the session as soon as you recognize that a participant may be under the influence. Whatever you do, do not confront the participant about being under the influence. You may be incorrect, but more importantly, you do not want a confrontation. Be discreet and polite ("Wow, you finished that task very quickly. That took less time than we expected. Thank you for all of your feedback!") and provide the incentive, if you have not already. Escort the participant back to the lobby, provide him with water, coffee, and/or snacks if possible, and encourage him to wait in the lobby if he is feeling "tired." If you are concerned about his ability to get home safely, offer to call a cab. Discretely inform both the receptionist and security of the situation and ask them to keep an eye on the participant. Discard any data you have collected, as it is not representative of users who are not under the influence.

Product Team/Observer Issues

The Team Changes the Product Midstudy

Situation: You are conducting a focus group for a product that is in the initial prototype stage. The team is updating the code while the focus groups are being conducted. In the middle of the second focus group, you discover the team has incorporated some changes to the product based on comments from the previous focus group. Should you continue the focus groups with the updated product or cancel the current focus group and bring in replacements so that all users see the same product? How do you approach the team with the problem?

Response: Ask the participants to take a break at the least disruptive opportunity and go to speak with the developers in attendance while your co-moderator attends to the group. This will give you time to determine whether the previous version is still accessible. If it is, use it. If the previous version is not available, it is up to you whether you would like to get some feedback on the new version of the prototype or you might attempt to continue the focus group with activities that do not rely on the prototype. Be sure to document the change in the final report. Meet with the team as soon as possible to discuss the change in the prototype. Make sure the team understands that this may compromise the results of the activity. If they would like to do an iterative design approach, they should discuss this with you in advance so that you may design the activity appropriately.

Make sure that you inform product teams of "the rules" before any activity. In this case, before the activity, you would inform them that the prototype must stay the same for all focus group sessions. Be sure to inform them why, so that they will understand the importance of your request. Let them know that you want to make design changes based on what all groups have to say, not just one. Remember that this is the product team's session, too. You can advise them and tell them the consequences, but be aware that they may want to change it anyway and it is your job to analyze and present the results appropriately (even if this means telling stakeholders that the data are limited because of a decision the team made).

In some cases, the team finds something that is obviously wrong in the prototype and changes it after the first session. Often this is OK, but they should discuss it with you prior to the session. If they do not discuss it with you and you find out during the session, it does not always invalidate the data if it is something that should be changed in any case. When working with a team, you must strike a balance between being firm but flexible.

Observers Make Themselves Known

Situation: You are interviewing a participant in the user room while the team is watching in the observation room. As time goes by, observers in the observation room begin talking louder and the team begins laughing. The participant appears to be ignoring it, but the noise is easily audible to you, so the participant must be able to hear it, too. All of a sudden, one of the team members decides to turn on a light because he is having trouble seeing. The observation room is now fully illuminated and the participant can see there are five people in the other room watching intently. Should you try to ignore it and hope it does not draw more attention or should you stop the interview and turn off the light?

Response: The participant should never be surprised to learn that people are in the observation room observing the activity. At the beginning of every activity, participants must be made aware that "members of our staff sometimes observe in the other room." It is not necessary to state the specific number of people in the other room or their affiliation (e.g., research group, development team). Participants should also be warned that they may hear a few noises in the other room, such as coughing or a door closing but they should just ignore it. Their attention should be focused on the activity at hand. Some people like to show the participants the observation room and the observers prior to the session. We typically do not adopt this approach because participants can become intimidated if they *know* that a large group of people are observing.

In the situation above, if the participant is not facing the other room and has not noticed the observers, do not call attention to it (someone may turn the light off quickly). However, if the participant has seen the observers, simply ask the observers to turn off the light and apologize to the participant for the disruption. After the participant has left, remind the team how one-way mirrors work and explain that it may affect the results if the participants see a room full of people watching them. Participants may be more self-conscious about what they say and may not be honest in their responses. If you notice that the participant's responses and behavior change dramatically after seeing the observers, you may have to consider throwing away the data.

To avoid this situation in the future, ask the observers to be quiet before you leave the observation room to conduct the interview and remind them how a one-way mirror works. It is also helpful to have another member of your team in the observation room (usually a notetaker) because that individual can prevent the situation from getting out of hand. If there are multiple sessions, observers may think that they have heard it all after the first participant. As a result, they start talking and ignoring the session. Explain to observers that *every* participant's feedback is important and that they should be taking note of where things are consistent and where they differ. Be nice but firm. You are in charge. Observers are rarely uncooperative.

We had the unfortunate situation once when a participant actually said, "I can hear you laughing at me." Despite assurances that this was not the case, the participant was devastated and barely spoke a word for the rest of the session. Amazingly, the observers in attendance were so caught up in their own conversation that they did not hear what the participant said!

Concluding Your Activity

At the conclusion of the study, you should thank participants for their time, give them a chance to ask any questions they may have, and remind them to keep the session confidential. If their participation was helpful and you think they might be qualified for future studies, ask them if they would be interested in participating in studies in the future. If so, add their name to your participant database (see Appendix A, Creating a Participant Recruitment Database). Escort participants out to the lobby or to the exit of the building and provide directions as needed or politely and quietly leave the field location.

Pulling It All Together

In this chapter, we have given you ingredients that will help you conduct any of your user research activities effectively. You should now be able to deal with participant arrivals, get your participants thinking creatively, moderate any individual or group activity, instruct your participants how to think aloud, and conclude a session successfully. In addition, we hope that you have learned from our experiences and that you are prepared to handle any awkward testing situation that may arise. In the following chapters, we delve into the methods of a variety of user research activities.

PART 3

THE METHODS

CHAPTER 8

Diary Studies

Introduction

Field studies (refer to Chapter 12) allow researchers to study users or customers in context and experience first-hand what the users experience; however, conducting field studies is expensive and time-consuming, and even the least privacy-sensitive individuals will rarely allow a researcher to observe them over many days or weeks. Even if you are lucky enough to conduct lengthy observations of participants, it is unlikely you can study a broad sample of your population, leaving one to wonder whether the observations are representative of the broader population.

Diary studies are one way to collect in situ, longitudinal data over a large sample. They "provide a record of an ever-changing present" (Allport, 1942) of the participant's internal and external experiences in his or her own words. This allows you to understand the user's experience as seen through his or her eyes, as described in his or her vernacular at the moment of occurrence. The diary can be **unstructured**, providing no specified format, allowing participants to describe their experience in the way they find best (or easiest). More often, though, diaries are **structured**, providing participants with a set of questions or probes to respond to. The beauty of diaries is that they can provide both rich qualitative and quantitative data without the need for a researcher to be present. They are ideal when you have a limited set of questions you want to ask participants, the questions are easy for participants to answer, and the experience you want to sample participants about is not so frequent that it will be disruptive for the participant to respond.

At a Glance

> Things to be aware of when conducting diary studies
> Diary study formats to choose from
> Sampling frequency
> Preparing for a diary study
> Conducting a diary study
> Data analysis and interpretation
> Communicating the findings

Things to Be Aware of When Conducting Diary Studies

Because participants self-report or provide the data without oversight of a researcher, you can never be sure if what you are receiving is complete, unbiased, or accurate. For example, participants are very likely to leave out embarrassing details that could be insightful for the researcher. Additionally, people are busy and will be going about their lives while participating in your diary study, so it should not be surprising that they will occasionally fail to enter useful information in their diaries. You risk disturbing the participant or altering his or her normal behavior if your diary study requires too much effort to participate. To help mitigate these effects, it is recommended that you keep your diary lightweight and instead follow up with other types of studies to probe deeper or

"You want to read my diary?"

Cartoon by Abi Jones

collect insights participants may have inadvertently or consciously left out. It may be impossible to know what a participant left out or what you may have missed in any study, regardless of the method; however, if you can collect data via multiple methods, you can obtain a more holistic view and fill in gaps any single method can miss. Follow-up interviews or field studies with a selection of participants can be especially insightful. You may want to follow up on areas that seem conspicuously absent like events during certain times of the day, specific locations, and activities you know are particularly difficult.

Diary Study Formats to Choose from

The original diary studies were done with pen and paper, but today, there are many additional options available, each with their own risks and benefits. Combining the methods ensures more variety in the data and flexibility for the participants; however, that means *you* must be flexible in your analysis to be able to handle multiple formats and monitor them all. Regardless of method, it is unlikely that participants will provide the level of detail in their entries that you would note if you were observing them. Making data entry as easy as possible for participants will increase the chances of good-quality data.

Paper

In paper-based diary studies, participants are provided instructions, a return-addressed, postage-paid envelope, and a packet of materials to complete during the study. Most often, the materials include a small booklet of forms to complete. In addition to completing the forms, participants may be asked to take photos throughout to visually record their experiences. With the ubiquity of digital photography, it is quite easy for participants to e-mail you their photos or upload them to your account in the cloud.

Benefits

- No hardware or software needed so anyone can participate
- Portable

- Low overhead to provide photos
- Cheap

Risks

- The overhead of mailing back the booklet is surprisingly high, even if a return-addressed, postage-paid envelope is provided. You may end up not collecting any data from a set of participants, even if they filled out some/most of the diary.
- Handwriting can be terribly difficult to read and interpret.
- For most analysis methods (see below), you will need to have the diaries transcribed. That takes time and money.
- Unless you ask participants to mail their entries back throughout the study, which requires more effort for the participants and more expense for you, you must wait for days or weeks until the study is over before you can begin any analysis. All other formats described below allow researchers to monitor data as they are entered and begin manipulating them (e.g., transcription, analysis) as soon as the study is over.

E-mail

Nearly everyone has access to an e-mail account (although this may not be the case in emerging market countries), so asking participants to periodically e-mail you their entries, include links to websites they visited, and attach digital photos, videos, etc., is doable by most potential participants. You can send a reminder e-mail with your questions/probes at set times (see "Sampling Frequency") for the participant to reply to.

Benefits

- Nearly everyone can participate
- No need to deal with paper and physical mail
- Everything is typed so no need to decipher someone's handwriting
- No need for transcription
- Instant submissions

Risks

- Not all user types access their e-mail throughout the day so they may wait to reply until the end of the day, or worse, the following morning, risking memory degradation.
- Depending on how participants take photos or videos, they may have to download them to a computer before they can attach them to e-mail, decreasing the likelihood of photos actually being included.
- You will miss out on participants who do not use e-mail. This could mean you undersample certain age groups (e.g., older adults who prefer paper mail or younger adults who prefer texting).

TIP

During recruitment, find out what tools your participant has access to. If you cannot support multiple formats of data collection, then you need to be sure that all of the participants have constant access to the tool you will use for your study (e.g., e-mail, social network, mobile app). Alternately, if you want to include a wide range of participants that do not have constant access to your study choice, you can ask them to take notes in a paper diary throughout the day and then type their entries into your tool at the end of the day. This adds overhead to the participant and introduces a sampling difference between your participants. You will want to compare your participants to see if there are qualitative or quantitative differences between those using your diary tool throughout the day and those entering only at the end of the day. For example, are there differences in the number of entries, word count, type of issues reported, etc.?

Voice

Allowing participants to leave voice messages of their entries can provide much richer descriptions along with indications of their emotional state at the time of the entry, although it can be difficult to interpret emotions (e.g., what sounds like excitement to you may actually be experienced as anxiety by the participant). Some voice mail services like Google Voice will provide transcripts, but these do not work well if the background is noisy or if the participant's dialect is difficult for the system to interpret. You can also just do voice recordings on a smartphone that can be e-mailed.

Benefits

- Low overhead for the participant to submit
- Richer data

Risks

- Participants may not be able to make phone calls when they wish to submit an entry (e.g., in a meeting), so they will have to make a note of it and call later. The emotion of the moment may have passed by that time.
- No voice mail system will be 100% accurate in its transcription. A human being will need to listen to every entry for accuracy and fill in what is missing or incorrect.

Video Diary Study

Video diaries are popular and can be an engaging method of data collection for both the participant and the researcher. A large percentage of the population can record video on their phones or tablets and many people in the US have desktops or laptops with a webcam. If you are interested in studying a segment of the population that does not have these tools available, you may choose to loan out webcams or cheap cell phones with video-recording capability.

Be aware that different user types prefer different video services (e.g., YouTube, Vimeo) so choose a service that you think your users are most likely to currently use.

Benefits

- Videos provide rich audio and visual data, making it excellent for getting stakeholders to empathize with the user.
- It is also easier to accurately detect emotion than from voice alone.

Risks

- Not all situations allow participants to record and submit videos at the moment (e.g., in a meeting, no Internet connection) so they may have to wait, risking memory degradation.
- Depending on bandwidth availability, some participants may have difficulty uploading their videos or may be charged a fee if attempting to do it via their mobile network rather than Wi-Fi. Speak with participants in advance to understand their situation and ways to work around them (e.g., download videos onto a portable drive and mail it to you, provide mobile data credits).
- Unless participants keep the instructions in front of them when creating the video entries, it is possible they may forget to answer all of the questions and include all of the information you are seeking. This format is also prone to digression so you may have additional content to sort through that is not helpful to your study.
- Transcription will be required for certain types of data analysis (see below), which requires time and money.

SMS (Text Message)

Like voice diaries, researchers can create a phone/message account to accept text messages (SMS messages). This option can be especially appealing to younger users that prefer texting over other forms of written communication.

Benefits

- Submissions are already transcribed.
- Easy for participants to quietly submit entries in nearly all situations.
- Photos can easily be sent via MMS if taken with one's phone.

Risks

- Depending on the participant's mobile plan, this can cost participants money to participate (and quite a lot, if the participant has overage fees). You will need to reimburse participants, on top of the incentive.
- Typing on a mobile phone may discourage lengthy explanations. Typos and bizarre autocorrections can make interpreting some entries difficult, although amusing!

TIP

We have found SMS diary studies to be particularly useful in quite a few instances. For example, in one case, we wanted to get input from participants who lived in rural West Africa. We were able to set up a local SMS number and collect data remotely. In another case, this time in the United States, we found that participants were willing to respond to text messages multiple times per day, perhaps because it fits into their daily routine where they already respond to text messages multiple times per day.

Social Media

Some user types spend a significant portion of their day on social networks so collecting diary study entries via Facebook, Google+, Tumblr, Twilio, or Twitter (just to name a few) can be ideal for real-time data collection.

Benefits

- You may be able to see their study entries alongside the rest of their content, providing additional context and insight to your participants.
- It is easy to include photos, videos, and links with their submissions.
- If participants are already on their social networks, it is less likely they will delay their diary submissions until later in the day.

Risks

- If participants are not sharing their entries privately (e.g., via Direct Messaging on Twitter), they may constrain what they tell you even more than via other formats because of what their followers may think, so it is important that you encourage private sharing.
- Some services limit the content that can be shared (e.g., tweets are limited to 140 characters), so you may miss out on important information.
- It is difficult to provide a specific format for participants to respond to.

Online Diary Study Services or Mobile Apps

Several online services and mobile apps have been developed to conduct diary studies. A web search for "online diary tool" and/or "diary app" will show you the most current tools available. Features vary between tools. Some integrate with Twitter, while others allow verbal or video entries to be submitted. Most tools have web UIs to monitor data collection.

Benefits

- Data are collected specifically for the purpose of analysis, so transcription is not needed.
- Notifications automatically remind participants when to submit their entries. All of the other methods listed require the researcher to manually (e.g., e-mail, SMS, phone call) remind participants to submit his or her entries.
- Participants who have smartphones can access these services or apps anytime, anyplace.
- You may be able to capture the participant's location at the time of his or her entry, but you need to be transparent about any data you are automatically collecting.

Risks

- Not all user types have smartphones, so you will need to offer additional data collection methods if you want to cover a representative sample of your population.
- Depending on your participant's data plan, submitting entries over his or her mobile network can be costly, so you will need to reimburse participants in addition to the incentives.

Sampling Frequency

Once you have decided the format for your study, you have to decide how often you want participants to enter data. Regardless of which format you choose, you should allow participants to submit additional entries whenever they feel appropriate. Perhaps they remembered something they forgot to mention in a previous entry or there was some follow-up consequence from a previous incident that they could not have known about at the time of their last entry. Allowing additional entries can provide immense benefit in understanding the participant's experience. If there are a minimum number of entries you are asking participants to submit per day, balance this with the length of the study.

End of Day

The quickest and lightest-weight method of data collection is to ask participants to provide feedback at the end of each day. Hopefully, they have taken notes throughout the day to refer to, but if they have not, it is likely participants will have forgotten much about what they experienced, the context, how they felt, etc. This is the least valid and reliable method.

Incident Diaries

Incident diaries are given to users to keep track of issues they encounter while using a product. Participants decide when it is appropriate to enter data (i.e., neither the researcher nor the tool to submit data notifies the participant when it is time to submit an entry). Worksheets may ask users to describe a problem or issue they encountered, how they solved it (if they did), and how troublesome it was (e.g., **Likert scale**). The purpose of incident diaries is to understand infrequent tasks that you might not be able to see even if you observed the user all day. In the example shown (see Figure 8.1), planning a vacation often happens over an extended period and

Planning Your Vacation Diary

ID: P1
Date: ______________

Describe what your goal was: ______________________________________

What website did you visit? Please provide the URL or address of the website.

____

Did you accomplish your goal? _____Yes_____No

Please explain: ______________________________________

Please describe any difficulties you encountered or anything you would have liked to do differently. ______________________________________

Other comments or thoughts: ______________________________________

Figure 8.1: Sample incident diary.

during unplanned times. You cannot possibly be there to observe on all of those occasions, and you do not want to interrupt their natural behavior:

- They are best used when problems or tasks are relatively infrequent. It is important to remember that frequency does *not* equate with importance. Some very important tasks happen rarely, but you need to capture and understand them. Frequent tasks can and should be observed directly, especially since participants are usually unwilling to complete diary entries every few minutes for frequent tasks.
- When you are not present, there is a chance that the participants will not remember (or want) to fill out the diary while they are in the middle of a problem. There is no way of knowing whether the number of entries matches the number of problems actually encountered.
- The participant may lack the technical knowledge to accurately describe the problem.
- User perception of the actual cause or root of the problem may not be correct.

Set Intervals

If you know the behavior you are interested in studying happens at regular intervals throughout the day, you may want to remind participants at set times of the day to enter information about that behavior. For example, if you are developing a website to help people lose weight, you will want to notify participants to submit entries about their food consumption during meal times. It is ideal if the participants can set the exact times themselves since it would be time-consuming for you to collect this information from each participant.

Random or Experiential Sampling

Experience sampling methodology (ESM) was pioneered by Reed Larson and Mihaly Csikszentmihalyi (Larson & Csikszentmihalyi, 1983). This method randomly samples participants about their experiences at *that moment* in time. You are not asking about what happened earlier in the day but rather what is happening right now and how the participant is experiencing it. Typically, the participant receives random notifications five to ten times per day. Because this is random, you may not "catch" the participant during an infrequent but critical moment. As a result, this sampling frequency may not be appropriate. However, if you want to learn about experiences that are more frequent or longer-lasting, this is ideal. For example, the case study in this chapter discusses Google's Daily Information Needs ESM study. People need information throughout their day, but these needs are often so fleeting that we are not even conscious of them. An ESM study is likely to catch participants during many of those information-need moments. By drawing the participants' attention to the need, they can describe their experiences (e.g., what triggered the need, where they are, where they are looking for the information).

Suggested Resources for Additional Reading

To learn more about ESM, check out

- Hektner, J. M., Schmidt, J. A., & Csikszentmihalyi, M. (2007). *Experience sampling method: Measuring the quality of everyday life*. Sage.

Preparing to Conduct a Diary Study

If a diary study will be part of a multiphase research plan including follow-up surveys or interviews, you will need to include enough time for a pilot study and analysis of the diary study data before proceeding to the next steps. No matter how large or small your study is, a pilot is *always* advised.

Identify the Type of Study to Conduct

The format of your diary study should be influenced by your user type, as well as the behavior you are studying. If your users do not have smartphones, loaning them a smartphone in order to ensure easy data collection via a diary study app may backfire when participants struggle with the technology rather than focus on the behavior you are trying to study. If you have a diverse population, you may need to collect data via multiple methods, so now is the time to figure out how you will combine the data from each method into one coherent data set for analysis.

Recruiting Participants

As with any research study, you need to be transparent with participants about what will be expected of them during the study. Communicate clearly the length of the study, how often they will need to submit information, how they need to submit it, and how much effort is expected of them. If you underestimate the time or effort required, participants may feel deceived and stop participating.

There is no guideline for the recommended number of participants in a diary study. Sample sizes in HCI studies are typically between 10 and 20 participants, but in the case study in this chapter, Google recruited 1200 participants. The sample size should be based on how variable your user population is and how diverse the behavior is that you want to study. The more diverse your population and behavior, the larger your sample size should be.

Diary Materials

List your research questions and then identify the ones that are *best* studied longitudinally and in the users' context. Are these questions that participants can actually answer (e.g., possess technical knowledge to describe what they experienced accurately)? Are they too personal or is there any reason a participant might not honestly or completely report? Is the phenomenon you wish to study too infrequent to capture over several days or weeks?

Identify the key questions you want to ask users in each report so you can study the same variables over time, for example (e.g., where they were at the time of the experience, how easy or difficult it was, who else was present at the time). To learn more about question design, refer to Chapter 9, Interviews and Chapter 10, Surveys. Remember that the more you ask, the less likely you will have a high compliance rate. Pilot testing is crucial to test your instructions, the tool you plan to use, the clarity of your questions, the quality of the data you are getting back, and the compliance rate of your participants.

Length and Frequency

As with field studies, you will want to know if the time you plan to study your users is indicative of their normal experience or out of the ordinary (e.g., holidays). You also need to determine how long it is likely to take for the participants in your study to experience the behavior you are interested in a few times. For example, if you are studying family vacation planning, you may need to collect diary entries over a period of weeks, rather than days. On the other hand, if you are studying a travel-related mobile app used at the airport, you may only need to collect diary entries for one day (the day of the flight). You will likely need to do some up front research to determine the right length of the study and how often to sample participants.

Fewer interruptions/notifications for entries will result in high compliance with the study because participants will not get burnt out. On the downside, because sampling is infrequent, you may miss out on good data. More interruptions may lead to a lot of data in the beginning of the study, but participants will burn out and may decrease the quality or quantity of data submitted over time. A pilot study should help you determine the right balance, but in general, five to eight notifications per day are ideal.

If you are able to collect data from a large sample of your population, you may wish to break up the data collection into waves. For example, instead of collecting data from 1000 participants during the same two-week period, you could conduct the study with 250 participants every two weeks, spread out over a two-month period. If you suspect that differences may arise during that two-month period, spreading out data collection can help you study that, assuming that participants are randomly distributed between waves and all other independent variables are constant.

Incentives

Determining the right level of incentives is tricky for longitudinal studies. Research ethics require that participants be allowed to withdraw *without penalty* from your study at any time. However, how do you encourage participants to keep submitting data for days or weeks? One option is to break the study into smaller pieces and provide a small incentive for every day that they submit an entry. You can provide a small bonus incentive to those that submit entries every day of the study. It should not be so large as to coerce participants into submitting incorrect entries just to earn the incentive. The actual incentive amounts can vary greatly depending on the amount of effort required and length of study (e.g., $25 to $200). If it is possible to go a whole day or several days without actually encountering the behavior you are studying (e.g., planning a vacation), then providing daily incentives is likely too frequent, so move to weekly incentives.

The amount of the incentive should be commensurate with the level of effort the study requires. Frequent, random notifications for information can be highly disruptive, so make sure the incentive is enough to be motivating. Periodic, personal e-mails thanking the participant for his or her effort can also go a long way!

Suggested Resources for Additional Reading

For more details on Diary Studies, check out

- Bolger, N., & Laurenceau, J. P. (2013). *Intensive longitudinal methods: An introduction to diary and experience sampling research.* Guilford Press.

Conducting a Diary Study

Train the Participants

When recruiting participants, you need to set expectations about the level of effort required for the study. You will also need to remind them in the instructions you send them when the study begins.

TIP

Some people learn best by reading, while others learn best by seeing or hearing instructions. Providing instructions in both a written document/e-mail *and* a video or phone call can increase your chances all the participants actually consume the instructions.

If you want participants to include photos in their diary entries, provide instructions about what the photos should be about. Give clear examples about what kind of photos are helpful and what kind are not. For example, "selfies" may be useful if you are studying user emotions or dieting but are unlikely to be helpful if you are studying information needs.

TIP

Have participants send a couple practice diary entries a day or two before the study begins to get in the habit, make sure the tool works, make sure the data participants are sending what you are expecting, and answer any questions they have before actual data are at risk.

Monitor Data Collection

If you are conducting the study electronically, do not wait until the study is over to look at the data. Check each day for abnormalities. If this is a study where you expect participants to submit entries multiple times every day, look for participants that are not submitting any data and check in with them. Is there a problem with the tool? Have they forgotten about the study or have they changed their mind about participating? Alternatively, does the data from some participants look … wrong? For example, the entries do not make sense or the fragments they are providing are simply not enough to be useful? Contact participants to give feedback about their participation (or lack thereof). If they are doing a great job, tell them to keep up the good work!

Data Analysis and Interpretation

Depending on the number of participants, number of daily notifications, and length of your study, you may have thousands of data points to analyze. There are a few options available depending on your data, time, and skill set.

Data Cleaning

As diligent as you may have been in preparing for data analysis, instructing participants, and testing your data collection materials, you will likely have some data that should be discarded prior to analysis. This might include participants that did not follow instructions and provided inappropriate responses, those that included personally identifying information (PII), such as phone numbers, or those that dropped out early in the study. Decide in advance what your rules are for excluding data and then write R, SPSS, SAS, etc. scripts or macros in Excel to clean your data.

Affinity Diagram

An affinity diagram is one of the most frequently used methods for analyzing qualitative data. Similar findings or concepts are grouped together to identify themes or trends in the data and let you see relationships. A full discussion of affinity diagrams is presented in Chapter 12, "Focus Groups" on page 363.

Qualitative Analysis Tools

Several tools are available for purchase to help you analyze qualitative data (e.g., diaries, interviews, focus groups, field study notes). These tools can help you look for patterns or trends in your data or quantify your data, if that is your goal. Some allow you to create categories and then search for data that match those categories, whereas others are more suited for recognizing emergent themes. A few can even search multimedia files (e.g., graphics, video, audio).

Because most of these programs require that the data be in transcribed rather than audio format, they are best used only when you have complex data (e.g., unstructured interviews) and lots of it. If you have a small number of data points and/or the results are from a very structured interview, these tools would be unnecessary and likely more time-consuming. A simple spreadsheet or affinity diagram would better serve your purposes.

Prior to purchasing any tool, you should investigate each one and be familiar with its limitations. For example, many of the products make statements like "no *practical* limit on the number of documents you can analyze" or "*virtually* unlimited number of documents." By "documents," they mean the number of transcripts or notes the tool is able to analyze. The limits may be well outside the range of your study, but investigate to be sure. The last thing you want is to enter in reams of data only to hit the limit and be prevented from doing a meaningful analysis. In addition, a program may analyze *text* but not *content*. This means that it may group identical words but is not intelligent enough to categorize similar or related concepts. That job will be up to you.

Below is a list of a few of the more popular tools on the market today:

- *ATLAS.ti®* supports qualitative analysis of large amounts of textual, graphical, audio, and video data.
- *Coding Analysis Toolkit (CAT)* is the only free, open-source analysis software in our list. It supports qualitative analysis of text data.
- *The Ethnograph* by Qualis Research Associates analyzes data from text-based documents.
- *HyperQualLite* is available as a rental tool for storing, managing, organizing, and analyzing qualitative text data.

- *NVivo10*™ by QSR is the latest incarnation of *NUD*IST*™ (Non-numerical Unstructured Data-Indexing, Searching, and Theorizing), a leading content analysis tool.
- *MAXQDA*™ supports qualitative and quantitative analysis of textual, graphical, audio, video, and bibliographic data.

Crowd Sourcing

You may have a taxonomy in mind that you want to use for data organization or analysis. For example, if you are collecting feedback from customers about their experience using your travel app, the categories might be the features of your app (e.g., flight search, car rental, account settings). If so, you can **crowd source** the analysis among volunteers within your group/company or people outside your company (e.g., Amazon's Mechanical Turk). You would ask volunteers to "tag" each data point with one of the labels from your taxonomy (e.g., "flight search," "website reliability"). This works well if the domain is easy for the volunteer to understand and the data points can stand alone (i.e., one does not need to read an entire diary to understand what the participant is reporting).

If you do not have any taxonomy in mind, you can create one by conducting an affinity diagram on a random subset of your data. Because this is a subset, it will likely be incomplete, so allow volunteers the option to say "none of the above" and suggest their own label.

If you have the time and resources, it is best to have more than one volunteer categorize each data point so you can measure **interrater reliability** (IRR) or **interrater agreement**. IRR is the degree to which two or more observers assign the same rating or label to a behavior. In this case, it is the amount of agreement between volunteers coding the same data points. If you are analyzing **nominal data** (see next section), IRR between two coders is typically calculated using **Cohen's kappa** and ranges from 1 to −1, with 1 meaning perfect agreement, 0 meaning completely random agreement, and −1 meaning perfect disagreement. Refer to Chapter 9, "Interviews" on page 254 to learn more about Cohen's kappa. Data points with low IRR should be manually reviewed to resolve the disagreement.

Suggested Resources for Additional Reading

There are actually multiple ways to calculate IRR, depending on the type of data and number of raters. To learn more about the types of IRR and how to calculate them, refer to the following handbook:

- Gwet, K. L. (2010). *Handbook of inter-rater reliability*. Advanced Analytics, LLC, Gaithersburg, MD.

Quantitative Analysis

Regardless of which method you use, if you are categorizing your data in some way, you can translate those codes into numbers for quantitative data analysis (e.g., diary entries about shopping equal "1," work-related entries equal "2"). This type of data is considered "**nominal data**." Additionally, if you included closed-ended questions in your diary, you can conduct **descriptive statistics** (e.g., average, minimum, maximum), **measures of dispersion** (e.g., frequency, standard deviation), and **measures of association** (e.g., comparisons, correlations). If your sample size is large enough, you can also conduct **inferential statistics** (e.g., t-tests, chi-square, ANOVA). A more detailed discussion of quantitative analysis can be found in the "Data Analysis and Interpretation" section in Chapter 10 on page 290.

Communicating the Findings

Preparing to Communicate Your Findings

The specific data that you communicate to product teams can vary depending upon the activity you conducted, but some elements of *how* you communicate the results are the same, regardless of the method. Because these strategies are common to all user research activities, they are discussed in detail in Chapter 15, Concluding Your Activity on page 450. We recommend that you read that chapter prior to relaying your results to your stakeholders. Topics discussed include the following:

- **Prioritization of your findings** (see page 450)
- **Creating an effective presentation** (see page 455)
- **Writing valuable reports for different audiences** (see page 463)
- **Ensuring the incorporation of your findings** (see page 469)

Because the data collected during diary studies are so rich, there are a wide variety of ways in which to present the data. For example, data may be used immediately for persona development, to develop an information architecture, or to inform product direction. There is no right or wrong answer; it all depends on the goals of your study, how your data stack up, and the method you feel best represents your data. In the end, a good report illuminates all the relevant data, provides a coherent story, and tells the stakeholders what to do next. Below, we offer some additional presentation techniques that work especially well for diary data. For a discussion of standard presentation techniques for any requirements method, refer to Chapter 15, Concluding Your Activity on page 450.

Three frequently-used methods for presenting or organizing your data are the **artifact notebook**, **storyboards**, and posters:

- *Artifact notebook.* Rather than storing away the photos, videos, and websites participants shared with you, create an artifact notebook. Insert each artifact collected, along with information about what it is and the implications for design. These can be print notebooks if your materials lend themselves well to that medium (e.g., photos), but they may work better as an electronic file. Video and audio files offer such a rich experience for stakeholders to immerse themselves in, so making these easy to access is critical. These can serve as educational materials or inspiration for the product development team.

- *Storyboards*. You can illustrate a particular task or a "day in the life" of the user through **storyboards** (using representative images to illustrate a task/scenario/story). Merge data across your users to develop a generic, representative description. The visual aspect will draw stakeholders in and demonstrate your point much faster. This is also an excellent method for communicating the emotion participants may have experienced in their submissions. Showing pure joy or extreme frustration can really drive home the experience to stakeholders.
- *Posters*. Create large-scale posters and post them around the office to educate stakeholders about the most frequent issues participants reported, photos they shared, insightful quotes, **personas** you developed based on the data, new feature ideas, etc.

Hackos and Redish (1998) provides a table summarizing some additional methods for organizing or presenting data from a field study, but this also works well for diary studies. A modified version is reproduced here as Table 8.1.

TIP

Do not let perfect be the enemy of good. Data analysis on large qualitative data sets can take time, and if you wait until all of your data are analyzed before you begin sharing it, you may lose any momentum or curiosity among your stakeholders. Prioritize your analysis and begin sharing insights in weekly newsletters, team meetings, fliers, etc. It will whet stakeholder appetites and increase the chances of your data having an impact on your product as soon as possible.

Table 8.1: Method for organizing or presenting data (Hackos & Redish, 1998)

Analysis method	Brief description
Lists of users	Examine the types and range of users identified during your study, including estimates of their percentages in the total user population and a brief description of each.
Lists of environments	Examine the types and range of environments identified during your study, including a brief description of each.
Task hierarchies	Tasks are arranged in a hierarchy to show their interrelationships, especially for tasks that are not performed in a particular sequence.
User/task matrix	Matrix to illustrate the relationship between each user type identified and the tasks they perform.
Procedural analysis	Step-by-step description examining a task, including the objects, actions, and decisions.
Task flowcharts	Drawings of the specifics of a task, including objects, actions, and decisions.
Insight sheets	List of issues identified during the field study and insights about them that may affect design decisions.
Artifact analysis	Functional descriptions of the artifacts collected, their use, and implications/ideas for design.

Pulling It All Together

In this chapter, we have discussed a way of collecting longitudinal data across a large sample of your population. Diary studies provide insights about how your target population lives and/or works in their own words. This information can be used to jump-start field studies, interviews, or other methods. They can also stand alone as a rich data set to develop personas and scenarios and inspire new feature creation.

Suggested Resources for Additional Reading

The following article is an excellent literature review of the diary study methodology with references to many other diary study presentations and peer-reviewed articles:

- Iida, M., Shrout, P. E., Laurenceau, J.-P., Bolger, N. (2012). In: H. Cooper, P. M. Camic, D. L. Long, A. T. Panter, D. Rindskopf, K. J. Sher (Ed.), *APA handbook of research methods in psychology, Vol 1: Foundations, planning, measures, and psychometrics* (pp. 277–305). Washington, DC, US: American Psychological Association, xliv, 744 pp. doi: 10.1037/13619-016.

CASE STUDY: *EXPLORING PEOPLE'S DAILY INFORMATION NEEDS*

John Boyd, Search User Experience Research Manager, Google

Fostering Innovation at Google

Henry Ford, an American industrialist, built his fortune by creating innovative processes and products. When asked about the creative process, Ford was reputed to have said, "If I had asked people what they wanted, they would have said a faster horse." More recently, Steve Jobs said, "You can't ask customers what they want and then try to give that to them. By the time you get it built, they'll want something new."

At Google, we take a somewhat different approach. We do not try to build exactly what people tell us they want, but we do respect our users' ability to tell us generally what they need. In fact, one reason for Google's success is that we have done an excellent job using what people tell us they want to improve search results. People tell us what they *want* millions of time a day by typing or speaking queries into search boxes. Teams then create new products and features that are often first tested in our usability labs and then live tested post-launch to ensure that the changes actually improve the user experience.

There is a subtle distinction between listening to our click stream and asking users what they want. In Ford's example, people want a specific solution to a general problem. A faster horse is a specific solution to a general need for faster transportation. In many cases with Google, people can articulate general needs, but not specific ways to meet them. For example, people may know that they are hungry. They typically do not know that they want go to a "Mexican restaurant near Mountain View that has 4+ stars." In response to a query like "restaurants," we provide a list of potential ways to meet their need and let them choose which one works best for them. Listening to our users is not our only source of innovation, but we believe that it can be a useful one.

One consistent ingredient of innovation is the identification of needs. In fact, Engelberger (1982) asserted that only three ingredients are needed for innovation: (1) a recognized need, (2) competent people with relevant technology, and (3) financial support. Google has incredibly talented, passionate, and hardworking people. We have technology that produces relevant results. And we have more than adequate financial support. Only the recognition of needs remains.

A first step toward innovation is thus the identification of needs that people have but that they do not currently enter into Google Search. We began to take tentative steps toward identifying needs in 2011 through what would come to be called "Daily Information Needs" (DIN) studies. The DIN method is predicated on the belief, built through experience with the query stream, that people are able to articulate at least some of their needs. It posits that even if Henry Ford was right that we should not ask users to design specific solutions, people can tell us about their *needs*, which should inform the solutions we design.

The DIN Method

Overview

Our DIN method is a modern interpretation of a traditional diary study methodology, Csikszentmihalyi's experience sampling method (ESM) (Larson & Csikszentmihalyi, 1983), and Kahneman's day reconstruction method (DRM) (Kahneman, 2011; Kahneman, Krueger, Schkade, Schwarz, & Stone, 2004). Traditionally, ESM studies capture rich time slices of how people experience everyday life. By randomly interrupting recruited participants during the course of their days during the study, ESM hopes to capture fleeting states, such as emotions, and to avoid confounds created by retrospective reconstruction and memory of daily experiences. We used an end-of-day (EOD) survey to capture the DRM component of our study. It gives participants the opportunity to see what they reported throughout the day and then elaborate or reflect further without getting in the way of ordinary life. DIN studies are also similar to diary studies in that self-reported data are collected from the same participants over multiple days.

DIN studies are not for the disorganized or the unmotivated. They require a large amount of work up front for planning and recruitment. Researchers and other team members must keep wayward participants on task, and during analysis, they must wade through the mountains of data that are collected. While a typical usability study may require 8-12 hours of interaction with participants over a couple days, DIN studies require consistent monitoring of participants over days, weeks, and even months. Literally dozens of people worked on each DIN study. Team members included internal recruiters, external recruiting vendors, product team members, software engineers, designers, and researchers. They helped at different times and in different ways, but we had at least one researcher coordinating activities full-time during the entire course of each study, which have lasted from several weeks to several months depending on the number of participants in the study. Without such a large and dedicated team, DIN studies would not be possible, at least not at Google scale.

We ran our first, much less ambitious DIN pilot study in 2011. Our goal was to capture information needs of real users that may not be reflected in query logs. We sought to minimize intrusiveness and maximize naturalism, which is what led us to our composite DIN methodology. We started with 110 participants in a three-day study. Each year, we have expanded the number of participants recruited and length of the study, so that our 2013 study (described below) involved data collected from 1000+ compensated participants across five contiguous days. We collected the data in waves over multiple months. Each year, we have improved the quality of the study, and we have expanded to some countries outside the US as well.

Participants

In a perfect world, participants would be a random sample from the population to which we planned to generalize results. In our case, this would have been a random sample of international web users. Due to multiple pragmatic, logistic, and technological constraints, we most often used a representative sample of US Internet users based upon age, gender, location, and other demographic/psychographic characteristics. To increase representativeness, some participants were recruited by Google recruiters, and some were recruited by an external recruiting agency. Participants were motivated to participate by a tiered compensation system that was tied to the number of daily pings to which they responded and the number of EOD survey responses they completed. Each person participated for five consecutive days. The start dates of participant cohorts were staggered so that needs were collected for each day of the week for approximately three months.

Tools

We used an open-source tool developed by Google engineer Bob Evans called the Personal Analytics Companion (PACO) app to collect data. This is a free tool anyone can download from Google Play and Apple iStore (see Figure 8.2). Working closely with Bob allowed us to customize the tool and data collected to meet our unique

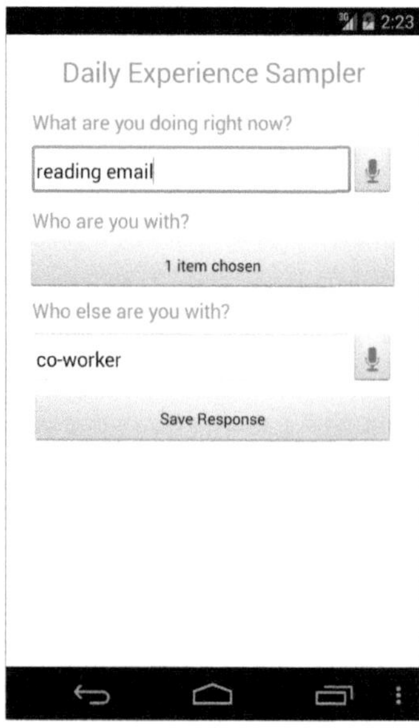

Figure 8.2: PACO form.

needs. Participants installed PACO (www.pacoapp.com) on their Android device and then joined the appropriate study. At the time of the study, the app was available only on Android devices.

We also created websites to support the needs of both Google research assistants and study participants. These sites included text instructions, video instructions, FAQs, and clear paths of escalation for issues that were not sufficiently addressed by site content. It took a lot of time and effort to develop the materials, but it was time well spent. The sites answered scheduling, study setup, and incentive-related questions and, in so doing, freed researchers to focus on more important tasks.

Procedure

DIN pings: Capturing the Experiencing Self

Participants were pinged by PACO at eight random times during normal waking hours during the five days of the study. Participants responded to pings by answering four simple questions on their mobile device: (1) What did you want to know recently? (2) How important was it that you find this information? (3) How urgently did you need the information? and (4) What is the first thing that you did to find this information? These questions were pretested to generate high-quality data and were designed to allow completion in about a minute. This was done via pilot testing and getting feedback from participants about the questions, what they were able to articulate about their experiences, what was difficult to answer, and which questions received the clearest, most useful data. In case participants missed pings, they were instructed to enter DIN as they occurred throughout the day. Participants could respond to pings by text or voice entry and could include pictures of their information need as well. Figures 8.3–8.5 show representative photos of actual needs submitted. (To protect participant privacy, these are not the actual photos submitted but replicas.)

EOD Survey Pings: Capturing the Remembering Self

At the end of each study day, PACO messaged and e-mailed participants reminders to complete the EODs. We recommended that participants completed the survey using a desktop or laptop computer because of the difficulty to view the form and respond with complete answers on a mobile device. The EOD survey included all of the DIN information that participants submitted during the day and asked them to elaborate on each need. Selected questions included the following:

1. Why did you need the information?
2. How did you look for the information?
3. How successful were you in finding the information?
4. Where were you when you needed the information?
5. What devices did you use to find the information?

Some of these questions were forced-choice, and some were free text.

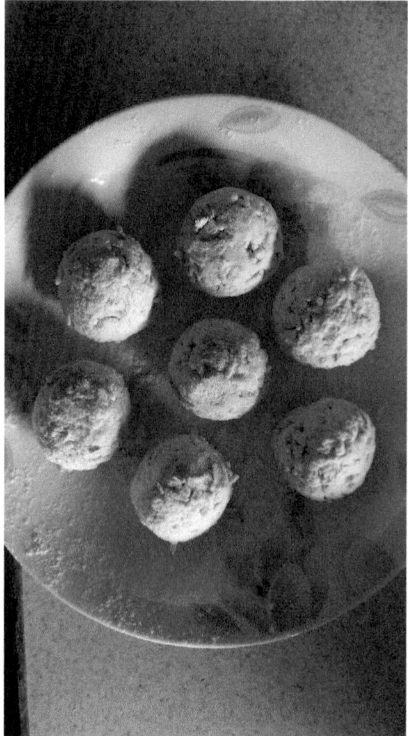

Figure 8.3: "What is this?"

Figure 8.4: "Will it snow tomorrow?"

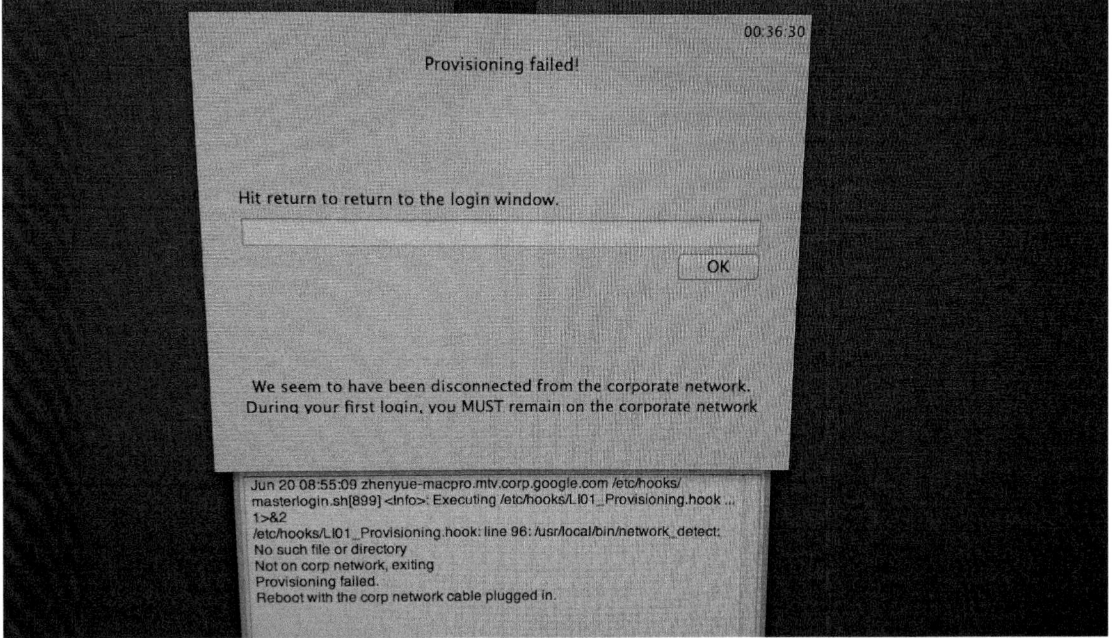

Figure 8.5: "What's wrong with my computer?"

Limitations

No study is perfect, and despite the assiduous work of our entire team, DIN is no exception. Some of the issues below are likely to be addressed in subsequent DIN studies, while others are inherent to the method itself. Different balances could be struck, but some limitations can never be completely eliminated.

Technological Limitations

One limitation of our early DIN studies is that PACO was available only for the Android operating system. We therefore were unable to collect needs from iOS users and cannot be sure that our data reflect the needs of all users. An iOS version of PACO is now available, and future DIN studies will address this limitation.

Incentive Structure

We created an incentive structure that we felt would provide an optimal balance between data quality and data quantity. We sought to motivate participants that had valid information needs to report the needs when they otherwise may not have, but we did not want to create so much motivation that participants would make up fake needs just so that they could earn the maximum incentive. After some trial and error, we settled on a tiered structure that provided incentives for initial study setup, response to a minimum number of pings, and submission of a minimum number of EOD surveys. Inspection of our data suggests that the tiered structure worked well for us, but we encourage to you to think carefully about what you want to maximize and to experiment with different structures. In the end, this limitation cannot be eliminated, but we feel that it can be managed.

Findings

We discovered several interesting findings in 2013. One area we examined was around the value of photos in ESM studies (Yue et al., 2014). Women and participants over 40 were significantly more likely to submit photos than others. Although many of the photos participants provided did not aid our analysis (e.g., selfies, photos that did not include information beyond what was in the text), we did find that text submissions that included photos were of better quality than those without photos. We compared the submissions of those that submitted photos versus those that did not and also looked within the submissions of those that submitted any photos. In both cases, responses that included photos included richer text descriptions.

The data collected in our annual study are a source of innovation for product teams across all of Google, not just within Search. For example, in Google Now (Google's mobile personal assistant application), DIN data led to 17 new notification cards and two voice actions, identified eight user-driven contexts, and improved 22 existing cards. Roles across the company including UX, engineering, product management, consumer support, and market research ask for the DIN data and use it to inform their work.

Lessons Learned

Pilot Studies

Although running a pilot study feels like a distraction from important preparation for the "real" study and takes serious time when you may be under pressure to begin collecting data, we strongly encourage you to run at least one. Pilots with team members and colleagues revealed typos, unclear instructions, technical installation issues with specific phone models, time zone logging issues, extraneous and missing pings, and other assorted issues. In addition, pilots with external participants were invaluable in refining the method and the creation of complete, accurate FAQs. Pilots saved time for us, when it really mattered with real participants.

Unfortunately, we did not do an analysis of the pilot data we collected and so we did not catch issues with data collection in a couple of the questions. This was caught during the data cleaning stage of our final analysis, but if it had been caught during the pilot, significant time and effort could have been saved in the cleaning phase.

Analysis

Preparation for DIN studies takes weeks. Running the studies takes days. Processing and analyzing the data takes months. This is due to the sheer volume of the data, the complexity of the data, and the numerous ways it can be coded and analyzed. There is seldom a "right" way to analyze qualitative data, but there are ways that are more and less useful, depending on your needs. Over the course of a literature review, several affinity diagramming exercises, and substantial hand coding, we developed a coding scheme that works for us, but it took time. Expect coding and analysis to take longer than planning and running the study combined.

Conclusion

Henry Ford and Steve Jobs' famous quotes are often used to justify the exclusion of users from the innovation process. We disagree and believe that users and user research can play a critical role. While it is clear that user wants and needs do not provide step-by-step instructions for innovation, user needs can provide important clues and data points that teams may not be able to get in any other way. For those of us for whom the understanding of needs and their solutions is less intuitive than for Ford and Jobs, DIN-like studies can be an important part of a data-driven innovation process. We hope that our experience encourages you to both adapt it to your needs and to avoid some of the mistakes we made while developing it.

CHAPTER 9

Interviews

Introduction

Interviews are one of the most frequently-used methods for understanding your users. In the broadest sense, an interview is a guided conversation in which one person seeks information from another. There are a variety of different types of interviews you can conduct, depending on your constraints and needs. They are flexible and can be used as a solo activity or in conjunction with another user research activity (e.g., following a card sort or in combination with a contextual observation).

In this chapter, we discuss how to prepare for and conduct an interview, how to analyze the data, and how to communicate the findings to your team. We spend a good deal of time concentrating on constructing good interview questions and how to interact with participants to get the best data possible. These processes are critical to a successful interview. Finally, we close this chapter with an illustrative case study about conducting interviews with children.

At a Glance

> Preparing to conduct an interview
> Conducting an interview
> Data analysis and interpretation
> Communicating the findings

Preparing to Conduct an Interview

Preparing for an interview includes selecting the type of interview to conduct, wording the questions, creating the materials, training the interviewer, and inviting observers. See Table 9.1 for a high-level timeline to follow as you prepare for an interview.

Table 9.1: Preparing for the interview session

When to complete	Approximate time to complete	Activity
As soon as possible	1–2 weeks	• Meet with team to identify Questions • Meet with team to develop user profile
After identification of questions and user profile	1 week	• Create and distribute activity proposal
After the proposal has been agreed to by all stakeholders	1–2 weeks	• Word questions appropriately and distribute to colleagues for review

Table 9.1: Preparing for the interview session—Cont'd

When to complete	Approximate time to complete	Activity
After development of the questions	2 weeks	• Identify and recruit users • Assign roles for the activity (e.g., notetaker, interviewer) • Prepare interview materials • Acquire location • Acquire incentives • Prepare documentation (e.g., confidentiality agreement, consent form)
1 week before activity	2 days	• Conduct pilot • Make necessary changes to questions and procedure based on pilot
Day before interview	1 hour	• Call and confirm with participant(s) • Remind stakeholders to come and observe the activity (if appropriate)
Day of interview	1 hour	• Set up location with all materials necessary

At a Glance

> Identify the objectives of the study

> Select the type of interview

> Decide now how you will analyze the data

> Write the questions

> Test your questions

> Players in your activity

> Inviting observers

> Activity materials

Identify the Objectives of the Study

When developing questions for interviews, it is easy to add more and more questions as stakeholders (i.e., product team, management, partners) think of them. That is why it is important for everyone to agree upon the purpose and objectives of the study from the beginning. These objectives should be included in your proposal to the stakeholders and signed off by all parties (see Chapter 6, "Creating a Proposal" section, page 116). As you and the stakeholders determine the type of interview to conduct and brainstorm questions for the interview, use the objectives of the study as a guide. If the type of interview suggested or the questions offered do not match the objectives that have been agreed upon, the request should be denied. This is much easier to do once the proposal has been signed off, rather than trying to get the agreement halfway through the process.

Select the Type of Interview

Interviews vary by the amount of control the interviewer places on the conversation. There are three main types of one-on-one interview:

- Unstructured
- Structured
- Semi-structured

An unstructured interview is the most similar to a normal conversation. The interviewer will begin with general goals but will allow the participant to go into each point with as much or as little detail and in the order he or she desires. The questions or topics for discussion are **open-ended** (see Chapter 10, "Response Format" section, page 275), so the interviewee is free to answer in narrative form (i.e., not forced to choose from a set of predetermined answers), and the topics do not have to be covered in any particular order. The interviewer is also free to deviate from the script to generate additional relevant questions based on answers given during the interview. When deviating from the script, it is important to be able to think on your feet so you can focus on getting the most important information, even if the question that will get you that information is not in the script. It is a good idea to have a list of carefully worded follow-up questions already prepared so you do not have to come up with these on the fly.

A structured interview, on the other hand, is the most controlled type because the goal is to offer each interviewee the same set of possible responses. The interview may consist primarily of **closed-ended questions** (see Chapter 10, "Response Format" section, page 275), where the interviewee must choose from the options provided. This presents a limit because a closed-ended question is only effective if the choices offered are complete and presented in the users' vernacular. Furthermore, participants tend to confine their answers to the choices offered, even if the choices are not complete. Open-ended questions may be asked, but the interviewer will not delve into the participant's responses for more details or ask questions that are not listed on the script. All possible questions and follow-ups are preplanned; therefore, the data gathered across participants are consistent. Thus, differences in results are attributable to real differences between participants rather than differences in measurement technique. This type of interview is similar to conducting a survey verbally but has the added benefit of allowing participants to explain their answers. It is used by organizations like the Census Bureau and Bureau of Labor Statistics.

TIP

When using only closed-ended questions, be sure to provide an "out" (e.g., "none of the above"). If participants have an opinion or experience different from the options offered, the participant will be forced to provide an inaccurate answer. Because closed-ended questions are more typical in surveys, you can find a discussion of the different types of closed-ended question and their uses in Chapter 10, "Response format" section on page 275.

A semi-structured interview is clearly a combination of the structured and unstructured types. The interviewer may begin with a set of questions to answer (closed-ended and open-ended) but deviate from the order and even the set of questions from time to time. The interview does not have quite the same conversational approach as an unstructured one.

When determining the type of interview to conduct, keep the data analysis and objectives of the study in mind. By first deciding the type of interview you plan to conduct, you know the type of questions you will be able to ask. As with any method, there are pros and cons to each type of interview (see Table 9.2).

In Person or Mediated?

Regardless of the type of interview you select, you have the option of conducting the interviews in an increasingly large number of ways, including (listed from the least mediated to the most mediated) in person, using video conferencing/video chat, over the phone, or via text chat. Some aspects of mediated interviews are easier than in-person interviews. For example, when conducting interviews via text chat, there is no need to have a conversation transcribed, because all data are already captured as text. It is also usually more convenient for both the participant and interviewer to conduct the interviews via a mediated channel so that less time is spent on travel. However, there are also disadvantages to conducting interviews that are not face-to-face:

- Participants may end interviews on the telephone before participants in face-to-face interviews. It can be difficult to keep participants on the phone for more than 20 minutes. If you are cold-calling participants (i.e., not a prescheduled interview), the biggest challenge may be keeping the participant's attention. If you do not have the participant in a quiet location, it is easy for his or her colleagues or children to come in during your interview for a "quick" question.

Table 9.2: Comparison of the three types of interview

Interview type	Type of data received	Pros	Cons
Unstructured	Qualitative	• Rich data set • Ability to follow up and delve deeper on any question • Flexible • Especially useful when you do not know what answers to expect	• Difficult to analyze • The topics and follow-up questions may not be consistent across participants
Semi-structured	Combination	• Provides both quantitative and qualitative data • Provides some detail and an opportunity to follow up	• Takes some additional time to analyze participants' comments • Not as consistent across participants as the structured interview
Structured	Quantitative	• Faster to analyze • Questions asked are consistent across participants • You can generally ask more questions than in an unstructured interview	• You may not understand why you got the results you did because participants were not given an opportunity to explain their choice

- Similarly, in all mediated interviews except video chat, both participants and the interviewer lack cues about identity and lack nonverbal communication cues. This may lead participants to take a more cautious approach to revealing sensitive information (Johnson, Hougland, & Clayton, 1989). It also means that you cannot watch the participant's body language, facial expressions, and gestures, which can all provide important additional information.
- Phones can be perceived as impersonal, and it is more difficult to develop a rapport with the participant and engage him or her over the phone.

An additional benefit of computer-mediated interviews rather than phone-mediated interviews is that you may show artifacts to participants if appropriate. Figure 9.1 provides a checklist that can help you determine which type of interview is most appropriate.

	Face-to-face	Video + audio	Audio (phone or VOIP)	Text (e.g., online chat)	Text (non-interactive)
The interview will take an exceptionally long time	✓				
The interviewer needs to be able to visually observe participants' reactions	✓	✓			
The interviewer needs to be able to include or exclude certain types of people based on their physical appearance or visible characteristics	✓	✓			
Participants are not able to type or are illiterate	✓	✓	✓		
The interviewer needs to be able to conduct an interactive session, including following up with unanticipated questions	✓	✓	✓	✓	
The interview task requires showing the respondent something.	✓	✓	✓*	✓*	
The respondents are spread across a wide geographic area, such that visiting them in person would pose great time and travel costs		✓	✓	✓	✓
There is a necessity for very rapid data collection			✓	✓	
There is a potential for psychological threat or intimidation of a personal encounter with an interviewer			✓	✓	✓
The nature of the questions are personal/sensitive so the participant may not feel comfortable revealing the answers to an interviewer				✓	✓

*If using Internet-based audio or video chat, it may be possible to show participants wireframes, prototypes, etc. using screen sharing programs.

Figure 9.1: Checklist to determine whether a face-to-face or mediated interview is most appropriate for your study.

TIP

Aim for one-hour interview sessions. If needed, two-hour sessions may be used. We do not recommend conducting interview sessions beyond two hours. Dedicated participants or customers may be willing to stay for longer interviews if you provide regular breaks and keep the session interesting.

Decide Now How You Will Analyze the Data

Whether you are asking closed-ended or open-ended questions, there are tools and methods available to help you analyze your data. For a discussion of how to analyze open-ended questions, see "Data Analysis and Interpretation" section on page 252. For a discussion of how to analyze closed-ended questions, refer to Chapter 10 on page 266.

However you choose to analyze your data, you should analyze some sample data from your pilot interviews to ensure that your analysis strategy is achieving the results you want and to help you understand whether you need to adjust your questions (see Chapter 6, "Piloting Your Activity" section, page 155). If you plan to use a new tool, be sure to allow time to purchase any necessary software and learn how to use it.

Identify the Questions

It is now time to identify all the questions to ask. You may want to do initial brainstorming with all stakeholders (members of the product team, UX, marketing). You will likely end up with questions that are out of the scope of the proposed activity or questions that are best answered by other activities. The questions that are out of the scope should be discarded, and the ones that are better answered by other activities should be put aside until the other activity can be performed. Even with limiting your questions in this way, you may still end up with more questions than you could possibly cover in a single interview. If this is the case, you will either need to conduct multiple sessions or focus on the most important topics, so you can trim down the number of questions to fit into a single session.

Write the Questions

Once you have a list of topics you are interested in, now is the time to write a first draft of the questions. One way to start this process is by making sure you have questions that fit each category of question necessary for the interview flow. Table 9.3 presents an overview of an idealized interview flow. The next step is to word the questions so that they are clear, understandable, and impartial. In the next section, we describe how to write good questions and provide examples and counter-examples.

Table 9.3: Idealized interview flow

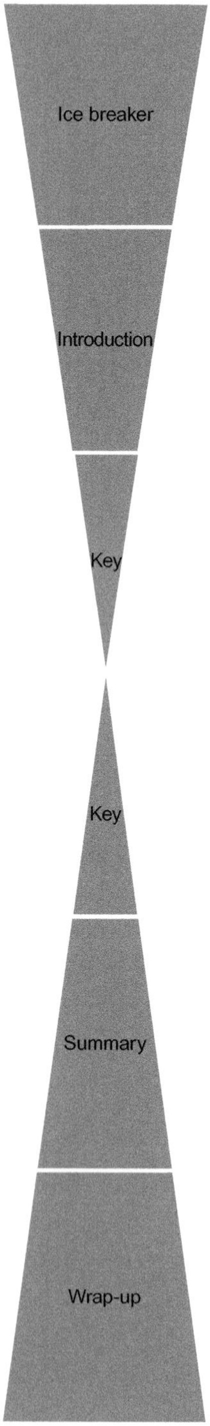

	Type of question	Purpose	Example question
Ice breaker	Ice breaker	Get participant talking, put participants at ease, create rapport	What's your name and where are you from?
Introduction	Introduction	Bring up topic, shift focus toward product	Tell me about a favorite place you've traveled.
Key	Key	Gather insight on areas of primary interest; achieve study goals	• How often do you book travel using only your smartphone? • Tell me about the most recent experience you had booking travel using your smartphone.
Summary	Summary	Consider key questions within a broader perspective	Considering everything we've talked about today, what's the one thing that's most important to you?
Wrap-up	Wrap-up	Bring closure to discussion	Is there anything we didn't talk about today that you'd like us to know?

"Next question: I believe that life is a constant striving for balance, requiring frequent tradeoffs between morality and necessity, within a cyclic pattern of joy and sadness, forging a trail of bittersweet memories until one slips, inevitably, into the jaws of death. Agree or disagree?"

© The New Yorker Collection 1989 George Price from cartoonbank.com. All rights reserved

Brevity

Questions should be kept short—usually 20 words or less. It is difficult for people to remember long or multiple-part questions. Break long, complex questions into two or more simple questions.

Wrong: "If you were waiting until the last minute to book a plane ticket to save money and the only seats available were on the red-eye flight or had two layovers, what would you do?"

Right: "If you were paying for the ticket on a four-hour airplane trip, would you take a late-night/dawn-arrival flight that cost half as much?<answer>Would you accept a change of planes with a two-hour delay?<answer>What if you saved a quarter of the direct-flight fare?"

Clarity

Avoid **double-barreled questions** that address more than one issue at a time. Introducing multiple issues in a question can be confusing. The example below addresses multiple issues: the frequency of traveling, the frequency of booking travel online, and the purpose for booking travel online. These should be asked separately.

> **Wrong**: "Do you regularly book your travel online to save money?"
>
> **Right**: "How often do you travel?<answer>What proportion of that do you book online?<answer>Why do you book travel online?"

Vague questions, too, can cause difficulty during an interview. Avoid imprecise words like "rarely," "sometimes," "usually," "few," "some," and "most." Individuals can interpret these terms in different ways, affecting their answers and your interpretation of the results.

> **Wrong**: "Do you usually purchase plane tickets online?"
>
> **Right**: "How often do you purchase plane tickets online?"

A final challenge to creating clear questions is the use of **double negatives**. Just as the name implies, double negatives insert two negatives into the sentence, making it difficult for the interviewee to understand the true meaning of the question.

> **Wrong**: "Do you no longer book travel on the TravelMyWay app because they do not offer travel rewards?"
>
> **Right**: "Tell me a little bit more about why you stopped using TravelMyWay app?<answer>What was the main reason?"

Avoiding Bias

As we mentioned earlier, there are a number of ways in which you might introduce bias into questions. One way is with **leading questions**. These questions assume the answer and may pass judgment on the interviewee. They are designed to influence a participant's answers rather than elicit the participant's true opinion.

Wrong: "Most of our users prefer the new look and feel of our app over the old one. How do you feel?"

Right: "How do you feel about the visual appearance of this app?"

Wrong: "Would you agree that it is more convenient to book travel using an app rather than through a travel agent?"

Right: "What is the greatest advantage to you of booking travel using an app?<answer>What is the greatest disadvantage?<answer>How does booking using an app compare to booking through a travel agent?"

Leading questions are rather obvious and easy to pick up on. **Loaded questions** are subtler in their influence. They typically provide a "reason" for a problem in the question. One example where loaded questions may be observed is in political campaigns. Politicians may use these type of questions in an attempt to demonstrate that a majority of the population feels one way or another on a key issue.

Wrong: "The cost of airline tickets continues to go up to cover security costs. Do you think you should have to pay more when you buy your ticket, or should the government start paying more of the cost?"

Right: "How much are you willing to pay for your plane ticket to cover additional security at the airport?"

The question above suggests that the reason for increasing travel costs is increased security costs. It is clear how the interviewer in the first (wrong) question would like the participant to answer. This is also an example of a question based on a false premise. The example implies that the government has not paid for additional security costs and should now start to do so. These types of questions begin with a hypothesis or assumption that may not be fully accurate or can be easily misinterpreted. Not only is this type of question unethical, but also the data you get in the end are not valid.

The final type of bias is **interviewer prestige bias**. In this case, the interviewer informs the interviewee that an authority figure feels one way or another about a topic and then asks the participant how he or she feels.

Wrong: "Safety experts recommend using a travel agent instead of booking your travel via an app. Do you feel safe using travel apps?"

Right: "Do you feel that booking travel via an app is more or less confidential than booking through a travel agent?"

Focus on Outcomes

Rather than asking your participants for solutions to problems or to identify a specific product feature that they might like, ask participants questions that help you ascertain the outcomes they need to achieve. People are often unable to know what works for them or what they may actually like until they have actual experience with a service or feature.

Wrong: "What are your thoughts about a new feature that allows you to instant message a travel agent with any questions as you book your travel?"

Right: "Would you like to correspond with a travel agent while you are booking travel?<answer>What are some ways that you would like to correspond with a travel agent while you are booking travel?"

The "wrong" question above would be a problem if the participant was unfamiliar with instant messaging. In that case, you would want to speak in broader terms and ask the participant to discuss communications methods with which he or she is familiar.

If you task customers with the responsibility of innovation, many problems can occur, such as small iterative changes rather than drastic, pioneering changes; suggestions that are limited to features available in your competitors' products (because these are what your participants are familiar with); and features that users do not actually need or use (most users use less than 10% of a software product). Focusing on outcomes lets you get a better understanding of what users really need. With a thorough understanding of what participants need, you can allow developers, who have more technical knowledge and desire to innovate than users, to create innovative solutions that meet these needs.

To do this, the interviewer must understand the difference between outcomes and solutions and ask the appropriate probes to weed out the solutions while getting to the outcomes.

Participant: "All the flight times presented on an iPhone." (Solution)

Interviewer: "Why would you like the flight time presented on an iPhone? What would that help you do?" (Probe for outcome)

Participant: "I travel a lot so I need to see when flight times change and I take my iPhone with me everywhere." (Outcome)

Interviewer: "So you would like to have access to flight times from anywhere?" (Rephrasing to confirm outcome)

Participant: "Exactly." (Confirmation)

Avoid Asking Participants to Predict the Future

Do not expect participants to be able to predict their future. Instead, focus on understanding what they want now. You will be able to translate that into what they will need in the future.

Wrong: "If we had a feature that let you communicate with all the other passengers on a plane using your smartphone, would you use it?"

Right: "Would you like to chat with other passengers while you are on a plane waiting for takeoff?"

Inaccessible Topics

You have screened your participants against the user profile, but you still may encounter those who cannot answer all of your questions. A participant may not have experience with exactly what you are asking about or may not have the factual knowledge you are seeking. In these cases, be sure a participant feels comfortable saying that he or she does not know the answer or does not have an opinion. Forcing a participant to choose an answer will only frustrate the participant and introduce error into your data.

Begin the interviews by informing participants that there are no right or wrong answers—if they do not have an opinion or experience with something, they should feel free to state that. Keep in mind that interviewees are often eager to please or impress. They may feel compelled to answer and therefore make a best guess or force an opinion that they do not actually have. Encourage them to be honest and feel comfortable enough to say they cannot answer a particular question.

Depending on Memory

Think about the number of times you have booked a rental car in the last three years. Are you confident in your answer? Interviewers and surveys often ask people how frequently they have done a certain task in a given period. If the question seeks information about recent actions or highly memorable events (e.g., your wedding, college graduation), it probably will not be too difficult. Unfortunately, people are often asked about events that happened many years ago and/or those that are not memorable.

What is key is the importance or salience of the event. Some things are easily remembered because they are important or odd and therefore require little effort to remember. Other things are unmemorable—even if they happened yesterday, you would not remember them. In addition, some memories that seem real may be false. Since most participants want to be "good" interviewees, they will try hard to remember and provide an accurate answer, but memory limitations prevent it. Underreporting and overreporting of events frequently happen in these cases.

In addition to memory limitations, people have a tendency to compress time. This response bias is known as **telescoping**. This means that if you are asking about events that happened in the last six months, people may unintentionally include events that happened in the last nine months. Overreporting of events will result in these cases.

To help mitigate these sources of error, you should avoid questions covering unmemorable events. Focus the questions on salient and easy-to-remember events. You can also provide memory aids like a calendar and/or provide specific instructions alerting participants to potential memory confusion and encouraging them to think carefully to avoid such confusion (Krosnick, 1999). Finally, if you are truly interested in studying events over a period of time, you can contact participants in advance and ask them to track their behaviors in a diary (see Chapter 8, "Incident Diaries" section, page 202). This means extra work for the participant, but the data you receive from those dedicated individuals who follow through will likely be far more accurate than from those who rely on memory alone.

Other Types of Wording to Avoid

Avoid emotionally laden words like "racist" and "liberal." Personal questions should be asked only if absolutely necessary and then with great tact. This includes questions about age, race, and salary. Figure 9.2 describes how to identify questions that might be perceived as threatening.

	Does the question:	Why this might be threatening
✓	Ask about financial matters?	Society judges people by what they earn and own
✓	Challenge mental or technical skill?	People fear looking stupid or inept
✓	Reveal self-perceived shortcomings?	People are highly sensitive to their inability to accomplish personally or socially desirable goals
✓	Discuss social status indicators?	Those with low-level educations, jobs, neighborhoods, and the like may be defensive
✓	Focus on sexuality, sexual identity or behavior?	Many people are embarrassed even by the mention of sex
✓	Refer to consumption of alcohol or illegal drugs?	Many will deny or understate such consumption or be insulted by the suggestion of use
✓	Focus on personal habits?	People do not like to admit their inability to form or to break personal habits
✓	Address emotional or psychological disturbance?	Such illnesses are considered even more difficult to discuss than physical ailments
✓	Focus on topics associated with the aging process?	Indicators of aging may arouse fear and anxiety among people of all ages
✓	Deal with death or dying?	Morbidity is often a forbidden topic that many refuse to even think about

Figure 9.2: Checklist to determine whether a question might be perceived as threatening (Alreck & Settle, 1995).

Jargon, slang, abbreviations, and geek speak should be avoided unless you are certain that your user population is familiar with this terminology. Speaking plainly and in the user's language (as long as you understand it) is important. And of course, take different cultures and languages into consideration when wording your questions (see Chapter 6, "Recruiting International Participants" section, page 147). A direct word-for-word translation can result in embarrassing, confusing, or misinterpreted questions. Figure 9.3 provides a checklist of dos and don'ts in question wording.

DO:

- Keep questions under 20 words
- Address one issue at a time
- Word questions clearly
- Keep questions concrete and based on the user's experience
- Limit questions to memorable events or ask participants to track their behavior over time in a diary
- Provide memory aids, such as calendars, to help participants remember previous events
- Use terms that are familiar to the user
- Use neutral terms and phrases
- Ask sensitive or personal questions only if necessary

DON'T:

- Force users to choose an option that does not represent their real opinion
- Ask leading questions
- Ask loaded questions
- Base questions on a false premise
- Use authority figures to bias questions
- Ask users to predict the future
- Ask users to discuss unmemorable events
- Use jargon, slang, abbreviations, geek speak
- Use emotionally laden words
- Use double negatives
- Ask sensitive or personal questions out of curiosity

Figure 9.3: Dos and don'ts in question wording.

Test Your Questions

It is important to test your questions to ensure that you are covering all the topics you mean to, to identify questions that are difficult to understand, and to ensure that questions will be interpreted as you intend. If you are conducting an unstructured interview, test your list of topics. If you are conducting a structured interview, test each of your questions and follow-up prompts. Begin with members of your team who have not worked on the interview so far. The team members should be able to summarize the type of information you are looking for in a question. If the colleague incorrectly states the information you are seeking, you need to clarify or reword the question. Find someone who understands survey and interview techniques to check your questions for bias. If no one in your organization has experience with survey and interview techniques, you may be able to ask a colleague in another organization to review your questions for bias, as long as the questions will not reveal proprietary information.

Once the questions have passed the test of colleagues, conduct the interview with a couple of actual participants. How did the participants react to the questions? Did they answer your question, or did it seem like they answered another question? Was everything clear? Were you able to complete the interviews within the allotted time frame?

Players in Your Activity

In addition to users (the "participants"), you will require three other people to run the sessions. In this section, we discuss the details of all the players involved in an interview.

The Participants

Participants should be representative of your existing end users or the users that you expect will be interacting with your system.

Number of Participants

We find in industry settings that a common sample size for interview studies is six to ten participants of each user type, with the same set of questions. However, there are several factors to take into consideration, including whether you are seeking qualitative or quantitative data and the size of the population of users. For qualitative studies, some researchers recommend that 12 participants are sufficient for discovering new themes (Guest, Bunce, & Johnson, 2006). On the other hand, other researchers suggest that thirty or more participants are needed for interviews seeking quantitative data (Green & Thorogood, 2009). See Chapter 6 on page 116 for a more thorough discussion of how many participants you should recruit for a user research activity.

The Interviewer

The task of the interviewer is to develop rapport with the interviewee, elicit responses from the participant, know what an adequate answer is to each question, examine each answer to ensure that the participant understands what he or she is really saying, and, in some cases, paraphrase the response to make sure that the intent of the statement is captured. In addition, the interviewer needs to know when to let a discussion go off the "planned path" into valuable areas of discovery and when to bring a fruitless discussion back on track. The interviewer needs to have sufficient domain knowledge to know which discussions are adding value and which are sapping valuable time. He or she also needs to know what follow-up questions to ask on the fly to get the details the team needs to make product decisions.

We cannot stress enough how important it is for interviewers to be well-trained and experienced. Without this, interviewers can unknowingly introduce bias into the questions they ask. This will cause participants to provide unrepresentative answers or to misinterpret the questions. Either way, the data you receive are inaccurate and should not be used. People new to interviewing may wish to take an interviewing workshop—in addition to reading this chapter—to better internalize the information. Another way to gain experience is to offer to serve as the notetaker for an experienced interviewer. We are always looking for an eager notetaker to help out, and you will get the opportunity to see how we handle various situations that arise.

We strongly recommend finding someone who is a skilled interviewer and asking him or her to review your questions. Then, practice interviewing him or her, and ask specifically for feedback on anything you may do that introduces bias. The more you practice this skill, the better you will become and the more confident you can be in the accuracy of the data you obtain. Co-interviewing with a skilled interviewer is always helpful.

Finally, although we all hate to watch ourselves on video or listen to audio of ourself, it is very helpful to watch/listen to yourself after an interview. Even experienced interviewers fall into bad habits—watching yourself on video can make you aware of them and help break them. Having an experienced interviewer watching or listening with you helps because he or she can point out areas for improvement. If you involve other members of the team, such as product managers, they may also be able to point out additional topics of interest or request that you focus on areas of concern. Ideally, this can be a fun, informative team-building activity.

The Notetaker

You may find it useful to have a colleague in the same room or another room who is taking notes for you. This frees you from having to take detailed notes. Instead, you can focus more of your attention on the interviewee's body language and cues for following up. Depending on the situation, the notetaker may also act as a "second brain" who can suggest questions the primary interviewer might not think of in context (see Chapter 7, "Recording and Notetaking" section on page 171, for more details on capturing the data.)

The Videographer

Whenever possible, video record your interview session (see Chapter 7, "Recording and Notetaking" section on page 171 for a detailed discussion of the benefits of video recording). You will need someone to be responsible for making the recording. In most cases, this person simply needs to start and stop the recording, insert new storage devices (e.g., SD cards) as needed, and keep an eye out for any technical issues that arise. He or she can also watch audio and light levels of the recording and suggest changes as needed. Be sure to practice with the videographer in advance. Losing data because of a video error is a common, yet entirely preventable, occurrence.

Inviting Observers

As with other user research techniques, we do not recommend having observers (e.g., colleagues, product team members) in the same room as the participant during the interview. If you do not have the facilities to allow someone to observe the interviews from another room but you do want stakeholders to be present, it is best to limit the observers to one or two individuals. Any more than this will intimidate the person being interviewed. The observers should be told explicitly, prior to the session, not to interrupt the interview at any time.

TIP

Spend some time prior to the interview informing the observers about the importance of asking unbiased questions and the impact different types of bias can have on the data you collect. You may even choose to do some role-playing with the observers, having them interview you. Identify any biased questions they ask and tell them how the question would be asked without bias. Once observers understand the difficulty of asking unbiased questions and the impact biased questions have on the data, you will find that they will be much more likely to respect your request for their silence.

It is up to you if you would like to invite observers to suggest questions for the participants. All questions observers suggest should follow the same guidelines discussed above (e.g., avoid bias, keep them brief). Since you cannot control what the observers say, we recommend asking them to write questions on paper and then pass them to you at the end of the session. This works well in cases where you do not have the domain knowledge to ask and follow up on technical questions. You then have the opportunity to reword a loaded or double-barreled question. Or you can work with the observers prior to the session to devise a set of follow-up questions that they may ask if time permits. You may also permit observers to view a session remotely and use a chat feature to suggest questions to you in real time. However, this can be difficult to manage since it requires you to keep an eye on the chat feature, be able to figure out the appropriate moment during the interview to ask the question, reword it on the fly, and know when to skip asking a suggested question.

Activity Materials

You will need the following materials for an interview (the use of these will be discussed in more detail in the next section):

- Protocol
- List of questions for interview
- Method of notetaking (laptop and/or paper and pencil on clipboard)
- Method of recording (video or audio recorder)
- Comfortable location for participant, interviewer, notetaker, and video equipment
- Memory aids (e.g., calendar) (optional)
- Artifacts to show the participant (optional)

Conducting an Interview

At a Glance

> Things to be aware of when conducting interviews
> The five phases of an interview
> Your role as the interviewer
> Monitoring the relationship with the interviewee
> Dos and don'ts

Things to Be Aware of When Conducting Interviews

As with all user research activities, there are some factors that you should be aware of before you jump into the activity. In the case of interviews, these include bias and honesty.

Bias

It is easy to introduce bias into an interview. Choice of words, your way speaking, and body language can all introduce bias. Bias unfairly influences participants to answer in a way that does not accurately reflect their true feelings. Your job as an interviewer is to put aside your ideas, feelings, thoughts, and hopes about a topic and elicit those things from the participant. A skilled interviewer will word, ask, and respond to questions in a way that encourages a participant to answer truthfully and without worry of being judged. This takes practice and lots of it.

Honesty

Individuals who are hooked on performance metrics or who question the value of "anecdotal" data may frown upon interviews. Sometimes, people ask how you know a participant is telling the truth. The answer is that people are innately honest. It is an extremely rare case that a participant comes into your interview with the intention of lying to you or not providing the details you seek.

However, there are factors that can influence a participant's desire to be completely forthcoming. Participants may provide a response that they believe is socially desirable or more acceptable rather than the truth. This is known as **social desirability**. Similarly, a participant may describe the way things are supposed to happen rather than the way things actually happen. For example, a participant may describe the process he or she uses at work according to recommended best practice, when, in actuality, the participant uses shortcuts and work-arounds because the "best practice" is too difficult to follow—but the participant does not want to reveal this. Make it clear that you need to understand the way he or she *actually* works. If work-arounds or shortcuts are used, it is helpful for you to understand this. And of course, remind the participant that all information is kept confidential—the employer will not receive a transcript of the interview.

A participant may also just agree to whatever the interviewer suggests in the belief that it is what the interviewer wants to hear. Additionally, a participant may want to impress the interviewer and therefore provide answers that increase his or her image. This is called **prestige response bias**. If you want the participant to provide a certain answer, he or she can likely pick up on that and oblige you. You can address these issues by being completely honest with yourself about your stake in the interview. If you understand that you have a stake in the interview and/or what your personal biases are, you can control them when writing questions. You can also word questions (see "Write the Questions" section, page 225) and respond to participants in ways that can help mitigate these issues (e.g., do not pass judgment, do not invoke authority figures). You should be a neutral evaluator at all times and encourage the participant to be completely honest with you. Be careful about raising sensitive or highly personal topics. A survey can be a better option than interviews if you are seeking information on sensitive topics. Surveys can be anonymous, but interviews are much more personal. Participants may not be forthcoming with information in person. On the other hand, if you are skilled at being a sympathetic listener and you are unafraid to ask questions that might be sensitive, interviews can be used. For more discussion on this topic, see "Asking the Tough Questions" section on page 242.

If the participant is not telling the complete truth, this will usually become apparent when you seek additional details. A skilled interviewer can identify the rare individual who is not being honest and disregard that data. When a participant is telling a story that is different from what actually happened, he or she will not be able to give you specific examples but will speak only in generalities.

TIP

With continued prodding, a dishonest participant will likely become frustrated and attempt to change the subject. If you doubt the veracity of a participant's responses, you can always throw away the data and interview another participant. Refer to "Know When to Move On" section on page 247.

You are now prepared to conduct an interview. In this section, we walk you through the steps.

First, Table 9.4 covers in general the sequence and timing of events to conduct an interview. It is based on a one-hour session and will obviously need to be adjusted for shorter or longer sessions. These are approximate times based on our personal experience and should be used only as a guide.

Interviewing is a skill and takes practice. You should observe the five phases of an interview and monitor the interviewing relationship throughout.

The Five Phases of an Interview

Whether the interview lasts ten minutes or two hours, a good interview is conducted in phases. There are five main phases to be familiar with.

Table 9.4: Timeline for a one-hour interview (approximate times)

Approximate duration	Procedure
5-10 minutes	Introduction (welcome participant, complete forms, and give instructions)
3-5 minutes	Warm-up (easy, nonthreatening questions)
30-45 minutes	Body of the session (detailed questions)
	This will vary depending on the number of questions
5-10 minutes	Cooling-off (summarize interview; easy questions)
5 minutes	Wrap-up (thank participant and escort him or her out)

The Introduction

This should not be too long. If it is over ten minutes, you are probably giving the participant too many instructions and other things to remember. This is the first opportunity you have to encourage participants to answer honestly and feel free to say when they cannot answer one of your questions. The following is a sample introduction:

Begin by introducing yourself. If there are other observers in the room, introduce them, too.	→	My name is Jane Doe and I work for TravelMyWay.
Thank the participants for coming.	→	Thank you for coming in today! We will spend the next hour talking about your experience booking travel online.
State the purpose of the interview and why the participant has been asked to participate.	→	I understand that you are a current user of the TravelMyWay app and that you signed up for our Customer Participation Program. We would like to learn how we could improve our site to better suit our customers' needs.
If there are people watching in another room, mention their presence in generic terms.	→	We have a couple members of the product development team in another room watching this session, and
Be sure to ask permission to audio or video record the session.	→	—if you do not mind—I would like to make a recording.
Say *why* you want to record the session.	→	This will allow me to go back at a later time and review your comments so that I am not distracted from our conversation by taking notes.
Help the participant understand that you think of them as the expert, that you are not invested in them liking any product or company, and that you will not judge their answers.	→	I am not a member of the product team. I am a neutral evaluator, so nothing you say today will hurt my feelings. Your honest opinions can only help us improve our product. If you do not have an opinion or cannot answer any of the questions I ask, please feel free to say so.
Explain any confidentiality agreements and consent forms that must be signed.	→	Since this product is not on the market yet, you will need to sign a nondisclosure agreement in which you promise not to discuss this product with anyone until it is put on the market or until two years from now.
Make sure participants understand they are not obliged to continue the session and may leave, without consequence, at any time.	→	You are free to leave at any time. Please stop me at any point if you have questions.

Warm-Up

Always start an interview with easy, nonthreatening questions where you are sure you will get positive answers to ease the participant into the interview. You can confirm demographic information (e.g., occupation, company), how the participant first discovered your product, etc. You may even allow the participant to vent his or her top five likes and dislikes of your product. The participant should focus his or her thoughts on your product and forget about work, traffic, the video cameras, and so on. This is best done with easy questions that feel more like a conversation and less like a verbal survey or test. It is best to avoid asking seemingly innocuous questions like "Do you enjoy working here?" or "Tell me about a recent problem you had." Negative questions or ones that might elicit a negative response tend to taint the rest of the interview.

Five to ten minutes may be sufficient for the warm-up, but if the participant is still clearly uncomfortable, this could be longer. However, do not waste the participant's time (and yours) with useless small talk. The warm-up should still be focused on the topic of the interview.

Body of the Session

Here is the place where you should ask the questions you wrote and tested (see "Write the Questions" section, page 225 and "Test Your Questions" section, page 233). Present questions in a logical manner (e.g., chronological), beginning with general questions and move into more detailed ones. Avoid haphazardly jumping from one topic to another. This should be the bulk (about 80%) of your interview time with the participant.

TIP

Another reason for practicing the interview questions early on is because it is not always obvious what will be "logical" in an interview. One trick is to have someone else read the interview script aloud. It is easier to notice a non sequitur when someone else is asking the questions than it is to notice them as you read your own writing.

Cooling-Off

Your interview may have been intense with very detailed questions. At this point, you may want to pull back and ask more general questions or summarize the interview. Ask any follow-up questions in light of the entire interview. One cool-off question we like in particular is "Is there anything else I should have asked you about?" This is a great trick that will often pivot an entire interview.

Wrap-Up

You should demonstrate that the interview is now at a close. This is a good time to ask the participant whether there are any questions for you. Some people like to do this by closing a notebook and putting away their pen (if they were taking notes), changing their seat position, or turning off the audio and/or video recorder. Thank the person for his or her time.

Your Role as the Interviewer

Think of your job as an interviewer as a coach that helps participants provide the information you need. "Active listening" means that you must judge if each response has adequately addressed your question, be on the lookout for areas of deeper exploration, and monitor the interviewing relationship throughout. Interviewing is an active process because you know the information you are seeking and must coax that information from the participant. Because of this, interviewing can be an intense activity for the interviewer.

Keep on Track

It is easy for unstructured interviews to go off track. The participant may go into far more detail than you need but not know that. A participant may also digress to topics that are outside the scope of the study. It is your job to keep the participant focused on the topic at hand and move on to the next topic when you have the information needed. Below are some polite comments to get participants back on track or to move them on to a new topic:

I can tell that you have a lot of detail to provide about this, but because of our time constraints, I need to move on to a new topic. If we have time at the end, I would like to come back to this discussion.

That's really interesting. I was wondering if we could go back to topic XYZ for a moment …

I'm sorry to stop you, but a moment ago, you were discussing XYZ. Can you tell me more about that?

Silence Is Golden

One of the most difficult skills in interviewing is patience. You never want to complete participants' thoughts for them or put words in their mouths. Give each participant time to complete his or her thoughts. If you do not have enough information after adequate silence, then follow up with another question or restate the participant's answer (see "Reflecting" section, page 248). Of course, if the participant is struggling with a word and you are sure you know what the participant is trying to say, offer the word or phrase the participant is searching for, especially if the participant says, "It's on the tip of my tongue. Do you know what I'm talking about?"

Think of silence as a tool in your tool belt. An interviewee may wonder how much detail you are looking for in response to a question. In that case, he or she will likely provide a brief answer and then wait to see whether you move on. If you do not, the participant has been "given permission" to provide more detail. Counting to five before either moving on to the next question or probing for more details can provide adequate time for the participant to continue. Counting to ten can seem uncomfortable to both you and the participant but can be a useful method for coaxing a response from a reticent interviewee. Always pay attention to the participant's body language (e.g., sitting forward, poised to make another statement) to determine whether he or she has more to say.

It is possible to go too far with your pauses and risk giving participants the silent treatment. That is why **acknowledgment tokens** are so important. Acknowledgment tokens are words like "oh," "ah," "mm hm," and "uh huh" that carry no content. Since they are free of content, they are unobtrusive and require almost no processing by the participant, so he or she can continue unimpeded with a train of thought. These devices reassure participants that you hear them, understand what is being said, and want them to continue. Speakers expect a reaction from listeners, so acknowledgment tokens complete the "conversational loop" and keep the interviewing relationship a partnership, rather than a one-way dialog. Tokens like "mm hm" and "uh huh" are called "continuers" because they are not intrusive or directive. Tokens like "OK" and "yeah" imply agreement, which you may not want to imply to participants, revealing your personal opinions (Boren & Ramey, 2000). However, this varies hugely from culture to culture. For example, in Japanese, if an interviewer failed to say "hai" (yes) often, it would be considered very rude.

Remain Attentive

Have you had the experience where someone has been talking for the past several minutes and you have no idea what he or she has been saying? If you are tired or bored, it is easy to zone out. Obviously, this is a faux pas in any conversation but particularly problematic in an interview. If you are tired or bored, there is a good chance that the participant is, too.

Take a break at a logical stopping point. This will give you a chance to walk around and wake up. Evaluate how much you have engaged the participant in the interview. If this is an unstructured interview, you should be engaging the participant frequently for clarification, examples, and reflection. If it is a highly structured interview, the interviewee's answers should be short, followed by your next question. In either case, you should be engaging in the interview (without interrupting the participant, of course). After the break, take a moment to ask the interviewee to briefly summarize his or her last response. This will help the interview pick up where it left off and get you back on track.

TIP

Running multiple interviews in one day may speed up the information gathering process, but it will also leave you exhausted and without adequate time to debrief with your notetaker and any other observers to discuss what you have learned. We recommend running no more than four one-hour interviews per day. Conducting more interviews per day for several days will likely leave you exhausted and degrade the quality of your data and lengthen the time it takes you to analyze those data.

If you are going from city to city conducting interviews and must conduct, for example, seven interviews in two days, you do not have much of a choice. In this case, we recommend bringing a colleague to tag-team the interviews with you. Alternating the roles of notetaker and interviewer can give you both a modest break. At least you will not have to be fully "switched on" for every interview (encouraging participants, following up on questions).

Also, be sure to allow a small break between interviews. The more time you can give yourself the better. You will need enough time to get up, stretch your legs, take a bathroom break, and grab a beverage. Allow yourself time to eat, too, because if you cram all of your interviews back to back, your energy is sure to run out. We hope it goes without saying, but *never* eat your lunch while interviewing a participant; that is rude and distracting.

If you have conducted several interviews on the same topic before, it is easy to assume that you have heard it all. What new information could the sixth participant provide? If you think you already know the answers to the questions, you can find yourself hearing what you want to hear or expect to hear, thereby missing new information. Every participant has something unique to provide—although it may not be significant enough to warrant additional interviews. If you have conducted several interviews and feel confident that you have gained the required information, do not recruit additional participants. However, once the participant is in the door, you owe him or her the same attention that you gave the very first participant. Keep an open mind and you will be surprised at what you can learn.

Asking the Tough Questions

To help determine if your questions are sensitive or embarrassing, run your questions by someone not connected with your project. Sometimes, you may need to ask questions that are embarrassing or cover sensitive topics. As we mentioned earlier, this may be better done via surveys, but if you think that there is a need to ask a difficult question in an interview, wait until you have developed a rapport with the participant. When you ask the question, explain why you need the information. This lets the participant know that you are asking for a legitimate reason and not just out of curiosity. The participant will be more likely to answer your question and relieve any tension. For example,

Say why you want the information and how you'll use it. →

This next question is about the range your salary falls in. I'm asking this only because we believe that people who fall within specific salary ranges are sometimes more or less likely to book their travel using an app. To help us understand this, we are asking everyone about their salary range—if they feel comfortable. Would you mind stating which of the following ranges your salary falls in?

Using Examples

No matter how hard you try to make your questions clear, a participant may still have difficulty understanding exactly what you are asking. Sometimes, rewording the question is not sufficient and an example is necessary for clarification. Since the example could introduce bias, you want to do this as a last resort. Having some canned examples for each question and then asking colleagues to check those examples for bias will help immensely.

Give the interviewee a moment to think about the question and attempt to answer it. If it is clear that the participant does not understand the question or asks for an example, provide one of the canned examples. If the participant still does not understand, you could either provide a second example or move to the next question.

Wrong: "What are some of the discount airlines, such as Jet Blue, that you prefer to travel on?"

Right: "Have you traveled on a discount (lower-fare) airline?<*User does not understand what you mean by discount airlines; read a complete list of discount airlines.*>If you have, which ones do you prefer to travel on?"

Watch for Generalities

Interviewees will often speak in general terms because they believe it is more useful to provide summary descriptions or typical situations rather than specific examples. This is usually the result of a generalized question (see below):

Interviewer: "Tell me what happens when you contact the agent on call."

Participant: "When you contact the agent on call, you wait and wait and wait. They don't pick up."

If you are looking for specific, detailed answers, do not ask generalized questions. Ask for **significant events**. Since the best indicator of the present is the past, ask the interviewee to describe a particular past event that best exemplifies the situation. Keep in mind our earlier discussion about memory limitations and telescoping (see page 231). Below is a sample interview asking for a significant event:

Generalized Question

Interviewer: "What has been your experience booking travel online?"

Participant: "Oh, I always have a terrible time. Either I can't remember my password or the session times out before I can make my decision so I have to start all over. It's always something."

Follow-up for a significant event

Interviewer: "Can you tell me what was particularly frustrating about the last time you tried to book travel online?"

Participant: "Well, the last time wasn't so bad. I know my session always ends up timing out before I can finish so this time I was prepared. I did research on the flight and hotel in advance so that I could enter in all the information quickly. I logged in, selected the airline I wanted, entered in the flight dates and times, and then chose the flight that I knew I wanted. That went very quickly. I couldn't book the hotel though. I knew which hotel I wanted but the dates I needed were not showing up as available. That annoyed me since I had already called the hotel to ask for availability. I ended up having to leave the site and just book the hotel over the phone. I didn't get any kind of discount, so that sucked."

Do Not Force Choices

Do not force opinions or choices from participants. If you ask an interviewee to make a choice from a list of options but he or she says that it does not matter or all of them are fine, take this as an opportunity to learn more about what the participant thinks about each option. By asking the participant to verbalize (and therefore think more about) each option, he or she may then show more of a preference for one option over others or at least help you understand *why* he or she feels the way he or she does. If the participant states that all options *are* equal, do not force him or her to make a choice. Likewise, if the participant states that he or she does not have an opinion on something, forcing him or her to elaborate will only generate annoyance (see example below).

Interviewer: "Which of the following customer rewards would you most like to receive when booking a certain number of trips with the TravelMyWay app?"

- 10% discount on your next plane ticket
- Free upgrade on a car rental or plane ticket
- Free night at the hotel of your choice
- 3% cash rebate

Participant may not have understood that a single response was desired →	**Participant**: "All of those sound good to me!"
Interviewer restates question →	**Interviewer**: "Do you have a preference for one over the other?"
	Participant: "No. They are all about equal."
Interviewer tries to determine if participant has a preference →	**Interviewer**: "Can you tell me the pros and cons you can see with each option?"

Watch for Markers

Sometimes, participants throw out **markers**. These are key events to the participant that you can probe into for more rich information. You should search for more details *only* if you believe it will provide relevant detail to your study—and not out of curiosity. Below is an interview excerpt with a marker and appropriate follow-up:

	Interviewer: "Can you tell me about a difficult time you had using the TravelMyWay app?"
Marker →	**Participant**: "Well, it was right after my aunt passed away. I needed to get a plane ticket back home quickly, but I couldn't get any on your site."
Interviewer detects marker and seeks relevant information →	**Interviewer**: "You mentioned your aunt had just passed away. What made it difficult to get a plane ticket at that time?"
	Participant: "I just knew I needed to get home quickly. Unfortunately, the seats would have cost a fortune since it was a last-minute travel. I heard that airlines offered bereavement discounts but I couldn't figure out how to do that on your site. I did a search on your site but I couldn't find anything. I was hoping that you had an on-call agent like WillCall.com, but you didn't."
	Interviewer: "What happened next?"
	Participant: "I was so stressed out that I ended up leaving your site and going to WillCall.com instead. They were able to get me the discount pretty quickly."

The participant provided the marker of her aunt passing away. That was critical to her. She was stressed out and could not find the information she needed. She wanted someone to personally help her and provide some support, but the app could not do it. Consequently, she now has a strong negative memory of the TravelMyWay app and a positive one of the competitor. Following up on that marker allows us to better understand the context of what happened and why the experience was so difficult for the participant. If the participant drops such a marker inadvertently and does not feel comfortable elaborating on it, he or she will let you know the topic is off-limits.

Select the Right Types of Probe

Probes are questions used to get interviewees to clarify or elaborate on responses. Your probes for detail should be as unbiased as your initial question to the participant. There are closed-ended and open-ended probes, just like the initial question you asked. A closed-ended probe would be something like "Were you using Chrome or Safari?" An open-ended probe might be "Tell me about the browser(s) you use." Keep all probes neutral and do not ask the participant to defend his or her choices.

Wrong: "Why did you do that?"

Right: "Can you tell me more about your decision?"

Table 9.5 provides an excellent comparison of different types of biased and unbiased probes and what makes each probe biased.

Some interviewers use the strategy of "playing dumb" to get more detail out of participants. By downplaying what you know, participants will be more explicit and may want to impress you with their knowledge. This may work in some cases, but if you slip and reveal in a question or probe that you know more than you are letting on, the participant can feel betrayed, duped, or patronized. This will clearly harm the interviewing relationship. As a result, we recommend being honest about what you know and understand while making it clear that your knowledge is limited and that the participant is there to increase your knowledge.

In that sense, adopting a beginner's mind and asking naive questions will help you be more open to what your participants have to say and instill confidence in them that they are the experts, not you.

Watch Your Body Language

Your tone and body language can affect the way a participant perceives your questions. Be alert to your biases. Is there an answer to your question that you would like the participant to provide? Is there an answer you expect? Your expectations and preferences can be conveyed in your tone, body language, and the way you phrase

Table 9.5: Biased and unbiased probes (adapted from Dumas & Redish, 1999)

Ask	Instead of	Why
Can you tell me what you are thinking right now? What are you trying to do?	Are you thinking ______? Are you trying to ______?	Even though you may think you know what they are thinking, your job is to get *them* to say it. Also, you do not want to put words into their mouths, because you may be wrong.
What are you thinking? Can you explain to me what you are trying to do?	Why are you ______? Are you trying to ______ because ______?	By asking participants why they are doing something, they may feel that you are asking them to justify their actions and, therefore, think that they are going about the task incorrectly.
Can you explain to me your train of thought right now? (After the task is ended) Why did you try to ______?	Are you trying to______?	It is, however, acceptable to ask participants why they went about a task in a certain way after the task has been ended or at the end of the test if future tasks have components similar to the task you are questioning them about.
Did you find the product easy or difficult to use? Were the instructions clear or confusing? Were error messages helpful or hindering?	Did you find the product easy to use? Did you find the product difficult to use? Were the error messages helpful?	Trying to get someone to express an opinion on a specific usability attribute is not always easy. Therefore, you may find that you need to guide participants by specifying the attribute you want them to react to. It is important to use both ends of the spectrum when you do this so that they do not perceive you as encouraging either a positive or negative answer. Also, by doing so, you will encourage a more informative response. Instead of responding "No (it was not easy)," they are more likely to say "I found it very difficult to use," or "It was pretty easy." You then can follow up by asking them "Why?"
What are you feeling? How did you feel when you were doing ______?	Are you feeling confused? Are you feeling frustrated?	Sometimes, participants need to stop and think. Though they may appear confused or frustrated, they may just be contemplating. Do not risk inserting your guess about how they are feeling.
Would you change anything about this (product, screen, design, etc.)?	Do you think______ would improve the product?	Unless the design team is considering a particular design change, you should never suggest what changes participants should talk about.
Are there any changes you would make to______ to make it easier to use?	If we changed ______to______, do you think that it would be easier to use?	If there is a design change that the design team wants to explore specifically, ask the participants to react to it *after* they have made their initial suggestions.

questions, probes, and summaries. For example, looking bored or not making eye contact when you disagree or sitting on the edge of your seat and nodding vigorously when the participant is confirming your suspicions will clearly reveal your biases. Your biases are even conveyed in the responses that you do not follow up on. Watching yourself on video can help you identify those biases. If you are alert to your biases, you can better control them. You can also use your body language to "hack your body for better interviews" (see http://www.gv.com/lib/how-to-hack-your-body-language-for-better-interviews for an overview).

Know When to Move On

Knowing when to let go is as important as knowing when to follow up. A participant may not be as forthcoming as you would like, or maybe, the person is just plainly lying. As rare as that is, you should know how and when to move on. Remember: this is an interview, not an interrogation. Even if you suspect that the participant is not being completely honest, continued badgering is as rude as calling the participant a liar. Once it is clear that the participant cannot provide the details you are looking for, drop the line of questioning and move on. If necessary, you can throw out that participant's data later. For ethical reasons, you must remember to treat the participant with respect, and part of that is knowing when to let a topic of discussion drop.

Reflecting

To verify that you understand what the participant has told you, it is essential to summarize, reword, or reflect the participant's responses. You are not probing for more details but confirming the detail you already have. It is not necessary to do this after every response, especially if the response is brief and straightforward as in structured interviews. However, if the participant's response has been lengthy, detailed, or not completely clear, you should summarize and restate what the participant has said to check for accuracy. A reflection of the earlier interview excerpt (see page 245) is provided below:

> **I just want to make sure that I have captured your experience correctly. You needed to purchase tickets for immediate travel, and you were looking for a bereavement discount. You couldn't find information on bereavement discounts or an agent to assist you using the TravelMyWay app, so you used the TravelTravel app because you knew they had an agent on call. They were then able to get you the tickets at a discount. Does that summarize your experience correctly?**

Reflections help build rapport by demonstrating that you were listening and understood the participant's comments. They can also be used to search for more information. The participant may clarify any incorrect information or provide additional information, when responding to your summary.

At no time should you insert analysis into your summary or in response to a participant's statement. In other words, do not try to provide a solution to a problem the participant has had and explanations for why the product behaved as it did or why you think the participant made a certain choice. In the example above, you would not want to inform the participant where she could have found the bereavement discount on your site. You are not a counselor, and you should not be defending your product. You are there to collect information from the interviewee—nothing more. Ask for observations, not predictions or hypotheses.

Empathy and Antagonism

When you are speaking with someone—even if it is someone you barely know—doesn't it make you feel better to know that the other person understands how you feel? A skilled interviewer is able to empathize with the participant without introducing bias. Keep in mind that this is not a conversation in the traditional sense; you are not there to contribute your own thoughts and feelings to the discussion. In the earlier example, the interviewer could have shown empathy by stating: "That [bereavement] must have been a difficult time for you." An inappropriate response would have been: "I know exactly how you feel. When my grandmother passed away, I had to pay an arm and a leg for my plane ticket." The interview is not about you. You do not have to be a robot, devoid of emotion, in order to prevent bias, but also know what is appropriate and what is inappropriate. Make eye contact and use your body language to show the participant that you are engaged, that you understand what he or she is saying, and that you accept the participant regardless of what he or she has said.

TIP

Do not correct participants. Rather, seek to understand *why* they believe what they believe. Refocus any urge you may have to correct a participant into an opportunity to understand why he or she perceives things differently from you.

Transitions

Your questions or topics for discussion should transition smoothly from one topic to another. This will allow participants to continue on a track of thought, and the conversation will appear more natural. If you must change to a new topic of discussion and there is not a smooth transition, you can state: "That's excellent information you've given me. While I make a note of it, can you think about how you would <*introduce different topic*>?" This lets the participant know that he or she should not be looking for a connection or follow-up from the last question. If the participant believes that you are trying to probe more deeply into the previous topic, he or she may get confused or misinterpret your next question. A simple transition statement gives closure to the last topic and sets the stage for the next one.

Avoid negative connectors like "but" and "however." These might signal to a participant that he or she has spoken too long or has said something incorrect. The person is likely to be more cautious when answering the following questions.

Monitoring the Relationship with the Interviewee

Like all user research activities, interviews are a giving and taking of information. Since it is one-on-one, the relationship is more personal. To get the most out of participants, it is important to monitor the relationship and treat the participant ethically. You want to make sure that the participant is comfortable, engaged, and trusting. If the participant does not feel you are being honest or is wondering what the motivation is behind your questions, he or she will be guarded and will not provide the full details you are looking for.

Watch the Participant's Body Language

Does the participant seem tense, nervous, bored, or angry? Is he or she looking at the clock or is his or her attention lapsing? Do *you* feel tense? If so, the participant likely feels tense too. You may have jumped into the detailed, difficult, or sensitive questions before you established a good rapport. If possible, go back to easier questions, establish the purpose and motivations of the study, and be sure that the participant is a willing partner in the activity. If a particular line of questioning is the problem, it is best to abandon those questions and move on. A break may help. Sometimes, a participant is just having a bad day and nothing you say or do will help. At that point, ending the interview can be the kindest act possible for the both of you.

Suggested Resources for Additional Reading

Although you should pay attention to a person's body language to determine whether he or she is tired, uncomfortable, or annoyed, we do not advocate ascribing meaning to it. Body language is ambiguous; a person may be staring at the floor because they are shy, rather than bored. It is more important to note *changes* in behaviors over time, rather than a singular action/behavior. To learn more about what people's gestures and body language might mean, refer to the following:

- Ekman, P. (2007). *Emotions revealed, second edition: Recognizing faces and feelings to improve communication and emotional life*. Holt Paperbacks.
- Pease, B., & Pease, A. (2006). *The definitive book of body language*. Bantam.

Fighting for Control

If you find yourself competing with the participant for control of the interview, ask yourself why. Is the participant refusing to answer the questions you are asking or is he or she interrupting before you can complete your questions? Just as the interview is not about your thoughts or opinions, it is not up to the participant to ask the questions or drive the interview. At some point, the participant misunderstood the guidelines of the relationship. Begin with polite attempts to regain control, such as the following:

Because we have a limited amount of time and there are several topics that I would like to cover with you, I am going to need to limit the amount of time we can discuss each topic.

If the participant refuses to be a cooperative partner in the interviewing relationship and you do not feel you are obtaining useful information, simply let the participant go on and then write off the data. In extreme cases, it is best for all parties to end the interview early. If you have recorded the session, watch or listen to it with a colleague to see whether you can identify where the interviewing relationship went awry and how you can avoid it in the future. Think of this as a learning opportunity where you can practice and improve your conversational control skills.

Hold Your Opinions

Even though the interview is not about you, if the participant directly asks your opinion or asks you a question, you do not want to seem evasive because it could harm the rapport you have established. If you believe your response could bias the participant's future responses, your reply should be straightforward:

Actually, I don't want to bias your responses so I can't discuss that right now. I really want to hear your honest thoughts. I would be happy to talk about my experiences after the interview.

If you are sure that the question and your response will not have an effect on the remainder of the interview, you can answer the question, but keep it brief.

Dos and Don'ts

We have provided many recommendations about how to conduct a successful interview. It takes a lot of sessions and being in a lot of different scenarios to be a good interviewer. Do not get discouraged. For easy referral, some of the key tips are summarized in Figure 9.4.

DO:

- Divide the interview into the five major phases
- Ask personal or sensitive questions only after you have developed a rapport with the participant and state why you need this information
- Use acknowledgment tokens to keep the participant talking
- For questions where you provide options, if the person says they do not have a preference, ask them to describe the qualities of each choice
- Provide background information only if necessary and keep that information factual
- Be alert to your biases and remain neutral
- Know when to stop probing for detail
- Reflect as accurately as possible what the participant has told you
- Empathize with the participant
- Provide transitions between different topics
- Monitor the interviewing relationship
- Keep the participant focused on the topic
- Choose an effective method for recording data
- Speak plainly

DON'T:

- Jump into detailed or sensitive questions without first developing a rapport with the participant
- Assume you know the participant's response
- Interrupt the participant, put words in his/her mouth, or complete his/her sentences
- Force participants to make choices or have an opinion
- Attempt to fill every silence
- Insert your own observations or analysis in the reflection
- Disagree with the participant or state that he/she is wrong
- Provide information about yourself, your opinions, or similar experiences
- Allow a poor interviewing relationship to continue unchecked
- Use jargon, slang, or geek speak

Figure 9.4: Dos and don'ts when conducting an interview.

TIP

If you look at a transcript of a bad interview, one of the first clues you might see is a one-to-one ratio of participant comments to interviewer comments/questions, especially in an unstructured interview. However, an abundance of participant comments does not necessarily indicate a successful interview. It is your job to keep the participant focused and not allow him or her to delve deeply into irrelevant topics or go beyond the scope of the study.

Data Analysis and Interpretation

Depending on the purpose of and outlet for your interviews, either you can wait until you have conducted all the interviews before analyzing the data, or you can do preliminary analysis following each interview. For UX professionals, we recommend the latter because it can give you insights for future interviews. You may want to delve into more detail on questions or remove questions that are not providing value. And as any UX professional can attest to, stakeholders often ask for results before a study is complete. It can help if you have something more substantial to give them than just a few interesting quotes that stand out in your mind. On the other hand, for some academic studies, conducting all the interviews prior to data analysis may be more appropriate because it increases standardization across interviews, which is often necessary for scientific publication.

As with any activity, the longer you wait to get to the analysis, the less you will remember about the session. The notes will be more difficult to interpret, and you will have to rely heavily on the recordings. The more you have to rely on the recordings, the more time it will take you to analyze the data. Either way, hold a debrief session as soon as possible with your notetaker and any other observers to discuss what you learned. Review the recording to fill in any gaps or expand on ideas if necessary, and add any additional notes or quotes. If the session is still fresh in your mind, it will not take as long to review the recording.

Transcription

For some interview studies, you may want to have the audio recordings transcribed into text (e.g., if it is critical to have the exact words your participant uses recorded, if you want to publish your findings in some scientific venues). Transcription is typically done in one of three ways: verbatim, edited, or summarized. *Verbatim* transcripts capture a record of exactly what was done by both the interviewer and respondent including "ums," "ahs," and misstatements. For some types of analysis (e.g., linguistic analysis), these word crutches are important. When such detail is not necessary, you may choose an edited or summarized transcript. *Edited* transcripts typically do not include word crutches or misstatements. *Summarized* transcripts typically contain an edited and condensed version of the questions asked or topics raised by the interviewer since these are known in advance, along with the respondent's comments.

Depending on whether you conducted a structured, semi-structured, or unstructured interview, you will have different types of data to analyze.

Structured Data

If you are conducting structured or semi-structured interviews, begin by tallying the responses to closed-ended questions. For example, how many people so far have selected each option in a multiple-choice question or what is the average rating given in a **Likert scale** question? Structured data from an interview are equivalent to survey data, with the exception that you may have to refer to recordings rather than data from paper or online forms. Chapter 10 has a detailed discussion of closed-ended question data analysis (see "Data Analysis and Interpretation" section, page 290).

Unstructured Data

Unstructured data are more time-consuming to analyze, in our experience so much so that it often goes unanalyzed. We recommend three strategies for analyzing unstructured data: categorizing and counting, affinity diagramming, and qualitative content/thematic analysis.

Categorizing and Counting

If you are conducting unstructured interviews, you can begin by identifying potential categories in the text as a whole. What is the range of responses you are getting? What is the most frequent response? Once you have identified categories, you can count the number of instances each category is represented in the data and organize this by participant or as represented in the interviews overall. After you have tallied the most frequent responses, select some illustrative quotes to represent each category of response.

Affinity Diagram

An affinity diagram is a method for analyzing interview data quickly. Similar findings or concepts are grouped together to identify themes or trends in the data. A detailed discussion of what an affinity diagram is, how to create one, and how to analyze the data from one is provided in Chapter 12 on page 340.

Qualitative Content/Thematic Analysis

Content analysis is a method of sorting, synthesizing, and organizing unstructured textual data from an interview or other source (e.g., survey, screen scrape of online forum). Content analysis may be done manually (by hand or software-assisted) or using software alone. When done manually (by hand or software-assisted), researchers must read and reread interviewee responses, generate a scheme to categorize the answers, develop rules for assigning responses to the categories, and ensure that responses are reliably assigned to categories. Because these rules are imperfect and interpretation of interviewee responses is difficult, researchers may categorize answers differently. Therefore, to ensure that answers are reliably assigned to categories, two or more researchers must code each interview and a predetermined rate of interrater reliability (e.g., Cohen's kappa) must be achieved (see How to Calculate Interrater Reliability [Kappa] for details).

Several tools are available for purchase to help you analyze qualitative data. They range in purpose from quantitative, focusing on counting the frequency of specific words or content, to helping you look for patterns or trends in your data. If you would like to learn more about the available tools, what they do, and where to find them, refer to Chapter 8, "Qualitative Analysis Tools" section on page 208.

HOW TO CALCULATE INTERRATER RELIABILITY (KAPPA)

To determine reliability, you need a measure of **interrater reliability** (IRR) or **interrater agreement.** Interrater reliability is the degree to which two or more observers assign the same rating, label, or category to an observation, behavior, or segment of text. In this case, we are interested in the amount of agreement or reliability between volunteers coding the same data points. High reliability indicates that individual biases were minimized and that another researcher using the same categories would likely come to the same conclusion that a segment of text would fit within the specified category.

The simplest form of interrater agreement or reliability is $\left(\text{agreements} / \left(\text{agreements} + \text{disagreements}\right)\right)$. However, this measure of simple reliability does not take into account agreements due to chance. For example, if we had four categories, we would expect volunteers to agree 25% of the time simply due to chance. To account for agreements due to chance in our reliability analysis, we must use a variation. One common variation is Krippendorff's Alpha (KALPHA), which does not suffer from some of the limitations of other methods (i.e., sample size, more than two coders, missing data). De Swert (2012) created a step-by-step manual for how to calculate KALPHA in SPSS. Another very common alternative is **Cohen's kappa**, which should be used when you are analyzing **nominal data** and have two coders/volunteers.

To measure Cohen's kappa, follow these steps:

Step 1. Organize data into a contingency table. Agreements between coders will increment the diagonal cells and disagreements will increment other cells. For example, since coder 1 and coder 2 agree that observation 1 goes in category A, tally one agreement in the cell A, A. The disagreement in observation 3, on the other hand, goes in cell A, B.

Raw data:

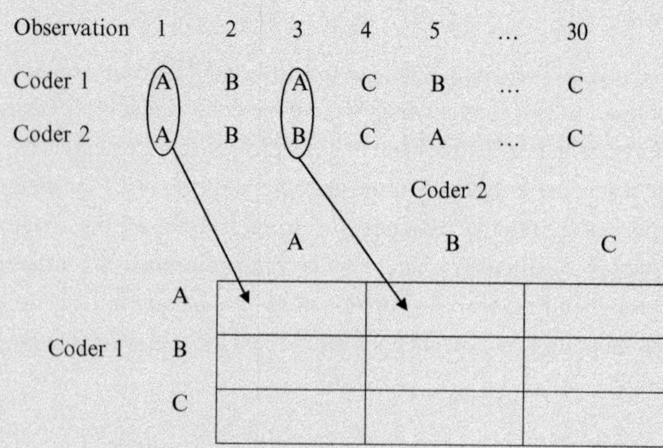

Step 2. Compute the row, column, and overall sums for the table. The row, column, and total should be the same number.

		Coder 2			
		A	B	C	
	A	6	2	1	9
Coder 1	B	1	9	1	11
	C	1	1	8	10
		8	12	10	30

Step 3. Compute the total number of actual agreements by summing the diagonal cells:

$$\sum \text{agreement} = 6 + 9 + 8 = 23$$

Step 4. Compute the expected agreement for each category. For example, to compute the expected agreement for "A," "A":

$$\sum \text{expected agreement} = \frac{\text{row total} \times \text{column total}}{\text{overall total}}$$

Step 5. Sum the expected agreements due to chance:

$$\sum \text{expected agreement} = 2.4 = 4.4 = 3.3 = 10.1$$

Step 6. Compute Cohen's kappa:

$$\text{Kappa} = \frac{\sum \text{agreement} - \sum \text{expected agreement}}{\text{total} - \sum \text{expected agreement}}$$

Step 7. Compare Cohen's kappa to benchmarks from Landis and Koch (1977):

<0.00	Poor
0.00-0.20	Slight
0.21-0.40	Fair
0.41-0.6	Moderate
0.61-0.80	Substantial
0.81-1.00	Almost perfect

In our example, Cohen's kappa of 0.746 falls within the "substantial" benchmark category. Generally, Cohen's kappas of greater than 0.7 are considered acceptable.

Step 8. Resolve disagreements among coders by having coders discuss the reasons they disagreed and come to an agreement.

Communicating the Findings

In this section, we discuss some of the ways in which interview data can be effectively communicated. There are a few different ways that you can present the data. It all depends on the goals of your study and the method you feel best represents your data. In the end, a good report illuminates all the relevant data, provides a coherent story, and tells the stakeholders what to do next (see Table 9.6 for sample recommendations based on interview data).

Over Time

Your interview may cover a period of time, such as asking a travel agent to describe his or her day from the first cup of coffee in the morning through turning off the computer monitor at the end of the day. Or you may ask someone a series of questions that cover the first six months of training on the job.

If your questions cover a period of time, it makes sense to analyze the data along a timeline. Use the results from your initial categorization to start filling in the timeline. In our travel agent example, what is the first thing that the majority of travel agents do in the morning? What are the activities that fill their days? Then, use individual anecdotes or details to fill in gaps and provide interesting information that does not fit neatly into a category. It can be those additional details that provide the most value.

By Topic

Your questions may not follow a timeline but simply address different topics related to a domain or user type. In these types of interviews, you may wish to analyze and present the data by question. Provide the range of answers for each question and the average response. Alternatively, you can group the data from multiple questions into larger categories and then discuss the results for each category. An affinity diagram is helpful in these types of interviews to identify higher-level categories, if they exist (see "Affinity Diagram" section, page 253).

Table 9.6: Sample table of recommendations

Issue	Recommendation
Search team should work with the UI group to identify methods for improving the search engine and display of search results	• The most frequently stated difficulty participants had with our site was finding information using our search facility.
Nine out of ten participants asked for an on-call agent to help when they had a difficulty	• Conduct a usability evaluation of site to improve overall usability. • Provide a FAQ based on the results of the interviews and questions we have received via e-mail to date. • Investigate the feasibility of providing on-call agents.
When asked for additional services we can provide, half the users suggested being able to arrange transportation to and from the airport (taxi, hotel shuttle, etc.)	• Investigate the feasibility of purchasing shuttle tickets from our site. • Ask associated hotels that provide shuttles to and from airports whether we can arrange this service online.

By Participant

If each participant and his or her results are widely different, it can be difficult to categorize the data. This may be the result of difficulties with your user profile and recruiting, or it may be intentional in the case where you want to examine a variety of user types. It may make more sense to summarize the results per participant to illustrate those differences. Similarly, you may choose to analyze the data per company (customer), industry, or some other category membership.

Pulling It All Together

We began by discussing the best uses for interviews and the different types of interviews (structured, unstructured, and semi-structured). Proper wording of questions in interviews was then discussed in detail. If the questions in an interview are constructed poorly, the results of your study will be biased or will not provide the information you need. We also discussed how to conduct an interview, including the five phases of an interview, your role as an interviewer, and recording the data from the interviews. Finally, methods for analyzing the data and presenting your results were discussed.

The results from your interviews can be incorporated into documentation such as the Detailed Design Document. Ideally, additional user research techniques should be used along the way to capture new requirements and verify your current requirements. To summarize, below we list a few tips for conducting your next interview.

Interview Tips

- Begin with general questions and follow up with specific questions. Asking specific questions first may lead the participant into talking about only what he or she thinks you want to hear about.
- Unless using a structured interview, do not feel you need to ask every question on your list. Let the participant talk, and then, follow up with those that are most interesting for the purposes of your study.
- Videotape everything, if possible. Audiotapes are insufficient in situations where participants constantly refer to things with vague references. Be sure to get permission from the participant before any recording (audio or video).
- Involve your product team early and often. Encourage team members to accompany you and debrief after each visit with those who do. This will increase their buy-in to the need for research. Also, understanding what they are taking away from the interview will help you understand their priorities better.
- Understand your own notetaking skills in deciding whether or not to type or write. Taking notes on the laptop may save a step, but slow or inaccurate typing drags down the interview. Additionally, the second step of typing up notes is a great double-check.
- At the beginning of each recording, say the date, time, and participant number and remind the participant that you are recording the interview. For example, say, "Today is March 14th, 2015, and this is participant number 9. The red light is now on and the voice recorder is now recording." Giving the date and participant number will help you keep track of your data and participants and help anyone who transcribes your audio data for you

as well. Showing the participant a visual indicator of recording and reminding them that you are recording will provide clear information to your participant about when you are and are not recording the interview.

- Check and recheck your equipment. For voice recorders, is the light on, indicating that it is recording? Replay sections of the recordings during breaks. If you find that audio or video was not recorded, the conversation should be fresh enough in your mind that you can jot down a few notes to fill in the blanks.

Suggested Resources for Additional Reading

The books below are a detailed resource for anyone conducting interviews. The authors provide lots of sample interviews and indicate good and bad points in the interviewers' techniques. We recommend them for anyone wanting a stand-alone resource for interviewing.

- Wilson, C. (2013). *Interview techniques for UX practitioners: A user-centered design method.* Morgan Kaufmann.
- Portigal, S. (2013). *Interviewing users: How to uncover compelling insights.* Rosenfield Media.

CASE STUDY: *CONNECTING FAMILIES: IMPORTANCE OF INCLUDING CHILDREN AS STAKEHOLDERS*

Lana Yarosh, Assistant Professor, University of Minnesota

Children and parents in modern families may spend significant periods of time living apart. According to the US Census, 30% of the children in the United States do not live in the same household with both of their parents, primarily due to divorce or separation of parents (Census, 2008). In another 15% of families, a child may spend temporary periods of a month or more living away from his or her parent (Census, 2006). Reasons for temporary separation include military deployment, travel for work, incarceration, and visitation travel after divorce. Continued meaningful contact with parents correlates strongly with positive outcomes for the child on measures of emotional, social, academic, and even physical well-being (Amato, 2000). Technology may be able to help parents achieve this meaningful contact even if they live apart from the child (Shefts, 2002). As a researcher in the domain of human-centered computing, I was interested in investigating the opportunities for novel communication technology to help separated families stay connected. To design for this context, I first sought to understand the needs of separated families. In this case study, I describe two interview studies with families, providing concrete examples of why it is important to include children in the interview process and providing strategies for interviewing young participants.

I conducted two in-depth semi-structured interview studies to understand the needs of separated families. In the first investigation, I interviewed five children (aged 7-14) and five residential and five nonresidential parents from divorced families (Yarosh, Chew, & Abowd, 2009). In the second study, I interviewed 14 pairs of parents and children (aged 7-13) from families separated by military deployment, business travel, or academic travel (Yarosh & Abowd, 2011). In this case study, I limit myself to providing evidence for why it is important to include children as stakeholders and specific advice for doing so successfully.

When seeking to understand families and children, it is critically important to include children in any user research activity. While it may be tempting to use parents as proxies for gauging the family's needs, I have found that this is insufficient for understanding the complexities of the family dynamic. As I conducted interviews with parents and children, I was frequently surprised by their divergent motivations, goals, and descriptions of the same situation. Here, I highlight the importance of including children directly by providing three examples of nonconsensus or instances where parents thought that their children thought one thing and children reported a different thing, from my interview studies. In these cases, using the parent as a proxy would have led to an incomplete understanding of the context:

1. In the study of divorced families, the parents' estimates of the child's awareness of conflict frequently diverged significantly from the child's account. The majority of the parents thought that their child was probably not aware of the competition over their time and affection between the parents. However, when asked about what was most difficult about staying close to both parents, children said things like the following:

   My mom has a way to make her voice sound like she doesn't care, but at the same time, you know that it's not true, and it really always hurts to hear that voice. And whenever I want to call my dad she always uses it saying, "Oh, so you're calling him?"

   Clearly, children's perceptions of the situation were different than the adults' models of their perceptions.

2. In work-separated families, parents and children use conflicting strategies to manage temporary separation, particularly disagreeing on what constitutes an appropriate amount of communication with the remote parent. The need to *increase* contact is a characteristic common of traveling parents. However, spending more time communicating with the remote parent interfered with the strategies used by children to cope with the separation, which frequently focused more on contact with collocated family members rather than seeking remote contact. While this does not mean that designers should not build systems to encourage parent-child communication, it is important for designers to consider the obligation to communicate that their system may impose on the child and what may happen if the parent's expectations for communication are not met. Again, excluding children from interviews would have led to an incomplete understanding of this context.

3. Lastly, in both studies, "the family" was too ambiguous to serve as a unit of analysis. When asked to list the people that they consider to be part of their family, many participants from the same household gave divergent responses. For example, younger children in divorced families typically

included biological and stepparents; older children sometimes did not list stepparents; the parents themselves did not include the child's other parent as part of their family. This "reflexive"—always referring back to the individual who is listing its members—definition of family is amplified in divorced families but is not unique to them. In intact families, in-laws are the classic example of persons that may be included in one member's family but not in another's. There are consequences for design when two individuals' definitions of family do not overlap, such as privacy considerations. Without interviewing all the stakeholders, it can be easy to fail to consider these issues in design.

These three examples of nonconsensus in families show that interviewing all stakeholders, including children, is necessary to achieve a more nuanced understanding of the context.

While it is easy to agree that including children as stakeholders is important, actually doing so can be a challenge. Even school-age children are still developing the communication competencies to understand the finer points of language, such as abstraction or metaphor (Stafford, 2004). Many children may also feel uncomfortable speaking with an unfamiliar adult. However, I offer six specific strategies to help manage these challenges:

1. Working with children requires **special considerations while preparing the protocol and assent documents**. Children are not able to give informed consent, which will have to be obtained through their parents, but the assent procedure gives them the opportunity to understand their rights and what will happen in the interview. It is important to emphasize to the child that he or she can withdraw from the study, decline to answer any question, or take a break at any time (for more on informed consent and research ethics, refer to Chapter 3). In designing both the assent document and interview protocol, it is important to keep specific developmental milestones associated with age in mind. In my experience, while I have tried interviewing children as young as three, I have only started getting useful data with children around age six. However, you should take care to check the comprehension level of your protocol by piloting the protocol with friendly participants in the target age group and by using Flesch-Kincaid Grade Level test (available online and built into many word processors, including Microsoft Word). While this test has its limitations and should not be substituted for piloting, it can serve as the first step to point out questions where you may want to simplify wording or take extra care to ensure that the child understands the question. For more on working with special populations like children, see Chapter 2.
2. To encourage children to be open and honest, the researcher should actively work to **equalize power between the child and the researcher**. Children spend their lives in situations where adults expect the "right" answer from them. To encourage the child to share honest opinions and stories, the researcher needs to break through this power differential. There are a number of details to consider here: choose an interview setting where the child has power (e.g., playroom), dress like an older sibling rather than as a teacher, encourage use of first names, and let the child play with any technology that will be used (e.g., audio recorder) before starting the interview. Above all, emphasize that you are asking these questions because you do not yet know the answers, that the child is "the best at being a kid," and that there is no wrong way to answer any of the questions.

3. Parents make the decisions in a study that concerns their children, which introduces a unique constraint in situations of nonconsensus between the parent and child. As a researcher, you will have to respect the parents' decisions: you may not be able to interview the child separately and you cannot promise the child that anything will be kept private from the parents. However, you can **explain to the parents why it is important for the child to have a chance to state his or her perspective in private**. In my experience, most parents are willing to provide that private space, especially when the study is being conducted in their home where they worry less about the child's comfort. Nonconsensus may introduce other ethical and methodological factors to consider, and I address these issues in more depth in Yarosh (2014).
4. Children may struggle with abstraction, so **ask for stories about specific situations**. For example, instead of asking "How do you and your dad talk on the phone when he's traveling?" ask "What did you tell your dad last time he called you?" It may take more questions to get at all the aspects you want to discuss, but it is much easier for children to discuss things they recently *did* rather than provide an overall reflection. This is most important with younger children but is a good place to start with any participant.

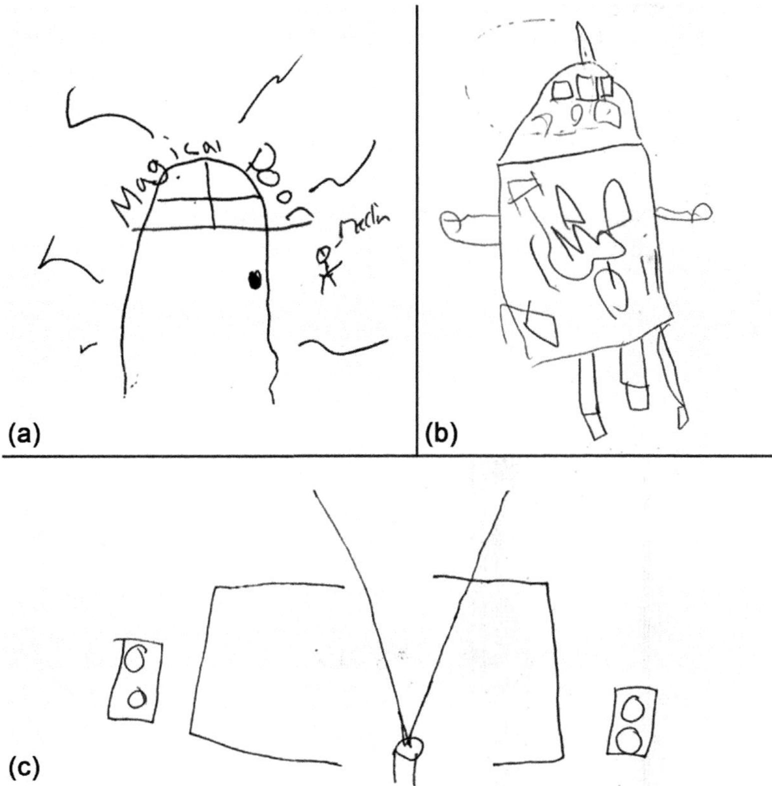

Figure 9.5: Children's drawings of magical objects to help them stay in touch with their nonresidential parents: (a) a magical door that lets the dad enter the child's room to say good night; (b) a robot for carrying secret messages between a boy and his father; and (c) a system with speakers and a holographic projector that lets the parent and child speak whenever they want.

5. Additional effort may be necessary to engage a shy child, and one way to do so is to **encourage the child to show-and-tell.** For example, "Show me where you usually are when you think about your mom." or "Show me some apps that you use with your dad on your phone." Use the places and objects shared as stepping-stones to ask more nuanced questions about feelings, strategies, and preferences.
6. Lastly, **incorporating drawing and design activities into the interview** may help the child get into the "open-ended" nature of the study, be willing to be a little silly, and reveal what may be most important to him or her. For example, I asked children, "What might future kids have to help them stay in touch with their parents?" These drawings are not meant to produce actionable designs, but will reveal important issues through their presentation. Listen for key words (e.g., "secret" = importance of privacy), look for underlying concepts (e.g., "trampoline" or "swimming pool" = importance of physical activity), and attend to common themes such as who would be interacting with their future device, where, and how often. See Figure 9.5 for example drawings.

There are many different ways to successfully include children as participants; however, the strategies above have worked well for me in encouraging and empowering children. They may be a good starting point for researchers who are new to this space.

The main takeaway of this case study goes beyond work with separated families: **when designing sociotechnical systems, make sure important stakeholders (such as children) are not left out of the process.** It can be a challenge to interview children, but they frequently provide a different view than their parents. Speaking with the parent is not a replacement for speaking with the child. The two biggest tips for interviewing children to take away from this case study are (1) work to **equalize power between children and adults** and (2) keep questions as concrete as possible by **asking the child to tell stories, show-and-tell, and draw**. Keeping these strategies in mind will go a long way toward creating an atmosphere where children can make their point of view heard.

CHAPTER 10

Surveys

Introduction

Surveys can be an extremely effective way to gather information from a large sample in a relatively short period of time. The problem is that a valid and reliable survey can be very difficult to design; yet surveys are *perceived* as very easy to create. It is just a bunch of questions, right? Well yes, but the questions you choose and how you ask them are critical. A poorly designed survey can provide meaningless or—even worse—inaccurate information. Additionally, how you choose your survey respondents will greatly impact the validity and reliability of your data. In this chapter, we hope to enlighten you about this process. Surveys can provide you with great data, but you must be familiar with the rules of creation and collection and the particulars of analyzing survey data, which is very different from log files or behavioral data. In this chapter, we cover the key topics that are important to consider when designing a survey and analyzing the data. Our primary focus is on web surveys because that is the most common survey format today; however, we also discuss paper and telephone surveys, as they offer unique benefits. In addition, we share an industry case study with you to show how Google uses surveys to track user sentiment over time.

At a Glance

> When should you use a survey?
> Things to be aware of when using a survey
> Creating and distributing your survey
> Data analysis and interpretation
> Communicating the findings

When Should You Use a Survey?

Whether it is for a brand-new product or a new version of a product, a survey can be a great way to start your user research. In the case of a new product, surveys can be used to:

- Help you identify your target user population
- Help you identify current pain points and opportunities that your product could fulfill
- Find out at a high level how users are currently accomplishing their tasks

In the case of an existing product, a survey can help you to:

- Learn about your current user population and their characteristics
- Find out the users' likes/dislikes about the current product and track user sentiment over time
- Learn how users currently use the system

Also, whether it is for a new or existing product, surveys are a way to reach a larger number of people than other methods typically allow. Surveys can be provided to users as a standalone research activity or as a supplement to other user activities (e.g., following a card sort).

Suggested Resources for Additional Reading

Because survey creation is so complex, *many* books have been written solely on the subject of survey creation and analysis. In this chapter, we are unable to dive into the details those books cover. So, if you are brand new to survey design or would like to learn more after reading this chapter, below are four books we recommend.

If you plan to conduct a survey that is very complex or will have large financial impact, we strongly urge you to read these books before creating your survey. We cannot stress enough how complex survey creation can be. **Intercept surveys**, for example, can be extremely tricky to code and implement. Making a mistake on your survey could cost you or your company significant revenue. Each book dives into all the details associated with a more complex survey. Such topics include sample selection methods, statistical analyses, and the use of surveys following usability evaluations.

- Albert, W., & Tullis, T. (2013). *Measuring the user experience: Collecting, analyzing, and presenting usability metrics*. Newnes.
- Fowler, F. J. (2014). *Survey research methods* (5th ed.). Sage, Thousand Oaks, CA.
- Groves, R. M., Fowler, F. J., Couper, M. P., Lepkowski, J. M., Singer, E., & Tourangeau, R. (2009). *Survey methodology* (2nd ed.). Wiley.
- Nardi, P. (2013). *Doing survey research. A guide to quantitative methods* (3rd ed.). Paradigm, Boulder, CO.

Things to Be Aware of When Using a Survey

As with any user research technique, there are always factors that you must be aware of before you conduct a survey. Here, we describe several types of bias you need to be aware of and ways to mitigate them.

Selection Bias

Some users/customers/respondents are easier to contact and recruit than others. You can create a **selection bias** (i.e., the systematic exclusion of some unit from your data set) by conducting **convenience sampling** (i.e., recruiting based on convenience). These might be people who have signed up to be your participant database, students and staff at your university, friends and family, colleagues, etc. Obviously, getting responses only from those that are most convenient may not result in accurate data.

Nonresponse Bias

The unfortunate reality of surveys is that not everyone is going to respond and those that do choose to respond may be systematically different from those who do not. For example, very privacy-conscious individuals may be unlikely to respond to your survey, and this would be a real problem if you are interested in feedback on your privacy policy. Experienced survey researchers give response rate estimates of anywhere between 20% and 60%, depending on user type and whether incentives are offered or not. In our experience, you are likely to get a response rate closer to 20%, unless you have a very small, targeted population that has agreed to complete your survey ahead of time. However, there are some things you can do to improve the response rate:

- *Personalize it.* Include a cover letter/e-mail or header at the top of the survey with the respondent's name to provide information about the purpose of the study and how long it will take. Tell the respondents how important *their* feedback is to your organization. Conversely, incorrectly personalizing it (e.g., wrong name or title) can destroy your response rate.
- *Keep it short.* We recommend 10 minutes or less. It is not just about the number of questions. Avoid long essay questions or those that require significant cognitive effort.
- *Make it easy to complete and return.* For example, if you are sending surveys in the mail, include a self-addressed envelope with prepaid postage.
- *Follow up with polite reminders via multiple modes.* A couple of reminders should be sufficient without harassing the respondent. If potential respondents were initially contacted via e-mail, try contacting nonrespondents via the phone.
- *Offer a small incentive.* For example, offering participants a $5 coffee card for completing a survey can greatly increase the response rate. At Google, we have found that raffles to win a high-price item do *not* significantly increase response rates.

Satisficing

Satisficing is a decision-making strategy where individuals aim to reach satisfactory (not ideal) results by putting in just enough effort to meet some minimal threshold. This is situational, not intrinsic to the individual (Holbrook, Green, & Krosnick, 2003; Vannette & Krosnick, 2014). By that, we mean that people do not open your survey with a plan to satisfice; it happens when they encounter surveys that require too much cognitive effort (e.g., lengthy, difficult-to-answer questions, confusing questions). When respondents see a large block of rating scale questions with the same headers, they are likely to **straight-line** (i.e., select the same choice for all questions) rather than read and consider each option individually. Obviously, you want to make your survey as brief as possible, write clear questions, and make sure you are not asking things a participant cannot answer.

Your survey mode can also increase satisficing. Respondents in phone sureys demonstrated more satisficing behavior than in face-to-face surveys (Holbrook et al., 2003) and online surveys (Chang & Krosnick, 2009). However, within online samples, there was greater satisficing among probability panels than nonprobability panels (Yeager et al., 2011). **Probability sampling** (aka **random sampling**) means that everyone in your desired population has an equal, nonzero chance of being selected. **Nonprobability sampling** means that respondents are recruited from an opt-in panel that may or may not represent your desired population. Because respondents in nonprobability panels pick and choose which surveys to answer in return for an incentive, they are most likely to only pick those they are interested in and comfortable answering (Callegaro et al., 2014).

Additionally, you can help avoid satisficing by offering an incentive, periodically reminding respondents how important their thoughtful responses are, and communicating when it seems they are answering the questions too quickly. When you test your survey, you can get an idea for how long each question should take to answer, and if the respondent answers too quickly, some online survey tools allow you to provide a pop-up that tells respondents, "You seem to be answering these questions very quickly. Can you review your responses on this page before continuing?" If a respondent is just trying to get an incentive for completing the survey, you should notify him or her that he or she will not be able to do it quickly. He or she may quit at this point but it is better to avoid collecting invalid data.

Acquiescence Bias

Some people are more likely to agree with any statement, regardless what it says. This is referred to as **acquiescence bias**. Certain question formats are more prone to bring out this behavior than others and should be avoided (Saris, Revilla, Krosnick, & Shaeffer, 2010). These include asking respondents if or how much they agree with a statement, any binary question (e.g., true/false, yes/no), and, of course, leading questions (e.g., "How annoyed are you with online advertising?"). We will cover how to avoid these pitfalls later in the chapter.

Creating and Distributing Your Survey

One of the biggest misconceptions about a survey is the speed with which you can prepare for, collect, and analyze the results. A survey can be an extremely valuable method, but it takes time to do it correctly. In this section, we will discuss the preparation required for this user research method.

At a Glance

> Identify the objectives of your study

> Players in your activity

> Compose your questions

> Determine now how you will analyze your data

> Building the survey

> Considerations when choosing a survey distribution method

> Distributing your survey via the web, e-mail, or paper

> Pilot test your survey and iterate

Identify the Objectives of Your Study

Do not just jump in and start writing your survey. You need to do some prep work. Ask yourself the following:

- Who do we want to learn about? (refer to Chapter 2, "Learn About Your Users" section, page 35)
- What information are you looking for (i.e., what questions are you trying to answer)?
- How will you distribute the survey and collect responses?
- How will you analyze the data?
- Who will be involved in the process?

It is important to come up with answers to these questions and to document your plan. As with all user research activities, you should write a proposal that clearly states the objectives of your study (refer to Chapter 6, "Creating a Proposal" section, page 116). The proposal should also explicitly state the deliverables and include a timeline. Because you normally want to recruit a large number of participants, it can be resource-intensive to conduct a survey. There are more participants to recruit and potentially compensate, as well as more data to analyze than for most user research activities. As a result, it is important to get your survey right the first time and get sign-off by all stakeholders. A proposal can help you do this.

Players in Your Activity

A survey is different from the other activities described in this book because—unless it is a part of another activity—you are typically not present as the survey is completed. As a result, there is no moderator, no notetaker, no videographer, etc. The players are your participants, but now, we will refer to them as respondents.

The first thing to determine is the user population (refer to Chapter 2, "Learn About Your Users" section, page 35). Who do you plan to distribute this survey to? Are they the people registered with your website? Are they using your product? Are they a specific segment of the population (e.g., college students)? Who you distribute your survey to should be based on what you want to know. The answers to these questions will impact the questions you include.

Number of Respondents

You must be sure that you can invite enough people from your desired user population (e.g., current users, potential users) to get a **statistically significant** response. That means that you can be confident that the results you observe are not the product of chance. If your sample is too small, the data you collect cannot be extrapolated to your entire population. If you cannot increase your sample size, do not despair. At that point, it becomes a **feedback form**. A feedback form does not offer everyone in your population an equal chance of being selected to provide feedback (e.g., only the people on your mailing list are contacted, it is posted on your website under "Contact Us" and only people who visit there will see it and have the opportunity to complete it). As a result, it does not necessarily represent your entire population. For example, it may represent only people that are fans and signed up for your mailing list or customers that are particularly angry about your customer service and seek out a way to contact you. On the other hand, you do not need (nor want!) to collect responses from everyone in your population. That would be a **census** and is not necessary to understand your population.

TIP

Feedback forms are a powerful way to hear from your customers whenever they want to share their experiences. Although they may not represent how your entire population feels, they do represent a segment of your population, and that is important. They can also be an insightful source for new feature ideas and ways to improve your product or service.

To determine how many responses you need, there are many free sample-size calculators available online. To use them, you will need to know the size of your **population** (i.e., the total number of people in the group you are interested in studying), the **margin of error** you can accept (i.e., the amount of error you can tolerate), desired **confidence interval** (i.e., the amount of uncertainty you can accept), and the expected **response distribution** (i.e., for each question, how skewed do you expect the response to be). If you do not know what the response distribution will be, you should leave this as 50%, which will result in the largest sample size needed. Let us continue with our travel example. If we are interested in getting feedback from our existing customer base, we need to identify how large that population is. We do not know what our response distribution is, so we will set it at 50%. If our population is 23,000 customers and we are looking for a margin of error of ±3% and confidence interval (CI) of 95%, we will need a **sample size** (i.e., number of completed responses) of 1020. This is the minimum number of responses you will want to collect for your desired level of certainty and error, but of course, you will have to contact far more customers than that to collect the desired number of completes. The exact number depends on many factors, including the engagement of your population, survey method (e.g., phone, paper, web), whether or not you provide an incentive, and how lengthy or difficult your survey is, among other factors. (Note that sample sizes do not increase much for populations above 20,000.)

Probability Versus Nonprobability Sampling

As with any other research method, you may want or need to outsource the recruiting for your study. In the case of surveys, you would use a survey panel to collect data. These are individuals who are recruited by a vendor based on the desired user characteristics to complete your survey. Perhaps you are not interested in existing customers and therefore have no way to contact your desired population. There are many survey vendors available (e.g., SSI, YouGov, GfK, Gallup), and they vary in cost, speed, and access to respondents. The key thing you need to know is whether they are using **probability** or **nonprobability sampling**. Probability sampling might happen via a customer list (if your population is composed of those customers), intercept surveys (e.g., randomly selected individuals who visit your site invited via a link or pop-up), random digit dialing (RDD), and address-based sampling (e.g., addresses are selected at random from your region of interest). In this case, the vendor would not have a panel ready to pull from but would need to recruit fresh for each survey. Nonprobability sampling involves panels of respondents owned by the vendor that are typically incentivized per survey completed. The same respondents often sign up for multiple-survey or market research panels. The vendors will weight the data to try to make the sample look more like your desired population. For example, if your desired population of business travelers is composed of 70% economy, 20% business, and 10% first-class flyers in the real world but the sample from the panel has only 5% business and 1% first-class flyers, the vendor will multiply the responses to increase the representation of the business and first-class flyers while decreasing the representation of the economy flyers. Unfortunately, this does not actually improve the accuracy of the results when compared with those from a probability-based sample (Callegaro et al., 2014). In addition, nonprobability-based samples are more interested in taking surveys and are experts at it.

Suggested Resources for Additional Reading

To learn more about probability sampling versus nonprobability sampling, check out the publications below. The authors have deeply researched this topic and cite years' worth of data.

- Blair, E. A., & Blair, J. E. (2015). *Applied survey sampling*. Los Angeles: Sage.
- Callegaro, M., Baker, R. P., Bethlehem, J., Göritz, A. S., Krosnick, J. A., & Lavrakas, P. J. (Eds.). (2014). *Online panel research: A data quality perspective*. John Wiley & Sons.

Compose Your Questions

Previously, you identified the objectives of your survey. Now, it is time to create questions that address those objectives. Recommendations in this section will also help increase completion rates for your survey. This stage is the same regardless of how you plan to distribute your survey (e.g., paper, web). However, the formatting of your questions may vary depending on the distribution method. The stage of "building" your survey and the impact of different distribution methods are discussed later in this chapter.

At a Glance

> Identify your research questions and constructs to measure

> Keep it short

> Asking sensitive questions

> Question format and wording

Identify Your Research Questions and Constructs

For each objective, you need to identify your research question(s) and the constructs you want to measure to answer those questions. We recommend creating a table to help with this. Table 10.1 is a sample table of what you might create for TravelMyWay.com. This is your first draft and you will likely need to iterate on it but working from this table will help avoid questions that are not directly tied to your objective, track branching logic, and help you group similar questions to avoid redundancy.

Keep It Short

One of the key pieces of advice is to *keep the survey short*. If you ignore this rule, you are doomed to fail because no one will take the time to complete your survey.

There are several ways to keep your survey short:

- *Every question should be tied to an objective and (ideally) be actionable.* One of your objectives may be to understand your user population or their context of use. You may want to track this over time. It is not necessarily actionable, but it can still be an important objective of the survey. Work with your stakeholders to find out the information they need to know and throw out "nice to know" or "curiosity" questions.

Table 10.1: Sample table of objectives, constructs, and questions

Objective	Construct	Question	Options
Track user satisfaction over time	Satisfaction	How satisfied are you with TravelMyWay.com?	7-Point scale (Extremely dissatisfied to Extremely satisfied)
Get feedback on new feature	Use	How often have you used the new Agenda Planning feature? (include screenshot)	• Never • Once • More than once
Get feedback on new feature	Satisfaction	(If "Once" or "More than once" is selected, ask) How satisfied are you with the Agenda Planning feature?	7-Point scale (Extremely dissatisfied to Extremely satisfied)
Get feedback on new feature	Open feedback	What are your thoughts about the Agenda Planning feature?	(Open text)
Understand demographics of respondents	Frequency of use	How many times have you booked travel on TravelMyWay.com in the last six months? You can check this by clicking on the "Account" link in the upper right corner and looking at your history	• 0 • 1 • 2 • More than 3 times
Understand demographics of respondents	Customer length	How long have you been using TravelMyWay.com? You can check this by clicking on the "Account" link in the upper right corner and looking at your history	• Less than a month • 1-6 months • 6-11 months • 1-2 years • More than 2 years

- *Use branching logic.* Not every question will apply to every respondent. If a respondent has not used a feature, for example, do not ask him or her about his or her satisfaction with the feature. Adding "If you have used feature X" at the beginning of the question does not help. You are taking up valuable space and time by making the respondent read it, and there is a good chance that the respondent will answer it anyway. A user's satisfaction with a feature he or she does not use is not helpful in making decisions.
- *Do not ask questions that respondents cannot answer validly.* Just like you do not want to ask people about features they do not have experience with, you do not want to ask them to predict the future (e.g., How often would use a feature that does X?) or to tell you about things that happened long ago, at least not without assistance. If you want to know if a respondent is a frequent customer based on how often he or she uses your product, you can ask him or her how often he or she has used the product in a given time frame, as long as there is an easy way for him or her to find this information (e.g., provide instructions for how to look in his or her account history).
- *No essay questions.* You do not need to avoid open-ended questions (OEQs) but use them only when appropriate and do not seek lengthy, detailed responses. See the discussion on writing OEQs on page 276.
- *Avoid sensitive questions.* This is discussed in the next section, but the general rule is to avoid asking sensitive questions unless you really need the information to make decisions.
- *Break questions up.* If you have a long list of questions that are all critical to your objective(s), you have a couple options for shortening the survey. One is to divide the questions into a series of shorter surveys. This works well if you have clearly defined topics that make it easy to group into smaller surveys; however, you will lose the ability to do analysis across the entire data set. For example, if you want to know about the travel preferences for those that travel by train and plane, you could divide the questions into a train survey and a plane survey, but unless you give the survey to the same sample and are able to identify who completed each survey, you will not be able to join the data later and see correlations between those that travel by train and plane. Another option is to randomly assign a subset of the questions to different respondents. You will need a much larger sample size to ensure that you get a significant number of responses to every question, but if you are successful, you will be able to conduct analysis across the entire data set.

If you can adhere to these rules, then your survey will have a much greater chance of being completed.

Asking Sensitive Questions

Both interviews and surveys have pros and cons with regards to asking sensitive questions. In an interview, you have the opportunity to develop a rapport with the respondent and gain his or her trust. But even if the respondent does trust you, he or she may not feel comfortable answering the question in person. If your survey is anonymous, it is often easier to discuss sensitive topics that would be awkward to ask face-to-face (e.g., age, salary range). However, even in anonymous surveys, people may balk at being asked for this type of information or you may encounter **social desirability bias** (i.e., people responding with the answer they think is most socially acceptable, even if it is not true for them).

Ask yourself or your team whether you *really* need the information. Demographic questions (e.g., age, gender, salary range, education) are often asked because it is believed that these are 'standard' questions, but behavioral factors (e.g., how frequently they use your product, experience with a competitor's product) are usually more predictive of future behavior than demographic data. If you are convinced that the answers to sensitive questions will help you better understand your user population and therefore your product, provide a little verbiage with the question to let respondents know *why* you need this information, for example, "To help inform decisions about our privacy policy, we would like to know the following information."

Clearly mark these questions as "optional." Never make them required because either respondents will refuse to complete your survey or they may purposely provide inaccurate information just to move forward with the survey if you offered an incentive for completion. Finally, save these questions for the end of the survey. Allow participants to see the type of information you are interested in, and then, they can decide if they want to associate sensitive information with it.

Question Format and Wording

Once you have come up with your objectives, constructs, and list of questions, you will need to determine their wording and format. By "format," we are referring to how the respondents are expected to respond to the question and the layout and structure of your survey. Participants are far more likely to respond when they perceive your survey as clear, understandable, concise, of value, and of interest.

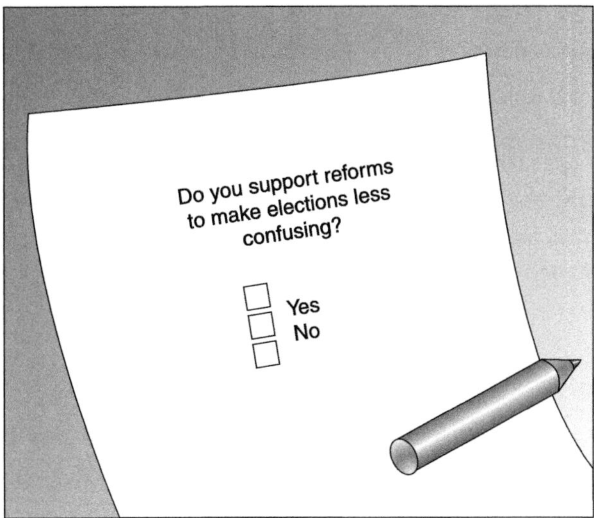

Based on an Illustration from The Christian Science Monitor (www.csmonitor.com)

Response Format

For each of your questions, you must decide the format in which you want the participant to respond: either from a set of options you provide or through free response. OEQs allow the respondents to compose their own answers, for example, "What is one thing you would like to see changed or added to TravelMyWay.com?" **Closed-ended questions** require participants to answer the questions by either:

- Providing a single value or fact
- Selecting all the values that apply to them from a given list
- Providing an opinion on a scale

There are several things to keep in mind with OEQs:

- Data analysis is tedious and complex because it is qualitative data that must first be coded before you can analyze them.
- Because respondents use their own words/phrases/terms, responses can be difficult to comprehend and you typically will not have an opportunity to follow up and clarify with the person who responded.
- They can make the survey longer to complete, thereby decreasing the return rate.

The bottom line is do not ask for lengthy OEQs. They are best used when:

- You do not know the full universe of responses to write a closed-ended question. You can conduct your survey with a small sample of respondents, analyze the answers to the OEQ in this case, and then categorize them to create your options for a close-ended question for the rest of your sample.
- There are too many options to list them all.
- You do not want to bias respondents with your options but instead want to collect their top-of-mind feedback.
- You are capturing likes and dislikes.

Clearly labeling OEQs as "optional" will increase the likelihood that respondents will complete your survey and only answer the OEQs where they feel that have something to contribute. Forcing respondents to answer OEQs will hurt your completion rate, increase satisficing, and may earn you gibberish responses from respondents that do not having something to contribute.

TIP

The size of the text box sends a signal to the respondent about how long of an answer you are looking for. If all of your OEQs have text boxes for a paragraph of text, that can scare respondents away. If you are looking for only a number or a few words, make sure your text box is small. However, if you expect a sentence or more, make the text field large enough to accommodate it without forcing the respondent to scroll to see what he or she wrote. With many survey tools, you can limit the word count, if desired; however, if respondents have a lot of feedback to share, why would you want to limit it? Additionally, respondents may feel frustrated if they have to count the number of words or characters to express their feedback and simply quit.

There are three main types of closed-ended question responses to choose from: multiple choice, rating scales, and ranking scales. Each serves a different purpose but all provide data that can be analyzed quantitatively.

Multiple-Choice Questions

In multiple-choice questions, respondents are provided with a question that has a selection of predetermined responses to choose from. In some cases, respondents are asked to select multiple responses, and in other cases, they are asked to select single responses. In either case, make sure that the options provided are either randomized to avoid a **primacy effect** (i.e., respondents gravitate to the first option they see) or, if appropriate, placed in a logical order (e.g., days of the week, numbers, size) (Krosnick, Li, & Lehman, 1990).

- *Multiple responses*. Participants can choose more than one response from a list of options. This is ideal when the real world does *not* force people to make a single choice. See example:

What types of travel have you booked online? Please select all that apply.

- ☐ Airline tickets
- ☐ Train tickets
- ☐ Bus tickets
- ☐ Car rental
- ☐ None of the above

- *Single response*. Participants are provided with a set of options from which to choose only one answer. This is ideal in cases where the real world *does* limit people to a single choice. See example below:

How often do you book travel online?

- ☐ Once a month
- ☐ four to six times per year
- ☐ one to three times per year
- ☐ I never book travel online

- *Binary*. As the name implies, the respondent must select from only two options, for example, "yes/no," "true/false," or "agree/disagree." With binary questions, you are forcing participants to drop all shades of gray and pick the answer that best describes their situation or opinion. It is very simple to analyze data from these types of questions, but you introduce error by not better understanding some of the subtleties in their selection. Additionally, these types of questions are prone to **acquiescence bias**. *As a result, you should avoid using binary questions.*

Rating Scales

There are a variety of scale questions that can be incorporated into surveys. Likert scale and ranking scale are two of the most common scales.

The **Likert scale** is the most frequently-used rating scale. Jon Krosnick at Stanford University has conducted lengthy empirical research to identify the ideal number of scale items, wording, and layout of Likert scales to optimize validity and reliability (Krosnick & Tahk, 2008).

- **Unipolar constructs** (i.e., units that go from nothing to a lot) are best measured on a 5-point scale. Some example unipolar constructs include usefulness, importance, and degree. The recommended scale labels are Not at all […], Slightly […], Moderately […], Very […], and Extremely […].
- **Bipolar constructs** (i.e., units that have a midpoint and two extremes) are best measured on a 7-point scale. The most frequently used bipolar construct is satisfaction. The recommended scale labels are Extremely […], Moderately […], Slightly […], Neither […] nor […], Slightly […], Moderately […], and Extremely […].

In both cases, move from negative (e.g., Not at all useful, Extremely dissatisfied) to positive (e.g., Extremely useful, Extremely satisfied). The negative extreme is listed first to allow for a more natural mapping to how respondents interpret bipolar constructs (Tourangeau, Couper, & Conrad, 2004).

Providing labels on all points of the scale avoids ambiguity and ensures that all of your respondents are rating with the same scale in mind (Krosnick & Presser, 2010). These particular labels have been shown to be perceived as equally spaced and result in a normal distribution (Wildt & Mazis, 1978). Do not include numbers on your scale, as they add visual clutter without improving interpretation. Below is an example of a fully-labeled Likert scale.

Overall, how satisfied are you with your experience on TravelMyWay.com?						
o	o	o	o	o	o	o
Extremely dissatisfied	Moderately dissatisfied	Slightly dissatisfied	Neither satisfied nor dissatisfied	Slightly satisfied	Moderately satisfied	Extremely satisfied

Another type of rating scale question asks users to give a priority rating for a range of options, for example:

Rate the importance of each of the following features in a travel site from 1 to 5, with 1 being Not At All Important and 5 being Extremely Important.

- Low prices
- Vast selection
- Chat and phone access to a live travel agent
- A rewards program for purchases

In this rating question, you are not comparing the options given against one another. As a result, more than one option can have the same rating.

Ranking Scales

This type of scale question gives participants a variety of options and asks them to provide a rank for each one. Unlike the rating scale question, the respondent is allowed to use each rank only once. In other words, the respondent cannot state that all four answers are "most important." These questions can be cognitively more taxing. To make it easier, break it into separate questions. For example, first ask "What is your most preferred method for booking travel?" and then follow up with "What is your second most preferred method for booking travel?" and remove the option that the respondent selected in the previous question.

The ranking scale differs from a rating scale because the respondent *is* comparing the options presented *against* one another to come up with a unique ranking for each option.

Other

Avoid including "other" as an option in your closed-ended questions unless you are not sure you know the complete list of options a respondent may need. It is cognitively easier to choose it than to match the answer they have in mind to one of the options in your question. If "other" receives more than 3% of your total responses, categorize the responses and add additional options to your question.

Question Wording

Your choice of words for survey questions is critical. Regardless of the format, avoid vague options like "few," "many," and "often." Participants will differ in their perception of those options, and it will be difficult for you to quantify them when you analyze the data. Avoid jargon and abbreviations for similar reasons. Not all respondents may recognize or interpret it the way you intended.

Double-barreled questions are a common pitfall. This is when two questions are combined as one, for example, "How satisfied are you with the customer support you received online and/or over the phone?" The problem is that respondents may have different answers for each piece of the question, but you are forcing them to pick a single answer. In that case, the respondents must choose if it is better to provide an average of how they feel, provide the best rating or the lowest rating, or simply satisfice and pick an option that does not accurately represent how they feel.

Statements Versus Questions

As mentioned earlier, binary (e.g., yes/no, true/false, agree/disagree) questions and statements lead to **acquiescence bias**. Instead of providing statements for respondents to reply to (whether binary or a rating scale), it is best to identify the construct you are interested in and then write a question to measure it. For example, instead of asking "How strongly do you agree with the statement 'I prefer to fly rather take a train'?" or "True or False: 'I prefer to fly rather than take a train,'" you should identify the construct of interest. In this case, it is mode of travel preference. You could measure this by asking the respondents to rank their modes of travel by preference or ask them how satisfied they are with each mode of travel.

Determine Now How You Will Analyze Your Data

Those who are new to survey methodologies have a tendency to wait until the data have been collected before they consider how they will be analyzed. An experienced researcher will tell you that this is a big mistake. You may end up collecting data that are unnecessary for you to answer your research questions or, worse, not collecting data that *are* necessary. Once your survey is closed, it is too late to get the data you need without launching another survey, and that is both expensive and time-consuming.

By thinking about your data analysis *before* you distribute your survey, you can make sure the survey contains the correct questions and options. Ask yourself the following questions:

- What kind of analysis do you plan to perform (e.g., descriptive statistics, inferential statistics)? Go through each question and determine what you will do with the data. Identify any comparisons that you would like to make and document this information. This can impact the question format.
- Are there questions that you do not know how to analyze? You should either remove them, do some research to figure out how to analyze them, or contact a statistics professional.
- Will the analysis provide you with the answers you need? If not, perhaps you are missing questions.
- Do you have the correct tools to analyze the data? If you plan to do data analysis beyond what a spreadsheet can normally handle (e.g., descriptive statistics), you will need a statistical package like *SPSS*™, *SAS*™, or *R*. If your company does not have access to such a tool, you will need to acquire it. Keep in mind that if you must purchase it, it may take time for a purchase order or requisition to go through. You do not want to hold up your data analysis because you are waiting for your manager to give approval to purchase the software you need. In addition, if you are unfamiliar with the tool, you can spend the time you are waiting for the survey data to come in to learn how to use the tool.
- How will the data be entered into the analysis tool? This will help you budget your time. If the data will be entered manually (e.g., in the case of a paper survey), allot more time. If the data will be entered automatically via the web, you may need to write a script. If you do not know how to do this, make time to learn.

By answering these questions early on, you will help ensure that the data analysis goes smoothly. This really should not take a lot of time, but by putting in the effort up front, you will also know exactly what to expect when you get to this stage of the process, and you will avoid any headaches, lost data, or useless data.

Building the Survey

Now that you have composed your questions, you can move on to the next stage, which is building the survey in the format in which it will be distributed (e.g., paper, web, e-mail). There are a number of common elements to keep in mind when building your survey, regardless of the distribution method. These will be discussed first. Then, we look at elements unique to each distribution method.

Standard Items to Include

There are certain elements that every survey should contain, regardless of topic or distribution method.

Title

Give every survey a title. The title should give the respondent a quick sense of the purpose of the survey (e.g., TravelMyWay.com Customer Satisfaction Survey). Keep it short and sweet.

Instructions

Include any instructional text that is necessary for your survey as a whole or for individual questions. The more explicit you can be, the better. For example, an instruction that applies to the whole survey might be "Please return the completed survey in the enclosed self-addressed, postage-paid envelope." An instruction that applies to an individual question might read, "Of the following, check the *one* answer that most applies to you." Of course, you want to design the survey form and structure so that the need for instructions is minimized. A lengthy list of instructions either will not be read or will inhibit potential respondents from completing the survey.

Contact Information

There are many reasons why you should include contact information on your surveys. If a potential respondent has a question prior to completing the survey (e.g., When is it due? What is the compensation? Who is conducting the study?), he or she may choose to skip your survey if your contact information is not available. However, you should make every effort to include all relevant information in your survey, so respondents will have no need to contact you. Participants also have the right to be fully informed before consenting to your research so you are ethically obligated to provide them with a way to ask you questions.

If your survey was distributed via mail with a self-addressed envelope, it is still wise to include the return address on the survey itself. Without a return address on the survey, if the return envelope is lost, people will be unable to respond. And last but not least, providing your contact information lends legitimacy to the survey.

Purpose

In a line or two, tell participants why you are conducting the survey. Ethically, they have a right to know (refer to Chapter 3, "The Right to Be Informed" section, page 70). Also, if you have a legitimate purpose, it will attract respondents and make them want to complete the survey. A purpose could read something like the following:

> TravelMyWay.com is conducting this survey because we value our customers and we want to learn whether our travel site meets their needs, as well as what we can do to improve our site.

Time to Complete

People will want to know at the beginning how long it will take to finish the survey before they invest their time into it. You do not want respondents to quit in the middle of your 15-minute survey because they thought it would take five minutes and now they have to run to a meeting. It is only fair to set people's expectations ahead of time, and respondents will appreciate this information. If you do not provide it, many potential respondents will not bother with your survey because they do not know what they are getting into. Worse, if you understate the time to complete, you will violate the respondent's trust and risk a low completion for the current survey and lower response rate for future surveys.

Confidentiality and Anonymity

You are obligated to protect respondents' privacy (refer to Chapter 3 "Privacy," page 66). Data collected from respondents should always be kept confidential, unless you explicitly tell them otherwise (refer to Chapter 3, "Anonymity," page 66). **Confidentiality** means that the person's identity will not be associated in any way with the data provided. As the researcher, you may know the identity of the participant because you recruited him or her; however, you keep his or her identity confidential by not associating any personally identifying information (PII) with his or her data. You should make a clear statement of confidentiality at the beginning of your survey.

Anonymity is different from confidentiality. If a respondent is anonymous, it means that even *you*, the researcher, cannot associate a completed survey with the respondent's identity, usually because you did not collect any PII in the first place or you do not have access to it, if it is collected. Make sure that you are clear with respondents about the distinction. Web surveys, for example, are typically confidential but not anonymous. They are not anonymous because you could trace the survey (via an **IP address** or panel member ID number) back to the computer/individual from which it was sent. This does not necessarily mean that the survey is not anonymous because someone may use a public computer, but you cannot make this promise in advance. Be sure ahead of time that you can adhere to any confidentiality and/or anonymity statements that you make. In addition to informing respondents of whether their responses are confidential or anonymous, you should also point them toward your company's privacy policy.

Visual Design

How your survey is constructed is just as important as the questions it contains. There are ways to structure a survey to improve the response rate and reduce the likelihood that respondents will complete the survey incorrectly.

Responsive Design

Increasingly, people are accessing information on mobile devices rather than desktop or laptop computers. This means that there is a good chance respondents will attempt to complete your survey on their phone or tablet. Using responsive design means that your online survey will scale to look great regardless of the size of the device. Check your survey on multiple mobile devices to ensure everyone can complete your survey with ease.

Reduce Clutter

Whether you are creating your survey electronically or on paper, avoid clutter. The document should be visually neat and attractive. Be a minimalist. Include a survey title and some instructional text, but avoid unnecessary headers, text, lines, borders, boxes, etc. As we mentioned earlier, it is imperative that you keep your survey short. Provide sufficient white space to keep the survey readable and one question distinguishable from another. A dense two-page survey (whether online or on paper) is actually worse than a five-page survey with the questions well spaced. Dense surveys take longer to read and it can be difficult to distinguish between questions.

Font Selection

You may be tempted to choose a small font size so that you can fit in more questions, but this is not advisable. A 12-point font is the smallest recommended. If you are creating an online survey, choose fonts that are comparable to these sizes. For web surveys, set relative rather than absolute font sizes so that users can adjust the size via their browsers. Remember that some respondents may complete your survey on a smartphone rather than a large computer monitor.

Font style is another important consideration. Choose a font that is highly readable. Standard sans serif fonts (fonts without tails on the characters, such as **Arial** or **Verdana**) are good choices. Avoid decorative or whimsical fonts, for example, *Monotype Corsiva*, as they tend to be much more difficult to read. Choose one font style and stick with it. NEVER USE ALL CAPS AS IT IS VERY DIFFICULT TO READ.

Use a Logical Sequence and Groupings

Surveys, like interviews, should be treated like a conversation. In a normal conversation, you do not jump from one topic to another without some kind of segue to notify the other person that you are changing topics. This would be confusing for the other person you are talking to, and the same is true in interviews and surveys. If your survey will cover more than one topic, group them together and add section headers to tell respondents you are moving on to a new topic.

Start with the simple questions first and then move toward the more complex ones to build a rapport. As discussed earlier, if you must include sensitive or demographic questions, leave them until the end of the survey and mark them as "optional." Confirm during your pilot testing that the flow of the survey makes sense, especially in the case of surveys that include significant branching.

Considerations When Choosing a Survey Distribution Method

This section discusses a variety of factors that apply to each of the distribution methods. This information should enable you to make the appropriate distribution choice based on your needs.

Cost per Complete

There are several collection costs one must keep in mind when considering which survey method to use. Unique costs per method are shown in Table 10.2.

Table 10.2: Costs per survey method

	Labor for stuffing envelopes, addressing	Printing	Postage	Labor for phone interviews	Labor for data entry	Online survey tool
Phone				✓	✓	
Postal mail	✓	✓	✓		✓	
Online						✓

TIP

Most large survey vendors conduct regular **omnibus surveys** that combine a few questions from many clients and send them to a broad sample of users on their panels. It is kind of like carpooling, but instead of sharing a car, you are sharing a survey instrument. This is a cheap and efficient method if you have just a few questions you want to ask a general population. Just make sure you are aware of the sample that is being used and which questions come before yours to ensure that respondents are not being predisposed to a certain mindset. For example, if the questions before yours are about privacy policies on the web, the respondents will be very mindful of privacy-related issues by the time they get to your questions. This may have no impact on your questions or it may completely skew your results, depending on your topic.

Respondents

If you have a customer list, regardless of which method you use, there are no upfront costs for getting access to your desired population. If not, you must pay a vendor to recruit respondents. For a full discussion about selecting research vendors, refer to Chapter 6, "Recruiting Participants" section on page 126. The response rate is often higher when contacting your own customers because customers feel invested in improving the product or service they use. However, it is important to realize that your customer list may not be up-to-date. People move, change phone numbers (work and personal), and sometimes give "junk" e-mail addresses to avoid getting spam. To get an idea of what your overall response rate will be before contacting every customer in your database, send your survey through your desired means (i.e., e-mail invitation, phone, mail) to 100 customers and see how many respond. You may be surprised how many "bounced" e-mails or disconnected phone lines you encounter. If you have a well-developed marketing department that communicates with your customers via e-mail using tools, such as *MailChimp* or *Constant Contact*, they should have a good idea of the health and activity of your mailing list.

Labor

Labor costs of data analysis will be the same regardless of the method you choose. Until now, we have not talked a lot about the use of telephone surveys using RDD or a customer list. Phone surveys require labor costs to conduct the interviews over the phone and enter the data, whereas paper-based surveys require costs for paper and printing, labor costs to stuff and label the envelopes, postage (both to the respondent and back to you), and entering the data.

Time

Paper-based and phone surveys require more time to prepare and collect data. Allow time in your schedule to make copies of your paper-based survey and to stuff and address a large number of envelopes. Data entry also takes significant time. Do a trial data entry early on using one of your completed pilot surveys, so you can get a sense of just how long this will take. It is also wise to have a second individual check the data entry for errors. Experienced researchers can tell you that this always takes longer than expected. It is better to be aware of this ahead of time, so you can budget the extra time into your schedule.

Tools

Online surveys will most likely require the purchase of a license for an online survey tool, although some basic ones are free (e.g., Google Forms). However, there are no additional costs over the other methods. Phone and e-mail surveys can be created cheaply using any word processing document; however, you will likely want to use a survey tool for phone interviewers to directly enter responses and skip the data entry step later.

Response Rate

The upfront costs are not the only thing to consider when deciding which method to choose. Your response rate will vary depending on the survey mode you choose, so what you are really interested in calculating is the **cost per complete** (i.e., total costs divided by the number of completed responses). Additionally, different modes are better at reaching different types of respondents. As a result, researchers who really need to get results from a representative sample of their entire population will often conduct mixed-mode surveys (i.e., conducting a survey via more than one mode) to enhance the representativeness of respondents. Mixed-mode surveys reduce **coverage bias** (i.e., some of your population is not covered by the sampling frame) and nonresponse errors and increase response rates and the overall number of respondents. Unfortunately, they are more expensive and laborious to manage. Several studies have been conducted comparing the costs, response rates, and composition of respondents (Dillman, Smyth, & Christian, 2009; Greenlaw & Brown-Welty, 2009; Groves, Dilman, Eltinge, & Little, 2002; Holbrook, Krosnick, & Pfent, 2007; Schonlau et al., 2004; Weisberg, 2005). One recent study (Crow, Johnson, & Hanneman, 2011) found mixed benefits in using mixed-mode surveys. Costs per complete were highest for phone ($71.78) and then for postal mail ($34.80) and cheapest for online ($9.81). They knew the demographics of their population and could conduct an analysis of nonresponse. They found that multiple modes improved the representativeness of gender in the sample but actually made the sample *less* representative of the citizenship and college affiliation of the overall population. At this time, it is unclear if mixed-mode surveys are worth the added cost and effort required to conduct them.

Suggested Resources for Additional Reading

If you are interested in mixed-mode surveys, the following resources will be helpful to review:

- Callegaro, M., Lozar Manfreda, K., & Vehovar, V. (2015). *Web survey methodology*. London: Sage.
- Dillman, D. A., Smyth, J. D., & Christian, L. M. (2014). *Internet, phone, mail, and mixed-mode surveys. The tailored design method* (4th ed.). Hoboken: Wiley.
- Holbrook, A., Krosnick, J. A., & Pfent, A. (2007). The causes and consequences of response rates in surveys by the news media and government contractor survey research firms. *Advances in telephone survey methodology*, 499–528.

Interactivity

E-mail and paper-based surveys do not offer interactivity. The interactivity of the web provides some additional advantages.

Validation

The survey program can check each survey response for omitted answers and errors when the respondent submits it. For example, it can determine whether the respondent has left any questions blank and provide a warning or error message, limit the format of the response based on the question type (e.g., allow only numbers for questions requiring a number), and give a warning if the respondent is answering the questions too quickly.

Allow for More Complex Designs

With careful design, a web-based survey *can* help you to make a detailed or large survey simple from the users' point of view. Online, you have the ability to include branching questions without the respondent even being aware of the branch (see Figure 10.1).

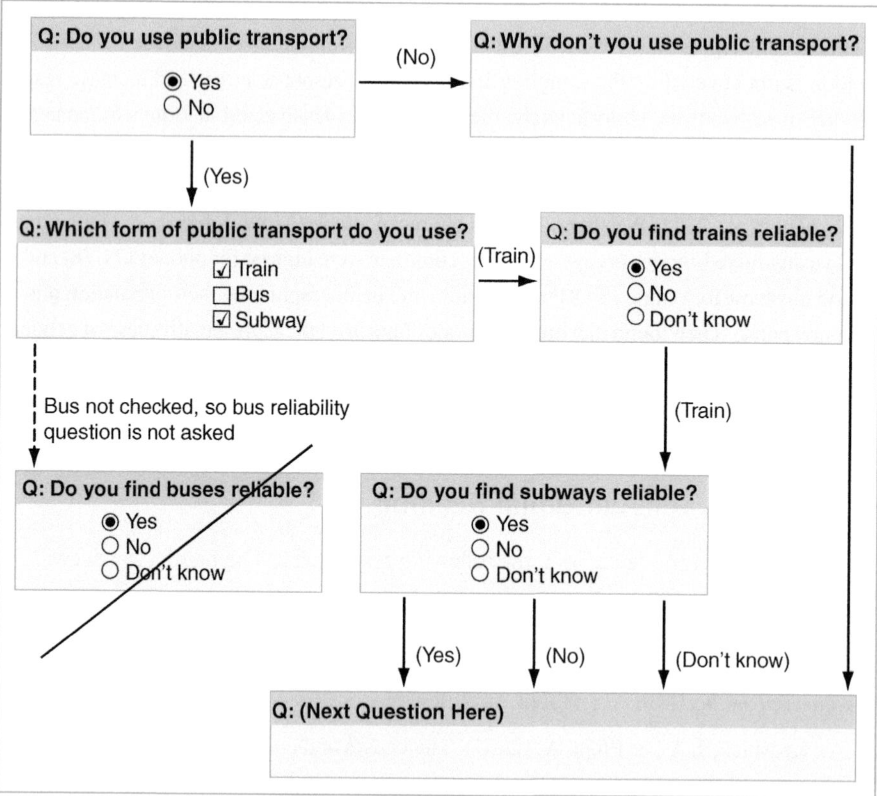

Figure 10.1: Survey with branching.

For example, let us say that the question asks whether a participant uses public transit and the response to this question will determine the set of questions the person will be required to answer. You could choose a design where once respondents answer the question, they are required to click "Next." When they click "Next," they will be seamlessly brought to the next appropriate set of questions based on the response they made on the previous page. The respondents will not even see the questions for the alternative responses. This also prevents respondents from answering questions they should not based on the experience (or lack thereof).

More Intuitive Design

Web widgets can help make your survey more intuitive. Widgets such as droplists can reduce the physical length of your survey and can clearly communicate the options available to the user. Radio buttons can limit respondents to one selection, rather than multiple, if required (see Figure 10.2).

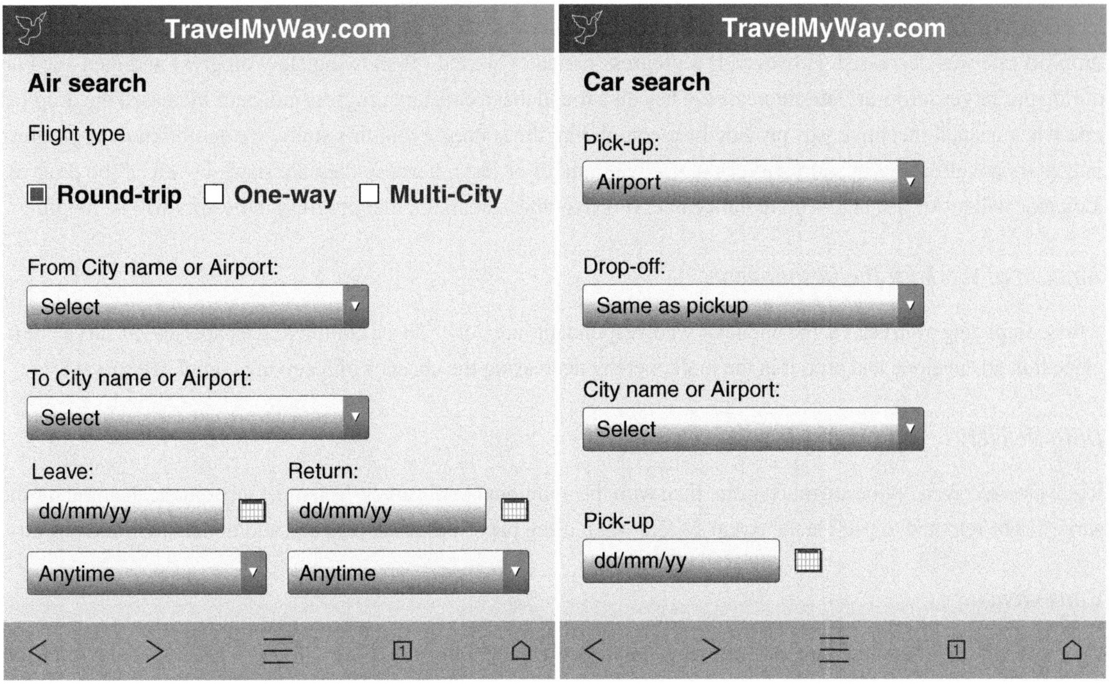

Figure 10.2: Examples of web widgets.

TIP

Scrolling droplists should be avoided. They hide the list of answers, and some people will visually focus on the top couple of entries without noticing a more suitable answer lower on the list. Avoid long lists of radio buttons that would force the user to scroll back and forth to view all of the options. Instead, break these questions in smaller questions by grouping similar options, if possible.

Progress Indicators

If a survey is broken into multiple pages online, progress indicators are often included to let respondents know how far along they are and how many more questions they have left to complete (see Figure 10.3). The belief is that this decreases the **drop-off rate** (i.e., respondents exiting the survey before completing it). However, a meta-analysis of 32 studies of medium to long length (10 minutes or more) on the effectiveness of progress indicators found that "overall, using a constant progress indicator does not significantly help reduce drop-offs and that effectiveness of the progress indicator varies depending on the speed of indicator …" (Villar, Callegaro, & Yang, 2013). If a progress

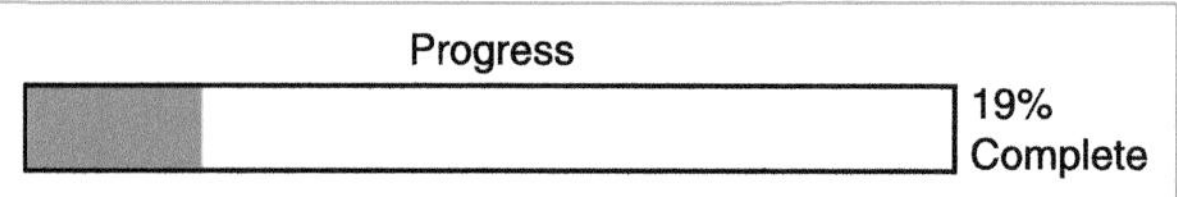

Figure 10.3: Progress indicator.

indicator started off showing quick progress and then slowed down as one progressed through the survey, the drop-off rate was decreased. However, if a progress indicator started off showing slow progress and then sped up during the survey, drop-off rates increased. They also found that a constant progress indicator increased the drop-off rate when a small incentive was provided for completing the survey. From this study, we do not know if progress indicators are effective for short surveys (e.g., five minutes or less); because they are short, however, the progress indicator will move fast and is more noticeable. It is hypothesized, then, that progress indicators will be helpful.

Amount of Work for the Respondent

After completing a survey via the phone or web, respondents are done. Those completing a paper-based survey must place it in an envelope and drop it in the mail, thereby decreasing the chances of receiving completed surveys.

Data Delivery

Responses received online are much faster than with the traditional mail survey. You must incorporate the time for the survey to be returned to you via the postal system when using paper-based surveys and additional time for data entry.

Consistency

By the term "consistency," we are referring to how the participant sees the survey. This is not an issue for paper-based surveys because you have total control over the way the questions appear. In the case of online surveys, your survey may look and behave differently depending on the device (e.g., desktop, laptop, tablet, smartphone) and browser used to open it. Ideally, you want your survey to render well regardless of device and browser. Test your survey across browsers and devices before launching to ensure the ideal user experience, or you may find lower completion rates for a portion of your sample.

Privacy

Respondents may be hesitant to complete your survey because they are concerned about their privacy. This can be manifested by lower completion rates (discussed above) and by the amount of **satisficing** and **social desirability bias** observed. This is usually not an issue for paper-based surveys since the person can remain anonymous (other than the postmark on the envelope). One study (Holbrook et al., 2003) comparing telephone to face-to-face surveys found that respondents in the telephone survey were more likely to **satisfice**, to express suspicion about the interview, and to demonstrate **social desirability bias**. Another study found more **satisficing** and **social desirability bias** in the telephone surveys than online surveys. Remember that you are ethically obligated to protect the respondents' privacy (refer to Chapter 3, "Privacy," page 66). Inform respondents in the beginning if the survey will be confidential or anonymous and point them to your company's privacy policy.

Computer Expertise/Access

Obviously, computer expertise and/or access is not an issue for paper-based surveys, but it is an issue for online surveys. If your respondents have varying levels of computer experience or access to the web, this could impact your survey results. You should also determine if your survey tool is accessibility-compliant. If it cannot be completed with a screen reader or without the use of a mouse, for example, you will be excluding a segment of your population. You can increase the representativeness of your sample by conducting a multimode survey, but ideally, your tools should also be universally accessible.

Pilot Test Your Survey and Iterate

The value of running a pilot or pretesting your user research activity is discussed in Chapter 6 "Preparing for Your Activity" (refer to "Piloting Your Activity" section, page 155). However, testing your survey is so important to its success that we want to discuss the specifics here in more detail. Keep in mind that once you send the survey out the door, you will not be able to get it back to make changes—so it is critical to discover any problems before you reach the distribution stage.

You may be thinking, "Well, my survey is on the web, so I can make changes as I discover them." Wrong. If you catch mistakes after distribution or realize that your questions are not being interpreted in the way intended, you will have to discard the previous data. You cannot compare the data before and after edits. This means that it will take more time to collect additional data points and cost more money.

When running your pilot, you want to make sure that you are recruiting people who match your user profile, not just your colleagues. Colleagues can help you catch typos and grammatical errors, but unless they are domain experts, many of the questions may not make sense to them. Using people who fit the user profile will help you confirm that your questions are clear and understandable. You will want to look for the following:

- Typos and grammatical errors.
- The time it takes to complete the survey (if it is too long, now is your chance to shorten it).
- Comprehensibility of the format, instructions, and questions.
- In the case of a web survey, determine (a) whether there are any broken links or bugs and (b) whether the data are returned in the correct or expected format.

A modified version of a technique referred to as **cognitive interview testing** (or **cognitive pretest**) is critical when piloting your survey. We say a "modified version" because formal cognitive interviewing can be quite labor-intensive. It can involve piloting a dozen or more people through iterative versions of your survey and then undertaking a detailed analysis. Unfortunately, in the world of product development, schedules do not allow for this. The key element of this technique that will benefit you in evaluating your survey is the **think-aloud protocol**.

Think-aloud protocol—or "verbal protocol" as it is often called—is described elsewhere in this book (refer to Chapter 7, "Using a Think-Aloud Protocol" section, page 169). If you have ever run a usability test, you are likely familiar with this technique. When applied to survey evaluation, the idea is that you watch someone complete your survey while literally thinking aloud, as you observe. As the participant reads through the questions, he or she tells you what he or she is thinking. The person's verbal commentary will allow you to identify problems, such as questions that are not interpreted correctly or that are confusing. In addition, during the completion of the survey, you can note questions that are completed with incorrect answers, skipped questions, hesitations, or any other behaviors that indicate a potential problem understanding the survey. After the completion of the survey, you should discuss each of these potential problem areas with the pilot respondent. This is referred to as the **retrospective interview**. You can also follow up with the pilot respondent and ask for his or her thoughts on the survey: "Did you find it interesting?" "Would you likely fill it out if approached?" This is sure to provide some revealing insights. Do *not* skip the cognitive pretest or retrospective interview, no matter how pressed for time you may be! If participants do not interpret your questions correctly or are confused, the data collected will be meaningless.

Suggested Resources for Additional Reading

If you would like to learn more about cognitive interviewing as applied to survey development, check out the following book:

- Miller, K., Chepp, V., Wilson, S., & Padilla, J. L. (2014). *Cognitive interviewing methodology*. Hoboken, NJ: Wiley.

After you have completed your cognitive pretesting, you will want to conduct a pilot study with a dozen or so respondents and then analyze the data exactly as you would if you were working with the final data. Obviously, this is too small of a sample to draw conclusions, but what you are checking is whether the data are all formatted correctly, there are no bugs (in the case online surveys), and you have all of the data you need to answer your research questions. Many people skip this step because it is viewed as not worth the time or effort, and stakeholders are usually anxious to get data collection started; however, once you experience a data collection error, you will *never* skip this step again. Save yourself the pain and do an analysis pilot!

Data Analysis and Interpretation

You have collected all of your survey responses, so what is next? Now, it is time to find out what all of those responses are telling you. You should be well prepared if you did an analysis pilot.

Initial Assessment

Your first step (if this did not happen automatically via the web) is to get the data into an electronic file. Typically, the data will be entered into a spreadsheet or .csv file. Attach to this file metadata about your survey (e.g., researcher, dates the survey was conducted, panel used, screening criteria). Having these data embedded as the first few lines of your file means that you (or researchers after you) will *always* know important details about how the data were collected without having to track down a separate report or presentation.

TIP

Make a copy of your original file and then make any changes to the *copy*. Never edit the original data file!

Microsoft® Excel®, *SPSS, SAS,* and *R* are some of the well-known programs that will enable you to accomplish your analyses. The rows will be used to denote each participant, and the columns will be used to indicate each question. Some statistical packages allow you to enter only numeric values, so you may need to do some coding. For example, if you asked people how they booked their most recent travel, you would not be able to enter "web," "travel agency," or "other" into the spreadsheet; you would have to use a code for each response, such as "web = 1," "travel agency = 2," and "other = 3." Figure 10.4 illustrates a sample of data entered in a spreadsheet format. For the same reason, these tools cannot handle the text responses respondents enter for "other." You will be able to see how many respondents chose "other," but you will need to use a qualitative analysis tool (refer to Chapter 8, "Qualitative Analysis Tools" section, page 208) or affinity diagram (refer to Chapter 12, "Affinity Diagram" section, page 363) or to manually group the responses yourself.

Participant no.	*Q1—Gender*	*Q2—Salary*	*Q3—Age*	*Q4—Years of web experience*
1	1	55,000	34	9
2	1	65,000	39	5
3	2	100,000	41	4
4	2	58,000	22	5
5	1	79,000	33	7

Figure 10.4: Sample data entered into a spreadsheet.

Once you have your data in the spreadsheet, you should scan it to catch any abnormalities. This is manageable if you have 100 or fewer responses, but it can be more difficult once you get beyond that. Look for typos that may have been generated at your end or by the participant. For example, you might find in the age column that someone is listed as age "400," when this is likely supposed to be "40." Some quick descriptive statistics (e.g., mean, min/max) can often show you big errors like this. If you have the paper survey to refer to, you can go back and find out whether there was a data entry error on your part. If data entry was automatic (i.e., via the web), you cannot ethically make any changes. Unless you can contact that respondent, you cannot assume you knew what he or she meant and then change the data. You will have to drop the abnormal data point or leave it as is (your stats package will ignore any empty fields in its calculation). You may also find that some cells are missing data. If you entered your data manually, the ideal situation is to have a colleague read out the raw data to you while you check your spreadsheet. This is more reliable than "eyeballing" it, but because of time constraints, this may not be possible if you have a lot of data.

Types of Calculation

Below, we discuss the most typical forms of data analysis for closed-ended questions. You should review Section "Qualitative Analysis Tools" in Chapter 8 on page 208 for a discussion of qualitative data analysis for OEQs.

Many of the types of calculation you will carry out for most surveys are fairly straightforward, and we will describe them only briefly here. There are many introductory statistics books available today, in the event that you need more of a foundation. Our goal is not to teach you statistics, but to let you know what the common statistics are and why you might want to use them. These types of calculations can be illustrated effectively by using graphs and/or tables. Where appropriate, we have inserted some sample visuals.

Suggested Resources for Additional Reading

If you would like to learn more about survey data analysis, we recommend the following:

Heeringa, S. G., West, B. T., & Berglund, P. A. (2010). *Applied survey data analysis*. CRC Press.

At a Glance

> Descriptive statistics
> Measures of dispersion
> Measures of association
> Inferential statistics
> Paradata

Descriptive Statistics

These measures *describe* the sample in your population. They are the key calculations that will be of importance to you for closed-ended questions and can easily be calculated by any basic statistics program or spreadsheet.

Central Tendency

- *Mean:* Average of the scores in the population. It equals the sum of the scores divided by the number of scores. See Figure 10.5.
- *Median:* The point that divides the distribution of scores in half. Numerically, half of the scores in your sample will have values that are equal to or larger than the median, and half will have values that are equal to or smaller than the median. This is the best indicator of the "typical case" when your data are skewed.
- *Mode:* The score in the population that occurs most frequently. The mode is *not* the frequency of the most numerous score. It is the value of that score itself. The mode is the best indicator of the "typical case" when the data are extremely skewed to one side or the other.

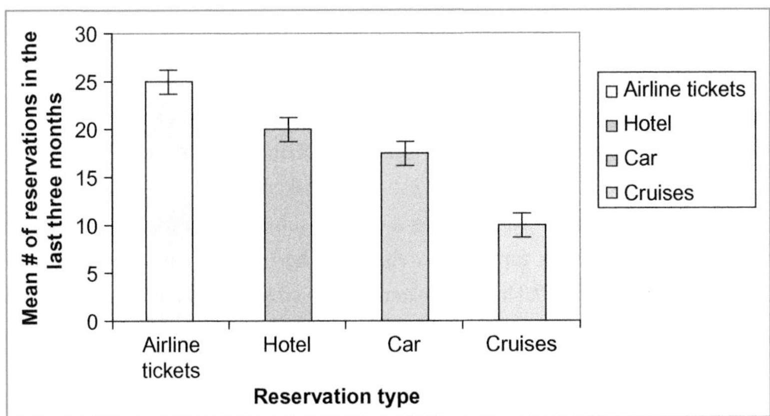

Figure 10.5: Graph of mean number of bookings in the last three months.

- *Maximum and minimum:* The *maximum* indicates how far the data extend in the upper direction, while the *minimum* shows how far the data extend in the lower direction. In other words, the minimum is the smallest number in your data set and the maximum is the largest.

Measures of Dispersion

These statistics show you the "spread" or dispersion of the data around the mean.

- *Range:* The maximum value minus the minimum value. It indicates the spread between the two extremes.
- *Standard deviation:* A measure of the deviation from the mean. The larger the standard deviation, the more varied the responses were that participants gave.
- *Frequency:* The number of times that each response is chosen. This is one of the more useful calculations for survey analysis. This kind of information can be used to create graphs that clearly illustrate your findings. It is nice to convert the frequencies to percentages (see Figure 10.6).

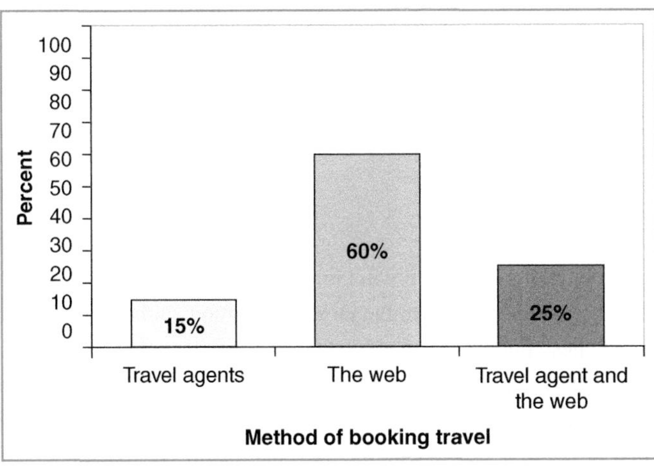

Figure 10.6: Graph of frequencies for the methods of booking travel.

Measures of Association

Measures of association allow you to identify the relationship between two survey variables.

- *Comparisons:* Comparisons demonstrate how answers to one question are related to the responses to another question in order to see relationships. For example, let us say we had a question that asked people whether they made hotel reservations via the web. Imagine 73% had and 27% had not. As a comparison, we want to see whether the answer to this question relates to whether or not they book cars on the web. So, of the 73% that have booked a hotel online, how many of them have also booked a car online? This is an example of a cross tabulation. You can graph it to see the relationships more clearly (see Figure 10.7). Pivot tables are one way to conduct this analysis.

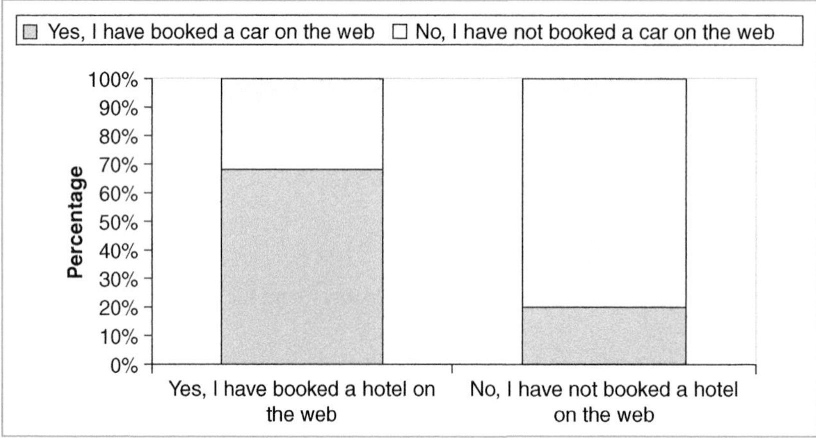

Figure 10.7: Graph comparing people who book hotels and cars on the web versus those who do not.

- *Correlations:* They are used to measure the degree to which two variables are related. It is important to note that correlations do not imply causation (i.e., you could not state that the presence of hotel deals caused people to book a hotel). Correlation analysis generates a correlation coefficient, which is the measure of how the two variables move together. This value ranges from 0 (indicating no relationship) to ±1. A positive number indicates a positive correlation, and the closer that number is to 1, the stronger the positive correlation. A "positive correlation" means that the two variables move in the same direction together, while a "negative correlation" means that the two variables move in the opposite direction.

Inferential Statistics

Like the name implies, these measures allow us to make inferences or predictions about the characteristics of our population. We first need to test how generalizable these findings are to the larger population, and to do that, we need to do tests of **significance** (i.e., confirming that these findings were not the result of random chance or errors in sampling). This is accomplished via T-tests, Chi-squared, and ANOVA, for instance. Other inferential statistics include factor analysis and regression analysis, just to name a few. Using our TravelMyWay.com example, let us imagine your company is trying to decide whether or not to do away with the live chat feature. If you conducted a survey to inform your decision, you would likely want to know if the use of the live chat feature is *significantly* correlated with other measures like satisfaction and willingness to use the service in the future. To answer this question, inferential statistics will be required. Refer to the "Suggested Resources" if you would like to find a book to learn more about this type of analysis.

Paradata Analysis

Paradata is the information about the *process* of responding to the survey. This includes things like how long it took the respondent to answer each question or the whole survey, if he or she changed any answers to his or her questions or went back to previous pages, if the respondent opened and closed the survey without completing it (i.e., partial completion), and how he or she completed it (e.g., smartphone app, web browser, phone, paper). It can be enlightening to examine these data to see if your survey is too long and confusing, if there are issues completing your survey via one of the modes (e.g., respondents that started the survey on a smartphone or tablet never submitted), or if you have a set of respondents that are flying through your survey far too quickly. It is unlikely you can collect much of these data for phone or paper surveys, but you can via some web survey tools and vendors.

Suggested Resources for Further Reading

If you would like to learn more about collecting and analyzing survey paradata, check out:

- Kreuter, F. (Ed.). 2013. *Improving surveys with paradata: Analytic uses of process information.* Hoboken, NJ: Wiley.

Communicating the Findings

As fascinating as you might find all of the detailed analyses of your survey, it is unlikely that your stakeholders will be equally fascinated by the minutia. You cannot present a 60-slide presentation to your stakeholders covering all of your analyses, so you really need to pick a few *critical* findings that tell a story. Once you have identified what those few critical findings are, you can begin to create your presentation (e.g., report, slides, poster, handouts).

An important thing to keep in mind when presenting survey results is to make them as visual as possible. You want those reviewing the findings to be able to *see* the findings at a glance. Bar charts and line graphs are the most effective ways to do this. Most statistics packages or *Microsoft Excel* will enable you to create these visuals with ease.

Obviously, you will need to explain what the results mean in terms of the study objectives and any limitations in the data. If the results were inconclusive, highly varied, or not representative of the true user population, state this clearly. It would be irresponsible to allow people to draw conclusions from results that were inaccurate. For example, if you know your sample was biased because you learned that the product team was sending only their best customers the link to your survey, inform the stakeholders that the data can be applied only to the most experienced customers. It is your responsibility to understand who the survey is representing and what conclusions can be drawn from the results. Sometimes, the answer is "further investigation is needed."

Pulling It All Together

In this chapter, we have illustrated the details of creating an effective survey. You should now be able to create valuable questions and format your survey in a way that is easy to understand and that attracts the interest of the potential respondents. You should also be equipped to deploy your survey, collect the responses, and analyze and present the data. You are now ready to hit the ground running to create a survey that will allow you to collect the user research you need.

CASE STUDY: *GOOGLE DRIVE'S HAPPINESS TRACKING SURVEY (HaTS)*

Hendrik Müller, Senior User Experience Researcher, Google, Sydney, Australia
Aaron Sedley, Senior User Experience Researcher, Google, Mountain View, USA

Introduction

At Google, we decided to implement surveys as a valuable user experience research method. By quantifying users' attitudes and tracking their experiences longitudinally, surveys complement other human computer interaction (HCI) research methods used to understand behaviors and needs. As Google expanded its product offerings beyond Search, we established Happiness Tracking Surveys (HaTS) as a survey research model yielding high-quality, high-value data across products. To provide unique insights for product design and development, we designed HaTS with two primary goals in mind: (1) to reliably measure and track changes in users' attitudes and perceptions about products over time, and (2) to explicitly collect open-ended feedback from a representative sample of the product's user base.

By inviting users to the survey as they are using the product, HaTS yields timely metrics and insights. HaTS applies best practices in sampling and questionnaire design, informed by decades of academic research, to optimize data validity and reliability. HaTS also uses consistent sampling and standardized results reporting to enhance its scalability. Launched in 2006, HaTS has expanded to many of Google's products, including Google Search, Gmail, Google Maps, Google Docs, Google Drive, and YouTube. Surveys now play an important role as a user-centric method to inform product decisions and measure progress toward goals.

In the remainder of this case study, we will take a closer look at how we use HaTS for the Google Drive product, discussing its approach to sampling and respondent invitation, the questionnaire instrument, and some of the insights it has provided to the team.

Sampling and Invitation

The essence of surveying is sampling, a way to gather information about a population by obtaining data from a subset of that population. Depending on the population size and the number of survey respondents, we can estimate metrics at a certain level of precision and confidence. HaTS uses a probability-based sampling approach, randomly selecting users to see a survey invitation.

Each week, we invite a representative set of Google Drive's users to take HaTS. An algorithm randomly segments the entire user base into distinct buckets. Each bucket may see the survey invitation for a week; then, the invitation rotates to the next bucket. Randomizing based on individual users, instead of page views (e.g., choosing every *n*th visitor), reduces bias toward users that visit the product more frequently. To avoid effects of survey fatigue, users shown an invitation to HaTS are not invited again for at least 12 weeks. The target sample size (i.e., the number of survey completions) depends on the level of precision needed for reliable estimates and comparisons. For Google Drive's HaTS, as commonly used for such research, we aim for at least 384 responses per week, which translates to a ±5% margin of error with 95% confidence.

One of the fundamental strengths of HaTS is that people are invited to the survey as they are using the product itself; therefore, the responses directly reflect users' attitudes and perceptions in context of their actual experiences with the product. We invite potential respondents through a small dialog shown at the bottom of the product page (see Figure 10.8). The invitation is visually differentiated from other content on the page and positioned so that it is easily seen when the page loads. Note that HaTS does not use pop-up invitations requiring users to respond before they can continue to the rest of the site, as that would interrupt users' normal workflows. The invitation text is "Help us improve Google Drive" with a "Take our survey!" call to action; this neutral wording encourages all users equally, not only those with especially positive or negative feedback.

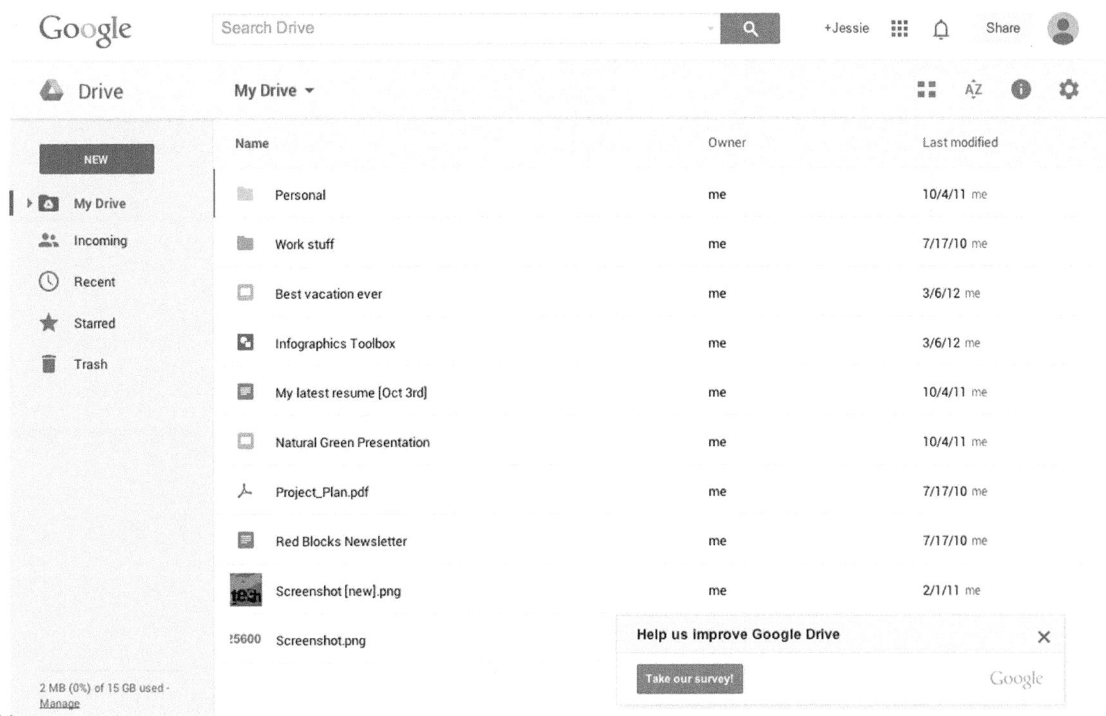

Figure 10.8: HaTS invitation in the Google Drive web interface.

Questionnaire Instrument

We designed the HaTS questionnaire following established guidelines to optimize the reliability and validity of responses (Müller, Sedley, & Ferrall-Nunge, 2014). HaTS minimizes common biases such as satisficing (Krosnick, 1991; Krosnick, Narayan, & Smith, 1996; Krosnick, 1999), acquiescence (Smith, 1967; Saris et al., 2010), social desirability (Schlenker & Weigold, 1989), and order effects (Landon, 1971; Tourangeau et al., 2004). It also relies on an extensive body of research regarding the structure of scales and responses options (Krosnick & Fabrigar, 1997). We optimized the visual design of the HaTS questionnaire for usability and avoid unnecessary and biasing visual stimuli (Couper, 2008).

The core of Google Drive's HaTS lies in measuring users' overall attitudes over time, by tracking satisfaction. We collect satisfaction ratings by asking, "Overall, how satisfied or dissatisfied are you with Google Drive?" (see Figure 10.9)

Google **Google Drive Survey**

Thank you for offering your feedback on Google Drive.
Understanding your experiences and opinions helps Google make this product better for you and other users.

You **must be at least 18 years old** to participate in Google user research. We will only use your personal information for purposes of Google user research. For details on how Google treats personal information from users, read our privacy policy which you will be taken to have agreed to when you submit your information in this form to us.

If you use Google Drive with multiple accounts, respond to this survey for the account from which you got here.

Overall, how satisfied or dissatisfied are you with Google Drive?

Extremely dissatisfied	Moderately dissatisfied	Slightly dissatisfied	Neither satisfied nor dissatisfied	Slightly satisfied	Moderately satisfied	Extremely satisfied
○	○	○	○	○	○	○

(Optional)
What, if anything, do you find frustrating or unappealing about Google Drive?
What *new* capabilities would you like to see for Google Drive?

(Optional)
What do you like best about Google Drive?

CONTINUE »

© 2014 Google

Figure 10.9: The first page of Google Drive's HaTS with questions on overall satisfaction, areas of frustrations, and areas of appreciation.

referring to the concept of satisfaction in a neutral way by calling out both "satisfied" and "dissatisfied." As satisfaction is a bipolar construct and we have sufficient space in the user interface, a 7-point scale is used to optimize validity and reliability, while minimizing the respondents' efforts (Krosnick & Fabrigar, 1997; Krosnick & Tahk, 2008). The scale is fully-labeled without using numbers to ensure respondents consistently interpret the answer options (Krosnick & Presser, 2010). Scale items are displayed horizontally to minimize order biases and are equally spaced (Tourangeau, 1984), both semantically and visually (Couper, 2008): "Extremely dissatisfied," "Moderately dissatisfied," "Slightly dissatisfied," "Neither satisfied nor dissatisfied," "Slightly satisfied," "Moderately satisfied," and "Extremely satisfied." Note the use of "Neither satisfied nor dissatisfied" instead of "Neutral" as the midpoint, which reduces satisficing (Krosnick, 1991). Furthermore, the negative extreme is listed first to allow for a more natural mapping to how respondents interpret bipolar constructs (Tourangeau et al., 2004). The satisfaction question is the only required question within HaTS, since without a response to this question, the primary goal of HaTS is not achieved.

Another critical goal of ours for Google Drive's HaTS is to gather qualitative data about users' experiences. Through two OEQs (see Figure 10.9), we ask respondents to describe the most frustrating aspects of the product ("What, if anything, do you find frustrating or unappealing about Google Drive?" and "What new capabilities would you like to see for Google Drive?") and what they like the most about the product ("What do you like best about Google Drive?"). Even though the former question may appear as double-barreled in its current design, through experimentation, we determined that asking about experienced frustrations and new capabilities in the same question increased the response quantity (i.e., a higher percentage of respondents provided input) and quality (i.e., responses were more thoughtful in their description and provided additional details) and also reduced analysis efforts. Respondents are encouraged to spend more time on the frustrations questions since they are listed first, and their answer text field is larger (Couper, 2008). These questions are explicitly labeled as "(Optional)," ensuring that respondents do not quit the survey if they perceive an open-ended response as too much effort and minimizing random responses (e.g., "asdf") that slow down the analysis process. We have consistently received response rates between 40% and 60% for these OEQs when applying this format.

Even though this case study only concentrates on HaTS' first-page questions about the respondent's overall attitudes and experiences with the product, the HaTS questionnaire contains further pages. On the second page, we explore common attributes and product-specific tasks; on the third page, we ask about some of the respondent's characteristics; and we reserve the fourth and last page for more ad hoc questions.

Applications and Insights

We have used HaTS in a variety of ways within the Google Drive team to aid product development and optimize users' experiences. One successful application of HaTS has been to measure the short- and long-term effects of user interface changes on users' attitudes, a phenomenon known as "change aversion" (Sedley & Müller, 2013). For one of Google Drive's major interface changes, we compared average satisfaction levels in the weeks prior to and following their launch, showing the intensity, duration, and resolution of attitudinal changes due to users' initial experiences with the modified product. By identifying the degree to which users react negatively to the way changes are introduced, we helped the product team to refine their launch strategy and to see whether certain changes are fundamentally degrading users' experiences beyond a natural adjustment period. Figure 10.10 shows the trends in satisfaction across two significant product changes. Identifying and measuring change aversion across products has

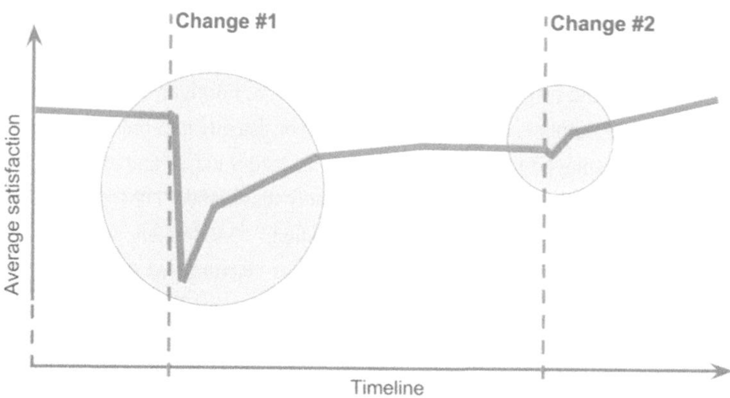

Figure 10.10: Trends in Google Drive's user satisfaction before and after two significant product changes.

led to the development and adoption of a framework that helps in minimizing users' pain and improves launches' prospects for success when transitioning from one to the next version of a product (Sedley & Müller, 2013).

Though tracking users' satisfaction is valuable, such attitudinal data in isolation only provides limited insights. Attitudinal shifts are further illuminated by coupling satisfaction data with an analysis of responses to the two OEQs, revealing the "why" behind the "what." The OEQs in HaTS provide a clear, quantifiable view of users' positive and frustrating experiences. In fact, these often represent the most insightful and actionable data being collected. We usually manually code hundreds of users' responses and then frequency-sort them, providing both a reliable prioritization of dissatisfaction causes and areas of appreciation. For example, after launching significant product changes, in several cases, we have analyzed these data and provided the team with explanations for changes in satisfaction. While the sources of frustration are often the most actionable, with a frequency-sorted list of areas of appreciation, we highlight aspects of the product team's efforts that were particularly successful. These insights allow the team to make informed decisions regarding the rollout process and the prioritization of postlaunch improvements. Furthermore, when we analyze HaTS' open-ended responses independent of a launch, they provide a wide range of views to inform product decision making. Contrasting with traditional "Send feedback" links that typically attract users who are particularly motivated to report good or bad experiences, with HaTS, we survey a representative set of users and can provide a more balanced set of responses. Through insights from such analyses, we repeatedly informed prioritization and product strategy for Google Drive.

Conclusion

As demonstrated in this case study, HaTS for Google Drive has successfully been used to measure change aversion throughout product updates and to understand top frustrations and areas of appreciation to inform product strategy. However, in other contexts, we have used HaTS to compare attitudes toward different product versions, to gauge users' awareness of specific product features, and to measure relationships between attitudes and usage characteristics. The described HaTS questions with their approach to sampling have proved to be an actionable, high-quality method for measuring, tracking, and comparing users' attitudes at scale.

This method can effectively be adopted by others who aspire to improve their products through a better understanding of their users' attitudes and experiences, both within and external to Google. We recommend to shift existing surveying practices to collecting data periodically from a random sample of users and to prepare analyses on a regular basis. Furthermore, to increase reliability and validity of the collected data, we recommend practitioners to explore ways to survey their products' users in the context of use, even if it may just be a link within the product pointing to a validated questionnaire implemented using one of the many available survey platforms.

Although the theoretical underpinnings of HaTS are solid and continual improvements have further strengthened this model, several challenges remain that inform our future work. As the manual analysis of large quantities of open-ended feedback is time-consuming, we need to explore approaches for full or partial automation of this analysis. Furthermore, even though HaTS is based on random sampling among active users, the self-selected nature of survey participation warrants a thorough investigation of potential nonresponse bias and consideration of options to address such bias.

CHAPTER 11

Card Sorting

Introduction

Card sorts show how people think content should be organized and named. Card sorts are often used to generate an **information architecture**. Information architecture refers to the organization of a product's structure and content, the labeling and categorizing of information, and the design of navigation and search systems. Information architecture can refer to software or websites or physical organization (e.g., controls on the dashboard of a car, the fruit stand at your local farmers' market). A good architecture helps users find information or items and accomplish their tasks with ease. Card sorting is one method that can help you understand how users think the information and navigation should be within your product. Information architecture is "all about three things: (1) organizing content or objects, (2) describing them clearly, and (3) providing ways for people to get to them" (Spencer, 2010, p. 4).

This method involves writing objects that are in—or proposed to be in—your product (e.g., hotel reservation, rental car agreement) on cards and asking users to sort the cards into groups that make sense to them. The objects are pieces of information or tasks that are—or will be—in your product. You want to understand how the users think those objects should be organized. There are no right or wrong groups; rather, a card sort helps you elicit from your participants the groups that already exist in their minds. You then strive to replicate these groupings in your product. By doing so, users will be able to easily find what they are looking for when using your product.

In this chapter, we discuss the uses of card sorting, how to prepare for and conduct a card sort, and how to analyze and present the information. Finally, a case study by Jenny Shirey is offered so that you may see an example of a successful card sort.

At a Glance

> Things to be aware of when conducting a card sort
> Preparing to conduct a card sort
> Conducting a card sort
> Data analysis and interpretation
> Communicating the findings

Things to Be Aware of When Conducting a Card Sort

There are a number of questions that you need to answer before starting your card sort. For example, will you use an open or a closed card sort procedure? Do you want participants to sort physical cards or use a computerized card sort program? If you are conducting a computerized card sort, will participants be remote (i.e., participating online from a location of their choice) or in person (i.e., in whatever location you choose to meet them, for example, your company's user research facility)? If you are conducting an in-person sort, will you conduct an individual (only one participant at a time) or simultaneous (more than one participant at a time) card sort exercise?

Open vs. Closed Sort

An open card sort is one where participants are allowed to generate as many categories of information as they want and name each of those categories however they please. A closed card sort is one where participants are given a set of cards *and* a set of predetermined categories and asked to place the cards into those preexisting categories. The two primary benefits of an open card sort are: (1) Participants have more flexibility to express how items are grouped in their minds, and therefore the outcome of the study may more accurately reflect an intuitive grouping; and (2) participants are asked to provide names for the groups they create, and therefore you get additional data about participants' vernacular. For these reasons, open sorts can be particularly useful early in the research process (e.g., at the concept stage, page 308). On the other hand, a closed card sort may be more appropriate when trying to improve the information architecture of an existing product. Open card sorts take more time to conduct and analyze because participants have more work to do (e.g., generate category names) and because the analysis can require more steps than a closed sort.

Physical Cards or Computerized Sort?

There are tools available that allow users to sort virtual cards on a computer rather than using physical cards. Computerized card sorting can save you time during the data analysis phase because the sorts are automatically saved in an immediately usable format. Another advantage is that, depending on the number of cards, users may be able to see all of the cards available for sorting at the same time. Unless you have a very large work surface for users to spread their physical cards on, this may not be possible for physical card sorts. Computerized sorting also has its disadvantages. First, you may need to provide a brief training session to explain how to use the software, and even with training, the user interface may be difficult for novice users to get the hang of. Second, if you run a simultaneous or group session, you will need a separate computer for each participant. This means money and potential technical issues.

Remote (Online) or In-Person Sort?

If you choose to conduct a computerized sort, some tools support remote online testing (see Remote card sort tools, page 317). Remote testing means that participants can participate in the card sort using an online tool or via a website that they access from their own computer. The advantage of this is that it allows you to gather data from users anywhere, without you having to travel. This means that you may be better able to get a geographically diverse population of participants. Furthermore, because the tests can be conducted simultaneously and do not require your active involvement, you can test a large number of participants in a short amount of time. However, the downside is that users may have a more difficult time without a facilitator in the room to answer questions, and therefore the quality of your data may suffer. You will also be less able to easily to capture think-aloud data using a remote sort.

TIP

Be sure to consider the privacy of your participants and/or your company when choosing to use remote/online services. Many remote testing providers have clauses in their Terms of Service that say they cannot promise that the data gathered using their tools will be kept private and secure. Even when providers assure privacy and security, you can never be sure that their servers will not be hacked and your data leaked. Therefore, if the product you are testing is confidential or the data you are collecting from participants are sensitive, you may be better off choosing to conduct your research in person, where you are in control of where data are stored and how data are protected.

Individual or Simultaneous Card Sort?

If you choose to conduct an in-person sort, you need to decide whether to conduct your card sort with several participants at once or one at a time. We often conduct sessions with several participants simultaneously because this allows us to collect large samples of data in a shorter time period. You can conduct an in-person card sort with as many people at a time as you can physically accommodate in your space. Even though we have a group of participants in the same room at the same time, they are not working together—they are each working individually.

The disadvantage with running several participants simultaneously is that you cannot collect think-aloud data (see Chapter 7, "Using a Think-Aloud Protocol" section, page 169), so you do not know why the users grouped the data the way they did. Although think-aloud data are helpful, participants typically provide enough information in their description of each group so the need to collect data quickly and from large samples may outweigh the benefit of having think-aloud data.

Some people dislike running a group card sort because they feel that the participants turn it into a race. In our experience, this has not been a problem. We encourage people to take their time because we will be there for as long as they need to sort the cards.

If you have the time, a hybrid approach works quite well: after collecting data from a group of participants, run one or two individual card sorts to collect think-aloud data. This additional data can help you better understand the groupings.

Preparing to Conduct a Card Sort

Now that we have presented when and why to conduct a card sort, we will discuss how to prepare for one.

At a Glance

> Identify or create objects and definitions for sorting
> Activity materials
> Additional data collected in a card sort
> Players in your activity
> Inviting observers

Identify or Create Objects and Definitions for Sorting

There are several ways to obtain your objects (i.e., pieces of information or tasks) and definitions for sorting. The way you choose will depend on whether you have an existing product or your product is still in the conceptual stage.

Existing Product

If a version of the product already exists and you work for an organization that has an information architect or content strategist, consult him or her to see if there is an existing content inventory. If your goal is to re-architect an existing product that does not have an existing content inventory, you and the team can together identify the possible areas to re-architect. Once you have done this, you can make a list of all the objects contained within these areas. If there are objects that will be omitted in the next release, you should omit these from the card sort. Conversely, if there are new objects that the product team intends to add to the product, you should certainly include these.

The most frequent method is to work with the development team to identify the objects and then develop clear definitions. The creation of definitions can be surprisingly time-consuming since the development team may define things in terms of the way the back-end or technical components of the product works. It is your job to make sure the definitions are clear and easy for participants to understand. Without those definitions, you cannot be sure that you and the participants are on the same page, speaking the same language.

TIP

The way you name your cards will influence how your participants group the items. In a recent card sort Kelly conducted to understand how patients group potential recipients of medical information (e.g., insurance companies, doctors, family members), we encountered a surprising finding. We anticipated that patients would group "Health Educators" with other potential recipients such as "Dieticians" because both "Health Educators" and "Dieticians" are medical providers that counsel patients and recommend strategies for helping patients achieve their health goals. However, we found that participants often grouped "Health Educators" with "Educational or Medical Researchers." "Educational or Medical Researchers" are scientists who most often do not interact with patients to provide care, but rather conduct scientific research to contribute new medical knowledge. We realized that the patients in our study grouped "Health Educators" with "Educational or Medical Researchers" because both cards contained the stem "educat-." Based on think-aloud data and the names participants assigned to groups of cards, we were able to understand how this occurred and account for it during analysis.

Concept

In cases when your product is still in the conceptual stage, you may not have determined a list of content or tasks for the product. While still working with the development team, you may need to supplement your knowledge with input from the marketing department or a competitive analysis (see Chapter 2, "Learn About Your Product" section, page 25). You may find it beneficial to do an interview or survey to learn about the information or tasks users would like to have in your product and the words they use to describe this information. You will need to ensure that you clearly understand what each idea means so that you can write complete definitions for your card sort.

Free-listing

Finally, you can also obtain objects for a card sort by asking participants to free-list all the items associated with a given domain (i.e., participants write down every phrase or word associated with a particular topic, domain, etc.). In **free-listing**, participants are asked to name every "item" they can think of that is associated with a domain—not just the ones they want for a given product or system. Using our travel example, we might want to ask participants to name every piece of information they can think of that is associated with making travel reservations. Some responses might be the following: plane ticket, car rental, hotel room, confirmation number, and frequent-flyer miles. The biggest benefit of free-listing is that you obtain information about the users' terminology because they are offering their ideas in their own language.

How Many Cards?

We have found that it is best to limit the number of objects to be sorted at 90 or less. However, there are published studies where researchers have successfully used more than 90 cards. One study we found used 500 cards (Tullis, 1985)! We would not recommend this unless you are an expert at conducting card sorts and have a good reason for doing so. Keep in mind that the more cards there are, the longer it will take for the participants to sort, and therefore you run the risk of fatiguing and overwhelming them. In addition, sorts with large numbers of cards can take considerably longer to analyze.

TIP

If you plan to conduct a computerized sort and analyze the data using specialized software or an online tool, check for any limit to the number of cards or users it can handle. There often is a limit. Sometimes, this information is buried in the "Release Notes" or "Known Bugs."

If possible, run a pilot session for a card sort before you have finalized your protocol. This will help you find typos or identify confusing definitions and terms. In addition, a pilot can help you get a sense of how long it will take for participants to complete the sort and determine whether you missed any objects.

Activity Materials

You will need the following materials for an in-person card sort:

- 3×5 in index cards (different-colored cards are helpful)
- Printer labels (optional)
- Stapler
- Rubber bands
- Envelopes
- Plenty of workspace for a participant to spread out the cards

And the following materials for a computerized card sort:

- A subscription to a remote card sort service, a computer program that offers card sort functionality, or a web-facing server hosting a card sort program you have created
- Participants who have access to a computer and/or the Internet

Create Cards for an In-Person Sort

To create the cards, type the name of the object, a blank space, and the definition of the object either directly on card stock or on a sticky printer label (see Figure 11.1). You can also add an example of the object, if you feel it will help users understand the object. Make sure that you use at least a 12-point font. It is easy to create a file of the objects and then print out several sheets. You can then quickly stick labels on the cards. Alternatively, you could buy sheets of punch-out index cards and print directly onto the sheets; however, we have found them only in white.

The number of index cards needed (C) can be computed by multiplying the number of objects in the sort (O) by the number of participants you intend to recruit (P):

$$C = O \times P$$

So, if you have 50 objects and ten participants, you will need 500 index cards. We recommend providing about 20 blank cards per participant for labeling their groups and in case they want to add an object.

TIP

To save time during data collection, card sorts can be conducted in groups. If you are running the sort as a group, you will need three different colors of index cards. When participants are sitting next to each other, it is easy for cards to get mixed up. You do not want to hear participants ask, "Are those my cards or yours?" Alternate the colors of the cards between users sitting next to or across from each other.

Airplane
A fixed-wing aircraft that flies in the air; commercial flights.

Yacht
A large, usually luxurious, vessel that travels in water.

Bicycle
A two-wheeled, self-propelled vehicle for use on ground.

Taxi
A hired automobile with a driver.

Figure 11.1: Example cards for a card sort exercise.

Primary Data Collected in a Card Sort

The main type of data you will collect in a card sort (both open and closed) is how participants group items. In a closed sort, since your categories are predetermined, you will collect only information about which cards participants assign to which categories. In an open sort, since participants create the categories, in addition to which cards participants think would go together, you will also gather how many groups participants think there should be for the set of items and how they name these groups. These data give insight into how content is organized in the participants' minds and the vocabulary they associate with the organized content.

Additional Data That May Be Collected in an Open Card Sort

There are five types of changes participants may be able to make to the cards you provide when you conduct an open card sort:

- Delete an item
- Add a new item
- Rename an item
- Change a definition
- Place an item in multiple groups

Some of these options may not be available in a computerized card sort depending on the design of the program. Furthermore, all of these changes must be analyzed manually (see "Data That Computer Programs Cannot Handle" section, page 325). Often, the additional information that you obtain by allowing participants to make these changes justifies the additional work, but be sure to consider this in your planning.

Delete an Object

If a participant does not think an object belongs in the domain, he or she can remove it. For example, if you have the object "school bus" in a card sort for your travel app, a participant may want to remove it because in that person's experience, school buses are never provided as an option on travel apps.

Allowing participants to remove cards reveals whether you are providing users with content or tasks that are unnecessary—which represent "noise" for the user to deal with. It can also reveal whether you (or the development team) have an incorrect perception of the domain (e.g., providing school buses on a travel app). However, you may have a product where all of your features must be included for business reasons. If this were the case, you would not want to allow participants to create a "discard" pile. Deleting an object may not be an available option for a computerized card sort.

Add a New Object

As participants read through the cards, they begin to understand the depth and breadth of information or tasks your product supports. They may realize that certain information or tasks are missing from the sort and therefore from your product. Using our travel example, a participant may notice that "airport code" is missing from the sort and add it in. Perhaps this was left out because the development team thought that the full name of the airport was more helpful and the airport code is unnecessary. Allowing participants to add cards points out information or tasks that users expect to have in your product. You should also ask users to define any objects they add and state why they are adding them. Again, adding items may not be an available option in a computerized card sort.

Rename Objects

As we mentioned at the beginning of the chapter, you can collect information about terminologies in a card sort. You might present participants with an object they are familiar with, but in their opinion, the name of the object and definition do not match up. Sometimes, differences exist between companies and different parts of the country, or there is an industry standard term that you were not aware of. Technical jargon or abbreviations that we are not aware of are sometimes used in the workplace, or users may simply have another term for the object in their workplace. By allowing participants to change the names of your objects, you collect information about terminologies that you may not have had before.

Change a Definition

Providing a definition for each term ensures that everyone is on the same page. This is important when asking participants to organize information. If everyone has a different understanding of the objects he or she is sorting, there will be no consensus in the organization of the cards. Sometimes, the definitions provided are incomplete or not quite right, so allow participants to make additions, deletions, or word changes to the definitions.

Place an Object in Multiple Groups

Sometimes, participants tell you that a single object belongs in multiple locations. In order to do this, a participant would need to create a duplicate card. This adds some complexity to the data analysis but you may want to collect this information (see "Data Analysis and Interpretation" section, page 318). You want to understand where an object *best* fits, so ask participants to place the card provided in the best group. Then, ask them to create as many duplicate cards as necessary and place them in the additional locations and note this to be analyzed separately.

Players in Your Activity

You will need users to take part in either an in-person or a remote card sort. For an in-person card sort, you will also require other people to help conduct the activity. In this section, we discuss the details of all the players involved in a card sort session.

The Participants

Users may not always have optimal mental models (Nielsen & Sano, 1994). Designing a system based on flawed user mental models can clearly hamper user performance. For this reason, you should avoid including users in your card sort with no or little experience in the domain of interest. Obviously, if a user does not understand a domain well and have experience in it, that person's mental model will not be as efficient or even correct as that of others who do.

All participants should meet the same **user profile** (see Chapter 2, "Learn About Your Users" section, page 35). It is not advisable to mix user types. If different user types sort information differently, you may need to create a different interface for each user type. Mixing the user types in the same sort washes out those differences and could result in an interface that no one can use. If you wish to compare user types (e.g., novice versus expert), we recommend running six or eight of each type, analyzing the data, adding a couple more, seeing how the groups change, and then determining whether more participants are needed as described in the next section. Refer to Chapter 6, "Recruiting Participants" section on page 126 for more information.

How Many Participants?

Aiming for 15 participants is a safe bet. A study with 168 participants revealed that a card sort with 15-20 participants can yield a correlation of 90% with the full data set (Tullis & Wood, 2004), meaning that at about 15 participants, you get a pretty good idea of how another 150 or so participants would group items. In the same study, Tullis and Wood reported that beyond 30 participants, you get diminishing returns, meaning that you get less information for your time and effort. In academic studies, rather than industry studies, we often get to run 30 participants.

In practice in industry, we often end up running one or two group sessions with 10-12 participants of the same user type. If you are on a time and resource budget, however, run six or eight participants and analyze the data. Add an additional couple of participants and see whether the addition of each new user changes the groupings (this is a good time to collect think-aloud data). If the results are stable and the major groups do not change, there is no need to run additional participants.

How many participants are needed for the free-listing activity? The answer is, "It depends." The best way to determine the appropriate number is to conduct the activity with five or six participants, tally the results to see the number of participants identifying each object, and then see how those results change by adding one or two new participants. If the results are stable, no further participants are needed.

The Facilitator

For an in-person card sort, a facilitator is needed for the activity. If you run participants as a group, it helps to have a colleague as an extra pair of hands, but that is optional. The job of the facilitator is to provide initial instructions, distribute the materials, answer any questions along the way, and then collect the materials. If run as a group, the majority of the session is spent sitting quietly, answering any questions, and making sure people are not comparing their sorts. If run individually, the facilitator must be familiar with the think-aloud protocol and how to instruct participants in it (see Chapter 7, "Using a Think-Aloud Protocol" section, page 169). The facilitator will also need to take notes of what a participant is thinking and record the session, in case you miss something or if you want to analyze the think-aloud results in more detail.

The Videographer

If you are conducting the card sort in a group setting, there is no discussion to video record, but if conducting the sort individually, it is beneficial to record so that you can capture the think-aloud data. You will find a detailed discussion of videotaping tips and the benefits of video recording in "Recording and Notetaking" section on page 171 in Chapter 7. If you plan to record, make sure that someone takes responsibility for this task. It is ideal if you can have someone to monitor the video equipment during the session in case something goes wrong, but if that is not possible, set up the shot, hit "Record," and hope that nothing goes wrong. We have found that a useful video angle for card sorts, in particular, is over the shoulder of the participant. This way, you capture the way the participant moves the cards into groups and how he or she points to them as he or she thinks aloud.

Inviting Observers

If you are conducting the card sort in a group setting or remotely, there is nothing for an observer to see except for either a room full of people silently grouping cards or data flowing in from the remote sort program. If the session is conducted individually and in person, stakeholders will find it interesting to hear why people group objects the way they do (see Chapter 7, "Inviting Observers" section on page 161 for more information).

Conducting a Card Sort

You have prepared for the card sort and now you need to actually conduct the session. The timeline in Table 11.1 shows the sequence and timing of events to conduct a card sort.

Activity Timeline

The times in Table 11.1 are *approximate* times based on our personal experience and should be used only as a guide. The overall length of the session will obviously depend on the number of cards to be sorted and whether you are having participants think aloud. Participants can typically sort 50-70 cards in a one-hour session when not asked to think aloud. For remote sessions, we have found it is best to limit the sort to 30 minutes, which may require you to limit the number of cards.

Table 11.1: Timeline for conducting a card sort

Approximate duration	Procedure
3 minutes	Welcome participants (introductions, forms)
5 minutes	Conduct a card sort practice
3 minutes	Instructions
30-100 minutes	Card sorting
5 minutes	Wrap-up (thank participants, escort them out)

For both remote and in-person card sorts, the basic idea is that you present people with cards (either a paper card or a virtual card on a computer) and ask them to group those cards in the way that makes the most sense to them, and then, in an open sort, to give the groups they create a name that makes sense to them. Because the basic activities in an in-person card sort using physical cards can be used as a basis for other types of sorts, we describe that process in detail here. Variations on this procedure, including using remote computerized sorts, can be ascertained by leaving out various portions of the activities described here or modifying them. For example, in a remote sort, there is no need to greet participants and offer snacks, but you could easily modify the sample script presented on page 315 to create the instructions screen for a remote computerized sort. We describe the elements unique to conducting a computerized sort separately on page 317.

In-Person Card Sort Using Physical Cards

At a Glance

> Welcome the participants
> Practice
> Card review and sorting
> Labeling groups

Welcome the Participants

This is the time during which you greet your participants, allow them to eat some snacks, ask them to fill out paperwork, and get them warmed up and settled in (see Figure 11.2). The details of these stages are described in Chapter 7, During Your User Research Activity, "Welcoming Your Participants" section on page 163.

Figure 11.2: The action! As you can see, participants do not need a lot of space.

Practice

Upon their arrival, explain to the participant(s) that the purpose of the activity is to gain an understanding of how people group a set of concepts. We then begin with a practice exercise so that they understand exactly what we will be doing (see Figure 11.3). We typically write about 12-15 types of zoo animals on a flip chart or whiteboard (e.g., grizzly bear, ape, polar bear, monkey). We then ask participants to call out animals that they think belong in the same group (e.g., polar bear and grizzly bear). We circle the items and then ask them to name that group (e.g., bears).

Card Review and Sorting

Once everyone is comfortable with the concept, distribute the cards and provide some instructions. You can use the following sample script:

> **We are currently designing<*insert product description*>and we need to understand how to best organize the<*information or tasks*>in the product. This will help users of the product find what they are looking for more easily.**
>
> **On each of the cards, we have written a<*piece of information or task*>in our proposed product, along with a description of it. Please read through all of the cards and make sure both the terms and definitions make sense. If the terms or definitions do not make sense, please make corrections directly on the cards. Use the blank line to rename the object to something that makes more sense to you. In addition, please let me know what changes you are making so I can be sure that I understand what you are writing.**
>
> **Once you have reviewed all the cards, you may begin sorting them into groups that belong together. There are no right or wrong answers. Although there may be multiple ways you can group these concepts, please provide us with the groupings that you feel make the most sense. When you**

Figure 11.3: A card sort demonstration exercise.

are sorting, you may place any cards that do not belong (or that you do not use, do not understand, etc.) in a discard pile, and you may use the blank cards to add any objects that are missing. If you feel that a particular card belongs in more than one location, please place the card provided in the best location you believe it fits. Use the blank cards to create as many duplicate cards as necessary and place those in the secondary groups.

When you have completed your sort, use the blank cards to name each of your piles.

You may wish to give participants a rough idea of how many groups of cards you expect. For example, you may say:

We expect you to end up with between seven and 11 groups of cards. It is OK if you end up with more or less, but feel free to use these numbers as rough guidelines.

If there are multiple participants in one room, add:

Please do not work with your neighbor on this. We want to understand how you think these cards should be grouped. We do not want a group effort—so please do not look at your neighbors' cards.

If this is an individual sort, state:

I would like for you to think aloud as you work. Tell me what you are thinking as you are grouping the cards. If you go quiet, I will prompt you for feedback.

Whenever participants make a change to a card, we strongly encourage them to tell us about it. It helps us to understand why they are making the change. In a group session, it offers us the opportunity to discuss the change with the group. We typically ask questions like:

Spencer just made a good point. He refers to a "travel reservation" as a "travel booking." Does anyone else call it that?

or

Keisha noticed that "couples-only resorts" is missing. Does anyone else book "couples-only resorts?"

If anyone nods in agreement, we ask him or her to discuss the issue. We then ask all the participants who agree to make the same change to their card(s). Participants may not think to make a change until it is brought to their attention; otherwise, they may believe they are the only ones who feel a certain way and do not want to be "different." Encouraging the discussion helps us decide whether an issue is pervasive or limited to only one individual.

Participants typically make terminology and definition changes while they are reviewing the cards. They may also notice objects that do not belong and remove them during the review process. Most often, adding missing cards and deleting cards that do not belong are not done until the sorting stage—as participants begin to organize the information.

Labeling Groups

In an open sort, once the sorting is complete, the participants need to generate a name for each of the groups they have created. Give the following instructions:

> **Now I would like for you to name each of your groups. How would you describe the cards in each of these piles? You can use a single word, phrase, or sentence. Please write the name of each group on one of the blank cards and place it on top of the group. Once you have finished, please staple each group together, or if it is too large to staple, use a rubber band. Finally, place all of your bound groups in the envelope provided.**

TIP

We prefer to staple the groups together because we do not want cards falling out. If your cards get mixed with others, your data will be ruined, so make sure your groups are secured and that each participant's groups remain separate! We mark each envelope with the participant's number and seal it until it is time to analyze the data. This prevents cards from being confused between participants. Another option is to immediately photograph all cards along with the labels on the table where the participant has performed the sort. This way, you could reuse card sets since you do not need to store them together for data entry, because you can simply use the photograph. This can also come in handy when participants lay out the groups of cards in relation to each other (e.g., these groups are the most similar; these the least).

Computerized Card Sort

Depending on which computerized card sort program you choose and whether that sort will be conducted in person or remotely, the steps to set up the card sort will differ slightly. Generally, you will need to set up the computerized program by telling it how many participants you would expect, by telling whether your participants will be participating in an open or closed card sort, by entering the names and definitions of the text you would like to appear on each card, and by entering the instruction text that you would like each participant to see. Each computerized card sort program will include specific instructions on how to set up and run a card sort using its platform.

Computerized Card Sort Programs

There are a variety of free, freemium, and pay computerized card sort programs available for either in-person or remote studies. For example,

- *UXSORT* (free)
  (https://sites.google.com/a/uxsort.com/uxsort/home)
- Optimal Workshop's *OptimalSort* (freemium)
  (http://www.optimalworkshop.com/optimalsort.htm)

- NIST's *WebCAT®* (free)
  (http://zing.ncsl.nist.gov/WebTools/WebCAT/overview.html)
- *uzCardSort* (free; open source)
  http://uzilla.mozdev.org/cardsort.html
- *xSort* (free)
  http://www.xsortapp.com/
- UserZoom (subscription-based; in 2015, $1000 for two months and $9000 for one year)
  http://www.userzoom.com

Tom Tullis also keeps a useful and updated list of tools to analyze card sort data at http://measuringuserexperience.com/CardSorting/index.htm.

Data Analysis and Interpretation

There are several ways to analyze the data you collect during a card sort, such as simple summary, cluster analysis, factor analysis, multidimensional scaling, and path analysis. The goal of all of these methods is to understand the similarity between items and determine how to group the most similar items together based on your participant data.

Simple Summary

When testing a small number of participants (four or less) and a limited number of cards, some evaluators simply summarize or even "eyeball" the card groupings. While this is not precise and can quickly become unmanageable when the number of participants increases, it may be useful for pilot tests and/or situations where the number of participants and the number of cards are very small and your time for analysis is extremely limited.

For example, see the card sort results presented in Figure 11.4. You could ascertain the following based on "eyeballing" the groupings:

1. Two participants created five categories, one participant created four categories, and one participant created three categories.
2. All participants grouped the following items together:
   a. Sea/Water/Boats
      i. Yacht
      ii. Sailboat
      iii. Ferry

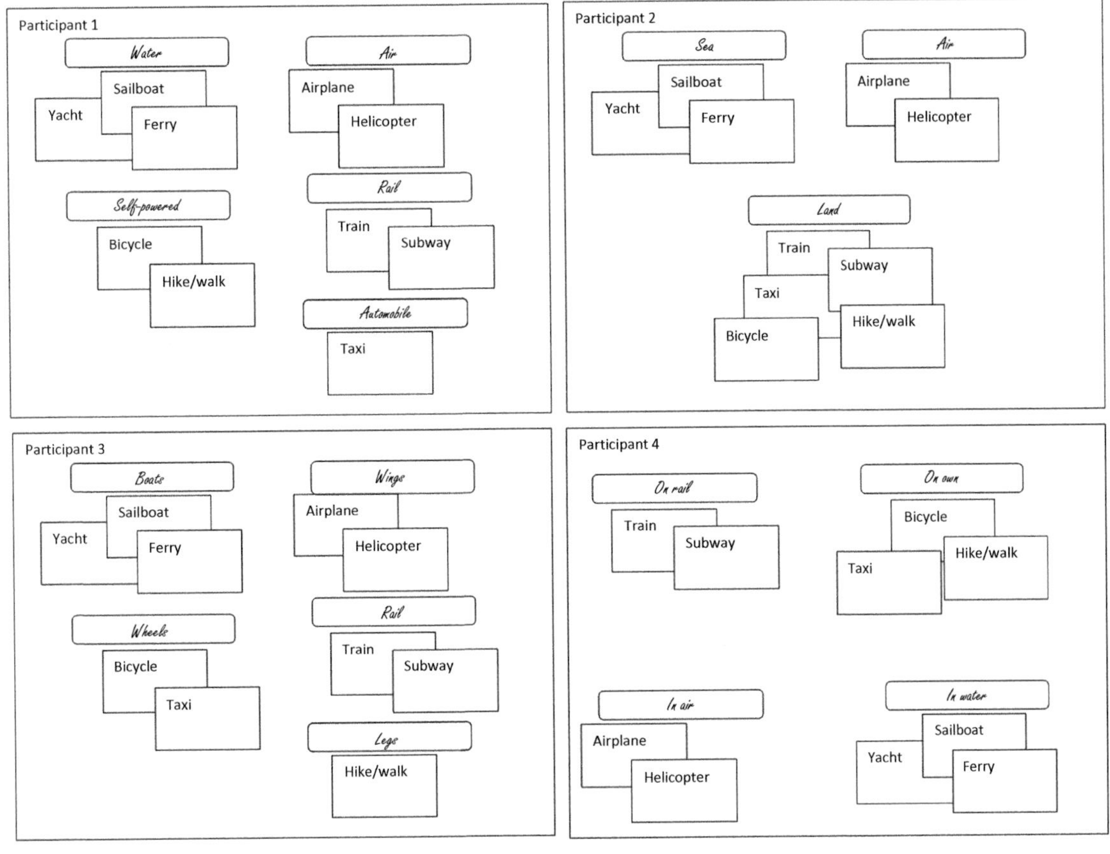

Figure 11.4: Raw card sort data.

   b. Air/Wings
      i. Airplane
      ii. Helicopter
3. Participants disagreed on groupings for the following item:
   a. Taxi

This type of informal analysis could help you figure out areas where you needed to pay more attention and/or continue your investigation. In the example above, you would want to pay more attention to the Taxi item because there was disagreement around this item and less attention to the Sea/Water/Boats items because participants agreed those should usually go together.

	Airplane	Bicycle	Sailboat	Ferry	Hike/walk	Helicopter	Subway	Train	Taxi	Yacht
Airplane	-	0	0	0	0	1	0	0	0	0
Bicycle		-	0	0	1	0	0	0	0	0
Sailboat			-	1	0	0	0	0	0	1
Ferry				-	0	0	0	0	0	1
Hike/walk					-	0	0	0	0	0
Helicopter						-	0	0	0	0
Subway							-	1	0	0
Train								-	0	0
Taxi									-	0
Yacht										-

Figure 11.5: Similarity matrix for participant 1.

Similarity Matrix

A similarity matrix, also known as a distance matrix, will allow you to understand how similar or far apart each pair of items is from the participants' perspective. For example, based on the data presented in Figure 11.5 and our eyeball analysis, we might expect "airplane" and "helicopter" to be very similar or close together conceptually while "yacht" and "hike/walk" to be dissimilar or far apart conceptually.

To investigate this quantitatively, we need to generate a simple matrix. To generate the matrix, create a spreadsheet (e.g., in Excel, OpenOffice Calc, or Google Drive; see companion wesbite for downloadable worksheet [booksite.elsevier.com/9780128002322]) that is set up as follows:

- Create a single sheet for each participant and one summary sheet.
- On the *x* axis, list all items.
- On the *y* axis, list all the items again in the same order.
- In each cell, put a 0 if the participant did NOT group the intersecting set of items together.
  - For example, for participant 1, put a "0" in the cell where "airplane" and "bicycle" intersect, since he or she did *not* group those cards together (see Figure 11.5).
- In each cell, put a 1 if the participant *did* group the intersecting set of items together.
  - For example, for participant 1, put a "1" in the intersection between "airplane" and "helicopter" since he or she grouped those cards together (see Figure 11.5).
- In the summary sheet, sum the numbers for each intersecting set of items.
  - For example, participants 1, 2, and 4 grouped "hike/walk" and "bike" together, but participant 3 did not. So, we would add the 1 (participant 1), 1 (participant 2), 0 (participant 3), and 1 (participant 4) = 3 for the summary intersection of "hike/walk" and "bike" (see Figure 11.6).

Now that the data are quantified and organized in a matrix, you can see which items are most commonly grouped together (items with a higher number) and which items are rarely grouped together (items with a lower number). The number in each cell represents the number of participants who grouped each item together. You can also analyze these data further using cluster analysis, a specialized card sort program, a statistical package, or a spreadsheet package.

	Airplane	Bicycle	Sailboat	Ferry	Hike/walk	Helicopter	Subway	Train	Taxi	Yacht
Airplane	-	0	0	0	0	4	0	0	0	0
Bicycle		-	0	0	3	0	1	1	3	0
Sailboat			-	4	0	0	0	0	0	4
Ferry				-	0	0	0	0	0	4
Hike/walk					-	0	1	1	2	0
Helicopter						-	0	0	0	0
Subway							-	4	1	0
Train								-	1	0
Taxi									-	0
Yacht										-

Figure 11.6: Similarity matrix summary (for all four participants).

Cluster Analysis

Cluster analysis allows you to quantify and understand your card sort data by calculating the strength of the perceived relationships between pairs of cards, based on the frequency with which members of each possible pair appear together. In other words, it allows you to answer the question: Which items are often grouped together and therefore perceived to be similar, and which items are rarely grouped together and therefore perceived to be dissimilar (or "distant")? The results are usually presented in a tree diagram or **dendrogram** (see Figure 11.7).

Reading a dendrogram is relatively straightforward. All items in your sort will be listed vertically. The order of the items reflects the similarity between items; that is, items placed next to each other vertically are more similar than items placed further apart. The lines extending horizontally from each item and then joining other items vertically show where items are grouped at higher levels of relationship. For example, in Figure 11.7, Taxi joins Hike/walk and Bicycle, after Hike/walk and Bicycle have already been joined.

The actual math behind cluster analysis can vary a bit, but the technique used in most computer programs is called the "amalgamation" method. Clustering begins with every item being its own single-item cluster. Then every item's difference score with every other item is computed (i.e., considered pair-by-pair), as demonstrated in the

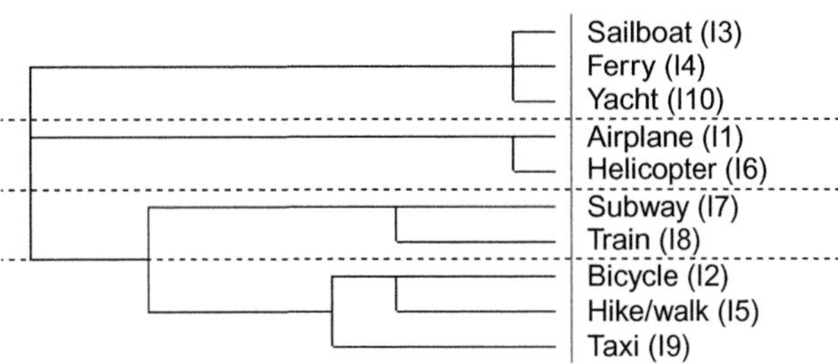

Figure 11.7: Example SynCaps dendrogram.

similarity matrix section (see page 320). Those with the closest (smallest) difference scores are then joined. The more participants that paired two items together, the shorter the distance.

There are several different amalgamation (or linkage) rules available to decide how groups should next be clustered, and some programs allow you to choose the rule used. Single linkage is also called the "nearest neighbor" method because it takes only two near neighbors to join both groups. Single linkage is useful for producing long strings of loosely related clusters. It focuses on the similarities among groups. Complete linkage (or "furthest neighbor") is effectively the opposite of single linkage and considers the most dissimilar pair of items when determining whether to join groups. This is useful for producing very tightly-related groups. For most cases, we recommend using average linkage, as this method attempts to balance the two methods above by taking the average of the difference scores for all the pairs when deciding whether groups should be joined.

Suggested Resources for Additional Reading

If you would like to learn more about advanced analysis methods including cluster analysis and factor analysis, you can refer to the following:

- Capra, M. G. (2005). Factor analysis of card sort data: An alternative to hierarchical cluster analysis. *Proceedings of the human factors and ergonomics society 49th annual meeting*, 691–695.
- Romesburg, C. H. (1984). *Cluster analysis for researchers*. Belmont, CA: Lifetime Learning Publications (Wadsworth).

Analysis with a Card-Sorting Program

Whether you have collected data in person or using a computerized card sort program, we recommend using a computer program to analyze card sort data. Data analysis using these tools has been found to be quicker and easier than using manual methods (Zavod, Rickert, & Brown, 2002). In our experience, these methods are also easier than using either a statistics package (e.g., R, SPSS) or a spreadsheet (e.g., Excel). While availability and prices of these programs change rapidly, at the time of publication, the following programs for analyzing card sort data are available for free on the Web:

- Syntagm's *SynCaps*

  (http://www.syntagm.co.uk/design/cardsortdl.shtml)
- NIST's *WebCAT®*

  (http://zing.ncsl.nist.gov/WebTools/WebCAT/overview.html)

Some of the programs (see "Computerized Card Sort Programs" section, pp. 317-318) also include analysis capabilities. For example, UXSORT automatically generates results including a dendrogram from card sort data collected using the UXSORT tool.

Example Analysis of Open Card Sort Data Using SynCaps

Imagine you have collected the data presented in Figure 11.4 in an in-person open card sort and you want to generate a dendrogram that shows how these items (modes of travel) cluster based on participants' perceptions.

Prepare the Data

SynCaps only accepts data from a simple .txt file. To create this file, create a new .txt file and enter the data as follows:

Items—list all items with an "I" preceding each item.

Participant—list each participant number, preceded by a "P."

Groups—list each group the participant creates, preceded by a "G."

Item numbers—list each item number the participant has included in a group (e.g., I2, I4).

Figure 11.8 presents the travel data in this format.

```
IAirplane (I1)
IBicycle (I2)
ISailboat (I3)
IFerry (I4)
IHike/Walk (I5)
IHelicopter (I6)
ISubway (I7)
ITrain (I8)
ITaxi (I9)
IYacht (I10)
P1
G1Water
I3
I10
I4
G2Air
I1
I6
G3Self-powered
I2
I5
G3Rail
I8
I6
G4Automobile
I9
...
```

Figure 11.8: Step 1 of import process in SynCaps; data entry/preparation for participant 1.

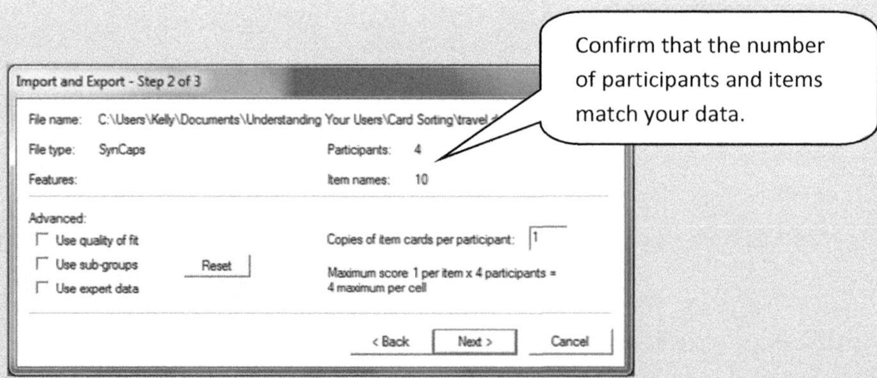

Figure 11.9: Step 2 of import process in SynCaps.

Analyze Data

Next, open SynCaps and import the data from the .txt file you have created. Be sure to check the "step 2" import screen to make sure that SynCaps recognizes the correct number of participants and item names (see Figure 11.9).

SynCaps will now display a dendrogram with your items grouped (see Figure 11.7). Items that are similar will be displayed close to each other, and items that are dissimilar will be displayed further apart. Examining the dendrogram further, you can see that some items in the tree are grouped very far to the right (close to the items); this indicates that they were often grouped together. The further to the left the lines connecting the items merge, the less often they were grouped together. By default, SynCaps also suggests cut points or places to group items. In this case, SynCaps has suggested four categories: (1) sailboat, ferry, and yacht; (2) airplane and helicopter; (3) subway and train; and (4) bicycle, taxi, and hike/walk (see Figure 11.7). SynCaps lets you edit the number of categories to create using the "groups" drop-down function. A guideline to use in determining how many categories to create is to use the mean number of groups created by your participants. In this example, our participants created 5, 3, 5, and 4 groups, so the mean number of groups is 4.25, which rounds down to 4.

You may use the same process described here to analyze closed card sort data.

Analysis with a Statistics Package

Statistical packages like *R*, *SAS*, *SPSS*, and *STATISTICA* are not as easy to use as specialized card sort programs when analyzing card sort data. If you are familiar with these packages or you have a card set that is too large for a specialized card sort program, you may use them to conduct hierarchical cluster analysis, multidimensional scaling, or path analysis. Alan Salmoni has an excellent piece on analyzing data from an open card sort using a combination of Excel and R available at http://www.uxbooth.com/articles/open-card-sort-analysis-101/.

Analysis with a Spreadsheet Package

Again, sophisticated analysis beyond simple similarity with a spreadsheet package is not as easy as with specialized card sort software. If you do not have funds to pay to use a commercial card sort analysis tool and the free options presented in this chapter are not available or appealing to you, it is possible to analyze your data using a spreadsheet. You can find excellent, step-by-step descriptions of analyzing the data with a spreadsheet tool at http://boxesandarrows.com/analyzing-card-sort-results-with-a-spreadsheet-template/ (mirrored at: http://www.joelamantia.com/html/projects/card_sort_template_ba.xls and rosenfeldmedia.com/blogs/card-sorting/card-sort-analysis-spreadsheet/).

Data That Computer Programs Cannot Handle

Computer programs dedicated to card sort analysis can be great, but they often do not do all of the analysis for you. Below are some of the issues we have encountered when using various programs. Although the data analysis for these elements is a little awkward, we think the value that the data bring makes them worth collecting.

Adding or Renaming Objects

One of the basic requirements of cluster analysis is that all participants must have the exact same set of cards in terms of name and number. If participants renamed any of the objects or if they added any cards, you will not be able to add this information into the program. You will need to record this information for each participant and analyze it separately. The number of cards added or changed tends to be very small but it is an extra step to take. Note each addition or renaming suggestion down and then tally the number of other participants who did the same thing. At the end, you will likely have a small list of added and renamed objects, along with the number of participants who made those changes. Based on the number of participants who added it, you can assess its importance.

Group Names

The group names that participants provide are not presented in the analysis. You will need to record the pile names that participants suggested and match them to the resulting categories. One option is to record the names of each group for each participant and look for similarities. How many participants created a "Boats" group? How many created an "Air" group? When examining the dendrogram, you will notice clusters of objects. See if there is a match between those clusters and the names of the groups that participants created. Alternatively, for a more systematic approach, especially with a large number of participants, you can use a word frequency analysis tool to count how many times participants associated certain words with each category. The more times a word appears with a given category, the more likely it would serve as a good name for that category.

Duplicate Objects

As we discussed earlier, sometimes participants ask to place an item in multiple locations. Because the computer programs available do not allow you to enter the same card more than once and you must have the same number of cards for each participant, include the original card in the group the participant placed it. The duplicate cards placed in the secondary groups will have to be examined and noted manually.

Deleted Objects

Many computer programs cannot deal with deleted cards. For these programs, if you have allowed participants to create a discard or miscellaneous pile of cards that they do not believe belong in the sort, there is a work-around you need to do. You cannot enter this collection of discarded cards as a group into a computer program, since the cluster analysis would treat these cards as a group of objects that participants believe are related. In reality, these cards are not related to any of the other cards. Place each rejected card in a group by itself to demonstrate that it is not related to any other card in the cluster analysis. For example, if participants placed "Taxi" and "Bicycle" in the discard pile, you should enter "Taxi" in one group and "Bicycle" in a second group.

Interpreting the Results

You now have a collection of rich data. The dendrogram displays groups of objects that the majority of participants believe belong together. Interpreting the dendrogram is straightforward—you can see visually represented which items participants considered conceptually similar. However, changes that participants make to cards can make interpretation of the results tricky. When a deleted object is repeatedly placed in a group by itself, you may see it on a branch by itself or loosely attached to a group where it really does not belong. Additionally, if participants place an object in multiple groups, they may not have agreed on the "best" location to place it. Consequently, you may find that the object is living on a branch by itself or loosely attached to a group where it does not belong. You must use your knowledge of the domain or product to make adjustments when ambiguity exists. Use the additional data you collected, such as new objects, group names, changed terminology, and think-aloud data to help interpret the data.

Let us walk through our travel example and interpret the results of the dendrogram shown in Figure 11.7. Using our domain knowledge and the group labels participants provided in the card sort, we have named each of the clusters in the dendrogram (see Figure 11.10). We appear to have four groups: "Sea," "Air," "Rail," and "Ground."

Tab name	Items to be located within the tab
Sea	Sailboat Ferry Yacht
Air	Airplane Helicopter
Rail	Subway Train
Ground	Taxi Hike/walk Bicycle

Figure 11.10: Travel card sort table of recommendations.

It is important to note that the card sort methodology will not provide you with information about the *type* of architecture you should use (e.g., tabs, menus). This decision must be made by a design professional. Instead, the tree diagram demonstrates how participants expect to find information grouped. In the case of a mobile app with tabs, the tree may present the recommended name of the tab and the elements that should be contained within that particular tab.

Now you should examine the list of changes that participants made (e.g., renamed cards, additional cards) to discover whether there is high agreement among participants.

- What objects did participants feel you were missing?
- What objects did participants feel did not belong?
- What are all of the terminology changes participants made?
- What definitions did participants change?
- What items did users want in multiple locations?

Use this information to determine whether your product needs to add or remove information or tasks to be more useful to participants. You may recommend to the team that they conduct a competitive analysis (if they have not already) to discover whether other products support such functionality. Similarly, use the information about deleted objects to recommend that the team examine whether specific information or tasks are unnecessary.

Terminology can be specific to a company, area of the country, or individual. With each terminology change, you will need to investigate whether it is a "standard"—and therefore needs to be incorporated—or whether there are several different possible terms. When several terms exist, you will want to use the most common term.

Finally, examine the definition changes. Were the changes minor—simply an issue of clarification? If so, there is not anything to change in your product. If, however, there were many changes, you have an issue. This may mean that the product development team does not have a good grasp of the domain or that there is disagreement within the team about what certain features of the product do.

Communicating the Findings

When we present the results of a card sort analysis to executives or teams, we present the actual dendrogram generated by the application (as in Figure 11.7) and a simple table to review (see Figure 11.10). We also present a table of changes that participants made to the cards (added objects, deleted objects, terminology changes, and definition changes) and any sketches the designers may have produced to illustrate the recommendations (see Chapter 15, "Reporting Your Findings" section, page 463).

Suggested Resources for Additional Reading

For a more thorough introduction and reference on card sorting than we provide in this chapter, please see:

• Spencer, D. (2009). *Card sorting designing usable categories*. ISBN 1-933820-02-0.

Pulling It All Together

In this chapter, we have discussed what a card sort is, when you should conduct one, and the things to be aware of. We also discussed how to prepare for and conduct a card sort, along with several modifications. Finally, we have demonstrated various ways to analyze the data and used our travel example to show you how to interpret and present the results.

CASE STUDY: *CARD SORTING WITH COLLEAGUES: HOW WE ADAPTED BEST PRACTICES TO FIT OUR NEEDS*

Jenny Shirey, Lead Product Designer, Citrix

This case study describes how a team at Citrix used a combination of quantitative and qualitative card-sorting methods to develop a new information architecture for the company intranet. Highlighting the successes of the project as well as important lessons learned, this case study will both educate and inspire teams looking to adapt card-sorting best practices to fit their unique situations and needs.

The Project

In 2012, the CEO of Citrix asked the Customer Experience group to lead a redesign of the company intranet. Our vision for the redesigned intranet was to apply user-centered and design thinking methods to create a space that would serve as the online heart of Citrix.

The core team was made up of about 15 people from several functional areas, as well as stakeholders from IT, facilities, and human resources. This not only gave the team the advantage of having a diverse set of experiences and perspectives but also posed challenges related to differences in process and collaborating effectively across time zones and locations. What the team shared, however, was a desire to create an intranet that was not merely functional but design-driven and based on the real needs and desires of Citrix employees.

The Challenge

During our research on intranets, we found that Citrix suffered from many of the same problems that other corporations face. Our intranet had evolved over time without a holistic design process, and the information architecture, or IA, was based on organizational departments, rather than where users would naturally think to seek out content.

After conducting a heuristic evaluation of the site, we found that it was extremely difficult to find content using the existing navigation. Part of this was due to too many choices. For example, the main navigation contained 35 menu items accessible from the top level alone. To help users access certain content and tasks, a well-intentioned team had created a list of quick links along the right-hand side of the home page. However, this list had become excessively long—in some cases, containing up to 50 items. The most useful content, such as benefits information, quarterly updates, or holiday calendars, was often buried deep within several levels of navigation or duplicated across many pages.

For this reason, we knew the IA needed to be redesigned from scratch. To ensure that the new structure would be based on users' mental models, we decided to conduct a card sort with users to test our new IA.

Our Approach

Choosing a Methodology

With card sorting, the recommended best practice is to conduct an open sort, during which participants sort content into groups and then name the groups (Spencer, 2009). Because we were on a tight time and fiscal budget, we created the initial first- and second-level categories as a team. While coming up with the categories, we focused on making key tasks easy to find, based on tasks users had mentioned in previous interviews (see "List of Key Tasks"). In addition, we referred to research on intranet IA best practices while writing the category labels (Nielsen Norman Group, 2014).

After we created the initial IA, our UX designers and user researchers developed a closed card sort study to test our proposed categories with a broader sample of employees.

Study Goals

Our main goal with the card sort was to find out whether our categories would enable employees to complete key tasks quickly and easily. In addition, we wanted to validate whether the labels we had chosen in our group exercise were mutually exclusive—that is, specific enough that an employee would look for a piece of content in one category and not another. We defined the accuracy of our IA by the percentage of users who sorted a card into a specific category. For example, if nine out of ten participants placed "Retirement and 401k" into "Benefits & Pay," we would call this 90% accuracy.

We tried to avoid creating cognitive overload whenever possible. For this reason, we decided to compare the performance of one-word versions of our category labels against multiword labels. In addition, we planned to measure improvement by comparing the accuracy of our new IA with the original categories. This resulted in a total of three card sorts: one baseline test and two versions of our new IA (see Figure 11.11).

Study Details

We planned to conduct the card sort with a large number of users to ensure a high level of stakeholder confidence. At the time, Citrix was made up of nearly 9000 employees, and we aimed to reach about 1% of the population, or at least 100 users, to conduct each sort. Because we were targeting users in many different locations, we created

Figure 11.11: Categories used in card sorts. Note that the baseline, IA 1, and IA 2 were tested at the same time. IA 3 (a slightly modified version of IA 2) was tested separately afterward.

Information Architecture (IA)	Top-level categories
Baseline IA	• Business Resources • Company Information • Employee Resources • Policies & Procedures • myITSupport
IA 1	• Benefits • Career • Support • Travel • Workplace
IA 2	• Benefits & Pay • Career & Training • Company & Campus • Support • Travel & Expenses
IA 3 *(also used for in-person card sorts)*	• Benefits & Pay • Career & Training • Company & Campus • IT Support

the card sort online using the tool OptimalSort, which provided reporting capabilities and the ability to include tooltip explanations on the cards.[1]

To keep the number of cards manageable, we had users sort types of content, rather than individual items. For example, we combined medical insurance, dental insurance, and vision insurance into one card. This method is sometimes called "sorting by topic," as opposed to detailed content (Spencer, 118). We also wrote a tooltip explanation for each card to give more details about the content.

Finally, we ran a pilot test with several employees to ensure that the online card sort tool was working properly and that our data collection plan was sufficient. As a result of this pilot test, we adjusted some card labels. For example, we changed "internal transfers" to "employee relocation information" because our testers were confused by the first term.

First Round of Testing and Iterations

Around 130 employees participated in the first round of testing, with an average of 100 participants completing each sort. We sent participants an e-mail with links to the three card sorts, targeting groups that represented various company functions and locations. Participants were encouraged to take all three sorts and were not told

[1]http://www.optimalworkshop.com/optimalsort.htm

which sort was which. Each sort contained the same cards but different categories (the baseline IA, IA 1, and IA 2). We included a short demographic survey to ensure that we had a representative ratio of managers to individual contributors and US- to non-US-based employees. After completing each card sort, participants had the opportunity to provide comments.

When we compared the results from the three variations, we found that our new IA worked better than the baseline, with the more descriptive labels resulting in an overall accuracy rate of 76% (see Figures 11.12–11.14). We also noticed that "Support" was not specific enough to be mutually exclusive. For this reason, we renamed this category "IT Support" and validated the change by sending out a final card sort (IA 3) to a new group of participants.

Qualitative Testing

In addition to the quantitative study, we tested the final IA variation with a few employees in person, in order to understand why participants were sorting cards the way they did. Eight employees participated individually with a facilitator. They conducted the sort on a computer with OptimalSort using think-aloud protocol.

The in-person sorts helped us to gain a deeper understanding of how participants were interpreting our categories. For example, we found that "Company & Campus" was considered a "general" category that participants would use for cards that did not seem to belong anywhere else. Half of the participants also suggested that "Company & Campus" needed subcategories, such as "Facilities" or "Policies." This showed us that we needed to conduct further research on the best labels for that section.

We also used these sessions as a way to follow up on cards that previous participants had placed into multiple categories, for example, items such as "Tuition Assistance," "Service Awards," and "Employment Verification Letter" (see Figure 11.14). In some cases, we found that participants felt content could belong in two different places, making these items ideal candidates for cross-linking.

Overall, the in-person card sorts enhanced the findings from the quantitative card sorts. They also helped us gain insights that we later drew upon when we began to redesign and rewrite the content for each section.

Final Results

In the end, we were very pleased with the quantitative card sort results, as we found that the final variation of our top-level IA had an average accuracy rate of 84% overall (compared with only 60% accuracy with the baseline). Even better, the most commonly accessed content, according to our list of key tasks, had an accuracy rate of 97% (see Figure 11.15).

Although the categories worked well, we found that the single-word labels were not as successful as the more descriptive labels. "Workplace" and "Career" in particular were considered vague (based on

	Business resources	Company information	Employee resources	Policies & procedures	myITsupport
Creative & writing guidelines & templates	42%	12%	19%	22%	4%
Facility services	38%	29%	14%	8%	11%
Building & Workspace Maintenance	37%	25%	12%	11%	14%
Office Locations	7%	87%	5%	1%	
Department lists	16%	79%	5%		
Org Chart	14%	78%	8%		
Global employee survey	13%	59%	20%	8%	
Global day of impact (GDI)	7%	47%	36%	10%	1%
Workplace amenities	16%	46%	31%	5%	2%
Career planning	8%	3%	89%	1%	
Retirement & 401(k)	3%	1%	88%	8%	
Family Matters	1%	1%	86%	12%	
Life Changing Events	2%	3%	86%	10%	
Health & Wellness	2%	6%	86%	7%	
Medical, Dental, Vision Insurance	1%	2%	84%	14%	
Life Insurance & Disability	3%	1%	83%	13%	
Coaching Conversations	10%		82%	8%	
Pay & Compensation	6%	5%	81%	8%	
Employee Stock Purchase Program (ESPP)	5%	3%	79%	13%	
Education & Training	19%	2%	75%	3%	1%
Employment verification letter	10%	3%	75%	13%	
Tuition assistance	5%	1%	75%	19%	
Time Off & Holidays	3%	11%	64%	22%	
Employee relocation information	8%	4%	64%	23%	1%
Legal aid and Immigration services	14%	3%	64%	19%	
Service awards	8%	24%	57%	9%	3%
Financial services	25%	5%	54%	14%	2%
Internal Job Postings	11%	35%	53%	1%	1%
Trip Planning tools and policies	23%	3%	15%	58%	
Corporate guidelines	8%	42%	1%	50%	
Purchasing & Procurement	32%	6%	6%	46%	10%
Bring Your Own Device (BYOD)	6%	1%	17%	38%	38%
Expense Reports	34%	3%	26%	36%	1%
WorkAnywhere and Workshifting	19%	11%	30%	35%	6%
Hardware, Software & System Help	2%			1%	97%
Software downloads	3%	1%			96%

Figure 11.12: Baseline IA results (118 participants). Note: The baseline IA category names were taken from the actual site at the time of the study. Numbers in the cells show the percentage of participants who placed a card into a certain category. Blue-highlighted cells show the category that the majority of participants placed a card into. Images were taken from an OptimalSort report.

	Benefits	Career	Support	Travel	Workplace
Employee Stock Purchase Program (ESPP)	97%	1%	1%		1%
Medical, Dental, Vision Insurance	96%		2%		1%
Life Insurance & Disability	96%	1%	1%	1%	1%
Retirement & 401(k)	92%	5%	1%	1%	1%
Family Matters	86%	2%	10%	1%	1%
Health & Wellness	83%	1%	3%	2%	11%
Time Off & Holidays	80%	4%	1%	3%	11%
Tuition assistance	76%	19%	5%		1%
Financial services	73%	1%	19%	1%	5%
Pay & Compensation	67%	24%	1%	1%	6%
Life Changing Events	67%	12%	12%	2%	7%
Legal aid and Immigration services	61%	4%	27%	4%	5%
Employee relocation information	33%	21%	21%	11%	13%
Career planning	1%	97%	1%		1%
Internal Job Postings	1%	88%	1%		9%
Coaching Conversations	1%	87%	4%		7%
Education & Training	13%	73%	7%		7%
Employment verification letter	25%	39%	26%		10%
Service awards	36%	37%	7%	1%	19%
Hardware, Software & System Help			94%	1%	5%
Software downloads	1%		82%		17%
Purchasing & Procurement	1%		55%	4%	39%
Creative & writing guidelines & templates	1%	14%	44%		41%
Trip Planning tools and policies	1%		3%	93%	2%
Expense Reports	1%	3%	13%	61%	21%
Office Locations	1%		11%	7%	81%
Workplace amenities	17%	1%	3%		79%
Corporate guidelines	4%	5%	13%	1%	78%
Department lists		7%	17%		76%
Org Chart		18%	10%		72%
Global employee survey	4%	16%	10%		70%
WorkAnywhere and Workshifting	25%	4%	5%	2%	64%
Global day of impact (GDI)	32%	1%	3%		64%
Building & Workspace Maintenance	1%		37%		61%
Facility services	4%		44%		53%
Bring Your Own Device (BYOD)	29%	1%	32%	1%	37%

Figure 11.13: IA 1 results (135 participants).

	Benefits & pay	Career & training	Company & campus	Support	Travel & expenses
Employee Stock Purchase Program (ESPP)	99%	1%			
Medical, Dental, Vision Insurance	98%	1%	1%	1%	
Life Insurance & Disability	96%	1%	2%	1%	1%
Retirement & 401(k)	94%	3%	1%	2%	
Pay & Compensation	91%	6%	3%		
Health & Wellness	84%	2%	11%	2%	
Family Matters	84%	1%	2%	11%	2%
Time Off & Holidays	81%	3%	7%	2%	6%
Life Changing Events	72%	10%	4%	12%	2%
Legal aid and Immigration services	67%	2%	5%	19%	7%
Tuition assistance	64%	31%	1%	4%	
Financial services	63%		7%	17%	13%
Employee relocation information	42%	14%	24%	11%	9%
Service awards	39%	35%	21%	4%	
Employment verification letter	36%	31%	11%	20%	1%
Career planning	1%	99%			
Education & Training	3%	93%	2%	1%	
Coaching Conversations	5%	90%	3%	2%	
Internal Job Postings		85%	12%	2%	
Office Locations			97%	2%	1%
Department lists		2%	94%	4%	
Org Chart		7%	90%	2%	
Corporate guidelines	1%	7%	87%	6%	
Global employee survey	4%	10%	83%	3%	
Workplace amenities	14%		80%	6%	
Building & Workspace Maintenance	1%		64%	35%	
Global day of impact (GDI)	29%		63%	6%	2%
WorkAnywhere and Workshifting	25%	6%	56%	11%	2%
Facility services	2%		55%	43%	
Creative & writing guidelines & templates		27%	38%	35%	
Hardware, Software & System Help			4%	96%	
Software downloads	1%	2%	6%	92%	
Purchasing & Procurement	2%	1%	27%	45%	25%
Bring Your Own Device (BYOD)	34%	2%	22%	41%	1%
Trip Planning tools and policies	2%		2%	2%	94%
Expense Reports	4%	2%	3%	2%	89%

Figure 11.14: IA 2 results (122 participants).

	Benefits & pay	Career & training	Company & campus	IT support	Travel & expenses
★ Medical, Dental, Vision Insurance	100%				
★ Pay & Compensation	100%				
Life Insurance & Disability	100%				
Retirement & 401(k)	100%				
Employee Stock Purchase Program (ESPP)	96%		1%		3%
Family Matters	93%	5%			1%
Life Changing Events	92%	7%			1%
★ Time Off & Holidays	88%		12%		
Financial services	84%	1%	5%		10%
Health & Wellness	79%	5%	15%		
Legal aid and Immigration services	77%	15%	8%		
Tuition assistance	66%	33%			1%
Service awards	44%	29%	25%	3%	
Employee relocation information	42%	21%	26%		11%
★ Career planning		100%			
★ Education & Training	3%	97%			
★ Coaching Conversations	1%	96%	3%		
Internal Job Postings		89%	11%		
Employment verification letter	40%	47%	14%		
Office Locations			100%		
Department lists		1%	99%		
Corporate guidelines		4%	96%		
★ Org Chart		5%	95%		
Global employee survey	1%	11%	88%		
Building & Workspace Maintenance			86%	10%	4%
Facility services			86%	12%	1%
Workplace amenities	12%		85%	1%	1%
Global day of impact (GDI)	25%	4%	70%		1%
Creative & writing guidelines & templates		34%	63%	3%	
WorkAnywhere and Workshifting	30%	5%	53%	11%	
Purchasing & Procurement	3%	1%	47%	10%	40%
★ Hardware, Software & System Help			1%	99%	
Software downloads			4%	96%	
Bring Your Own Device (BYOD)	8%	4%	15%	73%	
★ Trip Planning tools and policies					100%
★ Expense Reports	3%		1%		96%

Figure 11.15: IA 3 results (97 participants). Note: starred items denote commonly accessed content, according to our list of key tasks.

comments from participants in the online survey). When combined with another word, however, categories seemed to be much clearer. For example, "Company & Campus," while not perfect, seemed to work better than "Workplace" because participants could assume that it related to company information and physical locations. "Support" on its own was not specific enough, but simply changing the label to "IT Support" seemed to make it clearer.

Lessons Learned

In looking back on the entire process, there are a few things that we might have done differently, as well as several recommendations that we can offer to other teams using card sorting.

One question we had was whether creating the groups as a team and then conducting a closed sort was the right approach or whether we should have pushed our timeline back and conducted an open sort with a small set of users first. While we would not necessarily recommend starting with a closed sort for all website redesigns, the approach worked well in our case for two reasons. First, we had a diverse multidisciplinary team with varying perspectives that we were able to use as a starting point. Second, as Citrix employees, we were able to refer to our own experiences as users of the site.

Based on our experience, we recommend that any large information architecture redesign include team members from a variety of backgrounds. When working on an intranet redesign in particular, it is best if the people designing the structure are not content owners. This avoids the common pitfall of making an IA based on the company organizational structure.

We also learned a few things about online card sorts in particular. During our in-person card sorts, we were surprised that the majority of our participants overlooked the tooltips in the OptimalSort UI. For this reason, we will be cautious about using tooltips during future card sorts.

In addition, the number of participants needed to obtain reliable quantitative results will vary. In our case, we watched the data as they came in and noticed that the trends did not change much beyond about 50 users. Because of this, teams that are compensating participants or on a limited budget could choose to watch the data trends and close the test when the changes appear to level out. This can be easily done using an online tool.

Finally, we highly recommend conducting at least a few card sorts in person, as this results in rich feedback on the "why" behind the "what" that cannot be captured from a survey alone. In our case, we received valuable insights from our in-person card sorts and found it extremely beneficial for us to hear participants describe which cards were difficult to sort and why.

The experience we gained from this study shows that there is no one "correct" way to conduct a card sort. The appropriate methods and resulting insights will vary depending on the content, team, and participants; thus, some level of experimentation and iteration will always be necessary. With card sorting, as with all user research, the most important things to remember are to be curious about users' point of view, open to surprises, and flexible enough to make adjustments along the way.

Appendix

List of Key Tasks

The following are the most common activities that employees use the Citrix intranet to complete, based on user and stakeholder interviews:

- Accessing the org chart
- Learning about and/or signing up for health benefits
- Reading company news
- Accessing IT services, such as filing a support ticket
- Entering quarterly career goals
- Viewing the holiday calendar
- Taking product training courses
- Booking a business trip
- Submitting expense reports

CHAPTER 12

Focus Groups

Introduction

A focus group is an interview where five to ten (ideally six to eight) people are brought together to discuss their experiences or opinions around topics introduced by a skilled moderator who facilitates an open, nonjudgmental atmosphere. The session typically lasts one to two hours and is good for quickly understanding user perception about a particular topic or concept. Focus groups are used in a variety of settings, including social science research (since the 1930s) and marketing research. In our experience, the focus group is a valuable methodology when done *correctly*. Key benefits of focus groups are that the group dynamic brings up topics you may never have thought to ask about, and the synergy of a group discussion can stimulate new ideas or encourage participants to talk about things they would not have thought about if interviewed alone. Focus group participants are often more willing and able to discuss their experiences candidly and use their preferred style of language with a group of peers than individuals with an interviewer. On the other hand, a drawback of the focus group method is that participants may be more susceptible to social influence and acquiesce to particularly influential group members (Schindler, 1992).

In this chapter, we present a common method for conducting a focus group, as well as several modifications (refer "Modifications" section, page 353). Finally, we discuss how to present the data, along with some of our lessons learned. A case study by Peter McNally is provided at the end to demonstrate an application of this method.

At a Glance

> Preparing to conduct a focus group
> Conducting a focus group
> Data analysis and interpretation
> Communicating the findings
> Modifications

Preparing to Conduct a Focus Group

Preparing to conduct a focus group study involves generating and refining the questions you will ask the group, determining the characteristics of the groups you are interested in studying, recruiting them to participate, inviting observers, and producing activity materials. Since a focus group is essentially a special case of an interview, we recommend you read Chapter 9, "Interviews," prior to planning your focus group.

At a Glance

> Create a discussion guide
> Players in your activity
> Inviting observers
> Activity materials

Create a Topic/Discussion Guide

A topic or discussion guide for a focus group is a tool that helps the moderator keep a session on track (see Table 12.1 for a sample). It contains the key topics that must be covered and specific questions to be posed to the group. While it is a guide rather than a script, and therefore moderators are free to deviate from it to follow participant interest and conversations on other topics, it does help the moderator maintain consistency across groups.

To create a discussion guide, you will need to identify the research questions you want to answer; generate, refine, and limit the topics and questions to be discussed; and finally, test the specific wording for each question.

Table 12.1: Sample discussion guide

Moderator:			
Date:			
Session:			
Topic	**Example questions**	**Duration**	**Goal**
Introduction (round-robin style)	Please tell us your name and where you're from.	<2 minutes	Get participants talking; participants get to know each other, help participants feel comfortable
Warm-up	What's your definition of (topic of interest)?	~5 minutes	Transition to the topic of interest; gauge participants' knowledge of topic
Key topic 1—typical travel destinations	What types of travel destinations have you been to in the last year?	10-15 minutes	Get answers to specific research question #1
Key topic 2—perceptions of travel app/useful and missing features	If you were telling a friend about the travel app, what would you say?	10-15 minutes	Get answers to specific research question #2
Key 3—barriers to using app/ reasons for abandonment	Tell me about the reasons you stopped using the travel app?	10-15 minutes	Get answers to specific research question #3
Wrap-up	"Of all the things we discussed, which one is most important to you?" (Krueger, 1998)	~5 minutes	Have participants reflect on discussion/ experience; bring closure to discussion
Summary	Does this summary capture what was said?	~5 minutes	Let participants validate/refute key findings
What's missing?	What did we *not* cover that we should have?	~5 minutes	Determine topics that were of interest to participants, but were not already covered

Identify the Questions You Wish to Answer

DILBERT © 2003 Scott Adams. Used By permission of UNIVERSAL UCLICK. All rights reserved.

By this point, you will already have a general idea of your research questions and have determined that a focus group is the most appropriate method for answering that question. You may still want to have a **brainstorming** session with all of your **stakeholders** (members of the product team, the UX group, marketing) to hone in on the most important questions to answer in your activity. You will likely end up with questions that are out of the scope of the proposed activity or questions that are best answered by other activities (e.g., behavioral questions). You may also end up with more questions than you could possibly cover in a single focus group session. If this is the case, you will either need to conduct multiple sessions or trim down the number of questions to fit into a single session.

TIP

Aim for a one-hour focus group session with the option to extend to two hours, if necessary. We do not recommend conducting sessions beyond two hours; however, dedicated participants or customers may be willing to stay for longer sessions if you provide regular breaks and keep the session interesting.

Writing the Focus Group Questions

Focus groups are particularly well suited to answering questions that explore attitudes, feelings, and beliefs about a topic, elicit concerns, answer a "why" question about quantitative or behavioral data, gather the local vocabulary used to talk about a topic, generate new ideas, and require answers from groups, rather than individuals. Questions in a focus group should be open-ended, worded clearly, impartial (e.g., not leading), and actually ask what you intended to ask.

As you can see in Table 12.1 (also see Table 9.3 on page 226), we list six types of questions: introduction, warm-up, key, wrap-up, summary and what's missing? Key questions are where you obtain the bulk of the information you will need to answer your research question.

Below, we list some types of questions that are suitable models of key questions:

- Review a user's "typical" day or the user's most recent day (e.g., at work, at home, depending on the context of interest).

- List questions. For example, list the tasks that users do and how they do them.
- The domain in general (e.g., terminology, standard procedures, industry guidelines).
- User's likes and dislikes and/or advantages or disadvantages.
- User's desired outcomes or goals.
- User's reactions, opinions, concerns, or attitudes toward a new product/concept.
- Desired outcomes for new products or features.

Krueger (1998) listed question types that are good for focus groups:

- Complete a sentence
- Create an analogy
- Use fantasy and daydream
- Use personification

Asking participants to discuss a "typical" day can give you a high-level overview of participants' perceptions about the way they work or activities they may do in general. Asking participants to tell you about their most recent day in a context (e.g., at work) gives you specific examples about tasks they have recently done. You can also understand how certain tasks are done at a high level, the challenges they face, and the things they enjoy. Asking participants to think back to a specific example is preferable to thinking about the future.

Similarly, you should be careful to avoid asking "why" questions. Why questions may encourage participants to generate a cause-effect relationship about a topic that does not exist and may make participants feel worried that they will have to justify their responses. Instead, choose "how" questions (Krueger, 1998).

Focus groups also offer the opportunity to learn about local terminology, guidelines, and industry practices. Participants can additionally describe desired outcomes in their activities or goals they want to achieve. Finally, you can gauge user reaction to concepts and brainstorm ideas for new products or features.

We strongly recommend reviewing the advice given in Chapter 9 for additional guidance in developing key questions (see "Write the Questions" section, page 225).

Example Question Design

Let us use our online travel app as an example and design some questions for a focus group. You know that college students sometimes attend professional conferences relevant to their major. You also know that college students are usually poor. Your company would like to offer "room sharing" via its app. People who are interested in sharing a hotel room in a particular hotel or city could sign up and specify preferences (e.g., females only, under $50/night, no more than three roommates, nonsmoking). Since you are not aware of any travel apps that offer this, you would like to learn more about people's attitudes toward signing up using an app to share a hotel room. A focus group seems like the best way to get a general feel for attitudes, biases, and new ideas in this area. This will be followed up with a survey and sent out to a few hundred current and potential customers. With a one-hour focus group and ten participants, you realize you can probably cover only about five or six questions. Some open-ended questions you might ask are as follows:

- How satisfied are you with the kind of accommodations your budget allows?
- How willing would you be to share a hotel room with someone you know to lower your costs and get a nicer room?
- How willing would you be to share a hotel room with someone you didn't know to lower your costs and get a nicer room?
- What would you want to know about a person with whom you might share a room?
- What would make you more likely to share a room with someone you didn't know?

Probes, Prompts, Pauses, and Checks

Probes, prompts, pauses, and checks are strategies to get participants to talk more about a topic of interest. Use one of these when you want participants to talk more about something you are interested in. We find the following probes particularly useful:

- Probes
  - Could you talk a little more about that (give me a little bit more detail)?
  - Could you tell me what you mean by that?
  - I'm not sure I understand.
  - Who else has an idea?
  - Are there other ways to look at this?
  - Could you give me an example?
- Prompts
  - Say "uh huh" and/or shake your head to encourage the participant to continue talking. Be careful not to provide any negative feedback that could be interpreted as you disagreeing with what a participant is saying.
  - Repeat the participant's question.
  - Repeat what the participant said in question format.
- Pauses
  - *Be quiet*—when you offer space to participants to speak, often they will.

- Checks
  - Is this correct?
  - So, if I understand correctly … (summarize) …

Question Types to Avoid

Sensitive or Personal Topics

Do not discuss extremely sensitive or personal topics like politics, sex, or morals in a focus group. These are topics that are sometimes uncomfortable or cause heated discussion between friends and family. It is not appropriate for you to ask participants to discuss them in front of strangers and in a way that will be recorded. Plus, you may end up wasting everyone's time if you ask but participants are not willing to tell.

Predictions

Studies have found that participants are not always good at predicting the features they would find useful in practice (Gray, Barfield, Haselkorn, Spyridakis, & Conquest, 1990; Karlin & Klemmer, 1989; Root & Draper, 1983). This is why we recommend against asking participants to "pretend" about things with which they have no experience. For example, it is completely appropriate for you to ask someone, "What is the biggest challenge you face in your job?" and then follow up the user's response with, "What would make that part of your job easier to do?" You are not asking the participant to pretend—the participant does that job and may encounter that challenge every day. You can be sure that the participant has thought on many occasions about ways the challenge could or should be addressed. Going back to our travel example in earlier chapters, a travel agent might say that her biggest challenge is when people call her to book a vacation but never have the information needed, like the maximum budget, the dates of travel, and desired destinations.

On the other hand, you should not ask the travel agent whether she would like using voice-activated input, if the agent has never seen or used such a system before. She may think the concept sounds really cool when you describe it, but once she begins using it at work, she hates it because everyone in the surrounding cubicles can hear every mistake she makes.

Test Your Topics/Questions

Before you use the topic/discussion guide in a focus group, it is important to pretest the topics and questions. Start by sending the questions out for review by the team. Say the questions out loud. Do they sound conversational when spoken? Ideally, you should have people from your target group review the questions and offer feedback. Will these questions elicit the type of information the team is looking for? Do they use local language? If not, you need to reword or create new questions.

Ordering Your Questions

Generally, questions should be ordered from general to specific. This order is beneficial for two reasons. First, the flow is natural for participants. As participants warm up to a topic and other participants bring up related topics, they tend to remember more details. As the focus group progresses, participants also become more comfortable with the moderator and other participants and are willing to reveal more. Second, conversations naturally flow from the general to the more specific. Ideally, a focus group feels like a conversation with one topic leading naturally to the next. In a focus group that goes really well, the participant, rather than the moderator, brings up the next topic on the discussion guide, without having ever seen it.

Players in Your Activity

Of course, you will need representative participants to take part in your session, but there are also three additional roles that need to be filled to conduct a successful focus group: moderator, notetaker, and videographer.

Participants

Because focus groups are a group activity, in addition to considering who your participants should be, you also have to consider how many you will interview per group and how to form the groups.

Number of Participants

Since the group dynamic is an important component to this method, we recommend six to eight participants per session; however, groups as small as four can still provide valuable information (Krueger & Casey, 2000 pp. 73-74 suggest a range of 4-12 per group). Groups with more than ten participants can be difficult to manage, and with a large group, it is unlikely that everyone will have an opportunity to speak. It may seem like two additional participants will not make a big difference, but when you are trying to get multiple perspectives to multiple questions, it will.

TIP

Recruit 10 participants per focus group session. That way, when one or two do not show up to the session, you will still have the ideal number of participants!

Number of Groups

The recommended number of groups per participant type is three to four (Krueger & Casey, 2000, pp. 26-27). If you are restricted on the number of participants you can recruit, then opt to run multiple smaller groups rather than one large group. For example, run two groups with five participants each rather than one group with ten participants. This is because group dynamics can vary. You do not want one dominating participant to influence all of the participants in the session. In addition, you may learn information in one focus group that you never thought about and would like the opportunity to develop new questions for a second focus group. If you put all your participants in one basket, you lose the opportunity to revise your questions. Of course, if you change your questions between sessions, you cannot compare the answers across groups, but you do have the opportunity to cover more ground.

Participant Mix

Participants in a single focus group are typically similar in some way that is relevant to your research question. For example, if you were interested in getting input from both novice and expert users, you might group participants into these separate groups for sessions. Speaking with especially effective or expert users can provide a wealth of ideas since these "lead" users can often be a source of innovation. However, you should also recruit novice and average users since expert users may request features or services that are too sophisticated from the majority of the user population. By speaking with each user type individually, you can quickly understand the needs and issues for a broad spectrum of your population.

Some user types should not be placed together because they may negatively influence comfort and disclosure. For example, managers and their direct reports should never be placed in the same group because the direct reports may not be honest or may defer to their managers. Managers may even feel it necessary to "take control" of the session and play a more dominant or expert role in the activity to save face in front of their employees. The issues are similar when you mix user types of different levels within a hierarchy, even if one does not report directly to the other (e.g., doctor and nurse). Refer to "Lessons Learned" section on page 368 for a discussion of how mixing user types of different levels in a hierarchy can cause real problems.

The Moderator

One moderator per session should facilitate the activity (see "Conducting a Focus Group" section on page 351 as well as "Moderating Your Activity" section on page 165 in Chapter 7 for the details of being an effective moderator). The moderator's job is to elicit meaningful responses from the group, manage the group dynamics (e.g., draw out quiet participants), examine each answer to ensure he or she understands what the participant is really saying, and then paraphrase the response to make sure the intent of the statement is captured. Finally, the moderator needs to know when to let a discussion go off the "planned path" into valuable areas of discovery and when to bring a fruitless discussion back on track.

To do all this effectively, the moderator needs to have sufficient domain knowledge to know which discussions are adding value and which are sapping valuable time. He or she also needs to know what follow-up questions to ask on-the-fly to get the details the team needs to make product decisions (see " Lessons Learned" section, page 368). Finally, the moderator should make participants feel at ease and create an atmosphere where participants feel free to express diverse opinions. Moderators who adopt a nonjudgmental, open, encouraging, and respectful mindset will be particularly successful at putting participants at ease. It is also important that they encourage all participants to adopt this attitude as well. Participants should not critique one another's ideas.

If you have never run a focus group before, we recommend you gain experience by participating in (not moderating) several different focus groups. You can go to online community boards or search job listings for companies in your area that are looking for focus group participants. Also, observe different moderators in action to learn what worked and what did not. You may also identify a certain style that you would like to emulate. Once you have been a participant and observed other moderators, it is essential that you practice moderating a focus group rather than just jumping in feet first. You do not want to learn "on the job" when expensive data collection is at stake.

Figure 12.1 is a moderator's checklist. For a detailed discussion of the art of moderating, refer to "Moderating Your Activity" section on page 165 in Chapter 7.

- ☐ **Have personality.** Be personable and approachable. Also, remember to smile!
- ☐ **Ask questions.** There is no point collecting data that you do not understand. Ask questions throughout. You should also be clarifying what you hear and delving into user responses for more details.
- ☐ **Stay focused.** Small diversions, if relevant, are appropriate, but try to get back on track quickly. Asking participants to turn off all cell phones at the beginning of the session will also go a long way to keeping them focused on the activity at hand.
- ☐ **You are not a participant.** Ask the questions and let participants answer them. Also, do not offer your opinions because you could bias your participants' responses.
- ☐ **Keep the activity moving.** You need to control the direction of the activity and level of detail participants are providing or else you will never finish your activity.
- ☐ **Keep the participants motivated and encouraged.** A little encouragement goes a long way. Also keep an eye on your participants' energy levels.
- ☐ **No critiquing.** As a moderator, you should never challenge what a participant has to say. It's OK for a participant to disagree with a fellow participant, but remind everyone that there are no wrong ideas—there are simply different experiences and perspectives.
- ☐ **Everyone should participate.** In a group activity, it can take a great deal of energy to draw out the quiet participants, but it is important to do so. This can be done by calling on individuals by name and making eye contact, or by asking for information in a round-robin format.
- ☐ **No one should dominate.** When you notice a participant is beginning to dominate the group, try to call on others in the group to balance things out and use body language to quiet down the dominant participant (e.g., turning your back to the participant, not making eye contact). If things don't improve, gently address the overbearing participant and, in the worst case, escort the participant out.

Figure 12.1: Moderator's checklist.

The Notetaker

A notetaker is needed to help the moderator. The moderator has a big job and should not be worried about taking detailed notes. The sole job of the notetaker is to write down notes from the session. It is important for the notetaker to have domain knowledge so that he or she knows what points are important to capture and what comments can be left out, as well as to ensure that the notes make sense. (See "Lessons Learned" section on page 368 to read more about the importance of domain knowledge.) You will find a detailed discussion of notetaking tips and strategies in Chapter 7 (see "Recording and Notetaking" section, page 171).

The notes can be displayed for the group (including the moderator) to see. This can be done on a laptop and projecting the image or by writing the notes on flip charts at the front of the room. Obviously, reading someone's handwriting is not an issue when using a laptop, but if your notetaker is not a fast or good typist, you may want to go with the handwritten notes. An obvious advantage of typing the notes during the session is that you can send out the notes to stakeholders immediately following the session.

Taking notes for the group to see has a few advantages and disadvantages. One advantage is that it can help the participants to avoid repeating the same information, and it shows the participants that their comments have been captured (otherwise, participants may ramble on to be sure you captured what was said). If the notetaker captured a comment incorrectly, the participant can correct him or her immediately. Finally, the moderator can refer back to the notes during the session to follow up on a particular comment or to direct the group to a different line of discussion.

One disadvantage to having the notes displayed for all to see is that you may not be able to use a lot of shorthand because the participants will not understand it. Additionally, the notetaker should not include design ideas or notes about the participants, comments, or session for all to see.

Whether or not the notes are being displayed to the group, the big benefit to having a notetaker is to avoid the need to watch the entire focus group on tape for later data analysis. As soon as the session is over, you have data at hand to begin analyzing. If there are areas where the moderator feels that the notes do not make sense, he or she can go back and watch just that portion of the session. This cuts down significantly on the time it takes to analyze the data. Finally, the notetaker can help you analyze your data. Since the notetaker was there for the entire session, he or she understands the data as well as you, and it is always helpful to have an extra pair of eyes and a different perspective to analyze the data.

Some focus group moderators prefer to have their sessions transcribed by professionals. People working in highly regulated fields (e.g., the pharmaceutical industry regulated by the FDA) may be required to have precise documentation of any user research activity they conduct, since the information learned in such sessions provides data for making product design decisions. Transcribing focus group sessions is extremely time-consuming and expensive. It can take six hours to transcribe one hour of tape. If multiple voices are involved, such as in a focus group, it will likely take longer. Transcription services charge $1-$4 per *minute* of audio. Shorter turnaround time often costs even more.

The Videographer

Whenever possible, you will want a video recording of your session. This recording can be useful for your analysis and can be shared with stakeholders who may not be able to attend a live session. You will need someone to be responsible for recording. In most cases, this person simply needs to start and stop the recording and keep an eye out for any technical issues that arise. This task can be combined with notetaking. For more information on the benefits of video recording, refer to "Recording and Notetaking" section on page 171 in Chapter 7.

Inviting Observers

If you have the facilities to allow stakeholders to view these sessions, you will find it highly beneficial to get them involved (see Chapter 4, "Lab Layout" section, page 87). Stakeholders can learn a lot about what users' like and dislike about the current product or a competitor's product, the difficulties they encounter, what they want, and why they think they want it.

If you take a break during the session, you can ask the observers if they have any questions they would like answered or areas they want to delve into further. You should not promise you will be able to cover them, but if time and opportunity permit, it is good to have these additional questions available. If the questions the observers suggest are clearly biased or would derail the focus group, you can always state, "Those are questions that we might want to consider for another activity."

Activity Materials

A basic focus group requires very few materials. Options include:

- Laptop/computer or whiteboard or flip chart
- Computer projector and screen (if using laptop/computer)
- Blue or black markers (if using whiteboard or flip chart)
- Materials for creativity exercises
- Paper and pens for participants to take notes
- Prototype or other artifact to stimulate discussion (optional)
- Large room conducive for a group activity
- Name tents or nametags
- Recording equipment

We prefer to use a laptop and display each question using a projector (see Figure 12.2). This looks professional and the questions are easy to read. A whiteboard or flip chart will work just as well. Remember to write clearly and with large letters in blue or black marker.

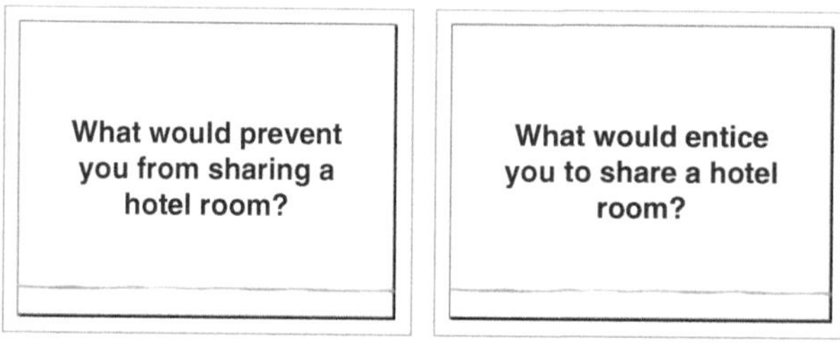

Figure 12.2: Sample focus group question slides.

It is valuable to provide paper and pens for the participants. If multiple people wish to speak at the same time, you may have to ask them to "hold their thoughts." Sometimes, people forget what they wanted to say when they hear someone else speaking. It can be frustrating for both you and the participant if good ideas are lost. Allowing participants to jot a quick note on paper can help save those great ideas.

Finally, presenting a prototype, a competitor's product, or a video (if appropriate) can help encourage discussion and focus thoughts. You do not want to bias participants' answers, but it is often helpful to show examples of the product (yours or a competitor's) during the discussion. Make sure that all participants can easily see whatever you are presenting.

Conducting a Focus Group

You are now prepared to conduct a focus group. In this section, we walk you through the steps to conduct your session.

Activity Timeline

The timeline in Table 12.2 covers in detail the sequence and timing of events to conduct a focus group. It is based on a one- to two-hour session and will obviously need to be adjusted for shorter or longer sessions. These are *approximate* times based on our personal experience and should be used only as a guide.

Now that you know the steps involved in conducting a focus group at a high level, we will discuss each step in detail.

Table 12.2: Timeline of a focus group session

Approximate duration	Procedure
5 minutes	Welcome participants (introductions and forms)
5 minutes	Creative exercise/participant introductions
45-100 minutes	Discussion
5 minutes	Wrap-up (thank participants and escort them out)

At a Glance

> Welcome the participants

> Introduce the activity and discussion rules

> The focus group discussion

Welcome the Participants

This is the time during which you greet your participants, allow them to eat some snacks, ask them to fill out paperwork, and get them warmed up for your activity. It is helpful to begin with a creative exercise such as designing name tents. Alternatively, you can discuss likes and dislikes of the current system or a competitor's product. The details of these stages are described in "Warm-Up Exercises" section on page 165 in Chapter 7.

Introduce the Activity and Discussion Rules

Once all forms are complete, introductions are made, and the participants are warmed up, the rules for discussion should be provided. The rules are simple: "All ideas are useful and please speak one at a time." It is important to explain to participants that their individual experiences may be different and those differences should be expressed—but they should not critique each other's ideas or perceptions. Write the rules "All ideas are correct" and "Please speak one at a time" on a flip chart and have it visible during the entire session. This will help tell participants that you are interested in everyone's opinions and that they should be respectful of the thoughts and expressions of the other members of the group. If anyone breaks the rules, the moderator can point to it as a polite reminder. Now is also a good time to remind participants that you will be recording the activity and give them an idea of how long you expect the session to last.

The Focus Group Discussion

Participants should feel that the focus group session is free-flowing and relatively unstructured. You have your discussion/topic guide and possibly a list of questions to be covered during the session, but you may discover interesting insights by allowing a conversation to progress down an unexpected path. Group interaction is the key benefit of focus groups, so it is important to be open to new topics and allow the conversation to flow; otherwise, you may as well do a series of individual interviews. If your questions are presented on slides (see Figure 12.3), that does not mean you are locked into asking the questions in that order. If a topic comes up out of turn, feel free to go with the flow. Just make sure you come back to the other questions so all your questions are answered by the

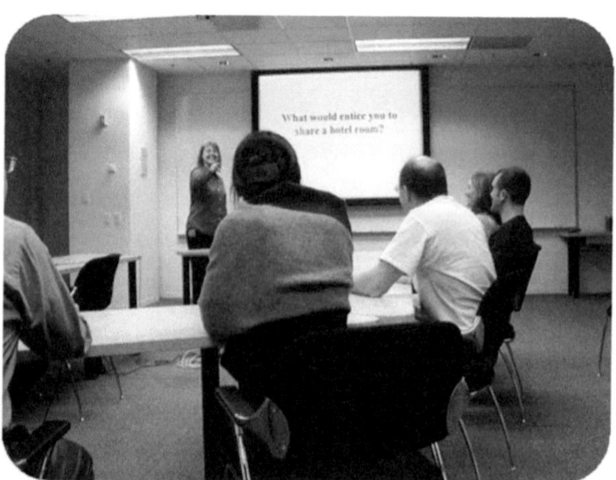

Figure 12.3: A focus group in action. The question has been projected so that everyone can read it easily. The tables are in a "U" formation so that everyone can see each other and the moderator easily.

end of the session. Create a parking lot flip chart, if a topic comes up that is out of scope. You can capture it and indicate that you will get back to these after the session, if time permits.

Everyone Should Participate. No One Should Dominate

It is your job as moderator to engage all the participants in the discussion. This is typically done by containing any overbearing participants and drawing out quiet participants. It can take a great deal of energy to draw out the quiet members, but it is worth the effort to do so. If you have a focus group of ten people and only five are contributing, that essentially cuts your effective participant size in half. You must get everyone involved and the sooner you do this, the better. Call quiet members out by name and ask them their thoughts: "Jane, what do you usually do next?" If things do not improve, you could try moving toward a round-robin format (i.e., everyone participates in turn). If you start off doing a round-robin, you may not need to continue it for the whole activity; just a couple of turns may help people feel more comfortable about speaking up.

It can also take a great deal of skill to handle an overbearing participant who dominates the group and spoils the group dynamic. When you notice that a participant is beginning to dominate, call on others in the group to balance things out. Use body language to discourage the dominant user and encourage the quiet members. Turn your body or eyes away so that the dominant one cannot get your attention and focus fully on a quieter participant. If things do not improve, gently thank the overbearing person for earlier ideas and let him or her know that now, other participants need to contribute. If this does not work, you can ask participants to raise a hand before speaking and to have an assistant note any hand that goes up to make sure that everybody gets called on eventually.

If it is clear that the participant will not work with others, give the group a break. Take the dominant member to the side and remind him or her that this is a *group* activity and that everyone should participate equally. Alternatively, you can thank the user and provide a graceful exit. It is certainly the exception and would only be used as a last resort (e.g., if the participant is being rude or offensive), but it is good to have a plan of action in mind just in case.

We have noticed that highly trained or technical users tend to have more dominating personalities. If you will be conducting a group activity with highly skilled users, beef up your moderations skills by practicing with your colleagues. Consider having a colleague assist you, since two people correcting the overbearing participant may be more effective.

Modifications

Because focus groups have been in use for so many years, there are a plethora of different modifications that you can try. Many of them involve providing users with exposure to the product or concept under development in different ways so that users have some base of experience from which to draw.

Including Individual Activities

While the purpose of a focus group is to understand perspectives from a group, this does not preclude also collecting data from individuals. For example, you could ask participants to rank options individually or ask participants to vote for their preference. Rather than asking everyone to vote by raising their hand (and risk **groupthink** or **evaluation apprehension**), you can ask people to vote on paper. You can have the questions preprinted and distribute each question at the time you would like to vote. This prevents users from filling out all the questions in advance rather than paying attention to the group discussion. You may also choose to give a survey prior to or following a focus group in order to address questions that you do not have time to address in the focus group itself.

You may also ask **closed-ended questions.** These are questions that provide a limited set of responses for participants to choose from (e.g., yes/no; agree/disagree; option a, b, or c), rank a series of options, or vote for a preferred choice. You can also poll the participants (i.e., determine how many people agree with a statement). The benefit of collecting this type of data during a focus group rather than on a survey (where it is typically collected) is that you can ask individuals to discuss *why* they made the selection(s) they did. In fact, it is best to think about ratings and polls as providing an opportunity to have a discussion rather than as a quantitative measure of a preference or attitude. **Live polling** allows you to ask closed-ended questions and gather real-time results using text messaging, a smart phone app, or other handheld input device (e.g., "clicker"). Those results can then be displayed immediately to the group without the moderator having to tally results.

Task-Based Focus Groups

In task-based focus groups, participants are presented with a task (or scenario) and asked to complete it with a prototype or the actual product. If your product is a software or web application, this will obviously require several computers. After participants have completed their task(s), they are brought together to discuss their experiences.

It is best to give the participants the same set of core tasks, so they can share common experiences. For example, in one study, participants were asked to look up information in a user's manual and describe how confident they were that the answer they gave was right (Hackos & Redish, 1998). Similar focus groups have been conducted for car owner's manuals, appliance manuals, and telephone bills (Dumas & Redish, 1999). Keep in mind, however, that a focus group is not a substitute for a usability test.

Similarly, you can present participants with multiple activities or artifacts during a single focus group. Participants may start off with a brief group discussion, but then, they work individually for the majority of the session. Multiple facilitators are needed for this activity. Each facilitator works with a participant one-on-one and completes a different activity (e.g., brainstorming new ways of solving a problem, viewing a prototype). After all the participants have gone through all of the activities, the group reconvenes to discuss experiences. Ideally, all participants will have completed all of the activities.

An excellent example of this methodology began with each of five focus groups photographing participants holding phone handsets to assess gripping styles (Dolan, Wiklund, Logan, & Augaitis, 1995). Participants then rank-ordered six conventionally-designed handsets and six progressively-designed handsets according to several ergonomic and emotional attributes (after having experience with each). Finally, participants critiqued the handset designs according to personal preference, and each built a clay model of his or her ideal handset. By giving participants exposure to a wide range of experiences with the potential product or domain area, participants do not need to "imagine" what a product would be like. They can discuss their actual experiences with the product or domain and determine whether or not the product would support their desired outcomes or goals. The activities can also spark new ideas for you to draw upon.

The same type of questions can be asked in task-based and nontask-based focus groups. The benefit of task-based focus groups is that follow-up discussions are richer when participants have the opportunity to actually use the product than when they must simply imagine it or remember when they used it last. With this technique, participants can reference the tasks they just completed to provide concrete examples, or the tasks may trigger previous experiences with the product.

The cost of doing such a study is that you must have several sets of your product available so that participants can work with them simultaneously. You will also need several facilitators to help, and the prep time to develop such a focus group will be longer than for traditional focus groups, since you need to create the materials for several activities. It can also be more expensive because more materials are needed. However, the added benefit of giving participants something to experience and work with is worth the cost and should be done whenever possible!

Day-in-the-Life

You can create a "day-in-the-life" video to demonstrate how someone would use your product and then discuss participants' impressions of what they have seen. Participants can get a better idea of what the product is really like without having to imagine it. This is perfect for situations where you cannot give participants direct exposure to the product or domain (e.g., because it would require significant training, there are safety issues, it would be financially infeasible).

It is important to show someone realistically using the product (warts and all!) since providing an idealized image will not result in valid user impressions. This allows users an opportunity to determine whether what they are seeing would address their desired outcomes. It takes additional time to create the video and may even require you to develop a prototype of the product to work with, if a real version does not exist. The benefit of getting all the participants on the same page and enabling them to share your vision is worth it!

Iterative Focus Groups

With iterative focus groups, you begin by presenting a prototype to participants and getting feedback from them. This can be specific design suggestions or just general impressions. Once the prototype is updated to reflect the feedback from users, the same participants are called back to participate in a second focus group. The new prototype is presented and additional feedback is collected. You could continue this iterative process as long as participants return, until you feel comfortable with the design, or until you run out of money.

The benefit is that you can see whether you are on the right track and understand the participants' requests. It also takes less time to recruit since you are not looking for new participants each time. On the other hand, this modification is useful only in cases where you have enough information to build a prototype and you have the time and resources to make regular changes and conduct additional focus groups. The downside is that it takes time and resources to make changes to a prototype and run additional sessions.

The Focus Troupe

The "focus troupe" is an interesting twist on the focus group (Sato & Salvador, 1999). Members of the UX or development group—or even the participants themselves—perform dramatic vignettes demonstrating the new product, feature, or concept in use (participants would follow a script). The play should demonstrate the implications, operations, and expectations of what the product would do. A discussion among the group is then initiated.

As with some of the modifications listed earlier, participants can gain experience with the product or domain and this will limit their need to "pretend." They can think of concrete examples of "using" the product while they provide their reactions, opinions, and alternative suggestions. The additional cost of using this modification is the time it takes to write the script(s) and—if you use colleagues in your troupe—the additional people involved. However, if you are unable to create a working prototype, this is the next best option.

Online or Phone-Based Focus Groups

Smaller focus groups (i.e., six or fewer participants) can be conducted via video chat, using VoIP or over the phone. This is more convenient for participants, and you can recruit people from outside your geographic region. You can also save money because participants will often participate for less, since they do not have to leave the comfort of their home or office. However, you need a video-conferencing system or phone system that allows multiple people to call and clearly hear everyone speak.

There are several disadvantages to this modification. **Social loafing** (i.e., the tendency for individuals to reduce the effort they make toward some task when working together with others) is potentially high because participants are not held accountable by their peer group or the moderator if they do not contribute. A participant can surf the web or text without others seeing it. Doing a "round-robin" can help because everyone knows they will be called on to contribute to the question, so they are less likely to slack off. It is also helpful to ask all participants to say their name before responding. It will be more obvious if, during an hour-long focus group, you never hear Ritee announce his name. In that case, you call on Ritee directly to reply.

Another problem is that the moderator cannot read the body language of the participants. There is no way to know whether a participant is silent out of disagreement or boredom or because he or she has nothing to add. Queue jumping by overbearing participants can also be a problem. It is hard to know who is speaking (even if you ask people to announce themselves before they speak) or if someone wants to speak but cannot get a word in edgewise!

Figure 9.1 in the "Interviews" chapter on page 224 can help you further determine whether it is better to conduct the session in person or over the phone. Overall, we recommend computer-mediated groups when you have geographically diverse users, when you do not need to demonstrate a product, when you are tight on resources, and when you have a high-quality phone conferencing system available.

Brainstorming/Wants and Needs Analysis

A possible component of focus groups is brainstorming. A wants and needs (W&N) analysis is an extremely quick, and relatively inexpensive, **brainstorming** method to gather data about user needs from multiple users simultaneously. Brainstorming with users is the key component of the W&N analysis, but the analysis has an added benefit compared to brainstorming alone because it incorporates a prioritization step that allows you to identify the most important wants and needs from the entire pool of ideas that were generated.

This method is ideal when you are trying to scope the features or information that will be included in the next (or first) release of the product. It enables you to find out what your users want and need in your product. Finally, by adding features based on the prioritized list, product teams can prevent **feature creep** (i.e., the tendency to add in more and more features over time).

Your goal is to gain an understanding of what the users want and need in the product. Rather than allowing the participants to brainstorm about anything they would like, it is more effective to ask the question so that it targets content, tasks, or characteristics of your product. Based on this assumption, the W&N question can be asked in three different forms:

- *Information.* You can ask a question that will tell you the information that users want and need to be found in, or provided by, the system. A typical content question might be: "What kind of information do you need from an ideal online travel app?" You might receive answers, such as hotels available in a given area, hotel prices, airline departure and arrival time, etc.
- *Task.* You can ask a question that will tell you about the types of activities or actions that users expect to be performed or supported by the system. A typical task-based question might be: "What tasks would you like to perform with an ideal hotel reservation system?" Some of the answers you receive might be as follows: book a hotel, compare accommodations between hotels, create a travel profile, etc.
- *Characteristic.* You can ask questions that will provide you with traits users want or need the system to have. For example, "What are the characteristics of an ideal system that lets you book travel online?" Some responses you might receive are "reliable," "fast," and "secure."

The question you ask should mention "the ideal system" because you do not want participants to be limited by what they think technology can do. You want participants to think about "blue sky."

However, one should be aware of the following:

- People do not always know what they *really* would like and are not good at estimating how much they will like a single option.

- There are always variables that people do not take into consideration.
- What people say they do and what they actually do may be different.

That is why the questions you ask users should not be for:

- Ill-defined problems (e.g., problems that are broad or unclear)
- Complex emotions (e.g., hatred)
- Things with which users have no experience

In the W&N analysis, you are asking users what they want or need, but the questions are well defined and about things users already have some amount of experience with.

It is critical to note that a W&N analysis is only the beginning, not the end. It should be used as a jumping-off point and not as your sole source of information.

Introduce the Activity and Brainstorming Rules

After a warm-up, we jump into a brief overview of the goal and procedure of the activity. We say something along these lines:

> **We are currently designing *<product description>* and we need to understand what *<information, tasks, or characteristics>* you want and need in this product. This will help us make sure that the product is designed to meet your wants and needs. This session will have two parts. In the first part, we will brainstorm *<information, tasks, or characteristics>* of an ideal system; and then in the second part of the activity, we will have you individually prioritize the items that you have brainstormed.**

After the brief overview, the rules the participants must follow during the brainstorming session are then presented. We always write these on a flip chart and have them visible during the entire session. If anyone breaks one of the rules, the moderator can point to the rule as a polite reminder.

The brainstorming rules are as follows:

1. This is an *ideal* system so all ideas are correct/useful. Do not edit yourself or others.
2. There is no designing, so do not try to build your system.
3. The moderator can ask about duplicates.
4. The notetaker writes down only what the moderator paraphrases.

Rule 1: Ideal System, No Wrong Answers

In the brainstorming phase, we want everyone thinking of an *ideal* system. Sometimes, users do not know what is possible. Encourage them to be creative and remind them that we are talking about the ideal. Because this is the ideal system, all ideas are correct. Something may be ideal for some users and not for others—and that is OK. Do not worry about unrealistic ideas, as they will be weeded out in the prioritization phase.

Rule 2: No Designing

Some users are steeped in the latest technology and will want to spend the entire session designing the perfect product. Users do not make good graphical or navigational designers, so do not ask them to design.

Rule 3: Moderator Checks for Duplicates

Another job of the moderator is to check for duplicates. Sometimes, users forget that someone made the exact same suggestion earlier. When you point it out to them, users will respond that they had forgotten about it or not seen it. However, there are times when the user *is not* asking for the exact same thing; it just sounds like it. This is where you must probe for more details and learn how these two suggestions are different from each other so that you can capture what the user is really asking for. It is important to mention this to the participants as a rule, so they do not think you are challenging their idea—you are simply trying to understand how it differs from another idea.

Rule 4: Notetaker Writes Down Only What the Moderator Paraphrases

This rule is important to set the participants' expectations. Participants may not understand why the notetaker is not writing down verbatim everything they are saying. It is not because the notetaker is rude and does not care what the participants are saying. It is because the moderator must understand what the participants really want with each suggestion. What the participant initially says may not be what he or she really wants. The notetaker needs to give the moderator time to drill down and get at what the participant is asking for before committing it to paper. Once participants understand this, they will understand that the notetaker is not being rude but is simply waiting for "the final answer."

Brainstorm

After about 40 minutes or so of brainstorming, you will notice that the number and quality of ideas tend to decrease. When you ask for additional suggestions, you will probably be met with blank stares. At this point, ask everyone to read through the list of ideas and make sure none are missing. If you are still met with silence, the generation phase is over. It is now time for the prioritization phase.

Prioritization

In the prioritization phase, users spend about 15 minutes picking the most desired items from the pool of brainstormed ideas. They are asked: "If you could have *only* five items from the brainstormed list, what items would you pick?" We ask for five choices because we have found that this will elicit the "cream of the crop." We also like asking for five because we often ask two W&N questions during a two-hour session. For example, during the first hour, we may ask about information desired in an ideal system, and in the second hour, we may ask about the tasks desired in that same ideal system. By asking for the top five at the end of each brainstorming portion of the session, it keeps the evening to two hours and it does not exhaust the participants. Choosing the top selections is quite an exhausting procedure for the participants, so the more choices you ask for, the more time and effort it takes.

Participants fill in their answers in a "Top five booklet." The booklet asks users to name the item they are choosing, describe it, and state why that item is so important to them (see Figure 12.4). We ask for this additional information to be sure that we are capturing what the users are *really* asking for. People may choose the same item from the brainstormed list but have completely different interpretations of these items. The descriptions and "why is it important" paragraph will help you detect these differences in the data analysis phase. A brief set of instructions is provided for users:

- Write only one item per page. If more than one answer is provided per sheet, the second answer will be discarded.
- Indicate the number of the item from the brainstorming flip chart.
- The five are not ranked and are of equal weight.
- No duplicates are allowed. If anyone votes for the same item more than once, the second vote will be discarded.
- Provide a description of the item.
- State why it is important to you.

Figure 12.4: Typical page of a wants and needs booklet.

Please identify the top five tasks you would like to do with an ideal hotel reservation system.

Idea #: ____

Idea name: ____________________

Describe it: ____________________

____

____

Why is it important to you? ____________________

____

____

Brainstorming Tips

The most effective brainstorm sessions follow some key recommendations. We have adopted a set of strategies that are used by many who conduct user research and market research studies (Kelly, 2001).

Hone the problem

This is the development and fine-tuning of your question. Work with the product team to develop a question that summarizes the problem and keeps your brainstorming focused.

Warm-up: Relax

As with other group activities, the warm-up is very important. This is particularly important when the group has not worked together before and most of the group does not have much brainstorming experience. Ideas for creativity exercises can be found in "Warm-Up Exercises" section on page 165 in Chapter 7.

The sky is the limit

You want to encourage creativity during your session. You want people to think "blue sky"—anything they want! Do not worry; the prioritization step of this technique will ensure that ideas such as "booking your airline travel ticket through osmosis" will not end up in your software requirements document.

Capture and number the ideas

As ideas are being captured on paper, it is useful to number them. This will make it easier for people to refer to points already on the list. It is also extremely helpful in the second stage when the participants are prioritizing their choices. It will also give you a sense of how many ideas you have generated during the session. As an approximation, you can use the rate of 100 ideas per hour as a brainstorming rate guideline.

Keep up the momentum

This is referred to as "build and jump." You need to be able to keep the brainstorming alive. One way to do this as a moderator is to help participants "build" on ideas. You can do this by probing further when you think there is more to be uncovered. For example, if we are brainstorming about features in an ideal airline travel site, someone might say that they want to be able to search by price. Well, there are lots of other things people might want to search on, so you should try to build on this idea and ask: "Is there anything else you think you might want to search on?"

Conversely, you also want to be able to "jump." If people are continuing to focus on a certain issue and are getting buried in the minutia, you will want to jump to another topic. Let us say people are getting bogged down in every kind of search criterion they want. This would be a good opportunity to say: "OK, I think we understand that it is important for you to be able to search, but let us now think about what features would help you make your decision of which flight(s) to buy." It can be hard to think of nonbiasing questions on the spot. It is best to speak with the team and come up with a list of areas the team would like more information about. Once you have that list, you can write "jump" questions that are nonbiasing and then refer to them as needed during the session.

The Doomed Brainstorm

Just as there are ways to have an effective brainstorming session, there are also ways to have an ineffective session. Here are some of the things that you do not want to do when acting as moderator (Kelly, 2001).

Do not be too serious

Yes, your report at the end of the day should be serious, but the brainstorming should not adopt this mood. You need to let people be creative. You want them to think about the ideal. Do not suffocate their creativity by telling them that ideas are silly or impossible. With the silly will come the serious. Let people have fun. All ideas are good ideas and all should be treated equally! Ideas that are a little far-fetched at the moment might be within the realm of possibility in the future.

Do not document every detail

Documenting every detail will not get you very far. It will interrupt the natural quick-paced flow of the session. You need to learn to summarize the points of interest and move on. The participants should not be required to take any notes: that is the job of the notetaker. The participants should focus on the generation of great ideas, not the documentation of them.

Do not limit your session to the elite

Experts can make great contributions, but do not always limit your participants to groups of experts. People who are new to a particular field or who do not have experience, but are interested, make great participants for a brainstorming session. Sometimes, the expert is the first person that comes to mind to recruit, but you should keep the average user in mind, too. Make sure you identify who will be using your product at the end of the day. Is the person who travels weekly going to be the predominant user of your travel app, or will it be the "average Joe" who travels once or twice a year? If you think that both the expert and novice will use your product, then you should consider including users with a range of experience in your sessions or conduct multiple sessions with different experience criteria.

Avoid too much structure

Yes, you want to encourage everyone to get involved, but do not make the discussion overly structured. For example, going around the room giving each person time to speak (e.g., round-robin) is going to kill the brainstorming. This approach may work initially if you want to get everyone warmed up (or in other activities, such as focus groups), but in a true brainstorming session, ideas are generated spontaneously. Jim says one thing and it makes Sarah think of something related (**synergy**). If you make Sarah wait until "her turn," she might be side-tracked by the next person's idea and/or the idea may be lost (**production blocking**). Encourage people who are quiet to speak and those who are speaking too much to settle down—but do not force it. The only exception to the round-robin is if your brainstorming has been done individually on paper (see "Modifications" section, page 353).

Tame the dominator

An overbearing person who insists on doing all of the talking and/or loves to interrupt others will surely ruin your session. You will need to get this person in check quickly (see Section "Moderating Your Activity" section on page 165 in Chapter 7 for tips on how to deal with this and other difficult moderating situations).

Data Analysis and Interpretation

Data analysis and interpretation of focus group data are similar to methods for other types of interview data. Therefore, refer to "Data Analysis and Interpretation" section on page 252 in Chapter 9 for additional information on how to analyze data.

Debrief

Ideally immediately following, but certainly within 24 hours of the focus group session, we recommend getting together with your notetaker (and any other team members who may have attended) to have a debriefing session. Review the questions asked and note the key points from the session. Were there any unexpected findings? What did each observer identify as the key takeaway from the session? Are there any trends that can be identified at this point? Fill in areas of the notes that may not be clear while everything is still fresh in your mind. You should also decide whether another session is necessary with the same user type. If so, determine if you would like to change the questions based on what you learned in the previous session.

Types of Focus Group Data

Focus group data consist primarily of notes from the session, audio recordings, and video recordings. Specifically, you may draw upon the following as you analyze the results:

- Notes taken by the notetaker
- Notes taken by observers (they can have different insights on the participants' comments)
- Notes taken during the debriefing session(s)
- Audio/videotapes of the sessions
- Transcripts of the sessions (if available)
- Notes participants may have made during the sessions

Affinity Diagram

A Japanese anthropologist, Jiro Kawakita, developed a method of synthesizing large amounts of data into manageable chunks based on themes that emerge from the data itself. It is known as the "K-J method," following the Japanese custom of placing the family name first. It has become one of the most widely used of the Japanese management and planning tools.

In the west, a very similar method known as "affinity diagramming" was developed based on the K-J method. An **affinity diagram** is a relatively quick and useful method for analyzing qualitative data, including open-ended participant responses from a focus group, as well as a diary study, interview study, or field study. It can also be used to group characteristics when building personas (Chapter 2, page 24) or to analyze findings from a usability test.

Figure 12.5: Large affinity diagram exercise in action

To create an affinity diagram, a researcher takes the data from each participant, pulls out key points (e.g., participant comments, observations, questions, design ideas) and writes each one individually on an index card or sticky note. The cards are then shuffled to avoid any preexisting order and each card/sticky note is placed on a wall or whiteboard. Similar findings or concepts are physically grouped together (on the wall or whiteboard), thus providing visual cues that allow the researcher(s) to identify themes or trends in the data. Figure 12.5 shows an large affinity diagraming process.

It is important to enter the analysis with an open mind and not preconceived categories within which that the data must fit. The structure and relationship will *emerge* from the data. Once the groups have emerged, you should label each group. What do these comments have in common? Why do they belong together?

When Should You Use an Affinity Diagram?

There are many situations when an affinity diagram is an appropriate and useful analysis method:

- An affinity diagram is an excellent method for sharing the results of your study with **stakeholders** as the study progresses. They can look at the physical diagram to see evolving trends, as well as individual pieces of data. It also allows for quick data analysis once the study is complete (see step 7).
- It can add structure to a large or complicated issue. You are able to break down a complicated issue into broader categories or more specific, focused categories.
- It helps you to identify issues that affect multiple areas because those same issues belong in multiple groups. It can also help you identify areas where you are missing information and the scope of issues that need to be addressed.

- When using an affinity diagram, you can see that the design/product ideas are based on direct user data. If you recommend solution A, you can point to a group of data points (each with an associated participant ID) that informed your recommendation.
- Because individual issues, requests, or problems are grouped into higher-level themes, the team can respond on a broad scale rather than trying to address each one individually. This leads to a holistic rather than piecemeal solution.
- It can help with innovation because you are not working from preconceived categories. New ideas emerge from the data.
- By working as a team with the raw data, you can gain agreement on an issue. It can also help unify a team because the product development team can take part in the analysis, alongside the person who led the study.

Things to Consider When Using an Affinity Diagram

Using an affinity diagram requires one to enter with an open mind and be creative. Some people are uncomfortable with using the gut feeling and feel more comfortable adding in structure. This often results in an attempt to create categories *a priori* (i.e., before the sorting). That defeats the purpose of using an affinity diagram. Make sure your team members understand the purpose of affinity diagram and the benefits to its approach before the analysis begins.

Creating an Affinity Diagram

Below are the steps to create your own affinity diagram. If you have never used an affinity diagram before, the process may be slow at first. With each analysis session, the team will get faster.

Step 1: Find a space

You can create an affinity diagram on any wall or whiteboard in your office, a lab, or a conference room. Obviously, the amount of space needed depends on the amount of data you collected. Since you will likely work on it for the duration of your study, be sure the diagram is in a secure location where colleagues or cleaning staff will not undo your hard work.

Step 2: Assemble your team

Following each user research session, bring together the members of the team that took part in the session (e.g., moderator, notetaker, videographer). We strongly recommend updating your diagram after each session while the data are fresh in your mind; however, if this is not possible, then complete the diagram as soon as you have finished running all sessions for your activity.

As with the K-J method, affinity diagramming works best as a team approach. Your notetaker, videographer, and/or fellow field study investigator(s) should take part in this exercise. If a product team member was a part of the session, be sure to get him or her involved as well. Not only will that speed data analysis, but also the additional point of view is helpful. This is information that should be discussed and examined from multiple angles and used to pose hypotheses. Creativity should be encouraged, and there should be no criticism of people's ideas or hypotheses.

Ground Rules for Creating an Affinity Diagram

1. Everyone is equal—there is no leader.
2. There will be no criticism of ideas—all ideas have merit.
3. There are no preconceived categories—they will emerge from the data.
4. Small groups can be merged and large groups can be broken apart, as appropriate.
5. Cards can be duplicated to live in multiple groups, if necessary.
6. Cards or groups of cards can be moved, if necessary. Cards are not locked in one place.

TIP

Write the ground rules for creating an affinity diagram on the board. Make sure everyone understands them and agrees to them. If anyone breaks them, you can simply point the offender back to the rules. This will save a good deal of bickering.

Step 3: Create the cards

As a team, write key points of information from the data on index cards or sticky notes. Participant quotes, observations, hypothesis, questions, design ideas, pain points, etc., can all be included. You may choose to color-code your data by using different-colored cards or notes for each participant or for each type of data (e.g., quotes are green, hypotheses are blue, questions are pink). Depending on the length of your user research session and/or number of participants, you can generate 50-100 cards or more. You may want to indicate other things on the cards like the participant number, task, or site (in the case of a field study) associated with that data point.

Step 4: Sort the cards

Once all the cards are created for a session, the cards should be shuffled and divided among the members of the team. As each card is posted to the wall, the team member should say what is on the card out loud. When grouping similar cards, you do not have to state *why* you think those cards belong together. This can be a gut feeling. Do not try to label your categories early on. If you find an identical (or very similar) issue, problem, request, or quote, stack those cards on top of each other. You will be able to tell at a glance that the thicker stacks indicate recurring issues. You can also duplicate cards if you feel the item belongs in more than one group. To indicate that one issue or data point lives in multiple groups (and therefore affects multiple areas), you may want to create that duplicate issue on a different-colored index card or sticky note. This will help the duplicated issues stand out.

Step 5: Label the groups

After about three research sessions (e.g., interviews, focus groups, field study visits), you will see the categories emerging. At this point, you can begin to label each group with a tentative title or description.

Step 6: Regroup

As the sorting proceeds with data from more sessions, look for duplicate groups. If you have a lot of data, sometimes duplicate groups are created; combine these. Also, look for smaller groups. Do they belong with larger groups? They may not, but it is useful as you progress to look for higher-level groups emerging. Conversely, larger groups may need to be broken down into more meaningful subgroups.

Step 7: Walk through the diagram

After all research sessions are complete, the team should verbally walk through the diagram together. You may want to audio record this discussion or have a notetaker take notes, because the discussion will be useful when writing up the results of your study. The team should try once again to identify high-level groups and break larger groups into more meaningful subgroups. They should also make sure they are in agreement with descriptions for each group. Members are free to add cards with clarifying information, new insights, design ideas, and questions for further investigation.

TIP

Placing a time limit on the sorting phase (e.g., one hour) can prevent team members from overanalyzing every placement. You *can* move cards or groups of cards later on. Place the card either by itself, near another card, or with a card quickly and move on to the next card.

TIP

Take a digital picture of the final affinity diagram. It can demonstrate to stakeholders the wealth of data you collected and how it all came together. Include this in your report to better describe how you analyzed your data. Many product developers and executives will be unfamiliar with affinity diagramming and a picture of the final result can better convey what it is. Even though they will be unable to read all the details, it will help to give them a sense of what you did.

Figure 12.6 shows an affinity diagram for a series of TravelMyWay focus groups conducted during a hypothetical mobile app field study. The intention of this figure is to give you a visual sense of what an affinity diagram might look like. As a result, we have not focused on the details of what could be written on each sticky note. The squares represent sticky notes with participant responses. Each participant is a different color. When the same participant made similar comments, the sticky notes were stacked on top of each other yielding rectangles, rather than squares. You will notice that some sticky notes cross the lines between categories. This means that the comment fell into more than one category and demonstrates related issues. The actual affinity

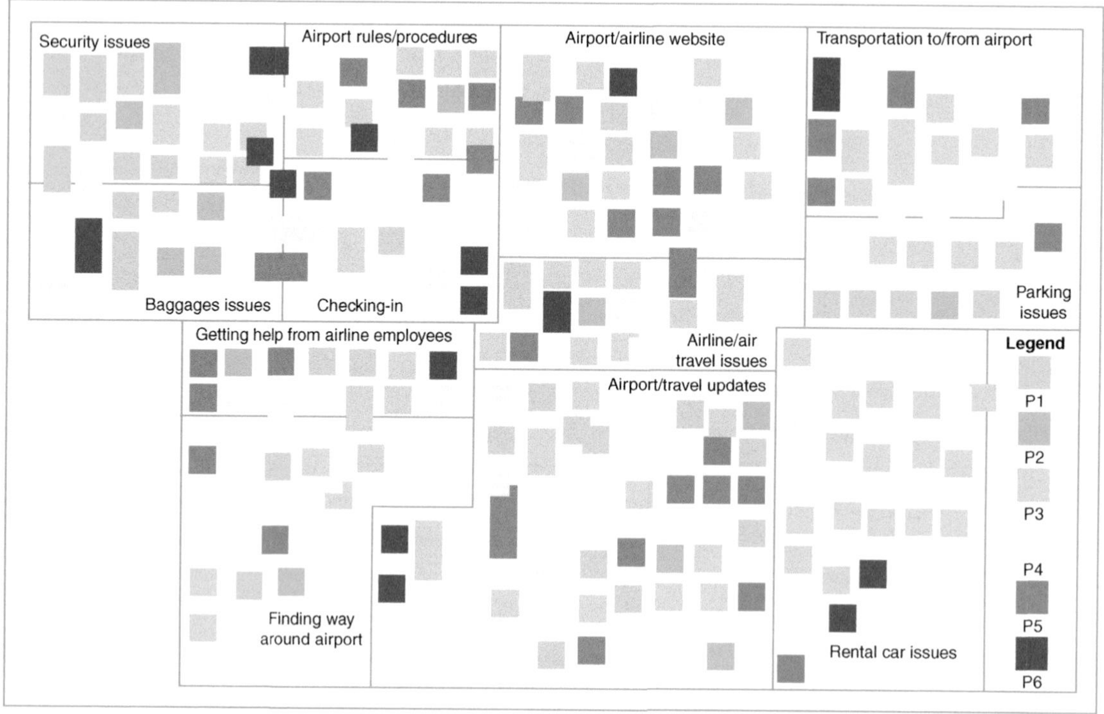

Figure 12.6: Fictional affinity diagram for TravelMyWay app focus group.

diagram can be recreated in any drawing application so that the high-level groupings can be visually displayed in a report. More detail can be added than is shown here so that a poster can be created to display the results for all to see.

Communicating the Findings

Depending on the complexity of the data you collected, you can create a simple bullet list of information you learned during the focus group, a table comparing the answers between two or more user types, or a summary paragraph for each of the questions you asked users. Figure 12.7 is an example of a portion of a report.

Lessons Learned

Below are three lessons we have learned with regard to user composition, moderating, and notetaking for focus groups.

We advised earlier not to mix user types of different levels in a hierarchy. The first lesson learned demonstrates why. Also, as we indicated earlier, it is important for a moderator to have good domain knowledge to follow up on user comments, but it is also important for the notetaker. The moderator also needs to know how to handle difficult users, even to the point of removing a user to save the session.

Question asked:

What would entice you to share a hotel room?

When the concept was initially introduced, participants expressed reluctance at the idea of sharing a hotel room with a stranger. Once participants began discussing possible merits of room sharing, the attitude of each group became more positive. Money was the most obvious benefit, regardless of user type. In addition, all participants wanted to ensure that a reputable agency was responsible for matching the guests. They would feel more comfortable that "dangerous" or "questionable" guests would be screened out, as well as ensuring that people with similar interests and habits (e.g., smoking versus non-smoking) would be matched.

In general, women expressed positive benefits that were more social in nature. This includes having someone to do things with, such as going to dinner, sightseeing, and sharing common experiences. Female participants stated one of the outcomes of travel was to see and learn about a new city, but they were rarely satisfied they met their goal because they do not like sightseeing alone. They also mentioned increased safety as a positive benefit. Most female participants said they would be more likely to explore new cities and go out in the evening if they had someone to go with. Finally, the majority of female participants made it clear that they would be interested in sharing a room only with other females.

Adult male budget travelers, on the other hand, discussed the networking benefits of sharing a room, particularly if they were on travel for related business (e.g., a common conference). Male college students stated having someone to hang out with would be "cool," but the social aspect was not of primary importance. None of the male participants mentioned increased safety as a possible benefit (or outcome) from sharing a room. Male participants also did not mention the gender of the guest as a concern. This does not mean that the gender of the guest will not matter to male customers; it simply means that gender was not one of the primary concerns for them when deciding whether or not to share a room.

Overall, participants in college (male and female) were much more enthusiastic about the concept of room sharing than people who were not in college because, for them, the outcome of sharing a room is to save money—and that is their primary concern.

Figure 12.7: Portion of a report summarizing the results of one question across multiple sessions and user types.

Mixing User Types

A series of focus groups were conducted to learn about the use of "patient problem lists" (PPL) by nurses and physicians. The goal of a PPL is to bring a provider up to speed regarding a patient's healthcare or medical history without having to review the patient's entire chart. Both doctors and nurses use it, so the development team wanted to combine the two user types in the same session to reduce the number of sessions needed and to hear a discussion of their different perspectives. Because the type of work they do is different, and because the relationship between doctors and nurses can be antagonistic, we insisted on separating the two user types.

During one of the sessions with the physicians, the participants began insulting nurses over the way they maintain their paperwork and the notes they take. A development team member who happened to be a registered nurse was watching from another room and nearly leapt through the one-way mirror when she heard the physicians' comments! Although both user types would have likely been on their best behavior if combined, we would not have gotten their *honest* opinions. The physicians' comments may have seemed mean-spirited at the time of the session, but the point was clear that the notes the nurses take (and find valuable in *their* job) clearly do not meet the needs of the physicians. Everyone on the product development team realized that it was far safer and more enlightening to keep those user types separated in future user research activities, even if it meant running additional sessions.

Removing the Difficult Participant

During the same healthcare focus group discussed in the first lesson learned, we covered an amazing ten questions in each session. Each question was presented and then we completed a "round-robin" so that each participant had adequate time to contribute. After everyone had a chance to speak, people were free to add additional thoughts. This worked extremely well for nurses. Once we reviewed the ground rules for participation, we never had to refer to them again.

The physician sessions were more difficult to moderate. The participants did not stick to the "round-robin" format, interrupted each other frequently, disagreed with each other, and by the end of the session were speaking quite loudly in order to be easily heard over the others. The ground rules had to be referred to regularly. One outspoken physician in particular insulted the comments and ideas provided by another soft-spoken physician. Despite continued instructions of "everyone is right" and "do not critique the thoughts of others," the domineering physician only got worse, and the soft-spoken physician stopped speaking altogether. The negative vibe rubbed off on the other participants and they all began criticizing each other's ideas.

We realized that even with a great deal of experience moderating groups, it is easy to lose control of a session. Once you let one negative or overbearing participant take control of a group, the rest of the group will either behave similarly (e.g., insulting each other) or bow out of participating all together. Sometimes, humor and polite reminders will not work. It takes a strong hand to get a session back on track. In this case, it meant taking the participant to the side and asking him either to quit criticizing others or to leave altogether. This is uncomfortable to do; but for the well-being of your participants and for the sake of good data collection, it is critical that you intervene as soon as you realize the session is headed for a downward spiral.

For more tips and information on moderating activities, see "Moderating Your Activity" section on page 165 in Chapter 7.

Suggested Resources for Additional Reading

For the beginning focus group researcher, we recommend the following book that covers everything from planning and conducting focus groups to analyzing the data:

- Krueger, R., & Casey, M. A. (2008). *Focus groups: A practical guide for applied research* (4th ed.). London: Sage Publications.

The next book is filled with multiple, short case studies. Each chapter addresses how you can use focus groups to address specific needs (e.g., market research, participatory design, scenario-based discussions):

- Langford, J., & McDonagh, D. (Eds.), (2003). *Focus groups: Supporting effective product development.* London: Taylor & Francis.

Two websites are also very useful in finding information about focus groups:

- www.groupsplus.com/pages/articles.htm. This site also includes an overview of the focus group process, organized as a calendar of events.
- http://www.stcsig.org/usability/topics/focusgroups.html.

Pulling It All Together

In this chapter, we have discussed what a focus group is, when you should conduct one, and things to be aware of. We also discussed how to prepare for and conduct a focus group, along with several modifications. In the following case study, Peter McNally discusses the use of focus groups for better user experience in the financial services industry.

CASE STUDY: *DESIGN CONCEPTS FOCUS GROUPS*

Peter McNally, User Experience Center, Bentley University

Overview

This case study highlights a series of three focus groups conducted to collect feedback on several online design concepts for a US financial services firm. The initial planning will be discussed, including participant recruiting, logistics, and discussion guide development. The structure and facilitation of the focus groups will be discussed in detail, including techniques to break the ice and get everyone to participate and ways we brought user experience techniques into a traditional marketing methodology.

Background

The financial services client approached the User Experience Center at Bentley University in 2013, seeking feedback on several design concepts related to retirement planning. Initially, we considered usability testing methods. We initially thought the client would be further along in the design process and be able to provide wireframes for their design concepts. When it became clear the client had mostly one graphic or high-level mock per design concept and their primary research goal was to determine if customers would be receptive to the concept, we recommended using the focus group method. Furthermore, since the client was looking for opinions on the usefulness of the concepts and not on the usability of the interaction, an individual feedback session, such as usability testing, would not be appropriate or cost-effective because it would take over a week to listen to the same number of participants. The project duration from kickoff meeting to final report presentation took about four weeks.

Initial Planning

We started with a kickoff meeting with the client project manager, the creative director, user experience designer, and several others from the client's design agency to define the goals, the schedule, and the general approach for recruiting and concepts to be evaluated. The first step was participant recruiting.

Participant Recruiting

The client wanted to get feedback on five concepts across three different user groups: financial planners, consumers nearing retirement, and consumers early in their careers.

The same design concepts would be shown to all three groups. Ideally, it is best to hold at least two focus group sessions per user group in order to limit any bias from one session. However, in this case, since all three user groups would see the same design concepts and to complete the project within the client's budget and schedule, we felt limiting the scope to one focus group session per user group would still provide valuable insights.

The recruiting process was similar to what we use for usability testing. We developed a screener for each focus group and hired a recruiting firm to recruit the participants. We recruited 10 participants for each focus group for two reasons: first, any more than this number makes it hard to facilitate the discussion, and second, if one or two participants canceled, we felt we could still have a good discussion with eight or nine participants.

Discussion Guide Development

With participant recruiting under way, we had several meetings with the client over two weeks to develop the discussion guide. The critical part of developing the discussion guide was to understand what the client wanted to get feedback on. We were given the design concepts from the client and their design agency. Word format was used initially to rough out the focus group flow. Eventually, the discussion guide was converted into three separate PowerPoint documents to facilitate presentation.

Housekeeping

During the first portion of the focus group, we introduced the moderator/participants, set ground rules and expectations, and obtained informed consent. Next, we did introductions. As part of the introduction process, I asked participants to tell me about a website or mobile app they currently use that is really good, fun, or entertaining. The site or app could be anything and did not have to be related to retirement planning. Responses varied from Twitter, to Instagram, to Words with Friends. The good thing about an icebreaker like this is that participants can piggyback on other comments, and before you know it, the group is sharing their experiences with you. Next, we explained how the focus group would be structured. Lastly, we spelled out specific ground rules to help the session run smoothly:

- I'll ask lots of questions!
- There are no right or wrong answers.
- Honesty is appreciated.
- Would like to hear from everyone.
- I may cut you off politely for the sake of time!
- All ideas are good. But we expect varied opinions. Feel free to agree and disagree with one another.
- Provide constructive feedback.

Incorporating UX into the Focus Group

We showed several design concepts, spending about 15 minutes per concept. Each design concept consisted of one slide providing a high-level overview with a bulleted list of features and one or more slides with a high-level design or graphic giving a visual representation. However, rather than jumping straight into the features of the design concept, we provided a scenario setting the use case or problem. Providing a scenario gave the participants context and focused them on a goal or problem to be solved with the concept. For example, for a retirement savings calculator, we used the following scenario:

> **You need to save more for retirement, but you have a lot of other competing priorities, such as rent or the mortgage, car payments, and other expenses. You hear everyone saying you need to save more for retirement, but what is a realistic number for you?**

When participants saw the design concepts, they referred back to the scenario during the discussion. In addition, for design concepts that showed any kind of user interface, we had the participants conduct a usability test either individually or as a group. For example, one design concept had two screens, the first displayed a main menu and the second screen displayed the expanded menu. While showing the first screen, we asked a participant to describe what he or she would expect to see under each main menu item. We also let other participants describe their expectations. For the retirement savings calculator, we asked what kind of specific information they would expect to have to input. We then discussed the inputs and got their reaction and what did or did not meet expectations. While this approach will not offer the same level of detail as a usability test, it can provide early insights into any major gaps before they become part of the design. By incorporating some scenario-based activities, it helped participants walk through the concepts and made it more (or less) real. This also helped the client realize the importance of user research as he or she moved into the design process.

Logistics

Over the course of three days, we held three 90-minute focus groups. We scheduled our focus groups in the evening to maximize participation. One hundred dollars and a light dinner was provided for focus group participants. In order to give participants enough time to arrive, eat, and get settled before the session started, we asked participants to arrive 20-30 minutes early. Even though the actual time for the focus group was 90 minutes, we set expectations that the session would take two hours.

We used our three-room suite lab, which we use for both usability testing and focus groups. For these focus groups, the participants sat around a table and the moderator stood at one end. We also had one notetaker present in the participant room to assist the moderator. See Figure 12.8 for an example of participants in the UXC participant room.

The design concepts and other material were presented on an overhead projector. We also provided printouts of the material so participants could have an alternative way to follow along.

Analysis and Report

After running the focus group sessions, we took several days to review our notes and analyze the data. In our analysis, we were looking for trends and patterns within each design concept, across each focus group (user group) and global findings across all design concepts and focus groups. We produced a report in PowerPoint format. As a quick snapshot of the focus groups, we presented a table summarizing the overall impression for each design concept across each user group giving the client a glance at how the sessions went (Table 12.3).

Design concept 4 fared the worst. We made the recommendation that the concept should be reexamined. The rest of the report went into more detail about each design concept. We dedicated one slide per design concept, describing the overall impression by focus (user) group (e.g., main reasons they would or would not find it

Figure 12.8: Focus group setup at the User Experience Center, Bentley University.

Table 12.3: Design concept snapshot

Concept	Consumers near retirement	Consumers in early career	Financial planners
(1) Design concept 1	Positive	Positive	Positive
(2) Design concept 2	Very positive	Very positive	Very positive
(3) Design concept 3	Fair	Positive	Fair
(4) Design concept 4	Poor	Fair	Poor
(5) Design concept 5	Positive	Positive	Poor

useful) with supporting user quotes. For example, for one design concept, participants were positive, but wanted the ability to chat with an advisor. We also made several recommendations to improve the design concept based on all the participant feedback. Finally, we ended the report with key takeaways and recommendations. We also provided overall recommendations when designing for each user group, regardless of design concept.

Key Takeaways When Running Focus Groups

For UX professionals that mostly use one-on-one research methods, such as usability testing and interviews, focus groups can seem a bit daunting; however, once you get the participants engaged and talking, you will find it a good technique for early research/brainstorming. I recommend using focus groups during the following instances:

- Validating a concept before the design phase. You may learn that the concept needs to be tweaked or moved in a different direction.
- Brainstorming with users in order to develop new ideas/concepts. Sometimes, you need to talk to users/customers/prospects to just understand the "what if."

Of course, if you have an interactive prototype, I would recommend individual usability testing.

Recruiting and Logistics

- Make sure the facility is accessible and inquire if any participants need any accommodations for accessibility.
- If you use an outside recruiter, make sure you know whether the client/sponsor of the focus group should be hidden from participants (e.g., if confidentiality is required).
- Inquire about any dietary restrictions for the snack/meal. Avoid loud snack options such as potato chips, as this may be distracting during the focus group.

Facilitation

- Run at least one pilot session with a small number of friendly colleagues to run through timing. Practice any interactive techniques. We ran a pilot for this focus group, and it helped us refine our techniques and timing and increased our confidence before the first focus group.
  - Test out all recording equipment during the pilot.

- Pay attention to focus group best practices, especially in encouraging everyone to participate and not letting one participant dominate the discussion.
  - Set the ground rules early—make sure everyone sets his or her mobile phone to vibrate.
  - Use tent cards, so you can call on people by first name.
  - If the focus group is more than an hour, provide a 5-minute break to use the restroom, etc.
- Incorporate interactive activities where appropriate. This can also serve as a good way to break up the focus group or mix things up. Some examples include the following:
  - Collaborative usability testing or cognitive walk-through is a great way to incorporate task-based usability techniques into a traditional marketing methodology.
  - A small group card-sorting activity with two or three participants is another great activity where participants have to group items/concepts into buckets and name them. This can provide some early research into the appropriate information architecture. After each small group is finished, have one person summarize his or her work. This can lead to some great large-group discussions. We did not do this activity during these focus groups, but when appropriate, it can be valuable.

Analysis and Reporting

- Provide an executive summary, so the client gets a quick overview of the results.
- Structure the report around the client/customer/business sponsor's goals.
- Include user quotes to back up key findings and/or recommendations.

General

Know when to use focus groups. As discussed, task-based techniques such as collaborative usability testing can be used to augment a focus group, but the main purpose is gathering user opinion. Some clients or customers think focus group and usability testing serve the same purpose, but they do not. If you need to understand if users can successfully interact with a prototype or system, usability testing is probably a better fit.

CHAPTER 13

Field Studies

Introduction

Field studies refer to a broad range of data-gathering techniques conducted at the user's location, including observation, apprenticeship, and interviewing. Collecting data in the field (i.e., in your user's environment) is also sometimes referred to as a "site visit." However, "site visit" is a broad term and can include other interactions with customers while not necessarily collecting data (e.g., conducting a sales demo). Other names for visits to collect data about users in their environment are "ethnographic study," "contextual inquiry," and "field research."

A field study can be composed of one, a few, or several visits to the user's environment and can be conducted in any environment in which a user lives, works, commutes, vacations, plays, visits, exercises, eats, hangs out, etc. Often, field studies are conducted in people's homes or offices, but the right place for a field study is the place where a technology will eventually be used. For example, researchers observed users in a vineyard to develop a ubiquitous computing system for agricultural environments (Brooke & Burrell, 2003). Sounds like fun!

Depending on the goals, resources, and specific methods of the study, a field study can last on the order of minutes, hours, days, or weeks. The biggest advantage of a field study is that you get to observe users completing tasks in their environment. You can directly observe their task flows, their inefficiencies and challenges, and their delights. This information can then be used to help you discover terminology, understand unmet user needs, and see how your product can fit into the context of users' lives.

You will notice that this chapter is designed a little differently from the other method-related chapters. In the previous chapters, we presented one primary way to conduct a specific method and then a few modifications. There is no one best way to conduct a field study—it depends on the goals of your study and your access to users. Consequently, we will provide you with several variations from which to choose. In this chapter, we discuss different types of field studies available to enable you to go into your user's environment to collect data, how to select the best method to answer your questions, special considerations, how to analyze the data you collect, and how to present the results to **stakeholders.** Finally, a case study demonstrates the value of a field study "in the wild."

At a Glance

- > Things to be aware of when conducting field research
- > Field study methods to choose from
- > Preparing for a field study
- > Conducting a field study
- > Data analysis and interpretation
- > Communicating the findings

Things to Be Aware of When Conducting Field Research

There are several challenges you may face when proposing a field study. There are also challenges you could face while conducting the study. Below are some specific issues to be aware of when deciding to conduct a field study.

Gaining Stakeholder Support

It can be difficult to convince people with limited time and budgets to support field studies. Products must be developed on tight budgets and deadlines. It can be easier to convince product teams or management to support an interview or usability test because the materials needed are few and the time frame for delivering results is short. It can be much more difficult to get that same support for longer-term, off-site studies with existing customers or potential end users.

However, for understanding users' context, no short-term, lab-based study can compare to observing users in their own environment. Write a detailed proposal to demonstrate the information you plan to collect and when. Also, include estimated cost and immediate and long-term benefits. You may also want to show documented cases where products went wrong and could have been saved by conducting a field study. Better understanding of your users can also provide a competitive edge. When time is the biggest issue, you can point out that schedules slip and field studies are beneficial over time, not just in the short term. Even if you cannot get information in time to influence an upcoming release of a product, there will be future releases where your data can be used. You want your information to make an impact as soon as possible, but do not let schedules prevent you from collecting data altogether. Finally, you will likely need to educate stakeholders on the empirical nature of user research, how the information you collect on-site with users differs from lab-based data, and how the data you collect in field studies can provide a competitive edge.

Other Things to Keep in Mind

Once you have convinced stakeholders that a field study is a good idea, there are a few other things to keep in mind when designing and conducting field studies.

Types of Bias

There are two types of bias, in particular, to be aware of when conducting field studies. The first is introduced by the investigator/moderator and the second by the participant.

If the investigator is a novice to the domain, he or she may have a tendency to conceptually simplify the expert users' problem-solving strategies while observing them. This is not done intentionally, of course, but the investigator does not have the complex mental model of the expert, so a **simplification bias** results. For example, if an investigator is studying database administrators and does not understand databases, he or she may think of a database as nothing more than a big spreadsheet and misinterpret (i.e., simplify) what the database administrator is explaining or demonstrating. It is important for you to be aware of this bias. One way to minimize this bias is by talking with a subject matter expert before you begin your study. He or she can help you understand the topic before you speak with users. Another way to minimize this bias is to ask users or a subject matter expert to review your notes/observations. He or she can identify areas where you have oversimplified or incorrectly captured information.

The other type of bias is called a **translation bias.** Expert users will attempt to translate their knowledge so that the investigator can understand it. The more the expert translates, the more potential there is for them to distort their knowledge, skills, etc. One way to avoid this is to ask the expert user to train you or speak to you as if you had just started a job working for them. If you are missing the background knowledge necessary to understand everything the user is saying, you may either ask probing questions or bring a **subject matter expert** (SME) with you to "translate." However, it is to your advantage to learn as much as you can prior to your visit so that you have some background knowledge and vocabulary of what you are observing. You should be enthusiastic about learning the domain and become well-versed yourself, but with a "usability hat" on, so you can identify opportunities for improvement. This is different from coming in with preconceived notions. You should have a good base of knowledge but try not to think about solutions yet.

The Effect of Being Observed

Participants behave differently when observed; this is known as the **Hawthorne effect** (Landsberger, 1958). They will likely be on their best behavior (e.g., observing standard operating procedures rather than using their usual shortcuts). It can take some time for users to feel comfortable with you and reveal their "true behavior." Users cannot keep up a façade for long, so you can expect aspects of the Hawthorne effect to diminish over time; the longer you spend observing participants and the better rapport you are able to establish with them, the lesser this effect will be.

Logistics Can Be More Challenging

Field studies can be very simple when you are conducting pure observation. All you need is a pen and paper. Depending on the location (e.g., in a public place), you may not even need anyone's permission to observe.

However, most field studies done for product development are more complex because you are not only observing but also interacting with people (e.g., recruiter, salesperson, site contact, other observers, participants, legal departments, etc.) and because more things can potentially go wrong on-site (e.g., broken equipment, missing forms, late arrival, dead batteries). For these reasons, field studies are much more challenging (but also more rewarding!) to conduct than most other techniques described in this book. Even though your equipment may fail in the lab, you are in a better position to replace/repair it than when you are traveling to an unfamiliar location. You cannot possibly take duplicates of every piece of equipment. In addition, directions to your site may be poor and driving in unfamiliar areas can be stressful. Being detail-oriented, creating a well-thought-out plan in advance, and piloting everything can help you avoid many problems, but there will always be some surprises along the way.

Field Study Methods

While field studies are conducted in many different disciplines ranging from biology to economics, the field study methods most widely used in user research communities come to us from anthropology and are sometimes called "ethnographic studies." However, even within the user research community, there is debate about what constitutes "ethnography" versus a "field study." For an introduction to the debate, see the "Field Study Versus Ethnography" callout. Generally, classic ethnographic practice requires one to enter a situation with an open mind, a nonegocentric perspective, no preconceived notions or biases, and no focus on solutions. You begin by observing the user, the tasks, and the environment before you ever formulate your first question or study goal.

Field Study Versus Ethnography

If you participate in the user experience research community, you have likely heard colleagues in a heated debate question whether a study being reported as ethnography actually fits the bill or not. What is ethnography? Can only people with a PhD in anthropology be ethnographers? If you typically use a quantitative approach to research, are you barred from the ethnography club? When is a study a field study versus an ethnography?

Dumas and Salzman (2006) defined ethnography as a form of field study and describe the key difference as what/who drives the goal of the study. In field studies, the product team drives the goals and thus the topic of the results, whereas in ethnographies, the participants drive the data obtained. Because of this nature, they argue that "ethnographic studies are best used for exploratory purposes, to help define requirements, and to inspire design ideas." Other types of field studies are more appropriate for answering specific questions about specific products.

Kirah, Fuson, Grudin, and Feldman (2005) provided a history of the use of ethnography in the software industry (e.g., PARC through Intel). They say, "The ethnographer's goal when working for a software company is to experience the world of technology from the people's perspective instead of the perspective of the software company. Ethnographers observe people in their own environments, where the activities the participants choose to do have meaning and have a direct impact on their daily lives. The translation of this experience and application of this learning into product design and development so that the products and features will be meaningful and appeal to 'real people' is the key. In essence, ethnographers bring the voice of the customer into product development" (p. 416).

They also say that "Ethnography is a form of qualitative research that is done in a natural setting ... Participant observation and interviews are core ethnographic methodology and are best described as participating in and observing as much as possible the daily lives of the individuals who are being observed."

Finally, they say, "A crucial part of the ethnographic data collection is learning the skill of understanding the 'native' point of view without imposing one's own ideas, frame of reference, or conceptual framework on top of the participant's point of view" (p. 418).

Here, we see the necessity of skills that are not trivial and require a great deal of training, vigilance, and practice. Just as in a quantitative approach, where practitioners must be aware of potential statistical design issues and participant and researcher biases, practicing ethnography that adheres to these standards takes a great deal of education and effort. The right education for this task may be a degree in anthropology, sociology, or another social science and/or field experience.

As Stokes Jones, principal researcher at Motorola Mobility, eloquently put this, "ethnography done **right** has a bias toward 'discovery', rather than strong pre-conceptions of what counts like a positivistic 'only the facts' point of view, common in human factors or usability."

To summarize, there is disagreement within the user research community about what is and is not ethnography. While both ethnographies and field studies are always conducted in the context of the user, some potential distinctions are the following:

Ethnography	Field Study
Bias toward discovery	Bias toward answering questions of interest
Exploratory	Guided
Emergent	A priori
Derive design inspiration	Answer specific questions about products
Participant drives topics/results	Product team drives topics/results
Holistic and data-driven	Goal-/question-driven
Point of view: participant	Point of view: product team
Longer immersion (e.g., 3 months-6+ years)	Shorter immersion (e.g., 1 day-6 weeks)

Some researchers have stopped using the term "ethnography" altogether because of these debates. As Ken Anderson, anthropologist at Intel states: "Ethnography is whatever people want it to be. Ethnography is not a copyrighted term. For me, ethnography is the outcome, not the method. Ethnography as an outcome is a narrative about a way of living. As such, it is primarily limited to graduate students in anthropology and sociology. What is often described as 'ethnography' is usually just 'participant observation.' I strongly feel it is a disservice to practitioners and academics to create this false separation of 'academic ethnography,' and 'non-academic ethnography.' The difference is in what is produced, for whom, and how. This is the key separation—it is a matter of audience."

Before you can begin preparing for a field study, you need to understand the techniques available to you. Methods range from pure observation to becoming a user yourself. Table 13.1 provides a comparison between the techniques.

Since there is no standard method, we will consider a range of techniques. The goal of each method is the same: to observe users and collect information about their tasks and the context in which they are done. The cost for each method

Table 13.1 Comparison chart of field study methods

Method	Synopsis	Advantages	Level of effort	
Pure observation	When you are unable or do not wish to interact with the user, you simply observe from a distance	• Flexible • Low resources	• Minimal • Place yourself in a good vantage point and observe as many users/sites/tasks as you feel appropriate • Continue to conduct observations until you feel you have a good understanding of the domain or areas of focus	Observation only
Deep hanging out	This method is similar to pure observation but provides more structure by suggesting focus areas and things to observe	It has more structure than pure observation so you can do a more detailed level of data analysis and compare data collected across multiple sites	• Moderate • Because there is more structure, it takes more effort than pure observation • You are "on" at all times, which can be tiring • It is also valuable to become a user yourself (if possible) and collect artifacts along the way	Observation only
Contextual inquiry	Interview, apprentice with, and interpret the resulting data with users	• Contextual inquiry is more focused and context-dependent than the previous methods • At the end, you walk away with actionable items	• High • The effort level is higher than for observation-only techniques. You must develop an observation guide, observe users, apprentice with them, and discuss your observations with them	Interacting with users
Process analysis	Capture the task sequence for a process that may span several days	Because it is more focused than contextual inquiry, it is also much faster	• Moderate • You need to stay focused on the process at hand to help users walk you through the process of interest	Interacting with users
Condensed ethnographic interview	Use the results of semi-structured interviews to guide observations	This technique takes considerably less time than some of the other techniques described here, because the interviews scope what you observe; but it also limits the data you collect	• Moderate • This takes more work than observation-only techniques because you must plan and conduct interviews and then observe users and collect artifacts	Interacting with users

Continued

Table 13.1 Comparison chart of field study methods—Cont'd

	Method	Synopsis	Advantages	Level of effort
Method supplements	Artifact walk-throughs	Collect all the artifacts used by participants and determine what triggers their use, when they are used, and for what	Quick and easy to conduct	• Minimal • Low level of effort to review artifacts with participants and make/collect copies of them
	Incident diaries	Worksheets the user takes home or to work to collect ongoing data rather than one-time performance or opinions	No observation is required. You are able to understand more issues than what can be observed in the lab or during a single visit	• Moderate • Low effort level to create and distribute diaries • Moderate effort to analyze data across multiple diaries. There will be a time lag between when you distribute the diaries and when you receive the data • You are depending on the participants to follow through
	Photographs	Capturing artifacts and the environment using a camera	Easy to do and can be very helpful during data analysis and for presenting results	• Minimal • Quick and easy to accomplish as long as participants do not mind you taking photos
	Observing while you are not present	Recording users in action when space, time, or restrictions prevent you from being there in person	If you have multiple video cameras, you can view several users simultaneously	• Moderate • Low effort to set up cameras and record • Moderate effort to meet with user again and review tapes • Moderate effort to categorize and index behavior

is also very similar (e.g., your time to collect and analyze the data, recording equipment, potential recruitment fees, and incentives). The differences arise in the way you collect data and some of the information you are able to collect.

The techniques described here are divided into three categories: observation only, interacting with the user, and method supplements. *The most important thing to remember when designing a field study is to be flexible*. Select the method(s) that will best address the goals of your study and the time and resources available to conduct it. Collect several types of data (e.g., notes, audio, video, still pictures, artifacts, sketches, diaries) to obtain a richer data set. Finally, and regardless of the type of study you conduct, do not focus on solutions before or during data collection. Doing that may bias your observations and needlessly limit the information you collect. You can conduct follow-up visits to investigate hypotheses, but—at least in the initial visit—focus on the data collection and keep an open mind.

At a Glance

> Observation only
- Pure observation
- Deep hanging out

> Interacting with the user
- Contextual inquiry
- Process analysis
- Condensed ethnographic interview

> Method supplements
- Artifact walk-throughs
- Photographs
- Observing while you are not present

Observation Only

Techniques that do not involve interacting with users are ideal in situations when you cannot interact with participants because doing so would take attention away from a critically important primary task (e.g., a doctor in surgery, a trader on the stock exchange floor). Observation-only techniques have their limits in terms of the information that can be collected, but they are typically less resource-intensive.

Pure Observation

The pure observation technique is valuable in situations where you cannot interact with the users. Perhaps you cannot speak with the end user for privacy or legal reasons (e.g., hospital patients), or it is an environment where you cannot distract the user with questions (e.g., emergency room doctors). In pure observation studies, users may or may not know they are being studied. If you wanted to observe people's initial reaction to a self-serve kiosk at an airport, you might sit quietly at a well-positioned table and simply record the number of people who saw the kiosk, looked at it, and then used it. You might also capture information such as facial expressions and overheard comments. If you do not need photographs or video recordings and you are in a public place and it is ethically appropriate, you may not necessarily need to inform participants of your presence. In most situations, however, you will need to inform individuals that you are observing them (e.g., in office settings). Refer to Chapter 3 on page 66 for information about informed consent and appropriate behavior with participants.

Obviously, with this technique, you do not interact with the participant. You do not distribute surveys, interview the user, or ask for artifacts from the user. This technique is simply about immersing yourself in the environment and developing questions along the way. From here, you may go back to your product team and management to recommend additional areas of focus.

If you are new to observing people, the following things to consider may help you:

- What language and terminology do people use?
- If you are observing the use of an existing system, how much of the system/software/features do users actually use?
- What barriers or stop points do people encounter?
- If what you are interested in is task-focused:
  - How much time do people devote to accomplishing a task?
  - What questions do people have to ask to accomplish a task?
  - What tools do users interact with as they are trying to accomplish a task?

Travel Example

TravelMyWay.com has decided that they want to build a mobile app that lets users view their itineraries for their hotel, car, and airline bookings; holds electronic tickets; and allows access to online help. Before the company actually invests money in such a venture, you would like to better understand travelers' needs and how they behave at the airport. You do not know exactly what you are looking for at this time, but you know that it is wise to observe users in the context where this app will be used.

You have spent the week walking around the airport, observing people being dropped off and picked up, checking in bags, picking bags up, asking the information desk for directions, going through security checkpoints, and interacting with mobile phone apps offered by various airlines. During this time, you observed that several people spent a couple of minutes looking at their mobile phones near the security line but then went to an airline kiosk to check in. This appears to be a trend across the different companies' kiosks. You do not know why they abandoned the mobile app and instead used a kiosk to check in, but this clearly provides a question for a follow-up study. What is it about the mobile app that makes some people use a self check-in kiosk after only a few minutes, and how can your company avoid that problem?

Because you do not interact with participants during pure observation, the information that you can obtain is obviously limited. You are not able to follow up on an interesting observation with a question that may help you understand why a participant engaged in a certain action. This is particularly challenging in situations where you are new to the domain and you may not understand much of what you are seeing. In addition, you cannot influence events; you get only what is presented and may miss important events as a result. Consequently, it is essential to have a good **sampling plan.** The sampling plan should include days/times you anticipate key events (e.g., the day before Thanksgiving Day or bad weather at an airport) and "normal" days. However, regardless of how good your sampling plan is, you may still miss infrequent but important events (e.g., a bad weather closure at the airport or multiple traumas in the ER). Nevertheless, the information that you can obtain is worthwhile and will bring you closer to understanding the user, tasks, and environment than you were when you began. As Yogi Berra said, "You can see a lot just by watching."

Deep Hanging Out

"I'm ready for some deep hanging out"

Cartoon by Abi Jones

A more structured form of observation is referred to as "deep hanging out." The key differences between deep hanging out and pure observation are that in deep hanging out, (1) you become a user yourself, and (2) there is a formal structure that organizes the observation process. Researchers from Intel developed this method by applying anthropological techniques to field research (Teague & Bell, 2001). Their method of deep hanging out includes structured observation, collection of artifacts, and becoming a user (i.e., in the travel example, you would actually travel and use the app yourself). However, you do not interview participants, distribute surveys, or present design ideas for feedback.

To make this data collection manageable, the system/environment is divided into ten focus areas, as shown in Table 13.2. The foci are intended to help you think about different aspects of the environment. Because these foci are standardized, you can compare data across multiple sites in a structured manner (to be described in detail later).

Breadth can be important, even at the expense of depth, when first learning about an area. One use of the list in Table 13.2 is to remind you to focus on a large number of areas and not focus on just one small (easy to collect) area. This list is particularly useful for a novice—to appreciate all the areas to look at and to understand that depth in every area is not that important.

Another key use of the list is to help teams who are doing research together to come away with better findings. Many times, a group of four to five people go out and conduct observations independently, but they all come back with pretty much the same findings. This can be frustrating for everyone involved and may cause stakeholders to question the value of having so many people involved in the study or the value of the study *period*. Using the list of foci and giving each person a specific focus area help to ensure that the team examines multiple areas. In addition, it gives individuals some direction and ownership and makes their insight a unique contribution to the team.

Table 13.2: Focal points for deep hanging out (Teague & Bell, 2001)

Focal point	Some questions to ask
Family and kids	Do you see families? How many children are there? What are the age ranges? What is the interaction between the kids? Between the parents and the kids? How are they dressed? Is the environment designed to support families/kids (e.g., special activities, special locations, etc.)?
Food and drinks	Are food and drinks available? What is being served/consumed? Where is it served/consumed? When is it served? Are there special locations for it? Are people doing other things while eating? What is the service like? Are only certain people consuming food and drinks?
Built environment	How is the space laid out? What does it look like? What is the size, shape, decoration, furnishings? Is there a theme? Are there any time or space cues (e.g., clocks on the walls and windows to show time of day or orientation to the rest of the outside)?
Possessions	What are people carrying with them? How often do people access them? How do people carry them? What do they do with them? What are people acquiring?
Media consumption	What are people reading, watching, and listening to? Did they bring it with them or buy it there? Where do they consume the media and when? What do they do with it when they are done?
Tools and technology	What technology is built-in? How does it work? Is it for the customers or the company? Is it visible?
Demographics	What are the demographics of the people in the environment? Are they in groups (e.g., families, tours)? How are they dressed? How do they interact with each other? How do they behave?
Traffic	What is the flow of traffic through the space? Was it designed that way? What is traveling through the space (e.g., people, cars, golf carts)? Where are the high-/low-traffic areas? Why are they high-/low-traffic areas? Where do people linger?
Information and communication access	What are the information and communication access points (e.g., pay phones, ATMs, computer terminals, kiosks, maps, signs, guides, directories, information desks)? Do people use them, and how often? How do people use them? Where are they located (e.g., immediately visible, difficult to access)? What do they look like?
Overall experience	Don't forget the forest for the trees. What is the overall environment like? What is the first and last thing you noticed? What is it like to be there? How is it similar or different from similar environments? Are there any standard behaviors, rules, or rituals? (Think high level and obtain a holistic view, rather than concentrating on details.)

Numerous studies at Intel demonstrated that, regardless of the system, users, or environment they studied, these ten foci represented the domain and supported valuable data collection. The technique is intended to be flexible. There is no minimum number of foci to collect data about or recommended amount of time to spend observing each focus area. However, even if a particular focal point does not seem appropriate to your study, you should still try to collect information about it. The lack of information about that particular focal point can be just as enlightening! For example, you may think that the "family and kids" focal point is not appropriate when you are studying users in their office environment. Who brings their family to work with them? But, you may observe that a participant is constantly getting calls from a spouse and messages from the kids. Perhaps, they are complaining because your participant is never home or is late for the daughter's recital. Maybe this means that the participant is so overwhelmed with work that problems with the family life are spilling over into work, and vice versa. Even if you do not think a particular focal point is applicable to your study, go in with an open mind and expect to be surprised.

Just as with pure observation when creating your sampling plan, we recommend collecting data at different times during the day and on different days of the week. For example, you would likely observe different things if you went to the airport at 8 am on Monday, 8 am on Saturday, and 6 pm on Wednesday.

Deep hanging out stresses that you are "on" at all times. Using our earlier travel example, you would begin your observations from the time you travel to the airport. Observe the experience from the very beginning of the process, not just once you are inside the airport. Pay attention to the signs directing you to parking and passenger pickup. The intention is to obtain a holistic view of the system/environment that goes beyond contextual inquiry (discussed on page 393).

While you are observing the users and environment, create maps (see Figure 13.1). Identify where actions occur. If your focus is "family and kids," identify locations designed for families or kids (e.g., jungle gym, family bathroom). Where do families tend to linger? In addition to creating maps, collect maps that the establishment provides. Collect every artifact you can get your hands on (e.g., objects or items that users use to complete their

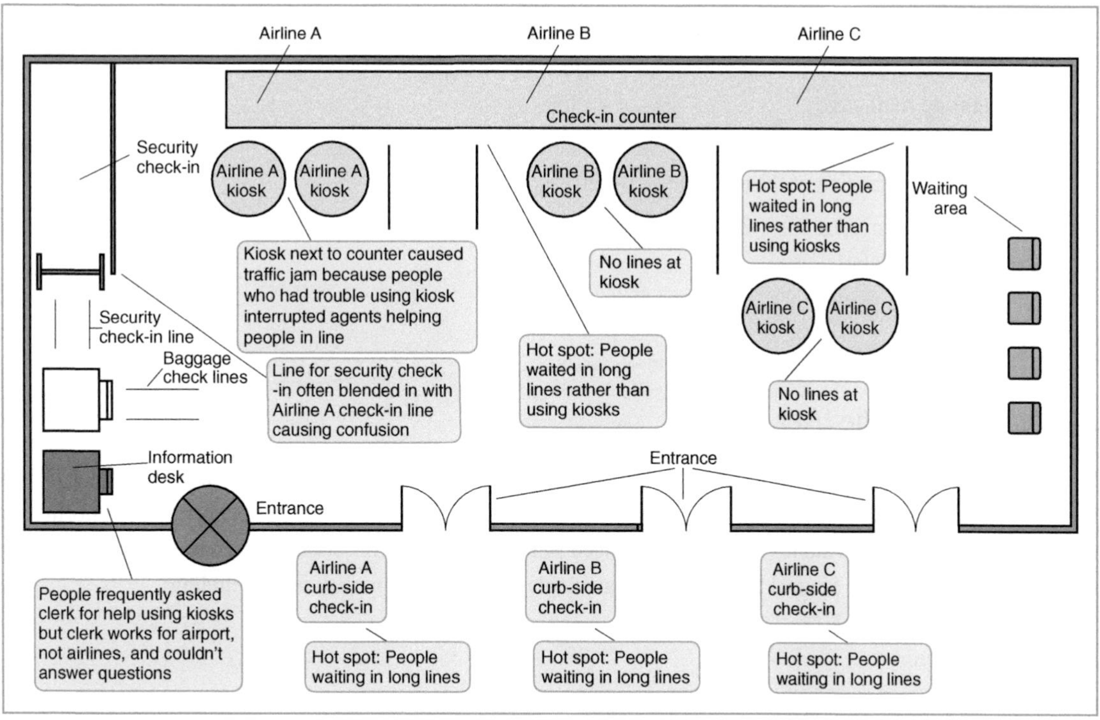

Figure 13.1: Map from an airport kiosk study—hot spot areas and other issues are noted on map.

tasks or that result from their tasks). If allowed, take photos or videos of the environment, though keep in mind that you may need to obtain permission first.

Finally, involve yourself in the process by becoming a user. If you are interested in designing a mobile app for use at an airport, use each mobile app available for use during check-in, but never mistake yourself for the actual end user. Involving yourself in the process helps you understand what the users are experiencing, but it does not mean that you *are* the end user.

TIPS

Here are some other tips to keep in mind when conducting pure observation or deep hanging out (Teague & Bell, 2001):

- *Maintain a low profile.* Do not announce your presence and what you are doing. Stay out of everyone's way and be quiet.
- *Act like everyone else—or not.* You can either blend in (e.g., clothing, behavior, language) or stand out to see people's reactions. How would people react if you did not observe their rituals (e.g., dressing inappropriately)? Perhaps, certain taboos are not actually taboos. You will not know until you test them.
- *Find an appropriate notetaking method.* You do not want to draw attention to the fact that you are observing people and making notes about their behavior. Find a method that allows you to take useable notes but is not obvious. This may be as simple as bringing a pocket-sized notepad, or you may find an isolated corner where you can dictate notes into an audio recorder (see Chapter 9 on page 220 for a discussion of notetaking methods).
- *Think "big picture."* Do not think about solutions or focus on just one interesting finding. You are going for a holistic understanding of the environment, users, and tasks.
- *Pay attention to signs.* There is a reason why signs are posted. What is the important point that needs to be conveyed, and why?

Interacting with the User

For actual product development (not just learning about a domain or preparing for another user research activity), it is almost *always* better to interact with users rather than just observe them. You will not get enough information to design from observation alone. You frequently need to follow up on an observational study with an interaction study or combine the two. Several techniques are available to you to accomplish this, including:

- Contextual inquiry
- Process analysis
- Condensed ethnographic interview

Contextual Inquiry

Beyer and Holtzblatt (1998) wrote the book on contextual inquiry (CI) and contextual design. In this chapter, we introduce you to the basics of this very popular and useful method. If this is a method you plan to use often, we highly recommend reading the book. There are four main parts to contextual inquiry:

- *Context*. You must go to the user's environment to understand the context of his or her actions. Contextual inquiry assumes that observation alone or out-of-context interviews are insufficient.
- *Partnership*. To better understand the user, tasks, and environment, you should develop a master-apprentice relationship with the participant. Immerse yourself in the participant's work and do as he or she does. Obviously, this is not possible with many jobs (e.g., surgeon, fighter pilot), so you have to be flexible.
- *Interpretation*. Observations must be interpreted *with the participant* to be used later. Verify that your assumptions and conclusions are correct.
- *Focus*. Develop an **observation guide** to keep you focused on the subject of interest/inquiry.

Unlike in pure observation, in contextual inquiry, the user is very aware of your presence and becomes a partner in the research. It *can* be faster, taking only a few hours or a day. At the end, you walk away with actionable items to begin designing a product, your next user research activity (e.g., tasks for a usability test, questions for a survey), or areas for innovation and future research.

The process begins by developing an observation guide (see Figure 13.2). This is a list of general concerns or issues to guide your observations—but it is *not* a list of specific questions to ask. You may want to refer to the foci listed in Table 13.2 to build your observation guide. Using a mobile travel app observation example, some issues to look out for might be sources of frustration for mobile app users, points where travelers could use the app instead of a self-check-in kiosk or airline agent, points where travelers abandon using the app, and length of time spent interacting with the app. This observation guide would obviously be influenced by the goals of your study and what you want to learn.

- Observation Guide: Mobile Travel App
- Issues:
    - Interactions between people traveling together (e.g., handing bags to one another to hold)
    - Interactions between groups of travelers (e.g., information seeking while waiting in line)
    - Length of time using mobile app functions
        - Searching for reservation
        - Checking in
        - Noting baggage, if any
    - Types of in-person interactions
        - Issues due to failed check in
        - Checking baggage
        - In the security line
    - Busy and slow periods (i.e., hurry up and wait)

Figure 13.2: Example of a portion of an observation guide for a mobile travel app study.

Next, you carefully select representative users to observe and apprentice. Beyer and Holtzblatt recommend 15-20 users, but our experience is that four to six are more common in industry practice. The number of participants used should be based on the question you are trying to answer. The more focused (or narrow) the question and the more consistency across users, tasks, and environments, the fewer participants are necessary. For example, if you are interested in studying only one particular task that travelers who are "frequent fliers" engage in during a trip at one particular airport, rather than the entire airport experience for all travelers at all airports, you could observe fewer participants and feel more confident in the reliability of the results (refer "How Many Participants" section, page 402).

Context

Work with participants individually. Begin by observing the participant in action. The goal is to collect ongoing and individual data points rather than a summary or abstract description of the way the participant works. It is best to have two researchers present who can switch roles between notetaker and interviewer quickly. Often, an interviewee will have better chemistry with one researcher or the other. Having the flexibility to switch roles quickly can improve the quality of the data you collect. You can ask the participant to think aloud as he or she works (see Chapter 7, "Using a Think-Aloud Protocol" section, page 169), or you may choose to ask the participant clarifying questions along the way. You may even decide not to interrupt the participant at all but wait until he or she has completed a task and then ask your questions. Your choice should depend on the environment, task, your goals, and user.

For example, air travelers may not be able to think aloud as they go through airport security. It may also be difficult for you to observe them during this time due to restrictions on your presence and the use of recording devices in airport security areas. It is best in that case to wait until the traveler has completed the security checks to ask your questions. Task clarification questions in the case of an airport security line might include "How did you determine which line to use?" "Why did you ask the security personnel whether you could keep your shoes on?" and "How did you use the app to determine security line wait time?"

Partnership

Once the participant is comfortable with your presence and you have developed a rapport (see "Monitoring the Relationship with the Interviewee" section on page 249 in Chapter 9 to learn about developing a rapport with participants), you can introduce the master-apprentice relationship. As long as the company approves it and you have considered potential ethical and legal issues (see Chapter 3, page 66), the participant becomes the master and instructs you (the apprentice) on how to complete a given task. Despite limitations in some environments (e.g., you may not be able to join a pilot in the cockpit of a plane), the participant can always instruct you on *some* aspect of his or her activities (e.g., perhaps, you *can* sit in a flight simulator with a pilot).

It is easy for certain types of relationships to develop during this time. You should avoid the three relationships listed below because they are not conducive to unbiased data collection:

- *Expert-novice*. Because you are entering the environment as a "specialist," the user may see *you* as the expert. It is important for you to remind the participant that he or she is the expert and you are the novice.

- *Interviewer-interviewee*. Participants may assume that this is an interview, and if you are not asking questions, you already understand everything. Stress to the participant that you are new to the domain and need to be instructed as if you were a new employee starting the job. The user should not wait for questions from you before offering information or instruction.
- *Guest-host*. You are a partner with the user and should be involved with the user's work. The user should not be getting you coffee, and you should not be concerned about invading the user's personal space. Get in there and learn what the user knows.

TIPS

This may sound *painfully* obvious, but remember to bring your own water and snacks. Do not let your growling stomach derail the interview. Anticipate if you will need caffeine along the way and schedule coffee breaks. Make sure you have a plan in place for lunch. If you wish to eat lunch with the participant—so that you can fully experience his or her day—ask the participant's permission first. Do not assume that you are welcome at what is considered "personal" time.

Interpretation

A key aspect of contextual inquiry is to share your interpretations with participants and have them verify that your interpretations are correct. You do not have to worry that users will agree with an incorrect interpretation just to please you. When you create a solid master-apprentice relationship, the user will be keen for you to understand the process and will correct any misconceptions you have. He or she will often add to your interpretations as well, extending your knowledge and understanding beyond what you have observed.

Remember what your teacher told you: "The only dumb questions are the ones you don't ask." Do not be afraid to ask even simple questions; just remember to phrase them correctly (see Moderation Tips, chapter 7, Table 7.3, page 166). In addition to increasing your own knowledge, you can make the participants think more about what they would consider "standard practices" or the "that's just the way we have always done it" mentality to help you understand the why (see "Your Role as the Interviewer" section on page 240 in Chapter 9 for tips about communicating with users and helping them provide the information you are seeking).

Focus

During the entire process, you want to keep the inquiry focused on the areas of concern. You began by developing an observation guide for the inquiry (see Figure 13.2). Refer to this guide throughout the process. Since the participant is the master, he or she will guide the conversation to points he or she finds interesting. It is essential for you to learn what the participant finds important, but it is also critical that you get the data necessary to guide your design, the next user research activity, or innovation. The user may find it more interesting to cover all topics at a high level, but your focus should uncover details in the areas that you believe are most important. Remember that the devil is in the details; if you do not uncover the details, your interpretation of the data will be inadequate to inform design, the next user research activity, or innovation (see "Your Role as the Interviewer" section on page 240 in Chapter 9 to learn more about guiding the participant's conversation).

Process Analysis

A process analysis is a focused type of field study targeted at understanding the task sequence for a process that may span several days. It is similar to contextual inquiry, but unlike a contextual inquiry, you begin the process analysis with a series of questions and you do not necessarily apprentice with the user. At the end of a process analysis, you develop a process map that visually demonstrates the steps in a process. (Figure 13.3 illustrates a very simple process map for a traveler using a mobile app.) Because process analysis is more focused than contextual inquiry, it is also much faster to conduct.

The following are questions to answer during a process analysis:

- When does the first task in the process happen?
- What triggers it?
- Who does it?
- What information does the person have when the task begins?
- What are the major steps in the task?
- What information comes out of it?

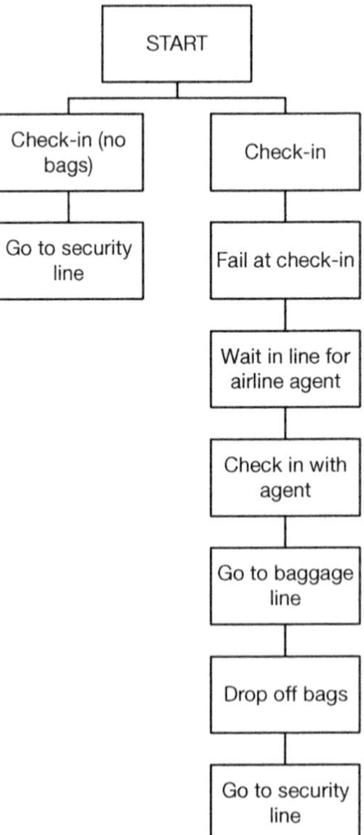

Figure 13.3: Process map for a traveler's typical airline check-in experience.

- Who is the next person in the chain of the process?
- When does the next task happen? (repeat for each task in the process)
- How do you know when the process is complete?
- Does this process connect to other processes?
- Is this process ever reopened, and if so, under what circumstances?
- What errors can be made? How serious are they? How often do they occur?
- What are the major roadblocks to efficient performance?

Condensed Ethnographic Interview

Based on the cognitive science model of expert knowledge, the condensed ethnographic interview employs the standardization and focus of a **semi-structured interview** (see Chapter 9, page 220) along with the context of observations and **artifacts.** Users are first interviewed to ask them how they accomplish a task and other information surrounding their work. Users are then observed doing the task(s) in question, focusing on processes and tools. Artifacts are collected and discussed. Rather than a general observation guide, investigators use a standard set of questions developed specifically for the questions they are interested in to guide the visits but remain flexible throughout.

This approach is characterized as "top-down"—in contrast to contextual inquiry's "bottom-up" approach—because the interviews form a general framework from which to interpret specific observations. This technique takes considerably less time than some of the other techniques described above, but it also limits the data you collect because the framework acts as a guideline.

Method Supplements

There are four activities that you can conduct in addition to the above methods or use as stand-alone techniques: artifact walk-throughs, photographs, observing while absent, and dairies. A sample incident diary is presented in Figure 13.4; see Chapter 8 on page 194 for a thorough discussion of diary studies. Each of the other supplements are discussed below.

Suggested Resources for Additional Reading

The book and book chapters below offer good examples of condensed ethnographic interviewing:

- Dewalt, K & Dewalt, B (2011). *Participant observation: A guide for fieldworkers, 2nd Edition.* Plymouth, UK AltaMitra Press.
- Bauersfeld, K. & Halgren, S. (1996). You've got three days! Case studies in field techniques for the time-challenged. In D. R. Wixon & J. Ramey (eds), *Field methods casebook for software design*, pp. 177–195. New York: John Wiley & Sons.
- Wood, L. (1996). The ethnographic interview in user-centered work/task analysis. In D. R. Wixon & J. Ramey (eds), *Field methods casebook for software design*, pp. 35–56. New York: John Wiley & Sons.

Planning Your Vacation Diary

ID: P1
Date: ____________

Describe what your goal was: ______________________________

What app did you use? ______________________________

Did you accomplish your goal? ____Yes ____No

Please explain: ______________________________

Please describe any difficulties you encountered or anything you would have liked to do differently. ______________________________

Other comments or thoughts: ______________________________

Figure 13.4: Sample incident diary.

Artifact Walk-throughs

Artifact walk-throughs are quick and easy but provide indispensable data. Begin by identifying each artifact a participant leverages to do a particular task. Artifacts are objects or items that users use to complete their tasks or that result from their tasks. These can include the following:

- "Official" documents (e.g., manuals, forms, checklists, standard operating procedures)
- Handwritten notes
- Documents that get printed out as needed and then discarded
- Communications (e.g., interoffice memos, e-mails, letters)
- Outputs of tasks (e.g., confirmation number from travel booking)
- Text messages

Next, ask participants to walk you through how the artifacts are used. You want to understand what triggers the use of each artifact: when is it used and for what. Whenever possible, get photos or copies of each artifact. If there are concerns about sensitive or private information (e.g., patient information, credit card numbers), ask for a copy of the original, redact the sensitive data by marking it out with a Sharpie, make a copy, and return the original to the owner or shred it. This takes a little extra time, but most participants are willing to help wherever possible and appreciate your willingness to preserve their privacy. You can also sign a company's nondisclosure agreement, promising that you will keep all data collected confidential (refer to Chapter 3, page 66). The information obtained during an artifact walk-through will be essential if you want to conduct an artifact analysis (see "Data Analysis and Interpretation" section, page 415).

Photographs

Another supplement that can be useful is to collect photographs of artifacts (e.g., printouts, business cards, notes, day planners) and the environment. This is a method that is commonly used in Discount User Observation (DUO; Laakso, Laakso, & Page, 2001). In this method, two researchers help with data collection. The first is a notetaker and is responsible for taking detailed, time-stamped notes (see Figure 13.5) during the visit and asking clarifying questions. The second researcher acts as a photographer. Since digital cameras typically include automatic time stamps, we find that these make reconciling the time-stamped notes with the time-stamped photos easy and provide a timeline of the user's work. Following data analysis, a summary of the results is presented to users for verification and correction (see "Data Analysis and Interpretation" section, page 415). The goal is to understand the complex interdependencies of tasks, interruptions, and temporal overlaps (i.e., two actions occurring at the same time) without having to spend significant amounts of time transcribing, watching videos, or confusing raw data with inferences and interpretations.

Observing While You Are Not Present

You can observe users even when you are not present by setting up a video camera and then leaving. This is an excellent way to understand detailed steps a user takes, especially in small environments where observers cannot fit or critical jobs where you do not want to interrupt or distract the user. For example, if you wanted to study how drivers and passengers interact with their dashboard during a road trip but you either did not physically fit in the car or did not want to alter the behavior of the driver and passenger during the drive, you could set up a camera to record their activities and then view the recordings later. Researchers have used this technique to formulate questions and then set up another appointment with the participants a few days later to view the recordings together while the participants provided a running commentary (called "retrospective think aloud" or "stimulated recall;" Ramey, Rowberg, & Robinson, 1996). This technique is referred to as "stream-of-behavior chronicles." In this technique, interviewers insert questions along the way, and to analyze the data, they categorize and index specific behaviors.

....

1:35 starts looking for reservation on mobile app
1:36 cannot find reservation on mobile app
1:37 frustrated by inability to find reservation, user closes app and restarts
1:38 looks for reservation again; unsuccessful
1:40 finds line for manual check-in with agent
1:50 checks in with airline agent

....

Figure 13.5: Sample of time-stamped notes.

Preparing for a Field Study

Now that you are familiar with some of the techniques available to you, it is time to plan and prepare for your field study. Although some of the details may vary slightly depending on the data-collecting technique selected, the preparation, participants, and materials remain constant.

At a Glance

> Identify the type of study to conduct
> Players in your activity
> Train the players
> Develop your protocol
> Schedule the visits
> Activity materials
> Summary

Identify the Type of Study to Conduct

To identify the type of study you would like to conduct, use the decision diagram in Figure 13.6.

Scope your study appropriately. You may not have time to learn everything you would like to or be able to visit all the sites you are interested in. It is critical to the success of your study to plan carefully. Create a realistic timetable for identifying the sites, recruiting the users, collecting the data, and then analyzing the data. You will have questions later on (usually during the analysis stage). If possible, leave enough time to conduct follow-up interviews. There is nothing more frustrating than running out of time and not being able to analyze all the data you have! And remember, it always takes longer than you think—so include enough extra time in case you run into snags along the way.

Write a proposal (see Chapter 6, "Creating a Proposal" section, page 116) that establishes the objectives of the study and identifies the user and site profile, the timeline, the resources needed (e.g., budget, materials, contacts, customers) and from whom, and how the information you collect will benefit the company, the product, and the design.

Players in Your Activity

In addition to participants to observe, there are a few other roles you may need to fill for your study. Each one is described below.

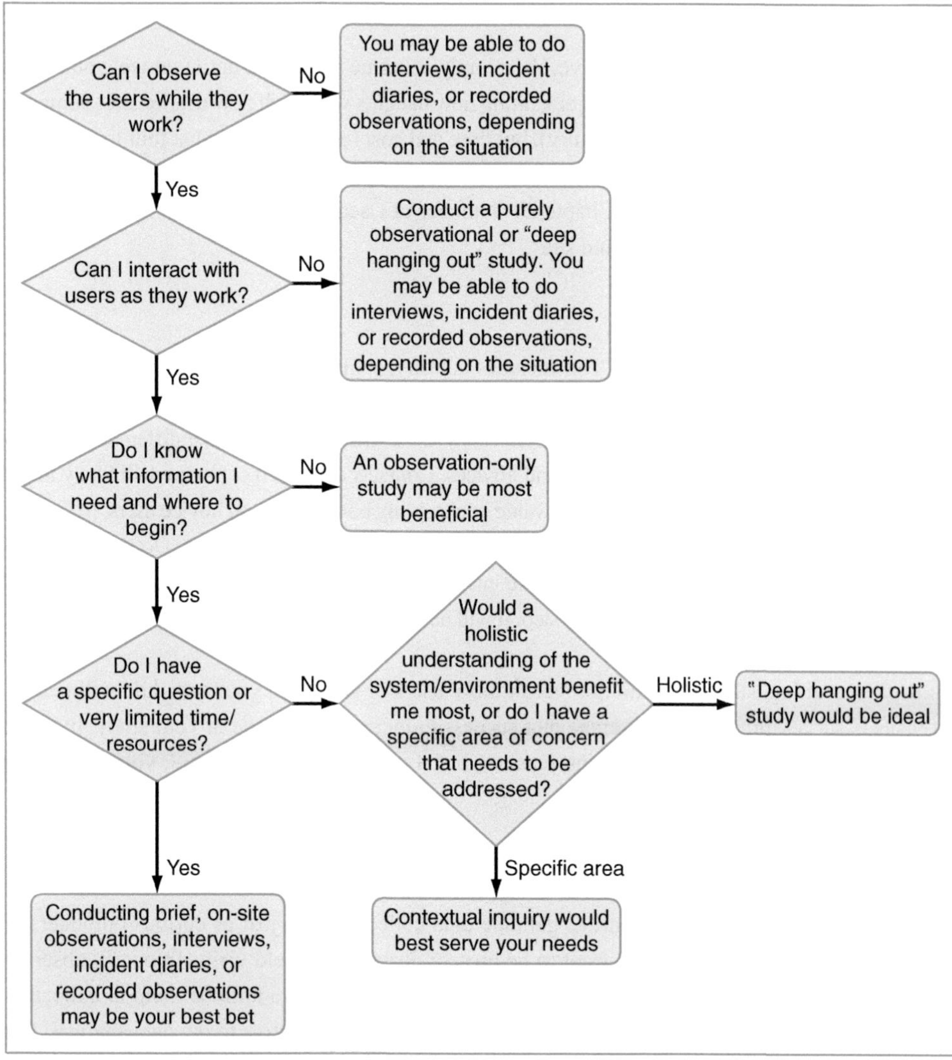

Figure 13.6: Decision diagram to determine the type of study that would best suit your needs.

The Participants

Once you know the type of study you would like to conduct, you need to identify the user type to investigate (see Chapter 2, "Learn About Your Users" section, page 35). As with any of the techniques described in this book, the data you collect are only as good as the participants you recruit.

Create a screener to guide your recruitment (see Chapter 6, "Recruitment Methods" section, page 139), and make sure everyone is in agreement before you start recruiting participants.

How Many Participants?

There is no set number of users or sites to observe. You simply continue to observe until you feel you understand the users, tasks, or environment and you are no longer gaining new insights with each new user or site. Some researchers recommend 15-20 users (e.g., in contextual inquiry), but time and cost restraints mean that four to six (per user type) is more common in industry practice. In academic settings, the number of participants depends on whether or not you are planning to conduct statistical tests (see Chapter 5, "Number of Users" section, page 104). Other factors to keep in mind are getting a diverse range of users and sites.

Diverse Range of Users and Sites

Get a broad representation of users and sites. This includes industry, company size, new adopters, and long-time customers, as well as geographic location, age, ethnicity, and gender diversity. Try to get access to multiple users at each site. They may be doing the same task, but each person may do it differently and have different ideas, challenges, work-arounds, etc. You also want a mix of experts and novices. Contacts at a given company will likely introduce you to their "best" employees. Explain to the contacts the value in observing both expert and novice users. In the end, though, politics and people's availability may determine your choice of sites and users to observe. Do everything you can to ensure that participants and sites meet the profile you are interested in. Stakeholders often have the contacts to help you identify sites and users, so get them involved in this step. It will help you and also help stakeholders buy in to the process.

When you begin recruiting, start small; do not recruit more users or sites than your schedule will permit. If your first set of visits is successful, you can leverage that success to increase the scope of your study. In addition, you may need to start with local sites for budgeting reasons, but if your study is successful, you could be given the opportunity to expand later.

The Investigators

Begin by identifying who wants to take part as genuine data collectors, not just as curious onlookers. You may be surprised to discover how many people want to be present during your field visits. In purely observational or deep hanging out studies, this is not a big issue. You should welcome some additional help in collecting data. It will speed the process, and an additional set of eyes can bring a fresh perspective to the data analysis. Expect and encourage people to get involved, but be aware of some of the issues surrounding inexperienced investigators.

You may want to establish a rule that anyone present at the site must participate in the data collection and follow a set of ground rules (see "Train the Players" section, page 404). This is where you must establish yourself as the expert and insist that everyone respect your expertise. Sometimes, you need to be diplomatic and tell a stakeholder that he or she cannot attend a particular visit, without ruining your relationship with that stakeholder.

Once you have a list of people who want to take part in the study, look for those who are detail-oriented and good listeners. For studies that involve some level of interaction, we recommend working in teams of just two, because that is less overwhelming for the participant being observed. Each team should consist of an investigator and a notetaker and a videographer/photographer (page 403). Since the video camera can usually be set up in the beginning and left alone, either the investigator or notetaker can do this. Either the notetaker or investigator can double up as photographer. Mixed-gender teams can help in cases where a participant feels more comfortable relating to one gender or another. For safety reasons, we recommend never conducting field studies in people's home or other private spaces alone.

The job of the investigator is to develop rapport with the participant, and if applicable, conduct the interview and apprentice with him or her. The investigator is the "leader" in the two-person team. In cases where you lack a great deal of domain knowledge, you may not know enough about what you are observing to ask the user follow-up questions. You may wish to create more of a partnership with a developer or product manager. You can begin by asking participants each question, but the domain expert would then follow up with more detailed questions. Just be sure that one of you is capturing the data! Alternatively, you can bring a "translator" along with you. This may be a user from the site or an expert from your company who will provide a running commentary while the participant is working. This is ideal in situations where the participant cannot provide **think-aloud** data and cannot be interrupted with your questions. In a healthcare field study we conducted, we asked a member of the product team who was a former registered nurse to act as a translator for us. She pointed out observations that were interesting to her and that we would not have noticed. She also explained the purpose of different artifacts when users were not available to discuss them. Her help was priceless!

If you have more potential investigators than you have roles, you may choose different investigators for each site. This can lower **interrater reliability** (i.e., the degree to which two or more observers assign the same rating or label to a behavior; see page 254), but it may also be necessary if individual investigators do not have the time to commit to a series of visits. Having a single person who attends all visits (i.e., yourself) can ensure continuity and an ability to see patterns or trends. Having a new investigator every few visits provides a fresh set of eyes and a different perspective. It also breaks up the workload and allows more people to take part in the study. You are sharing the knowledge, and important stakeholders do not feel excluded.

If time is a serious issue for you, it may be wise to have more than one collection team. This will allow you to collect data from multiple sites at once, but you will need to train several people and develop an explicit protocol for investigators to follow (see "Develop Your Protocol" section, page 405). If there is more than one experienced user experience professional available, pair each one up with a novice investigator. Having more than one collection team will mean that you will lose that consistent pair of eyes, but it may be worthwhile if you are pressed on time but have several sites available to you.

The Notetaker

In addition to an investigator, a notetaker is required. The investigator should be focused on asking questions and apprenticing with the user (if applicable), not taking detailed notes. You will find a detailed discussion of notetaking tips and strategies in Recording and Notetaking on page 171. The notetaker can also serve as a timekeeper, if that is the information you wish to collect. You may also wish to have the notetaker serve as the videographer/photographer (page 404). Lastly, it is also important to have an additional pair of hands on-site to set up equipment, and the notetaker can serve this purpose. If it is not possible to have a notetaker, one alternative is to record the session, and then, the investigator can take notes after the session is over. We do not recommend this, however.

TIP

It is extremely beneficial to have your notetaker present during data analysis. Having someone as a sounding board and additional pair of eyes is invaluable!

The Videographer/Photographer

Whenever possible, you will want to video record your field study. You will find a detailed discussion of tips for recording video and the benefits of video recordings in Recording and Notetaking (page 171). In most cases, this person simply needs to start and stop the recording, insert new media (e.g., SD card) as needed, and keep an eye out for any technical issues that arise.

You may also want someone to take photographs. (Again, the notetaker can often take on the roles of videographer and photographer.) Capturing visual images of the user's environment, artifacts, and tasks is extremely valuable. It helps you remember what you observed, and it helps stakeholders who were not present to internalize the data. Even if you do not plan to include pictures of participants in your reports or presentations, they can help you remember one participant from another. A digital camera with a screen is advantageous, because if the user is nervous about what you are capturing, you can show him or her every image and get permission to keep it. If the user is not happy with the image, you can demonstrate that you deleted it.

Account Managers

The **account manager** or sales representative is one person who may insist on following you around until he or she feels secure in what you are doing. Since this is the person who often owns the sales relationship with the customer and must continue to support the customer after you are long gone, you need to respect his or her need for control. Just make sure the account manager understands that this is not a sales demo and that *you* will be collecting the data. We have found that account managers are so busy that they will often leave you after an hour or less.

Train the Players

You are entering someone's personal space; for some users, this can be more stressful for the user than going to a lab. You will also likely need to leverage multiple skill sets such as interviewing, conducting surveys, observing, and managing groups of people. If you or a colleague has not conducted a field study before, we recommend reviewing "Moderating Your Activity" section on page 165 in Chapter 7 for a foundation in moderating. You may also want to sign up for a tutorial at a conference hosted by a professional organization to get hands-on training for one of the particular techniques. (EPIC, UPA, ACM SIGCHI, and HFI often offer workshops on field studies led by experts in the field, such as Susan Dray, David Siegel, and Kate Gomoll.) Shadowing an experienced user research professional is another option, but it is more difficult to do, since the primary investigator will want to reduce the number of observers to an absolute minimum.

Even if the people available to collect data are all trained user research professionals, you want to ensure that everyone is on the same page—so a planning and/or training session is essential. Begin by identifying roles and setting expectations. If you need the other investigator to help you prep (e.g., copy consent forms, QA equipment), make sure he or she understands the importance of that task. You do not want to get on-site only to find that you do not have the consent forms because of miscommunication or because the other investigator was annoyed at being your "assistant." Also, make sure that everyone is familiar with the protocol that you will be using (see Chapter 6, "Creating a Protocol" section, page 153).

If you will be observing participants use your products in the field, make it clear to all investigators that they are not there to "help" the participant. It is human nature to want to help someone who is having difficulty, but all the investigators need to remember that they will not be there to help the user later on. One humorous user experience professional we know keeps a roll of duct tape with him and shows it to his coinvestigators prior to the visit. He informs them that he will not hesitate to use it should they offer inappropriate help or comments during the visit. It gets a laugh and helps colleagues remember the point.

If this will be an ongoing field study (rather than a one-time visit), you may want inexperienced investigators to read this chapter, attend workshops, practice during mock sessions, or watch videos of previously conducted field studies. Develop standardized materials (see "Activity Materials" section, page 407) and review them with all investigators. Additionally, everyone should know how to use each piece of equipment and how to troubleshoot problems with the equipment. Practice setting up and packing up equipment quickly. Labeling cords for easy identification will make setting up much faster. Finally, identify a standard notetaking method and shorthand for easy decoding.

Develop Your Protocol

By now, you have selected the type of field study you will conduct. Now, you need to identify your plan of attack or protocol. This is different from your observation guide (a list of concerns or general areas to observe). A **protocol** can include how you will interact with users (the observation guide is part of that), how much time you plan to spend observing each user/area, and what instructions you will give users (e.g., think-aloud protocol) if you are interacting with them. You should also identify any activities that you want other investigators to participate in. The answers to these and many other questions need to be spelled out in a protocol (see Chapter 6, "Creating a Protocol" section, page 153). Without a protocol, you do not have a script for everyone to follow, and each investigator will do his or her own thing. Even if you are doing the study alone, you risk standardization in your data collection because you may end up conducting each visit differently, forgetting some questions, haphazardly adding in others. A protocol allows you to collect the data in the most efficient and reliable manner possible. It also allows you to concentrate on the data collection, not trying to remember what you forgot this time.

Schedule the Visits

After you have selected your investigators, get commitment from each one and include them in scheduling discussions. They must agree to be present at the visits they are scheduled for, and they must be willing to receive training. If they do not have time for either of these, it is best to find someone else.

Below are some things to consider when scheduling your visits. The questions below may seem obvious, but when you are in the middle of creating the schedule, many obvious details are forgotten.

- Where is the site? How long will it take to get there? If there will be a significant drive and traffic will likely be a problem, you do not want to schedule early morning appointments.
- Have you checked to see if your contact or the user's manager should be called or scheduled as part of the visit?
- Do you plan to visit more than one site per day? How far apart are they? Will there be traffic? What if you are running behind schedule at the other site? If you must visit more than one location per day, put in plenty of pad time between sites.
- Include breaks between users or sites in your schedule. This will allow you to review your notes, rest, eat a snack, check your messages, etc. You do not want a growling stomach to interrupt your quiet observations.
- Make sure you are refreshed for each visit. If you are not a morning person, do not schedule early morning appointments. Or if your energy tends to run out at the end of the day, schedule interviews early in the day and catch up on e-mail in the afternoon. You do not want the user to see you yawning during the interview.
- Consider the user's schedule:
  - Lunchtime may either be good or bad for users. Find out what they prefer and what their workload might be during that time (see next point).
  - Some users want you there when work is slow so you will not disturb them. You want to be there when things are busy! Make sure that the time the user suggests for your visit will allow you to observe what you are interested in.
  - Consider the cyclical nature of work. Some tasks are done only during certain times of the year. If you are interested in observing the harvest, for example, there is a limited window in which you can observe.
  - Some days of the week are worse than others (e.g., Monday and Friday). As a general rule, avoid Monday mornings and Friday afternoons. Also, find out if there are standard "telecommuting" days at your user's site.
  - Be prepared to compromise. Your users have lives to live and your study is likely low on their priority list. You may have to change your original plan or schedule, but stay open-minded and thankful that some data are better than none.
- Do not forget the other investigators. Ask them for their availability. Find out whether they are morning or evening people. It is not any less offensive for the notetaker to be yawning during an interview.
- Find out how to make copies or print files if you do not want to ship paperwork. Can you use the user's facilities, or will you have to find a local copy shop?
- Finally, consider the haphazard schedule of some occupations (e.g., surgeons, flight crew). They may agree to participate but be pulled away to activities you cannot observe. Be prepared to wait long periods of time. Bring other work with you to do and/or have a list of things to observe that do not require interacting with participants. Also, be prepared to take advantage of sudden opportunities.

TIP

Get detailed directions to each site and verify them with the participant. Do not simply trust the directions on your cell phone map app or GPS. Some of our researcher colleagues found while doing field studies in Tokyo that their map programs had each recommended different directions to a participant's home. Unfortunately, none of the directions were correct, and they became completely lost. They resorted to calling the participants to ask for directions. It is a good idea to ask the participants to warn you about typical traffic or public transport conditions, tell you about the best routes or shortcuts, and warn you of any detours, etc.

The final thing to keep in mind when scheduling is *burnout*. Burnout is a risk for extended studies. Field studies are intense activities where you must be "on" at all times. It is time- and energy-consuming to conduct each visit and analyze the data. You can also suffer from information overload. All of the sites or users tend to blur together after a while. And travel can be stressful. Take the "fatigue factor" into consideration when scheduling the visits and determining the timeline for analyzing data. Unfortunately, you may be placed in the situation where you must visit six sites in three days and there is no way around it. Alternating the roles of notetaker and interviewer between yourself and your colleague can give you a break and help build more novice team member's skills. At least, you will not have to be "on" for every participant (e.g., encouraging participants to think aloud, following up on questions, and apprenticing). You will still be exhausted, but you will get a small "break" every other participant.

TIP

Find out the appropriate dress code. You cannot assume that most places have the same dress code as a Silicon Valley start-up. If a workplace is quite conservative, you will look out of place in your khakis, and people may not take you seriously. On the other hand, if it is an extremely casual environment, people may be afraid to approach you or talk to you if you are dressed in a suit and tie. If in doubt, dress a little nicer than you think is necessary—but wear comfortable shoes. And check with your teammates to make sure you are on the same dress code page.

Activity Materials

You may have many materials to take to each site; it depends on the type of study you are conducting and what is permitted on-site. Below is a list of suggested materials for most types of studies, but you should tailor this for your own study and include more detail in your own checklist. This is the best way to stay organized and keep your study running smoothly from one site to the next. Without your checklist, you will likely forget at least one thing each time.

Checklist of All Materials and Equipment Needed

- Contact information for each participant
- Directions and map to site
- Consent forms and confidentiality agreements
- Protocol

- Observation guide
- Visit summary template
- Schedule
- Method of notetaking (audio recorder and/or paper and pencil)
- Peripherals (e.g., batteries, SD cards, extension cords, power strip)
- Method for collecting artifacts (e.g., accordion folder, notebook, hole puncher)
- Method for carrying all the equipment (e.g., small suitcase, luggage cart)
- Thank-you gift for participant(s)
- Business cards for participants to contact you later with questions or additional information
- Video recorder or camera and audio recorder (if permission has been obtained to record)

TIPS

- Conduct a check of your equipment prior to every visit. Are the batteries still good? Did you bring all the cords back from your last visit? Is everything behaving as it should? Practice to make sure you know how everything works and needs to be set up. Do not wait until you are in the user's cubicle to find out the battery to the video recorder is dead or you did not bring the right power cord.
- Label all cords and make sure they are correct. Many black cords tend to look alike but are not interchangeable.
- Use your checklist!

We recommend providing an incentive for participants (see Chapter 6, "Determining Participant Incentives" section, page 127). We also recommend getting a small token gift for anyone who helped arrange your access to the site or users (e.g., account/product manager). This individual may have spent significant time finding people in the company to match your user profile or helping you to arrange your visit. It never hurts to show your appreciation, and it can also help if you ever need to access that site again. When selecting the gift, keep in mind that you

TIP

If you are flying from one site to another and you have the time between sites, shipping materials to your hotel can save your back and your sanity. You do not want to lug 30 pounds of recording equipment onto a plane, only to find that there is no overhead bin space left. Watching luggage handlers throw your expensive equipment onto the plane with the rest of the check-in baggage can ruin your entire flight (and visit!). When you ship equipment, you can purchase additional insurance for a small fee. If any damage is done to your equipment, you will be reimbursed with less hassle than most airlines will give you. Make sure you have a tracking number so you can track the progress of your shipment. After 15 years, our shipments have never been lost, damaged, or late. Yes, it costs more, but it is worth it!

must carry it along with the rest of your equipment. You do not want to carry around several shirts in each size or heavy, breakable coffee mugs. Instead, opt for a light, small, one-size-fits-all gift such as a USB drive with your company logo.

As we mentioned earlier, it is important to develop an observation guide (see Figure 13.2). This will help ensure you address each of the goals of your study. Next, use your observation guide to develop a **visit summary template** (see Figure 13.7). This is a standardized survey or worksheet given to each investigator to complete at the end of each visit. This helps everyone get his or her thoughts on paper while they are fresh. It also speeds data analysis and avoids reporting *only* odd or funny anecdotal data. Stakeholders who are eager for immediate results can read the summary worksheets and know what the key points are from each visit. They will appreciate being kept in the loop and will be less likely to insist on being present at each site if they feel you are promptly providing the information.

Mobile Travel App Study

Location: ______________________________
Participant ID: __________________________
Date: _________________________________
Investigator: ____________________________

Area I observed: __Curb-side check-in__ Ticket counter__ Baggage claim__Gate

Key observations:____
____
____
____

Participant job title: ___________________________
Years of experience: ___________________________

Summary of main points from interview with participant: ______________
____
____
____
____
____

Artifacts collected:__Audio tape of interview__Digital photos__Video recording
__Screenshots __Notes/documents from user

List any documents/notes/artifacts you collected from the user:
____
____
____
____
____

Recommendations for next visit/lessons learned:
____
____
____
____
____

Figure 13.7: Sample visit summary template.

TIP

Do you really need all that stuff? If you are traveling to six different cities in five days, you cannot possibly ship everything from one site to another. You want to be well-equipped, but you should also pack light. Buying gifts or incentives once you get on-site can lighten the load. Saving forms to the cloud or e-mailing yourself a copy and then printing them at a local copy shop or business center or creating digital versions will further relieve your burden. If you cannot pack it all in a bag and comfortably carry it around the office with you for 10 minutes, how will you ever lug it from site to site?

Although this can be the most thought-provoking information and can bring your users to life for stakeholders, it should not be the *only* data you report. The template should be flexible enough so that you can record data that you had not anticipated and avoid losing important insights. You may also further develop the template as you conduct more visits. Just make sure that everyone who views the summaries understands that he or she is viewing summary data from *one* data point. He or she should not begin building the product or making changes to his or her existing product based on his or her interpretations of that data.

TIP

If you are traveling internationally, find out about customs and/or customary restrictions that may apply to materials you bring in luggage or ship over. Some items may be seized in customs or taxed heavily, while others may simply cause you to encounter situations that you may not be used to. For example, a colleague was traveling in India recently and was asked for a bribe to get his video camera from officials. At some point, the bribe requested was larger than the cost of the equipment, so the colleague decided to buy a video camera locally rather than pay the bribe. Unfortunately, the tapes did not work on US equipment so another fee was required to convert the video to a usable format. In another case, when Kelly was traveling in Rwanda to conduct research, she had a large bag of equipment that had to travel with her on local public transportation. When she brought the bag on the public van, the driver made her pay for an additional seat because the bag took up as much space as a person would. The key to these situations is to realize that unexpected things will come up in the field and to be prepared and flexible, so you can enjoy these differences and learn from each experience.

Create any incident diaries, surveys, prototypes, or interview worksheets you may need during your study. You can also send any previsit activity materials before your visit to help you develop your observation guide (e.g., mailing out a survey in advance). Incident diaries are another valuable tool to send out prior to your visit. The surveys and diaries will be extremely useful if you know you will have limited time with each participant.

TIP

Identify back-up activities. In the event there is nothing to observe (e.g., no customer calls, no emergencies in the emergency room), you will want to do a different activity, such as an impromptu interview. If you are caught on the spot without an interview script, use the list of questions in "Deep Hanging Out" or do an artifact walk-through. Do not waste the precious time you have with users by waiting for a notable event.

- Create a proposal that establishes the objectives of the study, identifies the user and site profile, the timeline, the resources needed and from whom, and the benefits of the study.
- Get a mix of sites and users.
- Start small when recruiting, and use the success of those studies to expand.
- Gain the support of stakeholders before accessing a customer site.
- Seek the help of at least one other investigator to speed data collection, and get an additional perspective.
- Include stakeholders in identifying sites, users, and contacts, as well as data collection so they, too, have a stake in success of the study and feel part of the process.
- If you are lacking in domain knowledge, bring along a member of the product team to ask follow-up questions or a "translator" to provide a running commentary.
- Train all investigators to collect data in a standardized method, including how to operate all equipment.
- Develop standardized materials for all investigators, so the data are collected similarly across teams, users, and sites.
- Develop a detailed protocol, including an observation guide.
- Identify back-up activities in case there is nothing to observe.
- Conduct a pilot session to pilot your protocol and timeline, and use that data to practice analysis.
- Consider factors like traffic, distance to site, personal breaks, the "fatigue factor," the user's schedule, holidays, and other investigators' schedules when scheduling your visits.
- Create a checklist of the required materials and check everything off prior to each site visit.
- Use digital cameras and video recorders whenever possible.
- Do a QA check of all equipment prior to departing, and have everyone practice setting up the equipment.
- Develop a visit summary template for each investigator to complete, and send these out for stakeholders to keep apprised of the progress of your study.
- Take extra forms, batteries, tapes, and other materials in case any are lost or damaged.
- Save your materials on your laptop, a pin drive, and/or to cloud storage to make additional copies of paperwork on-site as necessary.

Figure 13.8: Recommendations for preparing for a field study.

Summary

We have provided a lot of information to help you prepare for your field study. Figure 13.8 summarizes the main points. Use this checklist when preparing for your study.

Conducting a Field Study

The specific procedure for your field study will vary depending on the type of study you conduct. We can offer some high-level tasks to conduct, regardless of the type of study. Just remember to remain flexible.

At a Glance

> Get organized
> Meet the participant
> Begin data collection
> Wrap-up
> Organize your data
> Summary

Get Organized

If the visit has been arranged (i.e., this is not a public location where you can observe users unnoticed), upon arrival, meet with your site contact. Familiarize yourself with the environment. Where is the bathroom, kitchen, copier, etc.? Where can you get food (if that has not been planned for you already)? If your site contact will not be with you throughout the visit, how will you get to your next appointment, and so forth? If there are multiple investigation teams, decide where and when you will meet up again. Arrive at least 15 minutes before your first scheduled appointment to take care of these details. Be prepared for some extra handshaking and time at this point. You may need to say "hello" to the contact's or user's boss. This is another good reason for being early.

Meet the Participant

Again, if your visit is arranged, go to your first scheduled appointment on time. Introduce yourself and any other investigators or observers with you. All participants should be aware of their rights, so ask them to sign a **consent form** at the beginning. Do not forget to make copies of those forms for the user, if he or she wants them (refer to Consent Forms, page 66, for more information).

Explain what you will be doing and your time frame. Also, state clearly that the participant is the expert, not you. Remind the participant that he or she is not being evaluated in any way. While you are going over the forms and explaining these points, the other investigator should be setting up the equipment. If you must invade a colleague's space, ask for permission and treat that person with the same respect you are showing your participant. This may sound obvious, but it is easy to overlook common courtesies when you are wrestling with equipment and trying to remember a million different things. This is when your protocol will come in handy.

TIP

When possible, it is always best to have all legal forms signed by you and/or the participants beforehand. This saves time and avoids that terrible situation of finding out the participant cannot sign your forms *after* you arrive.

Next, get a feel for the user's environment (e.g., take pictures, draw maps, record sticky notes, note lighting, equipment, background sounds, layout, software used). While the notetaker is doing this, the interviewer should begin developing a rapport with the user. Give the participant time to vent any frustrations about your product or his or her job in general. If the user has product-specific questions or enhancement requests, state that you can record these questions and take them back to the product team, but do not attempt to answer them yourself. Participants will be curious about you and the purpose of the study. They may also ask for help. State that you cannot give advice or recommendations and that you are there simply to observe. At the end of the session, you may choose to provide the user with help, both to repay the user and to learn more about why the user needed help in the first place. Throughout, be polite and show enthusiasm. Your enthusiasm will rub off on others and make the participant feel more comfortable.

If you plan to set up recording equipment and leave for a few hours, you should still review the consent form with the participant and have a discussion to make sure the participant is comfortable with being recorded. You may think that it is not necessary to establish rapport with the user; but if you want the participant to behave naturally, he or she needs to understand the purpose of your study and have the opportunity to ask questions. Enthusiasm is important, even if you will only be there for 10 minutes.

Begin Data Collection

Now, it is time to begin your selected data collection technique. Use an appropriate notetaking method. If you do not want people to notice you, select an inconspicuous method (e.g., a small notepad). If it is not necessary to de-emphasize your actions, a laptop and digital voice recorder may be better.

Suggested Resources for Additional Reading

Biobserve (www.biobserve.com) offers a number of tools for observing users and noting their actions. Although we have not used them ourselves, *Spectator* (software that records a large variety of events like movements and behaviors via user-definable keyboard shortcuts and records to .mpg or .avi files) and *Spectator Go*! (a mobile version of *Spectator*) appear to offer a lot of potential for recording observational data.

Know the Difference Between Observations and Inferences

It is very important to know the difference between capturing observations and making inferences. Observations are objective recordings based on what you have seen or heard, whereas inferences are conclusions based upon reasoning. For example, an observation may be that a flight attendant interacting with clients is always smiling and is very cheery and pleasant. This is good information to record, but do not infer from that observation that the flight attendant loves his job—he may feel extremely overworked but has learned to hide it with a smile. Unless you verify your interpretations with the participant, do not record your assumptions as facts.

TIP

Give the participant privacy as needed (e.g., personal phone calls, bathroom breaks). Tell the person up front that he or she can let you know when privacy is needed and that you will gladly respect that request. For example, if you are noting events, you might tell the user that any personal calls that he or she receives will be noted as just "a personal call," with no further details.

Wrap-Up

Once you have completed your selected data collection technique or when your time with the participant is up, wrap up the session. Make sure you leave time at the end to provide any help that you promised earlier and to answer additional questions the participant may have. While the interviewer thanks the participant and answers questions, the notetaker should be packing up all materials and equipment. You may wish to leave behind follow-up surveys or incident diaries. This is also a good time to schedule follow-up visits. You will often find during data analysis that you have unanswered questions that require a second visit.

TIP

When you return to your office, always send a simple thank you note to all participants. It just reminds them that the time they took away from their day is still appreciated. If you ever need to follow up with those same users, they will be more likely to welcome you, since they know you really appreciated their effort.

Organize Your Data

After the session, you will find it useful to compare notes, thoughts, and insights with your fellow investigators. Now is the time to get everything on paper or record the discussion on a digital voice recorder. You can complete the visit summary template individually or together. You may be tired after the session and just want to move on to the next appointment or wrap up for the day, but be sure to leave time to debrief with your team and document your observations right now. Doing this now will allow you to provide quick interim reports, and it will make data analysis much easier.

Now is also the time to label all data (e.g., digital recordings, surveys, artifacts) with a participant ID (but not his or her name, for confidentiality reasons), date, time, and investigation team. If you are keeping paper copies, you may want to have a large manila envelope to keep each participant's materials separate. It is a terrible feeling to get back to the office and not know which user provided a set of artifacts or who completed a certain survey.

When you return to the office, scan in artifacts, notes, and photos. In addition to sending out the visit summary report, you can include electronic files or physical copies of the artifacts to stakeholders without worrying about losing the originals. However, this is time-consuming if you have lots of artifacts. (We collected nearly 200 documents from one hospital during our healthcare field study!)

- Bring your own snacks and drinks.
- Audio record at a minimum.
- Maintain a low profile.
- Choose an appropriate notetaking method.
- Think "big picture" and obtain a holistic understanding of the environment, users, and tasks.
- Pay attention to signs and notes. Collect multiple types of data for a richer data set.
- Meet with your site contact upon arrival on-site.
- Familiarize yourself with the environment (e.g., bathrooms, kitchen, copier).
- If there are multiple investigation teams, decide where and when you will meet up again.
- Develop a rapport with the participant before delving into observation or interviews.
- Treat the participant's colleagues with the same respect you show the participant.
- If the participant asks for help, wait until the end of the study to provide it to avoid biasing your study.
- Show your enthusiasm and interest in the participant's work.
- Know the difference between capturing observations and inferences.
- Give the participant privacy when needed.
- Leave time at the end for the participant to ask questions and for you to wrap up (e.g., distribute incentives, pack up equipment).
- Send a thank-you note following the study.
- Take time to organize your data immediately after each visit.
- Scan in artifacts to share electronically with all stakeholders.

Figure 13.9: Recommendations for conducting a field study.

Summary

We have given a lot of recommendations about how to conduct a successful field study. For easy referral, they are summarized in Figure 13.9.

Data Analysis and Interpretation

At this point, you have a stack of visit summary worksheets and other notes and artifacts from your visits to wade through. The task of making sense out of all the data can seem daunting. Below, we present several different ways of analyzing the data. There is no one right way—you have to select the method that best supports your data and the goals of your study. The goal of any of these data analysis techniques is to compile your data and extract key findings. You do this by organizing and categorizing your data across participants. Before you begin your analysis, there are few key points to keep in mind:

- *It is all good data.* Some points may not seem to make sense or it may be difficult to bring it all together, but the more time you spend with the data, the more insight you will gain from it. In other words, your first impression will not be your last.
- *Be flexible.* If you planned to analyze your data with a qualitative data analysis tool but it is not working for you, consider an affinity diagram or a quantitative summary.

- *Do not present raw data.* It can be quite challenging to take the detailed data from each visit and turn them into actionable recommendations for the product team. However, neither designers nor product developers want the plethora of raw data you collected. You need to compile the information, determine what is really important, and highlight it for your audience.
- *Prioritize.* You will likely end up with a lot of data and may not have the time or resources to analyze them all at first. Analyze the data, first based on the goals of your study, and then, you can go back and search for other insights and ideas.
- *Frequency does not necessarily mean importance.* Just because a user does a task frequently, that does not necessarily mean it is critical to the user. Keep the context and goals of the user's actions in mind during analysis.

Recommendations for Conducting Family/Home Visits

It is just as important to begin on a professional foot when attempting to access users in their home environment as it is when accessing them at work. Stress that you are not attempting to sell them anything, and provide your contact information so they can call you back with additional questions or to verify your legitimacy. Also, provide information about all of the logistics up front, so they can make an educated decision.

When doing home visits, it is best to ask when the individual or family eats meals. You should either avoid those times or offer to bring food for everyone. The latter can provide an opportunity to socialize with your users and develop a rapport (just make sure that you approve the menu with everyone). Feel free to discuss the study and allow the participants to ask questions (if this will not bias the study). This is a time to develop rapport, not interview the participants. Since you are not collecting data at this time, do not tape discussions over dinner—you will kill the laid-back atmosphere.

The initial few minutes are critical to developing rapport and trust with your user(s). Start with introductions and state the purpose of your visit, even if this was stated during recruiting. It helps to find something in common to relate to (e.g., pets, kids' ages, collectables in the house, etc.). Review the consent form and confidentiality agreements (if necessary). Finally, ask permission to record the session and make it clear to the participants that they may ask to have the audio/video recorders turned off at any time. If they are embarrassed by the mess in the living room and do not want it photographed, respect their wishes. If the mess in the living room is important to your study, explain why a photograph of it would be valuable to your study. If they still object, do not pursue it further. You will only break down any trust you may have developed up to that point.

If your study involves the entire family, begin by interviewing or observing the children. Use their enthusiasm and curiosity to bring out more reserved parents. Parents will respect your attention to their children. Create an additional activity for the children to participate in while you speak with the parents (e.g., draw a picture of an airplane from the future). Since most kids love being the center of attention, you could have difficulty ending your interaction with the children and then collecting data from the parents. The additional activity will keep them occupied and prevent them from feeling left out for the rest of your visit.

Finally, if you plan to follow up with the family, it is particularly helpful to send a thank-you note. It is a nice idea to take a family photo at the end of each visit and send a copy to the family along with the card.

At a Glance

> Select your analysis method
> Affinity diagram
> Analyzing deep hanging out data
> Analyzing contextual inquiry/design data
> Qualitative analysis tools

Select Your Analysis Method

The method you select to structure or organize data should depend on the goals of your study and how you collected the data. Regardless of the data collection technique used (e.g., contextual inquiry), the data you collect in a field study are similar to the data you collect using other user research methods. Therefore, you can use many of the analysis techniques presented in other chapters (e.g., affinity diagram, coding qualitative data). Pick the analysis method that best fits your data or the goals of your study. We provide a brief overview of some of the most common analysis methods here.

Affinity Diagram

An affinity diagram is one of the most frequently-used methods for analyzing qualitative data. Similar findings or concepts are grouped together to identify themes or trends in the data and let you see relationships. A full discussion of affinity diagrams is presented on page 363 in Chapter 12.

Analyzing Deep Hanging Out Data

It is best to begin by going around the room and asking each person to provide a one-sentence summary for each focus area (refer back to Table 13.2 on page 390). Ask the following questions when analyzing the data:

- What were the biggest/most important findings?
- What were the immediate impressions?
- What sticks out or really grabs you?
- Are there themes/patterns/coherence?
- What's the *story?* What is the key takeaway?
- What surprised you and what didn't?
- What is the disruptive or challenging information?
- If you could go back again, what else would you do or what would you do differently?
- What do you wish you paid more attention to?

- If more than one person studied a focus area or observed a single user, what are the similarities and differences found?
- What's considered *normal* in this context? (And therefore, what kinds of patterns or behaviors would be considered aberrations?)

Upon answering these questions, you can begin organizing the data.

Analyzing Contextual Inquiry/Design Data

If you have conducted a contextual inquiry to prepare for another user research activity (e.g., identify questions for a survey) to better understand the domain or as an innovation exercise, you can choose the most appropriate data analysis technique for the type of data you have. If, however, you conducted a contextual inquiry to inform your design decisions, you are ready to move into contextual design. Contextual design is complex and beyond the scope of this book. We recommend referring to Beyer and Holtzblatt (1998) for information on contextual design.

Grounded Theory

Grounded theory is not only a form of analysis, but an approach to inquiry. The goal is to derive an abstract theory about an interaction that is grounded in the views of users (participants). In this method, researchers engage in constant comparison including coding, memoing and theorizing as data are collected, rather than waiting to examine data once it is all collected. The emphasis is on the emergence of categories and theories based in the data, rather than using a theory to derive a hypothesis which is then tested as in positivist inquiry. A complete discussion of grounded theory is outside of the scope of this book. We recommend referring to Creswell (2003) and Strauss and Corbin (1990) for more information.

Qualitative Analysis Tools

There are times when you need an analysis method that is more systematic and reproducible than an affinity diagram, the results of which may differ depending on who participates, instructions given, etc. In cases where you need this kind of rigor, we recommend employing qualitative analysis tools and checking the reliability of your coding using a measure of interrater reliability such as Cohen's kappa (see Chapter 9 "How to Calculate Interrater Reliability," page 254). There are a variety of tools available such as nVivo and maxQDA that you can use to code qualitative data. Refer to Chapter 8 on page 194 for a description of each tool and the pros and cons of using such tools.

Communicating the Findings

Because the data collected during field studies are so rich, there is a wide variety of ways to present the data. For example, data may be used immediately for persona development, to develop an information architecture, or to develop requirements for the project. Leveraging several of these techniques below will help bring stakeholders closer to the data and get them excited about your study. There is no right or wrong answer; it all depends on the goals of your study and the method you feel best represents your data. In the end, a good report illuminates all the relevant data, provides a coherent story, and tells the stakeholders what to do next. One way to present data is in a timeline (see Figure 13.10). Below, we offer some

Location	Time	Event
Curbside	2:15	Dropped off by airport shuttle
Airport lobby	2:19	Set bags down to find phone
Airport lobby	2:20	Open mobile app to check in
Airport lobby	2:21	Abandon mobile app for check-in
Self-check-in kiosk	2:25	Use self-check-in kiosk to check in
Baggage check	2:35	Present documents and bags to agent
Security line	2:50	Wait in line for security screening
Gate	3:15	Wait at gate for flight

Task 1: Getting to the gate

The majority of an air travelers' activities take place while they are getting to the gate where their plane will depart. While traveling to San Juan, Elisa abandoned the mobile app provided by her airline to check in for her flight because she was unable to locate her reservation.

Although she has used the app before and has successfully checked in, Elisa abandons the check-in process on her phone and uses the self-check-in kiosk provided by her airline.

Elisa at the airport

Elisa had hoped to get to her gate early so she could stand by for an earlier flight, but since she took extra time to check in at the kiosk, she missed the earlier flight and now must wait for the later flight. She does not open the mobile app during the rest of her travel experience. She has a great time in San Juan anyway.

Figure 13.10: Sample slide presenting the timeline and description of specific events observed of a traveler at the airport.

additional presentation techniques that work especially well for field study data. For a discussion of standard presentation techniques for any requirements method, refer to Chapter 15 on page 450.

Two frequently-used methods for presenting or organizing your data are the artifact notebook and **storyboards.**

- *Artifact notebook.* Rather than storing away the artifacts you collected in some file cabinet where people will not see them, create an artifact notebook. Insert each artifact collected, along with the information about how the artifact is used, the purpose, and the implications for design. Keep this notebook in an easily accessible location. You can create several of these and include them as educational material for the product development team.
- *Storyboards.* You can illustrate a particular task or a "day-in-life" of the user through **storyboards** (using representative images to illustrate a task/scenario/story). Merge data across your users to develop a generic, representative description. The visual aspect will draw stakeholders in and demonstrate your point much faster.

Hackos and Redish (1998) provided a table summarizing some additional methods for organizing or presenting data from a field study. A modified version is reproduced here as Table 13.3.

Table 13.3: Methods for presenting/organizing data (Hackos & Redish, 1998)

Analysis method	Brief description
Lists of users	Examine the types and range of users identified during your study, including estimates of their percentages in the total user population and a brief description of each
Lists of environments	Examine the types and range of environments identified during your study, including a brief description of each
Task hierarchies	Tasks are arranged in a hierarchy to show their interrelationships, especially for tasks that are not performed in a particular sequence
User/task matrix	Matrix to illustrate the relationship between each user type identified and the tasks he or she performs
Procedural analysis	Step-by-step description examining a task, including the objects, actions, and decisions
Task flowcharts	Drawings of the specifics of a task, including objects, actions, and decisions
Insight sheets	List of issues identified during the field study and insights about them that may affect design decisions
Artifact analysis	Functional descriptions of the artifacts collected, their use, and implications/ideas for design

Lessons Learned

In the course of conducting field studies over the years, we have learned some painful lessons. We describe a couple lessons here, in hopes you can avoid such situations.

Surprise Guests

Several years ago, Kathy and another colleague went on-site to several customers in the Atlanta area. It took almost three months to arrange the visits. The product team was invited to participate in the field study from the very beginning, but declined. We later learned that they were conducting their own "site visits" with customers along the east coast during the same time as our field study in Atlanta.

We were fortunate that our company's account manager for the Atlanta customers was open to our study, but it was clear that she was a bit nervous about our presence. She was relieved to hear that only two people would be conducting the visits. Upon arriving at our first site, the account manager came up to us and fumed, "I thought you said there were only two of you!"

We were stunned and did not understand what she was talking about. She replied that four other members of "our team" had already arrived and were waiting. When we walked around the corner, four product managers greeted us. Needless to say, we were astonished. They decided that, since they were so close, they might as well fly down and join us. Because we had sent the product team copies of all documents (including our agenda), they knew exactly where to go and who to contact. Unfortunately, they felt no need to inform us of their change in plans.

Since we did not expect the additional guests, we had not conducted any training sessions or even discussed the appropriate protocol. Our intended activity was a focus group with eight database administrators. We knew we could not delve into each question deeply, but we wanted to get an overall impression. We could then use the following individual interviews to learn more about the important issues that arose from the focus group. Unfortunately, the product managers were not on the same page. They drilled down into each question in such painful detail that a couple of users actually walked out of the session. We then decided to split up for the individual interviews. We suggested that the product managers interview one user while we interviewed another. It allowed the product managers to be involved, but they were not able to influence the data we were collecting during our interviews. The data the product managers collected were not incorporated into our data analysis because the questions they asked were quite different, being feature-oriented.

Considering our close relationship to the team before this activity, it was all the more shocking that they did not understand the inappropriateness of their behavior. The lesson learned here is that you should be prepared for anything! Have a back-up plan, and be ready to improvise. In this case, we split up so that the team could interview some participants while we interviewed others. We got the data we needed without alienating the product team, although our credibility with the account manager was a bit scuffed at the end.

Missing Users

At another location in Atlanta, we had difficulty finding our participants. The supervisor who had arranged for his employees to speak with us had an emergency at home and had to leave early. Unfortunately, no one knew which of his employees he wanted us to speak with. We walked around the floor, asking people whether they had been asked to participate in our study. We found only one participant. We now know to insist on getting the names and contact information for all participants, even if there is one point of contact that will take you to each participant.

Pulling It All Together

In this chapter, we have discussed the best uses for field studies and things to keep in mind when proposing them. We have presented a plethora of techniques for collecting, analyzing, and presenting the data. Considering the complexity of field studies, tips and recommendations have been provided throughout. Finally, painful lessons learned illuminate common mistakes we are all capable of making.

Suggested Resources for Additional Reading

The first book has a detailed discussion of how to convince your product team why a field study is of tremendous value and how to prepare for, conduct, and analyze data from field studies. It includes success stories and challenges throughout:

- Hackos, J. T. & Redish, J. C. (1998). *User and task analysis for interface design.* New York: John Wiley & Sons.

This second book provides 14 detailed case studies to demonstrate how practitioners adapted field methods to meet their needs:

- Wixon, D. R. & Ramey, J. (eds) (1996). *Field methods casebook for software design.* New York: John Wiley & Sons.

These books provide an anthropological/ethnographic perspective on field studies:

- Sunderland, P.L. (2010). *Doing znthropology in consumer research.* Left Coast Press.
- LeCompte, M.D. & Schensul, J.J. (2012). *Analysis and interpretation of ethnographic data: A mixed methods approach, 2nd Edition.* AltaMira Press.

This book is a nice "how-to" for ethnographic research:

- Emerson, R. M., Fretz, R. I., & Shaw, L. L. (2011) *Writing ethnographic fieldnotes.* University of Chicago Press.

CASE STUDY: *INTO THE WILD: UNCOVERING HOLISTIC MOBILE INSIGHTS*

Pamela Walshe, People & Client Experience, AnswerLab
John Cheng, UX Research Principal, AnswerLab

A large national bank engaged AnswerLab to help them understand their customers' mobile banking experiences across platforms. A wide range of stakeholders and business units were involved in this effort because the bank wanted to gather insights on the mobile website, the banking app, and text banking. We not only executed the research but also focused on creating buy-in and ownership of the findings by including key stakeholders as observers in the field. This helped to ensure the insights would be evangelized internally and would have a meaningful impact on product decisions and mobile strategy well into the future.

Research Objectives and Methodology

We collaborated with our client to identify four key objectives for our study:

1. Deepen understanding of overall mobile usage/behaviors in a broad range of contexts.
2. Observe and profile different types of mobile banking users.
3. Identify unmet customer banking needs.
4. Identify opportunities to improve existing offerings.

Conducting only in-home interviews would provide a limited view of what users were actually doing on their mobile devices. If the purpose of a field study is to observe and understand users in their natural environments and contexts, it would be impossible to understand mobile usage environments and contexts in a single interview. By definition, the mobile context is dynamic and constantly changing. AnswerLab recommended a solution that would incorporate more longitudinal, holistic feedback to obtain a more complete picture of customers' experiences and how their environments and lives impacted their mobile usage.

How AnswerLab Met the Research Objectives

Study Design. AnswerLab designed a two-part study to develop a clear picture of the holistic mobile customer experience.

Phase I: Diary study. To develop a baseline of not only understanding about the common tasks and routines for mobile customers—including banking—but also generally understanding mobile activities overall, we conducted a four-week diary phase that captured longitudinal data across a 30-day financial cycle (depositing paychecks, paying bills, etc.). We asked participants to record all of their financial-related behaviors across offline, online, and mobile channels.

Phase II: In-home interviews. To understand preferences between mobile devices and traditional desktop computers, we conducted in-home interviews with participants in two markets (San Francisco, CA, and Charlotte, NC). We used the diaries as a launching point for the interviews and asked participants to walk us through their past experiences, highlighting any pain points or examples of great experience along the way. We also probed on the banking experience across platforms and discussed when one might choose one platform over another.

Research subjects. We recruited 30 participants across two markets (San Francisco, CA, and Charlotte, NC), with a goal of interviewing a total of 20 customers who completed the four-week diary phase. Note that we purposefully designed the study to begin with a larger pool of diary contributors in order to allow for natural attrition and careful selection of in-home interview participants. Because the client had such a diverse customer base across a range of socioeconomic segments and a wide range of technical savviness, we included participants across a range of major mobile devices, including feature phones. We also ensured that all customers were active across a range of tasks in both online banking and mobile banking. While 20 final participants may initially appear to be a small number to work from considering such a wide customer base, we felt that it was sufficient for our research goals because we were still able to capture a wide variety of mobile use cases that served as a crucial starting point for understanding mobile behavior overall. In traditional qualitative usability testing, anywhere from four to eight users are recruited from a given segment in order to capture user issues, attitudes, and behaviors that may project to a broader user base.

Data collection and analysis. In-home interviews provide a great opportunity to capture rich data and artifacts from the field, but they can create a challenge for the research team to collate and organize field notes, self-reported data, and artifacts, such as photos or collected documents. Pulling together this mixed format material in a cohesive way is critical in order to facilitate analysis. The AnswerLab team used Evernote for this purpose, which allowed us to create a notebook for each participant containing diary data, artifacts (photos, sketches), and notes taken in the field. Because the client sought to preliminarily identify mobile banking personas, we began clustering the participants around three variables: tech savviness, level of financial complexity, and level of experience with mobile banking. We chose these three dimensions because we learned through the research that they were the most influential in terms of impacting the desire, need, and ability to utilize mobile banking offerings. Within each of these groupings, we enumerated the most common tasks and routines and their related pain points and areas of opportunities. Additionally, we identified the barriers and motivators to enabling customers to be even more active in the mobile channel. With our data collection approach, AnswerLab was able to deliver a set of user profiles, a mobile framework outlining distinct "modes" that users operate within that directly influence their mobile behaviors, and some specific, tactical recommendations to improve existing mobile offerings.

Key learning/surprises. One of the primary benefits of ethnographic research is that its exploratory approach provides the best opportunity to discover surprises—whether they be experience gaps, pain points, or new understandings that challenge previously held beliefs. These surprises are where the "magic" happens in terms of uncovering opportunities. In the mobile banking study, here are a few of our biggest surprises.

- *A new definition of "convenience."* We witnessed the tipping point when mobile switched from being a channel of "emergency"—when a computer was not accessible—to being the preferred channel of convenience even when one was available.
  When we conducted the research in 2010, the client's mobile banking channel was still fairly new with a relatively small customer base actively using it. Prior to our research, the assumption had been that mobile banking was more of a secondary channel that served emergency and ad hoc requests when users were away from their computers. In reality, users were checking their balances and paying their bills while they were cooking in the kitchen, sitting on buses, watching TV, waking up in the morning, or even using the restroom. They wanted or expected to bank on their mobile devices at any time of day and any place, even if a computer was available. The net effect to customers' lives was that it enabled a level of control and good decision-making that had not been as accessible or easy for customers in the past. For example, being able to check one's balance while in a store prior to making a purchase enabled customers to ensure they were not at risk for overdrafting and incurring fees. What this meant for the bank was that there was far greater opportunity to develop robust banking functionality beyond the simple ATM locator and viewing of balances that had formed the basis for their first launch. Furthermore, the "convenience" driver seemed to trump early concerns about security. This meant that while it was still somewhat mysterious and a bit scary for some customers to do banking by phone, the convenience factor of being able to quickly make a transfer or pay a bill during a commute was worth it.

- *Financial complexity—not tech savviness—drives mobile adoption.* Another assumption we had prior to research was that tech-savvy customers would be the primary target for mobile banking adoption. Instead, we found that there was a stronger correlation between someone's financial complexity—the need to keep track of multiple accounts and transactions—and the desire to have the kind of ready access to banking that the mobile channel provided. This insight directly impacted who the bank identified as their target audience.
- *People use their devices in unexpected ways.* Watching how people used their mobile devices in their natural environments proved to be an eye-opener on many levels and enabled us to understand external factors that influenced overall behavior and perception about ease of use. For example, a customer had a habit of checking several websites first thing in the morning while walking his dog, including his bank balance. He noted that the sites he felt had the best user experience were those that enabled him to interact with the site with one hand (since he had a leash in the other). It underscored the importance of simplicity in designing menus and overall site architecture.

What Worked Well

Three critical factors led to the overall success of this study: (1) capturing the right data, (2) keeping participants engaged, and (3) building buy-in with stakeholders. Here are the ways AnswerLab successfully addressed these important factors:

Capture the right data by requiring prework: In-home interviews are much more effective when the participant has done at least some level of prep work in advance. This preinterview task can be as simple as a homework assignment, such as summarizing common daily or weekly tasks when a diary study is not possible. Prework enables the researcher to get to know the participant in advance, to prepare targeted questions, and to establish rapport in the beginning by discussing the homework together. It also helps establish a high-level understanding of the participant's experience so that the time spent in the actual interview can be focused on delving more deeply into the issues rather than starting from scratch. This results in an overall richer and more complete data set for analysis and is crucial to teasing out the nuances that influence people's behavior.

Keep participants engaged by anticipating fatigue and repetitive feedback, and conduct a brief midpoint interview to reinvigorate them: We knew going in that 30 days was a long time for someone to log banking and mobile activities on a daily basis. Furthermore, frustrations from routine banking activities were likely to get repetitive. To prevent these factors from impacting the quality of user feedback, we scheduled a brief midpoint interview with each participant two weeks into the diary phase. During this 30-minute call, the moderator would answer any questions from the participants, provide encouragement, and, if necessary, give them a "nudge" to break them out of repeating the same frustrations and behaviors for routine activities. For example, one participant frequently complained about having to repeatedly enter her login credentials on her mobile phone and desired a more convenient way to check her balance. During her midpoint interview, the moderator encouraged her to learn about text banking and to report on her experiences, thus avoiding two more weeks of mobile login complaints.

Build buy-in with stakeholders by bringing them into the field: Since this foundational research was intended to inform initiatives across the bank, facilitating stakeholder participation in the field work was critical to the overall success of the study and the ability of the organization to internalize and act on the findings. At AnswerLab, we require all stakeholders to attend a preparatory training session prior to going into the field with the research team. This ensures that the observers know what to expect overall, establishes guidelines for behavior in the field, and helps them get the most out of the experience by sharing some basic principles about ethnographic research so they can be effective observers. Another key benefit to encouraging the participation of stakeholders is that this experience enables them to be true champions of the research findings when they return to the organization and begin to share their own personal observations with others.

Challenges and Strategies

One of the biggest challenges with field work is the complexity of the logistics involved, including planning travel and coordinating the internal research team (in our case, this included two researchers, a videographer, and a client observer). We will not focus on logistics here other than to underscore the fact that detailed planning is required to mitigate hiccups in the field and to think through contingency plans carefully. Do not underestimate the time needed in the planning phase. Give yourself at least two weeks to select, schedule, and coordinate your in-home interviews, assuming you will be traveling domestically.

Aside from logistics, each study has unique challenges. We highlight a few of them here, along with our successful strategies for overcoming them:

1. Privacy restrictions prevented us from directly observing secure banking sessions, so we used sketching and screenshots as tools for discussion.

Due to the sensitive nature of personal banking and the client's customer privacy policies, we were unable to observe any mobile banking tasks directly, nor were we able to track their banking behaviors through the client's database. Instead, we had to rely on self-reported experiences of our research participants. While firsthand observation would have been ideal, we were still able to get fairly detailed descriptions from our participants during in-person interviews using a couple of techniques.

(1) Sketching. We would frequently ask participants to sketch out a process or task they had completed. While these sketches may not have been technically accurate, they gave us insight into the participant's perception of what the experience was like.

(2) Using screenshots as guides. We were able to show participants screenshots that worked as visual aids to facilitate the interview and make sure that we understood what the participant was trying to describe.

2. Participants have varied preferences and skill levels depending on what device and platform they log their diary entries, so we offered a range of feedback channels.
   During the diary component of the study, we wanted to ensure participants could use the communication channel that was most convenient and natural for them, so we captured feedback from e-mail, text, and voice mail. This ensured that less tech-savvy or mobile-savvy users would not be disadvantaged in their ability to provide thorough, thoughtful feedback on their experiences. Overall, most participants opted to use e-mail for their diary feedback, while a few utilized voice mail and text intermittently.

3. Financial activities happen cyclically, so we supplemented our in-home interviews with a 30-day diary study to capture financial routines and habits during a standard billing cycle.
   Since the bank wanted to understand how customers were currently using mobile websites and apps versus the desktop website, the diary study was vital to helping us learn common behaviors and what types of tasks were best suited to completing on desktops versus mobile devices. If we had relied exclusively on interviews, we would not have had the visibility into the frequency of repetitive tasks, and we would have lost insight into the emotional frustration of some of the pain points that were reported.

How the Research Was Used for Decision Making

The research findings were used in three key ways to drive decisions for the business:

1. *The client's mobile roadmap was realigned:* Following the final presentation of findings and recommendations, AnswerLab led an interactive workshop with the client's mobile team and key stakeholders to revisit the mobile channel roadmap. Through this working session, the team decided to accelerate some projects that were currently in flight and to reprioritize others that were in the pipeline. For example, we learned from participants that there was a strong desire for more transactional capabilities (e.g., transfers, paying bills) rather than simply viewing account information on mobile devices. This helped the team convince the broader organization to accelerate the development of more complex tasks that had been previously assumed to be desirable for a very small subset of tech-savvy customers.

2. *Existing mobile experiences were redesigned:* After uncovering the fact that most users opted to use Google Maps rather than the mobile banking app to find the nearest ATM, the product team quickly streamlined the ATM experience both to reduce the number of steps in the process and to integrate more effectively with the native GPS functionality.
3. *Key mobile personas/early customer segments were identified and enabled a more targeted marketing strategy:* AnswerLab identified key profiles and attributes of mobile banking users, enabling the mobile team to conceptualize their audience more concretely and helping lay the groundwork for future development of user personas and segmentation. The insights from the research were also used by the client's customer insights team to develop personas and a mobile task model that became part of the user-centered design toolkit. This enabled the design team to ensure they continually applied the insights directly to the design challenges they faced.
4. *Mobile experiences were designed with an understanding of the mobile "modes" we identified:* Our research highlighted the fact that users often operate in distinct "modes" that directly influence behavior. For example, two contrasting modes included using their device passively in a "standby" mode (e.g., reacting to alerts or on-screen notifications) versus actively using their device to aid them in certain situations, problems, and events in day-to-day life. This insight enabled the design team to consider the most effective ways of creating an experience that would be in alignment with these modes. As a result, when designing the end-to-end experience of what happens when a customer had a low balance or overdrawn account, the team recognized that they needed to use push notifications to get the customers' attention and then to provide them with a path to correct the situation through a transaction such as making a transfer or finding an ATM to make a deposit.

Lessons Learned

Through our experiences managing and analyzing the data from this study, we were able to refine our approach for similar engagements in the future:

1. *Offering participants multiple feedback channels for the diary phase* (voice mail, e-mail, and text) *added complexity to data collection but not a lot of value, so we streamlined their use in the future studies.*
   We found that having to monitor three separate channels to review, code, and collate artifacts from 30 respondents across 30 days added more logistical complexity than it was worth. In subsequent diary studies, we have streamlined this process to accept only entries via e-mail; additionally, we use Evernote to automatically import and categorize submissions. This enables our researchers to spend more time on analysis, and less time on managing and organizing data.

2. *Participants tend to fall into routines for submitting diary feedback, so in later studies, we adjusted our incentive structure to encourage diversity.*
   Similar to banking activities becoming parts of customers' routines and day-to-day lives, contributing diary feedback was also incorporated into our participants' daily routines. In this particular case, participants were encouraged to submit both open-ended responses to daily questions and photos

relating their experiences or capturing their environments and would receive a small incentive for each day they provided any kind of contribution. As a result, several participants tended to contribute only one kind of feedback. In future studies, photos and e-mail responses were incentivized independently, and an additional bonus incentive was provided when both were submitted on the same day.

3. *We experienced higher than expected attrition and a smaller than expected pool of fully engaged, high-quality respondents in the diary phase, leading us to "the rule of thirds."*
The extended duration (30 days) and sensitive nature of personal finances and banking may have contributed to more users lapsing or "slipping" in the quality of their responses than other diary studies. In general, for a study of this nature, expect three roughly equal groups of diary study participants. One-third will lapse and contribute only infrequently, if at all. Another third will fulfill participation requirements through the duration of the study, but their contributions will be terse or repetitive and will not offer much insight into research objectives. The final third will be engaged throughout the diary study, offering thoughtful, comprehensive responses, going above and beyond participation requirements. For this reason, we recommend recruiting three times the number of desired interviewees in order to choose the most interesting and articulate research participants.

In Summary

Going into the field to interview users directly represents a significant investment in time and money, but the insights captured through this method simply cannot be captured through other means. The most impactful findings come from observing people in their natural environments, thereby uncovering unmet needs and pain points and adjusting internally held beliefs and assumptions based on real-world behavior.

Since the focus of in-home interviews and field studies is about uncovering behaviors, habits, and beliefs, those insights have a longevity or "shelf life" that can span years. For example, although the way people manage finances may change with new tools and technology, the overriding goals of being in control and avoiding negative consequences of being late on bills remain constant. In the case of our client, this foundational work continues to be referenced several years later, even as they continue to learn new insights and nuances from work that builds on personas and frameworks established with this study.

CHAPTER 14

Evaluation Methods

Usability evaluations can generally be divided into **formative** and **summative evaluations. Formative evaluations** are done early in the product development life cycle to discover insights and shape the design direction. They typically involve usability inspection methods or usability testing with low-fidelity mocks or prototypes. **Summative evaluations,** on the other hand, are typically done toward the end of the product development life cycle with high-fidelity prototypes or the actual final product to evaluate it against a set of metrics (e.g., time on task, success rate). This can be done via in-person or remote usability testing or live experiments. Table 14.1 lists several formative and summative evaluation methods. Each method mentioned in this chapter could fill an entire chapter, if not a book, devoted just to discussing its origins, alternatives, and intricacies. As a result, our goal is to provide an overview of the evaluation methods available and provide information about where to look to learn more.

Table 14.1: Comparison of evaluation methodologies

Method	Formative or summative	State of your product	Goal	Resources required
Heuristic evaluation	Formative	Low to high fidelity	Identify violations of known usability guidelines	Low
Cognitive walkthrough	Formative	Low to high fidelity	Identify low-hanging issues early	Low
Usability testing in-person	It depends	Any stage	Identify usability issues	Medium
Eye tracking	Summative	Very high fidelity to launched	Identify where users look for features/information	High
RITE	Formative	Any stage	Iterate quickly on a design	High
Desirability testing	Summative	Very high fidelity to launched	Measure emotional response	Medium
Remote testing	Summative	Very high fidelity to launched	Identify usability issues across large sample	Low to High
Live experiments	Summative	Launched	Measure product changes with large sample of actual users	High

Introduction

Just like with other research methods described in this book, none of the evaluation methods here are meant to stand alone. Each uncovers different issues and should be used in combination to develop the ideal user experience.

At a Glance

> Things to be aware of when conducting evaluations

> Evaluation formats to choose from

> Preparing for an evaluation

> Data analysis and interpretation

> Communicating the findings

Things to Be Aware of When Conducting Evaluations

It is ideal to have a third party (e.g., someone who has not been directly involved in the design of the product or service) conduct the evaluations to minimize bias. This is not always possible, but regardless of who conducts the evaluation, the evaluation must remain neutral. This means that he or she must:

- *Recruit representative participants,* not just those who are fans or critics of your company/product
- *Use a range of representative tasks,* not just those that your product/service is best or worst at
- *Use neutral language and nonverbal cues* to avoid giving participants any signal what the "right" response is or what you want to hear, and never guide the participants or provide your feedback on the product
- *Be true to the data,* rather than interpreting what he or she thinks the participant "really meant"

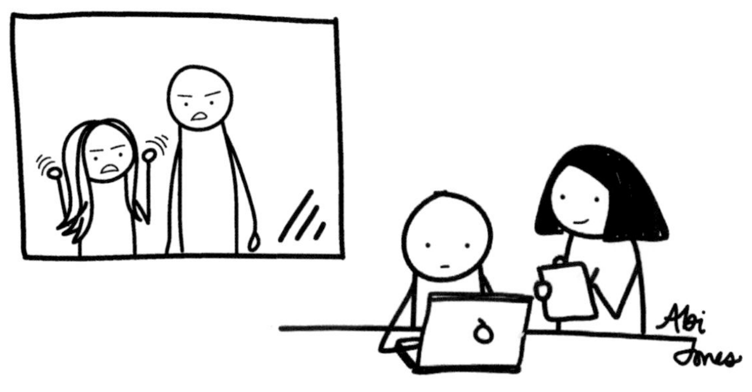

"No, don't click that!"
"That's not how I programmed it to work!"

Cartoon by Abi Jones

Evaluation Methods to Choose From

Depending on where you are in product development, what your research questions are, and what your budget is, there are a number of evaluation methodologies to choose from (see Table 14.1 for a comparison). Whether you choose a storyboard, paper prototype, low- or high-fidelity interactive prototype, or a launched product, you should evaluate it early and often.

Usability Inspection Methods

Usability inspection methods leverage experts (e.g., people with experience in usability/user research, subject matter experts) rather than involve actual end users to evaluate your product or service against a set of specific criteria. These are quick and cheap ways of catching the "low-hanging fruit" or obvious usability issues throughout the product development cycle. If you are pressed for time or budget, these methods represent a minimum standard to meet. However, be aware that experts can miss issues that methods that involve users will reveal. System experts can make incorrect assumptions about what the end user knows or wants.

Heuristic Evaluations

Jakob Nielsen and Rolf Molich introduced the **heuristic evaluation** as a "discount" usability inspection method (Nielsen & Molich, 1990). "Discount usability engineering" meant that the methods were designed to save practitioners time and money over the standard lab usability study (Nielsen, 1989). They argued that there are 10 heuristics that products should adhere to for a good user experience (Nielsen, 1994). Three to five UX experts (or novices trained on the heuristics)—not end users or subject matter experts (SMEs)—individually assess a product by walking through a core set of tasks and noting any places where heuristics are violated. The evaluators then come together to combine their findings into a single report of issues that should be addressed. Note that it is difficult for every element in a product to adhere to all 10 heuristics, as they can sometimes be at odds. Additionally, products that adhere to all 10 heuristics are not guaranteed to meet users' needs, but it is significantly less likely that they will face the barriers of poor design. Nielsen's heuristics are as follows:

1. *Visibility of system status:* Keep the user informed about the status of your system and give them feedback in a reasonable time.
2. *Match between system and the real world:* Use terminology and concepts the user is familiar with and avoid technical jargon. Present information in a logical order and follow real-world conventions.
3. *User control and freedom:* Allow users to control what happens in the system and be able to return to previous states (e.g., undo, redo).
4. *Consistency and standards:* Be consistent throughout your product (e.g., terminology, layout, actions). Follow known standards and conventions.
5. *Error prevention:* To the greatest extent possible, help users avoid making errors, make it easy for users to see when an error has been made (i.e., error checking), and give users a chance to fix them before committing to an action (e.g., confirmation dialog).
6. *Recognition rather than recall:* Do not force users to rely on their memory to use your system. Make options or information (e.g., instructions) visible or easily accessible across your product when needed.
7. *Flexibility and efficiency of use:* Make accelerators available for expert users but hidden for novice ones. Allow users to customize the system based on their frequent actions.
8. *Aesthetic and minimalist design:* Avoid irrelevant information, and hide infrequently needed information. Keep the design to a minimum to avoid overloading the user's attention.
9. *Help users recognize, diagnose, and recover from errors:* Although your system should prevent errors in the first place, when they do happen, provide error messages in clear terms (no error codes) that indicate the problem and how to recover from it.

10. *Help and documentation:* Ideally, your system should be used without documentation; however, that is not always realistic. When help or documentation is needed, make it brief, easy to find, focused on the task at hand, and clear.

We have provided a worksheet at http://tinyurl.com/understandingyourusers to help you conduct heuristic evaluations.

Cognitive Walkthroughs

Cognitive walkthroughs are a formative usability inspection method (Lewis, Polson, Wharton, & Rieman, 1990; Polson, Lewis, Rieman, & Wharton, 1992; Nielsen, 1994). Whereas the heuristic evaluation looks at a product or system holistically, the cognitive walkthrough is task-specific. It is based on the belief that people learn systems by trying to accomplish tasks with it, rather than first reading through instructions. It is ideal for products that are meant to be walk-up and use (i.e., no training required).

In a group of three to six people, your colleagues or SMEs are asked to put themselves in the shoes of the intended user group and to walk through a scenario. To increase the validity and reliability of the original method, Jacobsen and John (2000) recommended that you include individuals with a variety of backgrounds that span the range of your intended user audience to increase the likelihood of catching issues and create scenarios to cover the full functionality of the system and that your colleagues consider multiple points of views of the intended user group (e.g., users booking a flight for themselves versus for someone else). State a clear goal that the user wants to achieve (e.g., book a flight, check-in for a flight) and make sure everyone understands that goal. The individual conducting the walkthrough presents the scenario and then shows everyone one screen (e.g., mobile app, airline kiosk screen) at a time. When each screen is presented, everyone is asked to write down the answers to four questions:

1. Is this what you expected to see?
2. Are you making progress toward your goal?
3. What would your next action be?
4. What do you expect to see next?

Going around the room, the evaluator asks each individual to state his or her answers and provide any related thoughts. For example, if they feel like they are not making progress toward their goal, they state why that is. A separate notetaker should identify any areas where expectations are violated and other usability issues identified.

Conduct two or three group sessions to ensure you have covered your scenarios and identified the range of issues. When examining the individual issues identified, you should consider if the issue can be applied more generally across the product (Jacobsen & John, 2000). For example, your colleagues may have noted that they want to live chat with a customer service agent when booking their flight. You should consider if there are other times when users may want to live chat with an agent, and therefore, that feature should be made more widely available. Ideally, you would iterate on the designs and conduct another round to ensure you have addressed the issues.

Usability Testing

Usability testing is the systematic observation of end users attempting to complete a task or set of tasks with your product based on representative scenarios. In individual sessions, participants interact with your product (e.g., paper prototype, low- or high-fidelity prototype, the launched product) as they **think aloud** (refer to Chapter 7, "Using a Think-Aloud Protocol" section, page 169), and user performance is evaluated against metrics such as task success, time on task, and conversion rate (e.g., whether or not the participant made a purchase). Several participants are shown the same product and asked to complete the same tasks in order to identify as many usability issues as possible.

There is a lot of debate about the number of participants needed for usability evaluation (see Borsci et al. (2013) for an academic evaluation and Sauro (2010) for a great history on the sample size debate). Nielsen and Landauer (1993) found that you get a better return on your investment if you conduct multiple rounds of testing; however, only five participants are needed per round. In other words, you will find more usability issues conducting three rounds of testing with five participants each if you iterate between rounds (i.e., make changes or add features/ functionality to your prototype or product based on each round of feedback) than if you conduct a single study with 15 participants. If you have multiple, distinct user types, you will want to include three to four participants from each user type in your study per round.

There are a few variations on the in-person usability test that you can choose from based on your research questions, space availability, user availability, and budget.

Lab Study

This involves bringing users to a dedicated testing space within your company or university or at a vendor's site. If your organization does not have to have a formal lab space for you to conduct a usability study, you can create your own impromptu lab with a conference room, laptop, screen recording software, and (optionally) video camera. See Chapter 4, "Setting Up Research Facilities" on page 82 to learn more. An academic or corporate lab environment likely does not match the user's environment. It probably has high-end equipment and a fast Internet connection, looks like an office, and is devoid of any distractions (e.g., colleagues, spouses, or kids making noise and interrupting you). Although a lab environment may lack **ecological validity** (i.e., mimic the real-world environment), it offers everyone a consistent experience and allows participants to focus on evaluating your product.

Suggested Resources for Further Reading

The following books offer detailed instruction for preparing, conducting, and analyzing usability tests:

- Barnum, C. M. (2010). *Usability testing essentials: ready, set ... test!*. Elsevier.
- Dumas, J. S., & Loring, B. A. (2008). *Moderating usability tests: Principles and practices for interacting*. Morgan Kaufmann.

Eye Tracking

One variation on a lab study incorporates a special piece of equipment called an eye tracker. While most eye trackers are used on a desktop, there are also mobile eye trackers that can also be used in the field (e.g., in a store for shopping studies, in a car for automotive studies). **Eye tracking** was first used in cognitive psychology (Rayner, 1998); however, the HCI community has adapted it to study where people look (or do not look) for information or functionality and for how long. Figures 14.1 and 14.2 show desktop and mobile eye tracking devices. By recording participant fixations and saccades (i.e., rapid eye movements between fixation points), a heat map can be created (see Figure 14.3). The longer participants' gazes stay fixed on a spot, the "hotter" the area is on the map, indicated by the color red. As fewer participants look at an area or for less time, the "cooler" it gets and transitions to blue. Areas where no one looked are black. By understanding where people look for information or features, you can understand whether or not participants discover and process an item. If participants' eyes do not dwell on an area of an interface, there is no way for them to process that area. This information can help you decide if changes are needed to your design to make something more discoverable.

Figure 14.1: Tobii x1 Light Eye Tracker.

Figure 14.2: Tobii eye tracking glasses in a shopping study.

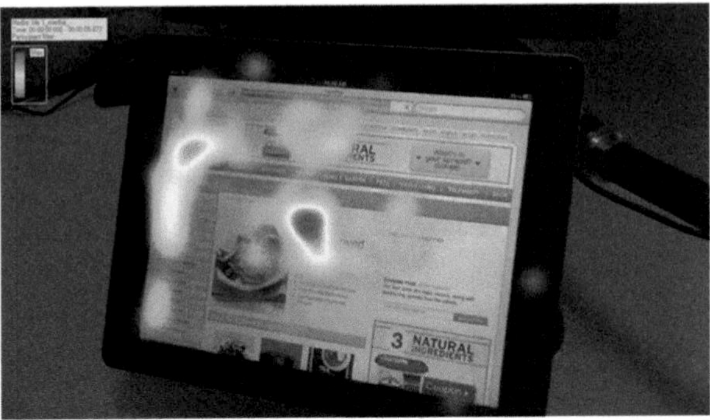

Figure 14.3: Eye tracking heat map.

Eye tracking studies are the one type of evaluation methodology where you do *not* want participants to **think aloud** as they interact with your product. Asking participants to think aloud will cause them to change their eye gaze as they speak with the evaluator or recall past remarks (Kim, Dong, Kim, & Lee, 2007). This will muddy the eye tracking data and should be avoided. One work-around is called the **retrospective think-aloud** in which participants are shown a video of their session and asked to tell the moderator what they were thinking at the time (Russell & Chi, 2014). A study found that showing participants a gaze plot or gaze video cue during the retrospective think-aloud resulted in a higher identification of usability issues (Tobii Technology, 2009). This will double the length of your study session so most researchers using this method will actually include half the number of tasks they normally would in order to keep their entire session at an hour.

Suggested Resources for Further Reading

Bojko, A. (2013). *Eye tracking the user experience: A practical guide to research.* New York: Rosenfeld Media.

Rapid Iterative Testing and Evaluation

In 2002, the Microsoft games division developed Rapid Iterative Testing and Evaluation (RITE) as a formative method to quickly address issues that prevented participants from proceeding in a game and evaluating the remaining functionality (Medlock, Wixon, Terrano, Romero, & Fulton, 2002). Unlike traditional usability testing that is meant to identify as many usability issues as possible and measure the severity of the issues in a product, RITE is designed to *quickly* identify any large usability issue that is preventing users from completing a task or does not allow the product to meet its stated goals. RITE studies should be conducted early in the development cycle with a prototype. The development team must observe all usability sessions, and following each session where a blocking usability issue is identified, they agree on a solution. The prototype is then updated and another session is conducted to see if the solution fixed the problem. If the team cannot agree on the severity of a problem, an additional session can be conducted before any changes are made. This cycle of immediately fixing and testing updated prototypes continues until multiple sessions are conducted where no further issues are identified. In contrast to traditional usability testing where five or more participants see the same design, in RITE, at most, two participants would see the same design before changes are made for the next session.

RITE sessions typically require more sessions and therefore more participants than a single, traditional usability study with five to eight participants. Additionally, because this method requires the dedication of the development team to observe all sessions, brainstorm solutions following each session, and someone to update the prototype quickly and repeatedly, it is a more resource-intensive methodology. Overall, this can be perceived as a risky method because a lot of resources are invested early, based on initially small sample sizes. However, if done early in the development cycle, the team can feel confident they are building a product free of major usability issues.

Café Study

At Google, when we need to make a quick decision about which design direction to take among several, we may conduct a 5-10-minute study with guests that visit our cafés for lunch. In only a couple of hours, we can get feedback from 10 or more participants using this formative method. Although the participants may be friends or family members of Googlers, there is surprising diversity in skills, demographics, and familiarity with Google products. We are able to collect enough data in a very short period of time to inform product direction and identify critical usability issues, confusing terminology, etc. You could do this at any café, in front of a grocery store, at any mall, etc. Of course, you need permission of the store manager or owner.

TIP

Buying and providing gift cards as incentives from the manager or owner of the establishment where you wish to conduct your study makes your study mutually beneficial to everyone.

In the Field

You can increase the **ecological validity** of your study by conducting evaluations in the field. This will give you a better sense of how people will use your product in the "real world." If your product will be used at home, you could conduct the study in the participants' homes, for example. See Chapter 13, "Field Studies" on page 380 for tips on conducting field research. This can be done either very early or much later in the product development life cycle, depending on your goals (i.e., identify opportunities and inform product direction or measure the product against a set of metrics).

Desirability Testing

To be successful, it is not enough for a product to be usable (i.e., users can complete a specified set of tasks with the product); it must also be pleasant to use and desirable. Don Norman (2004) argued that aesthetically-pleasing products are actually more effective. The games division at Microsoft introduced us to another new methodology in 2002, this time focusing on emotions, rather than usability issues (Benedek & Miner, 2002). Desirability testing evaluates whether or not a product elicits the desired emotional response from users. It is most often conducted with a released version of your product (or competitor's product) to see how it makes participants feel. The Microsoft researchers identified a set of 118 positive, negative, and neutral adjectives based on market research and their own research (e.g., unconventional, appealing, inconsistent, professional, motivating, intimidating). However, you may have specific adjectives in mind that you would like users to feel (or not feel) when using your product. You can add those to the list; however, be mindful to keep a balance of positive and negative adjectives.

To conduct the method, create a set of flash cards with a single adjective per index card. After interacting with the product, perhaps following your standard usability study, hand the stack of cards to participants. Ask them to pick anywhere from five to ten cards from the stack that describe how the product made them feel. Then, ask participants to tell you why they chose each card. The researchers suggest conducting this method with 25 participants per user segment. From here, you can do affinity diagramming on the themes participants highlighted. If your product does not elicit the emotions you had hoped for, you can make changes as needed (e.g., adding/removing functionality, changing the tone of messaging, adding different visuals) and retest.

Remote Testing

It is not always possible, or even desirable, to conduct evaluations with participants in person. For example, if you are based in any of the tech-savvy regions of the country, conducting only in-person sessions around your company will result in a **sampling bias**. You may also miss out on any region-specific issues users face (e.g., customer service hours are unfriendly to one or more time zones). Remote testing can help you gather data from participants outside of your geographic area. Another benefit of remote testing is that you can typically collect feedback from a much larger sample size in a shorter period of time, and no lab facilities are needed. Unfortunately, if you are conducting studies on hardware devices or with highly confidential products, you may still need to conduct studies in person.

There are two ways to conduct remote studies:

1. Use online vendors or services to conduct evaluations with their panels (e.g., *UserZoom, UserTesting.com*).
2. Use a service like *GoToMeeting, WebEx,* or *Hangouts* to remotely connect to the participant in his or her environment (e.g., home, office) while you remain in your lab or office. You will need to call or e-mail directions to the participant for how to connect your computer to his or her computer to share screens, and it may be necessary to walk participants through the installation step-by-step over the phone. Once you have done this, you can show the participant your prototype and conduct the study as you normally would in the lab. Alternatively, you can ask the participant to show you his or her computer or, using the web cam, show his or her environment, mobile device, etc. You will also need to leave time at the end of the session to walk participants through the process of uninstalling the application.

TIP

It is important to realize that not all participants will be comfortable installing something on their computers, so you will need to notify participants during the recruitment phase about what you will be asking them to install so they can ask questions and be completely informed when deciding whether or not to participate. Do not put the participant in the awkward position of having to say, "I'm not comfortable with that" at the very beginning of the session. You should also be prepared to help the participant with technical troubleshooting if the application causes problems for his or her computer. Do *not* leave the participant stranded with computer problems as a result of agreeing to participate in your study! This may mean getting on the phone with your IT department or customer support for the company whose application you are using to ensure the participant's issues are resolved.

Live Experiments

Live experiments, from an HCI standpoint, is a summative evaluation method that involves comparing two or more designs (live websites) to see which one performs better (e.g., higher click-through rate, higher conversion rate). To avoid biasing the results, users in industry studies are usually not informed they are part of an experiment; however, in academia, consent is often required. In **A/B testing**, a percent of users are shown one design ("A") and, via logs analysis, performance is compared against another version ("B"). Designs can be a variation on a live control (typically the current version of your product) or two entirely new designs. See Figure 14.4 for an illustration. **Multivariate testing** follows the same principle, but in this case, multiple variables are manipulated to examine how changes in those variables interact to result in the ideal combination. All versions must be tested in parallel to control for extraneous variables that could affect your experiment (e.g., website outage, change in fees for your service).

You will need a large enough sample per design in order to conduct statistical analysis and find any significant differences; however, multivariate testing requires a far larger sample than simple A/B because of the number of combinations under consideration.

There are a few free tools and several fee-based online services that can enable you to conduct live experiments. Simply do a web search for "website optimization" or "A/B testing," and you will find several vendors and tools to help you.

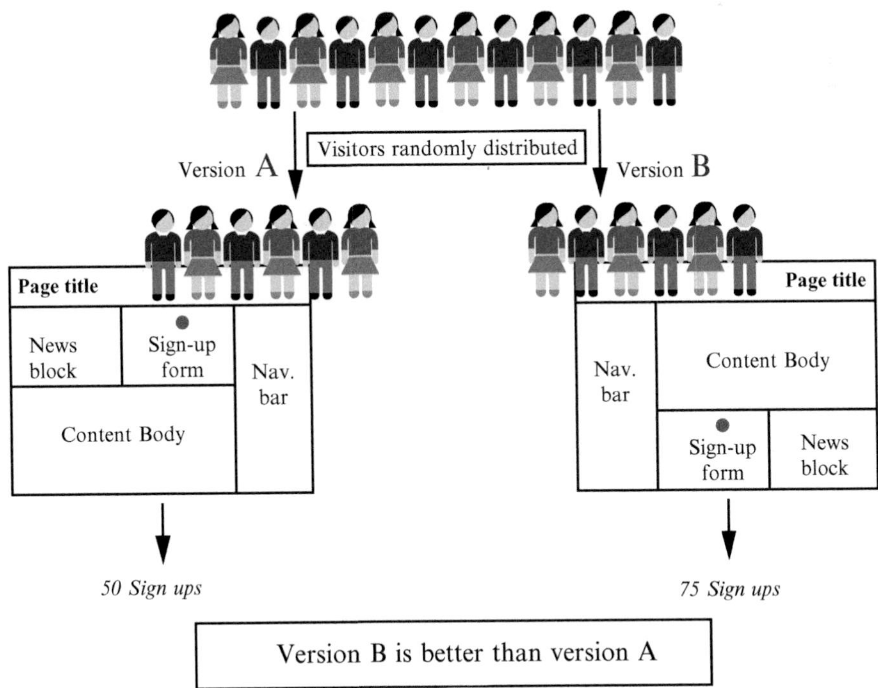

Figure 14.4: A/B testing.

Suggested Resources for Further Reading

Designing successful experiments is not an easy task. We recommend the two books below. The first offers a great introduction to this topic, and the second provides information about statistics for user research that will be extremely helpful when analyzing your data.

Siroker, D., & Koomen, P. (2013). *A/B testing: The most powerful way to turn clicks into customers*. John Wiley & Sons.

Sauro, J., & Lewis, J. R. (2012). *Quantifying the user experience: Practical statistics for user research*. Elsevier.

Data Analysis and Interpretation

In addition to identifying usability issues, there are a few metrics you may consider collecting in a summative evaluation:

- *Time on task:* Length of time to complete a task.
- *Number of errors:* Errors made completing a task and/or across the study.
- *Completion rate:* Number of participants that completed the task successfully.
- *Satisfaction:* Overall, how satisfied participants are on a given task and/or with the product as a whole at the end of the study (e.g., "Overall, how satisfied or dissatisfied are you with your experience? Extremely dissatisfied, Very dissatisfied, Moderately dissatisfied, Slightly dissatisfied, Neither satisfied nor dissatisfied, Slightly satisfied, Moderately satisfied, Very satisfied, Extremely satisfied").
- *Page views or clicks:* As a measure of efficiency, you can compare the number of page views or clicks by a participant against the most efficient/ideal path. Of course, the optimal path for a user may not be his or her preferred path. Collecting site analytics can tell you *what* users do but not *why*. To understand *why* users traverse your product in a certain path, you must conduct other types of studies (e.g., lab study, field study).
- *Conversion:* Usually measured in a live experiment, this is a measure of whether or not participants (users) "converted" or successfully completed their desired task (i.e., signed up, made a purchase).

In a **benchmarking study**, you can compare the performance of your product or service against that of a competitor or a set of industry best practices. Keep in mind that with small sample sizes (e.g., in-person studies), you should not conduct statistical tests on the data and expect it will be representative of your broader population. However, it can be helpful to compare the metrics between rounds of testing to see if design solutions are improving the user experience.

Suggested Resources for Further Reading

Albert, W., and Tullis, T. (2013). *Measuring the user experience: collecting, analyzing, and presenting usability metrics*. Morgan Kaufman.

Communicating the Findings

For all of the evaluation methods listed, you should document the design that was evaluated to avoid repeating the same mistakes in later versions. This might be as simple as including screenshots in a slide deck or maintaining version control on a prototype so it is easy to see exactly what the participant experienced.

In small sample size or informal studies (e.g., cognitive walkthrough, café study, RITE), a simple list of issues identified and recommendations is usually sufficient to communicate with your stakeholders. A brief description of the participants can be important, particularly if there are any caveats stakeholders should be aware of (e.g., only company employees participated for confidentiality reasons). These are meant to be fast, lightweight methods that do not slow down the process with lengthy documentation.

For larger or more complex studies (e.g., eye tracking, live experiment), you will want to include a description of the methodology, participant demographics, graphs (e.g., heat map, click path), and any statistical analysis. Different presentation formats are usually required for different stakeholders. For example, it is unlikely engineers or designers will care about the details of the methodology or statistical analysis, but other researchers will. A simple presentation of screenshots showing the issues identified and recommendations is often best for the majority of your stakeholders, but we recommend creating a second report that has all of the details mentioned above, so if questions arise, you can easily answer (or defend) your results.

Pulling It All Together

In this chapter, we have discussed several methods for evaluating your product or service. There is a method available for every stage in your product life cycle and for every schedule or budget. Evaluating your product is not the end of the life cycle. You will want (and need) to continue other forms of user research so you continually understand the needs of your users and how to best meet them.

CASE STUDY: *APPLYING COGNITIVE WALKTHROUGHS IN MEDICAL DEVICE USER INTERFACE DESIGN*

Arathi Sethumadhavan, Manager, Connectivity Systems Engineering, Medtronic, Inc.

Medtronic, Inc., is the world's largest medical technology company. As a human factors scientist at Medtronic, my goal is to proactively understand the role of the user and the use environment, design products that minimize use error that could lead to user or patient harm, and maximize clinical efficiency and product competitiveness by promoting ease of learning and ease of use. I have been conducting human factors research in the Cardiac Rhythm and Disease Management (CRDM) division of Medtronic, which is the largest and oldest business unit of Medtronic. In this case study, I describe how I used one human factors user research technique, a lightweight cognitive walkthrough, on a heart failure project at CRDM.

Heart failure is a condition in which the heart does not pump enough blood to meet the body's needs. According to the Heart Failure Society of America, this condition affects five million Americans with 400,000-700,000 new cases of heart failure diagnosed each year. Cardiac resynchronization therapy (CRT) is a treatment for symptoms associated with heart failure. CRT restores the coordinated pumping of the heart chambers by overcoming the delay in electrical conduction. This is accomplished by a CRT pacemaker, which includes a lead in the right atrium, a lead in the right ventricle, and a lead in the left ventricle. These leads are connected to a pulse generator that is placed in the patient's upper chest. The pacemaker and the leads maintain coordinated pumping between the upper and the lower chambers of the heart, as well as the left and right chambers of the heart. The location of the leads and the timing of pacing are important factors for successful resynchronization. For patients with congestive heart failure who are at high risk of death due to their ventricles beating fast, a CRT pacemaker that includes a defibrillator is used for treatment.

The *Attain Performa® quadripolar* lead is Medtronic's new left ventricle (LV) lead offering, which provides physicians more options to optimize CRT delivery. This lead provides 16 left pacing configurations that allow for electronic repositioning of the lead without surgery if a problem (e.g., phrenic nerve stimulation, high threshold) arises during implant or follow-up. Though the lead offers several programming options during implant and over the course of therapy long-term, the addition of 16 pacing configurations to programming has the potential to increase clinician workload. To reduce clinician workload and expedite clinical efficiency, Medtronic created *VectorExpress*™, a smart solution that replaces the 15-30-minute effort involved in manually testing all the 16 pacing configurations through a one-button click. *VectorExpress*™ completes the testing in two to three minutes and provides electrical data that clinicians can use to determine the optimal pacing configuration. This feature is a big differentiator from the competitive offering.

Uniqueness of the Medical Domain

An important aspect that makes conducting human factors work in the medical device industry different from non-healthcare industries is the huge emphasis regulatory bodies place on minimizing user errors and use-related hazards caused by inadequate medical device usability. International standards on human factors engineering specify processes that medical device manufacturers should follow to demonstrate that a rigorous usability engineering process has been adopted and risks to user or patient safety have been mitigated. This means analytic techniques (e.g., task analysis, interviews, focus groups, heuristic analysis) as well as formative evaluations (e.g., cognitive walkthrough, usability testing) and validation testing with a production-equivalent system with at least 15 participants from each representative user group is required to optimize medical device design. Compliance to standards also requires maintenance of records showing that the usability engineering work has been conducted. Though a variety of user feedback techniques were employed in this project as well, this case study will focus on the use of a lightweight cognitive walkthrough with subject matter experts, which was employed to gather early feedback from users on design ideas before creating fully functional prototypes for rigorous usability testing. Cognitive walkthroughs are a great technique to discover users' reactions to concepts that are being proposed earlier on in the product development life cycle, to determine whether we are going in the right direction.

Preparing for the Cognitive Walkthroughs

The cognitive walkthrough materials included the following:

- An introduction of the *Attain Performa quadripolar* lead and the objective of the interview session.
- Snapshots of user interface designs being considered, in a Microsoft PowerPoint format. Having a pictorial representation of the concepts makes it easier to communicate our thoughts with end users and, in turn, gauge users' reactions.
- Clinical scenarios that would help to evaluate the usefulness of the proposed feature. Specifically, participants were presented with two scenarios: *implant,* where a patient is being implanted with a CRT device, and *follow-up,* where a patient has come to the clinic complaining of phrenic nerve stimulation (i.e., hiccups). Data collection form is as follows: For each scenario, a table was created with "questions to be asked during the scenario" (e.g., "When will you use the test?" "How long would you wait for the automated test to run during an implant?" "Under what circumstances would you want to specify a subset of vectors on which you want to run the test?" "How would you use the information in the table to program a vector?") and "user comments" as headers. Each question had its own tabular entry in the table.

Conducting the Cognitive Walkthroughs

Cognitive walkthroughs were conducted at Medtronic's Mounds View, Minnesota, campus with physicians. A total of three cognitive walkthroughs (CWs) were conducted. Unlike studies that are conducted in a clinic or hospital where physicians take time out of their busy day to talk to us and where there is a higher potential of interruptions, studies conducted at Medtronic follow a schedule, with physicians dedicating their time to these sessions. Though three CWs at first glance seem like a small sample size, it is important to point out that we followed up with multiple rounds of usability testing with high-fidelity, interactive prototypes later on.

Each CW session included a human factors scientist and a research scientist. The purpose of including the research scientist was to have a domain expert who was able to describe the specifics of the *VectorExpress*™ algorithm. It is also good practice to include your project team in the research because this helps them understand user needs and motivations firsthand. Both the interviewers had printed copies of the introductory materials and the data collection forms. The PowerPoint slides illustrating the user interface designs were projected onto a big screen in the conference room.

The session began with the human factors scientist giving physicians an overview of the feature that Medtronic was considering and also describing the objective of the session. This was followed by the research scientist giving an overview of how the *VectorExpress*™ algorithm works—in other words, a description of how the algorithm is able to take the electrical measurements of all the LV pacing configurations. Then, using the context of an implant and follow-up scenario, the human factors scientist presented the design concepts and asked participants questions about how they envisioned the feature to be used. This was a "lightweight" CW, meaning that we did not ask participants each of the four standard questions as recommended by Polson et al. (1992). Time with the participants was extremely limited, and therefore, in order to get as much feedback about the design concepts as possible, we focused on interviewing participants deeply about each screen they saw. Both the interviewers recorded notes in their data collection forms.

Analyzing Information from Cognitive Walkthroughs

The human factors scientist typed up the notes from the CWs by typing in the responses to the questions in the data collection form. The "key takeaways" section was then generated for each CW session that was conducted. The document was then sent to the research scientist for review and edits. The report from each CW session was submitted to the cross-functional team (i.e., Systems Engineering, Software Engineering, and Marketing). Note that these one-on-one CW sessions were also preceded by a focus group with electrophysiologists to gather additional data from a larger group. After all of these sessions, we came together as a cross-functional team and identified key takeaways and implications for user interface design based on the learnings from the CWs and focus groups.

Next Steps

- The feedback obtained from the CWs helped us to conclude that overall, we were going in the right direction, and we were able to learn how users would use the proposed feature during CRT device implants and follow-ups. The CWs also provided insights on the design of specific user interface elements.
- In preparation for formative testing, we developed high-fidelity software prototypes and generated a test plan with a priori definition of usability goals and success criteria for each representative scenario. We worked with Medtronic field employees to recruit representative users for formative testing.
- We also conducted a user error analysis on the proposed user interface, to evaluate potential user errors and any associated hazards.
  - A formative test plan was generated with a priori definition of usability goals and success criteria for each representative scenario.
  - We worked with Medtronic field employees to recruit representative users for formative testing.

Things to Remember

- When conducting any research study, including CWs, flexibility is important. Research sessions with key opinion leaders rarely follow a set agenda. Sessions with highly-skilled users, such as electrophysiologists, involve a lot of discussion, with the physicians asking a lot of in-depth technical questions. Be prepared for that by projecting ahead of time the technical questions they might ask. I have in the past created a cheat sheet with a list of potential questions and answers to these. These cheat sheets should be developed with input from a technical expert.
- Involve cross-functional partners such as the project systems engineer or the research scientist (who are domain experts) in the user research process. They have a much more in-depth understanding of the system that becomes complementary to the role of a human factors engineer.
- Most research studies run into the issue of taking what users say at face value. It is important to question in depth the motivation behind a perceived user need before jumping to conclusions. In addition, it is important to triangulate the data with conclusions derived from other techniques, such as behavioral observations and formative testing.

PART 4

WRAPPING UP

CHAPTER 15

Concluding Final

Introduction

In earlier chapters, we have presented a variety of user research activities to fit your needs. After conducting a user research activity, you have to effectively relay the information you have collected to the **stakeholders** in order for it to impact your product. If your findings are not communicated clearly and successfully, you have wasted your time. There is nothing worse than a report that sits on a shelf, never to be read. In this, the concluding chapter, we show you how to prioritize and report your findings, present your results to stakeholders, and ensure that your results get incorporated into the product.

At a Glance

> Prioritization of findings

> Presenting your findings

> Reporting your findings

> Ensuring the incorporation of your findings

Prioritization of Findings

Clearly, you would never want to go to your stakeholders with a flat list of 400 user requirements. It would overwhelm them and they would have no idea where to begin. You must prioritize the issues and research you have obtained and then make recommendations based on those priorities. Prioritization conveys your assessment of the impact of the research findings. In addition, this prioritization shows the order in which the research findings should be addressed by the product team.

It is important to realize that **usability** prioritization is not suitable for all types of user research activities. In methods such as a card sort, the findings are presented as a whole rather than as individual recommendations. For example, if you have completed a card sort to help you understand the necessary architecture for your product (see Chapter 11, page 304), typically, the recommendation to the team is a whole architecture. As a result, the entire object (the architecture) has high priority. On the other hand, most other methods typically generate data that are conducive to prioritization. For example, if you conducted a product evaluation, you might encounter a number of issues from terminology to discoverability to task success. Rather than just handing over the list of findings to the product team, you can help the team understand which findings are the most important so that they can allocate their resources effectively. In this chapter, we will discuss how to do this. We also distinguish between usability prioritization and business prioritization. There is no one "right" answer regarding prioritization. Here, we will highlight a sequence of the prioritization activities where prioritization is broken into two phases. We have found this method effective, but close-knit teams with strong established relationships or teams with a strong understanding of user research can often accomplish prioritization in one phase. The two-stage process is highlighted in Figure 15.1.

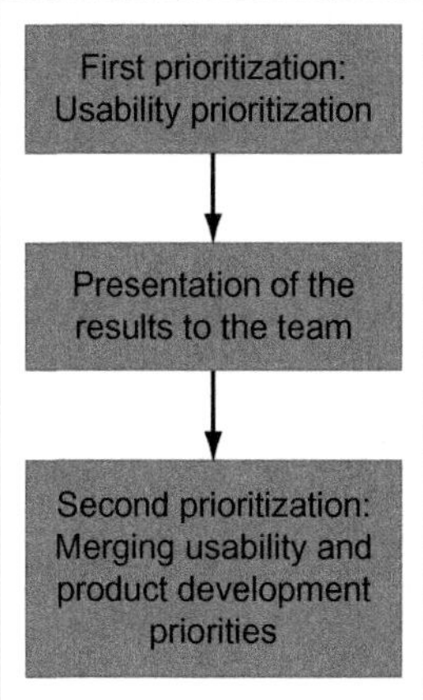

Figure 15.1: Prioritization sequence.

DILBERT © 2003 Scott Adams. Used By permission of UNIVERSAL UCLICK. All rights reserved.

First Prioritization: Usability Perspective

There are two key criteria (from a usability perspective) to take into consideration when assigning priority to a recommendation: impact and number.

- *Impact* refers to your judgment of the impact of the usability finding on users. Information about consequence and frequency is used to determine impact. For example, if a particular user requirement is not addressed in your product so that users will be unable to do their jobs, clearly this would be rated as "high" priority.
- *Number* refers to the number of users who identified the issue or made a particular request. For example, if you conducted 20 interviews and two participants stated they would *like* (rather than need) a particular feature in the product, it will likely be given a "low" priority. Ideally, you also want to assess how many of your true users this issue will impact. Even if only a few users mentioned it, it may still *affect* a lot of other users.

The reality is that prioritization tends to be more of an art than a science. We do our best to use guidelines to determine these priorities. They help us decide how to determine a rating of "high," "medium," or "low" for a particular finding. To allow stakeholders and readers of your report to understand the reasons for a particular priority rating, the description of the requirement should contain information about the impact of the finding (e.g., "the issue is severe and recurring," or "the requested function is cosmetic") and the number of participants who encountered or mentioned it (e.g., 20 of 25 participants).

Guidelines for the "high," "medium," and "low" priorities are as follows (keep in mind that these may not apply to the results of every activity):

High:

- The finding/requirement is extreme. It will be difficult for the *majority* of users to use the product and will likely result in task failure (e.g., data loss) without addressing it.
- The requirement will enhance how users do their work in a significant way—breakthrough idea.
- The finding/requirement has a large impact and is *frequent and recurring*.
- The finding/requirement is broad in scope, has interdependencies, or is symptomatic of an underlying infrastructure issue.

Medium:

- The finding/requirement is moderate. It will be difficult for *some* users to use the product as a result of the issue or without the required feature.
- The finding/requirement reflects an innovation that will aid users in accomplishing their tasks.
- A *majority* of participants will experience frustration and confusion when completing their work (but not an inability to get their work done) as a result of the finding or without the required feature.
- The requirement is less broad in scope and its absence *likely* affects other tasks.

Low:

- A *few* participants might experience frustration and confusion as a result of the issue or without the requirement.
- The requirement reflects a minor impact feature enhancement.
- The requirement is minor in scope and its absence will not affect other tasks.
- It is a cosmetic requirement.

If a requirement meets the guidelines for more than one priority rating, then it is typically assigned the highest rating.

Of course, when using these rating guidelines, you will also need to consider your domain. If you work in a field when any error can lead to loss of life or an emergency situation (e.g., a nuclear power plant, hospital), you will likely need to modify these guidelines to make them more stringent.

Second Prioritization: Merging Usability and Product Development Priorities

The previous section described how to prioritize recommendations of a user research activity from a usability perspective. The focus for this kind of prioritization is, of course, on how each finding impacts the user. In an ideal world, we would like the product development team to make changes to the product by dealing with all of the high-priority issues first, then the medium-priority, and finally the low-priority issues. However, the reality is that factors such as budgets, contract commitments, resource availability, technological constraints, marketplace pressures, and deadlines often prevent product development teams from implementing your recommendations. They may really want to implement all of your recommendations but are simply unable to. Frequently, user research professionals do not have insight into the true cost to implement a given recommendation. By understanding the cost to implement your recommendations and the constraints the product development team is working under, you not only ensure that the essential recommendations are likely to be incorporated but also earn allies on the team.

This type of prioritization typically occurs after you have presented the findings to the development team. After the presentation meeting (described later), schedule a second meeting to prioritize the findings you have just discussed. You may be able to cover it in the same meeting if time permits, but we find it is best to schedule a separate meeting. At this second meeting, you can determine these priorities and also the status of each recommendation (i.e., accepted, rejected, or under investigation). A detailed discussion of recommendation status can be found below (see "Ensuring the Incorporation of Your Findings" section, page 469).

It is valuable to work with the product team to take your prioritizations to the next level and incorporate cost. The result is a cost-benefit chart to compare the priority of a usability recommendation to the cost of implementing it. After you have presented the list of user requirements or issues and their impact on the product development process, ask the team to identify the cost associated with implementing each change. Because developers have substantial technical experience with their product, they are usually able to make this evaluation quickly.

The questions in Figure 15.2 are designed to help the development team determine the cost. These are based on questions developed by MAYA Design (McQuaid, 2002).

Average the ratings that each stakeholder gives these questions to come up with an overall cost score for each user research finding/recommendation. The closer the average score is to 7, the greater the cost for that requirement to be implemented. Based on the "cost" assignment for each item in the list and the usability priority you have provided, you can determine the final priority each finding or requirement should be given. The method to do this is described below.

In Figure 15.3, the *x*-axis represents the importance of the finding from the usability perspective (high, medium, low), while the *y*-axis represents the difficulty or cost to the product team (rating between 1 and 7). The further to the right you go, the greater the importance is to the user. The higher up you go, the greater the difficulty to implement the recommendation. This particular figure shows a cost-benefit chart for a focus group travel example.

The degree to which the finding (issue/requirement) is widespread or pervasive:

None						A great deal
1	2	3	4	5	6	7

The requirement requires more research or a major restructuring (information architecture, hardware, system architecture):

None						A great deal
1	2	3	4	5	6	7

The product development team has adequate resources to include the requirement:

A great deal						None
1	2	3	4	5	6	7

The key corporate stakeholders are interested in including the requirement:

Extremely						Not at all
1	2	3	4	5	6	7

The key product management stakeholders are interested in including the requirement:

Extremely						Not at all
1	2	3	4	5	6	7

The key marketing stakeholders are interested in including the requirement:

Extremely						Not at all
1	2	3	4	5	6	7

Figure 15.2: Questions to aid in prioritization (McQuaid, 2002).

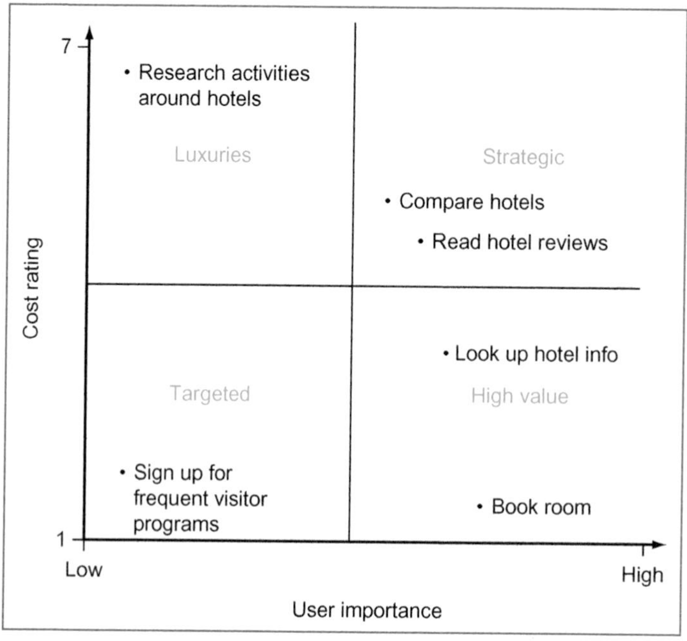

Figure 15.3: Sample cost-benefit chart from requirements from a focus group.

The Chart Quadrants

As you can see, there are four quadrants into which your recommendations can fall:

- *High value.* Quadrant contains high-impact issues/recommendations that require the least cost or effort to implement. Recommendations in this quadrant provide the greatest return on investment and should be implemented first.
- *Strategic.* Quadrant contains high-impact issues/recommendations that require more effort to implement. Although it will require significant resources to implement, the impact on the product and user will be high and should be tackled by the team next.
- *Targeted.* Quadrant contains recommendations with lower impact and less cost to implement. This may be referred to as the "low-hanging fruit:" They are tempting for the product development team to implement because of the low cost. The impact is lower, but they tend to be easy, so it is good to tackle some of these along with the "high-value" and "strategic" recommendations.
- *Luxuries.* Quadrant contains low-impact issues/recommendations that require more effort to implement. This quadrant provides the lowest return on investment and should be addressed only after recommendations in the other three quadrants have been completed, if at all.

By going through the extra effort of working with the product team to create this chart, you have provided them with a plan of attack. In addition, the development team will appreciate the fact that you have worked with them to take their perspective into account.

Presenting Your Findings

Now that you have collected your data and analyzed them, you need to showcase the results to all stakeholders. This presentation will often occur prior to the prioritization exercise with the product development team (i.e., you will have a usability prioritization, but it will not factor in the product team's priorities yet). The reality is that writing a user research report, posting it to a group website, and e-mailing out the link to the report are just not enough. User research reports fill an important need (e.g., documenting your findings and archiving the detailed data for future reference), but you must present the data verbally as well.

You really need to have a meeting to discuss your findings. This meeting will likely take an hour. In the case of in-depth research like field studies, you may require more time. The meeting ideally should be done in person. Then you can see for yourself the reaction of your audience to the results. Do they seem to understand what you are saying? Are they reacting positively with smiles and head nods, or are they frowning and shaking their heads? If this is not possible, use a web sharing app with cameras.

TIP

If you are an external consultant (i.e., not a full-time employee of the company), you will likely have to depend on an internal contact to set up the meeting and to set expectations about the meeting's scope. Be sure that your contact is clear about the agenda. Also, although the meeting room is important, as a consultant, you may have no control over its layout. You may not even know where it is. It important to get there early and set it up the way you want and figure out how to run the equipment.

At a Glance

> Why the verbal presentation is essential
> Presentation attendees
> Creating a successful presentation
> Delivering a successful presentation

Why the Verbal Presentation Is Essential

Since your time and the stakeholders' time are valuable, it is important to understand why a meeting to present your results and recommendations is so critical. No one wants unnecessary meetings in his or her schedule. If you do not feel the meeting is essential, neither will your stakeholders. What follows are some reasons for having a meeting and for scheduling it as soon as possible. When you schedule the meeting, be sure to insert a clear agenda with goals to set expectations.

TIP

If there is time, you should go over all your recommendations with a key member of the team *before* this meeting—to make sure that they are realistic and do-able. Otherwise, at the meeting, it may appear that you do not understand the findings or their complexity, which can set the meeting off course. It deteriorates into a discussion about why the recommendations cannot be followed. A premeeting can also enable you to get a sense of the team's other priorities.

Dealing with the Issues Sooner Rather Than Later

Product teams are very busy. They are typically on a very tight timeline and they are dealing with multiple sources of information. You want to bring your findings to the attention of the team as soon as possible. This is for your benefit and theirs. From your perspective, it is best to discuss the issues while the activity and results are fresh in your mind. From the product team's perspective, the sooner they know what they need to implement based on your findings, the more likely they are to actually be able to do this.

Ensuring Correct Interpretation of the Findings and Recommendations

You may have spent significant time and energy conducting the activity, collecting and analyzing the data, and developing recommendations for the team. The last thing you want is for the team to misinterpret your findings and conclusions. The best way to ensure that everyone is on the same page is to have a meeting and walk through the findings. Make sure that the implications of the findings are clearly understood and why they are important to the stakeholders. The reality is that many issues are too complex to describe effectively in a written format. A face-to-face presentation is key. Also, stepping the team though infographics, storyboards, and other visual assets is very helpful.

Dealing with Recommendation Modifications

It may happen that one or more of your recommendations are not appropriate. This often occurs because of technical constraints that you were unaware of. Users sometimes request things that are not technically possible to implement. You want to be aware of the constraints and document them. There may also be a case where the product is implemented in a certain manner because a key customer or contract agreement requires it. By having the stakeholders in the room, you can **brainstorm** a new recommendation that fulfills the users' needs and fits within the product or technological constraints. Alternatively, stakeholders may offer better recommendations than what you considered. We have to admit that we do not always have the best solutions, so a meeting with all the stakeholders is a great place to generate them and ensure everyone is in agreement.

Presentation Attendees

Invite all the stakeholders to your presentation. These are typically the key people who are going to benefit and/or decide what to do with your findings. Do not rely on one person to convey the message to the others, as information will often get lost in translation. In addition, stakeholders who are not invited may feel slighted, and you do not want to lose allies at this point. We typically meet with the product manager, the engineer(s), and sometimes the business analysts. The product manager can address any functional issues, the schedule, and budget issues that relate to your recommendations, while the development manager can address issues relating to technical feasibility and the time and effort required to implement your proposals. You may need to hold follow-up meetings with individual engineers to work out the technical implementation of your recommendations. Keep the presentation focused on the needs of your audience.

Creating a Successful Presentation

A timely presentation of results is one of the most important factors. We have seen far too many researchers let data get stale and take weeks to deliver findings to the stakeholders. At this point, the team may have moved on and made decisions without you. You also risk creating the perception that research takes too long to be useful and lose critical buy-in. As a part of any study, it is key to block most if not all of your time poststudy so you can quickly get findings to the team. There are some cases, such as a large field study, where this might not be possible; however, in that situation, you keep your stakeholders engaged throughout the process by sending out periodic updates, posts on a blog site, or video snippets. For the most part, you should shoot for one to three days to generate findings.

The format and style of the presentation is as important as the content that you are trying to relay. You need to convey the importance of your recommendations and do it in a way that is easy to understand and empathize with. Do not expect the stakeholders to automatically understand the implications of your findings. The reality is that product teams have demands and requirements to meet from a variety of sources, such as marketing, sales, and customers. User research is just one of these many sources. You need to convince them that your user findings are significant to the product's development. There are a variety of simple techniques that can help you do this.

One important element is to think about your presentation in its entirety from creation to delivery. Figure 15.4 below is a great illustration of many of the elements that you should consider in advance as you formulate your ideas all the way through follow-up.

Life cycle of a presentation

1. Start at the end	2. Core message	3. Storyboard	4. Choose a form	5. Make stuff	6. Rehearse & iterate	7. Prepare	8. Showtime!	9. Results
Who is your audience?	**Identify the top two to three things your audience needs to know**	**Brainstorm how to explain top two to three things**	**What is your audience most likely to consume?**	**Keep it simple**	**Rehearse on your own; rehearse in front of others**	**Don't tweak things at the last minute**	**Make it clear that you care deeply about your content**	**Follow up with key people**
What do you want them to do afterward?	Cut everything else	Consider stories, metaphors, diagrams, timelines, etc.	Consider videos, handouts, etc.	Big letters	Get feedback when it's still a draft	Get a good night's sleep	Double up your enthusiasm	Reinforce your message
Write an opinionated title			Don't play it safe with the usual format	Full-page images	Can they repeat your core message?	Exercise the morning of	Make eye contact	
				Simple diagrams		Block your calendar: arrive early, test room	Enjoy yourself!	
				One key idea per slide				

Action

Title · Mind map · Storyboard — Paper

Slides — Computer

Action

Figure 15.4: Life cycle of a presentation (by Jake Knapp, Jenny Gove, & Paul Adams, Google Inc.).

Chip Heath and Dan Heath popularized the term "sticky idea." They refer to a sticky idea as one that is understood and remembered and changes something. They believe all sticky ideas have six traits in common. We like their sticky framework and want to share it with you (Heath & Heath, 2007).

1. *Simple:* Simplicity is not about dumbing down; it is about prioritizing. (Southwest will be the low-fare airline.) What is the core of your message? Can you communicate it with an analogy or high-concept pitch?
2. *Unexpected:* To get attention, violate a schema. (The Nordie who ironed a shirt ...) To hold attention, use curiosity gaps. (What are Saturn's rings made of?) Before your message can stick, your audience has to want it.
3. *Concrete:* To be concrete, use sensory language. (Think Aesop's fables.) Paint a mental picture. ("A man on the moon ...") Remember the Velcro theory of memory—try to hook into multiple types of memory.
4. *Credible:* Ideas can get credibility from outside (authorities or anti-authorities) or from within, using human-scale statistics or vivid details. Let people "try before they buy." (Where's the beef?)
5. *Emotional:* People care about people, not numbers. (Remember Rokia.) Do not forget the WIIFY (What's in it for you). But identity appeals can often trump self-interest. ("Don't mess with Texas" spoke to Bubba's identity.)
6. *Stories:* Stories drive action through simulation (what to do) and inspiration (the motivation to do it). Think Jared. Springboard stories (see Denning's World Bank tale) help people see how an existing problem might change.

Use Visuals

Regardless of the tool you use to deliver your findings, you will want to make it visual.

Visuals can really help to get your points across, and we deem this to be one of the most important aspects of your presentation. Screenshots, photographs, results (e.g., **dendrogram** from a card sort), storyboards, personas, and proposed designs or architectures are all examples of visuals you can use. Insert them wherever possible to help convey your message. These are the elements that will bring your story alive and make it stick. Video and highlights clips can be particularly beneficial. Stakeholders who could not be present at your activities can feel a part of the study when watching video clips or listening to audio highlights. This can take some significant time and resources on your part, so choose when to use these carefully. For example, if the product team holds an erroneous belief about their end users and you have data to demonstrate it, there is nothing better than visual proof to drive the point home (done tactfully, of course).

The Delivery Medium

The way you choose to deliver your presentation can have an effect on its impact. Know your audience and what will be most impactful for them. Often we use a variety of formats, which may include some or all of the following:

Slides

PowerPoint can be an effective format to communicate your results. In the past, we used to come with photocopies of our table of recommendations and findings. The problem was that people often had trouble focusing on the current issue being discussed. If we looked around the room, we would find people flipping ahead to read about other issues. This is not what you want. By using slides, you can place one finding per slide so the group is focused on the finding at hand. Also, you are in control so there is no flipping ahead. There are also tools like *Prezi* that make for a more interactive presentation rather than the serial flow of a PowerPoint.

Posters

Posters are an excellent lingering technique that can grab stakeholders' attention and convey important concepts about your work quickly. You can create a different poster for each type of user, activity conducted, major finding, storyboard, design principles, etc. It obviously depends on the goals of your study and the information you want the stakeholder to walk away with. The poster can contain a photo collage, user quotes, artifacts collected, results from the activity (e.g., dendrogram from a card sort, charts from a survey), and recommendations based on what was learned (see Figure 15.5). Display posters in the hallways where the product team works so people will stop and read them. It is a great way to make sure that everyone is aware of your findings.

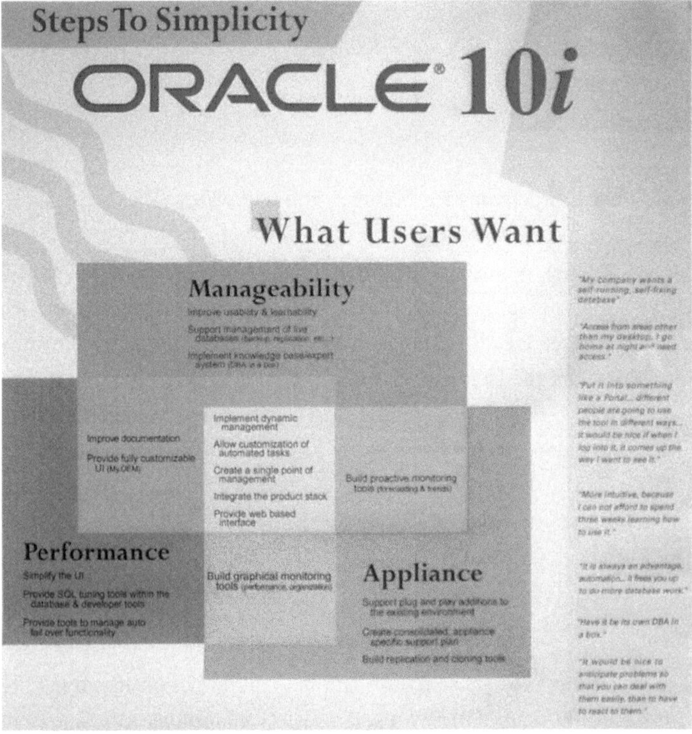

Figure 15.5: Sample findings poster for wall display.

Immersive Experiences

In some cases, it may merit creating a rich immersive experience. A large health insurance provider was faced with the challenge of getting thousands of employees to internalize their customers. The insurer took their user research and built an innovative and engaging mobile persona room and other creative learning experiences to help employees "walk in the shoes" of their customers. It was a huge success and went on a road show to many different sites.

Delivering a Successful Presentation

You have created your masterpiece and you are ready to go. Here are some things to consider during your presentation.

At a Glance

> Keep the presentation focused
> Start with the good stuff
> Prioritize and start at the top
> Avoid discussion of implementation or acceptance
> Avoid jargon

Keep the Presentation Focused

You will typically have an hour at most to meet with the team, so you need to keep your presentation focused. If you need more than an hour, you are probably going into too much detail. If necessary, schedule a second meeting rather than conducting a multihour meeting (people become tired, irritable and lose their concentration after an hour).

"As you can see on slide 387, participant interest declined sharply in the 4th hour of testing"

Cartoon by Abi Jones

You may not have time to discuss all of the details, but that is fine because a detailed user research report can serve this function (discussed later). What you should cover will depend on who you are presenting to and what it is you want to achieve from that meeting. Hopefully, the product team has been involved from the very beginning (refer to Chapter 1, page 4), so you will be able to hit the ground running and dive into the findings and recommendations (the meat of your presentation). The team should be aware of the goal of the activity, who participated, and the method used. Review this information at a high level and leave time for questions. If you were not able to get the team involved early on, you will need to provide a bit of background. Provide an "executive summary" of what was done, who participated, and the goal of the study. This information is important to provide context for your results.

TIP

Keep the meeting on track! You will have a lot of material to cover and you will not have time to get sidetracked. If someone moves away from the focus (e.g., discussing all of the detailed technical requirements necessary to implement a particular recommendation), table it for a follow-up discussion.

Start with the Good Stuff

Start the meeting on a positive note; begin your presentation with positive aspects of your findings. You do not want to be perceived as someone who is there to deliver bad news (e.g., this product stinks or your initial functional specification is incorrect). Your user research findings will always uncover things that are perceived "good news" to the product team.

For example, let us say you conducted a card sort to determine whether an existing travel website needed to be restructured. If you uncovered that some of the site's architecture matched users' expectations and did not need to be changed, while other aspects needed to be restructured, you would start out your discussion talking about the section of the product that can remain unchanged. The team will be thrilled to hear that they do not need to build from scratch! Also, they work hard and they deserve a pat on the back. Obviously, putting the team in a good mood can help soften the potential blow that is to come.

Everyone loves to hear the positive things that participants have to say, so when you have quotes that give praise to the product, be sure to highlight them at the beginning of the session.

TIP

If you are too pressed for time to create video or audio clips, be sure to include some quotes from your users to help emphasize your findings.

Prioritize and Start at the Top

It is best to prioritize your issues from a usability perspective prior to the meeting (refer "First Prioritization: Usability Perspective" section, page 451). It may sound obvious, but you should begin your presentation with the high-priority issues. It is best to address the important issues first because this is the most critical information that you need to convey to the product team. It also tends to be the most interesting. In case you run out of time in the meeting, you want to make sure that the most important information has been discussed thoroughly.

Avoid Discussion of Implementation or Acceptance

The goal of this meeting is to present your findings. At this point, you do not want to debate what can and cannot be done. This is an important issue that must be debated, but typically, there is simply not enough time in the presentation meeting. It will come in a later meeting as you discuss the status of each recommendation (discussed later). If the team states, "No, we can't do it," let them know that you would like to find out why, but that discussion will be in the next step. Remind them that you do not expect the research findings to replace the data collected from other sources (e.g., marketing and sales), but rather that the data should complement and support those other sources and you will want to have a further discussion of how all the data fit together. A discussion of when and how to determine a status for each recommendation can be found below (see "Ensuring the Incorporation of Your Findings" section, page 469).

Avoid Jargon

This sounds like a pretty simple rule, but it can be easy to unknowingly break it. It is easy to forget that terms and acronyms that we use on a daily basis are not common vocabulary for everyone else (e.g., "UCD," "think-aloud protocol," "transfer or training"). There is nothing worse than starting a presentation with jargon that no one in the room understands. If you make this mistake, you are running a serious risk of being perceived as arrogant and condescending. As you finalize your slides, take one last pass over them to make sure that your terminology is appropriate for the audience. If you must use terminology that you think will be new to your audience, define it immediately.

Next Steps

Be sure to convey the next steps. You do not want to leave the team with a pile of insights and walk away. The next step could be a variety of things depending on circumstances. For example, it might be generating a prototype to bring the findings to life, it might be a recommendation for a follow-up activity, such as a design sprint, or it could be a follow-up meeting to define the product requirement for the next release based on your findings. Whatever the next step, be explicit. You want to keep the momentum going and ensure your findings get used appropriately.

Suggested Resources for Additional Reading

- Duarte, N. (2010). *Resonate: Present visual stories that transform audiences.* Wiley.
- Heath, C., & Heath, D. (2010). *Switch: How to change things when change is hard.* Crown Business.
- Heath, C., & Heath, D. (2007). *Made to stick.* Random House.
- Reynolds, G. (2008). *Presentation Zen: Simple ideas on presentation design and delivery.* New Riders.

Reporting Your Findings

By this point, you have conducted your activity, analyzed the results, and presented the recommendations to the team, and now, it is time to archive your work. It is important to compile your results in a written format for communication and archival purposes. This could be in the form of a linear report or, if you have a lot of materials for stakeholders to consume (e.g., videos, photos, literature review, posters), a website may be more usable. After your deliverable is created and finalized, you should post it on the web for easy access. You do not want to force people to contact you to get the report or other deliverables or to find out where they can get it. The website should be well known to all stakeholders. The more accessible it is, the more it will be viewed. In addition to making it accessible online, we recommend sending an e-mail to all stakeholders with the executive summary (discussed below) and a link to your deliverables as soon as they are available.

Report Format

The format of the report should be based on the needs of your audience. Your manager, the product development team, and executives are interested in different data. It is critical to give each reader what he or she needs. In addition, there may be different methods in which to convey this information (e.g., the web, e-mail, paper). In order for your information to be absorbed, you must take content and delivery into consideration. There are three major types of report:

- The complete report
- The recommendations report
- The executive summary

The complete report is the most detailed, containing information about the users, the method, the results, the recommendations, and an executive summary. The other "reports" are different or more abbreviated methods of presenting the same information. You can also include items such as educational materials and posters to help supplement the report. These are discussed in "Creating a Successful Presentation" section on page 457.

The Complete Report

Ideally, each user research activity that you conduct should have a complete report as one of your deliverables. This is the most detailed of the reports. It should be comprehensive, describing all aspects of the activity (e.g., recruiting, method, data analysis, recommendations, conclusion).

At a Glance

> Value of the complete report

> Key sections of the complete report

> Complete report template

Value of the Complete Report

The truth of the matter is that not everyone creates a full report. The understanding of user research, the culture of your company, and the pace of work may not make this a reasonable or useful task. For many companies, the presentation deliverable may serve as the final report.

A full report can serve some important functions. Also, regulated industries (e.g., drug manufacturers) may be required for legal reasons to document everything they learned and justify the design recommendations that were made. We will present some additional reasons why it holds value, and you decide. See Appendix B for a sample report template.

The good news is that it is really not much extra work to pull a complete report together once you have a template (discussed later). Plus, the proposal for your activity will supply you with much of the information needed for the report. (Refer to Chapter 6, "Creating a Proposal" section, page 116.)

Archival Value

The complete report is important for archival purposes. If you are about to begin work on a product, it is extremely helpful to review detailed reports that pertain to the product and understand exactly what was done for that product in the past. What was the activity? Who participated? What were the findings? Did the product team implement the results? You may not be the only one asking these questions. The product manager, your manager, or other members of the user research group may need these answers as well. Having all of the information documented in one report is the key to finding the answers quickly.

Another benefit is the prevention of repeat mistakes. Over time, stakeholders change. Sometimes when new people come in with a fresh perspective, they suggest designs or functionality that have already been investigated and demonstrated as unnecessary or harmful to users. Having reports to review before changes are incorporated can prevent making unnecessary mistakes.

The detail of a formal, archived report is also beneficial to people that have never conducted a particular user research activity before. By reading a report for a particular type of activity, they can gain an understanding of how to conduct a similar activity. This is particularly important if they want to replicate your method.

TIP

Put all the reports in a searchable database. You can then search by a feature or a question and pull up all surveys/reports that contain keywords to find out whether that feature/question has ever been the subject of an activity.

Certain Teams Want the Details

Complete reports are important if the product team that you are working with wants to understand the details of the method and what was done. This is particularly important if they were unable to attend any of the session or view videotapes. They may also want those details if they disagree with your findings and/or recommendations.

Consulting

Experienced user researchers working in a consulting capacity know that a detailed, complete report is expected. The client wants to ensure that they are getting what they paid for. It would be unprofessional to provide anything less than a detailed report.

Key Sections of the Complete Report

The complete report should contain at least the following sections.

Executive summary

In this summary, the reader should have a sense of what you did and the most important findings. Try not to exceed one page or two pages maximum. Try to answer a manager's simple question: "Tell me what I need to know about what you did and what you found." This is one of the most important sections of the report, and it should be able to stand alone. Key elements include:

- Statement of the method that was conducted
- Purpose of the activity
- The product and version number your research is intended to impact (if applicable)
- High-level summary of the participants (e.g., number of participants, job roles)
- The key, high-level findings in one or two pages at most

Background

This section should provide background information about the product or domain of interest.

- What product was the activity conducted for? Or what domain/user type/question were you investigating?
- What is the purpose of the product?
- Were there any past activities for this product? Who conducted them and when?
- What was the goal of this activity?

Method

Describe in precise detail how the activity was conducted and who participated.

- *Participants*. Who participated in the activity? How many participants? How were they recruited? What were their job titles? What skills or requirements did an individual have to meet in order to qualify for participation? Were participants paid? Who contributed to the activity from within your company?

- *Materials*. What materials were used to conduct the session (e.g., survey, cards for a card sort)?
- *Procedure*. Describe in detail the steps that were taken to conduct the activity. Where was the session conducted? How long was it? How were data collected? It is important to disclose any shortcomings of the activity. Did only eight of your 12 participants show up? Were you unable to complete the session(s) due to unforeseen time restraints? Being up front and honest will help increase the level of trust between you and the team.

TIP

Do not to reveal participants' names, as this is considered personally identifiable information. You should never reveal a participant's identity. Refer to participants by a unique ID (e.g., user 1, P1, user's initials).

Results

This is where you should delve into the details of your findings and recommendations. It is ideal to begin the results section with an overview—a couple of paragraphs summarizing the major findings. It acts as a "mini" executive summary.

- What tools, if any, were used to analyze the data? Show visual representations of the data results, if applicable (e.g., a dendrogram).
- Include quotes from the participants. Quotes can have a powerful impact on product teams. If the product manager reads quotes like "I have gone to TravelMyWay.com before and will never go back" or "It's my least favorite travel site," you will be amazed at how he or she sits up and takes notice.
- Present a detailed list or table of all findings with recommendations. The level and type of detail will depend on the kind of activity you have conducted. For example, a usability test will have a list of issues with priorities and detailed recommendations, while a field study may be designed with personas as the final deliverable. If appropriate, include a status column to track what the team has agreed to and the priority. Document what recommendations they have agreed to and what they have rejected. Where possible, talk explicitly about the expected effectiveness of your recommendations once they are adopted (e.g., improved click-through rates, increased time on-site, decreased time on task, and reduced usability errors on subsequent usability tests). It adds credibility when you can speak to the expected impact.

TIP

Just as in a presentation, you want to highlight positive findings in your report as well. Often, we just think to deliver a laundry list of things to change or modify.

Conclusion

Provide the reader with a summary of the activity and indicate the next steps.

- How will this information aid the product?
- What do you expect the team to do with the data?
- Are there any follow-up activities planned or recommended?
- Are there any limitations to how the data can be used?

Appendixes

Here, include any documents that were a part of the process (e.g., the participant screener, the protocol that was used for the activity, any surveys that were given, etc.).

The Recommendations Report

This is a version of the report that focuses on the findings and recommendations from the activity and is ideal for activities that result in tactical recommendations like usability tests or card sorts. This report format is ideal for the audience that is going to be implementing the findings—typically the product manager or developer manager. In our experience, developers are not particularly interested in the details of the method we used. They want an action list that tells them what was found and what they need to do about it (i.e., issues and recommendations). To meet this need, we simply take the results section of the complete report (discussed above) and save it as a separate document.

We find that visuals such as screenshots or proposed architecture flows, where appropriate, are important for communicating recommendations. A picture is truly worth a thousand words. We find that developers appreciate that we put the information that is important to them in a separate document, saving them the time of having to leaf through a 50-page report. Again, the more accessible you make your information, the more likely it is to be viewed and used. You should also provide your developers with access to the complete report in case they are interested in the details.

The Executive Summary Report

The audience for this report is typically executive vice presidents and senior management (your direct manager will likely want to see your full report). The reality is that executives do not have time to read a formal user research report; however, we do want to make them aware of the activities that have been conducted for their product(s) and the key findings. The best way to do this is via the executive summary. We typically insert the executive summary into an e-mail and send it to the relevant executives, together with a link to the full report. (The reality is that your executives still may not take the time to read the full report, but it is important to make it available to them.) This is especially important when the changes you are recommending are significant or political. Copy yourself on the e-mail and you now have a record that this information was conveyed. The last thing you want is a product VP coming back to you and asking, "Why was I not informed about this?" By sending the information you can say, "Actually, I e-mailed you the information on June 10."

Report Supplements

You can create additional materials to enhance your report. Different people digest information best in different formats, so think of what will work best for your audiences. Educational materials and posters (as discussed above) are two ways to help relay your findings in an additional format. You normally would not create this additional content for every study, but it can be helpful for new teams or business-critical projects.

Ensuring the Incorporation of Your Findings

You have delivered your results to the stakeholders, and now you want to do everything you can to make sure the findings are acted upon. You want to make sure that the data are incorporated into user profiles, personas, functional documentation, and ultimately the product. As mentioned in the previous section, presenting the results rather than simply e-mailing a report is one of the key steps in making sure your results are understood and are implemented *correctly*. There are some key things you can do to help ensure your findings are put to use. These include involving stakeholders from beginning to end, becoming a team player, making friends at the top, and tracking outcomes.

At a Glance

> Stakeholder involvement

> Be a virtual member of the team

> Obtain a status for each recommendation

> Ensure the product team documents your findings

> Track outcomes

Stakeholder Involvement

A theme throughout this book has been to get your stakeholders involved from the inception of your activity and to continue their involvement throughout the process (refer to Chapter 1, page 4). Their involvement will have the biggest payoff at the recommendations stage. Because of their involvement, they will understand what the need was for the activity, the method used, and the users who were recruited. In addition, they should have viewed the session(s) and should not be surprised by the results of your study. By involving the product team from the beginning, they feel as though they made the user research discoveries with you. They have seen and heard the users' requirements firsthand. Teams that are not involved in the planning and collection processes may feel as though you are trying to shove suspect data down their throats. It can sometimes be a tough sell to get them to believe in your data.

If the team has not been involved in the user research process at all, start to include them now—better late than never! Work with them to determine the prioritization of your findings (see "Prioritization of Findings" section, page 450) and continue to do so as the findings are implemented. Also, be sure to involve them in planning for future activities.

Be a Virtual Member of the Team

As was mentioned earlier in this book, if you are not an organizational part of the team, you will want to become a virtual member. Be an active, recognized member of the product team from the moment you are assigned to the project (refer to Chapter 1, page 4). Take the time to become familiar with the product and with the product team priorities, schedule, budget, and concerns. You need to do your best to understand the big picture. You should be aware that usability data are only one of the many factors the team must consider when determining the goals and direction of their product (refer to Chapter 1, "A Variety of Requirements" section, page 12).

Recognizing this time investment, the product team will trust you and acknowledge you as someone who is familiar with their product and the development issues. This knowledge will not only earn you respect but also enable you to make informed recommendations that are executable because you are familiar with all the factors that impact the product's development processes. The team will perceive you as someone who is capable of making realistic recommendations to improve the product. In contrast, if you are viewed as an outsider with the attitude "You must implement all of the users' requirements and anything less is unacceptable," you will not get very far.

Obtain a Status for Each Recommendation

Document the team's response to your recommendations (e.g., accept, reject, needs further investigation). See Appendix B, the report template. This shows that you are serious about the finding and that you are not simply presenting them as suggestions. We like to include a "status" column in all of our recommendations tables. After the results presentation meeting (discussed above), we like to hold a second meeting where we can determine the priority of the results in terms of development priorities (see "Second Prioritization: Merging Usability and Product Development Priorities" section, page 453) and the status of each recommendation. If the team agrees to implement the recommendation, we document the recommendation as "Accepted." If the recommendation is pending because the product team needs to do further investigation (e.g., resource availability, technical constraints), we note this and state why. No matter how hard you try, there will be a few recommendations that the product development team will reject or not implement. You should expect this—not all requirements make sense for the business and/or are feasible. In these cases, we note their rejection and indicate the team's reasoning. Perhaps they disagree with what the findings have indicated, or they do not have the time to build what you are requesting. Whatever their reason is, document it objectively and move on to the next recommendation. We also like to follow up with the team after the product has been released to do a reality check on the status column. We let them know ahead of time that we will follow up to see how the findings were implemented. Did they implement the recommendations they agreed to? If not, why? Be sure to document what you uncover in the follow-up.

Ensure the Product Team Documents Your Findings

As mentioned in Chapter 1, Section "A Variety of Requirements," page 12 there are a variety of different kinds of product requirements (e.g., marketing, business, user research). Typically, someone on the product team is responsible for creating a document to track all of these requirements. Make sure your user research findings get included in this document. Otherwise, they may be forgotten.

As a reader of this book, you may not be a product manager, but encouraging good habits within the team you are working with can make your job easier. The product team should indicate each requirement's justification, the source(s), and the date it was collected. This information is key to determining the direction of the product, so it is important to have the documentation to justify the decisions made. If certain user research findings are rejected or postponed to a later release or sprint, this should also be indicated within the document. By referring to this document, you will be able to ensure that the user research is acknowledged—and if it is not incorporated, you will understand why. This is similar to the document that you own that tracks the status of each recommendation, but a product team member will own this document and it will include all of the product requirements, not just user requirements. If the team you work with uses a formal enhancement request system, make sure that your findings are entered into the system.

Track Outcomes

As was just discussed above, you should track the recommendations that the product development team has agreed to implement. If you are working as an external consultant, you may not be able to do this because your contract ends, but if you are an internal employee, it is important. We formally track this information in what we refer to as "the user research scorecard." Figure 15.6 illustrates the information that we maintain in our scorecard.

User Research Scorecard

We use this information for a number of purposes. If a product is getting internal or customer complaints regarding usability and the team has worked with us before, we like to refer to our tracking document to determine whether they implemented our recommendations. In some cases they have not, so this information proves invaluable. Executives may ask why the research group (or you) has not provided support or why your support failed. The tracking document can save you or your group from becoming involved in the blame game. If the product development team has implemented the recommendations, however, we need to determine what went wrong. The tracking document helps to hold the product team and us accountable.

We also find that the tracking document is a great way to give executives an at-a-glance view of the state of usability for their products. It helps them answer questions such as "Who has received user research support?" "When and how often?" and "What has the team done with the results?" We assign a "risk" factor to each of the activities, based on how many of the recommendations have been implemented. When a VP sees the red coding (indicating high risk), he or she quickly picks up the phone and calls the product manager to find out why they are at that risk category. It is a political tactic to get traction, but it works.

Product/ version #	Activity	Risk	Recommendations: Given	Accepted	Implemented	Product VP	Notes
TravelMyWay .com v1 – hotel UI	Card sort	High	38	10	5	John Adams	Team feels the user requirements do not match the marketing requirements of the product
TravelMyWay .com v1– airline reservation UI	Interviews	Medium	35	25	22	Karen McGuire	None
TravelMyWay .com v2 - airline reservation UI	Focus group	Medium	50	33	33	Karen McGuire	Technical investigations being conducted to assess unaddressed issues
TravelMyWay .com v2 – car rental UI	Interviews	Low	42	40	39	Jennifer Crosbie	None

Figure 15.6: A usability scorecard

It is important to note that this kind of tracking can be useful within many companies. However, you need to know your company culture. It may not work for you. For example, if you are a part of a small company or a startup, such level of detail and tracking may not be important, as teams are smaller and speed is of the essence.

Pulling It All Together

In this chapter, we have described the steps to take after you have conducted your user research activity and analyzed the data. You may have conducted several activities or only one. In either case, the results and recommendations need to be prioritized based on the user impact and cost to the product development to incorporate them. In addition, we have described various formats for showcasing your data, presenting the results, and documenting your data. It is not enough to collect and analyze user research; you must communicate and archive them, so they can live on long after the activity is done. Good luck in your user research ventures!

PART 5

APPENDICES

APPENDIX A

REQUIREMENTS FOR CREATING A PARTICIPANT RECRUITMENT DATABASE

There are several things you should know if you want to set up your own participant database for recruiting people for your activity. Unfortunately, the creation of a participant database does not happen overnight. It will take some work on your part to create and maintain it.

Develop a Questionnaire for Potential Participants

There are a variety of avenues you can pursue to add people to your database. After you have considered the ethical and legal implications of collecting participant information (see Chapter 3, page 66), the next thing you will want to do is develop a questionnaire for potential participants to complete. This is the information that you will enter into your database and use to query when you have an activity. (See Chapter 10, "Surveys" on page 266 to learn how to develop an effective survey.)

Some basic information you will want to include is the following:

- Name
- Address
- E-mail address
- Phone numbers (cell, home, work)
- Job title
- Age
- Gender
- Company name

- Company size
- Industry
- Technology experience
- How the person found out about your questionnaire (this can help you track the most effective methods for signing people up)

The rest of the details really depend on what is important for you to know when you are trying to recruit participants (Figure A.1).

Distribute Your Questionnaire

Now that you have your questionnaire, you need to distribute it to potential participants. Some distribution methods are described below.

User Research Participation Questionnaire

If you are interested in participating in our User Experience Program, please complete this questionnaire. It should take approximately 5 minutes to complete. All information will remain confidential. This information will not be sold to a third-party vendor. Thank you for your participation. If you have any questions please e-mail usability@travelmyway.com or call (800) 999-2222.

Contact Information

First Name: ______________________

Last Name: ______________________

Mailing Address:

Street or PO Box ______________________

____

City ______________________

State ______________________

Zip ______________________

Phone Numbers:

Daytime # (   ) ____________ Ext: ________

Evening # (   ) ____________ Ext: ________

E-mail Address: ______________________

Background Information

Highest Level of Education (*please choose one*):

O High School or Less

O Some College

Figure A.1 Sample participant database questionnaire.

- O Associate Degree
- O Bachelor's Degree
- O Graduate Degree

Age Group:

- O Under 18
- O 18–29
- O 30–44
- O 45–60
- O Over 60

Gender:

- O Male
- O Female
- O Prefer not to say

Do you own a cell phone?

O Yes   O No

If yes, is it web-enabled?

O Yes   O No

Occupational Information

Industry (*please choose one*):

- O Advertising / Marketing / PR
- O Aerospace
- O Architecture
- O Biotechnology
- O Chemical / Petroleum / Mining / Lumber / Agriculture
- O Education
- O Entertainment / Media / Film
- O Finance / Banking / Accounting
- O Government Services
- O Health / Medical
- O Insurance
- O Internet Provider
- O Legal
- O Manufacturing Design: Computer / Communications Equipment
- O Manufacturing Design: Software
- O Manufacturing Design: Other
- O Non-Profit Organization
- O Pharmaceuticals
- O Real Estate
- O Retail
- O Services: Business (non-computer)

Figure A.1 – Cont'd

Continued

O Services: Data Processing / Computer
O System Integrator
O Telecommunications
O Transportation / Freight / Shipping
O Travel
O Utilities / Energy-Related
O VAR / Distributor / Other Reseller
O Wholesale
O Other:____________________

Company's Name: ____

Size of Company:
O Small (1–49) O Medium (50–500) O Large (500+)

Job Function (*please choose one*):
O Executive / Senior Mgmt
O HR / Personal / Benefits
O Finance / Accounting
O Administration / Clerical
O Shipping / Receiving
O Marketing / Sales / PR
O Operations / General Mgmt
O Facilities / General Mgmt
O Manufacturing
O Purchasing / Procurement
O Consulting
O Other:__________________

Are you a manager?
O Yes O No

Job Title:____

Job Description: ____
____

Job Experience (*years*): ______________________

Employment Status (*please choose one*):
O Full Time
O Part Time
O Self-Employed
O Temp / Contract
O Unemployed

Thank you for your time!

Figure A.1 – Cont'd

Attend Trade Shows or Conferences

Attending trade shows or conferences where you think your users might be provides the opportunity to speak with end users in person and hand out your questionnaire. For example, if you are looking for Mac users, go to Macworld. If you are looking for electronics users, go to the Consumer Electronics Show. It is ideal if you can get a booth and offer people goodies for signing up or enter their name in a prize drawing if they sign up.

Visit Places Your Users Hang Out

Some businesses like coffee shops or grocery stores will allow you to set up a table on the sidewalk and distribute fliers. If possible, have a laptop or tablet handy to sign users up on the spot. You can even combine the sign-up effort with on-the-spot studies like quick interviews (see Chapter 9, page 220) or usability evaluations (see Chapter 14, page 432). This gives people an idea of what they are signing up for and they can receive an immediate incentive. Farmers' markets and community centers are also great locations to sign up a variety of people. In every case, make sure you obtain permission from the owner or manager of the location, as well as any applicable permits.

Put a Link on Your Company Website

Place a link to your web-based questionnaire on your company's website and in-product. The best locations are on a page that talks about your company's user research program and your company's home page.

Put a Link on an Electronic Community Bulletin Board

Just like an ad that you put up to recruit people for a specific activity, place an ad to invite people to sign up for your participant database. Costs vary depending on where you want to place the ad, but you can get a lot of responses by doing so.

Recruit People Who Participate in Your Activities

If you have participants who come in for activities from a source other than your participant database, invite them to join your database. (This may not be possible if the participants come from a recruiting agency—refer to Chapter 6, "Use a Recruiting Agency" section, page 140). You can do this at the end of your session, or you can send them a thank you note after the session and invite them to sign up.

Partner with Academic Centers That Are Engaged with the Community

If you are an academic researcher, it is likely that you work in an institution that already has a center that is engaged with the community you are interested in recruiting. For example, Clemson has the Institute for Engaged Aging that conducts workshops, seminars, and research with older adults. When Kelly is considering conducting user research with older adults, she reaches out to the director for guidance.

Technical Requirements for a Participant Database

There are some technical requirements to consider when planning your participant database. As with usability labs, you can build your participant database on the cheap or you can create an ideal participant database. Like everything else, there are pros and cons to each choice.

On the Cheap

Some companies offer databases with online forms (e.g., Knack, Zoho Creator, Google Forms) that enable you to create simple surveys.

Pros:

- It can be free or relatively cheap.
- The UIs make it easy to create a simple survey and database in a few minutes.
- Because it is available online, versioning is not a problem if multiple people will be accessing the database.
- You can quickly and easily search through your database for participants based on specific criteria.

Cons:

- Securing participant data on someone else's server means you must be aware of their security measures, privacy policies, and how the data are handled.
- Depending on the limits of the tool you choose, you may hit size limits for the database.

More Extensive and Expensive

You can create a very simple participant database in Microsoft Excel or Microsoft Access® or an open-source alternative. These are easy to acquire, but you will notice this approach has several limitations.

Pros:

- It is cheaper than using an enterprise database.

Cons:

- If multiple people in your group will be leveraging the participant database, versioning may become a problem.
- You will need to write macros to conduct searches for participants, based on certain criteria.
- You will likely need to hire an IT professional or hosting service to build and post your survey online, as well as design the database and maintain it.

Most Extensive and Expensive

If your company or institution has an enterprise database, many of the problems listed above will be solved, but new ones arrive.

Pros:

- Everything is included in one package (the database, scripting tools, the web server, and management, monitoring, and tuning tools).

- Versioning is not an issue.
- You can easily post your survey on the web and upload the results into your database.
- You can quickly and easily search through your database for participants based on specific criteria.
- You can create your infrastructure in the language of your choice (e.g., Perl, Java, SQL/PLSQL, C++) to run your form and get its contents into the database.

Cons:

- It is expensive.
- You will need the time of your organization's database administrator (DBA), system administrator, or software engineer to maintain your database and applications.

TIP

In each of these options, you need to be aware of how participant data are handled. You are responsible for keeping it secure. Speak with your IT department about their security measures or have them review the security measures of any company you use to host your survey or database.

Maintenance Requirements for Any Solution

Regardless of which database you go with, you will need to keep it up to date. This is critical; information that is out of date is useless. Maintenance includes the following:

- Removing or updating people whose contact information is no longer valid
- Removing people who no longer want to participate
- Adding new entries on a regular basis
- Tracking when each participant came in and how much he or she was paid (refer to Chapter 6, "Determining Participant Incentives" section, page 127)
- Adding comments about certain participants after activities ("great participant," "arrived late," etc.)
- Moving people to a watch list (refer to Chapter 6, "Create a Watch List" section, page 151)

Ideally, you want the people who sign up for your database to instantly update their own data and remove themselves, rather than having to submit their requests to someone else. In some states, you are legally required to remove individuals from your database within a specific time period of the individual making the request. By removing individuals automatically, rather than requiring someone at your company to manually do it, you can ensure you are adhering to the law.

APPENDIX B

REPORT TEMPLATE

This document is a report template. Its purpose is to demonstrate sample layout and content for a complete report. This particular template illustrates a card sort report, but the same basic sections can be modified and used for any user research activity.

Card Sort

Product Name *(version number, if applicable):*

<Department Name>

Author:
Creation date:
Test dates: *<mm/dd/yy—mm/dd/yy>*
Version: *<draft or final>*
Last updated: *<month, yyyy>*

Report contributor(s)

Name	Position	Role	Contact information
		Comoderator	
		Videographer	
		Designer	

Report reviewer(s)

Name	Position

Supporting documents

Document title	Owner

User research history

Activity	Author	Date of study

Executive Summary

Briefly introduce the product and the motivation for conducting this activity. Provide an overview of the number of participants, dates, purpose of the session(s), number of sessions, and a summary of the results of the study. If a particular design recommendation is being made, include an image of the proposed design.

Proposed Information Architecture or Menu structure <optional>

[Insert figure if available]

Travel Card Sort Table of Recommendations

In app tab name	Objects to be located within the tab
Resources	Tipping information Languages Currency Family-friendly travel information
News	Travel deals Travel alerts Featured destinations Weekly travel polls
Opinions	Read reviews Post and read questions on bulletin boards Chat with travel agents Chat with travelers Rate destinations
Products	Travel games Luggage Books Links to travel gear sites

Background

Provide a brief description of the product and the anticipated tasks that users will accomplish with it.

State the number and dates of the sessions. You can use the following paragraph to describe the purpose and goals of the card sort. You can also describe the rationale for conducting a card sort (e.g., to derive a new tab or menu structure for an application). Modify the following to your own specific needs.

Card sorting is a common user research technique used to discover the users' mental model of an information space (e.g., a website, app, or menu). It generally involves representing each piece of information from the information space on an individual card and then asking target users to arrange these cards into groupings that make sense to them.

Method

Participants

*Briefly describe the participants who were recruited, the number of participants, the method of recruitment (e.g., internal participant database, customers, recruiting agency), and the incentive (e.g., $100 AMEX gift card or a company logo mug). If conducting multiple group sessions, discuss the number of groups and composition of each group. Also, include recruitment criteria (*see Appendix B1*). Below is an example.*

Recruitment was based on specific criteria. The screening profile required that users:

- Could not work for a competitor
- Were over 18 years of age
- Demonstrated proficiency in the language used in the card sort

Detailed user profiles can be found in Appendix B2. Participants were recruited via ideal recruiting and were compensated with a $100 gift card for their time.

Materials

Describe the cards. For example, did the cards contain a description and/or a line for an alternative label? Descriptions and space for an alternative label are optional. Next, show a sample card. Below is an example.

Each card contained a label, a short description of the concept/label, and a space for participants to write in an alternative label. Figure B.1 shows a sample card from this activity.

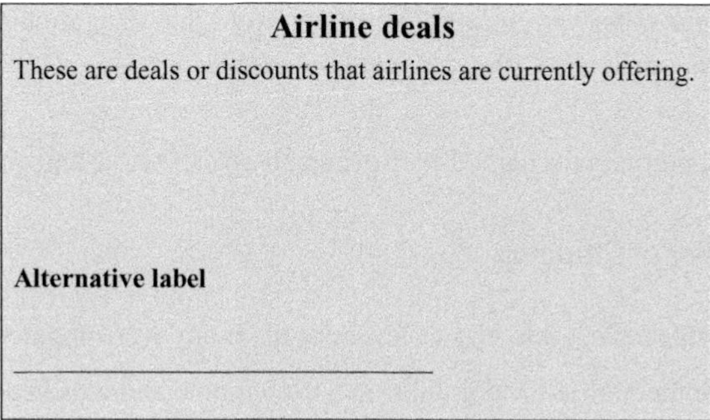

Figure B.1 Sample card.

Procedure

Participants read and signed informed consent forms and nondisclosure agreements. *<If you did a warm-up activity, mention it here.><Insert number>*Members of the UX group acted as moderators for the session. Moderators answered participants' questions and handed out and collected card-sorting materials.

Participants worked individually throughout the session. Each participant was given an envelope containing a set of*<Insert number>* cards in random order representing the concepts included in*<Insert product name here>*—see Appendix B3.

<Optional: The following text can be used as a boilerplate procedure for defining the subtasks. Customize it to your own needs.> The card sort activity involved three subtasks: card sort read/rename, card sort initial grouping, and card sort secondary grouping. Card sort subtasks were presented to the participants as separate and discrete steps. Instructions specific to each subtask were given separately. Participants were not told what they would be doing in the later steps because this might have biased their decisions. Details of each subtask are summarized below.

Part 1: Card-Sorting Read/Rename

- Participants read through each card to make sure they understood the meaning of the function. The test facilitator instructed participants not to order the cards.
- Participants renamed any cards they found unfamiliar or inappropriate by crossing out the original name and writing in an alternative(s).

Part 2: Card-Sorting Initial Grouping

First, participants sorted the cards into logical groups. When everyone had finished reading the cards, participants were instructed to

> **"Arrange the cards into groups in a way that makes sense to you. There is no right or wrong arrangement. We are interested in what you perceive to be the most logical or intuitive arrangement of the cards."**

*<Optional: Typically, there are no constraints on the number and size of groups that participants can create. If there are constraints, provide them here.>*Participants were told that they should make no more than*<Insert number>* groups, each with no more than*<Insert number>* cards.

After finishing the groupings, participants named each group on a Post-it note and attached the note to the groups.

Part 3: Card-Sorting Secondary Grouping

- Participants sorted the grouped cards into higher-level groups if any were apparent.
- Participants named each of the higher-level groups on a Post-it note and attached the note to the groups.

<Optional> See Appendix B4 for the complete instructions provided to the participants.

Results

Note that authors may choose to divide the results into several subsections dealing with sorting data, terminology, and user comments. Customize what follows according to your needs.

Sorting Data

The card-sorting data were analyzed using a cluster analysis program called *EZCalc* to derive the overall sort shown in Figure X. The figure shows the composite sort of all *<Insert number>* cards for all *<Insert number>* participants. The closer the concepts are to each other on the sorting diagram, the more conceptually related they are. *EZCalc* generates groups based on relationship strength between items.

Figure X: Sorting Results Diagram

- *<Optionally, include more images as needed.>*
- *<Optional: Insert callouts in the image to show the groupings and their names. Discuss how the sorting results can be translated into a UI design.>*

Figure X shows the suggested menu labels and menu content derived from these card-sorting data. This can be used as a guide for determining the new menu structure.

If the recommendations deviate from the EZSort *results, explain why. When appropriate, make your results as visual as possible. You can also use other kinds of images (schematics, tab layouts, etc.) to communicate your design recommendations.*

Travel Card Sort Table of Recommendations

This table provides the recommended architecture for the subtabs of the planning tab. The proposed architecture is considered high priority.

Tab name	Objects to be located within the tab	Status of recommendation
Resources	Tipping information Languages Currency Family-friendly travel information	Accepted
News	Travel deals Travel alerts Featured destinations Weekly travel polls	Accepted
Opinions	Read reviews Post and read questions on bulletin boards Chat with travel agents Chat with travelers Rate destinations	Accepted

Tab name	Objects to be located within the tab	Status of recommendation
Products	Travel games Luggage Books Links to travel gear sites	Pending. The team may not be adding this functionality to the first release

Terminology Data<section optional>

Optionally, add a subsection about terminology issues discovered during the card sort activity (e.g., relabeling, questions from participants to the session moderator). If relabeling occurred, include a table (see below) showing which concepts were relabeled, with what frequencies, and what the participant-generated labels were. A column with terminology recommendations should also be included.

Alternative Labels for Concepts<optional>

Current label	Concept description	Label provided by participants	Recommendations
Airline deals	These are deals or discounts that airlines are currently offering	Flight deals (six of ten participants)	Flight deals
....			
....			
....			

Participant Comments<section optional>

If a think-aloud protocol was used, or if you allowed users to make comments at the end of the activity, include a section highlighting participants' comments. Only include participant comments if those comments affected your recommendations.

Conclusion

Discuss the implications of the card sort data on the information architecture of the product. Do the data validate the current direction of the product? If not, discuss how the product team should change their designs to be more consistent with the users' mental model of the domain.

<Optional: Discuss future usability activities to be conducted as a follow-up.>

Appendix B1

Insert your screening questionnaire. For a sample, see Sample Screener on page 132.

Appendix B2

Participant profiles

Participant #	Employer	Job title	<Other requirement>	<Other requirement>	<Other requirement>

The following are some information to consider including in the table:

- *Company size*
- *Industry*
- *Line of business*
- *Experience with a particular domain, application, or product*

If applicable, gender, age, and disability may be included.

Appendix B3

Card Set

Show the complete set of cards used in the study. List the card names and definitions listed on the cards. Below are some examples:

Travel news
The latest news that relates to traveling

Travel deals
Travel specials or discounts offered by the website

Children's promotions
Travel specials or discounts offered by the website that relate to children

Vacation packages
Travel packages that include combinations of transportation, accommodations, and other features

Appendix B4

Participant Instructions

Show the complete instructions provided to the participants, including rules about relabeling, grouping, etc. Below is an example.

"The cards in front of you have pieces of objects/information that might be contained within a travel app.

1. Look over all of the cards.
2. If something is confusing, make a note on the card.
3. Sort the cards into groups that you would want or expect to find together.
4. Try to reduce them to four or fewer groups.
5. Each group cannot have less than three cards or more than 11 cards.
6. Use a blank card to give each group a name.
7. Staple each of the groups together.
8. Take the provided envelope and write your initials on the front. Put the stack of stapled cards in the envelope."

APPENDIX C

GLOSSARY

A

A/B testing—A percentage of users are shown a design (A) and, via log analysis, performance is compared against another version (B). Designs can be a variation on a live control (typically the current version of your product) or two entirely new designs.

Accessibility—The degree to which a product, device, service, or environment is available to as many people as possible.

Account manager—Within large corporations, an account manager is often someone who is devoted to managing a customer's relationship with his or her company. For example, if IXG Corporation is a large customer of TravelMyWay.com, an account manager would be responsible for ensuring that IXG Corporation is satisfied with the services they are receiving from TravelMyWay.com and determining whether they require further services.

Acknowledgment tokens—Words like "oh," "ah," "mm hm," "uh huh," "OK," and "yeah" carry no content. They reassure participants that you hear them, understand what is being said, and want them to continue.

Acquiescence bias—To easily agree with what the experimenter (e.g., in interviews, surveys, evaluations) or group (e.g., focus group) suggests, despite one's own true feelings. This may be a conscious decision because a participant wants to please the experimenter (or group) or it may be unconscious.

Affinity diagram—Similar findings or concepts are grouped together to identify themes or trends in the data.

Analysis of variance (ANOVA)—An inferential statistical method in which the variation in a set of observations is divided into distinct components.

Anonymity—Not collecting any personally identifying information about a participant. Since we typically conduct screeners to qualify participants for our studies, we know their names, e-mail addresses, etc. so participants are not anonymous.

Antiprinciples—Qualitative description of the principles your product does not intend to address.

Antiuser—Someone who would not buy or use your product in any circumstances.

Artifacts—Objects or items that users use to complete their tasks or that result from their tasks.

Artifact notebook—A book that a participant uses to collect all the artifacts during a diary study.

Artifact walkthrough—This is typically a session where stakeholders step through the artifacts collected to understand the users' experience

Asynchronous—Testing and/or communication that does not require a participant and a researcher to be working together at the same time. For example, e-mail is an asynchronous form of communication while a phone call is a synchronous method of communication. See also *Synchronous*.

Attitudinal data—How a participant or respondent feels (as opposed to how he or she behaves).

B

Behavioral data—How a participant behaves (as opposed to how he or she feels).

Benchmarking—Study to compare the performance of your product or service against that of a competitor or a set of industry best practices.

Beneficence—Concept in research ethics that any research you conduct must provide some benefit and protect the participant's welfare.

Binary questions—Questions with two opposing options (e.g., yes/no, true/false, agree/disagree).

Bipolar constructs—Variables or metrics that have a midpoint and two extremes (e.g., Extremely satisfied to Extremely unsatisfied).

Brainstorming—A technique by which a group attempts to find a solution for a specific problem or generate ideas about a topic by amassing all the ideas together without initial concern of their true worth.

Branching logic—Presenting questions based on responses to earlier questions.

Brand-blind study—Study in which the product branding is removed to avoid biasing the participant or to protect product confidentiality.

Burnout—In the case of a longitudinal study, participants become exhausted of participating.

C

Cache—Location where information is stored temporarily. The files you request are stored on your computer's hard disk in a cache subdirectory under the directory for your browser. When you return to a page you have recently visited, the browser can retrieve the page from the cache rather than the original server. This saves you time and saves the network burden of some additional traffic.

Café study—Research study (e.g., usability evaluation) that takes place in a café or other gathering spot in the wild to recruit people at random for brief studies (typically 15 minutes or less).

Card sorting—Research method in which participants group concepts or functionality based on their mental model. The data are analyzed across many participants to inform a product's information architecture.

CDA—See *Confidential disclosure agreement*.

Census—A survey that attempts to collect responses from everyone in your population, rather than just a sample.

Central tendency—The typical or middle value of a set of data. Common measures of central tendency are the mean, median, and mode.

Chi-squared—An inferential statistical test commonly used for testing independence and goodness of fit.

Click stream—Sequence of pages requested as a visitor explores a website.

Closed sort—Card sort in which participants are given a set of cards *and* a set of predetermined categories and asked to place the cards into those preexisting categories.

Closed-ended question—A question that provides a limited set of responses for participants to choose from (e.g., yes/no, agree/disagree, answer a/b).

Cluster analysis—Method for analyzing card sort data by calculating the strength of the perceived relationships between pairs of cards, based on the frequency with which members of each possible pair appear together.

Cognitive interference—The ability of one idea to interfere with another's ability to generate ideas.

Cognitive interview testing—This involves asking the target population to describe all the thoughts, feelings, and ideas that come to mind when examining specific questions or messages, and to provide suggestions to clarify wording as needed. Typically used to evaluate a survey prior to launch to determine if respondents understand the questions, interpret them the way you intended, and measure how long it takes to complete the survey.

Cognitive pretest—See *Cognitive interview testing*.

Cognitive walkthrough—A formative usability inspection method. It is task-based because it is based on the belief that people learn systems by trying to accomplish tasks with it, rather than first reading through instructions. It is ideal for products that are meant to be walk up and use (i.e., no training required).

Cohen's Kappa—Measure interrater reliability.

Communication speed—Whether one is speaking, writing, or typing, one can communicate an idea only as fast as he or she can speak, write, or type.

Competitive analysis—List of the features, strengths, weaknesses, user base, and price point for your competitors. It should include first-hand experience with the product(s) but can also include user reviews and analysis from external experts or trade publications.

Confidence interval—In statistics, it is a type of interval estimate of a population parameter. It is the range of values with a specified probability that the value of a parameter lies within it. In other words, it is the amount of uncertainty you are willing to accept.

Confidential disclosure agreement (CDA)—A legal agreement, which the participant signs and thereby agrees to keep all information regarding the product and/or session confidential for a predefined time.

Confidentiality—The practice of protecting participants' identity. In order to keep their participation confidential, do not associate a participant's name or other personally identifiable information with his or her data (e.g., notes, surveys, videos) unless the participant provides such consent in writing. Instead, use a participant ID (e.g., P1, participant 1).

Confound—A variable that should have been held constant but was accidentally allowed to vary (and covary) with the independent/predictor variable.

Conjoint analysis—Participants are presented a subset of possible feature combinations to determine the relative importance of each feature in their purchasing decision making. It is believed that relative values of attributes considered jointly can be better measured than when considered in isolation.

Consent form—A document that informs a participant of the purpose of the activity he or she is involved in, any risks involved, the expected duration, procedures, use of information collected (e.g., to design a new product), incentives for participation, and his/her rights as a participant. The participant signs this form to acknowledge that he or she has been informed of these things and agrees to participate.

Construct—The variable that you wish to measure.

Context of use—The situation and environment in which the task is conducted or product of interest is used.

Convenience sampling—The sample of the population used reflects those who were available (or those that you had access to), as opposed to selecting a truly representative sample of the population. Rather than selecting participants from the population at large, you recruit participants from a convenient subset of the population. For example, research done by college professors often uses college students for participants instead of representatives from the population at large.

Correlation—Relationship or connection between two or more variables.

Cost per complete—The amount you must spend in order to get one completed survey.

Coverage bias—Sampling bias in which certain groups of individuals are not represented in the sample for personal reasons or recruiting methods (e.g., households without a landline are not included in a telephone survey).

Crowd sourcing—In the case of data analysis, it is leveraging the services of groups of individuals not otherwise involved in the study to help categorize the study data.

Customer support comments—Feedback from customers or users about your product or service.

D

Data retention policy—An organization's established protocol for retaining participant data.

Data-logging software—Software that allows one to quickly take notes and automatically record data during a usability study.

Data saturation—It is the point during data collection at which no new relevant information emerges.

Debrief—The process of explaining a study to the participant once participation is complete.

Deep hanging out—Coined by anthropologist Clifford Geertz in 1998 to describe the anthropological research method of immersing oneself in a cultural, group, or social experience on an informal level.

Demand curve analysis—The relationship between the price of product and the amount or quantity the consumer is willing and able to purchase in a specified time period.

Dendrogram—A visual representation of a cluster analysis. Consists of many U-shaped lines connecting objects in a hierarchical tree. The height of each U represents the distance between the two objects being connected. The greater the distance, the less related the two objects are.

Descriptive statistics—These measures *describe* the sample in your population (e.g., measures of central tendency, measures of dispersion). They are the key calculations that will be of importance to you for close-ended questions and can easily be calculated by any basic statistics program or spreadsheet.

Design thinking—Human-centered design approach that integrates the people's needs, technological possibilities, and requirements for business success.

Desirability testing—Evaluates whether or not a product elicits the desired emotional response from users. It is most often conducted with a released version of your product (or competitor's product) to see how it makes participants feel.

Diary study—Longitudinal study in which participants respond to questions either in writing or via an app at specified times of a day.

Discussion guide—List of questions, discussion points, and things to observe in an interview.

Double negatives—The presence of two negatives in a sentence, making it difficult for the survey respondent or study participant to understand the true meaning of the question.

Double-barreled questions—A single question that addresses more than one issue at a time.

Drop-off rate—Respondents exiting the survey or remote, unmoderated study before completing it.

Droplist—Web widget that can expand to show a list of items to choose from.

E

Early adopters—People who start using a product or technology as soon as it becomes available.

Ecological validity—When a study mimics the real-world environment (e.g., observing users at the home or workplace).

ESOMAR—European Society for Opinion and Marketing Research. It provides a directory of market researchers around the world.

Ethnography—The study and systematic recording of the customs or behaviors of a people or culture.

Evaluation apprehension—The fear of being evaluated by others. Individuals with evaluation apprehension may not perform a specific task or speak truthfully for fear of another's negative opinion. The larger the group, the larger the affect.

Experience Sampling Methodology (ESM)—Diary-like study in which participants are pinged at random several times a day for several days and asked about their experience or what they are doing/thinking/feeling *right* now. It provides a reliable measure of the events occurring in the stream of consciousness over time.

Expert review—Usability inspection methods leverage experts (e.g., people with experience in usability/user research, subject matter experts) rather than actual end users to evaluate your product or service against a set of specific criteria. These are quick and cheap ways of catching the "low-hanging fruit" or obvious usability issues throughout the product development cycle.

Eye tracking study—An evaluation method that utilizes an eye tracker to record participant fixations and saccades (i.e., rapid eye movements between fixation points) to create a heat map of where people look (or do not look) for information or functionality and for how long.

F

Feasibility analysis—Evaluation and analysis of a product or feature to determine if it is technically feasible within an estimated cost and will be profitable.

Feature creep—The tendency for developers to add more and more features into a product as time goes by without clear need or purpose for them.

Feature-shedding—The tendency for developers to remove features from a product because of time constraints, limited resources, or business requirements.

Feedback form—A questionnaire that does not offer everyone in your population an equal chance of being selected to provide feedback (e.g., only the people on your mailing list are contacted, it is posted on your website under "Contact us" and only people who visit there will see it and have the opportunity to complete it). As a result, it does not necessarily represent your entire population.

Firewall—Computer software that prevents unauthorized access to private data on your computer or a network by outside computer users.

Focus troupe—Mini-workshop in which dramatic vignettes are presented to potential users where a new product concept is featured merely as a prop but not as an existing piece of technology.

Formative evaluation—Studies done early in the product development life cycle to discover insights and shape the design direction. They typically involve usability inspection methods or usability testing with low-fidelity mocks or prototypes.

Free-listing—Participants write down every word or phrase that comes to their mind in association with a particular topic, domain, etc.

Frequency—The number of times each response is chosen.

G

Gap analysis—A competitive analysis technique in which your product/service is compared against a competitor's to determine gaps in functionality. A value of "importance" and "satisfaction" is assigned to each function by end users. A single score is then determined for each function by subtracting the satisfaction from importance. This score is used to help determine whether resources should be spent incorporating each feature into the product.

Globalization—The process of expanding one's business, technology, or products across the globe. See also *Localization.*

Grounded theory—A form of inquiry where the goal of the researcher is to derive an abstract theory about an interaction that is grounded in the views of users (participants). During this form of inquiry, researchers engage in constant comparison to examine data with respect to categories as they emerge.

Groupthink—Within group decision-making procedures, it is the tendency for the various members of a group to try to achieve group consensus. The need for agreement takes priority over the motivation to obtain accurate knowledge to make appropriate decisions.

Guidelines—A general rule, principle, or piece of advice.

Guiding principles—The qualitative description of the principles the product stands by.

H

Hawthorne effect—Participants may behave differently when observed. They will likely be on their best behavior (e.g., observing standard operating procedures rather than using their usual shortcuts).

HCI—Acronym for human-computer interaction. Human-computer interaction is the field of study and practice that sits at the intersection of computer science and human factors. It is interested in understanding and creating interfaces for humans to interact successfully and easily with computers.

Heat map—Visualization created from an eye tracking study showing where participants looked at a website, app, product, etc. The longer the participants' gazes stay fixed on a spot, the "hotter" the area is on the map, indicated in red. As fewer participants look at an area or for less time, the "cooler" it gets and transitions to blue. Areas where no one looked are black.

Heuristic—A rule or guide based on the principles of usability.

Hits—The number of times a particular webpage is visited.

Human factors—The study of how humans behave physically and psychologically in relation to particular environments, products, or services.

I

Incentive—Gift provided to participants in appreciation for their time and feedback during a research study.

Incident diary—Participants are provided with a notebook containing worksheets to be completed on their own. The worksheets may ask users to describe a problem or issue they encountered, how they solved it (if they did), and how troublesome it was (e.g., via a Likert scale). It is given to users to keep track of issues they encounter while using a product.

Inclusive design—See *Universal design.*

Inference—A statement based on your interpretation of facts (compare to observation).

Inferential statistics—These measures allow us to make inferences or predictions about the characteristics of our population.

Information architecture—The organization of a product's structure and content, the labeling and categorizing of information, and the design of navigation and search systems. A good architecture helps users find information and accomplish their tasks.

Informed consent—A written statement of the participant's rights and any risks with participation presented at the beginning of a study. Participants sign this consent form saying they willingly agree to participate in the study.

Intercept surveys—A survey recruitment technique in which individuals are either stopped in person while completing a task (e.g., shopping in the mall) or online (e.g., booking a ticket on a travel site). When conducted online, the survey typically pops up and asks the user if he or she would like to complete a brief survey.

Internationalization—Process of developing the infrastructure in your product so that it can *potentially* be adapted for different languages and regions without requiring engineering changes each time.

Internet protocol (IP)—This is the method or protocol by which data are sent from one computer to another on the Internet.

Internet service provider (ISP)—A company that provides individuals or companies access to the Internet and other related services. Some of the largest ISPs include AT&T WorldNet, IBM Global Network, MCI, Netcom, UUNet, and PSINet.

Interrater agreement—See *Interrater reliability*.

Interrater reliability—The degree to which two or more observers assign the same rating or label to a behavior. In field studies, it would be the amount of agreement between observers coding the same user's behavior. High interrater reliability means that different observers coded the data in the same way.

Interviewer prestige bias—The interviewer informs participants that an authority figure feels one way or another about a topic and then asks the participant how he or she feels.

IP address—Every computer connected to the Internet is assigned a unique number known as an Internet protocol (IP) address. Since these numbers are usually assigned in country-based blocks, an IP address can often be used to identify the country from which a computer is connecting to the Internet.

Iterative design—Product changes are made over time based on user feedback or performance metrics to continually improve the user experience.

Iterative focus group—A style of focus group where the researcher presents a prototype to a group and gets feedback. Then, the same participants are brought back for a second focus group session where the new prototype is presented and additional feedback is gathered.

L

Laws—Rules set forth by the government and everyone must comply with them, regardless of where they work. Laws vary by country.

Leading questions—Questions that assume the answer and may pass judgment on the participant. They have the ability to influence a participant's answers.

Likert scale—A scale developed by Rensis Likert to measure attitudes. Participants are given a statement and five to seven levels along a scale to rate their agreement/disagreement, satisfaction/dissatisfaction, etc., with the statement.

Live experiments—From an HCI standpoint, this is a summative evaluation method that involves comparing two or more designs (live websites) to see which one performs better (e.g., higher click-through rate, higher conversion rate).

Live polling—An activity during a study in which participants are asked questions in order to get information about what most people think about something. Responses are collected and results are often displayed in real time.

Loaded questions—Questions that typically provide a "reason" for a problem listed in the question. This frequently happens in political campaigns to demonstrate that a majority of the population feels one way or another on a key issue.

Localization—Using the infrastructure created during internationalization to adapt your product to a specific language and/or region by adding in local-specific components and translating text. This means adapting your product to support different languages, regional differences, and technical requirements. But it is not enough to simply translate the content and localize things like currency, time, measurements, holidays, titles, standards (e.g., battery size, power source). You also must be aware of any regulatory compliance that applies to your product/domain (e.g., taxes, laws, privacy, accessibility, censorship).

Log files—When a file is retrieved from a website, server software keeps a record of it. The server stores this information in the form of text files. The information contained in a log file varies but can be programmed to capture more or less information.

Longitudinal study—Research carried out on the same participants over an extended period.

M

Margin of error—The amount of error you can tolerate in your statistical analysis.

Markers—Key events to the participant that you can probe into for richer information.

Measures of association—Using statistics, they allow you to identify the relationship between two survey variables (e.g., comparisons, correlations).

Measures of central tendency—Descriptive statistics that tell us where the middle is in a set of data (e.g., mean, median, mode).

Measures of dispersion—These statistics show you the "spread" or dispersion of the data around the mean (e.g., range, standard deviation, frequency).

Median—A measure of central tendency. When data points are ordered by magnitude, the median is the middlemost point in the distribution.

Mental model—A person's mental representation or organization of information.

Mixer—A video mixer/multiplexer will allow multiple inputs—from cameras, computers, or other inputs—to be combined into one mixed image. Some mixers will also allow creation of "picture in picture" (PIP) overlays. The output from a video mixer can be fed either directly into a screen (e.g., in the observation room) or into a recording device locally.

Mobile lab—See *Portable lab*.

Moderator—Individual who interacts with participant during a study.

Multimodal survey—Conducting a survey via more than one mode (e.g., online, paper, telephone, in person) to increase the response rate and representativeness of the sample.

Multiple-choice questions—Close-ended questions that provide multiple responses for the participant to choose from.

Multivariate testing—Follows the same principle as A/B testing but instead of manipulating one variable, multiple variables are manipulated to examine how changes in those variables interact to result in the ideal combination. All versions must be tested in parallel to control for extraneous variables that could affect your experiment (e.g., website outage, change in fees for your service).

N

N—In statistics, the size of a population or sample. Traditionally, N refers to the size of the population and n to the size of the sample.

NDA—See *Nondisclosure agreement*.

Negative user—See *Antiuser*.

Nominal data—Values or observations that can be assigned a code in the form of a number where the numbers are simply labels (e.g., male = 1, female = 2). You can count but not order or measure nominal data.

Nondisclosure agreement (NDA)—Legally binding agreements that protect your company's intellectual property by requiring participants to keep what they see and hear in your study confidential and hand over the ownership of any ideas, suggestions, or feedback they provide.

Nonmaleficence—In research ethics, this is the obligation that your research cannot do harm. Even stopping a study or intervention can actually cause harm, not just introducing the study or intervention.

Nonprobability sampling—Respondents are recruited from an opt-in panel that may or may not represent your desired population. There is not an equal chance (probability) for everyone in your user population to be recruited.

Nonresponder bias—People who do not respond to surveys (or participate in studies) can be significantly different from those who do. Consequently, missing the data from nonresponders can bias the data you collect, making your data less generalizable.

O

Observation—A statement of fact based on information obtained through one of the five senses (compare to an inference).

Observation guide—A list of general concerns or issues to guide your observations in a field study—but it is *not* a list of specific questions to ask.

Older adult—A person chronologically aged 65 years or more. This age is generally associated with declines in mental and physical capabilities and, in many developed countries, is the age at which people begin to receive pensions and social security benefits.

Omnibus survey—Most large survey vendors conduct regular omnibus surveys that combine a few questions from many clients and send them to a broad sample of users on their panels. It is kind of like carpooling but instead of sharing a car, you are sharing a survey instrument. This is a cheap and efficient method if you have just a few questions you want to ask a general population.

Open sort—Card sort in which participants are allowed to generate as many categories of information as they want, and name each of those categories however they please.

Open-ended question—A question designed to elicit detailed responses and free from structure (i.e., you do not provide options for the participant to choose from).

Outlier—A data point that has an extreme value and does not follow the characteristics of the data in general.

P

Page views—Number of users who visit a specific webpage.

Paradata—The information about the *process* of responding to the survey. This includes things like how long it took respondents to answer each question or the whole survey, if they changed any answers to their questions or went back to previous pages, if they opened and closed the survey without completing it (i.e., partial completion), how they completed it (e.g., smartphone app, web browser, phone, paper), etc.

Participant rights—The ethical obligations the researcher has to the participant in any research study.

Persona—An exemplar of a particular user type designed to bring the user profile to life during product development.

Pilot test—Study to evaluate the questions in your survey, interview, evaluation, or the methodology of your study to ensure you are measuring what you want to measure. It is typically done with a few individuals similar to your sample. It is an important step to ensure a successful study.

Policies—Guidelines set forth by your company, often with the goal of ensuring employees do not come close to breaking laws or just to enforce good business practices. Policies may vary by company.

Population—All of the customers or users of your current or potential product or service.

Portable lab—Set of equipment taken to the field to conduct a study (e.g., laptop, video recorder).

Power analysis—Statistical method that allows us to determine the sample size required to detect an effect of a given size with a given degree of confidence.

Prestige response bias—The participant wants to impress the facilitator and therefore provides answers that enhance his or her image.

Price sensitivity model—The degree to which the price of a product affects consumers' purchasing behaviors.

Primacy effect—The tendency for the first variable presented to participants (e.g., first item in a list, first prototype shown) to influence a participant's choice.

Primary users—Those individuals who work regularly or directly with the product.

Privacy—An individual's right to prevent others from knowing his or her personally identifying information.

Probability sampling—Recruiting method that ensures everyone in your population has an equal chance (probability) of being selected to participate in your study.

Procedural knowledge—Stored information that consists of knowledge of how to do things.

Process analysis—A method by which a participant explains step-by-step how something is done or how to do something.

Product development life cycle—The duration and process of a product from idea to release.

Production blocking—In verbal brainstorming, people are asked to speak one at a time. By having to wait in a queue to speak, ideas are sometimes lost or suppressed. Attention is also shifted from listening to other speakers toward trying to remember one's own idea.

Progress indicators—Online survey widget to let respondents know how far along they are and how many more questions they have left to complete.

Protocol—A script that outlines all procedures you will perform as a study moderator and the order in which you will carry out these procedures. It acts as a checklist for all of the session steps.

Proxy—Server that acts as a mediator between a user's computer and the Internet so that a company can ensure security, administrative control, and caching service.

Purposive sampling—Also known as selective or subjective sampling, this nonprobability sampling technique involves recruiting a nonrepresentative sample of your larger population in order to serve some purpose. This is typically done with you having a specific group in mind that you wish to study (e.g., small business owners).

Q

Qualitative data—Represents verbal or narrative pieces of data. These types of data are collected through focus groups, interviews, open-ended questionnaire items, and other less structured situations.

Quantitative data—Numeric information that includes things like personal income, amount of time, or a rating of an opinion on a scale from 1 to 5. Even things that you do not think of as quantitative, like feelings, can be collected using numbers if you create scales to measure them.

R

Random Digit Dialing (RDD)—Survey recruiting method in which telephone numbers are selected at random from a subset of households.

Random sampling—Each member within a population has an equal chance of being selected for a study.

Range—The maximum value minus the minimum value. It indicates the spread between the two extremes.

Ranking—This type of scale question gives participants a variety of options and asks them to provide a rank for each one. Unlike the rating scale question, the respondent is allowed to use each rank only once.

Rating scale—Survey question that presents users with an item and asks them to select from a number of choices along a continuum. The Likert scale is the most commonly used rating scale.

Reliable/reliability—Reliability is the extent to which the test or measurement yields the same approximate results when used repeatedly under the same conditions.

Research ethics—The obligation of the researcher to protect participants from harm, ensure confidentiality, provide benefit, and secure informed consent.

Response bias—In any study in which responses of some sort (e.g., answers to set questions) are required of participants, *response bias* exists if, independently of the effect of any experimental manipulation, the participants are more likely to respond in one way than in another (e.g., more likely, in a multiple-choice task, to choose option A than option B).

Response distribution—For each question, it is how skewed you expect the response to be.

Retrospective interview—An interview that is done after an event has taken place.

Retrospective think-aloud—Participants are shown a video of their session and asked to tell the moderator what they were thinking at the time.

S

Sample—A portion of the population selected to be representative of the population as a whole. Since it is typically unfeasible to collect data from the entire population of users, you must select a smaller subset.

Sample size—The number of participants in your study.

Sampling bias—The tendency of a sample to exclude some members of the sampling population and overrepresent others.

Sampling plan—A list of days/times to observe users. This should include days/times when you anticipate key events (e.g., the day before Thanksgiving, or bad weather at an airport), as well as "normal" days.

Satisficing—Decision-making strategy in which participants scan the available alternatives (typically options in a survey question) until they find the minimally acceptable option. This is contrasted with optimal decision making, which attempts to find the best alternative available.

Scenario—A story about a user. It provides a setting, has actors, objectives or goals, a sequence of events, and closes with a result. It is used to illustrate how an end user works or behaves.

Screen-capture software—Software that automatically records a computer desktop or other digital input (e.g., mobile device via HDMI cable).

Screener—Survey that captures data about potential participants in order to select which individuals to include in a study based on certain criteria.

Secondary users—Individuals that utilize the product infrequently or through an intermediary.

Selection bias—The selection of research participants for a study that is nonrandom and thus results in a nonrepresentative sample. Nonresponse bias and self-selection bias are two forms of selection bias.

Self-report—A form of data collection where participants are asked to respond and/or describe a feeling or behavior about themselves. These reports represent participants' own perceptions, but are subject to limitations such as human memory.

Self-selection bias—Bias that results because a certain type of person has volunteered or "self-selected" to be a part of your study (e.g., those people who have a special interest in the topic, those who really just want your incentive, those who have a lot of spare time on their hands, etc.). If those who volunteered differ from those who did not, there will be bias in your sample.

Semi-structured interview—The interviewer may begin with a set of questions to answer (closed- and open-ended) but deviate from that set of questions from time to time. It does not have quite the same conversational approach as an unstructured interview.

Significance testing—Statistical methods used to determine whether a claim about a population from which a sample has been drawn is the result of chance alone or the effect of the variable under study. Tests for statistical significance tell us the probability that a relationship we think exists is due only to random chance.

Significant event—A specific experience in a participant's past that either exemplifies specific experiences or that is particularly noteworthy.

Similarity matrix—A matrix of scores that represents the similarity between a number of data points. Each element of the similarity matrix contains a measure of similarity between two of the data points.

Simplification bias—If the researcher is a novice to the domain, he or she may have a tendency to conceptually simplify the expert user's problem-solving strategies while observing the expert. This is not done intentionally, of course, but the researcher does not have the complex mental model of the expert.

Snowball sampling—Nonprobability sampling method in which participants in one study are asked to recruit participants for future studies from their acquaintances.

Social desirability bias—Participants provide responses to your questions that they believe are more socially desirable or acceptable than the truth.

Social loafing—The tendency for individuals to reduce the effort that they make toward some task when working together with others. The larger the group, the larger the effect.

Social sentiment analysis—Analysis of text posted by customers or users on social media, online forums, product review sites, blogs, etc.

Sponsor-blind study—Study in which participants are not informed what organization is paying for the study.

Stakeholder—An individual or group with an interest (or stake) in your user requirements activity and its results. Stakeholders typically influence the direction of the product (e.g., product managers, developers, business analysts, etc.).

Standard deviation—A measure of dispersion, it calculates the deviation from the mean. The larger the standard deviation, the more varied the responses were that participants gave.

Statistically significant—The probability that the results you obtained were unlikely to have occurred by chance.

Storyboards—Illustrate a particular task or a "day-in-the-life" of the user using representative images to illustrate a task/scenario/story. Merge data across your users to develop a generic, representative description.

Straight-lining—In survey completion, participants select the same choice for all questions rather than read and consider each option individually.

Structured data—Data that reside in a fixed field within a record or file. This includes data contained in relational databases and spreadsheets.

Subject matter expert—Domain expert who is an authority on a given topic or domain.

Summative evaluation—Studies typically done toward the end of the product development life cycle with high-fidelity prototypes or the actual final product to evaluate it against a set of metrics (e.g., time on task, success rate). This can be done via in-person or remote usability testing or live experiments.

Surrogate products—These are products that may or may not compete directly with your product. They have similar features to your product and should be studied to learn about the strengths and weaknesses.

Surveys—Data collection technique in which a sample of the population is asked to self-report data via a questionnaire on paper or online or is interviewed in person or over the phone and a researcher completes a questionnaire for the respondent.

Synchronous—Testing and/or communication that requires a participant and a researcher to be working together at the same chronological time.

Synergy—An idea from one participant positively influences another participant, resulting in an additional idea that would not have been generated without the initial idea.

T

Task allocation—The process of determining who or what should be responsible for completing various tasks in a system. This may be dividing tasks among different humans or between human and machine based on specific criteria.

Telescoping—People have a tendency to compress time. So, if you are asking about events that happened in the last six months, people may unintentionally include events that happened in the last nine months. Overreporting of events will result.

Tertiary users—Those who are affected by the system or the purchasing decision makers.

Think-aloud protocol—A technique used during usability activities. The participant is asked to vocalize his/her thoughts, feelings, and opinions while working or interacting with the product.

Transfer of training—Transfer of learned skills from one situation to another. You are leveraging the users' current skill set so they do not have to learn everything new to use your product.

Translation bias—Expert users will attempt to translate their knowledge so that the researcher can understand it. The more experts translate, the more there is the potential for them to oversimplify and distort their knowledge/skills/etc.

Triangulation of data—Combining data from multiple methods to develop a holistic picture of the user or domain.

Trusted testers—A set of vetted evaluators given early access to a product or service to provide feedback. This nonprobability sampling recruiting method may not be representative of your broader population but is used when there are confidentiality concerns.

t-Test—Statistical test of two population means.

Two-way mirror—A panel of glass that can be seen through from one side but is a mirror on the other.

U

Unipolar construct—Variables or units that go from nothing to a lot (e.g., Not at all useful to Extremely useful).

Universal design—A product or service that enables everyone to access and use your product or service regardless of one's age, abilities, or status in life.

Unstructured data—Refers to information that does not reside in a traditional row-column database. As you might expect, it is the opposite of structured data—the data stored in fields in a database.

Usability—The effectiveness, efficiency, and satisfaction with which users can achieve tasks when using a product. A usable product is easy to learn and remember, efficient, visually pleasing, and pleasant to use. It enables users to recover quickly from errors and accomplish their tasks with ease.

Usability inspection method—Methods that leverage experts (e.g., people with experience in usability/user research, subject matter experts) rather than involve actual end users to evaluate your product or service against a set of specific criteria. These are quick and cheap ways of catching the "low-hanging fruit" or obvious usability issues throughout the product development cycle (e.g., heuristic evaluation, cognitive walkthrough).

Usability lab—Space dedicated to conducting usability studies. Typically contains recording equipment and the product you wish to get feedback on. It may contain a two-way mirror to allow the product team to view the study from another room.

Usability testing—The systematic observation of end users attempting to complete a task or set of tasks with your product based on representative scenarios.

User experience—The study of a person's behaviors, attitudes, and emotions about using a particular product, system, or service.

User profile—A list of characteristics and skills that describe the end user. It should provide the range of characteristics or skill levels that a typical end user may fall in, as well as the most common ones.

User requirements—The features/attributes your product should have or how it should perform from the users' perspective.

User-centered design (UCD)—A product development approach that focuses on the end users of a product. The philosophy is that the product should fit the user, rather than making the user fit the product. This is accomplished by employing techniques, processes, and methods throughout the product life cycle that focus on the user.

V

Vague questions—Questions that include imprecise terms like “rarely,” “sometimes,” “usually,” “few,” “some,” or “most.” Individuals can interpret these terms in different ways, affecting their answers and your interpretation of the results.

Valid/validity—The degree to which a question or task actually measures the desired trait.

Visit summary template—A standardized survey or worksheet used in field studies. It is given to each investigator to complete at the end of each visit. This helps everyone get his or her thoughts on paper while fresh in his or her mind. It also speeds data analysis and avoids reporting only odd or funny anecdotal data.

W

Warm-up activity—Activity for getting participants comfortable at the beginning of a study.

Web analytics—Measurement and analysis of web data to assess the effectiveness of a website or service.

APPENDIX D

REFERENCES

Chapter 1: Introduction to User Experience

Bias, R. G., & Mayhew, D. J. (2005). *Cost-justifying usability: An update for the Internet age* (2nd ed.). San Francisco, CA: Morgan Kaufmann Publishers.

Burns, M., Manning, H., & Petersen, J. (2012). *The business impact of customer experience, 2012. Business case: The experience-driven organization playbook*. Cambridge, MA: Forrester. http://www.forrester.com/The+Business+Impact+Of+Customer+Experience+2012/fulltext/-/E-RES61251.

Farrell, S., & Nielsen, J. (2014). *User experience career advice: How to learn UX and get a job*. Retrieved from, http://www.nngroup.com/reports/user-experience-careers/.

Forrester's North American Technographics Customer Experience Online Survey, Q4, 2011 (US).

Gould, J. D., & Lewis, C. (1985). Designing for usability: key principles and what designers think. *Communications of the ACM*, *2*(3), 300–311.

Hackos, J. T., & Redish, J. C. (1998). *User and Task Analysis for Interface Design*. New York: John Wiley & Sons.

IBM. (2001). *Cost justifying ease of use: Complex solutions are problems*. October 9, 2001. Available at www-3.ibm.com/ibm/easy/eou_ext.nsf/Publish/23.

Johnson, J. (2008). *GUI bloopers 2.0: Common user interface design don'ts and dos*. Morgan Kaufmann.

Keeley, L., Walters, H., Pikkel, R., & Quinn, B. (2013). *Ten types of innovation: The discipline of building breakthroughs*. Hoboken, NJ: John Wiley & Sons.

Lederer, A. L., & Prasad, J. (1992). Nine management guidelines for better cost estimating. *Communications of the ACM*, *35*(2), 51–59.

Manning, H., & Bodine, K. (2012). *Outside in: The power of putting customers at the center of your business*. New York: Houghton Mifflin Harcourt.

Marcus, A. (2002). *Return on investment for usable UI design, user experience, Winter, 25–31*. Bloomingdale, IL: Usability Professionals' Association.

Nielsen, J. (2000). *Why you only need to test with 5 users*. Retrieved from, http://www.nngroup.com/articles/why-you-only-need-to-test-with-5-users/.

Norman, D. A. (2006). Words matter. Talk about people: not customers, not consumers, not users. *Interactions*, *13*(5), 49–63.

Pressman, R. S. (1992). *Software engineering: A practitioner's approach*. New York: McGraw-Hill.

Rhodes, J. (2000). *Usability can save your company*. [Webpage] Retrieved from, http://webword.com/moving/savecompany.html.

Sharon, T. (2012). *It's Our Research*. Morgan Kaufmann.

Stone, M. (2013). Back to basics. [Blog post] Retrieved from, http://mariastonemashka123.wordpress.com/.

Weigers, K. E. (1999). *Software Requirements*. Redmond, WA: Microsoft Press.

Weinberg, J. (1997). *Quality Software Management. Vol. 4: Anticipating change*. New York: Dorset House.

Chapter 2: Before You Choose an Activity: Learning About Your Product Users

AARP. (2009). *Beyond 50.09 chronic care: A call to action for health reform*. Retrieved from, http://www.aarp.org/health/medicare-insurance/info-03-2009/beyond_50_hcr.html.

Benedek, J., & Miner, T. (2002). Measuring desirability: New methods for evaluating desirability in a usability lab setting. In *Proceedings of UPA 2002 Conference,* Orlando, FL.

Chavan, A. L., & Munshi, S. (2004). Emotion in a ticket. In *CHI'04 extended abstracts on human factors in computing systems* (pp. 1544–1544). New York, NY, USA: ACM.

Chavan, A. L., & Prabhu, G. V. (Eds.). (2010). *Innovative solutions: What designers need to know for today's emerging markets*. CRC Press.

Costa, T., Dalton, J., Gillett, F. E., Gill, M., Campbell, C., & Silk, D. (2013). *Build seamless experiences now: Experience persistence transforms fragmented interactions into a unified system of engagement*. Forrester. Retrieved from, http://www.forrester.com/Build+Seamless+Experiences+Now/fulltext/-/E-RES97021.

Department of Health and Human Services, Administration on Aging. (2010). *Trends in the older population using Census 2000, Estimates 2001–2009, Census 2010*. Retrieved from: http://www.aoa.gov/AoAroot/Aging_Statistics/Census_Population/census2010/docs/Trends_Older_Pop.xls.

Fisk, A. D., Rogers, W. A., Charness, N., Czaja, S. J., & Sharit, J. (2009). *Designing for older adults: Principles and creative human factors approaches* (2nd ed.). Boca Raton, FL: CRC.

Folstein, M. F., Folstein, S. E., & McHugh, P. R. (1975). Mini-mental state: A practical method for grading the cognitive state of patients for the clinician. *Journal of Psychiatric Research, 12*(3), 189–198.

Geert, H., & Jan, H. G. (1991). *Cultures and organizations: Software of the mind*. New York: McGraw-Hill.

Hall, E. T. (1989). *Beyond culture*. Random House LLC.

Mace, R. (1985). Universal design: Barrier free environments for everyone. *Designers West, 33*(1), 147–152.

McInerney, P. (2003). Getting More from UCD Scenarios. Paper for IBM MITE. Available at: http://www-306.ibm.com/ibm/easy/eou_ext.nsf/Publish/50?OpenDocument&../Publish/1111/$File/paper1111.pdf.

Pew Internet Research Project Social Networking Media Fact Sheet. Retrieved from: http://www.pewinternet.org/fact-sheets/social-networking-fact-sheet/ on April 27, 2014.

Plocher, T., & Chavan, A. (2002). User needs research special interest group. In *CHI'02 extended abstracts on human factors in computing systems*. ACM, New York, NY, USA.

Snider, J. G., & Osgood, C. E. (Eds.), (1969). *Semantic differential technique; a sourcebook*. Hawthorne, NY: Aldine Pub. Co.

Story, M., Mace, R., & Mueller, J. (1998). *The universal design file: Designing for people of all ages and abilities*. Raleigh, NC: Center for Universal Design, NC State University.

Chapter 5: Choosing a User Experience Research Activity

Bernard, H. R. (2000). *Social research methods*. Thousand Oaks, CA: Sage.

Creswell, J. W. (1998). *Qualitative inquiry and research design: Choosing among five traditions*. Thousand Oaks, CA: Sage Publications.

Fishbein, M., & Ajzen, I. (1975). *Belief, attitude, intention, and behavior: An introduction to theory and research*. Reading, MA: Addison-Wesley.

Food and Drug Administration. (2014). *Draft guidance for industry and Food and Drug Administration staff—Applying human factors and usability engineering to optimize medical device design*. Silver Spring, MD: U.S. Food and Drug Administration.

Green, J., & Thorogood, N. (2009). *Qualitative methods for health research* (2nd ed.). Thousand Oaks, CA: Sage.

Guest, G., Bunce, A., & Johnson, L. (2006). How many interviews are enough? *Field Methods*, *18*(1), 59–82. http://dx.doi.org/10.1177/1525822X05279903, Sage Publications.

Hektner, J. M., Schmidt, J. A., & Csikszentmihalyi, M. (2007). *Experience sampling method: Measuring the quality of everyday life*. Thousand Oaks, CA: Sage.

Hwang, W., & Salvendy, G. (2010). Number of people required for usability evaluation: the 10±2 rule. *Communications of the ACM*, *53*(5), 130–133.

Krueger, R. A., & Casey, M. A. (2000). *Focus groups: A practical guide for applied research*. Thousand Oaks, CA: Sage Publications Inc.

Morse, J. M. (1994). Designing funded qualitative research. In N. K. Denzin, & Y. S. Lincoln (Eds.), *Handbook of qualitative research* (2nd ed., pp. 220–235). Thousand Oaks, CA: Sage.

Nielsen, J. (1994). Estimating the number of subjects needed for a thinking aloud test. *International Journal of Human-Computer Studies*, *41*, 385–397.

Nielsen, J. (2000). Why you only need to test with 5 users. Alertbox. Available at: www.useit.com/alertbox/20000319.html.

Quesenbery, W., & Szuc, D. (2005). *Choosing the right usability tool*. Retrieved from: http://www.wqusability.com/handouts/right-tool.pdf.

Sauro, J., & Lewis, J. R. (2012). *Quantifying the user experience: Practical statistics for user research*. Burlington: Elsevier.

Sears, A., & Jacko, J. (2012). *The human-computer interaction handbook: Fundamentals, evolving technologies*. Boca Raton, FL: CRC Press.

Tullis, T., & Wood, L. (2004). How many users are enough for a card-sorting study? In *Proceedings UPA'2004* (Minneapolis, MN, June 7–11, 2004).

Chapter 6: Preparing for Your User Research Activity

Bohannon, J., 2011. *Science, 334*.

Buhrmester, M., Kwang, T., & Gosling, S. (2011). Amazon's mechanical Turk: a new source of inexpensive, yet high-quality, data? *Perspectives on Psychological Science*, *6*, 3.

Casler, K., Bickel, L., & Hackett, E. (2013). Separate but equal? A comparison of participants and data gathered via Amazon's MTurk, social media, and face-to-face behavioral testing. *Journal of Computers in Human Behavior, 29*(6), 2156–2160.

Dray, S., & Mrazek, D. (1996). A day in the life of a family: An international ethnographic study. In D. R. Wixon & J. Ramey (Eds.), *Field methods casebook for software design*. New York: John Wiley & Sons.

Kittur, A., Chi, E., & Suh, B. (2008). *Crowdsourcing user studies with Mechanical Turk*. In *Proceedings of the SIGCHI conference on human factors in computing systems* (pp. 453–456).

Chapter 7: During Your User Research Activity

Boren, M. T., & Ramey, J. (2000). Thinking aloud: Reconciling theory and practice. *IEEE Transactions on Professional Communication, 43*(3), 261–278.

Dumas, J. S., & Redish, J. C. (1999). *A practical guide to usability testing* (2nd ed.). Exeter, England: Intellect Books.

Nisbett, R. E., & Wilson, T. D. (1977). Telling more than we can know: Verbal reports on mental processes. *Psychological Review, 84*(3), 231–259.

Chapter 8: Diary Studies

Allport, G. W. (1942). *The use of personal documents in psychological science*. New York: Social Science Research Council.

Engelberger, J. F. (1982). Robotics in practice: Future capabilities. *Electronic Servicing & Technology magazine*.

Hackos, J. T., & Redish, J. C. (1998). *User and task analysis for interface design*. New York: John Wiley & Sons.

Kahneman, D., Krueger, A. B., Schkade, D., Schwarz, N., & Stone, A. A. (2004). A survey method for characterizing daily life experience: The day reconstruction method. *Science, 306*, 1776–1780.

Kahneman, D. (2011). *Thinking, fast and slow*. New York: Farrar, Strauss, Giroux.

Larson, R., & Csikszentmihalyi, M. (1983). The experience sampling method. In H. T. Reis (Ed.), *Naturalistic Approaches to Studying Social Interaction. New Directions for Methodology of Social and Behavioral Science: Vol. 15* (pp. 41–56). San Francisco: Jossey-Bass.

Yue, Z., Litt, E., Cai, C. J., Stern, J., Baxter, K. K., Guan, Z., et al. (2014, April). Photographing information needs: the role of photos in experience sampling method-style research. In *Proceedings of the 32nd annual ACM conference on human factors in computing systems* (pp. 1545–1554). ACM.

Chapter 9: Interviews

Alreck, P. L., & Settle, R. B. (1995). *The survey research handbook* (2nd ed.). Burr Ridge, IL: Irwin Professional Publishing.

Amato, P. R. (2000). The consequences of divorce for adults and children. *Journal of Marriage and the Family, 62*(4), 1269–1287.

Boren, M. T., & Ramey, J. (2000). Thinking aloud: Reconciling theory and practice. *IEEE Transactions on Professional Communication, 43*, 261–278.

Census, U. S. (2006). *Children living apart from parents—Characteristics of children under 18 and designated parents*.

Census, U. S. (2008). *Household relationship and living arrangements of children under 18 years, by age and sex*.

De Swert, K. (2012). Calculating inter-coder reliability in media content analysis using Krippendorff's Alpha, Available online: http://www.polcomm.org/wp-content/uploads/ICR01022012.pdf.

Dumas, J. S., & Redish, J. C. (1999). *A practical guide to usability testing* (2nd ed.). Exeter, England: Intellect Books.

Green, J., & Thorogood, N. (2009). *Qualitative methods for health research* (2nd). Thousand Oaks, CA: Sage.

Guest, G., Bunce, A., & Johnson, L. (2006). How many interviews are enough? An experiment with data saturation and variability. *Field Methods*, *18*, 59–82.

Johnson, T., Hougland, J., & Clayton, R. (1989). Obtaining reports of sensitive behavior: A comparison of substance use reports from telephone and face-to-face interviews. *Social Science Quarterly*, *70*(1), 173–183.

Krosnick, J. A. (1999). Survey research. *Annual Review of Psychology*, *50*, 537–567.

Landis, J. R., & Koch, G. G. (1977). The measurement of observer agreement for categorical. *Biometrics*, *33*, 159–174.

Shefts, K. R. (2002). Virtual visitation: The next generation of options for parent-child communication. *Family Law Quarterly*, *36*(2), 303–327.

Stafford, M. (2004). Communication competencies and sociocultural priorities of middle childhood. In *Handbook of family communication* (pp. 311–332). Mahwah, NJ: Lawrence Erlbaum Associates.

Yarosh, S., Chew, Y. C., & Abowd, G. D. (2009). Supporting parent-child communication in divorced families. *International Journal of Human-Computer Studies*, *67*(2), 192–203.

Yarosh, S., & Abowd, G. D. (2011). Mediated parent-child contact in work-separated families. In *Proc. of CHI* (pp. 1185–1194). ACM.

Yarosh, S. (2014). Conflict in families as an ethical and methodological consideration. In T. K. Judge & C. Neustaedter (Eds.), *Evaluating and designing for domestic life: research methods for human-computer interaction*. Springer Publishers.

Chapter 10: Surveys

Callegaro, M., Baker, R. P., Bethlehem, J., Göritz, A. S., Krosnick, J. A., & Lavrakas, P. J. (Eds.). (2014). *Online panel research: A data quality perspective*. John Wiley & Sons.

Chang, L., & Krosnick, J. A. (2009). National surveys via RDD telephone interviewing versus the Internet comparing sample representativeness and response quality. *Public Opinion Quarterly*, *73*(4), 641–678.

Couper, M. (2008). *Designing effective web surveys*. Cambridge: Cambridge University Press.

Crow, D., Johnson, M., & Hanneman, R. (2011). Benefits—and costs—of a multi-mode survey of recent college graduates. *Survey Practice*, *4*(5).

Dillman, D. A., Smyth, J. D., & Christian, L. M. (2009). *Internet, mail, and mixed-mode surveys: The tailored design method* (3rd ed.). Hoboken, NJ: John Wiley and Sons.

Greenlaw, C., & Brown-Welty, S. (2009). A comparison of web-based and paper-based survey methods testing assumptions of survey mode and response cost. *Evaluation Review*, *33*(5), 464–480.

Groves, R. M., Dilman, D. A., Eltinge, J. L., & Little, R. J. A. (2002). Survey nonresponse in design, data collection, and analysis. In R. M. Groves, D. A. Dilman, J. L. Eltinge, & J.A. Little Roderick (Eds.), *Survey nonresponse*. New York: John Wiley and Sons.

Holbrook, A. L., Green, M. C., & Krosnick, J. A. (2003). Telephone versus face-to-face interviewing of national probability samples with long questionnaires: Comparisons of respondent satisficing and social desirability response bias. *Public Opinion Quarterly*, *67*(1), 79–125.

Holbrook, A. L., Krosnick, J. A., & Pfent, A. (2007). Response rates in surveys by the news media and government contractor survey research firms. In J. Lepkowski, B. Harris-Kojetin, & P. J. Lavrakas (Eds.), *Advances in telephone survey methodology* (pp. 499–528). New York, NY: Wiley.

Krosnick, J. A., Li, F., & Lehman, D. R. (1990). Conversational conventions, order of information acquisition, and the effect of base rates and individuating information on social judgments. *Journal of Personality and Social Psychology*, *59*(6), 1140.

Krosnick, J. (1991). Response strategies for coping with the cognitive demands of attitude measures in surveys. *Applied Cognitive Psychology*, *5*, 213–236.

Krosnick, J., Narayan, S., & Smith, W. (1996). Satisficing in surveys: Initial evidence. *New Directions for Evaluation*, *1996*(70), 29–44.

Krosnick, J., & Fabrigar, L. (1997). Designing rating scales for effective measurement in surveys. In *Survey measurement and process quality* (pp. 141–164).

Krosnick, J. (1999). Survey research. *Annual Review of Psychology*, *50*(1), 537–567.

Krosnick, J. A., & Tahk, A. M. (2008). *The optimal length of rating scales to maximize reliability and validity*. California: Stanford University, Unpublished manuscript.

Krosnick, J., & Presser, S. (2010). Question and questionnaire design. In *Handbook of survey research*. (2nd ed., pp. 263–314). Bingley, UK: Emerald.

Landon, E. (1971). Order bias, the ideal rating, and the semantic differential. *Journal of Marketing Research*, *8*(3), 375–378.

Müller, H., Sedley, A., & Ferrall-Nunge, E. (2014). Survey research in HCI. In *Ways of knowing in HCI* (pp. 229–266). New York: Springer.

Saris, W. E., Revilla, M., Krosnick, J. A., & Shaeffer, E. (2010). Comparing questions with agree/disagree response options to questions with item-specific response options. *Survey Research Methods*, *4*(1).

Sedley, A., & Müller, H. (2013). Minimizing change aversion for the google drive launch. In *CHI'13 extended abstracts on human factors in computing systems* (pp. 2351–2354). ACM.

Schlenker, B., & Weigold, M. (1989). Goals and the self-identification process: Constructing desired identities. In *Goal concepts in personality and social psychology* (pp. 243–290).

Schonlau, M., Zapert, K., Simon, L. P., Sanstad, K. H., Marcus, S. M., Adams, J., et al. (2004). A comparison between responses from a propensity-weighted web survey and an identical RDD survey. *Social Science Computer Review*, *22*(1), 128–138.

Smith, D. (1967). Correcting for social desirability response sets in opinion-attitude survey research. *The Public Opinion Quarterly*, *31*(1), 87–94.

Tourangeau, R. (1984). *Cognitive science and survey methods*. In *Cognitive aspects of survey methodology: Building a bridge between disciplines* (pp. 73–100).

Tourangeau, R., Couper, M. P., & Conrad, F. (2004). Spacing, position, and order interpretive heuristics for visual features of survey questions. *Public Opinion Quarterly*, *68*(3), 368–393.

Vannette, D. L., & Krosnick, J. A. (2014). *A comparison of survey satisficing and mindlessness. The Wiley Blackwell handbook of mindfulness, 1, 312*. Wiley-Blackwell.

Villar, A., Callegaro, M., & Yang, Y. (2013). Where am I? A meta-analysis of experiments on the effects of progress indicators for web surveys. *Social Science Computer Review, 31*(6), 744–762.

Weisberg, H. F. (2005). *The total survey error approach: A guide to the new science of survey research*. Chicago: The University of Chicago Press.

Wildt, A. R., & Mazis, M. B. (1978). Determinants of scale response: Label versus position. *Journal of Marketing Research, 15*, 261–267.

Yeager, D. S., Krosnick, J. A., Chang, L., Javitz, A. S., Levendusky, M. S., Simpser, A., et al. (2011). Comparing the accuracy of RDD telephone surveys and Internet surveys conducted with probability and non-probability samples. *Public Opinion Quarterly, 75*(4), 709–747.

Chapter 11: Card Sorting

Nielsen, J., & Sano, D. (1994). SunWeb: User interface design for Sun Microsystem's internal web. In *Proceedings of the 2nd world wide web conference '94: Mosaic and the web,* Chicago, IL, 17-20 October (pp. 547–557). Available at, http://archive.ncsa.uiuc.edu/SDG/IT94/Proceedings/HCI/nielsen/sunweb.html.

Nielsen Norman Group. (2014). Intranet Design Annual: 2013. *Nielsen Norman Group. Web.* 27 March 2014.

Spencer, D. (2009). *Card sorting*: *Designing usable categories*. Brooklyn, New York: Rosenfeld Media, LLC. 82. Print.

Spencer, D. (2010). *A practical guide to information architecture*. Penarth, UK: Five Simple Steps.

Tullis, T. S. (1985). *Designing a menu-based interface to an operating system*. In: *CHI '85 proceedings, San Francisco, CA* (pp. 79–84).

Tullis, T., & Wood, L. (2004). How many users are enough for a card-sorting study? In *Proceedings of the Usability Professionals' Association 2004 conference,* Minneapolis, MN, 7-11 June (CD-ROM).

Zavod, M. J., Rickert, D. E., & Brown, S. H. (2002). The automated card-sort as an interface design tool: A comparison of products. In *Proceedings of the Human Factors and Ergonomics Society 46th annual meeting,* Baltimore, MD, 30 September-4 October (pp. 646–650).

Chapter 12: Focus Groups

Dolan, W., Wiklund, M., Logan, R., & Augaitis, S. (1995). *Participatory design shapes future of telephone handsets*. In *Proceedings of the Human Factors and Ergonomics Society 39th annual meeting. San Diego, CA, 9–13 October* (pp. 331–335).

Dumas, J. S., & Redish, J. C. (1999). *A practical guide to usability testing* (2nd). Exeter, England: Intellect Books.

Gray, B. G., Barfield, W., Haselkorn, M., Spyridakis, J., & Conquest, L. (1990). *The design of a graphics-based traffic information system based on user requirements*. In *Proceedings of the Human Factors and Ergonomics Society 34th annual meeting. Orlando, FL, 8–12 October* (pp. 603–606).

Hackos, J. T., & Redish, J. C. (1998). *User and task analysis for interface design*. New York: John Wiley & Sons.

Karlin, J. E., & Klemmer, E. T. (1989). An interview. In E. T. Klemmer (Ed.), *Ergonomics: Harness the power of human factors in your business* (pp. 197–201). Norwood, NJ: Ablex.

Kelly, T. (2001). *The art of innovation*. New York: DoubleDay.

Krueger, R. (1998). *Developing questions for focus groups*. Thousand Oaks, CA: Sage Publications.

Krueger, R., & Casey, M. A. (2000). *Focus groups: A practical guide for applied research*. London: Sage Publications.

Root, R. W., & Draper, S. (1983). Questionnaires as a software evaluation tool. In *Proceedings of the ACM CHI conference. Boston, MA, 12–15 December* (pp. 83–87).

Sato, S., & Salvador, T. (1999). Playacting and focus troupe: Theater techniques for creating quick, intense, immersive, and engaging focus groups sessions. *Interactions*, *6*(5), 35–41.

Schindler, R. M. (1992). The real lesson of new coke: The value of focus groups for predicting the effects of social influence. *Marketing Research: A Magazine of Management and Applications*, *4*, 22–27.

Chapter 13: Field Studies

Beyer, H., & Holtzblatt, K. (1998). *Contextual design: Defining customer-centered systems*. San Francisco: Morgan Kaufmann.

Brooke, T., & Burrell, J. (2003). From ethnography to design in a vineyard. In *DUX 2003 Proceedings, San Francisco, CA* (pp. 1–4). http://www.aiga.org/resources/content/9/7/8/documents/brooke.pdf.

Creswell, J. W. (2003). *Research design: Qualitative, quantitative and mixed methods approaches.* (2nd ed.).

Dumas, J. S., & Salzman, M. C. (2006). *Reviews of Human Factors and Ergonomics*, *2*, 109.

Hackos, J. T., & Redish, J. C. (1998). *User and task analysis for interface design*. New York: JohnWiley & Sons.

Kirah, A., Fuson, C., Grudin, J., & Feldman, E. (2005). Usability assessment methods. In R. G. Bias, & D. J. Mayhew (Eds.), *Cost-justifying usability: An update for an Internet age*.

Laakso, S. A., Laakso, K., & Page, C. (2001). *DUO: A discount observation method*. Available at: www.cs.helsinki.fi/u/salaakso/papers/DUO.pdf.

Landsberger, H. A. (1958). *Hawthorne Revisited*. Ithaca.

Ramey, J., Rowberg, A. H., & Robinson, C. (1996). Adaptation of an ethnographic method for investigation of the task domain in diagnostic radiology. In D. R. Wixon, & J. Ramey (Eds.), *Field methods casebook for software design* (pp. 1–15). New York: John Wiley & Sons.

Strauss, A. L., & Corbin, J. (1990). *Basics of Qualitative Research: Grounded Theory Procedures and Techniques*. Newbury Park, CA: Sage Publications.

Teague, R., & Bell, G. (2001). Getting Out of the Box. Ethnography meets life: Applying anthropological techniques to experience research. In *Proceedings of the Usability Professionals' Association 2001 Conference, Las Vegas, NV (Tutorial)*.

Chapter 14: Evaluation Methods

Benedek, J., & Miner, T. (2002). Measuring desirability: New methods for evaluating desirability in a usability lab setting. In *Proceedings of Usability Professionals Association, 2003* (pp. 8–12).

Borsci, S., Macredie, R. D., Barnett, J., Martin, J., Kuljis, J., & Young, T. (2013). Reviewing and extending the five-user assumption: A grounded procedure for interaction evaluation. *ACM Transactions on Computer-Human Interaction*, *20*(5), 29. http://dx.doi.org/10.1145/2506210. 23 pages, http://doi.acm.org/10.1145/2506210.

Jacobsen, N. E., & John, B. E. (2000). *Two case studies in using cognitive walkthrough for interface evaluation*. Pittsburgh, PA: Carnegie Mellon University, School of Computer Science, No. CMU-CS-00-132.

Kim, B., Dong, Y., Kim, S., & Lee, K. P. (2007). Development of integrated analysis system and tool of perception, recognition, and behavior for web usability test: With emphasis on eye-tracking, mouse-tracking, and retrospective think aloud. In *Usability and internationalization. HCI and culture* (pp. 113–121). Berlin, Heidelberg: Springer.

Lewis, C., Polson, P., Wharton, C., & Rieman, J. (1990). Testing a walkthrough methodology for theory-based design of walk-up-and-use interfaces. In *CHI '90 Proceedings* (pp. 235–242): ACM.

Medlock, M. C., Wixon, D., Terrano, M., Romero, R., & Fulton, B. (2002). *Using the RITE method to improve products: A definition and a case study*. Usability Professionals Association.

Nielsen, J. (1989). Usability engineering at a discount. *Proceedings of the third international conference on human-computer interaction on designing and using human-computer interfaces and knowledge based systems (2nd)*. Elsevier Science Inc, pp. 394–401.

Nielsen, J. (1994). Heuristic evaluation. In J. Nielsen, & R. L. Mack (Eds.), *Usability inspection methods*. New York, NY: John Wiley & Sons.

Nielsen, J., & Landauer, T. K. (1993). A mathematical model of the finding of usability problems. In *Proceedings of the INTERACT'93 and CHI'93 conference on human factors in computing systems, ACM* (pp. 206–213).

Nielsen, J., & Molich, R. (1990). Heuristic evaluation of user interfaces. In *Proceedings of the SIGCHI conference on human factors in computing systems, ACM* (pp. 249–256).

Norman, D. A. (2004). *Emotional design: Why we love (or hate) everyday things*. New York: Basic Books.

Polson, P. G., Lewis, C., Rieman, J., & Wharton, C. (1992). Cognitive walkthroughs: A method for theory-based evaluation of user interfaces. *International Journal of Man-Machine Studies*, *36*(5), 741–773.

Rayner, K. (1998). Eye movements in reading and information processing: 20 years of research. *Psychological Bulletin*, *124*(3), 372.

Russell, D. M., & Chi, E. H. (2014). Looking back: Retrospective study methods for HCI. *Ways of knowing in HCI*. New York: Springer, pp. 373–393.

Sauro, J. (2010). *A brief history of the magic number 5 in usability testing*. Retrieved from, https://www.measuringusability.com/blog/five-history.php.

Tobii Technology. (2009). *Retrospective think aloud and eye tracking: Comparing the value of different cues when using the retrospective think aloud method in web usability testing*. Retrieved from, http://www.tobii.com/Global/Analysis/Training/WhitePapers/Tobii_RTA_and_EyeTracking_WhitePaper.pdf.

Chapter 15: Concluding Final

Heath, C., & Heath, D. (2007). *Made to stick*. Random House.

McQuaid, H. L. (2002). Developing guidelines for judging the cost and benefit of fixing usability problems. In *Proceedings of the usability professionals' association 2002 conference (CD-ROM)*.

INDEX

Note: Page numbers followed by *f* indicate figures, *b* indicate boxes, and *t* indicate tables.

C

E

F

G

H

I

K

L

M

S

T

U

V

W

9780128002322